TEACHER'S WRAPAROUND EDITION

WRITER'S CHOICE

GRAMMAR AND COMPOSITION

Carmen Lomas Garza, *Cakewalk*, 1987

Consulting Author for Composition
Jacqueline Jones Royster

Grammar Specialist
Mark Lester

Visual-Verbal Learning Specialists
Ligature, Inc.

GLENCOE

McGraw-Hill

New York, New York   Columbus, Ohio   Woodland Hills, California   Peoria, Illinois

Glencoe/McGraw-Hill
A Division of The ***McGraw-Hill*** *Companies*

Cover, Co Rentmeester/The Image Bank, (inset) Aaron Haupt.

Send all inquiries to:
Glencoe/McGraw-Hill
936 Eastwind Drive
Westerville, OH
43081

ISBN 0-02-635872-7
(Student's Edition)
ISBN 0-02-635873-5
(Teacher's Wraparound Edition)

Printed in the United States of America.
4 5 6 7 8 9 10 071/046 03 02 01 00 99 98

Contents of Teacher's Wraparound Edition

Teacher's Wraparound Edition

The Teacher's Wraparound Edition provides an effective resource for presenting the lessons in Writer's Choice. *Each lesson plan has four parts: Focus, Teach, Assess, and Close. The margins offer additional information and strategies to meet a wide range of teaching situations.*

TEACH provides varied strategies for addressing the needs of basic-to-average, LD, and advanced learners.

FOCUS clearly sets the objective with writing, thinking, speaking, and listening skills as well as motivating activities for the lesson.

Strategies and background information support critical thinking, cultural diversity, students learning English, cross-curricular connections, fine art, and civic literacy.

Teacher's Classroom Resources lists ancillaries that extend and support the lesson.

UNIT 3
Lesson 3.2

TEACH

Guided Practice

Describing Work Situations
Challenge students to think of an interesting occupation in which note taking is important. Ask students: What kinds of details would a crime detective write in his or her notes? A reporter at a sports event? An insurance agent touring an area devastated by a hurricane? Have students pick an occupation and imagine a situation in which they'd take notes. With their detailed list, they then can write a page or two about the situation.

Independent Practice
For further stimuli for descriptive writing, see *Fine Art Transparencies*, 11–15.
Writing Process Transparencies 11–13B
Writing Across the Curriculum, p. 16
Cooperative Learning Activities, pp. 13–18

Skills Practice
Thinking and Study Skills, pp. 3, 6, 34–37
Composition Practice, p. 21
Composition Reteaching, p. 21
Composition Enrichment, p. 21

104

Vocabulary
Revising Tip
If you can't find just the right word when revising, turn to a thesaurus. A thesaurus is a reference book that groups together words with similar meanings.

Take Notes
Exploring the world aro... Make careful notes about i... notes can help you rememb... them with others later.
When you take notes o... about grammar, spelling, o... what you see, hear, touch, t... whatever details will help y...
Later, when you prepar... notes. Keep in mind that yo... you gathered. Choose thos... impression of the experien... for example, you might foc... describing a holiday dinner... and tastes.

Enabling Strategies

LEP Writing from Dictated Notes
Students learning English may have trouble using English to describe the different senses. Encourage them to communicate their sensory details orally to English-speaking students, who can jot down notes for them.

UNIT 3
Lesson 3.2

Setting the Purpose
Taking notes about the sensory details of one's own experiences can enrich written descriptions of scenes and events.

FOCUS

Lesson Overview
Objective: To take notes that will serve as a source of ideas for descriptive writing
Skills: observing events using all five senses; using vivid language to describe events
Critical Thinking: analyzing; comparing
Speaking and Listening: discussing; note taking

Bellringer
When students enter the classroom, have this assignment on the board: *Write down the name of a favorite movie. Jot down at least three reasons why you like it so much.*

Grammar Link to the Bellringer
Have students circle any action verbs they used in the Bellringer activity.

Motivating Activity
Ask students to imagine that a new movie has opened and they are deciding whether to see it. One person who has seen the film says, "The bad guy is scary." Another recalls, "The bad guy's voice sounds like fingernails scraping across a chalkboard. You'll be so scared that you'll want to run out of the theater." Ask students which person was more observant. Whose description would make you want to see the movie—the first or the second? How important are details when describing a film?

102

LESSON 3.2
Descriptive Writing
Observing and Taking Notes

Sensory details call up realistic images of taste, sound, smell, touch, and sight. These details ca... add richness to your description... of everyday things.

In the model below, Maya Angelou describes a picnic she remembers from her childhood. Notice the sensory details Angelou uses to help readers picture the scene.

Literature Model

The summer picnic gave ladies a chance to show off their baking hands. On the barbecue pit, chickens and spareribs sputtered in their own fat and a sauce whose recipe was guarded in the family like a scandalous affair. . . . Pound cakes sagged with their buttery weight and small children could no more resist licking the icings than their mothers could avoid slapping the sticky fingers. . . . On one corner of the clearing a gospel group was rehearsing. Their harmony, packed as tight as sardines, floated over the music of the county singers and melted into the songs of the small children's ring games.

Maya Angelou, *I Know Why the Caged Bird Sings*

102 Descriptive Writing: Picture This

3.2 Observing and Tak...

Teacher's Classroom Resources

The following resources can be used for planning, instruction, practice, reinforcement, assessment, reteaching, enrichment, or evaluation.

Teaching Tools
Lesson Plans, p. 22

Transparencies
Fine Art Transparencies, 11–15
Writing Process Transparencies, 11–13B

Blackline Masters
Thinking and Study Skills, pp. 3, 6, 34–37
Writing Across the Curriculum, p. 16
Cooperative Learning Activities, pp. 13–18
Composition Practice, p. 21
Composition Reteaching, p. 21
Composition Enrichment, p. 21

Assess...

ASSESS presents Writing Activities Evaluation Guidelines to help you critique and assess student writing.

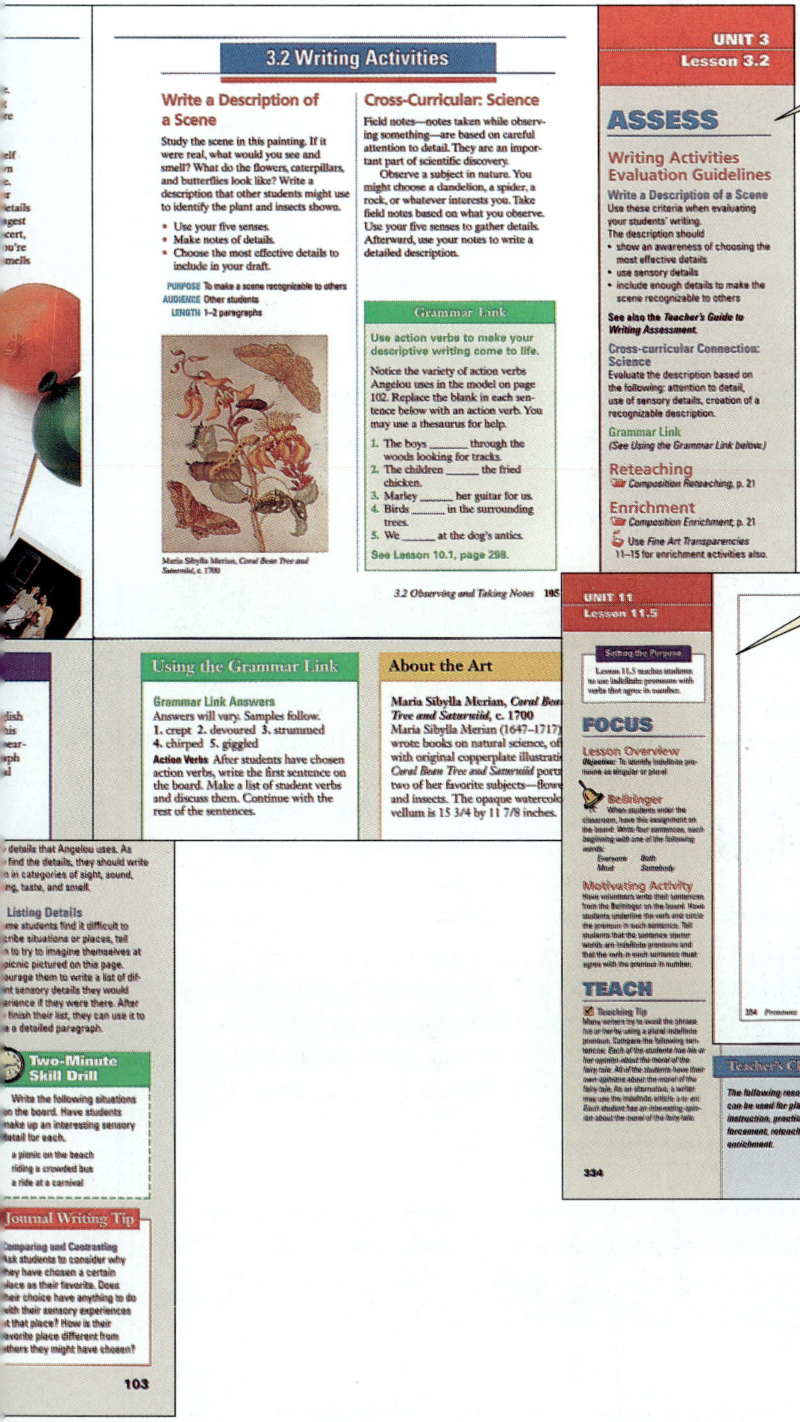

3.2 Writing Activities

Write a Description of a Scene

Study the scene in this painting. If it were real, what would you see and smell? What do the flowers, caterpillars, and butterflies look like? Write a description that other students might use to identify the plant and insects shown.

- Use your five senses.
- Make notes of details.
- Choose the most effective details to include in your draft.

PURPOSE To make a scene recognizable to others
AUDIENCE Other students
LENGTH 1–2 paragraphs

Maria Sibylla Merian, *Coral Bean Tree and Saturniid*, c. 1700

Cross-Curricular: Science

Field notes—notes taken while observing something—are based on careful attention to detail. They are an important part of scientific discovery.

Observe a subject in nature. You might choose a dandelion, a spider, a rock, or whatever interests you. Take field notes based on what you observe. Use your five senses to gather details. Afterward, use your notes to write a detailed description.

Grammar Link

Use action verbs to make your descriptive writing come to life.

Notice the variety of action verbs Angelou uses in the model on page 102. Replace the blank in each sentence below with an action verb. You may use a thesaurus for help.

1. The boys _______ through the woods looking for tracks.
2. The children _______ the fried chicken.
3. Marley _______ her guitar for us.
4. Birds _______ in the surrounding trees.
5. We _______ at the dog's antics.

See Lesson 10.1, page 298.

3.2 Observing and Taking Notes 105

UNIT 3 Lesson 3.2

ASSESS

Writing Activities Evaluation Guidelines

Write a Description of a Scene
Use these criteria when evaluating your students' writing.
The description should
- show an awareness of choosing the most effective details
- use sensory details
- include enough details to make the scene recognizable to others

See also the *Teacher's Guide to Writing Assessment.*

Cross-curricular Connection: Science
Evaluate the description based on the following: attention to detail, use of sensory details, creation of a recognizable description.

Grammar Link
(See Using the Grammar Link below.)

Reteaching
Composition Reteaching, p. 21

Enrichment
Composition Enrichment, p. 21
Use Fine Art Transparencies 11–15 for enrichment activities also.

Using the Grammar Link

Grammar Link Answers
Answers will vary. Samples follow.
1. crept 2. devoured 3. strummed 4. chirped 5. giggled

Action Verbs After students have chosen action verbs, write the first sentence on the board. Make a list of student verbs and discuss them. Continue with the rest of the sentences.

About the Art

Maria Sibylla Merian, *Coral Bean Tree and Saturniid*, c. 1700
Maria Sibylla Merian (1647–1717) wrote books on natural science, of... with original copperplate illustrati... *Coral Bean Tree and Saturniid* port... two of her favorite subjects—flow... and insects. The opaque watercol... vellum is 15 3/4 by 11 7/8 inches.

Listing Details

Two-Minute Skill Drill

Write the following situations on the board. Have students make up an interesting sensory detail for each.
a picnic on the beach
riding a crowded bus
a ride at a carnival

Journal Writing Tip

Comparing and Contrasting Ask students to consider why they have chosen a certain place as their favorite. Does their choice have anything to do with their sensory experiences at that place? How is their favorite place different from others they might have chosen?

103

Grammar units contain an abundance of practical suggestions for helping students master grammar and improve their writing.

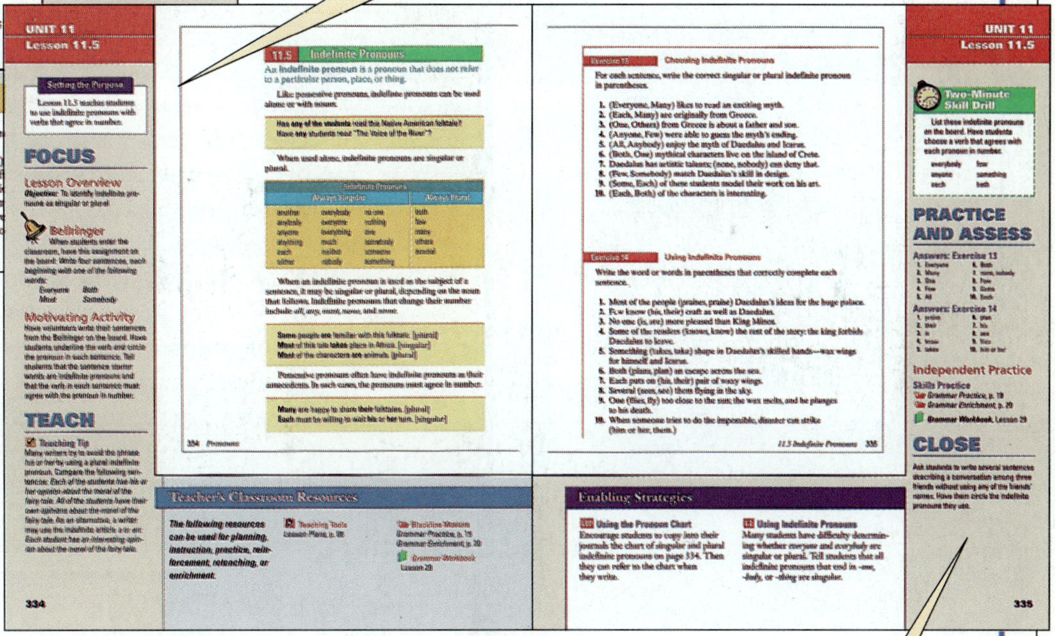

UNIT 11 Lesson 11.5

FOCUS

TEACH

11.5 Indefinite Pronouns

334 *Pronouns*

11.5 Indefinite Pronouns 335

Teacher's Classroom Resources

Enabling Strategies

UNIT 11 Lesson 11.5

Two-Minute Skill Drill

PRACTICE AND ASSESS

Independent Practice

CLOSE

335

CLOSE gives tips for reviewing, applying, and extending the lesson.

Language and Learning in Classrooms

by Jacqueline Jones Royster
Associate Professor of English and Director of the University Writing Center at The Ohio State University

What Do Our Students Need to Learn?

The last thirty years or more have been tremendously exciting times in English Studies at all educational levels. We have made thought-provoking discoveries that encourage us to imagine *all manner of possibilities for language and learning* in our classrooms. As teachers whose concerns are systemically intertwined with reading and writing, we have been privileged to see other educators come to perceive the centrality of such concerns in their endeavors as well.

Likewise, we are more attuned now than ever before to the intense demands placed on our students. Even the young ones, seemingly, must contend with complex forces and lead complicated lives. To operate reasonably on a daily basis, they need to be able to:

- read varieties of text well.
- use language well (as speakers, listeners, readers, and writers) in gaining access to various and sundry information and in being critical and creative as they construct ideas meaningfully for different audiences and different purposes.
- reflect critically on their own uses of language and on the uses of others.
- recognize how language, particularly within a multimedia environment, impacts on their daily lives.

The intersection of these two points of understanding

Writer's Choice provides all manner of student-friendly invitations and instruction for frequent writing:

- Every four-page lesson includes a journal activity.
- Every four-page lesson ends with a full page of Writing Activities.
- Remarkable variety of writing activities includes writing based on Case Studies, on literature, and on content areas.

often becomes a point of anxiety for us, however. When we actually face our students, so widely divergent in backgrounds and ability levels, in the systems of support available to them, in their desires, motivation, and aspirations, and in their responses to the highly pressurized contexts in which we all live, we can feel very much at sea. These realities across communities—urban, suburban, rural—place considerable demands on us to be, above all else, *flexible and creative* in both our theoretical and pedagogical constructs.

What Is Our Task as Teachers?

Classroom teachers must operate now from a constant need to keep the conversations with our students open and viable, asking good questions and not just giving our own answers, looking from multidimensional, not just one-dimensional, points of view. The imperative is to think beyond the specifics of discrete skills and knowledge and easily countable measures of achievement. The imperative is to look qualitatively and dynamically at how language works, how students learn, how learning and achievement can break new ground. The imperative is to use our knowledge, experiences, expertise, and imagination to help our students:

- create a central place for reading and writing in their lives.
- function competently on their own and in the company of others.
- feel capable as human beings who can recognize and solve problems.
- live positive and productive lives.

Our task is to *structure classroom environments* that are content-rich, that incorporate students' participation as active learners, and that invite risk and experimentation. A basic goal becomes helping students to develop keen skills by which they make observations and articulate their visions. The impetus is toward structuring classroom experiences that allow them to think variously about their lives, the lives of others, and the wonderfully rich range of texts that continue to emerge from the human experience, and to *use their skills, knowledge, and understanding as they construct and reconstruct their perceptions of reality*. These efforts seem to stand at the center of our concerns. Ongoing developments in both theory and practice seem to reaffirm these values constantly, and most of us remain hopeful that, despite the hard work that is inevitably demanded, our students will learn to *manage the array of complex language and writing skills* they need to face future and unknown worlds.

Writer's Choice enables both students and teachers to be flexible and creative by providing an engaging array of options:
- Composition lessons in a unit may be used in order, or lessons may be linked to particular writing needs.
- Writer's Choice pages offer a variety of workable assignments and degrees of guidance.
- Grammar instruction is delivered through a wealth of exercises, the Grammar Links, literature-based Grammar Reviews, and the Troubleshooter.

Writer's Choice is a structured environment for problem solving and success:
- Manageable lessons address specific writing situations with workable strategies.
- Writing assignments and Writing Process in Action lessons give substantial contexts and criteria for self-evaluation.
- Complete unit on sentence combining is based on structured sentences.

Writer's Choice presents skills in context to help students construct a unified experience of language:
- Composition lessons use annotated models to show specific skills in action.
- Writing Process Tips integrate composition with grammar and vocabulary skills.
- Grammar Reviews integrate grammar, usage, and mechanics with literature.

Writer's Choice helps students manage the complexity of language and writing tasks:
- Complete instruction in the writing process
- Writing Process Tips throughout composition lessons for help with writing process
- Writing Assignments—realistic writing prompts with real-world context
- Troubleshooter to help solve nine most common grammar, usage, and mechanics errors

The Middle School Concept

Writer's Choice is designed to capitalize on students' eagerness to explore possibilities:

- Wide variety of writing assignments gives students an array of choices and empowers them to draw on their own experiences.
- Contemporary design blends visual appeal with student-friendly text.
- Frequent Journal Writing activities provide opportunities for experimentation, reflection, and self-expression.

Writer's Choice reflects students' real-world consciousness:

- Case Studies of the writing process at work in real-world situations
- Student models by real student writers reflecting diverse populations
- Purpose, audience, and real-world context identified for writing assignments
- Readers Respond to the Model—actual student responses to literature
- Student Advisory Board ensuring student involvement in creation of the series

by Philip M. Anderson
Associate Professor, Department of Secondary Education and Youth Services, and Director of the English Education Program, Queens College, City University of New York

What Is Special About Middle School?

Anyone walking into a middle school can see what a special place it is: noisier, livelier, and simultaneously more disorienting and more interesting than either elementary or high school. Middle school students, while no longer children, are not ready to commit to the specialized, somewhat abstract, academic model of high school. But young adolescents ardently pursue knowledge about the world and *eagerly explore the possibilities* they now see before them.

Surveys of young adolescent educational interests reflect this *real-world consciousness*, reporting the following concerns:

- developing a personal identity
- dealing with questions encompassing morals and values
- securing a place of status in their peer group
- sorting out the maze of adult expectations
- anticipating their future lives (Paul S. George, et al., *The Middle School—and Beyond*, ASCD, 1992).

While some might perceive these social and psychological needs as impediments to academic learning, they embody powerful forces for motivating learning and ensuring interest in activities and outcomes. Meeting developmental needs (surveys of young adolescents' parents echo these concerns) provides a more productive learning environment for middle school students and more satisfying teaching conditions for their teachers.

How Is Middle School Organized?

The middle school is organized around student interests rather than administrative imperatives. Teachers of young adolescents structure the curriculum to respond to students' individuated needs while providing enough structure to foster learning and promote social development. Interdisciplinary learning, the pragmatic approach of extracting from academic subjects as needed, supplies an essential ingredient.

Interdisciplinary curriculum in the middle school develops from central themes, or problems, drawn from young adolescent interests. Curriculum projects devised from these themes provide activities and an intellectual focal point for the students. The unifying theme invites cooperative learning, while the interdisciplinary projects evoke useful connections between the academic disciplines.

Cooperative learning, the other key feature of middle school organization, typically involves heterogeneous groups of students working toward a common goal. Studies of cooperative learning in the middle school report higher achievement levels, greater use of high-level thinking, and increased self-esteem. Cooperative learning models also heighten the social imperatives of the students as a means for teaching interdependence and advocating collaboration.

How Do Middle School Students Learn?

Middle school students learn best through active involvement. They need time to read, write, and explore. Writing activities should encourage personal response while maintaining enough structure for developing, expressing, and organizing ideas. Reading activities should extend information, yet allow students to shape meaning through a variety of responses.

Learning content at this age means connecting it with one's own experience. Students must draw on their prior knowledge to integrate new learning experiences. Young adolescents desire knowledge about life's possibilities and wish to measure themselves against their new interpretations and perceptions of the world.

Middle school students do not learn useful skills well in isolation. *Activities connecting reading, writing, speaking, listening, and viewing* are more likely to produce successful learning of skill and content. The connected world view young adolescents seek, and their nascent perceptions of the relationships among ideas and actions, are not served by sequestered drill and a fragmented curriculum.

Middle schools provide a vision of responsive and responsible education for all ages. The noise in a middle school is the sound of learning; the seeming disorder is the commotion of a construction site bent on building a better world.

Writer's Choice encourages and provides help with interdisciplinary writing:
- Writing assignments cover such curriculum areas as art, science, mathematics, music, and, of course, literature.
- Case Studies explore and model how today's professionals write in a variety of fields.
- *Writing Across the Curriculum* blackline masters provide practical help for writing in content areas.
- *Research Paper and Report Writing* blackline masters offer cross-curricular support.

Writer's Choice incorporates practical, carefully planned cooperative learning activities:
- Writing Activities often include a choice of a cooperative learning activity with clear, step-by-step guidance.
- Teacher's Wraparound Editions include additional optional cooperative activities, such as Pairs Check, Round-robin, and Think-Pair-Share.

Writer's Choice integrates reading, writing, speaking, listening, and viewing for a unified learning experience:
- Case Studies that connect the world of writing with the world of everyday experience
- Manageable lessons with Journal Writing activities for response and reflection
- Writing Activities at the end of every lesson, with a variety of contexts, curriculum areas, and degrees of guidance
- Literature selections and models
- Speaking and Listening activities
- Visual/verbal graphic devices that teach as well as invite response

Integrating the Language Arts

by Denny Wolfe
Professor and Associate Dean of Darden College of Education at Old Dominion University in Norfolk, Virginia; formerly director of the Tidewater Writing Project

Why Integrate the Language Arts?

As English teachers, we have a unique responsibility: to assist students in their growth toward language maturity. Specifically, our challenge is to help students read, write, speak, and listen capably and effectively. To the extent we are successful in meeting this challenge, students learn to *think* critically and imaginatively.

Reading, writing, speaking, and listening are complementary processes. That is, growth in any one enhances growth in the others. We want students to achieve both *oracy* (speaking and listening competence) and *literacy* (reading and writing competence), and each feeds the other. Our curriculum, therefore, should function to give students *opportunities for total language growth*. By talking and by listening to others, students often are stimulated to read or write; during and after reading or writing, the *exchange of perceptions* through further oral and written activities both broadens and deepens students' understanding.

We must lead students toward a recognition of the *interdependence of all language processes*. Students can then become truly competent readers, writers, speakers, and listeners. The process works much like learning to drive a car. The competent driver must accomplish many tasks simultaneously—managing the steering wheel, operating the gas pedal, using the brake, looking ahead at the road, glancing behind through the rear-view mirror, paying attention to road signs. All of these are necessary to making the car work for us. Similarly, for language to work for us, we must use all the processes together, capitalizing on each to make the others meaningful.

Writer's Choice encourages total language growth through reading, responding, writing, and reflecting:
- Manageable lessons with Journal Writing activities
- Writing Activities at the end of every lesson, with a variety of contexts, curriculum areas, and degrees of guidance
- Literature selections
- Shorter literature models
- Writing process instruction that demonstrates how thinking and writing go hand in hand

Writer's Choice encourages the exchange of perceptions:
- Student models by real student writers
- Readers Respond to the Model—real student responses to literature
- Peer Editing built into writing assignments
- Cooperative Learning activities
- Speaking and Listening activities

Writer's Choice embodies the interdependence of all language processes:
- Literature integrated into composition—through literature selections and models
- Grammar integrated into composition—through the Troubleshooter and the Grammar Links
- Composition integrated into grammar—through the Writing Applications
- Literature integrated into grammar—through selections in Grammar Reviews

How Can We Integrate the Language Arts?

One conception of the English curriculum is that it is about literature—in both print and nonprint forms—and that it is about experience. *The world of literature* and the world of students' experience must be drawn together if the English classroom is to be an exciting, dynamic place. When we as teachers attempt to draw these two worlds together, we create conditions for integrating the language arts.

For example, a poet may write about a sunset. Before asking students to read the poem (or hear it read), we can invite them to talk or to write about a sunset—a memorable experience, a place or a person they associate with a sunset, or a generic description of one. We might relate an experience or two of our own. Afterward, when students approach the poem, they have established a mindset for reading it, and they are potentially able to relate to it in special ways. Upon finishing the poem, they might talk in groups about how the poem is different from or similar to their own experiences. Or they may be invited to make journal entries. Such discussions or personal reflections in journals may lead to a full, even formal, piece of writing on some interesting aspect of the poem, perhaps drafted several times and finally released to the teacher. In these ways, students practice reading, writing, speaking, and listening to clarify and to enhance their thoughts and feelings about a literary experience.

How Do Students Benefit from Integrating the Language Arts?

When students engage in experiences that invite reading, writing, speaking, and listening to be used in concert, they gain a sense of the wholeness of English. They cease to think of these language processes as discrete—reading as one thing, writing another, and speaking and listening something else. They develop *a sense of community* as they talk together, share perceptions from their reading, and respond to each other's written drafts. Most importantly, they grow *toward full language maturity*, recognizing that each language process contributes to the development of all others. Finally, they become better thinkers, a major goal of all instruction.

Writer's Choice is literature-rich:
- Literature selections from the finest contemporary writers
- Annotated Literature models to take the mystery out of writing well
- Writing About Literature lessons with practical instruction for specific writing situations
- Literature-based Grammar Reviews

Writer's Choice helps students develop a sense of community through the use of language in their own lives, in the classroom, and in the world at large:
- Case Studies—writing in the real world
- Journal Writing—for response and reflection
- Peer Editing—for shared responses
- Cooperative Learning—reading, writing, speaking, listening, and thinking toward common goals
- Readers Respond—students talking to students

Writer's Choice provides a framework for each student's growth toward full language maturity:
- Choice among writing assignments empowers students to draw on their own experiences.
- Writing Process in Action includes criteria for students' self-evaluations.
- Grades 11 and 12 include *The Elements of Style* by William Strunk Jr. and E. B. White.

Multiculturalism

by Arnold Webb
Senior Research Associate, Research for Better Schools, Philadelphia, Pennsylvania

What Is Multiculturalism?

Multiculturalism is one of those words to which we educators nod knowingly when we hear it. We nod, secure in righteous affirmation of a concept that is second only to motherhood and with which no one would dare disagree. We also believe that we are all using essentially the same definitional parameters and, therefore, can communicate with each other on this issue from a common (and enlightened) conceptual base.

As comforting as the above notion may be, it is not entirely accurate. Perceptions concerning what constitutes meaningful multiculturalism in our classrooms range from fostering and stressing a common culture to celebrating and supporting cultural diversity. Hardcore adherents to each of these views believe strongly that their approach is the only viable way to *channel the dynamic cultural and ethnic mix in our classrooms* into areas that support and strengthen our democratic society.

I agree with Asa Hilliard, who said:

> I do not believe that it is necessary to choose between (cultural) commonality and uniqueness. This is a false dichotomy. Human minds and systems are powerful and flexible enough to handle both.

The truth is that both are essential. We must provide an environment in which children can understand the world around them and their place (and responsibility) in that society as citizens and as contributors to the perpetuation of democratic precepts and ideals. We cannot do this, however, without empowering every child to recognize and value his/her individual worth. That empowerment for many children can occur only when they are in an educational environment that provides opportunities for them

Writer's Choice helps you channel the cultural mix in your classroom:

- Student Advisory Board ensures student involvement in creation of the series.
- Student models reflect diverse population.
- Literature, grammar exercises, and fine art present cultural variety.

to understand and appreciate the unique historic and ongoing contributions of their ethnic and cultural heritage to their land of origin and to the American dream.

How Do We Strike the Right Balance?

How does a teacher strike a balance between providing youngsters with a positive sense of self-worth through pride in their cultural heritage and still engender appreciation of our unique shared culture as Americans? It is a daunting task, but it must be accomplished. Perhaps one might begin by taking a self-administered test and responding candidly to the following questions:

- What do I believe about the children I teach? What are the bases of my expectations of them?
- What do I know about the history, mores, and culture of my students?
- How is this knowledge utilized in my planning and teaching?
- Does the curriculum I teach reflect *the truths of a pluralistic society*? In what ways?
- What opportunities are provided in my classroom for children to know, understand, and *relate to classmates from other backgrounds and cultures*?
- What skills are my students learning that enable them to *contribute positively to an evolving, diverse, and demanding democracy*?

Your answers to the questions posed above should provide some private insights for you into the impact of multiculturalism in your own classroom. Do not believe for a moment, however, that you are alone in the struggle to celebrate diversity and to make multiculturalism a viable aspect of our educational systems.

In the final analysis, we teachers (all of us) must be responsive to the needs and exigencies of our changing society. For example, the 1990 Census revealed that one of every four Americans is a person of color. It is projected that by the year 2000, this figure will be one of every three. This demographic and economic imperative must be dealt with realistically in America's classrooms. Cultural and ethnic diversity is endemic, and we can shy away from its impact to our detriment, or we can build upon its strengths and benefit us all. What happens in our classrooms as we address this issue will markedly affect the rest of the nation's response. It's up to us!

Writer's Choice reflects the truths of a pluralistic society:
- Contemporary photographs
- Fine art
- Cultural Diversity annotations in Teacher's Wraparound Edition

Writer's Choice helps students relate to people of other backgrounds:
- Cultural diversity in Case Studies and topics of assignments and exercises
- Cultural diversity in models and literature

Writer's Choice empowers students to learn the skills of civic literacy:
- Civic Literacy annotations in Teacher's Wraparound Edition pinpoint skills and concepts.
- Case Studies exemplify variety of social roles and contributions.

Teaching Students with Different Abilities

by Beverly Ann Chin
Professor of English, University of Montana; Director of the Montana Writing Project

How Can We Teach Writing to Students with Different Abilities?

Our students bring a wide variety of experiences, attitudes, learning styles, cultures, and languages to our classrooms. The diversity of abilities is most apparent when we teach writing. Many students learn English as a second language and are developing basic skills in speaking, listening, reading, and writing. Other students speak standard English as a second dialect.

In our classrooms, we may have students who seem unable to put their ideas on paper, as well as students who view themselves as writers and initiate their own writing. We also have students who differ in their abilities to write for different purposes. For example, the student who enthusiastically creates a historical narrative on Spanish exploration in the 1500s may have difficulty organizing a persuasive editorial on Columbus Day celebrations. On the other hand, another student may find the persuasive editorial easier to write than the historical narrative.

We can teach writing to students with different abilities when we create learning environments that immerse students in reading, writing, speaking, listening, and viewing. By *placing our students at the center of the curriculum*, we engage them as active learners and language users. We can meet the needs, interests, and abilities of our individual students if we respect our students' languages and if we are flexible in our teaching strategies.

Writer's Choice places students at the center of the curriculum by offering a coherent writing plan based on personal choice:
- Short, manageable lessons to meet specific writing needs and goals
- Wide variety of writing prompts with different degrees of guidance
- Journal writing and Portfolio keeping
- Alternative strategies for Basic Learners, Advanced Learners, and Limited English Proficiency Learners (Teacher's Wraparound Edition)

What Writing Strategies Work with Students of Different Abilities?

Here are some guidelines for teaching writing to students with different abilities:

1. Provide *frequent opportunities* for students to write, read, and reflect. Students need to engage in authentic communication and to discover the personal and social nature of writing and reading. Students also need to read literature by authors of diverse backgrounds and cultures.
2. Help students discover the relationship between oral and written language. By encouraging students to "talk out" their ideas before and during the writing process, we help students *understand the connections* among speaking, writing, listening, and reading. We can also stimulate creative thinking by teaching students a variety of prewriting strategies.
3. Vary the instruction and management of writing workshops. Students differ in the amount and type of writing instruction they need. When we allow students to choose their writing topics, we help students become responsible for focusing the purpose and audience for their writing. By structuring small group, partnership, and individual writing activities, we address differences in learning styles as well as language abilities.
4. Emphasize fluency and quality of ideas before correctness. We need to model appropriate ways for students to respond to each other's writing. We also need to teach grammar, usage, and mechanics in the context of the students' writing. As students write for authentic purposes and audiences, students discover how the conventions of written language affect communication.
5. Encourage all students to display, present, and publish their writing. By creating an environment in which all students share their writing, we recognize each student as a valued and unique member of *our learning community*. Students also learn to take pride and ownership in their writing.
6. Evaluate writing process as well as progress. Students need to see and value their growth as writers. Through a portfolio, students document and reflect upon their growth as writers, readers, decision-makers, and risk-takers. Through observations, anecdotal records, and conferences with students, we can assess our students' development as language users and language learners.
7. Above all, appreciate the diversity of students in the classroom. When we teach writing as a tool for learning, thinking, and communicating, we enable our students to discover and define their individual and social identities. By engaging our students in meaningful language activities, we empower the students as problem-solvers, decision-makers, and lifelong learners.

Writer's Choice is a program of frequent writing opportunities:

- Personal Writing beginning each book
- Journal Writing for reflection and self-expression
- Writing prompts with a variety of student-friendly contexts
- Writing Process in Action lessons
- Opportunities to respond to literature

Writer's Choice helps students understand the connections among speaking, writing, listening, and reading through the sheer variety of language experiences:

- Case Studies
- Literature discussion
- Student models
- Writing Conferences
- Journal Writing
- Writing Across the Curriculum
- Speaking and Listening opportunities
- Peer responses
- Cooperative learning activities

Writer's Choice includes all students as members of a literate community:

- Choices among lessons and array of contexts for assignments enable all students to feel involved.
- Case Studies, Student Models, and Readers Respond encourage participation by example.
- *Practice, Reteaching,* and *Enrichment* blackline masters meet individual needs.

Journal Writing

by Charleen Silva Delfino
English Coordinator, East Side Union High School-District, San Jose, California; Director of the San Jose Area Writing Project

Journals—What Is Their Purpose?

In the 1960s, when I began teaching high school, journal writing looked very different from the journal writing I use today. Students were given little structure or purpose for their writing. Journals sounded more like diaries, and students were encouraged to keep writing for an assigned amount of time even if the same word was repeated over and over again. The journals were often boring to write and boring to read. The exception occurred when the students used the journal as a diary and told me more than I ever wanted to know about their romantic life. I soon abandoned journals.

Today, I find journal writing to be an *integral part* of all of my teaching. The big difference is that students have a very specific purpose for their journals—the purpose varies, but it is always present for me in my planning and for students in their writing. Journals are a form of personal writing, sometimes shared, but the main audience is always the writer himself or herself. I find that for special education students, second language students, and all less verbal students, journals help to develop fluency. For many students, any writing can be a painful activity. They know that the fewer words they write, the fewer chances they have of making a mistake. They don't view writing as an opportunity to express their opinions (often, they don't value their own opinions or feel anyone else does); rather, they see writing as a trap to demonstrate their weaknesses and to show what they don't know. Consistent use of journals that focus on content and not on form can help students develop the fluency they have lacked.

Writer's Choice makes journal writing an integral part of a complete composition program:

- Personal Writing Unit, including lessons on Writing as Self-Discovery, Keeping a Writer's Journal, and Keeping a Commonplace Book
- Journal Writing—a brief prompt halfway through each composition lesson
- Writing Process in Action includes suggestions for journal writing as a means for students to reflect on their writing experiences

Are Journals Just for Special Students?

It is impossible for students to be wrong in a journal; consequently, they develop confidence in the student as a writer and as a learner. They help all students generate and validate ideas and beliefs. They enable students to explore ideas before writing a formal paper and to record impressions and reconstruct memories for personal writings. Journals enable students to bring prior knowledge and experiences to the study of a piece of literature and to respond as we read through a work of literature. Students may keep a double entry journal, recording words, phrases, or sentences that impress them on one side of a page, and then asking questions, responding, or debating them on the opposite side of the page. I often use journals to review previously learned materials and to check the effectiveness of a lesson. I also check on the effectiveness of my teaching by ending a class or starting the next one by asking what was the most interesting or important thing learned in the previous lesson. I can check for understanding in this manner as quickly as I can correct an objective test. Moreover, it is impossible for a student to fail a journal, and I have a better picture of my *students as learners*.

How Should We Respond to Student Journals?

No matter how effective journals may be, if responding to them becomes a burden, I won't use them. I never correct journals or other types of first draft writing. This decision saves me time and is based on sound teaching principles. When students write journals, I want them to concentrate on generating and exploring ideas and concepts; they can do this only if they are not concerned with form or correctness. Correctness is important, but not at this generating time. However, I do believe that it is important that students receive a response to their journals. Their ideas need to be validated. I vary the way I respond to all journals. Again, I never correct; sometimes, I read all journals and write one journal back to the whole class sharing some of the varying viewpoints I learned from my students. Other times, I use highlighters to identify key ideas in student journals that I found interesting, amusing, or challenging. Students can see that I have read their journals and know which part engaged me, yet I can read a whole class set in very little time.

Journals, as with all parts of the writing process, work most effectively in an atmosphere of trust and respect. The sharing of writing makes us vulnerable, but the sharing of personal writing where we are exploring new ideas makes us especially so. I have found that the best way for me to establish trust and a supportive atmosphere is for me to write with my students and to share my journals for their response. When they see me *thinking through new ideas*, *trying out various forms*, and exploring new concepts, I can truly establish a classroom that houses a community of writers who are trusting and open and willing to take risks.

Writer's Choice encourages journal writing as a tool for unifying students' educational experiences:

- Lessons on Writing to Learn, Keeping a Reader-Response Journal, and Using a Learning Log help students become more aware of themselves as learners.
- Cross-curricular writing prompts help students practice composition skills and transfer them to writing done in other classes and in the world of work.

Writer's Choice invites students to experiment, summarize, articulate, anticipate, synthesize, and evaluate:

- Journal Writing activities suggest a variety of relevant stimuli for helping students start out and set frameworks for problem solving, pose questions for follow-through, and engage higher-order thinking skills.

Portfolio Keeping

by Bonnie S. Sunstein
Associate Professor of English and Director of the Master of Arts in Teaching Program at Rivier College, Nashua, New Hampshire

How Do People Use Portfolios?

Artists, musicians, heads of state, and financiers use portfolios at intervals during their careers, gathering samples to represent depth and breadth in their work. They select different artifacts at different times, depending on who will be looking at their portfolios, and for what purposes. Over the last two centuries there is evidence that portfolios have appeared in tooled leather cases, carved wooden boxes, ornate display stands, and makeshift cloth carrying cases. The word *portfolio* derives from the Latin *portare* ("to carry") and *fogli* ("leaves or sheets of paper").

In the last decade, we've seen similarly colorful and energetic varieties of portfolios in schools and colleges. They appear on our classroom shelves in plastic boxes, shoe boxes, loose-leaf scrapbooks, neon-colored trapper-keepers, and metal drawers full of sedate manila folders. With homage to their heritage, all portfolios "carry" representative "leaves" of paper for the display of their owner's work. With portfolios, students can document their own histories as learners. They can *become their own authorities* rather than relying on external authorities to judge what's good or bad about their work. The use of portfolios to represent students' accomplishments is in its infancy, and the possibilities for learning from them are open and exciting.

Writer's Choice empowers students to become their own authorities:
- Reflection and Portfolio activities at the end of every composition unit
- Writing Portfolios for collecting student work

How Can Portfolios Help Students and Teachers?

As students, teachers, classes, and whole school systems experiment with portfolios, we are shifting our thinking about the terms *assessment* and *evaluation.* For students, a collection of writing over time can offer insights as they *write reflectively about their own learning.* For teachers, portfolios enable us to include our students in our evaluation process. When we keep our own portfolios along with our students, our own written reflections point out the time we devote to our students and to our own personal literacy.

Because evaluation is inextricably tied to instruction, portfolios teach us more about our teaching. For whole classes, teachers and students can view progress over time and make more informed decisions about curriculum coverage. For school systems, large-scale use of portfolios can offer new kinds of information and raise questions we've never been able to ask before. In other words, portfolios can help us to evaluate where we've been, assess where we are, and project where we want to go next. When we collect our reading and writing for display and analysis, we connect our present to our past and our future.

What Goes into a Portfolio—and Why?

As this is being written, there are as many kinds of portfolios as there are people working with them, and that's a healthy sign. Some are distilled folders, holding samples of students' "best" work. Deciding what's "best" becomes a negotiation between a teacher and a student in which they decide what is important in writing. The decisions may offer surprises as we discover what issues we most value in our evaluations. Portfolios offer us a multidimensional look at ourselves.

Portfolios complete with students' reflections—commentaries about why the paper is included—offer *opportunities for metacognition*—thinking about their own thinking and documenting it. A "best" paper might be the one with the fewest errors or one that follows the teacher's assignment perfectly. But a "best" paper might be the one in which the student took a risk, worked out a nagging question, researched and synthesized a new idea, reached beyond the teacher's assignment. This paper might not have followed the assignment exactly, but it might represent a new moment in a student's thinking.

Portfolios are not writing folders redone; they are documented collections of literary decisions made at certain times among certain people. They reflect our philosophies of reflection, evaluation, and learning. Portfolio keeping is decision making, and making decisions involves asking tough questions—of ourselves and our students—about what we value in writing and reading.

Writer's Choice encourages students to write reflectively about their own learning:

- Student models of writing to learn
- Journal Writing
- Unit Review

Writer's Choice offers opportunities for metacognition:

- Writing activities point the way at each stage of the writing process.
- Criteria for self-evaluation accompany every Writing Process in Action.
- The Unit Review helps students ask the right questions about their work.

Vision, Values, and Assessment

by Jacqueline Jones Royster
Associate Professor of English and Director of the University Writing Center at The Ohio State University

What Should Our Perspective Be?

Any discussion of assessment in the language arts must realistically begin with an articulation of what, within the context of current trends and practices, we have determined to be worthy of attention in effective teaching and learning. With a clarification of vision and values, we are much better positioned to begin a more meaningful discussion of what to measure, why, how, and when. From this perspective, we turn away from images of ourselves as failure detectives and language-use police. Objectives for learning take a rightful place as the linchpins for teaching and translate reflexively into measures of learning and achievement.

This perspective emphasizes the importance of having an appropriate interface between the theoretical base on which a curriculum or course is fashioned, the pedagogical frame within which learning happens, and the mechanisms for monitoring and measuring learning and achievement. It brings into question what assessment should be about and do in the interest of the educational process. It encourages us to see assessment as critical throughout the learning process, not just at the end of it, and to recognize a need to think well beyond ordinary techniques of testing and evaluation.

A reconsideration of the role of assessment in learning makes it possible to examine particular mechanisms for exactly what and how much they can tell us about the learning process and achievement. Inevitably, we are drawn to a need to measure many values and expectations in determining learning quality. We are drawn to a need for *multiple measures*, both quantitative and qualitative, and *alternative mechanisms.* The imperative is twofold: 1) to bring to clarity a fully developed picture of students' abilities to perform and their capacity to activate and maximize learning; 2) to select a range of

Writer's Choice offers both students and teachers multiple measures and mechanisms for assessment:

- Writing Process in Action assignments encourage peer response and editing.
- Guidelines for Evaluation in the Teacher's Wraparound Edition provide specific suggestions for giving students feedback.
- An array of Tests accompanies the program.
- *Teacher's Guide to Writing Assessment* offers additional models and guidelines for assessment.

mechanisms that reaffirm the values in learning that we seek to engender and also mirror both the ways we teach and the ways our students learn.

What Is the Role of Portfolios?

One promising strategy for addressing this twofold imperative is a portfolio system. While there are several models of portfolio assessment—some more product-oriented, some more process-oriented—the key is to select a model that is well rooted in the values, needs, and concerns of the specific learning environment. A usable definition for *portfolio* is that it is an assembly of evidence, a collection, a repertoire of writing or writing-related performances that illustrates a particular set of values, concerns, and expectations. As artifacts of talents, abilities, and performance, therefore, portfolios serve as a multidirectional mechanism for curriculum evaluation and development, for teaching, and for learning. Several features seem worthy of noting:

1. Conceived as either a product or a process, portfolios facilitate the development of a community of discourse within which to engage in ongoing dialogue about knowledge, learning, and performance.

2. In inviting a consideration of multiple measures, interpretations, and reading over time and across tasks, purposes, and genres, portfolios become the embodiment of learning and pedagogy, so that the curriculum is less likely to be driven by assessment and more likely to be driven by learning.

3. As an organic tool, portfolios focus on the acquisition, development, and demonstration of particular strengths as these strengths constitute consensus definitions of learning and achievement.

4. Portfolios make room for students in their own learning, offering them opportunities to develop a sense of their responsibilities as learners and a sense of authority over what, indeed, they have managed to learn.

5. Portfolios provide systematic moments at which both teachers and students, independently and collaboratively, can engage in the type of talk and reflection that maximizes the capacity for assessment to filter itself more productively and positively throughout the learning process.

The challenge, therefore, is really to reconceive *testing and evaluation as a multidimensional measurement of learning and achievement.* The push is to defuse the adversarial nature of the testing relationship so that teachers are in a position to identify, reaffirm, and reward growth, development, and achievement.

Writer's Choice helps students establish, maintain, and assess portfolios:

- Criteria for self-evaluation accompany Writing Process in Action.
- Reflection and Portfolio activities within the Unit Review end each unit.

Writer's Choice provides instruments for testing and evaluation in addition to portfolios:

- Tests include both objective forms and holistic forms.
- Composition tests include criteria for the student's self-evaluation.
- Pretests and Mastery Tests cover Grammar, Usage, Mechanics, and Resources.
- Tests are available in both print form and as *Test Generator* software (IBM, Apple, Macintosh).

Writing Across the Curriculum

Writer's Choice provides numerous opportunities for students to discover what they know, what they want to know, and what they've learned:

- Writing assignments cover art, science, social studies, mathematics, music, and, of course, literature.
- Case Studies explore and model how today's professionals write in the world of work.
- *Writing Across the Curriculum* blackline masters provide practical help for writing in content areas.
- *Research Paper and Report Writing* blackline masters offer cross-curricular support.

Writer's Choice encourages students to write to learn:

- Individual lessons cover such topics as Keeping a Learning Log, Writing to Learn, and Keeping a Reader-Response Journal.
- Annotations in the Teacher's Wraparound Edition identify points of intersection between English and other curriculum areas.

by Beverly Ann Chin
Professor of English, University of Montana; Director of the Montana Writing Project

What Is Writing Across the Curriculum?

Writing across the curriculum integrates subject area instruction with writing instruction. Teachers who implement a writing across the curriculum program view writing as a way to help students learn and think in different subject areas. When students write about specific subject area concepts, students *use writing as a means for discovering what they know, what they want to know, and what they've learned.* Through writing, we help students engage in the higher-level thinking skills of application, analysis, synthesis, and evaluation. We also encourage students to reflect on their feelings and progress as learners in the subject area.

In many writing across the curriculum programs, the terms "writing to learn" and "writing process" are intertwined. Writing to learn emphasizes the importance of writing as a tool for discovering ideas and gaining insights. When students engage in *writing to learn*, the writing becomes a vehicle for inquiry, hypothesis, and reflection. Often the writing is ungraded because the audience for the writing is the learner. The writing may or may not result in a "product."

Writing process refers to the recursive stages of prewriting, drafting, revising, editing, and publishing/presenting. Writing process teachers understand that students may vary in the amount of time needed for different writing projects. We also realize that all pieces of writing need not advance to the publishing stage. We value the learning that occurs in unfinished writing, and we celebrate the sharing that results from published writing.

Writing across the curriculum does not mean that "new" content is added to our subject areas. Rather, writing across the curriculum focuses our attention on "how" students learn and make sense of knowledge. When we use writing across the curriculum strategies in our teaching, students become better learners, and better communicators, in the different subject areas.

How Can We Help Our Students Use Writing to Learn in Different Subject Areas?

The most effective writing strategies are those that encourage students to write often and to reflect on their learning. One way of *inviting students to write* in any subject area is the journal. In the journal (or learning log), students enter their observations and feelings about subject area concepts. For example, in science, students record notes analyzing the data from an ongoing earth science experiment. In social studies, students create a chart on how different television stations report local news events during a one-week period. In English, students reflect on how an author creates suspense in an adventure novel they are reading. By making regular entries in their journals, students document their growth as thinkers.

The journal is also a place where students can do prewriting or drafting of an idea for a piece of writing. Students can share their journal ideas with classmates and use these ideas in future writing assignments.

Another important strategy in teaching writing across the curriculum is the creation of writing assignments that *reflect real-world writing.* When we write to communicate to other people, we have a clear purpose and audience for our writing. Writing assignments that incorporate writing purpose and audience create motivation for students to write. Helping students see themselves in different roles also gives students the opportunity to experiment with different voices. For example, an art writing assignment can ask students to imagine that they are museum curators. As museum curators, they must write a brochure that describes a new exhibit and that invites the community to see the exhibit. During a social studies unit on the California gold rush, students can imagine they are Chinese immigrants living in California in the mid-1800s. In a letter to their families in China, they describe their new life in the mining camps. Through these types of writing assignments, students reveal their insights into the subject area.

When we engage our students in writing across the curriculum, we motivate students to explore subject area knowledge as well as provide them with a powerful tool for lifelong learning.

Writer's Choice is a program of *invitation* and *instruction:*

- Journal Writing activities occur in every composition lesson.
- Annotated models invite student response.
- Case Studies and Literature selections invite student response.
- Guided Practice, Independent Practice, and Cross-Curricular activities invite the kinds of choices that generate student engagement.
- Writing Process in Action gives even more extended modeling and guidance.

Writer's Choice motivates students with real-world writing:

- Purpose, audience, and real-world context identified for writing assignments
- Case Studies of the writing process at work in real-world situations
- Student models by real student writers

Writing and Thinking

Writer's Choice is built on the belief that writing and thinking are closely connected:
- Clear, manageable lessons help students think through specific writing situations.
- Journal Writing activities support each composition lesson.
- A writing objective, as well as critical thinking and speaking and listening skills, is identified in the Teacher's Wraparound Edition for every writing lesson.

Writer's Choice involves students in the personal, active, and integrative processes of thinking:
- Student-friendly text and visuals
- Student models by real students
- Literature that engages contemporary readers
- Readers Respond to the Model pages that foster critical thinking
- Choices of assignments that enable students to draw on their own personal experiences and cross-curricular interests

by Philip M. Anderson
Associate Professor, Department of Secondary Education and Youth Services, and Director of the English Education Program, Queens College, City University of New York

How Can Writing Develop Thinking?

The *connections between writing and thinking* are not well established in schools. Allan Glatthorn's analysis of thinking skills programs found most rely on oral language, some ignoring written language altogether. Similarly, many "writing across the curriculum" programs give scant attention to thinking skills, instead restricting instruction solely to formal aspects of the term paper or note-taking techniques for lectures (in Frances Link, ed., *Essays on the Intellect*, ASCD, 1985).

Research conducted on thinking argues that cognitive processes must be taught, since they do not arise instinctively from social experience. Furthermore, students must strive to articulate tacit knowledge, i.e., personal knowledge residing below conscious levels of thinking (the phenomenon of "knowing more than we can say"). Tacit knowledge frequently establishes assumptions when we think about an issue or solve a problem.

In this regard, writing represents an important means for teaching thinking since it involves *personal, active, and integrative cognitive processes*. But, cognitive structures underlying writing need to be made explicit, allowing for a reciprocal relationship between growth in thinking and growth in writing.

How Can Thinking Be Taught During the Writing Process?

Many students perceive school writing as "knowledge telling"; they write all they know about a subject and stop. They expend little effort in expanding, analyzing, or reformulating that knowledge. As a result, academic writing frequently lacks coherence and rarely offers new understandings. However, teachers can remedy the situation by *emphasizing thinking*, and teaching cognitive structure, *throughout the recursive writing process.*

Journal writing provides a means for uncovering and examining tacit knowledge during prewriting. Reflection and reconstruction of ideas are encouraged when students articulate personal knowledge. Since the journal symbolizes recorded thought, opportunities to interact with one's own thinking over time are also accommodated.

Techniques such as graphic mapping (Venn diagram, e.g.) and thinking frames (compare/contrast, problem/solution, e.g.) enhance student thinking prior to writing and provide direction during the composing process. Structured prewriting assists student writers in organizing thought and determining means for completing the writing task.

Teachers can nurture student thinking during the writing process by "scaffolding" instruction. Scaffolding is a strategy in which teachers collaborate with students by carrying out parts of a task students temporarily need adult support to accomplish. Some forms of scaffolding include teacher modeling of process, frame categories and questions, changing misconceptions, and coaching (B. F. Jones, et al., *Teaching Thinking Skills: English/Language Arts*, NEA, 1987).

Scaffolded instruction may employ face-to-face interaction, such as conferencing during revision. Peer and teacher dialogue with the student writer during revision, if more than mere editing, must focus on meaning and organization of thought.

But, scaffolding is also employed when the teacher clearly spells out the writing assignment by defining key features of structure and content. Students then can assess and construe the goals of the assignment, both discourse form and intellectual organization, providing an appropriate response within supportive guidelines provided by the teacher.

Finally, teaching students about the process of composing and the author's situation serves a metacognitive (i.e., conscious control of thinking strategies) function within writing instruction. Some research even suggests that misconceptions about the purpose and function of composing may be the primary culprit in poor writing achievement.

Process models of composing and cognitive process instruction are not incompatible components of the school curriculum. Each can advance the improvement of the other, resulting in students who can *think clearly and independently as well as effectively.*

Writer's Choice emphasizes thinking throughout the recursive writing process:

- Writing Process Tips recur throughout composition lessons.
- Writing Process in Action reinforces "revisiting" of previous thinking and writing.
- Case Studies exemplify the recursive writing process in the real world.

Writer's Choice fosters independent thinking and writing:

- Writing Process in Action includes criteria for self-evaluation.
- Reflection and Adding to Your Portfolio in each Unit Review focus students' thoughts about their writing.
- Troubleshooter helps students help themselves.
- *Thinking and Study Skills* blackline masters provide additional practice and activities.

Cooperative Learning

Writer's Choice incorporates practical cooperative learning activities:
- Writing Activities often include a choice of a cooperative learning activity.
- Additional optional cooperative activities appear in Teacher's Wraparound Edition.
- Peer response and peer editing are encouraged.

by Charleen Silva Delfino
English Coordinator, East Side Union High School District, San Jose, California; Director of the San Jose Area Writing Project

Walking down the hallway, I heard voices coming out of F-22, and I smiled as I neared Mrs. Kennett's classroom. I knew that the noise I heard was the sound of eager students energetically discussing their friends' writing. Entering the room, I watched young writers asking questions, making suggestions, trying different options. When was the last time I had seen young people this engaged in the process of writing? Certainly, there weren't many models. Writing, especially in schools, is often a lonely enterprise entered into without great enthusiasm. What was different in F-22?

These students, representing many cultures—African American, Japanese, Hispanic, Filipino, Vietnamese, European American, Chinese—worked in groups of four responding to the historical fiction they had written based on a story of a family member who had moved to a new area. These stories were to be published in a class anthology about the immigrant experience. What was different? These students were engaged in a *practical cooperative learning activity.* They had a real audience and a real purpose for their writing. They had something to say because they cared about their own writing and they cared about the writing of the members of their group.

Isn't Cooperative Learning Just Group Work?

Certainly, cooperative learning is group work, but it is more than what is implied in "just group work." If a teacher tells students to get into groups and discuss their writing, the chances are very good that students will say something like, "I like your writing; it is really good." And then they will go on to discuss more pressing matters—like the dance Friday night or the basketball game after school. Students need to be *trained in a variety of ways of providing feedback* to each other about their writing. They need to learn how to ask questions that will give them the assistance they need. Certainly, this is not a natural gift that all students possess. They don't have the language to engage in these kinds of discussions (not many adults do either), but they can be trained.

Why Cooperative Learning?

Cooperative learning is not a panacea; it is not the answer to every problem. It is not the only method of instruction I employ, but it is certainly an important part of my classroom and my students' learning experience. With cooperative learning students need to be actively involved in their instruction; they are not passive participants in the learning process. Also, in the small group activities, students are more willing to participate and risk. If the group is constructed well, each student has a part and a contribution to make. The different learning styles and abilities of each student can be addressed. In heterogeneously grouped classes and classes with second language learners, these students' needs can be met. Students are forced to use the language to communicate with others.

What Makes Cooperative Learning Groups Work?

Careful planning is an essential step in making groups work. I have developed five rules that have made cooperative learning more successful for me:

1. Give clear directions, being sure that all students understand what is expected of them and what they are going to do.
2. Model with the whole class whatever you expect the students to do in their small groups.
3. Have students responsible for something concrete when they are finished.
4. Assign less time than you think they will need; it is easier to give more time than to take it away.
5. Vary the purpose and the activity of cooperative learning groups. Although students like some structure, too much repetition leads to boredom.

What is important is that learning be student-centered and that each student take an active role, making decisions and staying involved in the learning process.

Writer's Choice includes cooperative learning activities that fit a variety of purposes:

- Choices include brainstorming for prewriting, peer response for revision, responding to literature, responding to fine art, group problem-solving, and research for group writing.

Writer's Choice offers cooperative learning activities that are carefully planned and defined:

- Students are given clear, step-by-step guidance for cooperative activities.
- Teacher's Wraparound Edition provides detailed, concrete suggestions for additional cooperative activities, including round-robin, pairs check, three-step interview, think-pair-share, roundtable, partners, and co-op co-op.

Teaching Grammar and Usage

by Mark Lester
Professor of English, Eastern Washington University; formerly Chair of the Department of English as a Second Language, University of Hawaii

Why Do We Teach Grammar?

Children do not need to go to school to learn their native language, but they need to go to school to learn to think and talk about it. All native speakers of a language have a vast intuitive knowledge of the rules of their language. However, this knowledge is so deeply below the level of conscious awareness that native speakers cannot easily talk or even consciously think about how their own language works. Our language is a vehicle for conveying our thoughts; it is very difficult for us to learn to focus on the vehicle rather than on the meaning the vehicle conveys.

The study of grammar in school gives students the concepts and terms necessary for *talking and thinking about the vehicle of language.* A conscious knowledge of grammatical concepts and terms is also necessary for students to compare and contrast their use of language with other people's use of language and to explore alternative ways of expressing their own ideas.

Writer's Choice helps students learn to talk and think about the vehicle of language:
- Clear, manageable, two-page grammar lessons
- Visual/verbals that convey grammar concepts and examples graphically

How Can We Teach Grammar Effectively?

Research shows us that just teaching grammar terminology by itself is ineffectual. Grammar terminology is enormously abstract and loaded with hidden assumptions. Robert deBeaugrande compared grammar terminology to a ladder with the bottom rungs cut out—if you don't already know the concept underlying the terminology, the terminology itself will be of little use to you. For example, the definition of preposition as "a word that shows the relationship of a noun or pronoun to some other word in a sentence" is incomprehensible unless you already know that a preposition is part of a prepositional phrase, that prepositions have noun or pronoun objects, and that prepositional phrases function as adjective or adverb modifiers. In order to grasp grammar terminology, students first need *numerous examples and extensive practice sessions* to grasp the concepts underlying the term.

Two techniques that help students grasp grammatical concepts are sentence combining and paraphrase tests. Sentence combining shows students how sentences with multiple phrases and clauses are built from underlying simple sentences. Sentence combining also allows students to compare and evaluate the grammatical and stylistic effect of different ways of combining the same simple sentences. Paraphrase tests that tap into students' unconscious knowledge of their language are practical ways of identifying grammatical concepts. For example, the definition of a noun as the name of "a person, a place, a thing, or an idea" doesn't really tell the student what a noun is. After all, even though *blue* is the name of a color and thus appears to fit the definition of a noun, *blue* still isn't a noun. However, learning that nouns typically follow the definite article *the* and can be made plural gives students two simple tests that they can use to see if a word is a noun. Since we cannot say *The sky is the blue* or *The sky is blues*, *blue* cannot be a noun in these sentences.

How Can We Teach Usage Effectively?

Usage is the way that we use grammar. Grammar provides a vocabulary that students and teachers need in order to talk about usage problems. For example, talking to a student about the subject-verb agreement errors in the student's paper would be very difficult if the student did not know what the terms *subject* and *verb* meant. However, just teaching grammar by itself to students does not necessarily help students with their usage problems. Not surprisingly, grammar taught in isolation from the students' usage problems is learned in isolation from usage problems.

Good grammar programs constantly *connect grammar to usage problems in the students' own writing*. Probably the most effective way of dealing with usage problems is the following: (a) collect examples of the error from the students' own papers; (b) have the students discuss the error, focusing on what the error is and how it can be corrected; and (c) back up the discussion with relevant exercises on grammar and usage.

Writer's Choice provides numerous examples and extensive practice in grammar and usage:

- Thematic exercises that are a natural part of every Grammar, Usage, and Mechanics lesson
- Alternative strategies for students of all ability levels provided in the Teacher's Wraparound Edition

Writer's Choice connects grammar and usage to students' own writing:

- Writing Process Grammar Tips in the composition units to further the integration of grammar and writing
- Grammar Reviews at the end of every grammar unit to integrate grammar, writing, and literature
- Troubleshooter that offers students a handy self-help guide to grammar, usage, and mechanics

Visual Learning

by Josef Godlewski
Executive Design Director, Ligature, Inc., Chicago and Boston

and Daniel Rogers
Executive Editorial Director, Ligature, Inc., Chicago and Boston

Why Are Visual Learning Strategies Important?

To be truly literate in a modern technological culture, we need to comprehend and use both verbal and visual literacies." This claim, made by Richard Sinatra and Josephine Stahl-Gemake in *Using the Right Brain in the Language Arts*, has important ramifications for the English classroom. Clearly, English teachers consider the development of verbal literacy as central to their mission, but what do we mean by visual literacy? Loosely defined, visual literacy encompasses a set of skills that enable an individual to decode and interpret images and visual representations of concepts, to use images and visual representations to communicate effectively, and to understand and enjoy the creative works of visual artists.

In a culture permeated by television, computer games, and other electronic media, students come to school with a rich experience in receiving and interpreting messages that are at once both visual and verbal. Rather than presenting a cause for alarm, this experience offers an opportunity for effective instructional materials and strategies to meet the learning needs of all students.

We can begin to use visual strategies to enhance instruction by first acknowledging that *presentations which effectively combine visual and verbal elements* are more compelling than text alone, particularly for students who have grown up in a video culture. We know from brain research that visual messages are processed largely in the brain's right hemisphere, while the processing of verbal messages takes place mainly in the left hemisphere. In essence, then, the compelling nature of video derives in large measure from its dual message that simultaneously stimulates

Writer's Choice enhances instruction by effectively combining visual and verbal elements:

- Sparkling visuals that grab and hold students' attention
- Computer graphics that clearly illustrate concepts and processes
- Visual Thinking annotations in the Teacher's Wraparound Edition with strategies for improving students' thinking and writing

two discrete regions of the brain. In the classroom, visuals that relate instructionally to the text can engage students' attention and serve as a gateway to a concept or skill to be explored verbally. This function of engagement and connection to personal experience is a necessary first step in the learning process.

An integrated combination of visual and verbal presentations can also provide greater access to concepts and skills for students of varied learning styles. For example, graphic organizers are a particularly powerful means of representing processes and relationships. Not just visual learners but all students can benefit from using a flow chart to represent the steps in a process or a Venn diagram to highlight similarities and differences.

In addition, *a memorable graphic representation of a key concept or relationship* provides a useful mnemonic tool for all learners. Again, brain research indicates that visual memories are formed and retrieved very differently from verbal memories. Thus, the association of an image with a particular concept can enhance students' ability to recall and apply that concept.

Writer's Choice provides memorable graphic representations of key concepts and relationships:

- State-of-the-art graphics to help students see the connections between observing, thinking, and writing
- Visuals that offer an alternate mode of information delivery that is especially helpful for today's visually oriented students

How Can Visuals Promote the Development of Student Writing?

Photographs and fine art can provide *points of entry to writing through visual exploration.* At the most basic level, students can write a personal response to a visual just as they would to a piece of literature. Similarly, they can describe what they see, narrate the story depicted, or write persuasively about their aesthetic judgment of the painting or photo.

At a more significant level, however, students can explore analogies between the writing process and the creative processes of photography and painting. Opportunities to explore the process of composing a photograph or other visual message can help students discover principles that they can apply to their written compositions. Like a writer, a photographer must select a subject, a focus, and a point of view. Similarly, both photographers and writers create a mood—one through the choice of lighting and camera angles, the other through the choice of words and sentence structure.

The ultimate payoff from these visual-verbal approaches to instruction lies in helping students become more effective communicators and more discerning recipients of communication. As they come to recognize the parallels between written and visual communication, they become better equipped to apply critical thinking skills both in their reading and writing and in their viewing.

Writer's Choice provides points of entry to writing through visual exploration:

- Fine art and contemporary photography for stimulating thinking and writing
- Fine Art Overhead Transparencies for additional writing prompts
- Writing Process Overhead Transparencies for easy-to-use graphic organizers and revision models

WRITER'S CHOICE

GRAMMAR AND COMPOSITION

Student Advisory Board

Rose Vales

Socorro Ayala

John Moore

Chip Mulaney

April Andry

Magaly Fernandez

Kaeng Yang

Matt Cassel

WRITER'S CHOICE

GRAMMAR AND COMPOSITION

Pierre-Auguste Renoir, *The Reading,* 1892

Consulting Author for Composition
Jacqueline Jones Royster

Grammar Specialist
Mark Lester

Visual-Verbal Learning Specialists
Ligature, Inc.

GLENCOE

McGraw-Hill

New York, New York Columbus, Ohio Mission Hills, California Peoria, Illinois

Cover, Co Rentmeester/
The Image Bank, (inset)
Aaron Haupt.

Printed in the United States of America.

Send all inquiries to:
Glencoe/McGraw-Hill
936 Eastwind Drive
Westerville, Ohio
43081

ISBN 0-02-635872-7
(Student Edition)
ISBN 0-02-635873-5
(Teacher's Wraparound Edition)

3 4 5 6 7 8 9 10 VH/MCI 99 98 97 96

Consulting Author for Composition

Jacqueline Jones Royster is Associate Professor of English and Director of the University Writing Center at The Ohio State University. She is also on the faculty at the Bread Loaf School of English, Middlebury, Vermont. Dr. Royster's professional interests, besides improving the teaching of writing, include literacy studies and black feminist literature.

As Consulting Author, Dr. Royster guided the development of focused, modular lessons to engage middle school students in the writing process. She contributed to the articulation of the contents and objectives across all three levels, 6–8. Dr. Royster also prepared extensive critiques of lessons and features from initial outlines through all stages of development. In addition, Dr. Royster advised on elements of the accompanying teaching material, with special attention to assessment.

Grammar Specialist

Mark Lester is Professor of English at Eastern Washington University. He formerly served as Chair of the Department of English as a Second Language, University of Hawaii. He is the author of *Grammar in the Classroom* (Macmillan, 1990) and of numerous professional books and articles.

As Grammar Specialist, Dr. Lester reviewed student's edition material from Part 2: Grammar, Usage, and Mechanics and contributed extensively to the *Teacher's Wraparound Edition* for Part 2.

Composition Advisers

Philip M. Anderson is Associate Professor in the Department of Secondary Education and Youth Services at Queens College, City University of New York, where he is also Director of the English Education program.

Beverly Ann Chin is Professor of English at the University of Montana, where she is Director of Freshman Composition and Co-director of English Teacher Education. She is also Director of the Montana Writing Project and is active in NCTE, serving as President-Elect (1995–1996) and President (1996–1997).

Charleen Silva Delfino is District English Coordinator for the East Side Union High School District in San Jose, California. She is also Director of the Writing Project at San Jose University.

The advisers helped develop the tables of contents and determine pacing, emphasis, and activities appropriate for middle school students. They reviewed and commented on the manuscript for complete units.

Acknowledgments

Grateful acknowledgment is given authors, publishers, photographers, museums, and agents for permission to reprint the following copyrighted material. Every effort has been made to determine copyright owners. In case of omissions, the Publisher will make acknowledgments in future editions.
Continued on page 569

Humanities Consultant

Ronne Hartfield is Executive Director of Museum Education at the Art Institute of Chicago. Dr. Hartfield consults widely and is a nationally known expert in the areas of urban arts and multicultural education.

As Humanities Consultant, Dr. Hartfield suggested and critiqued works of fine art and folk art, pointing out esthetic matters (mentioned in the *Teacher's Wraparound Edition*) and suggesting activities for engaging the student's attention.

Visual-Verbal Learning Specialists

Ligature, Inc., is an educational research and development company with offices in Chicago and Boston. Ligature is committed to developing educational materials that bring visual-verbal learning to the tradition of the written word.

As visual-verbal and curriculum specialists, Ligature collaborated on conceiving and implementing the pedagogy of *Writer's Choice.*

Educational Reviewers

The reviewers read and commented upon manuscripts during the writing process. They also critiqued early drafts of graphic organizers and page layouts.

Toni Elaine Allison
Meridian Middle School
Meridian, Idaho

Amy Burton
Sterling Middle School
Fairfax, Virginia

Mary Ann Evans-Patrick
University of Wisconsin, Oshkosh
Oshkosh, Wisconsin

Marie Hammerle
Oak Creek Elementary School
Cornville, Arizona

Randy Hanson
Mapplewood Middle School
Menasha, Wisconsin

Geraldine Jackson
Mountain Gap Middle School
Huntsville, Alabama

Jeanne Kruger
Blair Middle School
Norfolk, Virginia

Diana McNeil
Pillans Middle School
Mobile, Alabama

Linda Miller
Lake Travis Middle School
Austin, Texas

Nadine Mouser
St. Thomas More School
Houston, Texas

Roslyn Newman
Woodland Middle School
East Meadow, New York

Evelyn Niles
Boys and Girls High School
Brooklyn, New York

Janet E. Ring
Dundee School District 300
Carpentersville, Illinois

Kathleen Oldfield
Main Street School
Waterloo, New York

Student Advisory Board

The Student Advisory Board was formed in an effort to ensure student involvement in the development of *Writer's Choice.* The editors wish to thank members of the board for their enthusiasm and dedication to the project.

The editors also wish to thank the many student writers whose models appear in this book.

Thanks are also due to *Merlyn's Pen* and *Cricket* for cooperation in providing student models.

Contents

Part 1 Composition

UNIT 1 Personal Writing

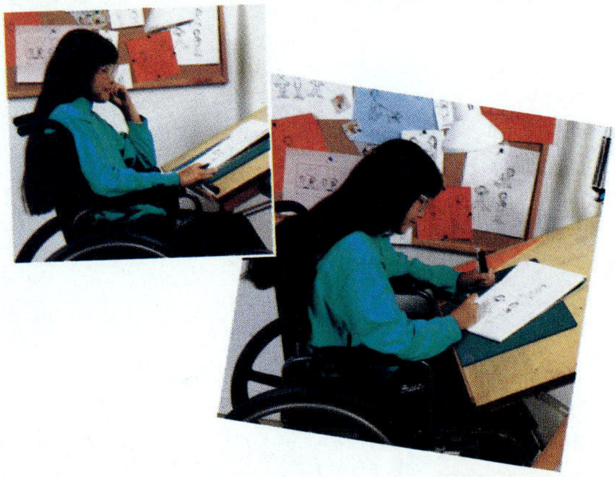

UNIT 2

The Writing Process

Grammar Link

Use correct punctuation at the ends of sentences.

Bernard put chicken and sausage into the gumbo. Is there a meatless version? . . . Those peppers even smell hot!

Write each sentence below, ending it with the correct punctuation mark.

1. Have you read the book *The Lion King*
2. How scary parts of it are
3. The book came out after the mo...

UNIT 3
Descriptive Writing

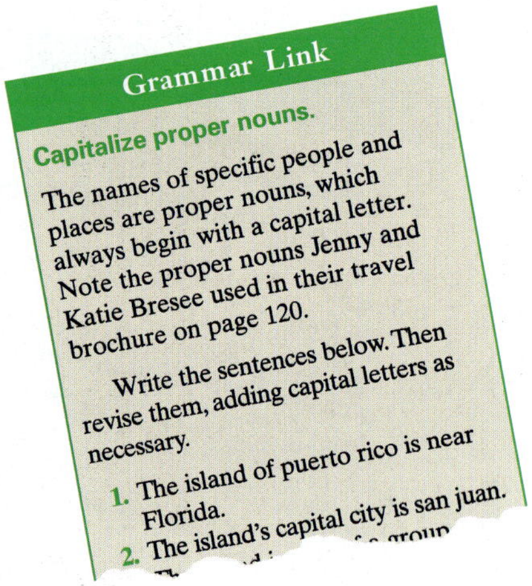
Grammar Link

Capitalize proper nouns.

The names of specific people and places are proper nouns, which always begin with a capital letter. Note the proper nouns Jenny and Katie Bresee used in their travel brochure on page 120.

Write the sentences below. Then revise them, adding capital letters as necessary.

1. The island of puerto rico is near Florida.
2. The island's capital city is san juan.

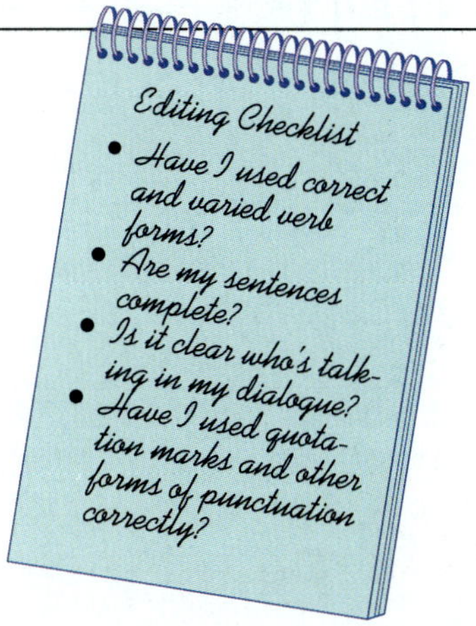

UNIT 4

Narrative Writing

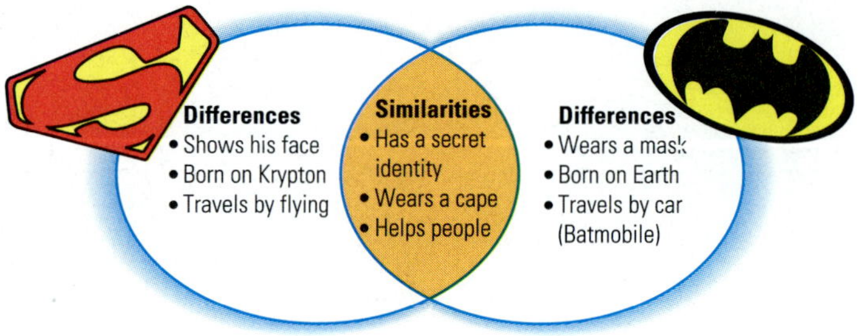

UNIT 5

Expository Writing

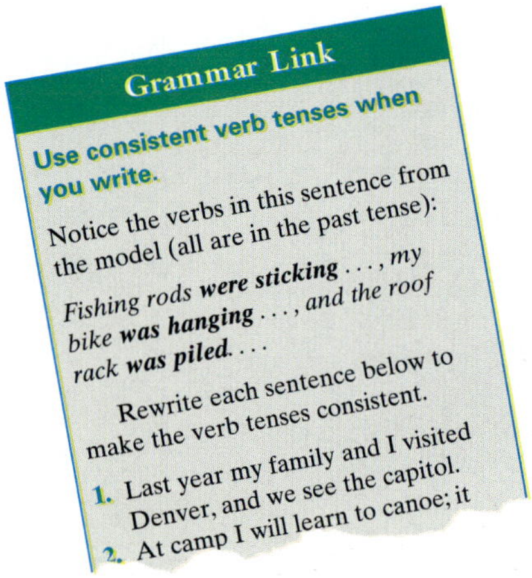
Grammar Link

Use consistent verb tenses when you write.

Notice the verbs in this sentence from the model (all are in the past tense):

*Fishing rods **were sticking** . . . , my bike **was hanging** . . . , and the roof rack **was piled**. . . .*

Rewrite each sentence below to make the verb tenses consistent.

1. Last year my family and I visited Denver, and we see the capitol.
2. At camp I will learn to canoe; it

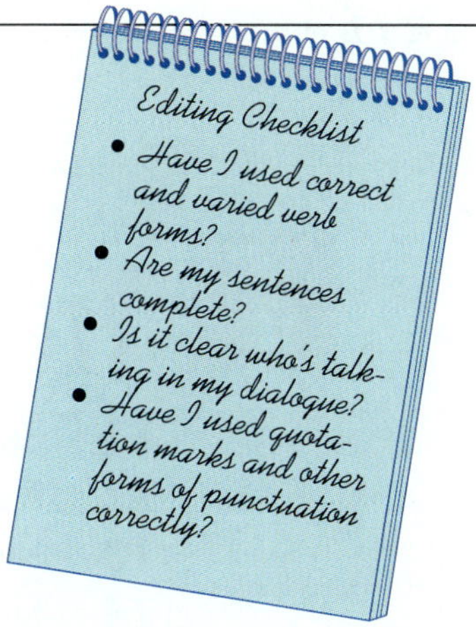

UNIT 6

Persuasive Writing

UNIT 7 Troubleshooter 241

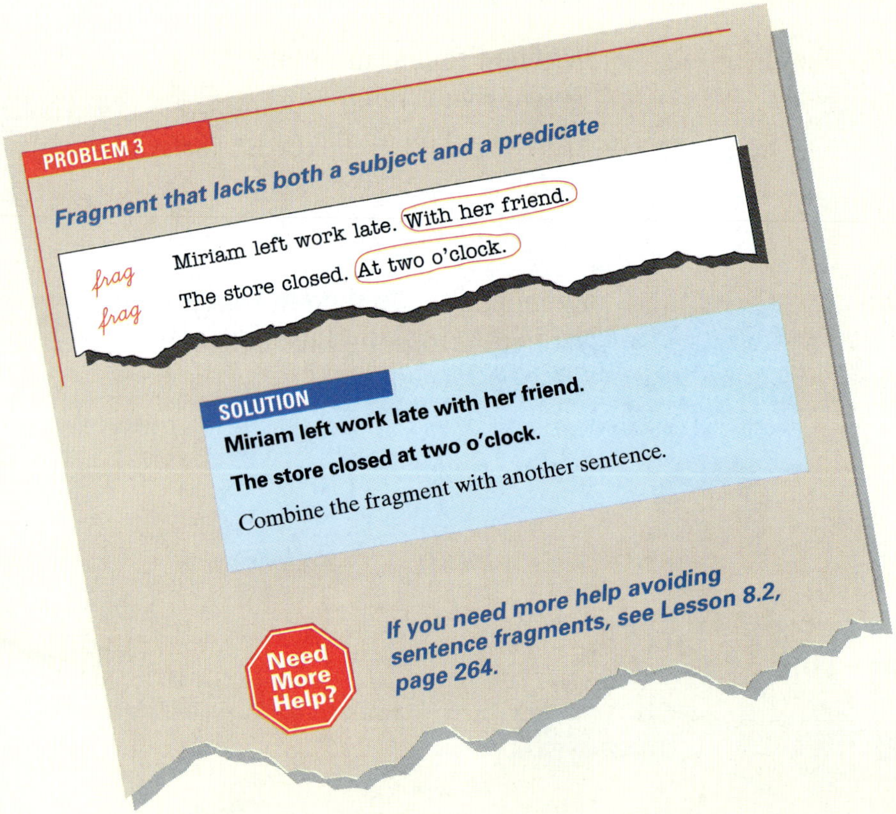

Part 2 Grammar, Usage, and Mechanics

UNIT 8 Subjects, Predicates, and Sentences 261

UNIT 9 Nouns 283

UNIT 10

Verbs

UNIT 11

Pronouns

Proofreading

UNIT 14 Prepositions, Conjunctions, and Interjections 379

UNIT 15 Subject-Verb Agreement 403

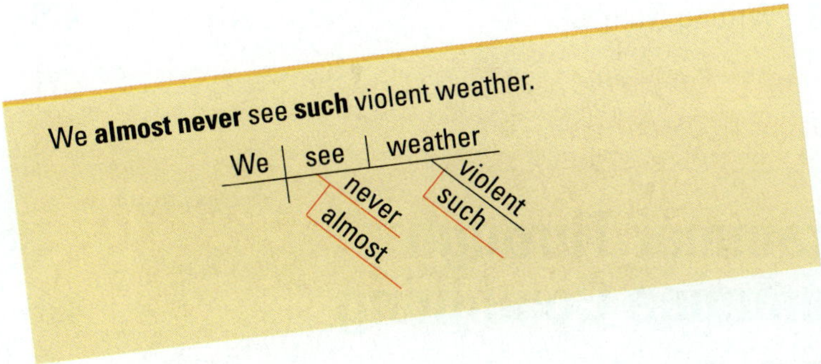
We **almost never** see **such** violent weather.
We
see
weather
never
almost
violent
such

Proofreading

UNIT 18 Capitalization 437

UNIT 19 Punctuation 453

UNIT 20 Grammar Through Sentence Combining 481

Part 3 Resources and Skills

Literature Models

Composition Models

Each literature selection is an extended example of the mode of writing taught in the unit.

Skill Models

Excerpts from outstanding works of fiction and nonfiction exemplify specific writing skills.

Language Models

Each Grammar Review uses excerpts to link grammar, usage, or mechanics to literature.

Fine Art

Fine art—paintings, drawings, photos, and sculpture—is used to teach as well as to stimulate writing ideas.

Case Studies: Writers at Work

Each case study focuses on a real writer working on a real-life writing project. Come on backstage!

Curtis Katz

Train Attendant
Travel Guide, *Katz Rides the* Empire Builder
Pages 38–43

Bill Pinkney

Adventurer
Travel Journal, *Pinkney Records a Round-the-World Voyage*
Pages 4–9

John Boulanger

Wildlife Biologist
Descriptive Writing, *Boulanger Describes Nunataks*
Pages 92–97

Julie Sheer, Steve Cvengros, and Dennis Odom

***Chicago Tribune* Team**
Expository Graphic, Tribune *Explores Hang Time*
Pages 172–177

Virginia Hamilton

Author
Biography, *Hamilton Narrates a Life*
Pages 134–139

Doug Anderson

Television Writer
Television Program, *Anderson Fights for the Planet*
Pages 210–215

Part 1

Composition

Part 1 Composition

UNIT
1 Personal Writing

Composition | **Lessons**

3

UNIT GOALS

The goal of Unit 1 is to help students, through example and instruction, to develop an understanding of themselves through personal writing. The lessons focus on a journal, a friendly letter, and a poem. In the Case Study, Bill Pinkney explores through personal writing his adventures on the high seas.

Unit Assessment

Tests with Answer Key
Unit 1 Choice A Test, p. 1
Unit 1 Choice B Test, p. 2
Unit 1 Composition Objective Test, pp. 3–4

Test Generator
Unit 1 Choice A Test
Unit 1 Choice B Test
Unit 1 Composition Objective Test

You may wish to administer either the Unit 1 Choice A Test or the Unit 1 Choice B Test as a pretest.

Key to Ability Levels

Enabling Strategies have been coded for varying learning styles and abilities.

L1 Level 1 activities are within the ability range of Learning Disabled students.

L2 Level 2 activities are basic-to-average activities and are within the ability range of average students.

L3 Level 3 activities are challenging activities and are within the ability range of above-average students.

LEP LEP activities are within the ability range of Limited English Proficiency students.

Setting the Purpose

In the Unit 1 Case Study, students examine the use of personal writing in a journal kept by a man sailing solo around the world. Students will explore and practice personal writing in the lessons that follow.

FOCUS

Lesson Overview

Objective: To explore how personal writing can be used to relate meaningful events from one's life
Skills: analyzing; discussing; writing journal entries
Critical Thinking: recalling; visualizing; evaluating; defining and clarifying
Speaking and Listening: discussing; questioning

Bellringer

When students enter the classroom, have this assignment on the board: *Write four sentences about four trips you have made. The trips might be to distant or nearby places.*

Grammar Link to the Bellringer

Ask students to consider how much a reader would learn from their sentences. Have they created clear pictures? Ask them to underline the nouns in their sentences and try to replace them with more specific nouns.

Motivating Activity

Invite students to reexamine their four sentences and decide which trip they would most like to write about. Ask these questions:
- Which trip meant the most to you personally?
- Can you recall your thoughts and feelings at the time?
- Could you put those thoughts and feelings into words?

UNIT 1 PREVIEW
Case Study

Personal Writing
in the Real World

Pinkney Records a Round-the-World Voyage

FOCUS: Just as explorers discover the world, writers explore life experiences in a personal journal.

On February 13, 1992, former Chicago businessman Bill Pinkney held a party like no party you've ever seen. Pinkney was the only person there—on board the *Commitment*, a 47-foot, single-masted sailboat. His party site? The rough seas between the stormy tip of South America and the northernmost finger of Antarctica.

Why was Pinkney celebrating? After more than a year alone at sea, he had just rounded Cape Horn. It was the last of the five southern capes he passed on his 32,000-mile, round-the-world voyage.

◄ *Adventurer Bill Pinkney*

4

Teacher's Classroom Resources

The following resources can be used for planning, instruction, practice, reinforcement, assessment, or evaluation.

Teaching Tools
Lesson Plans

Transparencies
Writing Process Transparencies 1–10

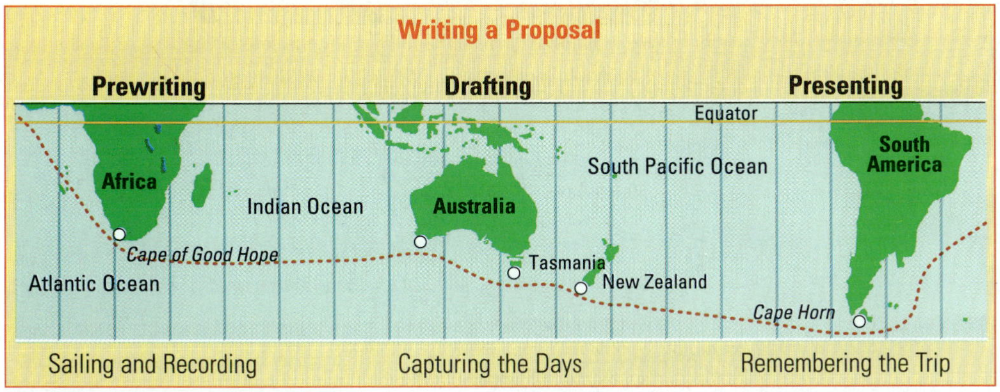

Prewriting

SAILING AND RECORDING

Pinkney set sail from Boston on August 5, 1990. Traveling southeastward, he rode the winds to Bermuda and Brazil. After crossing the Atlantic to the Cape of Good Hope, South Africa, he headed to Cape Leeuwin, Australia, and South East Cape, Tasmania. From there, Pinkney slipped around South West Cape, New Zealand. Across the Pacific was Pinkney's final goal—Cape Horn. Rounding Cape Horn is one of the most dangerous feats a solo sailor can perform. Once he rounded the Cape, Pinkney sprinted home, arriving 22 months after he began.

> *"I wanted to do something that would have a lasting effect on how I'm remembered. . . . The method I chose was to sail around the five great capes."*
>
> —Bill Pinkney

What was it like to sail this route all alone? "There was no such thing as a typical day," Pinkney said. Good weather or bad, Pinkney rarely became bored. He spent hours fixing sails, cooking, reading, and navigating. He also taped videos for friends, family, and

TEACH

Building Background

Warm-up:
Ask students to list as many occasions as they can in which personal writing might be used.

Personal Reports in Speaking:
Invite students to tell how they use personal reports in their everyday speech, such as when they recount a school triumph (or disaster) to their family at home or perhaps tell a friend about their first attempt at skateboarding.

Personal Reports in Writing:
Discuss any personal writing students have read. You might ask:

- Have you ever read a book or magazine article that told about personal experiences? Did it describe the author's feelings rather than just recite facts?
- Have you ever received a letter from a friend who was on vacation? Did it make the place vivid to you? Did it express your friend's reactions?

Preview the Case Study

Call students' attention to the title and focus of the case study. Point out that recording a trip or other adventure in a journal is one of the most interesting kinds of personal writing. Have students read the case study.

Blackline Masters
Cooperative Learning Activities, pp. 1–6
Thinking and Study Skills, pp. 2–3
Case Studies: Writing in the Real World, pp.1–4

Assessment

Teacher's Guide to Writing Assessment

TEACH

Discussion Prompts

- If you were recording a sailing adventure as Pinkney did, what could you show on a videotape that you couldn't tell in writing? What could you tell in a journal entry that you couldn't show on videotape?
- How would a daily journal create a more accurate picture of an adventure than a journal that recorded only exciting moments?

Friday, February 7 52° 56' S 85° 42' W
I sat in my cocoon (my bunk) and went through all the photos I have on board. The sights and memories made an otherwise grey day a warm and joyful time. It is difficult sometimes to grasp the full scope of the experiences, places and people that have filled my life over the last five to six years.

students in Chicago and Boston who were tracking his trip. Just as important, Pinkney kept a daily account of the trip.

Between Boston and Tasmania, Pinkney recorded most of his experiences on videotape. But in Tasmania a friend gave him "a very fancy daily diary book." From Tasmania onward, it was in this book that Pinkney wrote his daily journal entries.

Drafting

CAPTURING THE DAYS

▲ *Pinkney's travel-worn journal was a gift from a friend in Tasmania.*

After leaving Tasmania, Pinkney hit a string of rough days. Still a month from Cape Horn, he had rough weather and tense moments with the boat. He wrote about many of these moments in his journal. He usually wrote at the navigation station—the nerve center of the boat.

In his entry for January 15, 1992, Pinkney describes a problem with the mainsail. In stormy, dangerous seas he crawled onto the boom to sew a corner of the sail onto a slide in the mast. He also noted his sense of achievement in solving the problem.

In his journal entries Pinkney also recorded the

Beyond the Classroom

Setting Goals

When Pinkney addressed a welcoming crowd at the end of his trip, he mentioned the negative statistics about urban African American men: "I did this to disprove the statistical information. … I'm 57, but when I was 25, the odds were good that I'd be in jail, on drugs, or dead. The thing is, I didn't believe that." Pinkney is a good role model for people who wish to succeed despite the odds. Ask students to name other people they think of as role models. What goals of their own could students aim for?

latitude and longitude of his location. Sometimes, Pinkney says, he drew pictures "of events that happened on a regular basis." These included sightings of whales, dolphins, and ships.

As January eased into February, Pinkney neared Cape Horn, and conditions began to improve. On February 13, Pinkney's dream came true. That night, in pitch blackness, he rounded Cape Horn.

"The day wasn't very eventful," he recalled. "The anticipation of getting to the Cape was great, and I had in my mind exactly when I was going to arrive. But the weather was getting bad, and my radar went out. I wanted to pass close enough to be able to see the light; it's only visible for about five or six miles. But, because I lost my radar, I couldn't figure my distance, so I kept a general track in an area that would keep me well off. If I wasn't careful, the weather would have blown me up on the Cape."

Pinkney didn't see the Cape Horn light, but he did glimpse the Cape the next morning. "I was exhilarated," Pinkney recalled. "I had completed my mission—I had passed all five capes."

Later Pinkney entered the moment in his journal. "The dream is fulfilled," he wrote. "Not without pain, fear, depression, and anger. But also with love, faith, determination, and humor. I only caught a glimpse of the great 'Rock,' but it will stay in my mind forever."

For Bill Pinkney sighting Cape Horn was an unforgettable experience.

TEACH

Discussion Prompts

- Pinkney faced a challenge when his radar went out as he approached Cape Horn. Do you think he responded intelligently? What else might he have done? How might the outcome have been different?
- Pinkney recorded his rounding of Cape Horn in his journal at some length. What value is there—to the writer and to readers—in making a full record of thoughts and feelings rather than writing only a brief, factual report?

Connections Across the Curriculum

Science

Invite interested students to find out more about how sailors communicate over long distances while at sea (by radio satellite). Some students might look for information at the library and then share their findings with the class. Other students might wish to find out more about how sailors determine their position with the help of radar and loran. Have them look up *radar* and *loran* in the dictionary to learn how these words were coined. (***ra***dio ***d***etecting ***a***nd ***r***anging; ***lo***ng ***ra***nge ***n***avigation)

TEACH

Guided Reading

L2 Discussion
Stimulate a discussion of the case study. You may want to invite students to talk about

- whether they would prefer to take a long trip by land, sea, or air, and what types of experiences they would hope to have
- what books they would want to read on a long solo journey, and what music they would listen to
- whether they would keep a daily journal, write letters, or choose some other form of personal writing, and what sorts of experiences they would record
- how they might wish to make use of their personal writing when the journey was over

Independent Practice

Writing Process Transparencies 1–10
Case Studies: Writing in the Real World, pp. 1–4
Cooperative Learning Activities, pp. 1–6

Skills Practice
Thinking and Study Skills, pp. 2–3

Presenting

REMEMBERING THE TRIP

Sailing swiftly north from Cape Horn, Pinkney finished his trip about four months later. He arrived in Chicago to a hometown hero's welcome early in June 1992. Pinkney was the first African American to sail solo around the five capes.

In Pinkney's mind, commitment made his success possible. "Commitment is not only saying you're going to do something," Pinkney said. "It's also saying you're going to do it in spite of whatever else happens."

"When I started this trip, the object was to finish, and there were days when I would have liked to quit. But I knew that I owed it to myself to stick to my commitment, because once I had done it, no one could ever take the accomplishment away from me."

Thanks to his journal, Pinkney also knew he would never lose the moments that made up his life's greatest adventure. "Every time you read your journal you get to do the good things all over again," Pinkney said. "You're able to really take a portion of your life and your feelings and hold them for all time."

◄ *Pinkney named his boat* Commitment. *What would you name your boat? Why?*

Cooperative Learning

Sharing "Likes" and "Dislikes"
Divide the class into small groups. Ask the groups to discuss what they think they would like and dislike about traveling around the world alone in a sailboat. Students should take turns sharing their thoughts. Groups can complete a pair of lists, one of "likes" and one of "dislikes," which they can refer to as they write a pretend letter to Bill Pinkney. Ask volunteers to read their group's letter aloud to the class.

Responding to the Case Study

1. Discussion

Discuss these questions about Bill Pinkney's personal writing.

- How did Pinkney record his experiences during his long voyage? Why did he record them?
- What kind of information did Pinkney include in his journal?
- Name some emotions Pinkney felt during the voyage. What might have caused them?
- What value does Pinkney say the journal is to him now that his trip is over?

2. Personal Writing

Write a travel journal entry. Think about an overnight journey you have made, close to home or far away. The photos on this page may give you some ideas. Jot down what was most memorable about the trip. Write a travel journal entry for the most memorable day of your trip. Tell what you did or saw. Also tell how you felt about the experience. Draw some pictures if you can.

Grammar Link

Use specific nouns to create clear pictures.

Some nouns are not very specific. For example, the word *book* doesn't tell much. Bill Pinkney uses the specific nouns *diary* and *journal.*

In each sentence below replace two nouns or pronouns with more specific nouns. (You may need to make other changes, too.)

1. They went to the museum in a vehicle.
2. Plants lined the way to the building.
3. Inside, a woman helped them find places.
4. The adults liked an exhibit on weather.
5. The others liked the exhibits about animals best.

See Lesson 9.1, page 284.

ASSESS

Responding to the Case Study

1. Discussion

- in his journal and on videotape; to relive and share his experiences
- daily events, great moments, reactions, boat's location, drawings
- pain, fear, depression, anger, caused by danger, bad weather, aloneness; also exhilaration and sense of achievement caused by determination and final success
- lets him keep his adventures and feelings for all time

2. Personal Writing

Students' journal entries will vary but should reveal an individual point of view and should describe not only events but their reactions as well.

See also the *Teacher's Guide to Writing Assessment.*

Grammar Link

(See Using the Grammar Link below.)

Reteaching

Encourage students to talk to a close friend about a personal goal and how they hope to achieve it.

Enrichment

Invite students to trace Pinkney's route on the map on page 5, naming the continent in which each cape is located.

CLOSE

Have students discuss how they could use a journal to record a mental journey from confusion to understanding.

Closing Note

The Boy Who Sailed Around the World Alone, by Robin Lee Graham, has photographs and logbook entries.

Using the Grammar Link

Grammar Link Answers

Answers will vary, but samples are given below.

1. They went to the Science Museum in a school bus.
2. Tulips lined the sidewalk to the planetarium.

Using Specific Nouns Have students rewrite the following sentence to make it more specific: *The man in the boat ran into bad weather and had an accident.*

Setting the Purpose

Lesson 1.1 teaches students that personal writing can be an excellent vehicle for exploring one's thoughts and feelings and for sharing them with others. Students explore freewriting as a way of getting started.

FOCUS

Lesson Overview

Objective: To express thoughts and feelings in a piece of personal writing
Skills: using freewriting to explore ideas; expressing oneself
Critical Thinking: relating personal feelings; generating new information
Speaking and Listening: discussing

Bellringer

When students enter the classroom, have this assignment on the board: *List three activities that fit your personal idea of adventure, and list three thoughts or feelings that you associate with each of those activities. Examples:*

ski jumping—skill, thrill, fear;
reading fiction—understanding, escape, emotion

Grammar Link to the Bellringer

Ask students to substitute pronouns for nouns in the second of these two sentences: *Joseph tried ski jumping for the first time last winter. Joseph loved ski jumping.* Remind students to use pronouns in writing, just as they do in conversation.

Motivating Activity

Students will probably find that their personal ideas of adventure vary greatly. Tell them that, as with other activities they engage in, writing is a way of showing who they are.

LESSON 1.1

Personal Writing

Writing as Self-Expression

Your personal writing expresses the real you. Through personal writing, you can look at yourself, share your feelings with others, or explore your ideas.

You can show any side of yourself in your personal writing, just as you can among friends. Sometimes you might write just for yourself. At other times you might decide to share your writing with others.

Personal writing can also be a way to look at yourself on paper. As the model below shows, novelist Terry McMillan discovered that writing a poem could cheer her up.

Literature Model

I did not sit down and say, "I'm going to write a poem about this." It was more like magic. I didn't even know I was writing a poem until I had written it. Afterward, I felt lighter, as if something had happened to lessen the pain. And when I read this "thing" I was shocked because I didn't know where the words came from. I was scared, to say the least, about what I had just experienced, because I didn't understand what had happened.

Terry McMillan, *Breaking Ice*

Teacher's Classroom Resources

The following resources can be used for planning, instruction, practice, reinforcement, assessment, reteaching, enrichment, or evaluation.

Teaching Tools
Lesson Plans

Transparencies
Fine Art Transparencies 1–5
Writing Process Transparencies 1–10

Blackline Masters
Thinking and Study Skills, pp. 3, 5–6
Writing Across the Curriculum, p. 11
Cooperative Learning Activities, pp. 1–6
Speaking and Listening Activities, pp. 14–15

Write to Express Yourself

Sometimes personal writing can sound like talking to your best friend. When you write about your own experiences, ideas, and interests, just let your ideas come out naturally, as they do in a conversation. Here's one example.

How does Angie make her writing sound friendly?

What details does Angie use to create lively pictures for Sara?

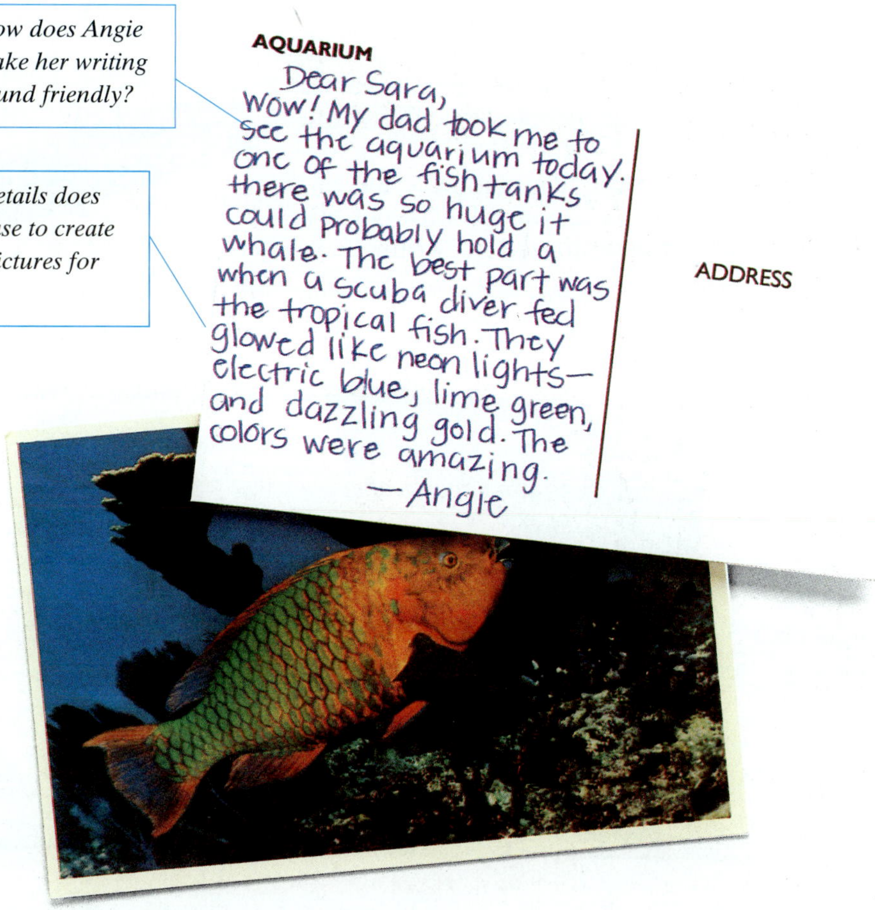

Like spending a night in the woods, personal writing can be an adventure. It can be a way of exploring the world around you. Best of all, writing can help you explore your own thoughts and feelings.

TEACH

Guided Practice

L2 Using the Model

Note for students that in the Literature Model on page 10, Terry McMillan honestly expresses her feelings. She says that her writing made her feel both "scared" and "shocked." Nevertheless, she made a discovery—that writing could make her feel better, too. Point out that students can use writing to make discoveries and explore their thoughts and feelings.

L1 Making It Personal

Call students' attention to the personal quality of the letter on page 11. Angie creates lively pictures by using vivid modifiers—"electric blue," "lime green," "dazzling gold." The use of "Wow!" as an exclamation and the inclusion of personal feelings makes her writing sound friendly.

Two-Minute Skill Drill

List these activities on the board. Have students list three or more ideas or feelings that each activity suggests to them.

watching movies	camping
beachcombing	flying

Journal Writing Tip

Identifying Topics Encourage students to identify the part of their writing that they personally find the most interesting. Remind them that that is likely to interest other readers, too, and may be the most effective way to write about themselves.

Composition Practice, p. 1
Composition Reteaching, p. 1
Composition Enrichment, p. 1

Unit Assessment

Teacher's Guide to Writing Assessment

Tests with Answer Key
Unit 1 Choice A Test, p. 1
Unit 1 Choice B Test, p. 2

Test Generator
Unit 1 Choice A Test
Unit 1 Choice B Test

You may wish to administer either the Unit 1 Choice A Test or the Unit 1 Choice B Test as a pretest.

TEACH

Guided Practice

L2 Using the Model

In the model on page 12, a student uses a favorite topic—volcanoes—to get him started freewriting. He is interested in the physical aspects of volcanoes as well as in the folklore surrounding them. Tell students that by exploring topics of personal interest, they'll find they have more to say.

L1 Getting Started

If students have difficulty thinking of a topic, remind them that freewriting lets them get their thoughts down on paper in whatever order they occur. If students get stuck, urge them to keep writing—even if they repeat themselves or write things that do not seem interesting. Assure them that one idea can lead to another and another until a good topic presents itself.

Independent Practice

For further stimuli for personal writing, see *Fine Art Transparencies* 1–5.

Writing Process Transparencies 1–10

Writing Across the Curriculum, p. 11

Cooperative Learning Activities, pp. 1–6

Skills Practice

Speaking and Listening Activities, pp. 14–15

Thinking and Study Skills, pp. 3, 5–6

Composition Practice, p. 1

Freewrite to Explore Ideas

One of the easiest ways to express yourself in writing is through freewriting. When you freewrite, you explore your thoughts on paper. You don't have to worry about punctuation, spelling, or even making sense. You just start writing—and keep writing, nonstop, for a few minutes. See where your thoughts lead you.

Ideas for freewriting can come from almost anywhere— games, movies, people, or your favorite activity after school. Take a look at the student model to the right. Can you tell what got this student started freewriting?

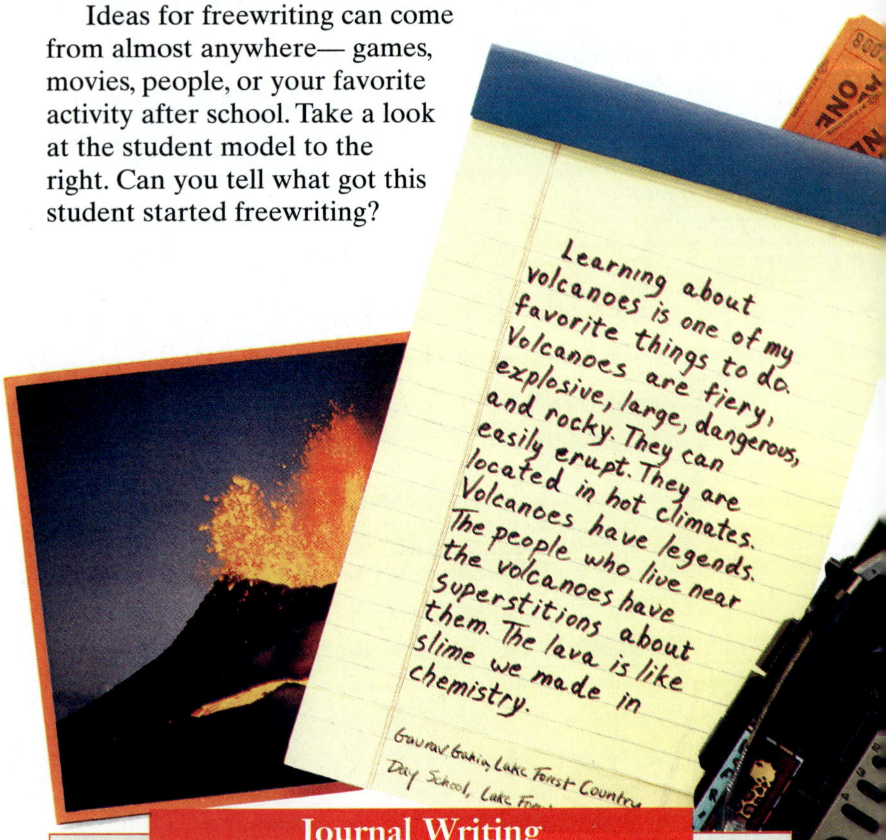

Journal Writing

Think back on something that happened to you today. Freewrite about it for five minutes. When you finish, look back over your writing. What ideas from your freewriting could you write more about?

Enabling Strategies

LEP Using Two Languages

Suggest that students who find writing in English difficult switch to their native language for a word or two if they get stuck during freewriting. Once they have found an interesting focus for their writing, encourage them to use English. Remind them that they do not need to worry about correct spelling or punctuation until they have finished the exercise. Then they can work with the teacher or another student to revise and edit the piece.

1.1 Writing Activities

Write a Personal Response

Study the people in the painting. What activities do you see them doing? Does the painting remind you of anything in your life? Freewrite for five minutes about whatever comes into your mind when you look at the painting.

- Write what you see.
- Write what you think and feel.
- Use words that create specific images.

PURPOSE To express personal thoughts and feelings
AUDIENCE Yourself
LENGTH Write for five minutes

Cross-Curricular: Geography

Pick a place on the globe that you've visited or would like to visit. Write a postcard or letter to a friend; describe your real or imaginary adventures there. Try to give a specific feeling of what the place is like.

Grammar Link

Replace nouns with the correct forms of pronouns in your writing.

The best part was . . . the tropical fish. ***They*** *[the fish] glowed . . . .*

Rewrite the sentences below, replacing the underlined words with pronouns.

1. Jeff and I went to the aquarium.
2. We looked at the tropical fish.
3. The fish were in huge tanks.
4. Jeff has his own tropical fish.
5. The fish were a present to Jeff.

See Lesson 11.1, page 326, and Lesson 11.2, page 328.

Maurcie Brazil Prendergast, *Promenade,* 1914–1915

ASSESS

Writing Activities Evaluation Guidelines

Write a Personal Response

Use these criteria when evaluating your students' writing.

- Does the student's writing clearly relate to the painting shown?
- Does the student's writing describe actual experiences and honest reactions?
- Does the student's writing create specific images?
- Does the student's writing give evidence of sustained writing for a five-minute period?

See also the *Teacher's Guide to Writing Assessment.*

Cross-Curricular: Geography

Consider the following as you evaluate each student's work.

- Does the writing sound like the student who wrote it?
- Are personal observations and experiences included?
- Does it give a feeling of what the place is like?

Grammar Link

(See Using the Grammar Link below.)

Reteaching

Composition Reteaching, p. 1

Enrichment

Composition Enrichment, p. 1

Use *Fine Art Transparencies* 1–5 for enrichment activities also.

CLOSE

Have volunteers read aloud postcards they wrote for the Cross-Curricular assignment. Have the class discuss whether the postcards give a good picture of the writer and whether they make the place interesting.

Using the Grammar Link

Grammar Link Answers

1. *We* went to the aquarium.
2. We looked at *them.*
3. *They* were in huge tanks.
4. *He* has his own tropical fish.
5. The fish were a present to *him.*

About the Art

Maurice Brazil Prendergast, *Promenade,* 1914–1915
Maurice Prendergast (1858–1924) often painted scenes of people in public places, especially at the seaside. This mural-sized work, 89-by-134 inches, hangs in the Detroit Institute of Art.

Setting the Purpose

Lesson 1.2 teaches students how to explore their ideas in a journal or learning log.

FOCUS

Lesson Overview

Objective: To begin a personal journal or learning log
Skills: keeping a journal; expressing ideas in writing
Critical Thinking: defining and clarifying; decision-making
Speaking and Listening: discussing, listening to oral reading

Bellringer

When students enter the classroom, have this assignment on the board: *List three good reasons why a person might want to keep a journal.*

Grammar Link to the Bellringer

Ask students to write sentences ranking their three reasons for keeping a journal. Which reason is good, which is better, and which is best?

Motivating Activity

Ask students if they have ever kept a journal. Encourage them to discuss the reasons they gave in the Bellringer for keeping journals. Explain that various kinds of journals are kept for different purposes. What most have in common is that they explore and record personal experiences, thoughts, and feelings. Tell students that, although journal writing may seem awkward at first, the more they do it, the more natural it will become.

LESSON **1.2**

Personal Writing

Writing with Confidence

A personal journal is meant just for you. You may choose to share it, however. Journal writing doesn't need to be formal. What is important is putting your thoughts on paper.

Like anything else you learn to do, writing seems more natural the more you do it. The more you write, the more confident you'll feel.

One way to build your writing confidence is to keep a personal journal. A journal is usually a notebook or a binder in which you write regularly. It is a place for you to write whatever you want. Look at the journal below. What kinds of things does this writer put in a journal?

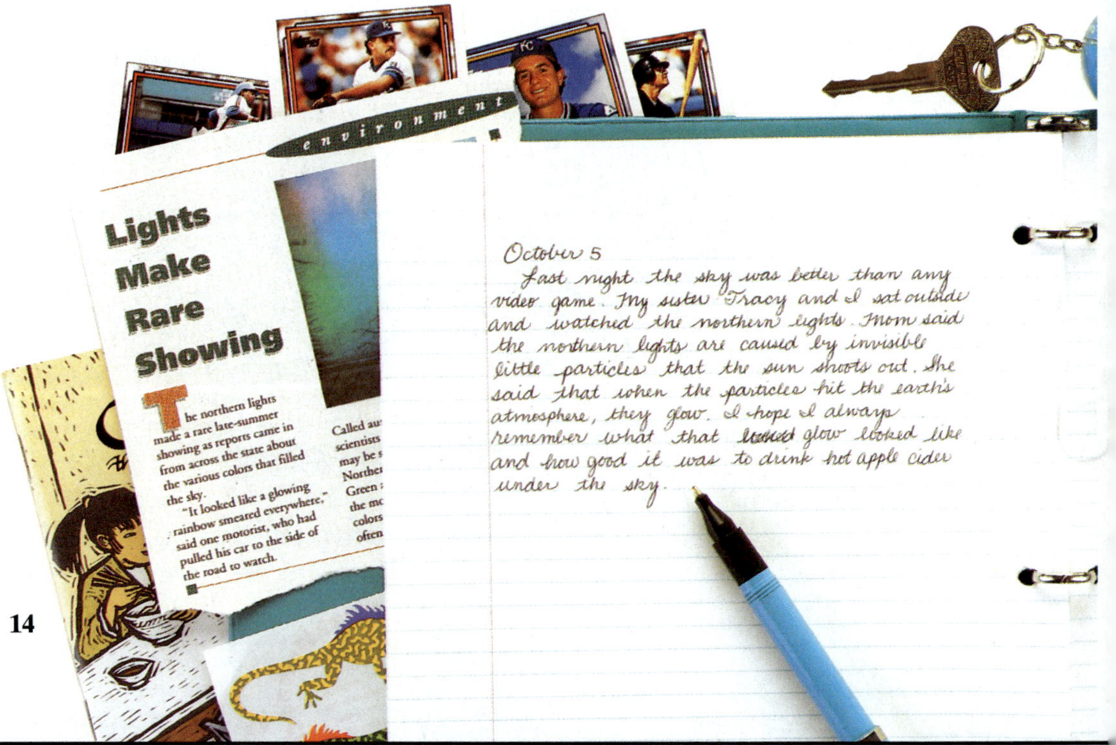

14

Teacher's Classroom Resources

The following resources can be used for planning, instruction, practice, reinforcement, assessment, reteaching, enrichment, or evaluation.

Teaching Tools
Lesson Plans

Transparencies
Fine Art Transparencies 1–5
Writing Process Transparencies 1–10

Keep a Journal

Your journal is a place where you can take risks with your writing. You might jot down notes about daily events, write poems, or just doodle. You might use your journal to collect things like photos, newspaper clippings, or ticket stubs. You can write about new and different ideas, personal feelings, and special memories. Sometimes you might invite others to share your thoughts and feelings. Here are a few suggestions on keeping a journal:

- Use a notebook or binder that you enjoy writing in.
- Write regularly, even if only for 10 minutes a day.
- Date each entry. Dates can help you find specific entries later.
- Write about whatever you want. Your journal is a place to think freely. Nobody is going to grade you on what you say or how you say it.

Journal Writing

Write down some ideas for things you could write about in a personal journal. They could be an activity you take part in, an experience you have had, or an idea you're thinking about. Remember, you can write about anything that is important to you.

TEACH

Guided Practice

L2 Using the Model

Ask students what may have prompted the journal entry on page 14 (seeing the northern lights, reading about the phenomenon). In this entry the writer reveals what made the experience special (beauty, seeing a rare event, sharing time with family).

Introduce the idea that students can make use of past journal entries when gathering ideas for new projects.

L1 Using Images

How to keep a journal is a personal choice. Students more comfortable with images than words may prefer to keep a scrapbook in which they draw and collect items of personal interest. They might then include brief captions for each item, working toward longer and longer written entries.

Two-Minute Skill Drill

List these events on the board. Have students write which they would use to record each: travel journal, personal journal, or learning log.

birthday party	music lessons
train trip	history class

Journal Writing Tip

Journal Options Remind students that journals can be used in many ways: To record daily events, reactions to a class, or thoughts about personal relationships; even to play with words, write stories, poems, or song lyrics.

Blackline Masters

Thinking and Study Skills, pp. 2, 5
Writing Across the Curriculum, p. 11
Cooperative Learning Activities, pp. 1–6
Speaking and Listening Activities, pp. 14–15
Composition Practice, p. 2
Composition Reteaching, p. 2
Composition Enrichment, p. 2

Assessment

Teacher's Guide to Writing Assessment

TEACH

Guided Practice

L2 Keeping a Daily Journal

If students find it difficult to write in their journals consistently, suggest that they keep the journal with them throughout the day, so they can jot down ideas as they occur. They might carry a pocket-sized notebook for this purpose. Or they could set aside a specific time for writing each day, such as during a free period or before bed. Suggest that they set a goal of writing for three minutes a day for the first week, six minutes for the next, working up to writing for ten minutes a day.

L3 Beginning a Learning Log

Invite students to select a school subject—perhaps the one that interests them most or one they find difficult—and begin a learning log, keeping it for two weeks or for the length of time that a particular topic is being taught. Then they can consider whether the learning log was useful enough that they wish to continue using it.

Independent Practice

- For further stimuli for personal writing, see *Fine Art Transparencies* 1–5.
- *Writing Process Transparencies* 1–10
- *Writing Across the Curriculum,* p. 11
- *Cooperative Learning Activities,* pp. 1–6

Skills Practice

- *Thinking and Study Skills,* pp. 2, 5
- *Speaking and Listening Activities,* pp. 14–15
- *Composition Practice,* p. 2

Use a Journal to Help You Study

You can use a type of journal called a learning log to help you study. A learning log is a place to write about what you are studying. It's just for you; no one else will read it.

Learning Log	
Purpose	**Entry**
Summarize.	After Herbert Hoover won the 1928 election, there were signs of economic problems. In 1929, the stock market crashed, marking the beginning of the Great Depression.
Highlight main ideas.	During this time, Americans were going too deeply into debt.
Define problems.	I still don't understand how the economy and the stock market are related.
Ask questions.	Why didn't anyone see the signs and do something before the market crashed?

Enabling Strategies

LEP Talking About Writing

Students whose first language is not English may benefit from talking about their writing with a friend. Some students might feel more comfortable paired with a student of similar linguistic background. Others might benefit more from talking with a classmate fluent in English.

1.2 Writing Activities

Write a Journal Entry

Think about all of the things that have happened to you yesterday or today—either in or out of school. Write a journal entry for one of those days. It might be an entry for a personal journal or it might be a learning log entry.

Begin your entry in any way you choose. If you wish, you may illustrate your entry with drawings or items similar to the ones mentioned on page 15.

- Write the date for the journal entry.
- Write about whatever you want.
- Use your own words.

PURPOSE To explore ideas through journal writing
AUDIENCE Yourself
LENGTH 2–4 paragraphs

COMPUTER OPTION

You may wish to keep your personal journal or your learning log on a computer. Many computer programs allow you to set up secured files. You can open secured files only with a secret password. Putting your journal entries in a secured file saves them "for your eyes only." The information that came with your software will provide directions for setting up a password.

Grammar Link

Use forms of *good* correctly in your writing.

The journal entry on page 14 begins with this statement:

Last night the sky was ***better*** *than any video game.*

Use *good*, *better*, or *best* to complete each sentence below.

1. Our soccer team is having a ______ year.
2. Of the three players, Jan is the ______ goalie.
3. I am quite ______ at defense.
4. Les is ______ than I am at long kicks.
5. The coach thinks we will do ______ than we did last season.
6. Saturday we play the ______ team in the league.
7. We hope to play ______ than we did last week.
8. Rosa is our ______ scorer.
9. Mr. Chen does a ______ job coaching the team.
10. We hope to end up with the ______ record in the league.

See Lesson 12.3, page 348, and Lesson 12.4, page 350.

ASSESS

Writing Activities Evaluation Guidelines

Write a Journal Entry

Use these criteria when evaluating your students' writing.

- Does the entry reveal personal thoughts and feelings?
- Does the entry show developing confidence in writing?
- Does the entry experiment with a personal writing style, perhaps including images or scrapbook items?
- Does the entry include a date?

See also the *Teacher's Guide to Writing Assessment.*

Computer Option

Encourage students to choose a password that will not be easily guessed but that they will not forget. Make sure they understand how to set up a secured file.

Grammar Link

(See Using the Grammar Link below.)

Reteaching

Composition Reteaching, p. 2

Enrichment

Composition Enrichment, p. 2

CLOSE

Invite volunteers to share their journal entries with the class. Have the class discuss the entries. Did they get any new ideas about journal writing? Did the students who shared their entries benefit from the feedback?

Using the Grammar Link

Grammar Link Answers

1. Our soccer team is having a *good* year.
2. Of the three players, Jan is the *best* goalie.
3. I am quite *good* at defense.
4. Les is *better* than I am at long kicks.
5. The coach thinks we will do *better* than we did last season.

Using Other Comparatives Other common modifiers have irregular comparative forms.

bad	worse	worst
many	more	most

Have students practice using these words in sentences.

Setting the Purpose

Lesson 1.3 teaches students that friendly letters can be used as a means of making and extending personal connections.

FOCUS

Lesson Overview

Objective: To write a friendly letter to share personal thoughts and feelings
Skills: expressing thoughts and feelings; writing the five main parts of a friendly letter
Critical Thinking: relating thoughts and feelings
Speaking and Listening: discussing

Bellringer

When students enter the classroom, have this assignment on the board: *Compare talking on the telephone to writing a letter to a friend. Write a short paragraph about why people might write letters and why people might use the telephone.*

Grammar Link to the Bellringer

Have students look over their paragraphs for correct capitalization and punctuation.

Motivating Activity

Ask students if they have ever received a friendly letter. Initiate a discussion about why people write letters, and why some people choose to communicate by letter instead of telephone. Discuss with students whether they would rather receive a letter or a phone call from a friend. Tell students that writing a letter, like writing in a journal, is a means of self-expression. Additionally, letter writing is an excellent way to make and maintain connections with other people.

LESSON 1.3

Personal Writing

Making Personal Connections

When you write a personal letter, you make a connection. You can tell what you are doing or share your thoughts and feelings. Whether you write a short note or a long letter, what you write should sound like you.

A personal letter is like a gift that lasts a long time. You can hold, reread, and keep a letter. It's not like a telephone call, where the words are gone when you hang up.

In the model below a boy is writing to share his delight about getting a new dog. The boy's name is Carl Davis III, and he's a character in a book by Rosa Guy.

Literature Model

Spots belongs to me! I'm bringing him home! You'll love him. Never in your life have you seen a dog so devoted, so intelligent. How lucky I am. To be seeing my mother, my father, my friend Selena, soon, and to have my very own dog, and to be able to visit Grandma whenever I wish. . . . My life just keeps opening and opening and opening. What a wonderful life.

Rosa Guy
The Ups and Downs of Carl Davis III

Teacher's Classroom Resources

The following resources can be used for planning, instruction, practice, reinforcement, assessment, reteaching, enrichment, or evaluation.

Teaching Tools
Lesson Plans

Transparencies
Fine Art Transparencies 1–5
Writing Process Transparencies 1–10

Write to Keep in Touch

The writing you send to friends and family can take many forms. You can send thank-you letters, get-well cards, or notes of apology. You can talk about things that interest you. You can ask questions. You can tell your experiences, thoughts, and feelings. Writing a letter is a special way to let other people know what you're doing. Also, if you send a letter, you might get one in return.

Read what one writer included in a letter to his grandfather.

Dear Grandpa,

Are you ready for a surprise? I just started saxophone lessons. I'm going to play you a song when I come visit. Right now my cheeks hurt from practicing so much. Sometimes the only sound I can make is a honk. It sounds like a weird bird. Unfortunately, it's really loud, but I'm working on that. I can't wait to see you.

Marvin

How does Marvin make his letter sound like a conversation?

What kinds of things does Marvin talk about that make his letter friendly?

Journal Writing

Think of a friend to whom you could write a letter. List some activities that both you and your friend enjoy. List some things that you've done lately that you'd like to share with your friend.

TEACH

Guided Practice

L2 Using the Model

Tell students that Carl Davis has been away from his parents and is about to join them. Ask students what feelings the writer expresses about his new dog (excitement, pride, sense of good luck). Carl also feels lucky and happy about being reunited with friends and family. Point out that people often write letters to share important experiences with friends and family.

L1 Writing a Note

Before they try writing a letter, give students a chance to write a simple note for inclusion on a birthday, thank you, or get-well card that they will send to someone they know. Students may create an illustrated card first. Suggest that they include at least three sentences in their note. Remind them that the note should show they are thinking about the other person.

Two-Minute Skill Drill

Have students list the five main parts of a friendly letter and briefly explain each.

Journal Writing Tip

Gather Information Students might prefer simply to list the activities they have in common with a friend. Students might title their list by writing "Activities my friend and I enjoy" at the top of a page and then numbering each activity.

Blackline Masters

Thinking and Study Skills, pp. 7, 9
Writing Across the Curriculum, p. 11
Cooperative Learning Activities, pp. 1–6
Speaking and Listening Activities, pp. 14–15
Composition Practice, p. 3
Composition Reteaching, p. 3
Composition Enrichment, p. 3

Assessment

Teacher's Guide to Writing Assessment

TEACH

Guided Practice

L3 Writing a Closing

Invite students to list as many different closings for a personal letter as they can. Encourage them to be inventive. Then have them name a real or imaginary person they might write a letter to using each closing. For example, they might use *Respectfully* on a letter to a favorite teacher and *Later, Dude* on a short note to a friend.

Independent Practice

For further stimuli for personal writing, see *Fine Art Transparencies* 1–5.

Writing Process Transparencies, 1–10

Writing Across the Curriculum, p. 11

Cooperative Learning Activities, pp. 1–6

Skills Practice

Thinking and Study Skills, pp. 7, 9

Speaking and Listening Activities, pp. 14–15

Composition Practice, p. 3

Write a Friendly Letter

Getting a letter is like getting a surprise package. It's fun to find out what's inside. Whatever the letter says, it will probably have five main parts: the heading, the greeting, the body, the closing, and the signature.

Look at the letter below. At the top is the heading, which includes the date and usually the writer's address. Next you'll see the greeting, a way of saying hello. Then comes the body, where the writer tells whatever he or she wants to say.

Finally, the writer says good-by with a closing such as *Your friend, Love,* or *Sincerely,* and then signs his or her name. No matter what a letter looks like, it's the thoughts and feelings that go into it that are the most important.

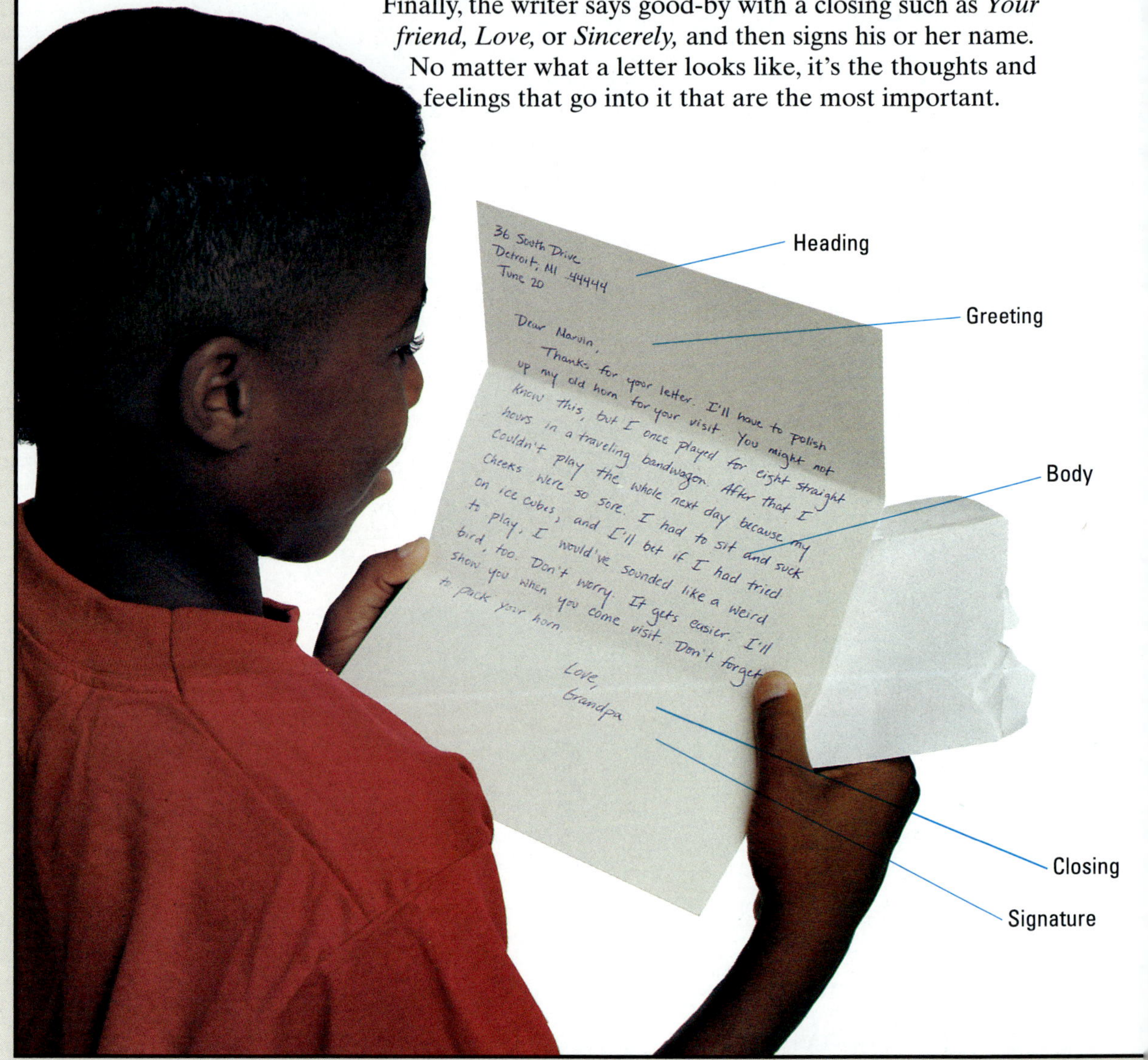

Enabling Strategies

LEP Writing a Short Note

Non-English-speaking students may benefit from working with a partner to prepare a short note. Have students first explain orally what they want to say. Then have them write a draft. Ask students to share this with a partner to correct errors and to determine if the note is clear and says what the student intended it to say.

1.3 Writing Activities

Write a Friendly Letter

Think of something that has happened to you recently. It could be an event such as receiving a gift, an experience at school or home, or going to a party. Write a brief letter to a relative or to your best friend.

- Tell what happened, say thank you, or apologize.
- Tell how you felt about it.
- Ask any questions you may have.
- Include the five main parts of a friendly letter.

PURPOSE To share personal thoughts and feelings
AUDIENCE A friend or relative
LENGTH 2–3 paragraphs

COMPUTER OPTION

You might compose your letter on a computer. After you write the letter, reread and change it until it suits you. If your computer has a spell checker, use it to find any misspellings. Then print out the letter.

If your computer is linked to a network of other computers, you may be able to send your letter electronically. Computers can also talk with each other by telephone through a device called a modem.

Grammar Link

Use clear punctuation and capitalization in letters.

Look at each section of the letter from Marvin's grandfather. Then correct the capitalization and punctuation in the friendly letter below. The letter contains 15 errors.

621 Norton avenue
portland OR 97216
September 18 1996

Dear aunt Lisa

I have just found out that we are going to Boulder, colorado, during the winter vacation. Father says I can bring my best friend, sung. She will be good company raul will be in school and can't come with us?

After we leave boulder, we will drive West. Maybe we can visit you. Will you be home then. I'll send more details as soon as we're sure of our plans.

Love

Maria

See Lesson 8.6, page 272; Lesson 18.1, page 438; Lesson 18.3, page 442; Lesson 19.1, page 454; Lesson 19.3, page 458; and Lesson 19.4, page 460.

ASSESS

Writing Activities Evaluation Guidelines

Write a Friendly Letter

Use these criteria when evaluating your students' writing.

- Does the student's letter include the five main parts of a friendly letter?
- Does the student's letter give detail about the writer's experience?
- Does the student's letter include personal feelings?
- Is the student's letter conversational?

See also the *Teacher's Guide to Writing Assessment.*

Grammar Link

(See Using the Grammar Link below.)

Reteaching

Composition Reteaching, p. 3

Enrichment

Composition Enrichment, p. 3

Use *Fine Art Transparencies* 1–5 for enrichment activities also.

CLOSE

Initiate a discussion about the different kinds of letters people write. Remind students that not every letter has to be about a momentous event. People often write about little events that happen during a typical day. They may write about new ideas they have come across, or whatever is on their minds. Tell students that such letters bring the writer and the recipient closer together.

Using the Grammar Link

Grammar Link Answers

1. Avenue
2. Portland
3. Portland, Oregon
4. September 18,
5. Aunt
6. Lisa,
7. Colorado
8. then?
9. Love,

Capitalization and Punctuation After students have corrected the capitalization and punctuation errors in the Grammar Link, have them check their own letters for errors.

Setting the Purpose

Lesson 1.4 teaches students how to focus their response to reading poetry and to produce original poetry of their own.

FOCUS

Lesson Overview

Objective: To write a poem in response to reading a poem
Skills: using specific adjectives
Critical Thinking: analyzing; contrasting; comparing
Speaking and Listening: discussing

Bellringer

When students enter the classroom, have this assignment on the board: *List the names of five poems or songs with words that you know and like.*

Grammar Link to the Bellringer

Have students think about the songs or poems they listed in the Bellringer. Have them identify any specific adjectives used in the song lyrics or poems.

Motivating Activity

Encourage students to tell what they like about the poems or songs they listed. Some students may have written their own poems or songs. Ask them if they think this type of writing is easier or more difficult than other kinds of writing. Explain that writing a poem, like journal writing, is a means of self-expression, a way to experiment with and explore personal thoughts, feelings, and experiences.

LESSON 1.4

Writing About Literature

Responding to a Poem

Poems are a way of sharing experiences and feelings. You can read poems, and you can write them. All you need is an idea or feeling to get started.

William Carlos Williams wrote the poem below. In addition to being a poet, he was a doctor. Frequently, he turned everyday experiences into poems.

Literature Model

This Is Just to Say

I have eaten
the plums
that were in
the icebox

and which
you were probably
saving
for breakfast

Forgive me
they were delicious
so sweet
and so cold

William Carlos Williams

Jot down your thoughts about the poem. How would you feel if you received it? Did it make you think of eating plums? What did it make you want to do?

Teacher's Classroom Resources

The following resources can be used for planning, instruction, practice, reinforcement, assessment, reteaching, enrichment, or evaluation.

Teaching Tools
Lesson Plans

Transparencies
Fine Art Transparencies 1–5
Writing Process Transparencies 1–10

Start with a Poem

One way of responding to a poem is to write. You might write your ideas about the poem in your journal or learning log. In the journal entry below, one student tells how Williams's poem made her feel.

When I read the poem, I felt like I had actually taken some plums that weren't mine out of the icebox. I have never done that, but I could almost feel what it was like to take something out of the icebox.

Once I stole one of my brother's cookies. He hadn't seen me, but he was so little that I felt bad. I apologized and he said he understood.

Jenny Jeep, O'Plaine Elementary School
Gurnee, Illinois

Another way to respond to a poem is to draw a picture. The student who drew this was inspired by the poet's description of the plums.

Journal Writing

Reread the notes you jotted down after reading "This Is Just to Say." Think about how you would respond. Would you write something, or would you draw a picture? Write or draw your response.

TEACH

Guided Practice

L2 Using the Model

Students having difficulty relating their own experiences to the poem might benefit from some prompts. Ask students if they have ever apologized for something; lost an item borrowed without permission; or tasted a sweet and delicious fruit. Questions like these can help students focus on an image or experience to use in their responses.

L1 Cooperative Learning

After students have responded to "This Is Just to Say," have them form groups for a cooperative learning activity. Each student in a group should share a response to the poem. Others should listen actively, and then comment or ask questions about the writer's response. These comments and questions can help students hone the images or ideas they used in responding.

Two-Minute Skill Drill

List these nouns on the board and have students choose an adjective to describe each.

plums	snow
breakfast	mountain
cookie	dogs

Journal Writing Tip

Responses to the Poem Remind students they can respond to any part of the poem that strikes them—a certain image, a line of words, the overall idea, or just the way the poem sounds.

Blackline Masters

Thinking and Study Skills, pp. 5, 22
Writing Across the Curriculum, p. 11
Cooperative Learning Activities, pp. 1–6
Speaking and Listening Activities, pp. 14–15
Composition Practice, p. 4
Composition Reteaching, p. 4
Composition Enrichment, p. 4

Assessment

Teacher's Guide to Writing Assessment

TEACH

Guided Practice

L2 Using the Models

Like the poem on page 22, both students' poems are about feeling sorry. Both students used Williams's poem as a "jumping-off" point for their own writing. Have students jot down responses as they read. That way any creative ideas prompted by the reading will not slip away. Point out that reading poems, and reading in general, is a good way for students to get their creative juices flowing.

L3 Responding with a Poem

Set aside a period for students to read and discuss poems they have found outside of class. Suggest that they bring in shorter poems so everyone can have a chance to read and respond. Have students respond to these poems by writing a poem of their own in their journals.

Independent Practice

For further stimuli for personal writing, see *Fine Art Transparencies* 1–5.

Writing Process Transparencies 1–10

Writing Across the Curriculum, p. 11

Cooperative Learning Activities, pp. 1–6

Skills Practice

Thinking and Study Skills, pp. 5, 22

Speaking and Listening Activities, pp. 14–15

Composition Practice, p.4

Respond with a Poem

Another good way to respond to a poem is to try a poem of your own. You might write about the same idea as in the poem you read. You could also write about a different idea.

Read the two poems below. What idea in Williams's poem do you think Shayne Bell is responding to? What different idea is Kim Myers writing about? What similarities or differences can you find between Kim's and Shayne's responses?

Can you tell how these two poems are similar?

I'm Sorry

I didn't mean
to make you mad.
I didn't mean
to hurt you.

I was just angry
that was all.
I said some things
I didn't mean.

Please forgive me.
Let's not fight.
The fight was not important.

Kim Myers,
Westfield School,
Winthrop Harbor, Illinois

For what I have done,
I will go out and find
the best plums in town.
I will even grow the plums
that will be as sweet as candy,
that will be sweeter and more delicious.
There will be enough for you to have
at least 10 a day for a year,
to tell you I'm so sorry I ate your plums.

Shayne Bell,
Wauconda Junior High,
Wauconda, Illinois

How does Shayne help her readers to understand what the plums taste like?

Poets often divide poems into sections called stanzas. Kim's poem has three stanzas, just like the poem on page 22.

Enabling Strategies

LEP Reading and Writing Poetry

Students with limited English proficiency will probably find the poem by Kim Myers easier to read. The shorter lines, use of repetition, and simple vocabulary and sentence structure make it a more accessible model. Have students look for words that are repeated within the poem. Note that the repeated use of *I* to start four of the lines underscores the writer's feeling of being sorry. As students write their own poems, point out that a graceful poem may use very simple words and have a simple structure.

1.4 Writing Activities

Write a Poem

William Carlos Williams wrote a poem about the painting on this page. He began with the lines below.

The Hunters in the Snow

The over-all picture is winter
icy mountains
in the background the return

from the hunt it is toward evening
from the left
sturdy hunters lead in

their pack the inn sign
hanging from a
broken hinge is a stag . . .

Write your own poem in response to the beginning of Williams's poem. Begin by freewriting about the painting and about the details that Williams chose.

- Make notes on your ideas about the poem.
- Make notes on how the poem makes you feel.
- Decide how your poem will be like or unlike Williams's poem.

PURPOSE To respond to a poem with a poem of your own
AUDIENCE Students your age
LENGTH 10 or more lines

Grammar Link

Use specific adjectives to create strong, clear images.

In "The Hunters in the Snow," William Carlos Williams uses specific adjectives: *icy, sturdy, broken.*

Add at least one specific adjective to each sentence below.

1. I ate an orange yesterday.
2. I found it in a basket on the table.
3. I peeled the skin.
4. I chewed up each section.
5. Then I wiped my hands and face.

See Lesson 12.1, page 344.

Pieter Brueghel the Elder, *Hunters in the Snow*, 1565

ASSESS

Writing Activities Evaluation Guidelines

Write a Poem

Use these criteria when evaluating your students' writing.

- Does the poem respond to some aspect of Williams's poem?
- Does the poem include specific details based on Williams's poem?
- Does the student use Williams's poem as a "take-off" point for details, thoughts, and feelings from his or her own experiences?
- Does the poem reflect the writer's personal thoughts and feelings?

See also the *Teacher's Guide to Writing Assessment.*

Grammar Link

(See Using the Grammar Link below.)

Reteaching

Composition Reteaching, p. 4

Enrichment

Composition Enrichment, p. 4

Use *Fine Art Transparencies* 1–5 for enrichment activities also.

CLOSE

Invite students to read the two student poems aloud. Discuss similarities between the poems (both are apologies) as well as differences. (Kim's poem emphasizes feelings and uses simple units of thought; Shayne includes many details and uses longer and more complex sentences.)

Using the Grammar Link

Grammar Link Answers

Answers will vary, but some suggestions are given below.

1. I ate a juicy orange yesterday.
2. I found it in a woven basket ....
3. I peeled the fragrant skin.
4. I chewed up each sweet section.
5. Then I wiped my sticky hands ....

About the Art

Pieter Bruegel the Elder, *Hunters in the Snow*, 1565
Bruegel was a close observer of nature. He captures the winter twilight in the gray-green sky and the dark tones of the trees and figures in this 46-by-64-inch painting that hangs in the Kunsthistorisches Museum, Vienna, Austria.

Setting the Purpose

Students have the opportunity to apply what they have learned about personal writing in Unit 1 to an independent writing project. They will use the stages of the writing process to create and present a finished piece.

FOCUS

Lesson Overview

Objective: To write a personal account of a special day
Skills: using the five stages of the writing process: prewriting, drafting, revising, editing, and presenting
Critical Thinking: recalling; main idea; summarizing
Speaking and Listening: discussing; note taking

Bellringer

When students enter the classroom, have this assignment on the board: *Write a few sentences about the most interesting place you have ever visited.*

Grammar Link to the Bellringer

Have students add specific adjectives to describe the nouns they wrote for the Bellringer.

Motivating Activity

Point out that special experiences and new places often go together, as in Yoshiko Uchida's account of visiting a farm for the first time on student page 27. Many students, however, may also remember special experiences they've had at home, at school, or in their community. Hitting a home run at the park, meeting a new neighbor—these are the sorts of special experiences that can happen anywhere. Invite students to discuss some special people, places, and experiences they have had.

UNIT 1

WRITING PROCESS IN ACTION

PERSONAL WRITING

In preceding lessons you've learned about various kinds of personal writing. You've expressed your own ideas and feelings in journal entries and personal letters. You've also had the chance to write your responses to poems. Now it's time to make use of what you've learned. In this lesson you're invited to write about a day that became special in your life.

• Assignment •

Context	*You have decided to submit your writing to Up, Up, and Away. This is a magazine that publishes student writing about special days, new experiences, or new feelings.*
Purpose	*To write a brief account of a special day or event in your life*
Audience	*The readers of Up, Up, and Away, ages 10–15*
Length	*1 page*

The following pages can help you plan and write your account. Read through them and then refer to them as you need to. Don't feel limited by them, however. You are in charge of your own writing process.

Teacher's Classroom Resources

The following resources can be used for planning, instruction, practice, reinforcement, assessment, reteaching, enrichment, or evaluation.

Teaching Tools
Lesson Plans

Transparencies
Writing Process Transparencies 1–10

Prewriting

Sometimes keying in on a few single words can help you focus your prewriting thoughts. For example, think of the words *usually*, *often*, and *always*. Those are words that describe everyday events. Now think of words like *once*, *seldom*, and *never*. Such words can help you identify the special day or experience that will make a good writing topic. The options graphic at the right will help you with these early, important steps.

Look at page 12 for suggestions on freewriting. Your goal is to choose a topic that fits the assignment and has meaning for you.

Option A
Explore your journal.

Option B
Brainstorm with a friend.

Option C
Freewrite for ideas.

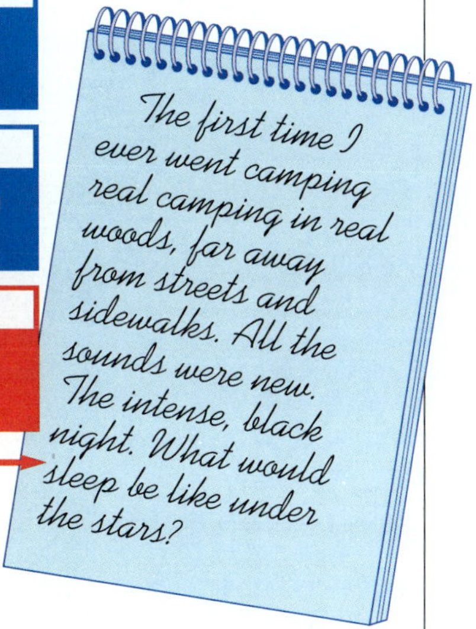

Drafting

As you go over your prewriting notes, think about the specific words and images that will make your readers aware of the special nature of your topic. For example, Yoshiko Uchida writes of riding through vineyards on her first visit to a farm—a wondrous experience for a city girl. Notice the language she uses to give the sense of discovering a new world.

Literature Model

I could hear crickets singing and frogs croaking and all the other gentle night sounds of the country. I felt as though I were in another more immense, never-ending world, and wished I could keep riding forever to the ends of the earth.

Yoshiko Uchida, *The Invisible Thread*

TEACH

Prewriting

L2 Developing Ideas for Personal Writing

Students preparing to freewrite may benefit from writing prompts. Offer some categories to help them focus their thoughts (the first time I—, the only time I—, the best time I had—, and so forth). Mention that these categories are just starting points, and that they should feel free to follow an idea wherever it leads them.

Drafting

L3 Adding Details

Uchida is aware of the singing crickets and other night sounds as she lies under the star-filled sky. These soft sounds provide a gentle music for the scene. Challenge students to list how sound played a part in their special day. Point out that they may wish to use details about music or musical sounds, as Uchida did, to give readers a sense of their experience.

Blackline Masters
Composition Practice, p. 7
Composition Reteaching, p. 7
Composition Enrichment, p. 7

Grammar Workbook
Lesson 30

Assessment
Teacher's Guide to Writing Assessment

TEACH

Revising

L2 Peer Editing

Students can work in writing conferences with peer editors before they revise their writing. You may duplicate the Peer Response forms in the *Teacher's Guide to Writing Assessment.* Suggest that peer editors discuss these questions: What did you like best about the writing? Were enough details provided?

L2 Cooperative Learning

Pairs of students can interview each other about the writing, taking turns as writer and reviewer. The writer prepares a list of questions for the reviewer. The reviewer asks questions about unclear things in the writing.

Editing

L2 Peer Editing

After students have edited their own work, have them edit another student's writing. Remind them to refer to the Editing Checklist on student page 29.

Presenting

Before students present their personal writing, discuss how to prepare their papers for publication. Emphasize the importance of the final draft and that it must be neatly done.

Independent Practice

Writing Process Transparencies 1–10

Skills Practice

Composition Practice, p. 7

Grammar Workbook, Lesson 30

Journal Writing Tip

Doing Things Differently Have students jot down things they might do differently the next time they write.

Drafting Tip

For help with getting a flow of your ideas down on paper, see Lesson 2.4, pages 56–59.

You can bring the same kind of amazement to your own writing if you keep your experience and feelings focused. What made this day important to you?

When you're ready to start your draft, take a deep breath and relax. The most important thing about drafting is to get your ideas down on paper. You can always change things later.

Revising

Revising Tip

For help with revising your writing, see Lesson 2.5, pages 60–63.

To begin revising, read over your draft to make sure that what you have written fits your purpose and your audience. Then have a **writing conference**. Read your draft to a partner or small group. Use your audience's reactions to help you evaluate your work.

Question A
Is my writing clear?

Question B
Does the writing sound like me?

Question C
Have I made effective use of details?

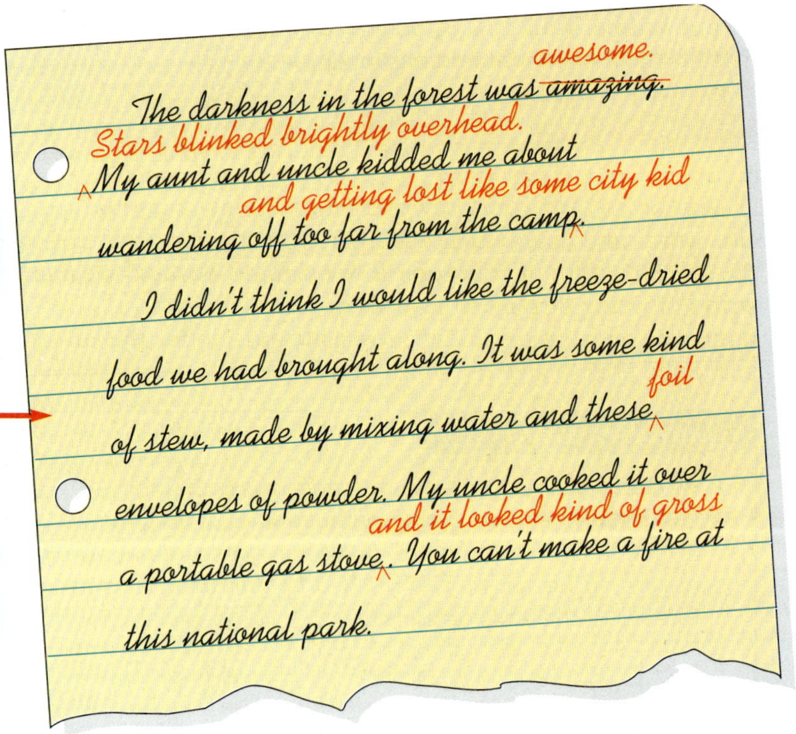
The darkness in the forest was ~~amazing~~ awesome.
Stars blinked brightly overhead.
My aunt and uncle kidded me about
wandering off too far from the camp and getting lost like some city kid.
I didn't think I would like the freeze-dried
food we had brought along. It was some kind
of stew, made by mixing water and these foil
envelopes of powder. My uncle cooked it over
a portable gas stove and it looked kind of gross. You can't make a fire at
this national park.

Enrichment and Extension

Follow-up Ideas

- Set aside time for students to celebrate the conclusion of their writing projects. Encourage them to share their finished pieces.
- Collect the finished pieces and illustrate, bind, and display the work.

Extending Personal Writing

Brainstorm with students ways they can use personal writing in other subject areas:

- a personal log of science experiments
- a journal of past experiences to be included in a time capsule

Editing

At the editing stage you put the finishing touches on your writing. A careful editing job shows your readers that you care about your work and don't want any errors to distract them from your ideas.

The checklist at the right will help you edit your writing. Usually writers **proofread** for only one kind of error at a time. Using this method means that you will read through your work several times, looking for only one kind of error each time.

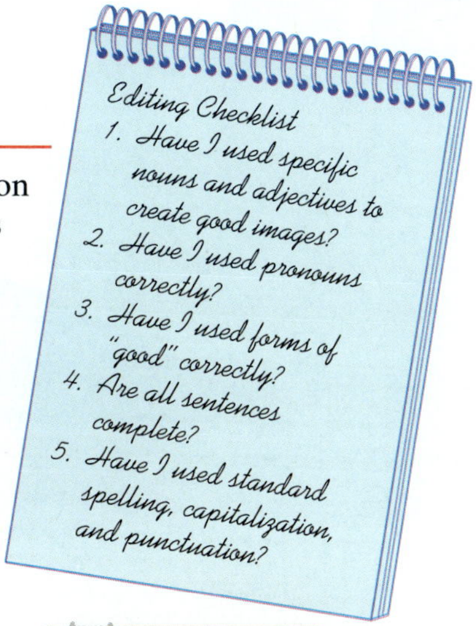

Proofreading

For proofreading symbols, see page 74.

Presenting

Maybe your class wants to make its own special edition of *Up, Up, and Away.* This would give you the chance to have other students read your writing. Likewise, you would have the chance to see how other students tackled this assignment.

Of course, you may not feel ready to share your work with anyone other than your teacher. That's OK. There is some risk involved in sharing with a wider audience. You decide what's best for you.

Journal Writing

Reflect on your writing process experience. Answer these questions in your journal: What do you like best about the personal account you wrote? What was the hardest part of writing it? What did you learn in your writing conference? What new things have you learned as a writer?

ASSESS

Evaluation Guidelines

Use the following questions to evaluate students' finished writing.

- Do prewriting notes explore a memorable personal experience?
- Does the draft build on the prewriting notes?
- Does it clearly communicate why the day or event was memorable to the student?
- Does it provide vivid details about the experience?
- Has the student ordered the account in a way that is easy to follow?
- Is the revision an improvement of the draft?
- Does the revision include language that is natural to the writer?
- Does the piece adhere to spelling and punctuation rules?
- Has the student used the questions on page 29 to edit his or her writing?

Refer to the *Teacher's Guide to Writing Assessment* for further help with evaluating student writing.

Reteaching

Composition Reteaching, p. 7

Enrichment

Composition Enrichment, p. 7

CLOSE

Ask students: What did you learn about yourself from the assignment? Have you changed the way you see your everyday experiences?

Speaking and Listening

Creating Dialogue

Tell students they may wish to incorporate dialogue into their accounts to help convey how they were feeling during their special experiences. Suggest that students try reading their dialogue aloud with a partner. Does the dialogue sound natural? Tell students that dialogue can convey personal feelings and capture the unique details of an experience.

Setting the Purpose

Students read a literature passage that illustrates in a very real way effective personal writing. Such readings serve as models for students as they create their own personal writing.

About the Author

Yoshiko Uchida, the daughter of Japanese parents, was born and grew up in California. *The Invisible Thread* is a memoir of her early life up to the time she completed her education and found her first job.

FOCUS

Lesson Overview

Objective: To read a passage to examine how a professional writer uses memorable details and lifelike characters in personal writing
Skills: reading comprehension
Critical Thinking: recalling
Speaking and Listening: discussing

Bellringer

When students enter the classroom, have this assignment on the board: *Write a few sentences about a place you visited for the first time.*

Motivating Activity

Ask students to think of a time when they left their everyday surroundings and went to a totally different kind of place. Maybe they took a school field trip, visited a relative in another city, or took a vacation in a place with different geography or climate. What new sights did they see? What new experiences did they have? How did the place and their experiences make them feel?

UNIT 1

Personal Writing
Literature Model

Yoshiko Uchida
from
The Invisible Thread

In her autobiography, The Invisible Thread, *Yoshiko Uchida focuses on the personal discoveries she made about people and places while growing up. As this passage opens, Uchida and her family are driving off for their first visit to a farm. As you read, note the personal details that the author uses to make her writing clear and appealing to her readers. Then try the activities in Linking Writing and Literature on page 35.*

As we turned off the main highway, it seemed as though we were driving through a vast ocean of vineyards[1] that spread out on both sides of the dusty road. Before long we could see the Okubo water-pump windmill sprouting up among the grapevines.

1 **vineyards** (vin′ yərdz) fields planted with grapevines

Teacher's Classroom Resources

The following resources can be used for planning, instruction, or practice.

Teaching Tools
Lesson Plans

Transparencies
Fine Art Transparencies 1–5

"There it is!" Keiko shouted. "There's the Okubo farm!"

She reminded Papa of his earlier promise and convinced him there was nothing on the deserted road that she could possibly hit. Papa knew he would never hear the end of it if he didn't give her a chance, so he stopped the car.

Keiko was in heaven as Papa let her slide over behind the wheel. But poor Mama was clutching my arm again.

"Careful, Kei Chan," she cautioned. "Be careful."

Keiko started slowly, like a tired turtle. But by the time she made the final turn toward the farm, she was feeling confident and picking up a little speed.

"Honk the horn to let them know we're here," Papa said.

At which point Keiko not only honked the horn, but simultaneously[2] crashed into Jick's dog house, knocked it over on its side, and stopped just inches short of the walnut tree.

"Look out, for heaven's sake," we all shouted. "Look out!"

Jick barked furiously at the sudden assault[3] on his territory, and the chickens scrambled in every direction, screeching and cackling as though the end of the world had come.

The startled Okubos rushed from their house, blinking in the sun, surveying with alarm what only moments before had been their peaceful yard.

Paul Cézanne, *Farmhouse and Chestnut Trees at Jas-de-Bouffan,* c. 1885

2 simultaneously (sī´ məl tā' nē əs lē) occurring at the same time

3 assault (ə sôlt') a violent attack

TEACH

L2 Guided Reading

To aid comprehension of the selection and understanding of personal writing, ask the following questions:

- How does the author let you know what Keiko is like? (Mama and Papa are reluctant to let Keiko drive but she is demanding and gets her way. She feels confident about driving. She's carefree, not worrying that she knocked over the doghouse and startled the chickens.)
- What words convey a sense of wide open farm country? ("a vast ocean of vineyards that spread out on both sides of the dusty road"; "nothing on the deserted road")

Blackline Masters

Speaking and Listening Activities, pp. 14–15

Thinking and Study Skills, p. 3

Assessment

Teacher's Guide to Writing Assessment

About the Art

Paul Cézanne, *Farmhouse and Chestnut Trees at Jas-de-Bouffan,* c. 1885
In this painting, French artist Paul Cézanne (1839–1906) celebrates the beauty of a simple scene. This oil painting, measuring 36 by 29 inches, is in the Norton Simon Museum.

TEACH

L2 Guided Reading

To aid comprehension of the selection and understanding of personal writing, ask the following questions:

- How do the author and her sister feel towards the Okubos? (They feel like family. The Okubos treat them like grandchildren. They call the Okubos Oji San and Oba San.)
- What is Oji San like? How do you know? (He is kind. You know this because he takes the time to show the girls how to drink from the well. He thinks about how they will feel about the outhouse. He's patient and lets them look for eggs in the henhouse.)

"We're here!" Keiko shouted, as if they needed to be told. "We're here!"

Because the Okubos' two grown daughters had already left home, they welcomed my sister and me as though we were their grandchildren, and we called them Oji San (uncle) and Oba San (auntie).

Oji San gave us a quick tour of the farm. He showed us how to pump water from the well and put our heads down to gulp the cold water that came gushing out. He pointed to the outhouse, saying, "I guess you've never used one of those before." We certainly hadn't. Whenever I had to use it, I held my breath and got out as fast as I could.

He also let us look for eggs in the henhouse, and took us to the barn where we staggered about in the hayloft, trying to pitch hay with forks that were bigger than we were.

Helen Oji, *Libellule (Memory of My Father)*, 1980

About the Art

Helen Oji, Libellule, *Memory of My Father*, 1980
In this piece, Helen Oji expresses aspects of her Japanese heritage. She used acrylics, rhoplex, and glitter on a kimono-shaped paper canvas. The work measures 60 by 72 inches, and is in the collection of the Prudential Insurance Company.

Genre and Style

Reading Personal Writing

In this selection, Uchida relates an episode from her childhood. Her vivid language gives the reader a sense of being at the farm. Uchida describes sights, tastes, sounds, and sensations.

He saved the best for last, taking us to a fenced enclosure where two dusty mules ambled over to greet us.

"Meet Tom and Jerry," he said. Then pulling some scraggly weeds by the fence, he told us to feed them to the mules.

I thrust some weeds at them and the mules grabbed them hungrily, showing their enormous yellow teeth. They seemed friendly enough, but I was rather glad they were on the other side of the fence.

"They like you," Oji San said. "Maybe they'll do something nice for you later on."

"Like what, Oji San?"

Oji San just grinned and smashed his felt hat down over his forehead. "You'll see," he said. "Wait and see."

Sitting on mats spread out under the walnut tree, we had a wonderful picnic supper of soy-drenched chicken and corn grilled over an outdoor pit. There were rice balls, too, sprinkled with black sesame[4] seeds that looked like tiny ants.

Oji San waited until the sun had dipped down behind the dusty grapevines and a soft dusky haze settled in the air. Then he announced he was taking us all on a moonlight ride through the vineyards. It was more than we'd ever hoped for.

Keiko took her usual place up front by Oji San, hoping for a brief chance at the reins. Mama and Papa chatted quietly with Oba San, and I lay stretched out in back, looking up at the enormous night sky.

There seemed to be millions and billions of stars up there. More than I'd ever imagined existed in the universe. They seemed brighter and closer than they were in Berkeley. It was as though the entire sky had dropped closer to earth to spread out its full glory right there in front of me.

I listened to the slow clop-clop of the mules as they plodded through the fields, probably wondering why they were pulling a wagonload of people in the dark, instead of hauling boxes of grapes to the shed under the hot, dry sun.

4 **sesame** (ses' ə mē) East Indian plant whose seeds are used for flavoring

TEACH

L2 Guided Reading

To aid comprehension of the selection and understanding of personal writing, ask the following questions:

- How does the author show you what she thinks and feels about the mules? (She says that at first she was afraid of them. She talks about their "enormous yellow teeth." Then she considers how the mules feel as they pull the people along, and tries to look at the event from the mule's point of view.)
- Even though it is Keiko's first time on a farm, the author says she "took her usual place up front." What does this mean? What does it tell you about Keiko? (In the car, Keiko sat up front with her father so that she could convince him to let her drive. She does the same on the mule cart. It means that Keiko likes to take control and try new things. She is brave.)

Writers and Writing

Celebrating Humanity

Uchida says that in her writing she tells about "the meaningful relationships between human beings, to celebrate our common humanity." Students may enjoy thinking about their personal experiences as somehow representative of the experiences of all people. That is, the specifics may differ, but many people have found and experienced a special place.

TEACH

L2 Guided Reading

To aid comprehension of the selection and understanding of personal writing, ask the following questions:

- What does the author say about Keiko that is consistent with her character? (Keiko is fearless and jumps right in the water.)
- What do you think made the farm seem special to the author? (She cherishes the country's gentle night sounds, the unfamiliar vastness of the night sky, the feeling of being close to family and friends in a new setting.)

Independent Practice

For further stimuli for personal writing, see *Fine Art Transparencies* 1–5.

Skills Practice

Speaking and Listening Activities, pp. 14–15

Thinking and Study Skills, p. 3

I could hear crickets singing and frogs croaking and all the other gentle night sounds of the country. I felt as though I were in another more immense,[5] never-ending world, and wished I could keep riding forever to the ends of the earth.

When we got back to the farm, it was time for an outdoor Japanese bath. Oji San built a fire under a square tin tub filled with water, banking[6] the fire when the water was hot and inserting a wooden float so we wouldn't burn our feet or backsides when we got in.

Oba San hung some sheets on ropes strung around the tub and called out, "*Sah, ofuro*! Come, Kei Chan, Yo Chan. The bath is ready. You girls go first."

Mama gave us careful instructions about proper bathing procedures. "Wash and rinse yourselves outside before you get into the tub," she reminded us. "And keep the water clean."

When we were ready to climb in, I saw steam rising from the water and was afraid I'd be boiled alive. "You go first," I told my sister.

As always, Keiko was fearless. She jumped right in and sank down in the steaming water up to her neck.

"Ooooooh, this feels wonderful!" she said.

I quickly squeezed in next to her, and we let the warm water gurgle up to our chins.

Keiko looked up at the glorious night sky and sighed, "I could stay here forever."

5 **immense** (i mens') without limits; vast

6 **banking** (bangk'ing) partially covering a fire with ashes so that it will burn more slowly and for a longer period of time

Cultural Diversity

Maintaining Traditional Ways

At their picnic, Uchida's family and the Okubos eat a Japanese meal and sit on Japanese tatami mats (mats made of rice straw). Ask students why immigrants and their descendants often maintain some of the traditional ways of their native country. (Observing these customs gives them a sense of who they are and where they come from. The traditions are a link with their past, their culture, and their families.)

Linking Writing and Literature

Readers Respond to the Model

What makes Yoshiko Uchida's personal writing enjoyable?

Form your response to Yoshiko Uchida's personal writing by answering these questions. Then read what other students liked about Uchida's autobiographical account.

1. How does Uchida give the reader a clear picture of the farm? Find some specific details.
2. Do the characters in Uchida's story seem lifelike? Explain.
3. What are some of the most memorable details that Uchida includes in the selection?
4. What did you like best about the story? Why?

I liked the beginning when Keiko yells, "There's the Okubo farm!" because it reminds me of family trips. When I was younger, I always got excited about seeing new places.

The part of the story I remember best is when Keiko drives the car. The author kind of hints something's going to happen when she writes that Keiko is getting comfortable and having fun. As soon as Keiko began to speed up, I knew she was going to crash.

I would like my friends to read this selection because a few of them have been on farms. I would like to ask them if the farm described in the story is anything like the farms they have visited.

John Moore

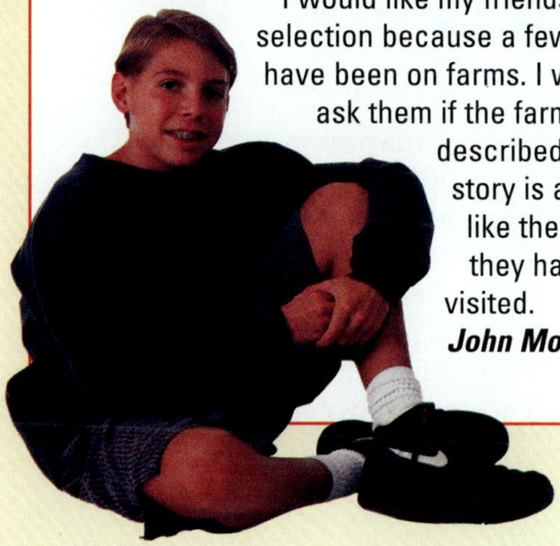

I really liked Keiko. She seemed daring and unafraid of anything. Because she wanted to drive, she also seemed like a normal teenager.

I enjoyed the description of the farm, too. The stars, the sunset, and the outdoor bath made it seem very beautiful.

April Andry

ASSESS

Evaluation Guidelines for Discussion

As your students discuss the selection, either in small groups or as a class, encourage them to begin with a personal response. The student responses on this page might be used as a starting point.

Look for evidence that students
- have read the selection
- can state some of the writer's ideas in their own words
- understand the writer's point of view
- have connected the content to their own knowledge and experiences
- understand the ideas and implications of the selection

Some possible responses to the discussion questions on this page:
1. There is a windmill rising up above the grapevines, vineyards on both sides of the road, dog house, walnut tree, and chickens cackling.
2. Yes, Keiko acts just like a teenager, and Mama seems real in the way that she clutches the author's arm.
3. Her sister knocking over the dog house, meeting the mules for the first time, looking at the night sky
4. I liked the part where she describes the stars in the night sky. I remember how I felt the first time I noticed how many stars there were like that.

CLOSE

Ask students to write a friendly letter to a character in *The Invisible Thread.* Students may comment on or ask questions about the Okubos' farm or the history of Japanese Americans. They may even want to write about a special personal experience.

Connections Across the Curriculum

History

When Japan bombed Pearl Harbor in 1941, Uchida was a senior at the University of California. In the aftermath of the attack she and her family, along with some 120,000 Japanese Americans, were sent to live in internment camps in the West. These camps, which were similar to prisons, have now been formally condemned by the United States Congress for violating the civil rights of Japanese Americans.

REVIEW

Reflecting on the Unit

You may have students respond to Reflecting on the Unit in writing or through discussion.

Writing Across the Curriculum

To help students organize their ideas and feelings about mathematics, you might lead them in a discussion about their mathematics experiences.

Adding to Your Portfolio

Suggest that students select writing samples that reflect who they are and what they care about. These samples might include writing that contains personal thoughts, feelings, and experiences. Mention that students need not share any parts of their journals that they consider private.

Portfolio Evaluation

If you grade the portfolio selections, you may want to award two marks—one each for content and form. Explain your assessment criteria before students make their selections. Commend

- experimentation with creative prewriting techniques
- clear, concise writing in which the main idea, audience, and purpose are evident
- successful revisions
- work that shows a flair for language

Unit 1 Review

Reflecting on the Unit

Summarize what you learned in this unit by answering the following questions.

- What are some ways to express your ideas and feelings through personal writing?
- How does writing in a personal journal build confidence in your writing skills?
- How can a learning log help you make sense of what you study?
- What are some important things to remember about writing a friendly letter?
- How can you express personal feelings in response to a poem?

Adding to Your Portfolio

Choose a selection for your portfolio. Look over the personal writing you did during this unit. Select a completed piece of writing to put into your portfolio. The piece you choose should show some or all of the following characteristics:

- grows out of a freewriting idea
- records your personal ideas, experiences, or feelings
- uses specific words that create clear images for your reader
- sounds like you

Reflect on your choice. Attach a note to the piece you chose, explaining briefly why you chose it and what you learned from writing it.

Set goals. How can you improve your writing? What skill will you focus on the next time you write?

Writing Across the Curriculum

Make a mathematics connection. Write down some of your ideas and feelings about mathematics. What do you like most about math? What do you dislike or find difficult? What kinds of math materials do you like to use? What skill or concept would you enjoy teaching to a younger child?

Teacher's Classroom Resources

The following resources can be used for planning, assessment, or evaluation.

Unit Assessment

Tests with Answer Key
Unit 1 Choice A Test, p. 1
Unit 1 Choice B Test, p. 2
Unit 1 Composition Objective Test, pp. 3–4

Test Generator
Unit 1 Choice A Test
Unit 1 Choice B Test
Unit 1 Composition Objective Test

You may wish to administer one of these tests as a mastery test.

UNIT

2

The Writing Process

Composition

Lessons

UNIT GOALS

The goal of Unit 2 is to help students, through example and instruction, to develop an understanding of the five-stage writing process (prewriting, drafting, revising, editing, and presenting) and an ability to apply the five stages to their own writing. The Case Study introduces travel announcement writer Curtis Katz and follows the steps of his writing process.

Unit Assessment

Tests with Answer Key
Unit 2 Choice A Test, p. 5
Unit 2 Choice B Test, p. 6
Unit 2 Composition Objective Test, pp. 7–8

Test Generator
Unit 2 Choice A Test
Unit 2 Choice B Test
Unit 2 Composition Objective Test

You may wish to administer either the Unit 2 Choice A Test or the Unit 2 Choice B Test as a pretest.

Key to Ability Levels

Enabling Strategies have been coded for varying learning styles and abilities.

L1 Level 1 activities are within the ability range of Learning Disabled students.

L2 Level 2 activities are basic-to-average activities and are within the ability range of average students.

L3 Level 3 activities are challenging activities and are within the ability range of above-average students.

LEP LEP activities are within the ability range of Limited English Proficiency students.

Setting the Purpose

In the Unit 2 Case Study, students examine how Curtis Katz used the writing process to create travel announcements for passengers on Amtrak's *Empire Builder* route. Students will explore and practice elements of the writing process in the lessons that follow.

FOCUS

Lesson Overview

Objective: To explore how the writing process is used to select and define a topic, collect and organize information, and draft and revise a manuscript

Skills: selecting and defining a topic; collecting and organizing information; drafting and revising a manuscript

Critical Thinking: analyzing; making generalizations

Speaking and Listening: informal speaking

Bellringer

When students enter the classroom, have this assignment on the board: *Write a paragraph describing a place that might be of interest to a person traveling through your community for the first time.*

Grammar Link to the Bellringer

Encourage students to check their paragraphs to make sure that they contain only complete sentences. How can they tell when a sentence is complete?

Motivating Activity

Ask students to imagine they are visiting their community for the first time. What kind of information about the area might they want or need to know?

UNIT 2 PREVIEW

Case Study

The Writing Process
in the Real World

Katz Rides the *Empire Builder*

FOCUS: Exploring your ideas—that's where the writing process begins.

For as long as he can remember, Curtis Katz has loved trains. Even as a young boy, he collected material about trains. Nowadays, Katz's lifelong hobby is a key part of his job as a coach attendant for Amtrak. Along the *Empire Builder* route, Katz tells stories to passengers about the facts and myths connected with the route. He's even written down his information to guide other coach attendants. His writing experience shows the various stages of the writing process.

The *Empire Builder* is an Amtrak long-haul route that runs from Chicago to Spokane. Katz makes the complete journey, a round trip that takes six days.

◄ *Coach attendant Curtis Katz*

Teacher's Classroom Resources

The following resources can be used for planning, instruction, practice, reinforcement, assessment, or evaluation.

Teaching Tools
Lesson Plans

Transparencies
Writing Process Transparencies, 1–10

Writing a Travel Guide

Collecting and Ordering Ideas | Writing the Manuscript | Polishing the Manuscript | Using the Guide

Prewriting

COLLECTING AND ORDERING IDEAS

Finding material about the *Empire Builder* route was no problem for Katz. First he collected information from train crew members. Carrying a small notebook on all his trips, Katz took notes from conductors and brake operators who lived along the route. During overnight stops, he went to used-book shops looking for stories and biographies about people and places in the area. "One thing led to another. I'd pick up an out-of-print book. That book contained lists of other books."

"I grew up in the East and never had been west of Chicago. Traveling by train, I realized I never had seen mountains before, and it was thrilling. As I learned more and more about the country I was traveling through, . . . I wanted to share that experience with people."

—Curtis Katz

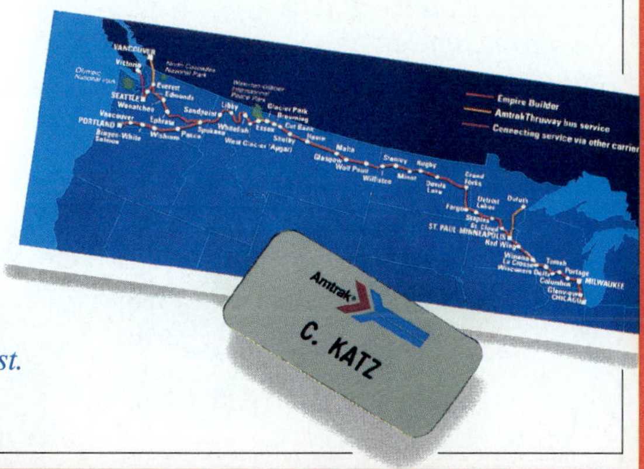

Katz's first train ride was on the Empire Builder *route. On that trip he was strongly influenced by the landscape of the Northwest.*

TEACH

Building Background

Warm-up:

Have students make a brief list of real-life situations in which they might organize information in a written presentation.

The Writing Process in Speaking:

Remind students that writers often use speaking as a part of the writing process. Writers use speaking when they discuss possible topics, gather information, review drafts, and give presentations.

Invite students to discuss instances in which speaking has aided them in the writing process.

The Writing Process in Writing:

Invite students to discuss various types of writing and the processes that might have produced them. Examples to consider might include the following:

- a descriptive essay
- a newspaper or magazine article
- a book report
- a travel guide
- a biography

Preview the Case Study

Have students preview the title and focus of the case study. Explain that Curtis Katz prepared his travel announcements by applying the writing process to information about an Amtrak train route in the western United States. Invite students to read the case study.

Blackline Masters

Cooperative Learning Activities, pp. 7–12
Thinking and Study Skills, pp. 1, 8, 11, 22
Vocabulary and Spelling Practice, p. 2
Case Studies: Writing in the Real World, pp. 5–8

Assessment

Teacher's Guide to Writing Assessment

TEACH

Discussion Prompts

- How might you make a "judgment call" when sources of information appear to conflict?
- When you find more information than you can possibly use in a writing project, how do you decide which information to include and which to set aside?

One bookstore visit uncovered details he'd been seeking about Chief Joseph. Katz first heard about Chief Joseph and the Nez Percé people when the train passed the Bear Paw Mountains. It was there that the chief had surrendered to U.S. troops after leading his people on a thousand-mile retreat. Katz used all of his sources to retell the tale of the Nez Percé's journey.

Railroad magazines, such as *Trains,* also provided information. Katz read about railroad history and recorded his ideas in his notebook. Even passengers offered stories, and often Katz heard several versions of one story. Later on, when drafting and revising, Katz needed "to make judgment calls when the facts were reported differently by different sources. Sometimes I included several versions."

Katz found that the sources of information were endless. His material covered subjects ranging from train robberies to mountain climbing.

Drafting

WRITING THE MANUSCRIPT

During the week-long breaks between trips, Katz wrote almost constantly. Surrounded by boxes of historical documents, his toy trains, and shelves full of books, it was easy to get involved in the material. Katz organized the manuscript to follow his route from west to

▼ *To give the mileage between locations, Katz researched old employee timetables and train maps.*

Cultural Diversity

Travel Writing

Remind students that travel writers often visit and write about cultures with which they are unfamiliar. Invite students to discuss why it is important to report accurately about an unfamiliar culture. Why might it be difficult to do so? What kinds of research might help a writer to depict a culture accurately? When writers finish a piece of cultural writing, how might they check to make sure the writing is accurate?

east. Passengers traveling east to west hear the manuscript in reverse. "I did it kind of straight ahead. From one end of the route to the other. I wrote each section in the order in which it occurred. It's not like a short story where you write from the middle out. This was strictly written by the way the railroad ran."

As he was drafting, Katz did some additional research, checking statistics, such as dates and mountain heights.

Writing the travel guide took several weeks. Katz continued to ride the *Empire Builder* for six days at a time, always gathering more information. To his route folder, he clipped notes and newspaper articles people gave him.

Revising/Editing

POLISHING THE MANUSCRIPT

Katz wrote the original manuscript by hand. Then he typed it. To revise and edit, he used the typed version, cutting and pasting the manuscript in the order he wanted. Then he combined the typewritten sections with revised or new inserts.

After retyping all of this material, Katz reread the manuscript. He made corrections in red ink and noted additions in black ink. "Even in the proofreading process," says Katz, "new information came to hand. I couldn't resist adding it."

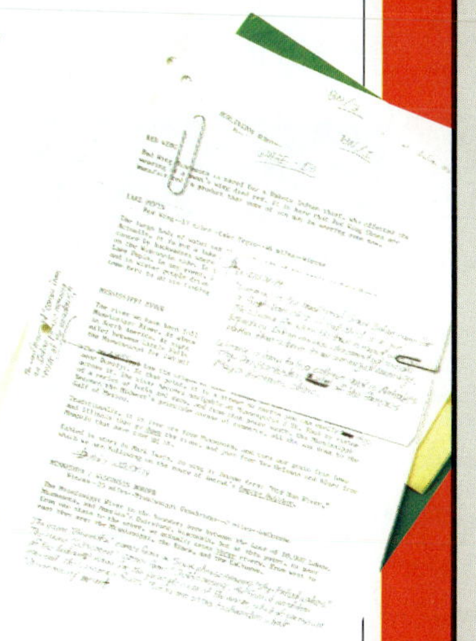

▲ *Katz wrote the travel announcements just in time for the* Empire Builder's *sixtieth anniversary.*

TEACH

Discussion Prompts

- How might a writer decide the order in which information is arranged and presented?
- How can statistics make writing more interesting and informative?

Connections Across the Curriculum

History

Railroads changed life in the West forever. They diminished isolation, brought consumer goods and new immigrants to the land, and enabled farmers and ranchers to send their products to markets in the East. Railroads also brought problems. They were often built at the expense of migrant laborers and contributed to the destruction of native cultures and the degradation of natural environments. Invite students to discuss the impact of railroads on the West.

TEACH

Guided Practice

L2 Discussion

Stimulate a discussion of the case study. You may want to invite students to talk about

- sources of information Mr. Katz used to prepare his travel announcements
- the use of peer reviewers in preparing manuscripts
- the importance of grammar in the writing process

Independent Practice

Writing Process Transparencies, 1–10

Case Studies: Writing in the Real World, pp. 5–8

Cooperative Learning Activities, pp. 7–12

Skills Practice

Thinking and Study Skills, pp. 1, 8, 11, 22

Vocabulary and Spelling Practice, p. 2

As the Empire Builder passes through the Bear Paw Mountains, Katz tells listeners about Chief Joseph and the Nez Percé.

Katz kept his audience in mind during the revision. Since other coach attendants would be learning the announcements, the guide needed to be easy to read. Katz says, "I tried . . . to make things grammatically correct. When you're speaking conversationally, you use phrases. This wouldn't go in a written version." He also checked for generalizations and corrected or added details. Finally, he asked his wife to read the revised version. "She asked me, 'Do you really want to say it that way?'"

Presenting

USING THE GUIDE

Katz's manuscript was distributed to his fellow coach attendants. In a cover letter, he encouraged them to have fun with the announcements: "Passengers can always tell the difference between someone reading over the loudspeaker and someone speaking." He also encouraged them to "embellish with your own style and material."

Katz has never stopped working on the guide, continuing to gather stories and update announcements. In his office is a photocopy of the "completed" manuscript. Throughout it, Katz has clipped notes for a later edition.

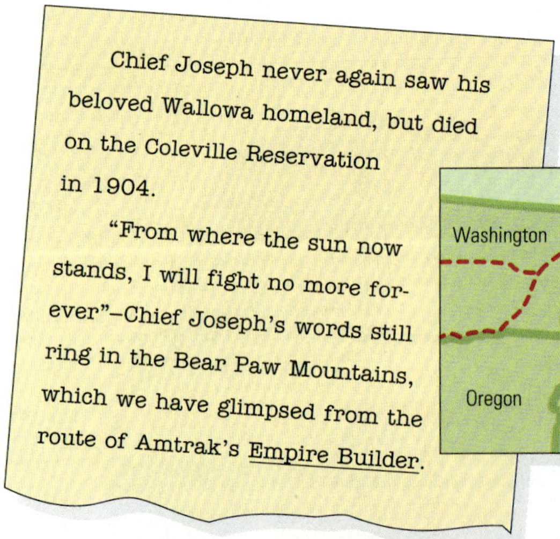

Chief Joseph never again saw his beloved Wallowa homeland, but died on the Coleville Reservation in 1904.

"From where the sun now stands, I will fight no more forever"–Chief Joseph's words still ring in the Bear Paw Mountains, which we have glimpsed from the route of Amtrak's Empire Builder.

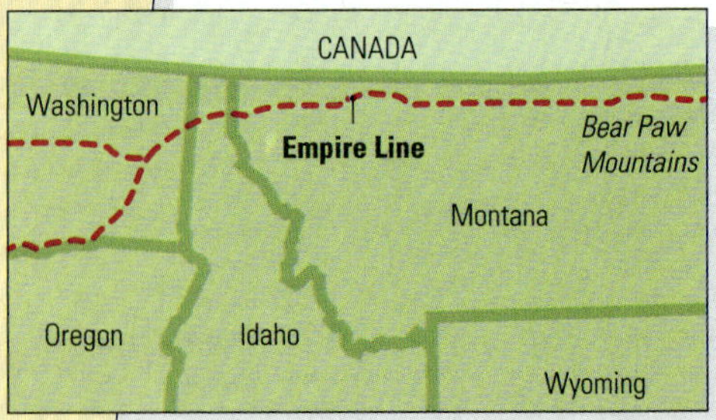

Visual Thinking

Using Photographs in Writing

Because photographs often recall the story of a place as well as words do, writers use photographs as note-taking tools. Have students bring in photographs of places they have visited. They can freewrite about a photo for five minutes and use their notes to write a travel announcement.

Responding to the Case Study

1. Discussion

Discuss these questions about Curtis Katz's writing process.

- What sources did Katz use to collect material for his travel guide?
- What order did Katz use to organize the information in his draft? Why do you think he chose this order?
- What did Katz do to make his guide easy for others to read?
- When did Katz add additional information to his guide?

2. Writing

Write a short paragraph for a travel guide.

A travel guide can be very helpful and entertaining. In addition to facts, it can include stories people tell about a place. Choose a place you know. It can be a place near your home or a place you have visited. Write a few paragraphs about the place. Tell its name, a fact or two, and something about its history or what people say about it. Look at Curtis Katz's entry on page 42 if you need ideas.

Grammar Link

Avoid sentence fragments when you write.

A fragment is a group of words that does not have all the parts that a complete sentence should. Curtis Katz used fragments in his notes, but in revising and editing his travel guide, he made sure that each sentence contained both a subject and a predicate.

Revise each fragment below so that it is a complete sentence.

1. the Lincoln Memorial in Washington, D.C.
2. statue of Abraham Lincoln
3. is a popular tourist attraction.
4. the words from the Gettysburg Address
5. the beautiful white building

See Lesson 8.2, page 264.

Using the Grammar Link

Grammar Link Answers

Answers will vary. Some suggestions follow.

1. We visited the Lincoln Memorial in Washington, D.C.
2. Using our new cameras, my sister and I photographed the statue of Abraham Lincoln.
3. Washington is a popular tourist attraction.
4. I read the words from the Gettysburg Address.
5. Rows of red flowers grew in front of the beautiful white building.

ASSESS

Responding to the Case Study

1. Discussion

- books, magazines, interviews
- order was based on the train route; to make travel announcements easy to use
- used correct grammar
- whenever he had new information

2. Writing

Answers will vary. A suggestion for the first paragraph is given below. Subsequent paragraphs should contain similar information.

When you visit Whitesville, don't forget to see the Johnson Iron Works. It's one of the most important businesses in the area, and one of the oldest.

See also the *Teacher's Guide to Writing Assessment.*

Grammar Link

(See Using the Grammar Link below.)

Reteaching

Invite students to read tourist brochures. How might the writers of these brochures have used the writing process?

Enrichment

Remind students to accurately record the comments of the people they interview.

CLOSE

Ask students to discuss the writing process. Which part of the process do they think is most important? Why? Which part do they most enjoy? Why?

Closing Note

For well-written travel writing, refer students to *National Geographic* or *National Geographic: Traveler.*

Setting the Purpose

In Lesson 2.1 students are guided through the stages of the writing process. The lesson teaches students how the process works and how to apply it to their own writing.

FOCUS

Lesson Overview

Objective: To identify attributes and components of the writing process and to use the writing process to generate or revise original writing

Skills: selecting and defining a topic; collecting and organizing information; drafting and revising a manuscript

Critical Thinking: analyzing; using a model

Speaking and Listening Activities: evaluating; questioning; discussing

Bellringer

When students enter the classroom, have this assignment on the board: *If you had to write a report about a favorite family recipe, what writing process would you follow? List the steps you would follow to write such a report.*

Grammar Link to the Bellringer

Ask students how many of them included checking punctuation as a part of their writing process. Why is checking punctuation important?

Motivating Activity

Invite students to discuss difficulties they have had writing reports or other documents. Explain that this lesson will provide them with a process that can make writing easier.

LESSON 2.1

The Writing Process

Exploring the Writing Process

The whole writing process includes five stages: prewriting, drafting, revising, editing, and presenting. This process can help you get from your first ideas to a finished piece of writing.

Maya, a reporter for her school newspaper, was stuck for a topic. While visiting her friend Bernard, Maya watched him cook a pot of gumbo for dinner. She thought that cooking was a topic that might interest other students. She pulled out her notebook and began taking notes.

Teacher's Classroom Resources

The following resources can be used for planning, instruction, practice, reinforcement, assessment, reteaching, enrichment, or evaluation

Teaching Tools
Lesson Plans

Transparencies
Fine Art Transparencies, 6–10
Writing Process Transparencies, 1–10

Blackline Masters
Thinking and Study Skills, pp. 2, 5
Writing Across the Curriculum, p. 4
Cooperative Learning Activities, pp. 7–12
Speaking and Listening Activities, pp. 6–7, 10–13

As soon as Maya got an idea and started taking notes, she had begun the prewriting stage of the writing process.

Begin with Ideas

Most writers take their work through all five of the stages you'll read about here. They often go through some stages more than oncc. Knowing about each of these stages will be helpful in completing your writing assignment.

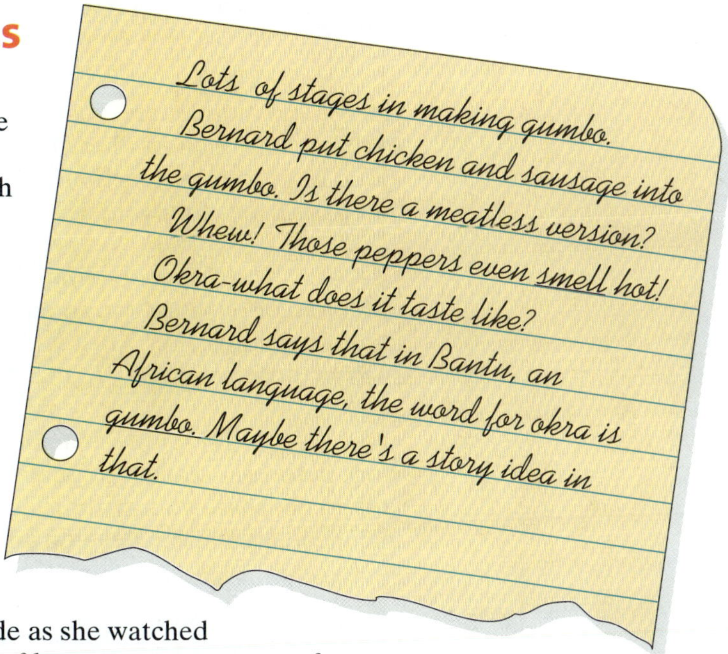

Prewriting Prewriting begins the moment you start to collect ideas. During this stage, writers explore and develop ideas into topics to write about. Look at the prewriting notes Maya made as she watched Bernard. Notice that some of her notes are sentence fragments. Notice that she wrote what Bernard did and what she thought. Notice where she wrote down words Bernard used.

Drafting Drafting involves developing your prewriting notes into connected sentences and paragraphs. During this stage, writers try new ideas and make connections. Sometimes they make some discoveries or even decide to change their topic. That's just part of the adventure of writing.

Journal Writing

What is your family's favorite recipe or food that has been handed down through the years? What is special about this recipe or food? Jot down ways to turn answers to these questions into a writing topic.

TEACH

Guided Practice

L2 Using a Writing Process Checklist

Students may equate the five stages of the writing process with a formula or prescription and, therefore, find it intimidating. To help eliminate such fears and make students more comfortable with the process, ask them to create a five-column chart with each of the five stages listed at the top of a column. Encourage students to use the chart when they write, making a check mark in the appropriate column when they recognize that they are in that stage of the process.

L2 Generating a Topic

Ask students to imagine that they are going to write a report about something they do in their spare time. Encourage them to spend ten minutes writing down ideas that might be included in a report. When students have finished, invite volunteers to read their lists of ideas. Work along with the class to help students focus their ideas into writing topics.

Two-Minute Skill Drill

Have students write as many ideas as they can think of for a written presentation entitled "The Musician I Admire Most."

Journal Writing Tip

Generating Topics When students write about family recipes, remind them to consider not only their own experiences and preferences but those of other family members.

Blackline Masters
Vocabulary and Spelling Practice, pp. 35–52
Composition Practice, p. 8
Composition Reteaching, p. 8
Composition Enrichment, p. 8

Unit Assessment

Teacher's Guide to Writing Assessment
Tests with Answer Key
Unit 2 Choice A Test, p. 5
Unit 2 Choice B Test, p. 6

Test Generator
Unit 2 Choice A Test
Unit 2 Choice B Test

You may wish to administer either the Unit 2 Choice A Test or the Unit 2 Choice B Test as a pretest.

TEACH

Guided Practice

L1 Revising a Manuscript

Help students to enhance their understanding of the revision process by looking for ways to improve another student's work. Invite students to work in pairs, exchanging draft copies and marking potential revisions. Help students to work through the comments their revision partners made, deciding which comments to incorporate in their final manuscripts.

L3 Using Different Presentation Formats

Encourage students to explore alternative methods for publishing and presenting their work. They might use computer technologies such as electronic mail or a disk to send their final manuscript to distant readers. The students might also augment a verbal presentation with video images or recorded audio effects.

Independent Practice

For further stimuli for using the writing process, see *Fine Art Transparencies* 6–10.

Writing Process Transparencies, 1–10

Writing Across the Curriculum, p. 4

Cooperative Learning Activities, pp. 7–12

Skills Practice

Thinking and Study Skills, pp. 2, 5

Speaking and Listening Activities, pp. 6–7, 10–13

Vocabulary and Spelling Practice, pp. 35–52

Composition Practice, p. 8

Follow Through

After getting your ideas on paper, you need to make sure they are clear. Look at the follow-through stages.

Revising The goal of revising is to make your writing clearer and more interesting to your audience. To revise, add or delete information where needed. Read your writing aloud to get others' reactions. Check to see that sentences and paragraphs fit together.

Editing The object of editing is to correct errors in spelling, grammar, or punctuation. To edit, read your draft, looking carefully for mistakes. Most writers use proofreading symbols such as those on page 74 to mark changes on their drafts.

Presenting Presenting includes everything from turning work in to your teacher to publishing a class book. Even if you do not share your writing, don't throw it away. It could include ideas you can develop and use later.

The Writing Process

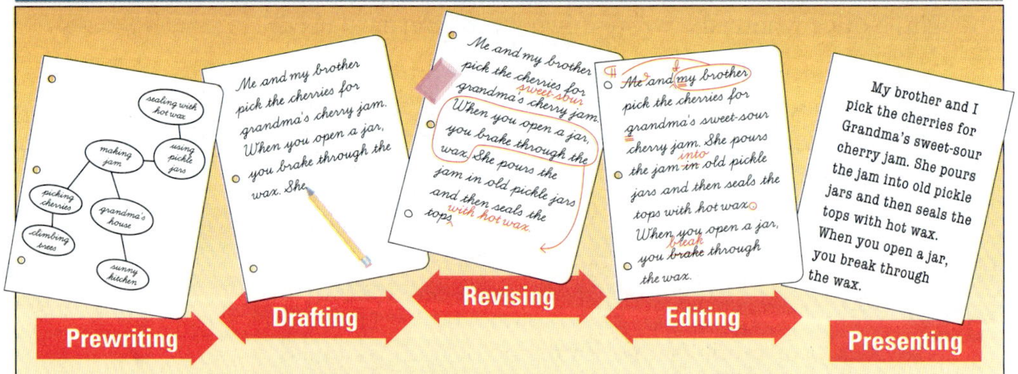

You can return to earlier stages before presenting your work.

Enabling Strategies

LEP Understanding the Writing Process

Students whose first language is not English can better understand the idea of *process* by thinking about the process of learning English. Students probably began learning the language by learning single words or phrases and slowly working these words into simple sentences. Then students worked step by step, increasing the complexity of their sentences as they became more familiar with the language.

2.1 Writing Activities

Write About Your Writing Process

Write a paragraph to explore your writing process. Follow the writing process for your own paragraph. Write about how you write now and what you might try in the future.

- Prewrite by making a list of what you do when you write. Organize your list.
- Draft a paragraph. Begin with a general statement about what you do when you write.
- Revise by reading your paragraph to yourself and to someone else and making changes to improve it.
- Edit your work by proofreading your paragraph.

PURPOSE To describe your own writing process
AUDIENCE Yourself
LENGTH 1 paragraph

COMPUTER OPTION

As you think about your own writing process, consider using a computer. Create a chart or table with five lists: one for prewriting, one for drafting, one for revising, one for editing, and one for presenting. Divide your notes among these lists.

Grammar Link

Use correct punctuation at the ends of sentences.

Bernard put chicken and sausage into the gumbo. Is there a meatless version? . . . Those peppers even smell *hot!*

Write each sentence below, ending it with the correct punctuation mark.

1. Have you read the book *The Lion King*
2. How scary parts of it are
3. The book came out after the movie
4. Read me the end of the story
5. Which character did you like best
6. Were you worried when the animals stampeded
7. What great special effects they made
8. The music was terrific
9. Do you think the voices fit the characters
10. *The Lion King* is the most popular animated film

See Lesson 19.1, page 454.

ASSESS

Writing Activities Evaluation Guidelines

Write About Your Writing Process

Use these criteria when evaluating your students' writing:
- Did students use the writing process to write their paragraphs?
- Were students' present and future writing processes detailed?
- Are paragraphs accurate in grammar, usage, and mechanics?

See also the *Teacher's Guide to Writing Assessment.*

Computer Option

If students are trying this option for the first time, make sure they know how to create the chart or table format.

Grammar Link

(See Using the Grammar Link below.)

Reteaching

Composition Reteaching, p. 8

Enrichment

Composition Enrichment, p. 8

Use *Fine Art Transparencies* 6–10 for enrichment activities.

CLOSE

Invite students to create sets of written guidelines to the writing process that they can use in future writing. You may wish to review students' individual guidelines to make sure they are accurate.

Using the Grammar Link

Grammar Link Answers

1. ?	6. ?
2. !	7. !
3. .	8. .
4. .	9. ?
5. ?	10. .

Using Correct Punctuation Suggest that students reread the paragraphs they wrote describing their own writing process. Did they vary the type of sentences they used? Would their paragraphs be more lively if they did? Remind students as they revise to check for correct punctuation.

Setting the Purpose

Lesson 2.2 teaches students to use questioning, listing, and clustering to generate writing topics.

FOCUS

Lesson Overview

Objective: To generate writing topics using questioning, listing, and clustering
Skills: listing writing ideas; using clusters
Critical Thinking: categorizing; classifying; generating new information
Speaking and Listening: discussing; questioning

Bellringer

When students enter the classroom, have this assignment on the board: *Imagine that you are writing an article for a student newspaper. You can pick any topic you want, but the article has to be of interest to ninth graders. Write a paragraph explaining how you would pick a topic.*

Grammar Link to the Bellringer

Invite students to list any possessive nouns in their Bellringer paragraphs. Help them to correct any punctuation errors in the possessive nouns.

Motivating Activity

Invite students to discuss problems they have had in coming up with interesting writing topics. What techniques might they suggest for students having difficulty choosing a topic? Explain that this lesson will provide students with strategies that make choosing a topic easier.

LESSON **2.2**

The Writing Process
Prewriting: Finding a Topic

Prewriting techniques can help you explore ideas and pinpoint possible topics that will interest readers. These techniques include listing, questioning, and clustering.

Think About a Topic

Sometimes it is difficult to nail down a topic that interests you. Once you do, you still need to know that your topic will be of interest to your readers.

Before Maya went to Bernard's house, she had struggled to find the right topic for her article. She needed a topic that would catch and hold the attention of her readers. She also wanted a topic she cared about. When people write about topics that truly interest them, that interest energizes the writing. This energy can be felt by the audience.

After her visit with Bernard, Maya knew she was close to pinning down her writing topic. She enjoys cooking, and she thought that others might be interested, too. However, she was not sure. She decided that she needed to do some research to find out if her audience would be as interested in cooking as she was.

Teacher's Classroom Resources

The following resources can be used for planning, instruction, practice, reinforcement, assessment, reteaching, enrichment, or evaluation.

Teaching Tools
Lesson Plans

Transparencies
Fine Art Transparencies, 6–10
Writing Process Transparencies, 1–10

Ask Questions

Prewriting techniques can help you explore topics that will interest both you and your readers. Maya combined questioning and listing in her prewriting. She asked herself the following questions:

- What do my friends like to learn about?
- What articles have appeared lately in the school newspaper?
- What things have I done recently?

Maya then took those three questions and made a list to answer each one. Read her notes.

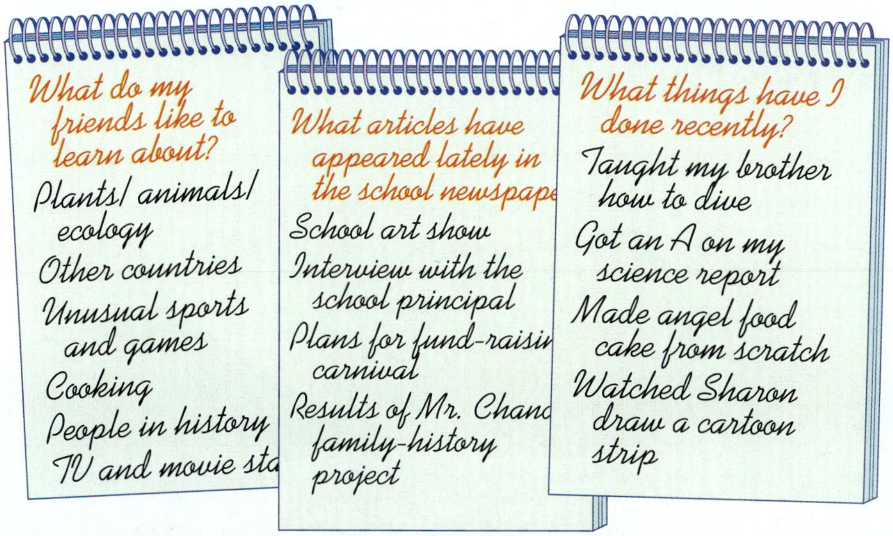

Journal Writing

Use Maya's lists as an example. Write three questions of your own. Create a list of ideas below each question. Then decide which three ideas might interest you most. Why would you want to write about these ideas? Answer this question in your journal.

TEACH

Guided Practice

L2 Using Visuals

Students who relate well to visuals may find it easier to generate writing ideas by looking through photo albums and magazines. Help them to group pictures with similar ideas. Students can then jot down ideas about one group of photos. Guide them to develop the ideas into a topic.

L1 Recording Discussions

Suggest that students use a tape recorder to find a writing topic. Help pairs of students to record a discussion about personal interests. In an interview-type format, one partner might ask: What do you like to do? What do you care about most? What do you like to read about? What are your friends interested in? Students can then listen to the tape as often as necessary to make a list of questions and answers. With your help, the students can use these questions and answers to find writing topics.

Two-Minute Skill Drill

Invite students to write a quick cluster around one of the following words:

science art music
sports computers

Journal Writing Tip

Answering Questions Remind students that a good way to start searching for a writing topic is to think about things they know or do well. What do they know or do that might interest someone else?

Blackline Masters

Thinking and Study Skills, pp. 1, 4–5, 7–8, 34–37
Writing Across the Curriculum, p. 5
Cooperative Learning Activities, pp. 7–12
Speaking and Listening Activities, pp. 6–7, 10–13
Vocabulary and Spelling Practice, pp. 35–52
Composition Practice, p. 9
Composition Reteaching, p. 9
Composition, Enrichment, p. 9

Assessment

Teacher's Guide to Writing Assessment

TEACH

Guided Practice

L2 Finding Topics

Ask students to give you examples of some objects or actions they saw on the way to school today. List these examples on the board. Then circle five of them. Ask the class to think of as many writing topics as possible for each circled item. Using the many writing topics listed on the board as an example, help students to see that writing topics are all around them.

L3 Using Clusters

Once students have decided on topics, they can use clusters to explore the topics. Direct them to write their topic in the center of their clusters and encourage them to take their clusters out as far as they can, including as much detail as they like. They can use words, phrases, or sentences to explore and expand their ideas. Point out that the more details they include, the more information they'll have to draw from when they write.

Independent Practice

For further stimuli for prewriting, see *Fine Art Transparencies* 6–10.

Writing Process Transparencies, 1–10

Writing Across the Curriculum, p. 5

Cooperative Learning Activities, pp. 7–12

Skills Practice

Thinking and Study Skills, pp. 1, 4–5, 7–8, 34–37

Speaking and Listening Activities, pp. 6–7, 10–13

Vocabulary and Spelling Practice, pp. 35–52

Composition Practice, p. 9

Use Cluster Diagrams

When Maya studied her lists, she noticed that some ideas fit together. A few involved collecting things. Others were about her friends' interests. Seeing these connections made Maya decide to write about her friends' hobbies.

Maya further explored her topic, using another prewriting technique called clustering. She began by writing "My Friends' Hobbies" in the center of a piece of paper. Then she drew a circle around the words. As Maya focused on that idea, details popped into her mind. Even though she knew she might not use all the ideas, she wrote them down anyway. She circled each idea, and drew lines to show where the details came from and how they were related.

As her cluster grew, Maya felt more confident about her topic.

50 *The Writing Process: Way to Go*

Enabling Strategies

LEP Using Translation Partners

Encourage students to use topic exploration as a way to practice and expand their English vocabulary. Remind students that they need not be concerned with grammatically correct construction when listing or clustering. Encourage them to write as many of their ideas as possible in English. They can then consult dictionaries or work with other students who are learning English to find English translations for their remaining ideas.

2.2 Writing Activities

Write to Explore a Topic

Gary Paulsen, author of many books for young adults, has given this advice: "Write about things that are real and important. Get loose, have a good time. Write about your fantasies. Write about what's happening that you don't like—or that you do like."

Review the three lists you created for this lesson's Journal Writing. Does Paulsen's quote describe the ideas in your list? Choose one of your journal ideas that really interests you. Apply prewriting techniques to explore the idea fully. Later in this unit you will develop the topic into a finished piece of writing.

- Ask yourself questions about your idea.
- Use clustering to explore your idea and collect details.
- Think about why the topic interests you and how you can interest your readers.

PURPOSE To apply prewriting techniques
AUDIENCE Yourself
LENGTH Lists and a diagram of varying lengths

COMPUTER OPTION

Consider using a computer drawing program to create your idea cluster. Use the Copy and Paste functions so that you don't need to redraw your cluster if you want to change it.

Grammar Link

Use possessive nouns correctly in your writing.

Possessive nouns describe ownership and are written with apostrophes.

***Mr. Chan's** project, or **my friends'** hobbies.*

Rewrite each sentence, using the correct possessive form of the noun in parentheses.

1. (Sally) hobby is swimming.
2. Sally swims on (Westville) swimming team.
3. Several of her (friends) hobbies also include swimming.
4. Her swim (team) colors are red and blue.
5. Sally's two swim (caps) colors are also red and blue.

See Lesson 9.3, page 288.

ASSESS

Writing Activities Evaluation Guidelines

Write to Explore a Topic

Use these criteria when evaluating your students' writing:

- Are details and ideas related to the topic?
- Is clustering used appropriately, including circles and lines linking related ideas?

See also the *Teacher's Guide to Writing Assessment.*

Grammar Link

(See Using the Grammar Link below.)

Reteaching

Composition Reteaching, p. 9

Enrichment

Composition Enrichment, p. 9

Use *Fine Art Transparencies* 6–10 for enrichment activities also.

CLOSE

Invite students to explain in their own words how techniques such as questioning, listing, and clustering can help them to decide on a writing topic. What tips would they offer other students working to choose a topic?

Using the Grammar Link

Grammar Link Answers

1. Sally's
2. Westville's
3. friends'
4. team's
5. caps'

Using Possessive Nouns Invite students to make a list of objects that they saw on the way to school or can see in the classroom. Help them to write possessive forms of the nouns: for example, *Tom's book, Ms. Chan's briefcase, Ellen's cat,* or *Adrienne's bicycle.*

Setting the Purpose

Lesson 2.3 teaches students how to organize ideas generated during the prewriting stage of the writing process.

FOCUS

Lesson Overview

Objective: To formulate questions about the purpose and audience for a piece of writing and to use purpose-determining questions to tailor a piece of writing to a specific audience
Skills: formulating questions; ordering information
Critical Thinking: defining and clarifying; categorizing; classifying
Speaking and Listening: discussing; questioning

Bellringer

When students enter the classroom, have this assignment on the board: *Write brief directions for how to make a cheese, lettuce, and tomato sandwich. Include the gathering of all ingredients and equipment in your directions.*

Grammar Link to the Bellringer

Have students reread directions for making their sandwiches and find phrases that include a past participle, such as "after you have added" or "when you have sliced." Work with them to make sure the past participles are used correctly.

Motivating Activity

Have several volunteers read their directions. Which directions are most effective? Why? Why is it important that directions for a process such as making a sandwich be in the proper order?

LESSON 2.3

The Writing Process
Prewriting: Ordering Ideas

Prewriting notes are much like a collection of baseball cards. These notes need to be ordered so that your readers will understand your message.

Organize Your Ideas

When you write, you can order your ideas in a variety of ways. Knowing your purpose for writing can help you decide what order to use. Most writing has one of four purposes.

- To tell an experience or story
- To describe how something or someone looks or acts
- To explain how something works or how to do something
- To persuade someone of something

Sometimes, one way of organizing works better than others for a certain purpose. For example, if you want to tell a story, you usually put events in the order in which they happened. If you want to convince someone of something, you might put your strongest argument last.

The passage on the opposite page tells about a boy and his mother walking down the street. They're exploring the town where they've just moved. Think about how the author organizes his details so that readers can picture what this town is like.

Teacher's Classroom Resources

The following resources can be used for planning, instruction, practice, reinforcement, assessment, reteaching, enrichment, or evaluation.

Teaching Tools
Lesson Plans

Transparencies
Fine Art Transparencies, 6–10
Writing Process Transparencies, 1–10

Literature Model

The first building we had seen when we turned the corner onto State Street was the church. Then we had come to a large house, followed by several stores. Some of the doors were closed, but one was open. There were men inside, talking. The whole next block was one long building. I stared up at all the windows.

David Kherdian, *Root River Run*

How do "first," "then," "followed by," and "next" help you know the order of details?

Journal Writing

Look through your journal for an entry that tells a story, describes something, explains something, or persuades someone. Is there a writing purpose you haven't tried yet in your journal? If so, make a list of possible topics for that writing purpose.

TEACH

Guided Practice

L2 Using the Model

The author describes the buildings in the order in which he passed by them. Encourage volunteers to discuss possible orders they might use to describe the buildings on their own street. Would they start with their house, or save it for later? Would they first describe a playground or a school? In how many different orders can they describe their street?

L3 Ordering a Story

Remind students that in stories the narrator often starts in the middle of the action and moves back and forth in time. Help students to come up with reasons why this type of ordering might be more interesting than relating events strictly in the order in which they happened.

Two-Minute Skill Drill

Ask students to write down the steps they took traveling to school that morning. Have them use the following words in their explanations:

first, before, finally, next, then

Journal Writing Tip

Observing As students identify different writing purposes in journal entries, ask them to notice the way their ideas are organized. Are ideas organized in similar ways for like purposes?

Blackline Masters

Thinking and Study Skills, pp. 2–4, 9, 20–21
Writing Across the Curriculum, p. 6
Cooperative Learning Activities, pp. 7–12
Speaking and Listening Activities, pp. 6–7, 10–13
Vocabulary and Spelling Practice, pp. 35–52
Composition Practice, p. 10
Composition Reteaching, p. 10
Composition Enrichment, p. 10

Assessment

Teacher's Guide to Writing Assessment

TEACH

Guided Practice

L2 Ordering from Clusters

Suggest an idea and help the class to create a cluster on the blackboard. Then break the class into small groups. Each group should create a list from one of the branches of the cluster, with each person in the group suggesting an item. The group should then order details in the way they would appear in a piece of writing. Groups should present their lists to the class and compare results with the other groups.

L1 Sorting Ideas

Students may find ordering ideas easier if they first sort the ideas into the categories "more important" and "less important" Help students to sort ideas from their clusters into these two categories. Then work with them to sort their ideas from these categories into a final order.

Independent Practice

- For further stimuli for writing, see *Fine Art Transparencies* 6–10.
- *Writing Process Transparencies,* 1–10
- *Writing Across the Curriculum,* p. 6
- *Cooperative Learning Activities,* pp. 7–12

Skills Practice

- *Thinking and Study Skills,* pp. 2–4, 9, 20–21
- *Speaking and Listening Activities,* pp. 6–7, 10–13
- *Vocabulary and Spelling Practice,* pp. 35–52
- *Composition Practice,* p. 10

Sketch a Plan

Maya looked back at her cluster diagram. Then she chose some of the details and added information to them. To organize her ideas, she made a list. Maya thought about her readers and her purpose for writing. Because she wanted to draw her readers into her article, she reordered her ideas in a way she thought would appeal to the readers. Below, you can see how Maya used her list to order her ideas.

To grab her readers' attention right away, Maya put what she thought was the most interesting hobby first.

This detail sounds interesting. Why didn't Maya number it?

Enabling Strategies

LEP Ordering By Example

Help students to understand the concept of ordering ideas by providing them with examples of well-ordered ideas in published writing. Articles that explain a process, computer manuals, and short stories are good sources of examples. Have students read carefully and take notes to record the order of ideas. Then have them discuss how ordered ideas helped make the writing understandable or enjoyable. Encourage students to apply what they have learned about order to their own work.

2.3 Writing Activities

Write an Ordered List

Review the cluster diagram that you prepared for your writing topic. Use it to help you plan the contents and the structure of your piece of writing.

- Choose details from the cluster diagram and list them.
- Add information about each detail.
- Organize the detailed list in the order you think will appeal to your readers.

PURPOSE To order details for writing
AUDIENCE Yourself
LENGTH 1 page

Eishōsai Chōki, *Catching Fireflies*, c. 1795

Grammar Link

Use past participles correctly in writing.

Past participles must be used with helping verbs.

The first building we ***had*** *seen . . .*

Rewrite each sentence below using the past participle form of the verb in parentheses.

1. Mr. Akito has (sketch) the scene with charcoal.
2. Earlier he had (make) a watercolor painting.
3. Our art teacher had (tell) us about the artist earlier.
4. We have (look) at much art.
5. What have you (like) best so far?

See Lesson 10.5, page 306.

ASSESS

Writing Activities Evaluation Guidelines

Write an Ordered List

Use these criteria when evaluating your students' writing:

- Does the list use details from the cluster diagram?
- Does it add information about each detail?
- Does it present ideas in a logical order?

See also the *Teacher's Guide to Writing Assessment.*

Grammar Link

(See Using the Grammar Link below.)

Reteaching

Composition Reteaching, p. 10

Enrichment

Composition Enrichment, p. 10

Use *Fine Art Transparencies* 6–10 for enrichment activities.

CLOSE

Have students work together to agree on general guidelines for ordering ideas in writing. Remind them that their rules may vary depending upon the type of writing.

Using the Grammar Link

Grammar Link Answers

1. has sketched
2. had made
3. had told
4. have looked
5. have you liked

About the Art

Eishōsai Chōki, *Catching Fireflies* c.1795

Catching Fireflies, a 15 by 10 inch woodblock with mica ground, is a famous *Ukiyoe* print, or "picture of the floating world." These prints depict everyday life in Japan between the seventeenth and nineteenth centuries.

Setting the Purpose

Lesson 2.4 teaches students how to get started writing and how to turn their prewriting ideas into a first draft.

FOCUS

Lesson Overview

Objective: To create a draft based on prewriting notes and ideas
Skills: developing details; organizing information; analyzing prewriting notes and ideas
Critical Thinking: analyzing; organizing; defining and clarifying; evaluating; elaborating
Speaking and Listening: discussing

Bellringer

When students enter the classroom, have this assignment on the board: *Write three questions related to the following statements:* Catamount is another name for a mountain lion. Mountain lions live in the United States. They are *hunters.*

Grammar Link to the Bellringer

Ask students what kind of sentences are written on the board for the Bellringer activity. (declarative) Then ask them what kind of sentences are the questions they wrote. (interrogative) Have students think of two other sentence types. (exclamatory, imperative) Can they give examples of these?

Motivating Activity

Lead a discussion comparing a first draft to a play rehearsal. Ask students if a rehearsal has to be perfect. Why not? (No audience is present and there is time to fix any problems.) Invite students to suggest ways in which a first draft is like a rehearsal.

LESSON 2.4

The Writing Process
Drafting: Getting It Down on Paper

Drafting is the stage when you turn ideas into sentences and paragraphs. When you draft, you just let the words flow. Later you can look for mistakes in grammar or spelling.

Maya couldn't wait to put her prewriting ideas into a first draft. She spread out her latest list, her cluster diagram, and the writing supplies she might need. Then she started to work.

Maya thought about some different ways she could organize. She also thought about some things she could say that would make her readers interested right away.

Teacher's Classroom Resources

The following resources can be used for planning, instruction, practice, reinforcement, assessment, reteaching, enrichment, or evaluation.

Teaching Tools
Lesson Plans

Transparencies
Fine Art Transparencies, 6–10
Writing Process Transparencies, 1–10

Start the Draft

The act of writing can make you think in new ways. When you begin to write, you may discover new ideas to add to your writing. You may also find that having prewriting notes can help you remember your original ideas and plan.

Maya made those same discoveries as she began to draft her article. Her cluster diagram and numbered list reminded her of the basics. She thought of ways to catch her audience's interest, and she talked to her friends about possibilities. Here's her introduction and part of her second paragraph.

> *It's time for a Wilson Elementary Wildcats Quiz! Who has attended bike-racing camp in Colorado? Who has boxes full of money in his closet? Whose gumbo can really make your mouth water? Whose name do you see in every edition of the school newspaper? They're all fellow Wildcats, students with some amazing hobbies.*
>
> *Take Jaime Sanchez, for example. He's been part of a local bike-racing club for two years.*

Which details do you recognize from Maya's cluster diagram and numbered list?

How does Maya make her readers want to go on reading the article?

Journal Writing

Look through your journal. Pick out two or three different types of topics. What might be an interesting introduction for each topic? Write your ideas in your journal.

TEACH

Guided Practice

L2 Using the Model

Ask students what Maya did to catch her readers' interest at the beginning of her article. Point out that Maya has incorporated details from her prewriting notes that refer to Jaime's interest in bike racing, Hector's coin collection, Bernard's gumbo, and Sharon's cartoons in the school newspaper. Ask students to think of some other ways that Maya might have captured the attention of her readers.

L1 Organizing Ideas

Students with learning disabilities might have trouble translating prewriting ideas into a structured paragraph form. These students may have more success if they try first to sketch each idea on a separate piece of paper. Tell students to arrange and rearrange the drawings until they are satisfied with the order of ideas. Then they can write a sentence for each drawing, using these sentences as the foundation for their draft.

Two-Minute Skill Drill

Ask students to write four kinds of sentences—declarative, exclamatory, interrogative, and imperative—including the word *window* in each.

Journal Writing Tip

Identifying Relationships and Patterns Remind students that when they review prewriting notes, they should look for related ideas.

Blackline Masters

Writing Across the Curriculum, p. 7
Thinking and Study Skills, pp. 7–13
Cooperative Learning Activities, pp. 7–12
Speaking and Listening Activities, pp. 6–7, 10–13
Vocabulary and Spelling Practice, pp. 35–52
Composition Practice, p. 11
Composition Reteaching, p. 11
Composition Enrichment, p. 11

Assessment

Teacher's Guide to Writing Assessment

TEACH

Guided Practice

L2 Thinking Critically

Ask students to find a piece of recorded music that features their favorite musical instrument. Play the recording in class, and then give a short explanation of why this music shows off their instrument so well. Tell them to refer to specific parts of the music to support their assertions. To help students think critically about the music, ask them, *Why does your instrument sound better in this music than another instrument would?*

L3 Discussing Writing Approaches

Tell students that every writer has a way to get started writing. Toni Morrison revealed, "I always know the ending; that's where I start." Ernest Hemingway said, "I rise at first light and I start by rereading and editing everything I have written to the point I left off." Ask students to list advantages and disadvantages of each approach. Discuss with students about which approach they feel most comfortable with, and why.

Independent Practice

- For further stimuli for writing a draft, see *Fine Art Transparencies* 6–10.
- *Writing Process Transparencies* 1–10
- *Writing Across the Curriculum*, p. 7
- *Cooperative Learning Activities*, pp. 7–12

Skills Practice

- *Thinking and Study Skills*, pp. 7–13
- *Speaking and Listening Activities*, pp. 6–7, 10–13
- *Vocabulary and Spelling Practice*, pp. 35–52
- *Composition Practice*, p. 11

Get Unstuck . . .

Maya got stuck on her introduction. She wasn't sure how to make it interesting. Two things helped. Maya had read that author Betsy Byars often begins writing in the middle of a story idea. So Maya began her draft by writing about Jaime and Sharon. As she wrote, she began to see how she might introduce them.

Maya also talked to her friend Stefan about her article. "Well, nothing makes me as curious as a question does," he told her. His comment helped Maya think of a way to draft her introduction. Maya's draft shows that she wrote her introduction using the advice from her friend. Most of the introduction is made up of questions that the rest of her draft will answer.

Sometimes it's hard to keep ideas flowing onto the paper. One or more of the following suggestions may help.

Getting Unstuck

Work on a different part of the piece. | Try other prewriting techniques. | Talk through your writing with a friend. | Take a break.

Enabling Strategies

LEP Choosing Words

To help students with a limited English vocabulary get started, give them several sentence starters to use in opening sentences. Some examples are *The most interesting/exciting/surprising thing about my new school/neighborhood is* ____ and *One of my favorite activities is* ____ *because it allows me to* ____ Explain that students can use these sentence starters in their first drafts. Later, when they revise, they can rewrite the sentences in their own words.

2.4 Writing Activities

Write a Draft

Review the ordered list you prepared about your topic. Use the list to write the first draft of your article or story. Let your ideas flow: don't worry about spelling and grammar at this point.

- Begin by writing an introduction that you think will catch your readers' attention.
- Write from your notes and add to them.
- If you get stuck, talk with a friend or use other techniques you learned in this lesson.

PURPOSE To write a first draft
AUDIENCE Yourself
LENGTH 2–3 paragraphs

Tina Dunkley, *Double Dutch Series: Keeping Time,* 1987

Grammar Link

Use different kinds of sentences when you write.

Using different kinds of sentences, as Maya did in her draft on page 57, makes writing more interesting.

Revise each sentence, writing it in the sentence type indicated in parentheses.

1. We will miss the bus. (interrogative)
2. Is everyone ready? (declarative)
3. We would like to go to the zoo. (exclamatory)
4. Will you please wait for me? (imperative)
5. Was this my favorite trip! (declarative)

See Lesson 8.1, page 262.

Cross-Curricular: Art

Write about your responses to the picture. What does it remind you of? How does it make you feel?

ASSESS

Writing Activities Evaluation Guidelines

Write a Draft

Use these criteria when evaluating your students' writing:

- Did students develop details by questioning, listing, or clustering?
- Did students incorporate details from prewriting into a draft?
- Did students arrange details in an order that makes sense?
- Did students keep the purpose and audience in mind?

See also the *Teacher's Guide to Writing Assessment.*

Cross-curricular: Art

Evaluate students' writing on the following elements: including personal responses; using specific details from the picture to clarify or explain; arranging details in a clear order.

Grammar Link

(See Using the Grammar Link below.)

Reteaching

Composition Reteaching, p. 11

Enrichment

Composition Enrichment, p. 11

Use *Fine Art Transparencies* 6–10 for enrichment activities.

CLOSE

Ask students what they would do if they got stuck while writing a draft. (for example, take a break, talk to a peer reviewer, or skip over the troublesome part) What else can students think of that might help keep ideas flowing? Remind them of the recursiveness of the writing process.

Using the Grammar Link

Grammar Link Answers

1. Will we miss the bus?
2. Everyone is ready.
3. Would we like to go to the zoo!
4. Please wait for me. (!)
5. This was my favorite trip.

About the Art

Tina Dunkley, *Double Dutch Series: Keeping Time*, 1987
This picture is batik on silk, 18-by-24 inches. Batik is a process of dying cloth. Wax is applied to the parts of the fabric not to be dyed. After the cloth is dipped in dye and dried, it is dipped in boiling water to remove the wax.

Setting the Purpose

In Lesson 2.5 students explore the revising stage of the writing process. Students will learn how to evaluate writing for unnecessary details and determine areas that need more information and organization.

FOCUS

Lesson Overview

Objective: To revise a piece of writing to address issues of purpose, audience, and clarity
Skills: selecting relevant information; organizing information; capitalizing proper nouns
Critical Thinking: analyzing; organizing; comparing; evaluating; clarifying
Speaking and Listening: discussing; interviewing; asking questions

Bellringer

When students enter the classroom, have this assignment on the board: *Write down these sentences in order of the most important fact to the least important fact (in your opinion):*

There were birds singing. Henry swam well Saturday. There were many people swimming. He broke his school speed record.

Grammar Link to the Bellringer

Have students underline the subject and circle the verb in each of the sentences they wrote for the Bellringer.

Motivating Activity

Ask students to imagine they are conducting a consumer opinion survey about a new video game. What questions might they ask? Tell them that manufacturers use such surveys to improve products. Introduce the idea that a similar process can be applied to writing.

LESSON 2.5

The Writing Process

Revising: Reviewing Your Ideas

The way you think about a piece of writing may change over time. After you've written a draft, you might think of a better way to say something. When you revise, you look for ways to make your draft better or clearer.

Writers aren't the only people who revise their work. While visiting her friend Sharon, Maya watched her study her latest cartoon sketch. Sharon erased a little here and added a little there. Taking a second look helped Sharon make her sketch funnier.

Teacher's Classroom Resources

The following resources can be used for planning, instruction, practice, reinforcement, assessment, reteaching, enrichment, or evaluation.

Teaching Tools
Lesson Plans

Transparencies
Fine Art Transparencies, 6–10
Writing Process Transparencies, 1–10

Step Back

When you finish your draft, put it away for a day or two if you can. Then, when you pick it up again, you may see that a point can be restated or that paragraphs can be rearranged.

A good way to check yourself is to ask questions. Read your draft as if you were a member of your audience. Then answer the five questions in the chart to the right.

Questions to Consider

1. Do I keep in mind what my audience knows or needs to know?
2. Do I stick to my topic? If not, why not?
3. Do I give my audience enough information?
4. Do I give my audience too much information?
5. Are the ideas in an order that makes sense?

The second step of revising is to have a conference to discuss your writing. Maya asked Stefan to comment on her article. His comments helped Maya see her work in a new way.

Working with a Peer Reviewer

1. Read your first draft aloud to a partner.
2. Discuss the draft with your partner.
3. Give your peer reviewer an evaluation form to fill out.

Journal Writing

In your journal, write about some times when you have changed your mind or revised your opinion. What caused the changes?

TEACH

Guided Practice

L2 Working with Peers

Have pairs of students work together on a piece of writing completed for an earlier assignment. Tell students that they will take turns reviewing and being reviewed. To begin, have students write a list of questions that they would like answered about their own piece of writing. These may include the Questions to Consider listed on this student page. Tell students to ask their partner these questions when it is their turn to be reviewed. Afterward, discuss with students how they think they can improve their work based on what they learned in the interviews.

L1 Peer Reviewing

When some students act as other students' peer reviewers, they may prefer to record their comments on a tape recorder rather than write them on an evaluation form. Ask writing partners to provide peer reviewers with lists of questions that they want answered during the review. Tell writers to include at least one positive leading question, such as, "What part did you like the most about my paper?"

Journal Writing Tip

Ordering Ideas Tell students that one way to approach their journal writing is first to list the reasons why they had the opinion, and then to list the reasons why they changed their mind.

Blackline Masters

Thinking and Study Skills, pp. 7, 9, 20–21
Writing Across the Curriculum, p. 8
Cooperative Learning Activities, pp. 7–12
Speaking and Listening Activities, pp. 6–7, 10–13
Vocabulary and Spelling Practice, pp. 35–52
Composition Practice, p. 12
Composition Reteaching, p. 12
Composition Enrichment, p. 12

Assessment

Teacher's Guide to Writing Assessment

TEACH

Guided Practice

L2 Using the Model

Ask students why Maya added this sentence to her draft: "She has been drawing pictures since she was three." Students should see that this is an interesting detail that adds new information. Ask students if there are any other details they might like to know about. (For example, How did Sharon learn to draw? Does she like to draw in pencil or ink?)

Two-Minute Skill Drill

List these common nouns on the board and have students write a proper noun for each (for example, *man, Mr. Smith*).

city
woman
street
teacher
country

Independent Practice

For further stimuli for writing, see *Fine Art Transparencies* 6–10.

Writing Process Transparencies, 1–10.

Writing Across the Curriculum, p. 8

Cooperative Learning Activities, pp. 7–12

Skills Practice

Thinking and Study Skills, pp. 7, 9, 20–21

Speaking and Listening Activities, pp. 6–7, 10–13

Vocabulary and Spelling Practice, pp. 35–52

Composition Practice, p. 12

Make a Mess

Taking a second look at your draft may have given you many new ideas. By asking questions you can decide if you want to make changes. For example, you may discover better ways to direct your writing to your audience. Mark changes on your draft, even if it makes the paper messy. After all, a draft is just a draft; it's not a final copy. Even the draft of the Declaration of Independence became messy when Thomas Jefferson revised it. Maya marked up the draft of her paragraph about Sharon, too.

SOS stands for Sharon Olivia Sanders. Someday you might see the initials SOS in your favorite comic strip. Sharon loves cartooning. She has her own room, which used to belong to her brother. He's away at college now. Sharon can draw animals and spaceships, ~~giraffes, shoes, dinner plates, chairs, fried eggs, toasters, or castles.~~ She can draw anything else you can imagine. Sharon makes cartooning look easy.

She has been drawing pictures since she was three.

Maya deleted these extra details. The phrase "anything else you can imagine" in the next sentence makes them unnecessary.

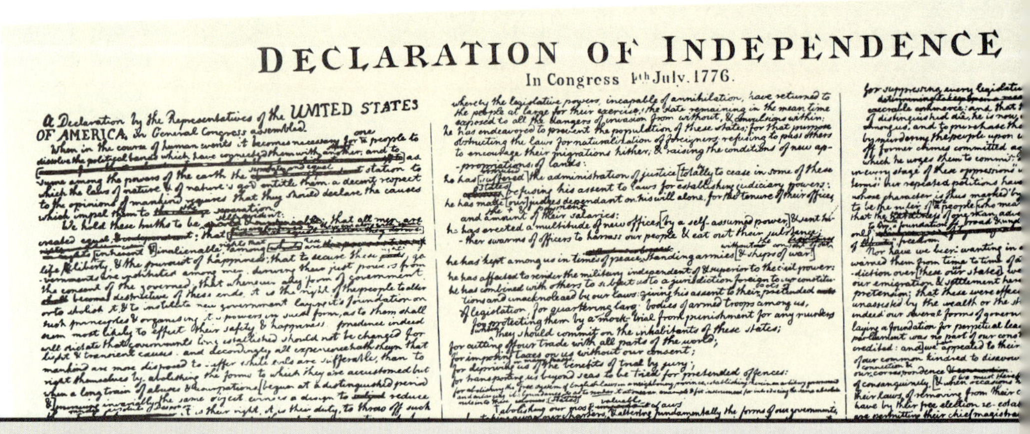

62

Enabling Strategies

LEP Asking Questions

Students acquiring English may benefit from peer reviews with students more proficient in English. Tell students that they are going to help each other with their writing. Have them select a piece of writing they are working on. Then have students write a list of questions they would like answered, such as, "What do you like best about my writing? What about my writing don't you understand? Is there anything I should write more about?" Have students form pairs, read each other's writing, and answer each other's questions.

2.5 Writing Activities

Write to Revise Your Draft

If possible, put your draft aside for a day or two before you begin this part of the writing process. Reread your first draft carefully. Think about its effectiveness.

- Ask yourself questions about your draft.
- Have a partner review and discuss the draft with you.
- Decide what changes you will make.
- Make all your changes directly on the first draft.

PURPOSE To revise a draft
AUDIENCE Yourself
LENGTH 2–3 paragraphs

COMPUTER OPTION

When you are ready to revise, use the Copy or Duplicate function to make copies of your draft. Keep your original unchanged, and experiment with changes on the copies. Compare each version with the original. Which version is best? Why?

Grammar Link

Capitalize proper nouns in your writing.

Read the first sentence of Maya's draft on page 62. Maya used capital letters for the initials and the full name of her friend. When you write, you often need to capitalize proper nouns that name particular people, places, or things.

Rewrite each sentence below. Use capital letters where needed.

1. We moved from san antonio to houston.
2. Our new home is on saddleback road.
3. My relatives, uncle jack and aunt jessie, live around the corner.
4. I started a new junior high school, huntington school.
5. My new teacher, mrs. lowery, made me feel welcome.

See Lesson 18.2, page 440 and Lesson 18.3, page 442.

ASSESS

Writing Activities Evaluation Guidelines

Write to Revise Your Draft

Use these criteria when evaluating your students' writing. If peer reviewers used evaluation forms, have them turn these in along with the piece of revised writing.

- Does the revision reflect changes suggested by the peer reviewer?
- Did the student revise with the audience in mind?
- Did the student add or delete information to make the ideas clearer?
- Does the order of the ideas make sense?

See also the *Teacher's Guide to Writing Assessment.*

Computer Option

Encourage students to use computers when drafting to make experimenting with changes easier.

Grammar Link

(See Using the Grammar Link below.)

Reteaching

Composition Reteaching, p. 12

Enrichment

Composition Enrichment, p. 12

CLOSE

Although peer reviewers are expected to be critical, tell students that it is also important for writers to know what works well. A peer reviewer should always begin by explaining what he or she liked about a piece of writing. Have students write down five positive things they might say to a writer. Give the following example: *excellent use of sensory details.*

Using the Grammar Link

Grammar Link Answers

1. San Antonio; Houston
2. Saddleback Road
3. Uncle Jack; Aunt Jessie
4. Huntington School
5. Mrs. Lowery

Capitalizing Proper Nouns Write the following proper nouns on the board, and have students rewrite them, correcting the capitalization.

t. l. bertolino	mrs. gomez
dr. price	kingsride avenue
clear lake, texas	gilroy, california
tokyo, japan	mount shasta

Setting the Purpose

Lesson 2.6 teaches students to revise paragraphs. It tells them how to identify main ideas, write topic sentences, and use transition words.

FOCUS

Lesson Overview

Objective: To revise paragraphs for unity and coherence
Skills: ordering sentences; using transition words; writing topic sentences; making subjects and verbs agree
Critical Thinking: analyzing; relating; visualizing; defining and clarifying
Speaking and Listening: discussing; speaking to a group

Bellringer

When students enter the classroom, have this assignment on the board: *Write two sentences that you think would be good beginnings for two pieces of writing.*

Grammar Link to the Bellringer

Ask students to rewrite the sentences they wrote for the Bellringer, beginning each sentence with either *Here* or *There.* Then ask students to underline the verb in each sentence.

Motivating Activity

Ask students to imagine they are watching a movie. The first scene shows a family traveling to Mars. The spaceship breaks down and the family is stranded in space. Next the scene shifts to children playing in a park. Then the movie shifts again to a recycling bin. How might the audience feel? What might they do? Why must a piece of writing, like a movie, stick to one main idea?

LESSON 2.6

The Writing Process

Revising: Getting Paragraphs into Shape

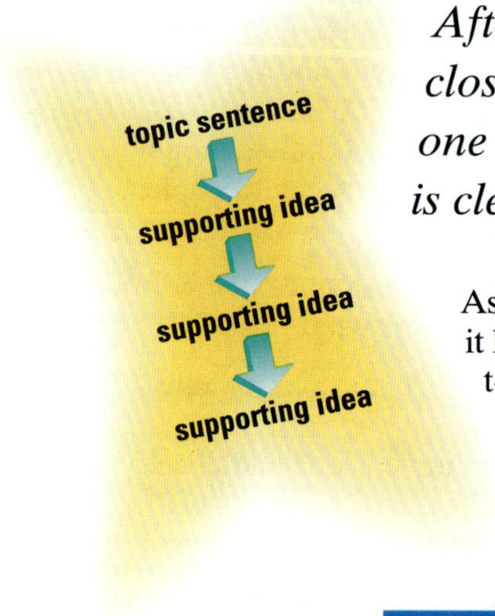

After you have revised your draft, look closely at each paragraph. Be sure each one expresses the main idea in a way that is clear to the reader.

Ask yourself these questions about each paragraph: Does it have a main topic? Does each sentence relate to the topic? Are the sentences in a sensible order? Without realizing it, you think about these questions when you read. When a paragraph is off track or unclear, you notice—it is difficult to understand. In the model below, how does the writer keep his idea on track?

Which sentence tells what this paragraph is about?

How do the other sentences help make the main idea easy to understand?

Literature Model

You will want several layers of clothing for backpacking. One reason for this is that temperatures can rise or drop several degrees in just a few minutes, particularly in thin mountain air. Stepping from sunlight into shadow can bring a drop of twenty degrees or more. Another reason is that [backpacking] is hard work. Your body will be hot as you hike, but when you stop you will cool off fast.

Richard B. Lyttle,
The Complete Beginner's Guide to Backpacking

Teacher's Classroom Resources

The following resources can be used for planning, instruction, practice, reinforcement, assessment, reteaching, enrichment, or evaluation.

Teaching Tools
Lesson Plans

Transparencies
Fine Art Transparencies, 6–10
Writing Process Transparencies, 1–10

Recognize a Paragraph's Shape

Every sentence in a paragraph should have a reason for being there. In Lyttle's paragraph, the main idea is expressed in a topic sentence. Some paragraphs begin with a topic sentence. Others build to a topic sentence that comes at the end. It is even possible to construct a strong paragraph without a topic sentence.

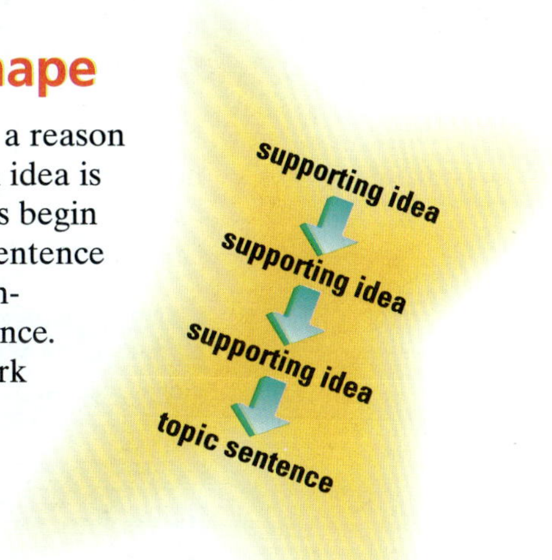

In a paragraph, all the sentences should work together to develop the main idea in a clear way. Lyttle's paragraph on page 64 *begins* with a topic sentence. Other sentences flow from the idea in the topic sentence. Vicki McVey's paragraph below *ends* with a topic sentence. Notice how the topic sentence ties together the sentences that lead to it.

Literature Model

The Pacific Ocean covers almost one third of the earth . . . and there are people who live on tiny islands in the middle of it. They can't see anything from horizon to horizon except water, and yet they set out in canoes for other tiny islands, . . . and get there. These are among the most amazing wayfinders of all time.

Vicki McVey, *The Sierra Club Wayfinding Book*

What do you learn about the people described in this paragraph?

Which sentence is the topic sentence?

Journal Writing

Read a few paragraphs in a library book or textbook, and answer these questions in your journal: Is there a topic sentence that tells the main idea in each paragraph? Where does the topic sentence appear? What do these answers tell you about writing paragraphs?

TEACH

Guided Practice

L2 Using the Model

Emphasize that the topic sentence in the model on page 65 comes at the end of the paragraph. Ask students the purpose of the first two sentences in the paragraph. (They offer supporting details.) Is this type of paragraph structure effective? Why or why not?

L2 Constructing a Paragraph

Find a well-constructed paragraph that has a topic sentence with a clearly stated main idea. Write the paragraph, starting each sentence on a new line. Then copy the paragraph, and cut the copies into separate sentences. Ask students to pair up with another student. Give all but the topic sentence to each pair of students. Ask them to construct a paragraph and then write a topic sentence that states the main idea. Partners can compare their completed paragraphs. Finally, read the original paragraph aloud so that students can compare their paragraphs to the original.

Two-Minute Skill Drill

Ask students to write a verb for each of the following sentences.

There _______ ducks.
Here _________ John.
There _______ a cloud.
Here _______ Tina and Lydia.

Journal Writing Tip

Topic Sentences For those paragraphs in library books with no topic sentences, ask students to write an appropriate main idea topic sentence.

Blackline Masters

Writing Across the Curriculum, p. 8
Thinking and Study Skills, pp. 7–9, 13
Cooperative Learning Activities, pp. 7–12
Speaking and Listening Activities, pp. 6–7, 10–13
Vocabulary and Spelling Practice, pp. 35–52
Composition Practice, p. 13
Composition Reteaching, p. 13
Composition Enrichment, p. 13

Assessment

Teacher's Guide to Writing Assessment

TEACH

Guided Practice

L1 Thinking Visually

Explain that a transition word is like a bridge that connects ideas. Ask students to summarize the message of the graphic on this page. (In a strong paragraph, each sentence gives an important detail about the main idea, and transition words provide smooth connections between ideas.) Ask students if they think the drawing is effective. Encourage students to draw other images to show the idea of a word or phrase linking two ideas.

L3 Writing Stories

Students might enjoy writing their own stories based on the weaving shown on page 67. Encourage them to research the geography and people of the Navajo reservation where Shiprock is located. Their research will provide them with authentic, realistic details for their stories and may give them ideas for a story plot. When they have finished their stories, they should use the comments and suggestions of peer reviewers to help them revise. Students may share stories.

Independent Practice

For further stimuli for writing, see *Fine Art Transparencies,* 6–10.

Writing Process Transparencies, 1–10

Writing Across the Curriculum, p. 8

Cooperative Learning Activities, pp. 7–12

Skills Practice

Thinking and Study Skills, pp. 7–9, 13

Speaking and Listening Activities, pp. 6–7, 10–13

Vocabulary and Spelling Practice, pp. 35–52

Composition Practice, p. 13

Shape Up Your Paragraphs

A strong paragraph has a clear main idea even if it does not have a topic sentence. These guidelines can help you find ways to make each paragraph you write stronger. Maya used them to make a few more changes on her draft.

Guidelines for Writing Stronger Paragraphs

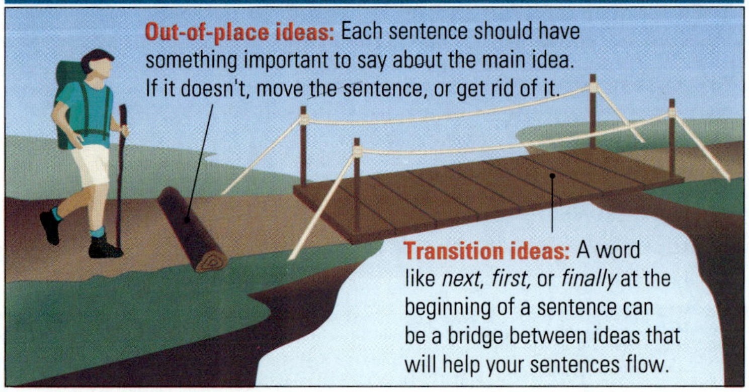

Maya switched the two sentences. She thought the second sentence would work better at the beginning of the paragraph.

Review the guidelines above. Why did Maya take out these two sentences?

Why did Maya change these two sentences?

SOS stands for Sharon Olivia Sanders. Someday you might see the initials SOS in your favorite comic strip. Sharon loves cartooning. She has been drawing pictures since she was three. ~~She has her own room, which used to belong to her brother. He's away at college now.~~ Sharon can draw animals, ~~and~~ spaceships, ~~She can draw~~ or anything else you can imagine. Sharon makes cartooning look easy.

Enabling Strategies

LEP Choosing Words

Students learning English may benefit from extra practice in using transition words. Write the following words on the board: *first, next, then, after, finally.* Model writing a simple paragraph in which each sentence starts with one of these words. The paragraph should describe a simple process, such as running a VCR. Next have students work in pairs to write their own paragraphs, beginning each sentence with a transition word. They can begin by verbalizing the steps in the process in their first language.

2.6 Writing Activities

Write Strong Paragraphs

Study your draft again. Make each paragraph stronger.

- Be sure that each paragraph is about one main idea.
- Take out any sentence that does not relate to the main idea.
- Put the ideas in the most sensible order.
- Use transition words to connect ideas.

PURPOSE To strengthen paragraphs
AUDIENCE Yourself
LENGTH 2–4 paragraphs

Artist unknown, Navajo, Shiprock rug, c. 1930

Cross-Curricular: Art

Look at the photo of a Navajo rug. Write a strong paragraph about what the weaver may have wanted to show. Express your main idea in a topic sentence. Support this sentence with details.

Grammar Link

Make subjects and verbs agree in sentences with *there*.

. . . *and there* ***are people*** *who live . . .*

Find the subject of each sentence below. Then write the correct form of the verb in parentheses.

1. There (is/are) a new skating rink at the mall.
2. There (is/are) many kids from our class who are good skaters.
3. There (has been/have been) times when the rink was not crowded.
4. There (is/are) a charge to rent skates.
5. There (is/are) two food stands next to the rink.

See Lesson 15.2, page 406.

ASSESS

Writing Activities Evaluation Guidelines

Write Strong Paragraphs

Use these criteria when evaluating your students' writing.

- Does each sentence contain a detail that relates to the main idea?
- Do sentences have transition words?
- Do the ideas flow?

See also the *Teacher's Guide to Writing Assessment.*

Cross-Curricular: Art

Evaluate the paragraph on the following: a topic sentence that clearly states the main idea; details from the art to support the main idea

Grammar Link

(See Using the Grammar Link below.)

Reteaching

Composition Reteaching, p. 13

Enrichment

Composition Enrichment, p. 13

Use *Fine Art Transparencies* 6–10 for enrichment activities also.

CLOSE

Write an idea for a topic sentence on the board, such as *Yesterday was the most wonderful day of my life.* Then ask for volunteers to think of sentences that give supporting details. Encourage students to use transition words. Write each sentence on the board. Then discuss with students how the sentences could be rearranged or changed to make the paragraph more coherent.

Using the Grammar Link

Grammar Link Answers

1. skating rink; is
2. kids; are
3. times; have been
4. charge; is
5. stands; are

About the Art

Artist unknown, Navajo, *Shiprock rug*, c. 1930
This rug of hand-spun wool, woven by an unknown Navajo weaver in the 1930s, depicts Shiprock, a geological formation located on a Navajo reservation in northern New Mexico. The 55-by-34-inch rug hangs in a private collection.

Setting the Purpose

Lesson 2.7 teaches students how to vary and combine sentences to create smooth-sounding paragraphs.

FOCUS

Lesson Overview

Objective: To use sentence variety
Skills: combining sentences; varying sentence beginnings; using connecting words
Critical Thinking: evaluating; patterning
Speaking and Listening: discussing; speaking to a group

Bellringer

When students enter the classroom, have this assignment on the board: *Combine any two of these sentences to make an interesting new sentence:*

The dog barked. The waves rolled in.
The sun shone. I found my towel.

Grammar Link to the Bellringer

Have students look at the new sentence they wrote for the Bellringer and underline the word or words they used to combine the original sentences.

Motivating Activity

Write the following sentences on the board, and then read them aloud: *The wind blew through the trees. The leaves fell to the ground. The children played in the park.* Ask students how the sentences sound. Help them recognize that their similar construction makes these sentences sound boring together. Discuss with students the idea that variety in sentence structure creates interest and adds to the reader's enjoyment.

LESSON 2.7

The Writing Process
Revising: Writing Sentences That Flow

Varying, or changing, the length of sentences can make your writing lively and a pleasure to read. When sentences are the same length, the writing sounds all the same and can be very boring.

In the model below, Marjorie Kinnan Rawlings describes a flock of whooping cranes that seem to be doing a strange dance. Read the paragraph aloud. Think about how sentence length affects the sound.

Would this sentence sound different if it were written as three sentences?

Literature Model

Two stood apart, erect and white, making a strange music that was part cry and part singing. The rhythm was irregular, like the dance. The other birds were in a circle. In the heart of the circle, several moved counter-clock-wise. The musicians made their music. The dancers raised their wings and lifted their feet, first one and then the other. They sunk their heads deep in their snowy breasts, lifted them and sunk again. They moved soundlessly, part awkwardness, part grace. The dance was solemn. Wings fluttered, rising and falling like out-stretched arms.

Marjorie Kinnan Rawlings, *The Yearling*

Teacher's Classroom Resources

The following resources can be used for planning, instruction, practice, reinforcement, assessment, reteaching, enrichment, or evaluation.

Teaching Tools
Lesson Plans

Transparencies
Fine Art Transparencies, 6–10
Writing Process Transparencies, 1–10

Write Notes to Yourself

As Maya wrote about her friend Hector Huang, she heard long and short sentences working together to create a pleasing pattern. Maya wanted to be sure that readers would hear this pattern, too.

With her readers in mind, Maya made a plan. She wrote some comments on her draft and put it aside for a day. Read what Maya wrote, and think about how a plan like Maya's might work for you.

Do you agree with Maya's question? How could you avoid repeating these words?

Should I use this word twice?

Too many "Hector's coins" Don't get boring

My friend Hector enjoys biking and canoeing. For his favorite hobby, though, he can stay indoors. You see, Hector is a numismatist, ~~A numismatist is~~ a coin collector. ~~Some of~~ Hector's coins are made of copper ~~The rest of Hector's~~ or coins are made of nickel. ~~Hector's coins~~ They flash white and gold in sunlight. Hector began his collection three years ago when his grandmother gave him a buffalo nickel.

Journal Writing

Choose a paragraph you wrote in a story or article some time ago, and read it aloud. Listen to the sound of your sentences. Think of ways to improve the sound without changing the meaning of your ideas. In your journal, experiment with different ways of revising your paragraph.

Blackline Masters

Thinking and Study Skills, pp. 9, 11, 38
Writing Across the Curriculum, p. 8
Sentence Combining Practice
Cooperative Learning Activities, pp. 7–12
Speaking and Listening Activities, pp. 6–7, 10–13
Vocabulary and Spelling Practice, pp. 35–52
Composition Practice, p. 14
Composition Reteaching, p. 14
Composition Enrichment, p. 14

Assessment

Teacher's Guide to Writing Assessment

TEACH

Guided Practice

L2 Using the Model

Ask students to rewrite the first sentence in the literature model on page 68 to make three or four separate sentences. Ask for volunteers to read their new sentences aloud, then discuss with students how these new sentences sound. Point out that breaking up the first sentence makes the prose sound choppy and dull and distracts from the image of the dance that Rawlings has created. Then ask students what they think of the original first sentence. Point out that the first sentence enhances the pleasant, rhythmic sound of the paragraph.

L2 Using the Model

Encourage students to explain whether or not Maya should repeat the word *numismatist*. Point out that Maya might revise to produce the following sentence: "You see, Hector is a numismatist, a coin collector." Ask students for other suggestions for ways to revise the sentence.

Two-Minute Skill Drill

Write these two sentences on the board and have students combine them using a connecting word or conjunction.

I love the sunshine. I don't like getting a sunburn.

Journal Writing Tip

Defining and Clarifying Problems Tell students that they can act as their own reviewers and write comments to themselves in the margin of the original paragraph.

TEACH

Guided Practice

L1 Revising Paragraphs

Encourage students to try reading their sentences into a tape recorder. Point out that when they play back the tape, they should listen carefully for short, choppy sentences and repeated words. Students can revise their paragraphs and record their revisions, listening to them to make sure the revisions improve the sound but do not change the meaning.

L3 Discussing Repetition

Tell students that occasionally repetition can be an effective tool—for example, in a political speech. Ask students why this might be, and encourage them to suggest other times when repetition might help a piece of writing. Ask for volunteers to imagine they are politicians and to write speeches using repetition. Ask students if they think the speeches are effective, and why or why not?

Independent Practice

For further stimuli for writing, see *Fine Art Transparencies* 6–10.

Writing Process Transparencies, 1–10

Writing Across the Curriculum, p. 8

Cooperative Learning Activities, pp. 7–12

Skills Practice

Thinking and Study Skills, pp. 9, 11, 38

Sentence Combining Practice

Speaking and Listening Activities, pp. 6–7, 10–13

Vocabulary and Spelling Practice, pp. 35–52

Composition Practice, p. 14

Think About Each Sentence

Maya noticed that her sentences were boring when certain words were repeated again and again. She studied her sentences and decided that she could make her writing smooth by combining some sentences. The point of sentence combining is to join sentences without changing the basic meaning. Combining should help the writing flow more smoothly and sound better.

Another way to make writing more interesting is to vary the beginnings of sentences. Writing also sounds boring if every sentence begins with *I* or *The*. Look at the chart below. How did Maya use these hints to change her writing?

Hints for Sentence Combining
1. Take out repeated words.
2. Use connecting words, such as *and, but,* and *or.*
3. Vary sentence beginnings.

Notice that changing the repeated words does not change the meaning of the paragraph.

My friend Hector enjoys biking and canoeing. For his favorite hobby, though, he can stay indoors. You see, Hector is a numismatist, ~~A numismatist is~~ a coin collector. ~~Some of~~ Hector's coins are made of copper, ~~The rest of Hector's coins are made~~ or of nickel. ~~Hector's coins~~ They flash white and gold in sunlight. Hector began his collection three years ago when his grandmother gave him a buffalo nickel.

Should I use this word twice?

Too many "Hector's coins" Don't get boring

How does using a connecting word here make the sentence easier to read?

Enabling Strategies

LEP Varying Sentence Length and Structure

Since English sentences might have a less-than-smooth sound for students who are learning English, these students may not be able to distinguish between the dull, choppy sound of many short sentences and the smooth, rhythmic sound created by a variety of sentence lengths. For these students you may want to focus on both correct sentence structure and variety in sentence length and structure.

2.7 Writing Activities

Write Smooth Paragraphs

Improve your draft by revising the sentences within each paragraph.

- Vary the length of sentences by combining some of them.
- Avoid unnecessary repetition.
- Use connecting words, such as *and, but,* and *or.*
- Vary sentence beginnings.

PURPOSE To improve paragraphs by revising sentences
AUDIENCE Yourself
LENGTH 2–4 paragraphs

Zhao Yixiong, *Jeep in the Desert,* 1981

Cooperative Learning

Work in a small group to describe the painting. Each member should write one sentence for a group paragraph. Then read your paragraph aloud and revise to improve the flow.

Grammar Link

Combine sentences for smoother paragraphs.

Combine the following pairs of sentences by writing compound subjects or compound verbs. See the Literature Model on page 68 for an example. Use the conjunctions in parentheses to combine the sentences.

1. My town is not too big. My town is big enough for me. (but)
2. Colorado has a good baseball team. Cincinnati has a good baseball team. (and)
3. My family can go hiking in the mountains. We can go camping. (or)
4. I like to go to the museum. My friend likes to go to the museum. (and)
5. We ski in winter. We swim in summer. (and)

See Lesson 20.2, page 484.

ASSESS

Writing Activities Evaluation Guidelines

Revise Sentences

Use these criteria when evaluating your students' writing.

- Do the sentences flow smoothly?
- Is unnecessary repetition avoided?
- Is there a variety of sentence lengths?

See also the *Teacher's Guide to Writing Assessment.*

Cooperative Learning

Evaluate each paragraph on the following: avoidance of unnecessary repetition; variety of sentence lengths; specific details about the painting.

Grammar Link

(See Using the Grammar Link below.)

Reteaching

Composition Reteaching, p. 14

Enrichment

Composition Enrichment, p. 14

Use *Fine Art Transparencies* 6–10 for enrichment activities also.

CLOSE

Tell students that paying attention to sentence patterns is very important when writing poetry, too. Ask students to write short poems of three to six lines about anything they like—perhaps something they enjoy doing, a pet, or even their favorite food. Tell them to pick a sentence structure pattern to use before they begin, such as short-long-short. Invite volunteers to share their finished poems with the class.

Using the Grammar Link

Grammar Link Answers

1. My town is not too big, but it is big enough for me.
2. We have a good basketball team and a winning baseball team.
3. My family can go hiking or camping in the mountains.
4. My friend and I like to go to the museum.
5. We ski in winter and swim in summer.

About the Art

Zhao Yixiong, *Jeep in the Desert*, 1981
In this painting Chinese artist Zhao Yixiong contrasts the old and the new China using the symbols of desert camels and a Jeep. This 4-by-4-foot oil painting is from the artist's own collection in Beijing, China.

Setting the Purpose

Lesson 2.8 teaches students how to edit a piece of writing for mechanical errors and to proofread using standard proofreading marks.

FOCUS

Lesson Overview

Objective: To identify sentence errors and mechanical errors in a piece of writing
Skills: editing; proofreading
Critical Thinking: establishing and evaluating criteria; making decisions
Speaking and Listening: discussing; note taking; listening accurately

Bellringer

When students enter the classroom, have this assignment on the board: *Rewrite this sentence correctly.*

johns father took us to a basketball game we seen famous players and eat popcorn.

Grammar Link to the Bellringer

Make a list of the types of errors that you found in the Bellringer.

Motivating Activity

Write a paragraph on the board that includes eight of the more common proofreading mistakes (misspelled words, missing punctuation, incorrect capitalization, incorrect possessives and contractions, wrong verb tense, sentence fragments, run-on sentences, and incorrect pronouns). Divide students into two groups. Each group should try to be first to find all eight mistakes and correct them on their paper. The group that wins should then correct the paragraph on the board.

LESSON **2.8**

The Writing Process
Editing: Checking Details

Your writing is not finished until you edit and proofread it. These two steps let you take care of the small details that show the pride you take in your work.

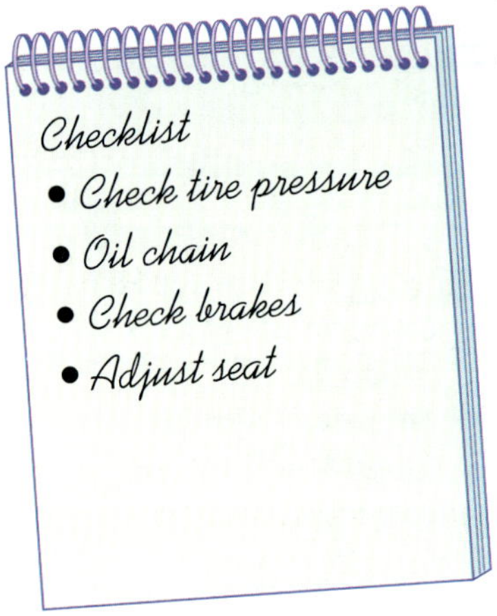

Maya's friends Jaime and Marta take their biking seriously. Maya watched Jaime and Marta tune up their bikes before a race. Marta showed Maya the checklist they were using. Marta explained that using a checklist gives them confidence during the race. They know they have checked everything and can concentrate on performing well. Maya was surprised. She uses a writing checklist for the same reason.

Teacher's Classroom Resources

The following resources can be used for planning, instruction, practice, reinforcement, assessment, reteaching, enrichment, or evaluation.

Teaching Tools
Lesson Plans

Transparencies
Fine Art Transparencies, 6–10
Writing Process Transparencies, 1–10

Polish Your Work

To make sure your sentences are clear, you need to edit your draft. Look for mistakes that might have slipped in. Think about the questions in the checklist on the right. You might want to read the draft one time for each question.

Look at Maya's second paragraph. She used the checklist to edit her draft. For each question she read through her work once. That way, she was more likely to catch errors. Maya will correct errors not covered by this checklist in a later reading.

Editing Checklist
1. *Do I have sentence fragments?*
2. *Do I have any run-on sentences?*
3. *Have I used correct punctuation and capitalization?*
4. *Are my verb forms and tenses correct?*

Take Jaime Sánchez for example. He and his sister Marta ~~loves~~ love biking. They both have been ~~Part~~ part of a local bike-racing club for too years. They've even ~~winned~~ won some amateur races. This spring, though, Jaime wanted to learn more about racing ~~they~~ His club sent him to a four-day racing camp sponsored by the United states Cycling Federation. This was JAime's first trip to Colorado.

Why did Maya change this sentence? Which question on Maya's list covers the problem?

There's more than one way to handle this run-on sentence. How else might you revise it?

Journal Writing

Have you made certain writing mistakes in your papers? In your journal list questions that can help you catch these mistakes. For more help, see page 74.

TEACH

Guided Practice

L2 Using the Model

Maya added a subject to make a complete sentence. She caught this mistake by asking herself if she had sentence fragments. Maya might have revised the run-on sentence this way: *Because Jaime wanted to learn more about racing, his club sent him to a four-day racing camp.*

L3 Using Fragments Deliberately

Students who read extensively may point out that some writers deliberately use fragments and run-on sentences in their work. Explain that writers occasionally do this for effect or to achieve a certain style. Suggest that students bring in published works that contain fragments and run-on sentences. Discuss the effects that fragments and run-ons have on the selections. Then have students "correct" the fragments and run-ons and discuss how their corrections change the feel of each work.

Two-Minute Skill Drill

Have students write this sentence correctly: *I went over to Jordan's house and together, we made cookies.* Ask students what question on the checklist on page 73 covers this type of error.

Journal Writing Tip

Write an Editing Checklist Students should look for mistakes that they are likely to repeat. Reviewing writing assignments that have been returned with teacher comments may help.

Blackline Masters

Thinking and Study Skills, pp. 20–21, 38
Cooperative Learning Activities, pp. 7–12
Speaking and Listening Activities, pp. 6–7, 10–13
Vocabulary and Spelling Practice, pp. 35–52
Composition Practice, p. 15
Composition Reteaching, p. 15
Composition Enrichment, p. 15

Assessment

Teacher's Guide to Writing Assessment

UNIT 2
Lesson 2.8

TEACH

Guided Practice

L2 Recognizing Fragments

Some students may need examples of fragments and run-on sentences in order to recognize them in their own writing. Provide review sheets with lists of fragments and run-on sentences. After students have checked their papers for fragments and run-ons, ask them if they would like partners who have mastered these concepts to check their papers.

L1 Using Proofreading Symbols

Some students may find proofreading symbols confusing. Explain that each symbol in the proofreading chart is a kind of shorthand used to edit writing. Ask students why these symbols might have been developed. (Symbols are easier to read than handwriting; they make editing more efficient; they make small mistakes easier to find and correct.) Write a few sentences with mistakes on the board. Have students copy and correct the sentences. Have them insert proofreading symbols in the text and, in the margin, write out what each symbol tells them to do.

Independent Practice

For further stimuli for writing, see *Fine Art Transparencies* 6–10.

Writing Process Transparencies, 1–10

Cooperative Learning Activities, pp. 7–12

Skills Practice

Thinking and Study Skills, pp. 20–21, 38

Speaking and Listening Activities, pp. 6–7, 10–13

Vocabulary and Spelling Practice, pp. 35–52

Composition Practice, p. 15

Use Proofreading Symbols

If you've traveled—by bike, by car, or on foot—you've seen road signs. Some road signs use words to communicate, but many others use pictures. Look at the picture on the left. What does the symbol on the sign tell you?

In a similar way, you can use signs when you edit. The chart below shows a few proofreading symbols. Use these symbols as you edit your writing. Study both parts of the chart. Then see how Maya used the checklist and the symbols to edit part of her draft.

Proofreading			
Symbols		Checklist	
∧	insert	1.	Does each sentence have the right punctuation?
ℓ	delete	2.	Are all words spelled correctly?
⊙	period	3.	Are possessives and contractions written correctly?
∧̦	comma	4.	Are capital letters used as needed?
≡	capital letter		
/	lower-case letter		

Take Jaime Sánchez, for example. He and his sister Marta love biking. They both have been part of a local bike-racing club for ~~too~~ two years. They've even won some amateur races. This spring, though, Jaime wanted to learn more about racing. His club sent him to a four-day racing camp sponsored by the United states Cycling Federation. This was JAime's first trip to Colorado.

Enabling Strategies

LEP Using Proofreading Marks

Once students understand how to use proofreading marks, they may find the symbols to be an effective way to identify errors. Have students work with partners to correct each other's writing using proofreading marks. Once they have applied symbols to their errors, encourage students to verbally explain the mistakes and their corrections to each other.

2.8 Writing Activities

Write a Well-Edited Story

Review your completed draft. This is the time to put into finished form. Read it through again, making any changes you want. Then edit carefully, checking for errors.

- Make sure forms of verbs and pronouns are correct.
- Look for mistakes in punctuation, capitalization, and spelling.
- Look for extra words or words that have been left out.
- Check for fragments and run-on sentences.

PURPOSE To apply editing techniques
AUDIENCE Yourself
LENGTH 2–4 paragraphs

COMPUTER OPTION

If your computer has a grammar checker or spelling checker, you might use the checker to check your drafts. It's always a good idea to have an extra set of eyes (even electronic ones) looking at your work. Still, the program will not catch everything. Make sure that you edit the draft yourself, too.

Grammar Link

Avoid fragments and run-on sentences in your writing.

Edit and rewrite the following sentences so that they are correct. For examples of fragments and run-ons, see Maya's draft on page 73.

1. Lee collects pictures of her favorite singers she has a large collection.
2. She even has some old pictures. Of the Beatles.
3. She goes to many concerts sometimes she gets autographs of the stars.
4. She has lots of pictures in her room it looks great.
5. Lee also has a good collection of tapes. From rock to hip-hop.

See Lessons 7.1, page 242; 7.2, page 244; 8.2, page 264; and 8.6, page 272.

ASSESS

Writing Activities Evaluation Guidelines

Write a Well-Edited Story

Use these criteria when evaluating your students' writing:

- Did the student use proofreading symbols correctly?
- Did the student find his or her errors and mark them accurately?

See also the *Teacher's Guide to Writing Assessment.*

Computer Option

If students are using spelling or grammar checkers for the first time, make sure they know how to access these features.

Grammar Link

(See Using the Grammar Link below.)

Reteaching

Composition Reteaching, p. 15

Enrichment

Composition Enrichment, p. 15

CLOSE

Stress to students that, like professional writers, they must edit and proofread any writing they intend others to read, whether the readers are teachers, parents, or friends. Ask students what message it sends to readers when a piece of writing contains errors. (The writer didn't care about what he or she wrote; the writer is sloppy.) Have students create two sets of proofreading checklists like the ones in the lesson, one to keep at school and one to keep at home. Then, whenever they want to edit a piece of writing, they will have their checklist questions at hand.

Using the Grammar Link

Grammar Link Answers

Answers may vary.

1. Lee collects pictures of her favorite singers. She has a large collection.
2. She even has some old pictures of the Beatles.
3. She goes to many concerts. Sometimes, she gets stars' autographs.
4. She has lots of pictures in her room. It looks great.
5. Lee also has a good collection of tapes, from rock to hip-hop.

Fixing Run-ons Correct this run-on: *Lee's parents think Lee's music is too loud Lee says the volume is fine.* (Answer: *…loud. Lee says…*)

LESSON **2.9**

The Writing Process
Presenting: Sharing Your Work

There are several ways to share your writing. Keep in mind, however, that some writing is private and not meant to be shared.

Maya chose to share her writing in the school newspaper. When she saw her article in print, she was very proud. She ran into her homeroom waving *The Wilson Chronicle*. Her friends were excited to see it, but Maya was the most excited of all.

Setting the Purpose

Lesson 2.9 teaches students to select an appropriate mode of presentation for a piece of writing.

FOCUS

Lesson Overview

Objective: To explore different modes of presentation for a piece of writing
Skills: planning a presentation
Critical Thinking: classifying; elaborating
Speaking and Listening: discussing; evaluating

Bellringer

When students enter the classroom, have this assignment on the board: *List three ways you can share your piece of writing with others.*

Grammar Link to the Bellringer

Have students rewrite their Bellringer response as a single sentence, inserting commas in the list of ways to share their writing.

Motivating Activity

Ask students to think of all the ways they have shared writing with other people. What other ways can they think of that they haven't tried? Encourage students to commit to a new mode of presentation for their next piece of writing.

Teacher's Classroom Resources

The following resources can be used for planning, instruction, practice, reinforcement, assessment, reteaching, enrichment, or evaluation.

Teaching Tools
Lesson Plans

Transparencies
Fine Art Transparencies, 6–10
Writing Process Transparencies, 1–10

Plan Your Presentation

You can present your writing in many different ways. Each way of presenting requires a different kind of final copy. Your teacher might want your name, the date, and the paper's title in the upper-right corner of your paper. A school newspaper might require that the final copy be typed with your name at the end.

No matter what the specific requirements are, any final copy should be clean and readable.The chart below offers some suggestions about presenting certain types of writing.

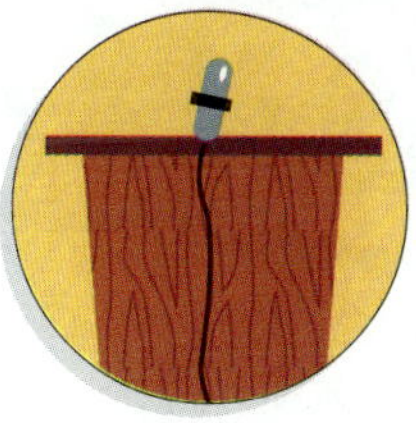

Oral Presentation
Almost anything you write can be shared aloud. Consider holding a group reading or using background music in your presentation.

Class Book
Collect copies of classmates' finished writing in a class book. You can keep it in class to enjoy, or you can donate it to the school library.

Newspaper
Items about local people and events are the heart of newspaper writing.

Literary Magazines
Literary magazines such as *Stone Soup* and *Cricket* publish poems and stories by students.

Journal Writing

In your journal, brainstorm ideas about different ways you might present your finished piece of writing. Which would be the most fun? The most exciting? How would you like to have your piece illustrated?

TEACH

Guided Practice

L2 Cooperative Learning

In a cooperative group activity, students can work together to produce a "Guide to Successful Presenting" booklet. Students can brainstorm a list of guidelines to help writers who want to share their stories, poems, and articles. Tips might cover such points as where to send articles, how to present a neat paper, and how to give an effective speech. Have students gather their tips into a group booklet.

L3 Getting Published

Encourage interested students to research the submission guidelines for different magazines and newspapers that publish children's writing, such as *Stone Soup, Cricket, New Moon,* and local newspapers. Point out that it is smart to read the publication they are planning to submit to in order to get an idea of the type of writing it publishes. Then encourage students to polish an appropriate piece of writing and submit it for publication.

Two-Minute Skill Drill

Ask students where the best place to present a piece of writing about how to raise puppies would be: in a cooking magazine, in a speech to an animal protection organization, or in a literary magazine.

Journal Writing Tip

Ways to Present As students brainstorm new and different ways for presenting, remind them to make sure that their ideas are appropriate for the piece and audience.

Blackline Masters

Thinking and Study Skills, pp. 7, 9, 17, 21
Writing Across the Curriculum, p. 1
Cooperative Learning Activities, pp. 7–12
Speaking and Listening Activities, pp. 6–7, 10–13
Vocabulary and Spelling Practice, pp. 35–52
Composition Practice, p. 16
Composition Reteaching, p. 16
Composition Enrichment, p. 16

Assessment

Teacher's Guide to Writing Assessment

TEACH

Guided Practice

L2 Presenting Creatively

The opportunity to present their work as part of a group may stimulate less motivated writers to share their writing with others. Many of these students may be able to suggest unique and interesting ways for the class to present its work, such as in a booklet of class quotes or humorous class stories. The more creative this effort appears to be, the more enthusiasm some students may have for writing and sharing what they write.

L1 Presenting Visually

Those students who are more skilled at communicating through visual images than through writing have several options for their presentations. For example, they can present their ideas in a cartoon strip with simple captions; through film, if they have access to a video camera; or through a series of photographs that tell a story. Encourage students to accompany their visual presentations with brief written explanations.

Independent Practice

- For further stimuli for writing, see *Fine Art Transparencies* 6–10.
- *Writing Process Transparencies,* 1–10
- *Cooperative Learning Activities,* pp. 7–12

Skills Practice

- *Thinking and Study Skills,* pp. 7, 9, 17, 21
- *Speaking and Listening Activities,* pp. 6–7, 10–13
- *Vocabulary and Spelling Practice,* pp. 35–52
- *Composition Practice,* p. 16

Prepare the Final Copy

Read this part of Maya's article as it appeared in *The Wilson Chronicle*. You can trace some ideas back to Maya's prewriting notes. Other ideas came up along the way.

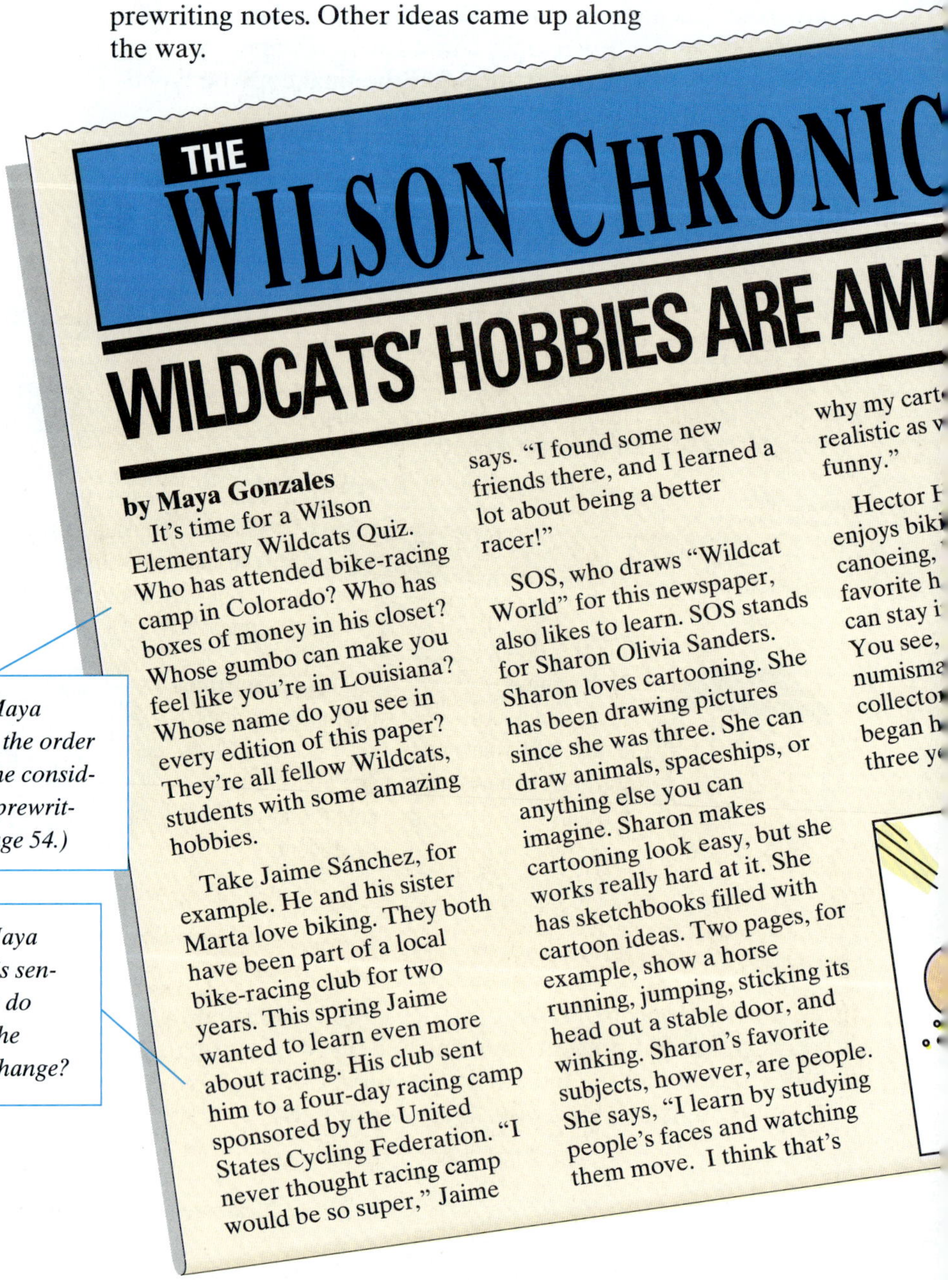
THE WILSON CHRONIC

WILDCATS' HOBBIES ARE AMA

by Maya Gonzales

It's time for a Wilson Elementary Wildcats Quiz. Who has attended bike-racing camp in Colorado? Who has boxes of money in his closet? Whose gumbo can make you feel like you're in Louisiana? Whose name do you see in every edition of this paper? They're all fellow Wildcats, students with some amazing hobbies.

Take Jaime Sánchez, for example. He and his sister Marta love biking. They both have been part of a local bike-racing club for two years. This spring Jaime wanted to learn even more about racing. His club sent him to a four-day racing camp sponsored by the United States Cycling Federation. "I never thought racing camp would be so super," Jaime says. "I found some new friends there, and I learned a lot about being a better racer!"

SOS, who draws "Wildcat World" for this newspaper, also likes to learn. SOS stands for Sharon Olivia Sanders. Sharon loves cartooning. She has been drawing pictures since she was three. She can draw animals, spaceships, or anything else you can imagine. Sharon makes cartooning look easy, but she works really hard at it. She has sketchbooks filled with cartoon ideas. Two pages, for example, show a horse running, jumping, sticking its head out a stable door, and winking. Sharon's favorite subjects, however, are people. She says, "I learn by studying people's faces and watching them move. I think that's why my cart… realistic as … funny."

Hector … enjoys biki… canoeing, … favorite h… can stay i… You see, … numisma… collecto… began h… three y…

Note that Maya stayed with the order of details she considered while prewriting. (See page 54.)

How has Maya changed this sentence? Why do you think she made this change?

78

Enabling Strategies

LEP Contributing with Pictures

Students might feel more confident about contributing to the class "Guide to Successful Presenting" booklet (see Cooperative Learning, page 77) if they are encouraged to use pictures. Some students might want to work with a partner and provide illustrations for their partner's tips. Others might write their own tips on presenting by making a cartoon strip. They can represent the tips in a series of drawings and add captions beneath each panel.

2.9 Writing Activities

Write to Present

Now that your writing is complete, decide how you will present it and to whom.

- Find out the requirements for the form of presentation you have chosen.
- Be sure your work is prepared properly.
- Present your work in the way you have chosen.
- Present it in another way, too, if you want.

Decide how you will present your writing. Prepare your final copy in the form necessary (see page 77).

- Plan your presentation.
- Prepare your final draft.
- Add a title, if possible.

PURPOSE To present a finished piece of writing
AUDIENCE Your choice
LENGTH 2–4 paragraphs

Cooperative Learning

In a small group, think about how you can start your own class book. Would it be illustrated? By whom? What kinds of writing would it have? How many pieces of writing would it include? What would be done with the class book after the class graduates to seventh grade? Would everyone in the class get a copy? Would you need to raise money to produce the class book? Pick two or three people to write up the group's ideas and suggestions. Then present them to the teacher or to the class.

Grammar Link

Use commas correctly in your writing.

Notice how Maya uses commas to set off interrupters.

*Take Jaime Sánchez, **for example**.*

*Sharon's favorite subjects, **however,** are people.*

Revise each sentence below, using commas to set off interrupters.

1. Maya's hobby as you can imagine is writing stories.
2. Not all of her stories however have been published.
3. Her favorite topics of course are people.
4. Several of her stories in fact tell about members of her family.
5. One story as you may know tells about her brother's trip to Chicago.

See Lesson 19.2, page 456.

ASSESS

Writing Activities Evaluation Guidelines

Write to Present

Use these criteria when evaluating your students' writing.

- presentation modes chosen are appropriate to the style and subject of their writing
- final copy is prepared with requirements of presentation form in mind
- writing is presented to an audience

See also the *Teacher's Guide to Writing Assessment.*

Cooperative Learning

Assess your students' ideas for a class booklet by evaluating their suggestions for its layout, content, production, and distribution.

Grammar Link

(See Using the Grammar Link below.)

Reteaching

Composition Reteaching, p. 16

Enrichment

Composition Enrichment, p. 16

CLOSE

Engage students in a reflection on the writing process. Have students compare the final copy of their writing to their prewriting notes. How did their ideas change? Ask volunteers to explain to the class the changes their writing went through in its different stages. Ask volunteers to share their favorite and least favorite parts of the writing process. What do students think were some of the best ideas for presentations?

Using the Grammar Link

Grammar Link Answers

1. Maya's hobby, as you can imagine, is writing stories.
2. Not all of her stories, however, have been published.
3. Her favorite topics, of course, are people.
4. Several of her stories, in fact, tell about members of her family.
5. One story, as you may know, tells about her brother's trip to Chicago.

Using Commas in Quotations Point out Maya's use of commas in direct quotations. Have students rewrite the following sentence, inserting commas as needed. "I had fun writing the article" Maya said "and it was exciting to see it in print!" ("I had fun writing the article," Maya said, "and it was exciting to see it in print!")

UNIT 2
Writing Process in Action

Setting the Purpose

Students now have the opportunity to apply what they have learned about the writing process to an independent writing project. They will use the stages of the writing process to create and present a finished piece.

FOCUS

Lesson Overview

Objective: To use interviewing and other prewriting techniques to explore the details of an outdated activity
Skills: using the five stages of the writing process: prewriting, drafting, revising, editing, and presenting
Critical Thinking: synthesizing
Speaking and Listening: interviewing; observing; note taking

Bellringer

When students enter the classroom, have this assignment on the board: *List some customary activities or pastimes that people seldom do anymore. You may have seen these customs in movies or heard of them from an older relative.*

Grammar Link to the Bellringer

Ask students if they used sentence fragments in their Bellringer response. Point out that we often use fragments when we take notes. Now have students rewrite their ideas in complete sentences.

Motivating Activity

Initiate a discussion about pastimes or activities that people no longer do. Ask students why people often enjoy reading, hearing, and watching stories about the past.

UNIT 2

WRITING PROCESS IN ACTION

THE WRITING PROCESS

In previous lessons you've learned about writers' tasks during each stage of the writing process. Now, you will practice more of what you've learned: prewriting, drafting, revising, editing, and presenting. You will also practice using the techniques used in Maya's article.

• Assignment •

Context	*You are going to send a piece of writing to a student publication called The Way Things Were, which publishes stories about pastimes or forgotten activities from earlier times.*
Purpose	*To remember for others a lost activity*
Audience	*Student readers of The Way Things Were*
Length	*1 page*

The pages that follow offer step-by-step advice on how to approach this assignment. You don't have to remember it all. Read through the pages before you start. Then refer to each stage if you need help while you work on your assignment.

Teacher's Classroom Resources

The following resources can be used for planning, instruction, practice, reinforcement, assessment, reteaching, enrichment, or evaluation.

Teaching Tools
Lesson Plans

Transparencies
Writing Process Transparencies, 1–10

Prewriting

What do machines do today that people did by hand a century ago? What was life like before microwave ovens, computers, and video games? Do you know anyone who has milked a cow or made soap?

Use one of the options at the right or an idea of your own to begin exploring a topic. You can develop your topic by freewriting.

Look at pages 48–55 for help with other kinds of prewriting and at pages 10–13 for freewriting suggestions.

Option A
Visit a living-history museum.

Option B
Read old magazines in the library.

Option C
Talk to older people.

Drafting

While you review your freewriting notes, think about how you can make the activity you're describing clear and interesting to your readers. Notice how author Betsy Byars uses questions and answers to explain a process.

Drafting Tip

To review ideas for getting "unstuck" when your drafting runs into a snag, see the chart on page 58 of Lesson 2.4.

Literature Model

He moved around the plane. "Look under the cowl. . . . Check the oil—the gas. The gas cap's up here."

"What's that wire sticking out of it?"

Pop unscrewed the cap. "That's the gas gauge. See, there's a cork on the end. The cork floats on the gas, and as the gas goes down, so does the cork and the wire."

Betsy Byars, *Coast to Coast*

TEACH

Prewriting

L2 Choosing a Topic

If students have trouble finding a topic, point out that many writers have made a career of writing how-to articles and books. There are how-to explanations available for almost every conceivable activity, from making a paper bag mask to building an airplane. Encourage students to look through newspapers, magazines, and how-to books in the library to get ideas for a writing topic.

Drafting

L2 Developing Interview Questions

Some students may have difficulty creating a list of interview questions that lead to a clear explanation rather than just a yes or no answer. Question words such as *who, what, when, where, why,* and *how* can help students form questions that require detailed answers. Students can practice asking questions with a partner, who will make up answers. Students should rephrase their questions until they are clear and precise. They can then use this prepared list of questions when they interview their subjects.

Blackline Masters
Thinking and Study Skills, pp. 3, 5, 23–24, 34–35
Composition Practice, p. 19
Composition Reteaching, p. 19
Composition Enrichment, p. 19

Grammar Workbook
Lessons 98–105

Assessment
Teacher's Guide to Writing Assessment

TEACH

Revising

L2 Peer Editing

Students can work in writing conferences with peer editors before they revise their writing. Suggest that peer editors respond to the following questions: Does the piece have a strong opening? Does the writer use vivid language? Is the explanation of the activity clear? Are there grammar and spelling errors?

You may want to duplicate the Peer Response forms in the *Teacher's Guide to Writing Assessment* for use in writing conferences.

Editing

L2 Peer Editing

After students have edited their own work, have them edit another student's writing. Remind them to refer to the Editing Checklist on the student page.

Presenting

Before students present their descriptive writing, discuss how to prepare their papers for publication. Emphasize the importance of the final draft and that it must be neatly done.

Independent Practice

Writing Process Transparencies, 1–10

Skills Practice

Thinking and Study Skills, pp. 3, 5, 23–24, 34–35

Composition Practice, p. 19

Grammar Workbook
Lessons 98–105

You can also use a question-and-answer format as you write your draft. Write out a few important questions that can be asked about your topic. What types of things would student readers of *The Way Things Were* ask about your topic? Respond to the questions with answers that help describe your topic. Use these questions as you complete your draft.

Revising

To begin revising, read over your draft to make sure that what you have written fits your purpose and audience. Then have a **writing conference.** Read your draft to a partner or a small group. Use your audience's reactions to help you evaluate your work.

Question A
Will readers understand what I'm writing about?

Question B
Have I varied the length of my sentences?

Question C
Are my paragraphs well constructed?

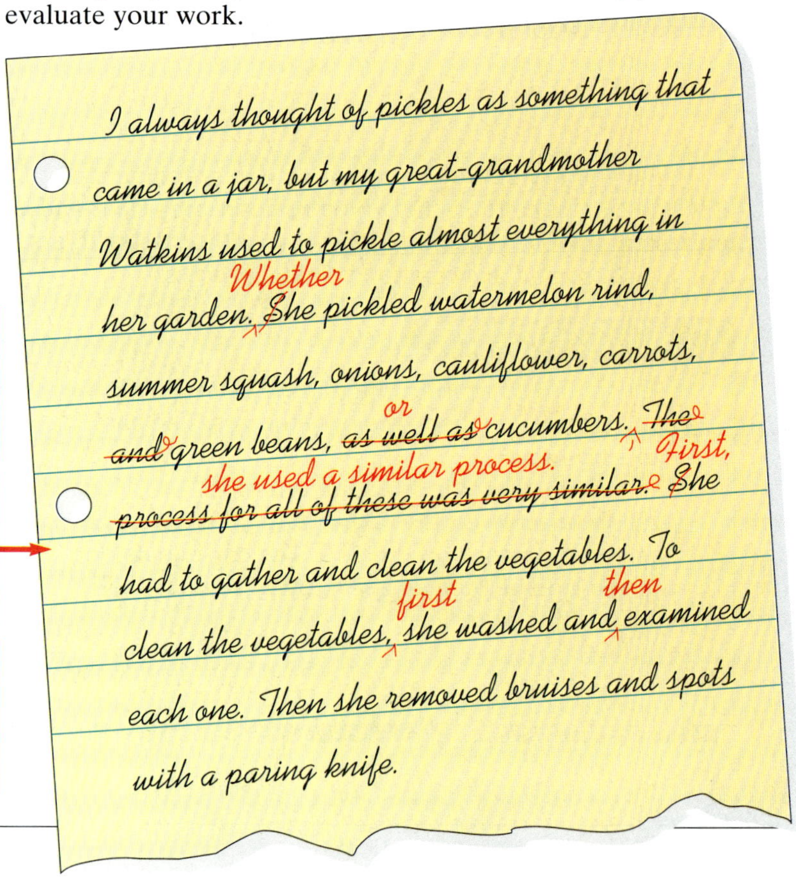

Enrichment and Extension

Follow-up Ideas

Set aside time for students to celebrate the conclusion of their writing projects. Encourage them to share their finished pieces with the whole class or in small groups.

Extending Explanation of a Process

Brainstorm with students ways they can use their expertise in writing to explain a process in other subject areas, such as describing the process of an election in the United States.

You can also set your writing aside for a day or two before you make revisions. Then you can read your work as a reader would. The questions in the boxes below can help both you and the listeners in your writing conference.

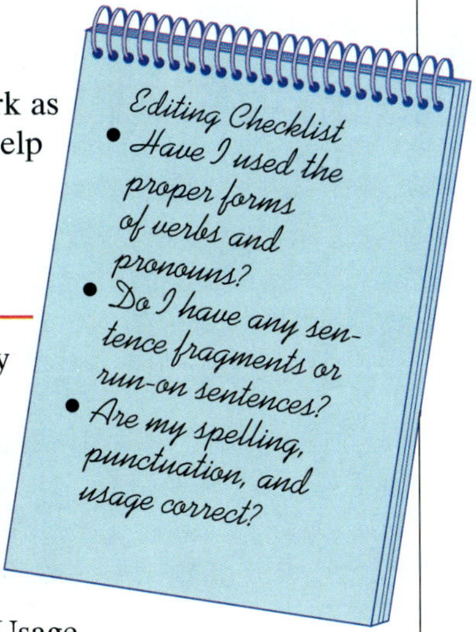

Editing

You've worked hard to decide what you want to say and how to say it well. You want your final draft to be free of errors. During the editing stage, you can get rid of any mistakes that distract readers from your ideas. The editing checklist at the right will help you catch errors. When you find one, mark it with the appropriate **proofreading** symbol. Read your work one time for each type of error. Use a dictionary and the Grammar, Usage, and Mechanics section of this book for additional help.

Proofreading

For proofreading symbols, see page 74.

Presenting

Make sure your explanation is neatly written or typed on clean white paper before submitting it to *The Way Things Were.* To help readers understand your subject, draw your own diagrams, or include clipped or photocopied illustrations.

If you have the opportunity to make an oral presentation, think about how you could demonstrate the activity in your writing. Use objects related to your subject, or simply act out the process.

Journal Writing

Reflect on your writing process experience. Answer these questions in your journal: What do you like best about your writing? What was the hardest part of writing it? What did you learn in your writing conference? What new thing have you learned as a writer?

ASSESS

Evaluation Guidelines

Use the following questions to evaluate students' finished writing.

- Does the article fulfill a clear purpose, centering on an outdated pastime?
- Does the article present the steps of an explanation in a clear and logical order?
- Does the writer address a specific audience?
- Does the writer use vivid language to create interest?
- Does the writer use grammar, usage, and mechanics correctly?

Refer to the *Teacher's Guide to Writing Assessment* for further help with evaluating student writing.

Journal Writing Tip

Reflecting on the Writing Process Suggest that students look back at their prewriting notes, their drafts and revisions, and their notes from peer conferencing in order to answer the questions.

Reteaching

Composition Reteaching, p. 19

Enrichment

Composition Enrichment, p. 19

CLOSE

Ask students to consider what they've learned about the way people worked or entertained themselves in the past. Do they think the activity they wrote about is more interesting than a similar activity today? Why? Discuss how the assignment has changed the way students look at their activities.

Setting the Purpose

Students read a literature passage that illustrates in a very real way the writing process. Such readings serve as models for students as they use the writing process.

About the Author

Betsy Byars (1928–) was born and grew up in Charlotte, North Carolina. She began writing for children when her own children were small. Byars gets her story ideas from things that happen around her, from events of her children's lives, and from newspaper and magazine articles. In *Coast to Coast,* Byars draws on her own interest in flying. She won the Newbery Award for *The Summer of the Swans* in 1971.

FOCUS

Lesson Overview

Objective: To discover how a writer's interests and experiences can inspire lively, realistic fiction
Skills: reading comprehension
Critical Thinking: recalling
Speaking and Listening: note taking; discussing; explaining a process

Bellringer

When students enter the classroom, have this assignment on the board: *Write down several topics that you know enough about to use in a story.*

Motivating Activity

Tell students they will be reading a passage by a writer who knows a lot about airplanes. Ask students if they have ever flown. What kind of experience was it? If they were able to see into the cockpit before takeoff, what was happening?

UNIT 2

The Writing Process
Literature Model

BETSY BYARS
from
Coast to Coast

Coast to Coast *tells the story of thirteen-year-old Birch, her retired grandfather, Pop, and what happens when Birch suggests that they fly his 1940 airplane cross-country. As you read, think about how the author gets and keeps her readers' attention. After reading, try the activities in Linking Writing and Literature on page 89.*

"I do. I want to do something. I can't explain it. I have to do something. And here is this perfectly good airplane." His jaws moved, chewing on the idea.

"What I meant about getting old, Pop, was that it's not getting pain in your joints or bad teeth. It's, like, not wanting to have fun."

Her grandfather got busy. He emptied the bucket and put the wet towels inside. "Help me push the plane back in the hangar. I'm tired of talking about my age."

"Yes, but it's my turn to pick. Remember? I picked being named for a tree, you picked flying in the war, now I pick this. I want to talk about you."

Teacher's Classroom Resources

The following resources can be used for planning, instruction, or practice.

Teaching Tools
Lesson Plans

Transparencies
Fine Art Transparencies, 6–10

Blackline Masters
Speaking and Listening Activities, pp. 12, 23
Thinking and Study Skills, pp. 3, 5, 9, 22
Vocabulary and Spelling Practice, p. 8

"Birch, the airplane is sold."

"You haven't got the money yet."

"I don't want to take any chances."

"See? Don't take any chances—that's exactly what getting old is. Don't step on the grass. Don't go out of the yard!"

"That's enough. I mean it."

Birch was silent for a moment. Then in a different voice, as if she were taking up a new topic, she said, "You never have taken me up."

Her grandfather glanced at the sky. Beneath her eyeshade, Birch's eyes narrowed. She knew she had him now.

"I really want to go!" As she said it, she realized it was true. She needed to get away from this world, and this was the way to do it. "What are we waiting for?"

Robert Delaunay, *Homage to Blériot*, c. 1913–1914

"I don't guess it would hurt to fly to the beach and back."

"Then get in! Let's go!"

"Don't get in too big a hurry." Her grandfather smiled. It was his first real smile of the afternoon.

Birch followed him around the plane. "What are you doing?"

"Well, right now, I'm doing a preflight inspection. I check the tires, the control surfaces, move them for freedom and cable looseness." He raised the aileron[1] and looked at the cable underneath. "I check the tail wheel springs . . . the stabilizer trim . . ."

"Does everybody do this? Or are you just extra careful?"

"There used to be a saying. 'Kick the tire. Twang the wire. Light the fire and let her go.' Nowadays a pilot checks everything—the prop for nicks, the cowling pins for security . . ."

1 **aileron** (ā′lə ron′) movable part on the back of an airplane wing

TEACH

L2 Guided Reading

- How would you describe the relationship between Birch and her grandfather? What in the story makes you feel as you do?
- How does the writer use dialogue to move the story along? Do readers get to know the characters through the dialogue?

Assessment

Teacher's Guide to Writing Assessment

About the Art

Robert Delaunay, *Homage to Blériot*, c. 1913–1914

In this collage, Robert Delaunay honors French aviator Louis Blériot, the first person to fly across the English Channel. Delaunay's 98¼-by-99-inch collage on canvas is on display in the Kunstmuseum in Basel, Switzerland.

UNIT 2
Literature Model

TEACH

L2 Guided Reading

- How does Betsy Byars use her own flying experiences and knowledge of planes to add realistic details to the story?
- Think about the preflight inspection as one of the first stages in a process. Which stage or stages in the writing process can be compared to the stage in the literature selection about preparing a plane for flight?

Henri Rousseau, *View of the Bridge at Sèvres,* 1908

He moved around the plane. "Look under the cowl—birds are very fond of building nests under cowls. Check the oil—the gas. The gas cap's up here."

"What's that wire sticking out of it?"

Pop unscrewed the cap. "That's the gas gauge. See, there's a cork on the end. The cork floats on the gas, and as the gas goes down, so does the cork and the wire."

Pop reached in the cabin and removed a clear plastic tube from the seat pocket. He drained some gas into the tube, checked it and threw it out. "Good! No water got in the gas from our wash job."

"How do you know, Pop?"

"Water's heavier than gas, so it would be on the bottom. And they look different."

"So can I get in now?" He nodded, and Birch stepped to the right side of the plane. "Do I sit in the front or back?"

"The pilot sits in the back."

"But how do you see the instruments?"

About the Art

Henri Rousseau, *View of the Bridge at Sèvres*, 1908
Henri Rousseau's 31½-by-39-inch oil painting *View of the Bridge at Sèvres* is on view at the Pushkin Museum in Moscow. This painting depicts an idyllic country scene at odds with the technological advances of the time.

Genre and Style

Using Precise Words

Coast to Coast is a novel based on the author's interest in flying and on her actual experience flying cross-country in a small plane. Technically precise words related to flying and airplanes punctuate the snappy dialogue and contribute to the realistic feeling of the story.

"I can see all I have to. Put your foot on the tire, not on the strut and . . . "

Birch pulled herself in and fastened the seat belt. "This is the first time I've been in a little airplane. Pop, your instruments are ancient."

"They're 1940, same as the plane." Her grandfather leaned into the cockpit. "This is the altimeter—it tells you how high you are. I'm setting that to the altitude of the field—it's about sea level so I set it on zero. Carburetor heat—off. Switch—off."

He moved the stick back and forth while looking at the tail, then from side to side while watching the wing. "Put your heels on the brake pedals."

"Oh, we both have brake pedals?"

"Yes, it's dual control."

She looked down at the pedals and positioned her feet so that her heels were on the smaller ones.

"I'm going to swing the prop to start the engine."

"You mean, like, it's going to start and I'm going to be sitting in here by myself with the engine going?"

Pop opened the throttle a half inch.

"Look at my feet, Pop, and make sure they're on the brakes."

"I did."

"Because I do not want to take off by myself. I saw that in an Abbott and Costello movie."

"This is the gas primer." Pop pulled out a knob and slowly pushed it back in. Then he stepped to the front of the plane and gave the prop a few turns. Birch listened to the clicks and watched the tip of the prop over the cowling.

"Now turn that overhead ignition switch on for me."

"This?"

"Right, and yell 'Contact' just before you do."

"Incidentally, I'm terrified. Contact!"

"Brakes?"

"Brakes!" she yelled, pressing her heels harder.

TEACH

L2 Guided Reading

- How do you think Birch feels when she climbs into the antique airplane? Is it realistic for Byars to make Birch seem excited and scared at the same time?
- How do you know that Birch has a sense of humor?

Connections Across the Curriculum

History

Remind students that older family members or friends can provide them with significant historical information. Some may remember when Charles Lindbergh crossed the Atlantic or when humans first journeyed into space.

Encourage students to discuss these and other historical events with older relatives and friends and to take notes in their journals. These notes can provide details for a future writing project.

TEACH

L2 Guided Reading

- Pop asks Birch not to tell her mom about the plane ride. Do you think her mom will find out? How will she react?
- Not many people can just hop on planes and fly away. What do you do when you need to "get away from this world," as Birch says?

Independent Practice

Fine Art Transparencies, 6–10

Skills Practice

Speaking and Listening Activities, pp. 12, 23

Thinking and Study Skills, pp. 3, 5, 9, 22

Vocabulary and Spelling Practice, p. 8

Pop came around and stood by the cabin. He reached forward with his right hand and gave the prop a quick downward pull. The engine caught. Pop leaned in and pushed the throttle back. The propeller turned slowly at idle, almost invisible against the blue sky.

Then he climbed in. "I got the brakes now," he yelled above the noise of the engine.

Birch took her feet off the pedals. "I feel a lot better with you in here."

The plane started forward. Following the yellow line on the pavement, they moved from the ramp down the taxiway and stopped just short of the runway.

"I'm revving up the engine now to check the magnetos[2] and carburetor heat."

"Check everything!"

He leaned forward. "Belt tight?"

"You bet. Let's go!"

"Birch?"

"What, Pop?"

"Let's don't say anything about this to your mom."

"Of course not! It's a secret mission." She put one hand on the window. "Aren't you going to close this?"

"We can close it later if you get too much wind."

"No, I like it open! Let's go!" And Birch's heart raced as Pop turned the J-3 onto runway nine.

2 **magnetos** (mag nē'tōz) small machines composed of magnets that provide the electric spark to make an engine start

Writers and Writing

Creative License

Point out to students that if dialogue is to be convincing, it must sound as if real people are speaking. A grammatically incorrect sentence such as "I got the brakes now" is something that students might hear in casual conversation. Stress that it can be acceptable to break a few grammar rules when writing dialogue, but only if doing so makes the dialogue sound more authentic.

Linking Writing and Literature

Readers Respond to the Model

How does Betsy Byars catch and hold her readers' attention?

Explore the way Betsy Byars uses the stages in the writing process by answering these questions. Then read what other students liked about the selection.

1. How is Betsy Byars's description of the process of starting an airplane like the stages of writing?
2. What might be some of the things the writer did during the prewriting stage? Why do you think so?
3. What order does Byars use to tell her story? How do you know?
4. What revising and editing steps do you think Byars took to make her characters more true to life?

My favorite character is Birch. The writer makes Birch real. She has feelings, and I could tell she loves her grandfather.

The scene I remember most clearly was when Birch was coaxing her grandfather to get in the plane.

I would recommend this literature selection to a friend who likes exciting adventures.

Rose Vales

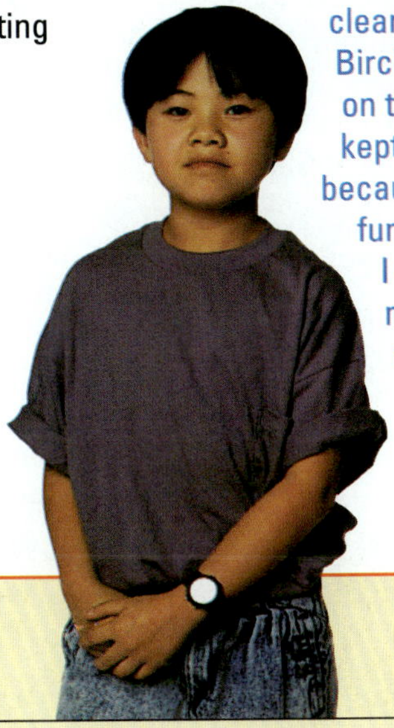

The writer made the character of Birch's grandfather seem real. He was old, but he could still fly an airplane. The scene I remember most clearly was when Birch was stepping on the brakes. It kept my attention because it was funny.

I would recommend this selection. You learn a little about airplanes.

Kaeng Yang

ASSESS

Evaluation Guidelines for Discussion

As your students discuss the selection, either in small groups or as a class, encourage them to begin with a personal response. The student responses on this page might be useful as a starting point.

Look for evidence that students
- have read the passage
- can state some of the writer's ideas in their own words
- understand the writer's point of view
- have connected the content to their own knowledge and experiences
- understand the ideas and implications of the passage

Some possible responses to the discussion questions on this page:

1. It is a process that has different steps that need to be done in a certain order.
2. When Byars was deciding on a topic to write about, she probably listed things she was interested in and knew a lot about. Her story is very well organized and her characters seem real, so she probably made an outline with ideas about things that might happen.
3. She uses time order. Everything happens in the present, and she tells you everything that Pop and Birch do, step by step.
4. She probably checked that what the characters said and did was realistic. She might have had friends of different ages read her story and give her suggestions.

CLOSE

Have students write the steps for performing a simple activity, such as baking a cake or changing a tire, as if they were explaining it to a younger student. Call on volunteers to read their steps to the class, and have students suggest improvements.

Enrichment and Extension

What Happens Next?

Challenge students to draft a scene in which they have a conversation with Birch after she returns from her flight to the beach with her grandfather. Students can use specialized or informal language in the conversation to make the scene more realistic. Then ask students to read the draft of their scenes aloud to the class. Students should offer suggestions for revising the scene.

REVIEW

Reflecting on the Unit

You may have students respond to Reflecting on the Unit in writing or through discussion.

Writing Across the Curriculum

To help students make a science connection, you may wish to guide a session in which students try to think of creative recreational uses for technology.

Adding to Your Portfolio

Ask students to consider the writing they have included in their portfolios. Students should write a short summary explaining how they used the writing process for each piece they have included. Students can then refer to these explanations for help with future projects.

Portfolio Evaluation

If you grade the portfolio selections, you may want to award two marks—one each for content and form. Explain your assessment criteria before students make their selections. Commend

- experimentation with creative prewriting techniques
- clear, concise writing in which the main idea, audience, and purpose are evident
- successful revisions
- work that shows a flair for language

Unit 2 Review

Reflecting on the Unit

Summarize what you learned in this unit by answering the following questions.

- What are the five steps of the writing process?
- What are the important elements of each step?
- What are some specific strategies you can use as you move through each step?

Adding to Your Portfolio

Choose a selection for your portfolio.
Look over the writing you did for this unit. Select a favorite piece for your portfolio. The writing you choose should show some or all of the following:

- ideas developed from prewriting
- a sensible organization of ideas
- a clear main idea supported by detail sentences
- interesting and varied sentences
- careful editing and proofreading

Reflect on your choice.
Attach a note to the piece you chose, explaining briefly why you chose it and what you learned from writing it.

Set Goals.
How can you improve your writing? What skill will you focus on the next time you write?

Writing Across the Curriculum

Make a science connection.
Describe a game or hobby you like. To do that, first use prewriting techniques to come up with an activity that uses technology or requires some up-to-the-minute information.

Draft a paragraph explaining how to do the activity, including your reason for writing about this activity. Revise, edit, and proofread your work. Decide how you would like to present it.

Teacher's Classroom Resources

The following resources can be used for assessment or evaluation.

Unit Assessment

Tests with Answer Key
Unit 2 Choice A Test, p. 5
Unit 2 Choice B Test, p. 6
Unit 2 Composition Objective Test, pp. 7–8

Test Generator
Unit 2 Choice A Test
Unit 2 Choice B Test
Unit 2 Composition Objective Test

You may wish to administer one of these tests as a mastery test.

UNIT
3 Descriptive Writing

Composition

Lessons

INTRODUCING
Unit 3

UNIT GOALS

The goal of Unit 3 is to help students, through example and instruction, to develop an understanding of descriptive writing based on observation. Students practice using all five senses to depict a scene, experience, event, or object. The lessons focus on the descriptive techniques of creating word pictures and observing, noting, and ordering details.

Unit Assessment

Tests with Answer Key
Unit 3 Choice A Test, p. 9
Unit 3 Choice B Test, p. 10
Unit 3 Composition Objective Test, pp. 11–12

Test Generator
Unit 3 Choice A Test
Unit 3 Choice B Test
Unit 3 Composition Objective Test

You may wish to administer either the Unit 3 Choice A Test or the Unit 3 Choice B Test as a pretest.

Key to Ability Levels

Enabling Strategies have been coded for varying learning styles and abilities.

L1 Level 1 activities are within the ability range of Learning Disabled students.

L2 Level 2 activities are basic-to-average activities and are within the ability range of average students.

L3 Level 3 activities are challenging activities and are within the ability range of above-average students.

LEP LEP activities are within the ability range of Limited English Proficiency students.

Setting the Purpose

In the Unit 3 Case Study, students examine the use of descriptive writing in a real-life situation. Students will explore and practice descriptive writing in the lessons that follow.

FOCUS

Lesson Overview

Objective: To examine how a naturalist uses descriptive details to make an unfamiliar place real to readers
Skills: observing; analyzing; writing descriptive details
Critical Thinking: comparing; visualizing
Speaking and Listening: discussing

Bellringer

When students enter the classroom, have this assignment on the board: *Use sentences to list five ways you could learn about a distant place you have never been to but would like to learn more about.*

Grammar Link to the Bellringer

Have students identify the subjects and verbs in the writing they did in the Bellringer activity. Do the subjects and verbs agree in number?

Motivating Activity

Ask students to describe an animal or object that they have observed in the natural world. Point out that good naturalists write two kinds of descriptions—precise, in-depth ones that assume background knowledge for people familiar with the subject, and more basic ones for people who may be unfamiliar with the subject. For example, ask students how they would describe a thunderstorm to someone who knows what one is or to someone who has never experienced one.

UNIT 3 PREVIEW

Case Study

Descriptive Writing
in the Real World

Boulanger Describes Nunataks

FOCUS: Before you can write a description of what you see, you must take a close look at the world around you.

▲ *Scientist John Boulanger explores a nunatak.*

On June 17, 1992, wildlife biologist John Boulanger boarded a small plane. He was bound for 19,850-foot Mt. Logan, the highest peak in Canada. From the plane window, Boulanger saw the green valleys and ridges of the northern Yukon give way to harsh mountains and rivers of ice—glaciers. For the next two months, Boulanger and six other scientists would call Mt. Logan home.

Here, beneath Mt. Logan, the team of seven scientists would ski across glaciers, looking for nunataks (nun′ ə taks′). Small islands in a sea of ice, the nunataks are home to all kinds of living things. There are butterflies and birds, wildflowers and tiny trees. On the nunataks the scientists would begin unlocking a mystery: How many different plants and animals live on nunataks? Where did they come from? How do they survive in this environment?

Teacher's Classroom Resources

The following resources can be used for planning, instruction, practice, reinforcement, assessment, or evaluation.

Teaching Tools
Lesson Plans

Transparencies
Writing Process Transparencies, 11–13B

Writing a Science Article

Observing a World — Writing the Article

Prewriting

OBSERVING A WORLD

Between mid-June and mid-August, the team covered more than a hundred miles and found many kinds of nunataks. Small ones looked like "someone's lawn." The biggest ones could cover nearly half a football field. Most amazing, though, was the variety of plants and animals the scientists found. They found grasses, willows, poppies, mosquitos, bees, and mouse-like animals called pikas.

As part of the scientific team, Boulanger collected facts about life on nunataks. He also took pictures and recorded information for an article in the magazine *International Wildlife.* Doing these jobs meant carefully observing this strange, cold world. "I was always trying to figure out ways that I could describe being up there to someone

Mt. Logan, the highest peak in Canada, is in the southwestern Yukon Territory.

TEACH

Building Background

Warm-up:
Have students list as many occasions as they can think of where descriptions are used.

Description in Speaking:
Remind students that they use descriptive language every day when they are speaking, such as telling a friend about a movie they recently saw, or describing how they felt when they lost a soccer game.

Description in Writing:
Discuss any descriptive writing students have read. Use prompts such as:

- Have you ever read an article in a magazine or newspaper about a place you have never been to before? Did the writer make you feel as if you were really there? How does a writer accomplish this?
- If you were visiting a city in another part of the country or the world and writing a postcard to a friend back home, what kinds of things would you describe to your friend?

Preview the Case Study

Have students preview the title and focus of the Case Study. Explain to students that Boulanger is a naturalist who described in detail a part of the world not often seen. Have students read the case study.

Blackline Masters

Cooperative Learning Activities, pp. 13–18
Thinking and Study Skills, pp. 3–9
Case Studies: Writing in the Real World, pp. 9–12

Assessment

Teacher's Guide to Writing Assessment

TEACH

Discussion Prompts

- Describe the process Boulanger used to take notes and to write his descriptions. What affected his decision about whether to write lengthy descriptions on the spot or to wait until later?
- Why did Boulanger feel that it would be more powerful to describe how a blizzard made him feel than to describe all the snow that was falling around him? Do you agree with him?

"Let's say you're caught in a blizzard. You can describe the white snow falling around you, but it's going to be more powerful if you talk about the white snow plastering your face, making you cold."

—John Boulanger

who had never been there before," Boulanger says. "For example, in one area we came to a place where gigantic glacial streams were running on either side of us." How would Boulanger describe the roaring streams? Could he compare them to something familiar? "Finally, it struck me that these streams were like water slides at an amusement park," he says.

Boulanger looked for different kinds of information as he sat on nunataks, watching the animals. When he spotted a pika, for instance, he noted its color, texture, size—details that would help him write a vivid word picture.

To be sure his notes were safe, Boulanger used a special reporter's notebook. It was made of paper that could get wet and not fall apart. Boulanger wrote with a pencil so his notes wouldn't blur if they fell into snow.

Boulanger wrote whenever something caught his eye. Usually, the team was moving and Boulanger had to dash off impressions. "I didn't pay that much attention to grammar," he says. "I'd just quickly spill my mind out and then use the notes later to remember."

▼ Boulanger's tools in the field included his special, sturdy notebook, a compass, an altimeter, mechanical pencil, binoculars, and a camera.

The pika has a grey coat with a white underside and is about the size of a guinea pig. Even though pikas are members of the rabbit family, they actually resemble mice with small ears and legs. Their fur is very thick and roughened, possibly from the long winter.

Cultural Diversity

Working Together

Explain to students that scientists from several countries often collaborate on a scientific research project. You can provide the example of the 1989–1990 Trans-Antarctic trek made by six men from six different nations. Elicit from students other examples of this kind of collaboration, such as space exploration. Discuss why this kind of cooperation benefits everyone.

Sometimes, he had time to write a full description. Confronted with the icy, roaring "water slides," Boulanger stopped and wrote. "That moment was so intense, I sat down and took ten or fifteen minutes to really try to describe it," he says.

At 8:00 or 9:00 P.M., after a full day of work, Boulanger often crawled into his sleeping bag and expanded his notes. In the far north at that time of year, the sun doesn't set until midnight. Even at 9:00 P.M., it's still light and often warm enough to write.

Some of Boulanger's longest entries were made at these quiet times. As he wrote, he searched for fresh ways to describe what he'd seen. Often he turned to comparisons, as he did in describing a tense moment in a pika colony.

"For the next twenty minutes I watch as the pika peers at me from nearby boulders, each time staring at me for a few seconds, then disappearing under the boulders. . . . At the meadow it grabs some grass and scampers back to the boulder. I wonder why these pikas are so jumpy in such an isolated location.

"My last question is answered when a new visitor appears, a weasel wandering through the colony attempting to surprise a pika and get breakfast. He is continuously moving in, over, and in between the rocks of the boulder field, resembling a snake."

▲ *Boulanger says, "When you're describing something, you have to think about ways to help people understand."*

TEACH

Discussion Prompts

- Boulanger observed a pika colony for twenty minutes. What did Boulanger learn about pikas that he could not possibly have learned if he had not taken the time to focus on the pikas' jumpy behavior?
- Why did Boulanger decide to write a lengthy description of the roaring streams? Have you ever experienced such an intense moment, such as seeing a deer dart across your path or watching an animal with its young? What kind of impact did such a moment have on you? Why do you remember it so vividly?

Connections Across the Curriculum

Visual Thinking

Many descriptions compare the object being described to a more familiar object. For instance, Boulanger compares the pika to a guinea pig and a mouse. He also compares a weasel to a snake and the roaring streams to water slides at an amusement park. Discuss with students how comparisons such as these help the reader visualize what is being described. Ask them to think of examples of comparing the unusual with the familiar.

TEACH

Guided Practice

L2 Discussion
Stimulate a discussion of the Case Study. You may want to invite students to talk about
- how they think Boulanger managed to reduce 200 pages of notes to one article.
- other writing topics that might require a great deal of note taking before starting on the drafting process.
- whether they think Boulanger considered his audience while writing his article. How would his audience influence what he wrote?

Independent Practice

Writing Process Transparencies, 11–13B

Case Studies: Writing in the Real World, pp. 9–12

Cooperative Learning Activities, pp. 13–18

Skills Practice

Thinking and Study Skills, pp. 3–9

Drafting

WRITING THE ARTICLE

Faced with so many amazing sights, Boulanger wrote more than 200 pages of notes. Rich in detail, they formed the basis of his science article.

Before starting to draft, Boulanger developed a plan for his article. After opening with a description of his thrilling plane ride into the wilds, he explained what the scientific team had set out to do. From there, Boulanger wrote his article like a field journal. He entered a date, then described the day's discoveries and listed his questions. The reader would learn along with the team.

Boulanger's major job was to boil down his notes into a short magazine article. "You have to be very selective," he explains. "I chose things I thought were interesting. That way, readers can live the experience with me, feel like they're there, too."

Boulanger's two months on Mt. Logan brought him many experiences. He published some of those experiences in his article for International Wildlife.

Civic Literacy

Protecting the Environment
Naturalists are aware that their work can interfere with nature. Most of them go out of their way to minimize their impact on the environment. Encourage students to make sure they infringe as little as possible on the areas that they are observing.

Responding to the Case Study

1. Discussion

Discuss these questions about John Boulanger's writing.

- When did Boulanger take notes?
- What was his main concern when he described something?
- Why and how did Boulanger use comparisons in his writing?
- What was Boulanger's major job when he turned his notes into an article?

2. Descriptive Writing

Write a description of an ordinary object. Choose something familiar—perhaps one of the items pictured here—and describe it for someone who has never seen it. First jot down a list of words, phrases, and comparisons you could use to describe your subject. Then use your list to write a descriptive paragraph.

Grammar Link

Make sure the subject and verb in a sentence agree, even when a phrase comes between them.

The *variety* of plants and animals *is* amazing.

Write the following sentences. In each one, underline the subject once and the verb twice. If they agree, write *correct.* If they do not agree, correct the verb.

1. The team of scientists skis across glaciers.
2. The nunataks, small islands in a sea of ice, is home to many living things.
3. John Boulanger, with other wildlife biologists, travel by plane to Mt. Logan.
4. Gigantic streams of glacial water is on either side of us.
5. A weasel in the pika colony hopes to catch his breakfast.

See Lesson 15.1, page 404.

ASSESS

Responding to the Case Study

1. Discussion

- whenever something caught his eye
- that he could describe it adequately to the reader
- by comparing the unusual to the familiar to help readers visualize what he was describing
- to reduce 200 pages of notes to a short magazine article

2. Descriptive Writing

Students' descriptions should

- create a clear picture of the object
- use comparisons that are relevant to students' lives
- use vivid, specific words rather than vague terms to describe the object

See also the *Teacher's Guide to Writing Assessment.*

Grammar Link

(See Using the Grammar Link below.)

Reteaching

As a group, create a list of places students want to read about.

Enrichment

Challenge students to write about why a natural object or area is valuable to the environment.

CLOSE

Ask students what they consider to be the most interesting phase of Boulanger's writing process. Why?

Closing Note

For further reading of descriptive writing, refer students to *National Geographic World.*

Using the Grammar Link

Grammar Link Answers

1. ski
2. are
3. travels
4. are
5. correct

Checking Subject-Verb Agreement Write the following verbs on the board: *survive, discover, collect, observe,* and *search.* Have students use either the singular or plural form of each of the verbs in a sentence about the case study. When they are finished, have them exchange papers with a partner, who will revise the sentences, making the singular verbs plural and the plural verbs singular.

Setting the Purpose

Effective descriptions use details that appeal to the senses and descriptive words and phrases that present a vivid picture.

FOCUS

Lesson Overview

Objective: To write a description that creates a clear picture for the reader
Skills: using colorful, effective language in written and oral descriptions
Critical Thinking: evaluating words and phrases for their effect
Speaking and Listening: taking notes on others' oral descriptions

Bellringer

When students enter the classroom, have this assignment on the board: *Write at least three sentences describing how a real or fictional person looks and acts. Try to make that individual come to life for your readers.*

Grammar Link to the Bellringer

Ask students to identify any possessive pronouns in their descriptions in the Bellringer. If their descriptions contain possessive nouns, have students replace the nouns with pronouns.

Motivating Activity

Invite volunteers to read their descriptions aloud. Have others identify the words or phrases that best help listeners picture the person being described. Discuss why the descriptions are effective.

LESSON **3.1**

Descriptive Writing
Painting a Picture with Words

An effective written description is one that presents a clear picture to your reader. An interesting description attracts the reader. Descriptions can present broad views or close-ups.

Good descriptive writing can take a reader anywhere. In the excerpt below, writer Jean Craighead George takes you to the Arctic. She describes the world of Miyax, an Inuit girl.

The writer sets the scene for the action by describing the sky and the landscape first.

Which precise details help you see what Miyax sees?

Literature Model

Miyax pushed back the hood of her sealskin parka and looked at the Arctic sun. It was a yellow disc in a lime-green sky, the colors of six o'clock in the evening and the time when the wolves awoke. Quietly she put down her cooking pot and crept to the top of a dome-shaped frost heave, one of the many earth buckles that rise and fall in the crackling cold of the Arctic winter. Lying on her stomach, she looked across a vast lawn of grass and moss and focused her attention on the wolves she had come upon two sleeps ago.

Jean Craighead George,
Julie of the Wolves

Teacher's Classroom Resources

The following resources can be used for planning, instruction, practice, reinforcement, assessment, reteaching, enrichment, or evaluation.

Teaching Tools
Lesson Plans

Transparencies
Fine Art Transparencies, 11–15
Writing Process Transparencies, 11–13B

Blackline Masters
Thinking and Study Skills, pp. 3, 9, 12, 20, 22
Writing Across the Curriculum, pp. 5, 16

Zoom In

Like George, you can use descriptive writing to help your reader see what you see, hear what you hear, and feel what you feel. In the paragraph below, George continues her description. Notice how she zooms in closer to the scene.

Which details help bring you closer to the wolf?

Literature Model

Amaroq [one of the wolves] glanced at his paw and slowly turned his head her way without lifting his eyes. He licked his shoulder. A few matted hairs sprang apart and twinkled individually. Then his eyes sped to each of the three adult wolves that made up his pack and finally to the five pups who were sleeping in a fuzzy mass near the den entrance. The great wolf's eyes softened at the sight of the little wolves, then quickly hardened into brittle yellow jewels as he scanned the flat tundra [plain].

Jean Craighead George, *Julie of the Wolves*

Compare the two paragraphs from *Julie of the Wolves.* In the first, George sets the overall scene. In the second, she moves in closer. She draws the reader into the wolf's world. She lets the reader see through the wolf's eyes.

Journal Writing

Having read the two descriptions from *Julie of the Wolves*, make a word picture of the scene. To start, list the descriptive details that made the scene clear to you. If you wish, draw a sketch of the scene.

TEACH

Guided Practice

L2 Using the Model

Jean Craighead George's vivid imagery describing the Arctic environment and wolves ("yellow disc in a lime-green sky," "dome-shaped frost heave") not only takes readers to the scene, it also places them with Miyax in her earnest observation of the wolves. Discuss why observation is so important to Miyax. (Information about a person's surroundings could be important for survival in such a challenging environment.)

L3 Using Metaphors

Write the last sentence in the model on the board. Ask students to identify the metaphor in the sentence. ("The great wolf's eyes...quickly hardened into brittle, yellow jewels....") Assign students to write one or two sentences using metaphors. For example, the wolf's fatherly attention to his family could be expressed by the metaphor "Amaroq was a sentry on duty as he kept watch over his cubs."

Two-Minute Skill Drill

Have students choose one of the ideas below and then write vivid words and phrases that could be used to describe that idea.

- busy playground
- active animal indoors or outdoors
- harsh weather or environment

Journal Writing Tip

Word Pictures After students complete their journal entries, ask them whether they discovered descriptive details that they missed on the first reading.

Cooperative Learning Activities, pp. 13–18
Composition Practice, p. 20
Composition Reteaching, p. 20
Composition Enrichment, p. 20

Unit Assessment

Teacher's Guide to Writing Assessment
Tests with Answer Key
Unit 3 Choice A Test, p. 9
Unit 3 Choice B Test, p. 10

Test Generator
Unit 3 Choice A Test
Unit 3 Choice B Test

You may wish to administer either the Unit 3 Choice A Test or the Unit 3 Choice B Test as a pretest.

TEACH

Guided Practice

L1 Using a Thesaurus
Students can expand the list of vivid words they made during the two-minute drill on page 99 by looking up some of their words in a thesaurus. For example, if they listed *run* for active animal, they might find words like *dash* and *race*.

Independent Practice

- For further stimuli for descriptive writing, see *Fine Art Transparencies* 11–15.
- *Writing Process Transparencies,* 11–13B
- *Writing Across the Curriculum,* pp. 5, 16
- *Cooperative Learning Activities,* pp. 13–18

Skills Practice

- *Thinking and Study Skills,* pp. 3, 9, 12, 20, 22
- *Composition Practice,* p. 20

Vocabulary
Drafting Tip
When you get ready to describe something, close your eyes and picture it. Then list words and phrases that tell how it looks, feels, smells, sounds, or tastes.

Look for Descriptive Writing

Books aren't the only place where descriptions are used. In fact, you probably use descriptions every day. For example, when you tell a friend about a new movie, you probably use description. When you take notes on a field trip, you probably use description for that, too.

Maybe you've taken a trip to the zoo. Did you notice the descriptive writing all around you? Signs at the zoo describe the animals. Posters describe new attractions. Advertisements describe food for sale. What examples of descriptive writing can you find in the illustration below?

Descriptive Writing

Enabling Strategies

LEP Choosing Words
Encourage students who have difficulty writing in English first to sketch a place they wish to describe. The setting can be a real or imaginary place. Urge them to include at least two elements in the sketch that show how the place looks or feels. (For example, a bright sun and drooping plants could illustrate a hot setting. A moon and shadowed trees could illustrate a dark, mysterious one.) Students can then "translate" their sketches into English words step by step.

3.1 Writing Activities

Write a Description of a Wolf

Write a description of a wolf for a group of younger students. Your description will help introduce them to this interesting animal that they'll see at the zoo.

- Look at the photo on page 99 or at other pictures of wolves.
- Then list details. How big is the wolf? What does it remind you of? What color is its coat? What color are its eyes?
- Use your list to write your description.
- To create a clear word picture of the wolf, zoom in on some details.

PURPOSE To describe an animal
AUDIENCE Younger students
LENGTH 1–2 paragraphs

Cooperative Learning

In a small group, take turns orally describing places that are familiar to you all—perhaps a specific place in or near your school. Describe these places without naming them. As each person tells about his or her place, other group members should write down the details that provide the best clues about what the place is.

After the oral presentations, discuss the details that made the presentations interesting. Each group member should then collect the notes written about the place he or she described. Use these notes to evaluate your own description and to help you decide what kinds of details are most effective for describing.

Grammar Link

Use possessive pronouns to show ownership of something.

Notice how Jean Craighead George uses possessive pronouns in the models on pages 98 and 99. For example, the phrase *her sealskin parka* shows that the parka belongs to Miyax. Unlike possessive nouns, such as *George's*, possessive pronouns do not contain an apostrophe.

Replace each underlined word or group of words with a possessive pronoun.

1. Miyax's attention was focused on the wolves.
2. The wolf's and Miyax's eyes met.
3. The wolf's eyes glittered in the light.
4. Three other adult wolves and five pups made up the wolf's pack.
5. Jean Craighead George's book *Julie of the Wolves* is an award-winner.

See Lesson 11.4, page 332.

ASSESS

Writing Activities Evaluation Guidelines

Write a Description of a Wolf

Use these criteria when evaluating your students' writing.

- Does the description of the wolf provide an overall picture that introduces the wolf to younger readers?
- Does it include some vivid details to help readers picture specific characteristics of the wolf?

See also the *Teacher's Guide to Writing Assessment*.

Cooperative Learning

Invite students to evaluate their own descriptions in writing or orally.

- Which parts of their descriptions were the best? Why?
- Which parts of their descriptions need more work? How can they be improved?

Grammar Link

(See Using the Grammar Link below.)

Reteaching

Composition Reteaching, p. 20

Enrichment

Composition Enrichment, p. 20

CLOSE

Invite students to share their favorite descriptions from this lesson and say why they chose them.

Using the Grammar Link

Grammar Link Answers

1. Her
2. Their
3. Its
4. its
5. Her

Using Possessive Pronouns Have students write five sentences with at least one possessive noun in each sentence. Pairs of students can exchange sentences and convert their partner's possessive nouns into possessive pronouns.

Setting the Purpose

Taking notes about the sensory details of one's own experiences can enrich written descriptions of scenes and events.

FOCUS

Lesson Overview

Objective: To take notes that will serve as a source of ideas for descriptive writing
Skills: observing events using all five senses; using vivid language to describe events
Critical Thinking: analyzing; comparing
Speaking and Listening: discussing; note taking

Bellringer

When students enter the classroom, have this assignment on the board: *Write down the name of a favorite movie. Jot down at least three reasons why you like it so much.*

Grammar Link to the Bellringer

Have students circle any action verbs they used in the Bellringer activity.

Motivating Activity

Ask students to imagine that a new movie has opened and they are deciding whether to see it. One person who has seen the film says, "The bad guy is scary." Another recalls, "The bad guy's voice sounds like fingernails scraping across a chalkboard. You'll be so scared that you'll want to run out of the theater." Ask students which person was more observant. Whose description would make you want to see the movie—the first or the second? How important are details when describing a film?

LESSON 3.2

Descriptive Writing
Observing and Taking Notes

Sensory details call up realistic images of taste, sound, smell, touch, and sight. These details can add richness to your descriptions of everyday things.

In the model below, Maya Angelou describes a picnic she remembers from her childhood. Notice the sensory details Angelou uses to help readers picture the scene.

Literature Model

The summer picnic gave ladies a chance to show off their baking hands. On the barbecue pit, chickens and spareribs sputtered in their own fat and a sauce whose recipe was guarded in the family. . . . Pound cakes sagged with their buttery weight and small children could no more resist licking the icings than their mothers could avoid slapping the sticky fingers. . . . On one corner of the clearing a gospel group was rehearsing. Their harmony, packed as tight as sardines, floated over the music of the county singers and melted into the songs of the small children's ring games.

Maya Angelou, *I Know Why the Caged Bird Sings*

Teacher's Classroom Resources

The following resources can be used for planning, instruction, practice, reinforcement, assessment, reteaching, enrichment, or evaluation.

Teaching Tools
Lesson Plans

Transparencies
Fine Art Transparencies, 11–15
Writing Process Transparencies, 11–13B

Angelou brings her description of the picnic to life by including details that help you see, hear, feel, taste, and smell the picnic. In your own descriptive writing, you can do the same thing. Just learn to pay attention to your senses.

Notice What's Around You

Whenever you see, hear, smell, taste, or touch, you learn something about the world around you. Look at the picture on this page. Then look at the list of sensory descriptive words alongside the picture. Which things in the picture relate to each sensory word?

Hot

Colorful

Sweet

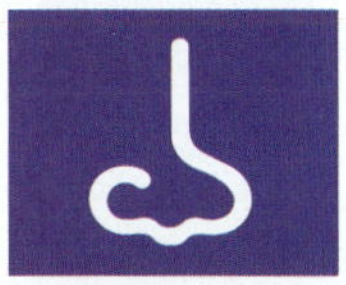

Smoky

Musical

Journal Writing

Recall one of your favorite places. Which senses do you use most when you're there? Make a list of details that you see, hear, touch, taste, and smell. Then circle the details that best describe your place.

TEACH

Guided Practice

L2 Using the Model

Maya Angelou's description comes from her mental notes of a picnic she attended. In just a few sentences, she uses dense layers of sensory details to re-create the scene for the reader. Have students make lists of the sensory details that Angelou uses. As they find the details, they should write them in categories of sight, sound, feeling, taste, and smell.

L1 Listing Details

If some students find it difficult to describe situations or places, tell them to try to imagine themselves at the picnic pictured on this page. Encourage them to write a list of different sensory details they would experience if they were there. After they finish their list, they can use it to write a detailed paragraph.

Two-Minute Skill Drill

Write the following situations on the board. Have students make up an interesting sensory detail for each.

a picnic on the beach
riding a crowded bus
a ride at a carnival

Journal Writing Tip

Comparing and Contrasting
Ask students to consider why they have chosen a certain place as their favorite. Does their choice have anything to do with their sensory experiences at that place? How is their favorite place different from others they might have chosen?

Blackline Masters
Thinking and Study Skills, pp. 3, 6, 34–37
Writing Across the Curriculum, p. 16
Cooperative Learning Activities, pp. 13–18
Composition Practice, p. 21
Composition Reteaching, p. 21
Composition Enrichment, p. 21

Assessment
Teachers Guide to Writing Assessment

TEACH

Guided Practice

L3 Describing Work Situations

Challenge students to think of an interesting occupation in which note taking is important. Ask students: What kinds of details would a crime detective write in his or her notes? A reporter at a sports event? An insurance agent touring an area devastated by a hurricane? Have students pick an occupation and imagine a situation in which they'd take notes. With their detailed list, they then can write a page or two about the situation.

Independent Practice

For further stimuli for descriptive writing, see *Fine Art Transparencies* 11–15.

Writing Process Transparencies 11–13B

Writing Across the Curriculum, p. 16

Cooperative Learning Activities, pp. 13–18

Skills Practice

Thinking and Study Skills, pp. 3, 6, 34–37

Composition Practice, p. 21

Composition Reteaching, p. 21

Composition Enrichment, p. 21

Vocabulary
Revising Tip

If you can't find just the right word when revising, turn to a thesaurus. A thesaurus is a reference book that groups together words with similar meanings.

Take Notes

Exploring the world around you can be an adventure. Make careful notes about important experiences. Taking notes can help you remember your experiences and share them with others later.

When you take notes on an experience, don't worry about grammar, spelling, or punctuation. Just ask yourself what you see, hear, touch, taste, and smell. Then jot down whatever details will help you remember the experience.

Later, when you prepare to write a draft, reread your notes. Keep in mind that you don't have to use all the details you gathered. Choose those details that create the strongest impression of the experience. If you're describing a concert, for example, you might focus on sights and sounds. If you're describing a holiday dinner, you might concentrate on smells and tastes.

Enabling Strategies

LEP Writing from Dictated Notes

Students learning English may have trouble using English to describe the different senses. Encourage them to communicate their sensory details orally to English-speaking students, who can jot down notes for them.

For instance, students learning English can describe the food pictured on this page—the taste, feel, smell, and appearance. Then they can write a paragraph using the notes taken from their oral descriptions.

3.2 Writing Activities

Write a Description of a Scene

Study the scene in this painting. If it were real, what would you see and smell? What do the flowers, caterpillars, and butterflies look like? Write a description that other students might use to identify the plant and insects shown.

- Use your five senses.
- Make notes of details.
- Choose the most effective details to include in your draft.

PURPOSE To make a scene recognizable to others
AUDIENCE Other students
LENGTH 1–2 paragraphs

Maria Sibylla Merian, *Coral Bean Tree and Saturniid*, c. 1700

Cross-Curricular: Science

Field notes—notes taken while observing something—are based on careful attention to detail. They are an important part of scientific discovery.

Observe a subject in nature. You might choose a dandelion, a spider, a rock, or whatever interests you. Take field notes based on what you observe. Use your five senses to gather details. Afterward, use your notes to write a detailed description.

Grammar Link

Use action verbs to make your descriptive writing come to life.

Notice the variety of action verbs Angelou uses in the model on page 102. Replace the blank in each sentence below with an action verb. You may use a thesaurus for help.

1. The boys _______ through the woods looking for tracks.
2. The children ______ the fried chicken.
3. Marley ______ her guitar for us.
4. Birds ______ in the surrounding trees.
5. We ______ at the dog's antics.

See Lesson 10.1, page 298.

ASSESS

Writing Activities Evaluation Guidelines

Write a Description of a Scene

Use these criteria when evaluating your students' writing.
The description should
- show an awareness of choosing the most effective details
- use sensory details
- include enough details to make the scene recognizable to others

See also the *Teacher's Guide to Writing Assessment.*

Cross-curricular Connection: Science

Evaluate the description based on the following: attention to detail, use of sensory details, creation of a recognizable description.

Grammar Link

(See Using the Grammar Link below.)

Reteaching

Composition Reteaching, p. 21

Enrichment

Composition Enrichment, p. 21

Use *Fine Art Transparencies* 11–15 for enrichment activities also.

CLOSE

Have students discuss using sensory details to describe. Ask students which senses they prefer to write about the most. Which help create the clearest picture?

Using the Grammar Link

Grammar Link Answers

Answers will vary. Samples follow.
1. crept **2.** devoured **3.** strummed **4.** chirped **5.** giggled

Action Verbs After students have chosen action verbs, write the first sentence on the board. Make a list of student verbs and discuss them. Continue with the rest of the sentences.

About the Art

Maria Sibylla Merian, *Coral Bean Tree and Saturniid*, c. 1700
Maria Sibylla Merian (1647–1717) also wrote books on natural science, often with original copperplate illustrations. *Coral Bean Tree and Saturniid* portrays two of her favorite subjects—flowers and insects. The opaque watercolor on vellum is 15 3/4 by 11 7/8 inches.

Setting the Purpose

Lesson 3.3 teaches students that effective description depends upon an ability to observe sensory details carefully during first and subsequent impressions and to re-create impressions using vivid nouns and modifiers.

FOCUS

Lesson Overview

Objective: To identify and observe details of objects and to use details gathered from both first and subsequent impressions in a description

Skills: observing objects; identifying details; using vivid adjectives

Critical Thinking: analyzing

Speaking and Listening: informal speaking; evaluating

Bellringer

When students enter the classroom, have this assignment on the board: *Write a short description of a car that you admire.*

Grammar Link to the Bellringer

Invite students to share with the class any parts of their description that include a series of items or characteristics. Did they include commas to punctuate their description? Invite a volunteer to write on the board part of a description that includes a series. Help the volunteer to use commas to punctuate the description properly.

Motivating Activity

Invite students to discuss a time when they've wanted to describe a place, a person, or an object to someone but had difficulty doing so. Why was it so hard to give a good description?

LESSON 3.3

Descriptive Writing
Focusing on the Details

With strong descriptions, you can help your readers see what you see. Use details that create that effect.

In the model below, Ian Fleming describes a wonderful car—a magical *Paragon Panther*—that has just been fixed up to look like new. Notice the details Fleming includes.

What details does the writer use to show readers that the car was flashy?

Literature Model

Every detail gleamed and glinted with new paint and polished chrome down to the snarling mouth of the big boa-constrictor horn. . . . from the rows and rows of gleaming knobs on the dashboard to the brand-new, dark-red leather upholstery; from the cream-colored collapsible roof to the fine new tires; from the glistening silver of the huge exhaust pipes snaking away from holes in the bright green hood to the glittering license plates that said GEN II.

Ian Fleming,
Chitty Chitty Bang Bang

Fleming focuses only on the details showing that the car looked new. By including these details and leaving out others, he presents a clear picture of the car.

Teacher's Classroom Resources

The following resources can be used for planning, instruction, practice, reinforcement, assessment, reteaching, enrichment, or evaluation.

Teaching Tools
Lesson Plans

Transparencies
Fine Art Transparencies, 11–15
Writing Process Transparencies, 11–13B

Pay Attention to First Impressions

Even an ordinary car has details that you can put into a description. All you have to do is look closely. Start with your first impressions—your first thoughts upon noticing something. In the notes on the right are the first impressions one writer had of the car shown on this page.

You might try thinking about your own first impressions as you walk down a street. What are the first things you notice? What details stick in your mind after you get home?

Journal Writing

Find three familiar objects in your classroom. Write down your new first impressions of them. Then write down the first three or four details you notice about each.

TEACH

Guided Practice

L2 Comparing First Impressions

Show students an object. Then ask them to close their eyes. What details can they remember about the object? Have them open their eyes and re-examine the object. Which details are still in their mind from their first impression? Students can compare observations and discuss why they chose the details they did.

L1 Exploring and Describing

Students may find it easier to talk about or sketch the details of an object before they write these details on a list. Tell them to observe an object you bring in. If possible, invite students to explore the object with their hands. Ask them questions that call attention to the object's details. Students may wish to sketch the object before making a list of its details.

Two-Minute Skill Drill

Ask students to list five words that describe a dog, cat, or other pet they have known.

Journal Writing Tip

Elaborating Ask students whether any of the details they have written describe something new they noticed about the object. Why do they think they noticed this new detail? Point out that concentration can increase their powers of observation.

Blackline Masters
Thinking and Study Skills, pp. 3, 5, 7, 9, 15, 17, 19
Writing Across the Curriculum, pp. 5, 7
Cooperative Learning Activities, pp. 13–18
Composition Practice, p. 22
Composition Reteaching, p. 22
Composition Enrichment, p. 22

Assessment
Teacher's Guide to Writing Assessment

TEACH

Guided Practice

L2 Sharpening Observation Skills

To help students recognize that familiar objects often contain previously unnoticed intriguing details, ask them to study two similar objects such as two desks, two shoes, or two books and try to list as many differences between the like objects as possible. Then students can discuss their observations.

L3 Practicing Observation

Encourage students to use their descriptive skills to create a written advertising brochure. They might describe a type of car, a pair of sneakers, a restaurant meal, or another item in their brochure. Remind students that the words in their brochures should both describe the object and entice customers to buy it.

Independent Practice

- For further stimuli for descriptive writing, see *Fine Art Transparencies* 11–15.
- *Writing Process Transparencies,* 11–13B
- *Writing Across the Curriculum,* pp. 5, 7
- *Cooperative Learning Activities,* pp. 13–18

Skills Practice

- *Thinking and Study Skills,* pp. 3, 5, 7, 9, 15, 17, 19
- *Composition Practice,* p. 22
- *Composition Reteaching,* p. 22
- *Composition Enrichment,* p. 22

Grammar
Editing Tip

Details listed in a series of three or more require commas to separate them. For more information, see Lesson 19.2, page 456.

Take a Closer Look

After noting your first impressions, start gathering details. One way is to identify the small things that help create each impression. For example, your first impression of a car might be "shiny." You might take a closer look and notice the polished chrome, freshly waxed paint, and gleaming hubcaps. All these details create the impression of "shiny."

Another way of gathering details is to reexamine your subject. Check for details you might have overlooked. Try to use all your senses. Maybe you forgot to describe the roar of the engine or the smell of the exhaust. Maybe you didn't notice how warm the hood was in the sun.

Enabling Strategies

LEP Describing Accurately

Invite students to observe an object. Next, ask them to write as much of a description as they can, first using English words and then words from their primary language. Then help them to complete their description in English, pointing out English meanings for their primary-language words when possible. You may wish to have students make a list of the new descriptive words they have learned along with the meanings of these words.

3.3 Writing Activities

Kenny Scharf, *Stellaradiola*, 1985

Write a Description of Art

Above is a photo of a very detailed piece of art. Examine the picture carefully. Describe the piece as if you were writing an article for your school newspaper.

- Start with one of your first impressions.
- Add the details that help create that impression.

PURPOSE To convey an impression by the use of details
AUDIENCE Readers of your school paper
LENGTH 2–3 paragraphs

Cross-Curricular: Geography

Landmarks can help people find their way. Large objects are good landmarks because they are easy to see. Pick an object you see on your way to school. Describe the object carefully enough so that a new student could use it as a landmark for finding the school.

Grammar Link

Use commas to separate items in a series.

Commas help readers keep descriptive details clear. A comma usually precedes *and* when there are three separate details. For example, *polished chrome, freshly waxed paint, and gleaming hubcaps*

Add commas to keep descriptive details separate in the following sentences. Write *correct* if a sentence needs no commas.

1. The art was humorous colorful and unique.
2. The front grill, headlight trim, and bumper were made of chrome.
3. The book is concise well written and informative.
4. The moth was grey soft and furry.
5. The car had black fat ugly tires.

See Lesson 19.2, page 456.

ASSESS

Writing Activities Evaluation Guidelines

Write a Description

Use these criteria when evaluating your students' writing:

- Do the details create a clear impression of the object?
- Are the details easy to understand?

Cooperative Learning

Evaluate the students' descriptions on the following: precise use of vivid nouns and modifiers; coherence in their overall impression

Grammar Link

(See Using the Grammar Link below.)

See also the *Teacher's Guide for Writing Assessment.*

Reteaching

Composition Reteaching, p. 22

Enrichment

Composition Enrichment, p. 22.

Use *Fine Art Transparencies* 11–15 for enrichment activities also.

CLOSE

Invite students to discuss improvements in their descriptive skills. Ask them to suggest tips for writing good descriptions.

Using the Grammar Link

Grammar Link Answers

1. The art was humorous, colorful, and unique.
2. correct
3. The book is concise, well written, and informative.
4. The moth was gray, soft, and furry.
5. The car had black, fat, ugly tires.

About the Art

Kenny Scharf, *Stellaradiola*, 1985
Kenny Scharf's pop-surrealist *Stellaradiola* consists of acrylic paint, jewels, plastic toys, and mirror figurines on a radio. Its dimensions are 16 by 29 by 7 inches. It is in the collection of Mr. and Mrs. K. Scharf.

Setting the Purpose

Lesson 3.4 teaches students that sensibly ordering elements and using transition words help to make their descriptions clearer.

FOCUS

Lesson Overview

Objective: To use appropriately ordered and linked details in a description
Skills: observing details; ordering details; using transition words
Critical Thinking: relating; visualizing
Speaking and Listening: discussing; evaluating

Bellringer

When students enter the classroom, have this assignment on the board: *Write a short description of this classroom.*

Grammar Link to the Bellringer

Ask volunteers to look for prepositional phrases such as *at the front, in the middle, on the right,* or *at the back* in their descriptions. How do these phrases make the descriptions easier to understand?

Motivating Activity

Ask students to discuss the image of their classroom that a stranger might have after reading their description. Invite students to discuss times in which people have described something to them and the object or place turned out to be much different from the description.

LESSON 3.4

Descriptive Writing

Ordering Descriptive Details

If details are presented in a sensible order, readers get a picture in their minds. Transition words help make the picture sharper.

In the model below, Freeman Hubbard orders details in his description of a circus parade in the early 1900s. Notice that Hubbard gives details in the order of their appearance in the parade. This makes it easy for readers to picture the scene.

Literature Model

The street was alive with noise as the first four lovely ladies on horseback, trumpets lifted to their lips, came into sight. They were always lithe and lovely, and the plumes they wore danced as their horses pranced. Then came the band, in red uniforms with gold braid, riding on a gilded band wagon that was sometimes drawn by as many as forty horses. The band never stopped playing: the big bass drum thumped steadily, the trumpets shrilled and blared, the cymbals flashed in the sun. Behind the band came great floats.

Freeman Hubbard, *Great Days of the Circus*

Teacher's Classroom Resources

The following resources can be used for planning, instruction, practice, reinforcement, assessment, reteaching, enrichment, or evaluation.

Teaching Tools
Lesson Plans

Transparencies
Fine Art Transparencies, 11–15
Writing Process Transparencies, 11–13B

Decide Where to Start

To order your own descriptive details, you might imagine your eye is a video camera lens. First, pick a starting point. Then pick a way to move your eye's camera across your subject. One way is to start at the front and move toward the back. Another way is to start at one side and move toward the other side. The order you use should be one that makes sense to your reader.

Drafting Tip

When you're drafting a description, make a quick sketch of the scene. The sketch can help you decide how to order your details.

Front to Back

At the front of the parade came the women on horseback. After them the band rode in on a wagon. The great floats rolled in behind the band.

Left to Right

On the left a tall blonde rider pranced on horseback. To the right came another rider draped with a banner. Two riders waving at the crowd were at the far right.

Journal Writing

Describe your classroom, using two different ordering methods. Compare the results. Which order makes more sense? Why?

TEACH

Guided Practice

L2 Ordering a Description

To help students understand how simple and natural it is to order elements in a description, encourage them to consider the route they travel to school. Tell them to picture in their minds everything they pass on the way to school. Then help them to list the different buildings, objects, and other landmarks, starting with the front door of their home and ending with the front door of the school building.

L2 Using Transitions

Freeman Hubbard gives readers a direct view, as if he were standing off to the side at the front, holding a movie camera to capture the players moving past him. Help students pick out phrases and sentences, such as "First four lovely ladies on horseback came into sight," "Then came the band," and "Behind the band came great floats." Point out that these phrases give clues to the arrangement and movement of the scene.

Two-Minute Skill Drill

Invite students to arrange the following objects on their desks and write a description of the arrangement:

a pencil, an eraser, a book, and a paper clip

Journal Writing Tip

Identifying Spatial Relationships
Invite students to describe the classroom or another area from several different vantage points.

Blackline Masters

Thinking and Study Skills, pp. 3, 11, 17
Writing Across the Curriculum, pp. 5, 7
Cooperative Learning Activities, pp. 13–18
Composition Practice, p. 23
Composition Reteaching, p. 23
Composition Enrichment, p. 23

Assessment

Teacher's Guide to Writing Assessment

TEACH

Guided Practice

L1 Experimenting with Order
Students may benefit by using transition words orally before writing them. Let some students take turns standing in various arrangements while other students describe these arrangements orally, for example "Anne is standing in back of Jerome," "Lorenzo is to the right of Susan," "Aaron and Kira are standing next to the door."

Independent Practice

For further stimuli for descriptive writing, see *Fine Art Transparencies* 11–15.

Writing Process Transparencies, 11–13B

Writing Across the Curriculum, pp. 5, 7

Cooperative Learning Activities, pp. 13–18

Skills Practice

Thinking and Study Skills, pp. 3, 11, 17

Composition Practice, p. 23

Grammar Editing Tip

Prepositional phrases, such as *in the middle,* can also tell position. For information about using commas with prepositional phrases, see Lesson 19.2, page 456.

Use Transitions

Words and phrases such as *after, on the left,* and *to her right* are called transitions. They show how the details in the descriptions are related. Transitions make the descriptions on page 111 easier to follow. Below is another example. Notice how the description changes when just the transition words are changed.

In back of the floats marched the drum major.

In front of the floats marched the drum major.

Transitions are powerful tools. Without them, you just have a list of details—not a description. Transition words can turn the details into vivid images. The chart below shows some additional transitions you can use.

Transitions		
in back of	beside	first
in front of	above	last
to the left of	below	then
to the right of	next	after

Enabling Strategies

LEP Listing Transition Words
Students learning English may find it helpful to prepare a list of common transition words that they can refer to as they write. Have students work with more fluent partners to develop two columns entitled *Spatial Transitions* and *Sequence Transitions.* Have students review lists of prepositions for words to include in each list, such as *beside* and *to the left.* Then have students look in this or another book for other examples of transitional phrases to write in their journals along with any necessary definitions, context, or sketches that will help them recall the meaning of the English word or phrase.

3.4 Writing Activities

Write a Description of a Scene

The painting on this page shows a farm. If you were at this farm and wanted to remember it in words, you could write a description of it. Start by listing the details. Use your list to write your description.

- Begin with the details that are closest to you.
- End with the details that are farthest away.
- Use transitions to make the order of your details clear.

PURPOSE To order details in a description
AUDIENCE Yourself, later
LENGTH 1–2 paragraphs

Grammar Link

Use prepositional phrases to show location.

Prepositional phrases, such as *at the front,* can clarify position.

Add a prepositional phrase to each sentence to show location.

1. The farm ______ belonged to the Kinsmans.
2. The barn ______ was painted red.
3. The cows stood calmly ______.
4. Mr. Kinsman was repairing the tractor ______.
5. Crops were growing ______.

See Lesson 14.2, page 382.

Louisa Matthiasdottir, *Sheep in Blue Landscape,* 1991

Cooperative Learning

Write a brief description of an object or place. Then read your description aloud to a small group. Group members should draw a picture of what they hear. Discuss why it was easy or difficult to draw the object or place. Revise your written description to avoid any confusion.

ASSESS

Writing Activities Evaluation Guidelines

Write an Ordered Description

Use these criteria when evaluating your students' writing:

- Are details in order?
- Are details used to describe accurately?
- Are transition words used?

See also the *Teacher's Guide to Writing Assessment.*

Cooperative Learning

Evaluate the revised description on the following: use of details to describe accurately.

Grammar Link

(See Using the Grammar Link below.)

Reteaching

Composition Reteaching, p. 23

Enrichment

Composition Enrichment, p. 23

Use *Fine Art Transparencies* 11–15 for enrichment activities also.

CLOSE

Encourage students to create a brochure for a recreational or commercial area of their community. The brochure can include a photograph or drawing of the area along with an ordered description. When students are finished with their brochures, invite them to compare their written descriptions. Why did the students choose the perspective they did? What could they do to make their descriptions of the area more accurate?

Using the Grammar Link

Grammar Link Answers

Answers will vary, but some suggestions are given below.

1. on the hill
2. beside the house
3. under the tree
4. in the barn
5. in the field

About the Art

Louisa Matthiasdottir, *Sheep in Blue Landscape,* 1991

The rich colors in *Sheep in Blue Landscape* help re-create the serene Icelandic landscape of Louisa Matthiasdottir's birth. This 14-by-21-inch oil-on-canvas painting is held by the Salander-O'Reilly Gallery.

Setting the Purpose

Lesson 3.5 teaches students how to observe, select details, and write a description of a place.

FOCUS

Lesson Overview

Objective: To observe and use details to write a description
Skills: choosing descriptive details; using common and proper adjectives
Critical Thinking: observing details; visualizing a place; identifying relationships and patterns
Speaking and Listening: discussing

Bellringer

When students enter the classroom, have this assignment on the board: *List five places you have seen in the last week.*

Grammar Link to the Bellringer

Have students add an adjective to describe each of the places on their lists.

Motivating Activity

The place Eric Garcia describes in the student model is a famous one—the Sierra Nevada mountains. Any place, though, qualifies as a subject for descriptive writing because it is the writer's perceptions that make it memorable to readers. Ask students to name places about which they could write. What are the most memorable details about these places?

LESSON 3.5

Descriptive Writing

Describing a Place

By using sensory details, writers are able to share images and experiences with their readers.

In the model below, Eric Garcia describes a place like the one shown in the photo. Notice how the details help you experience the place as if you were there, too.

What details does Eric include to appeal to the senses other than sight?

Details such as "clean air" and grass "soft like a waterbed" help create the impression of a pleasant and peaceful place.

Student Model

I am up in the Sierra Nevada mountains. I breathe clean air and smell the pine trees. I lie on grass, soft like a waterbed, high green trees around me blocking the sun. The forest animals are all around me making chirping noises. I feed birds and squirrels while I'm on the ground. They seem so peaceful when I am feeding them. When I feed them, they tickle my funny bone.

Eric Garcia, Emperor School,
San Gabriel, California

Teacher's Classroom Resources

The following resources can be used for planning, instruction, practice, reinforcement, assessment, reteaching, enrichment, or evaluation.

Teaching Tools
Lesson Plans

Transparencies
Fine Art Transparencies, 11–15
Writing Process Transparencies, 11–13B

Explore a Place

Choose a special place to write about. When you describe your own special place, include specific details as Eric did. Without details, readers might think your place is like the picture below—dark and uninteresting. To fill in the details, ask yourself questions.

Vocabulary Tip

Specific nouns and adjectives can help make your description more precise. For more information about adjectives, see Lesson 12.1, page 344.

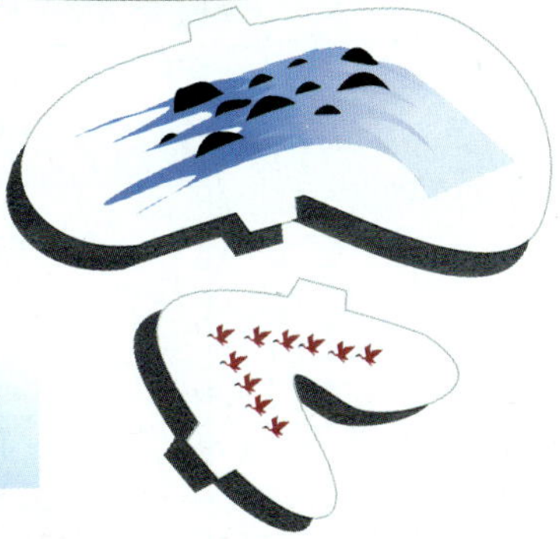

Questions	Answers
Q. What do I see?	**A.** A crane, some wading birds, jungle trees, and rapids
Q. What do they look like?	**A.** The crane is white. The flock of birds is scarlet. The jungle trees are dark green. The rapids make a waterfall.
Q. What sounds do I hear?	**A.** Water roaring over rocks

Journal Writing

Pick a place that you can observe and describe it. Ask yourself questions to generate details. List the details, and then underline the ones that show your place most clearly.

TEACH

Guided Practice

L1 Choosing Details

Students who feel uncertain about which impressions or details to choose may benefit by limiting the task. Ask them to think of a place and to list as many details as they can. From the list, have them choose one or two *sight* details. Next, have them choose one or two *sound* details. After choosing the details, they can write sentences describing what they see and hear.

L3 Writing for Radio

News reporters for radio or newspapers have to describe a scene more precisely than reporters on television, because a reading or listening audience cannot see a scene as television viewers do. Encourage students to watch a news story on television and to take notes on the setting of the story. Then tell them to write a one- or two-paragraph description that they would hear on the radio or read in the newspaper.

Two-Minute Skill Drill

List these nouns on the board and have students write descriptive adjectives for each.

garage	meadow
park	library
hilltop	attic

Journal Writing Tip

Evaluating Ideas Point out that generating questions and answers is only a first step in creating a vivid description. Good writers choose only the best details for their writing purpose.

Blackline Masters

Thinking and Study Skills, pp. 3, 9, 11, 20, 22
Writing Across the Curriculum, pp. 4–8
Cooperative Learning Activities, pp.13–18
Composition Practice, p. 24
Composition Reteaching, p. 24
Composition Enrichment, p. 24

Assessment

Teacher's Guide to Writing Assessment

TEACH

Guided Practice

L2 Using the Model

Armstrong Sperry's place description contrasts sharply with that of the previous writer. Mystery and drama replace the peaceful mood in the mountain scene. Encourage students to look at the model and write down specific words and phrases they could use to write about places.

Independent Practice

For further stimuli for descriptive writing, see *Fine Art Transparencies* 11–15.

Writing Process Transparencies, 11–13B

Writing Across the Curriculum, pp. 4–8

Cooperative Learning Activities, pp. 13–18.

Skills Practice

Thinking and Study Skills, pp. 3, 9, 11, 20, 22

Composition Practice, p. 24

Presenting Tip

Read your description to a friend. What questions does he or she have about it?

Describe the Scene

Once you've selected your details, use them to write a draft. What order should you use? Questions like the ones shown below can help you decide.

- Which details go together?
- Where are they located?
- Can you link the details with transitions?

- The rapids are on the right, between the rocks.
- The white crane is rising from the rocks.
- The flock of birds is flying through the dark green jungle.

As you draft your description, think about ways to draw your readers in. You might start by choosing one strong impression of your place. Then choose only those details that help create that impression vividly for your readers. In the model below, the writer describes a jungle river valley.

What words help you picture the location of the details?

Words like "witch's cauldron," "heavy wings," "scarlet," and "dark green" create a feeling of mystery and drama.

Literature Model

As the jungle valley broadened, the river became an archipelago [group] of islets [small islands]. To the right a gorge opened up, with rapids cascading between sheer walls of rock. The water boiled like a witch's cauldron. . . . From the rocks a white crane rose on heavy wings; a flock of ibis [tall wading birds] fled in a wedge formation, scarlet against a backdrop of dark green.

Armstrong Sperry, *Thunder Country*

Enabling Strategies

LEP Getting the Picture

Students learning English may benefit from the following exercise. Supply students with a picture or photograph of a place. Have students identify and label as many things in the picture as they can. Then have students think of adjectives to describe the items they have labeled. Encourage students to think about what they might see, hear, or feel if they were to visit the place. Students can then write sentences to describe the place in the picture.

3.5 Writing Activities

Write a Description of a Place

Pick a place that's special to you. It could be a neighborhood basketball court or a quiet corner of the library. It could even be the same place you picked for the Journal Activity in this lesson. Observe your place closely or just think about it. Then write a description of it for an issue of a student magazine called *Special Places.*

Try to show all the details that make your place special to you. Ask yourself: What colors do I see? What do I smell? What do I hear? What types of people, plants, and animals are there? What, if anything, changes from season to season?

- Decide which details go together.
- Think about where the details are located.
- Order your details to create a good picture of your place.
- Use transitions to link the details in a sensible order.

PURPOSE To describe a favorite place accurately
AUDIENCE Readers of a student magazine
LENGTH 2–3 paragraphs

COMPUTER OPTION

Some word-processing programs have a built-in electronic thesaurus. You might use the electronic thesaurus to help you choose interesting nouns and verbs. By carefully choosing your words, you can make your place description more vivid.

Grammar Link

Use adjectives to create clear pictures for readers.

Specific adjectives help to make descriptions vivid and precise. Notice the adjectives Armstrong Sperry uses to modify nouns in the model on page 116.

Add at least one adjective to each sentence below to make the statement clearer and more interesting.

1. The bird flew over the river.
2. The man wrote in his notebook.
3. We hiked on the trails.
4. The air nipped at our noses.
5. The wolf watched over the pups in the den.

See Lesson 12.1, page 344.

ASSESS

Writing Activities Evaluation Guidelines

Write a Description of a Place

Use these criteria when evaluating your students' writing.

- grouping of details by sensory categories
- ordering of details
- transition words used to link details
- a final description of neighborhood, integrating all details

See also the *Teacher's Guide to Writing Assessment.*

Grammar Link

(See Using the Grammar Link below.)

Reteaching

Composition Reteaching, p. 24

Enrichment

Composition Enrichment, p. 24

Use *Fine Art Transparencies* 11–15 for enrichment activities also.

CLOSE

Have students read their descriptions aloud to a partner. Ask the partners if they could picture the place in their minds based on the description. Discuss why it is or is not a good example of descriptive writing.

Using the Grammar Link

Grammar Link Answers

Answers will vary, but some suggestions are given below.

1. red-plumed
2. studious
3. rocky
4. frosty
5. wary

Descriptive Adjectives After students have finished, write the first sentence on the board. Underline the nouns and beneath them write students' adjectives. Have students rewrite the sentence using adjectives from the list. Discuss why one adjective may be more descriptive than another. Continue with the other sentences.

Setting the Purpose

Lesson 3.6 teaches students that descriptive literature can elicit an emotional response that they can elaborate on in their own writing.

FOCUS

Lesson Overview

Objective: To create a travel brochure
Skills: responding to a description; using details; capitalizing proper nouns
Critical Thinking: visualizing details; elaborating on an emotional response
Speaking and Listening: discussing; informal speaking; questioning

Bellringer

When students enter the classroom, have this assignment on the board: *List five places that you would like to visit some day.*

Grammar Link to the Bellringer

Have students check their lists for correct capitalization of proper nouns.

Motivating Activity

Tell students to freewrite for five minutes, describing the school cafeteria. Ask half the class to describe the negative characteristics of the cafeteria and the other half to describe the positive ones. Then have each side trade papers and write a response to what they read.

LESSON 3.6

Writing About Literature
Getting to Know a New Place

Descriptive writing can create strong feelings in a reader. Specific details help to set a mood.

Descriptive writing can also bring out new feelings. In the model below, a young city girl finds herself in the woods for the first time. Think about your own feelings as you read Nicholasa Mohr's description.

Details like "sweet fragrance" and "warm sunlight" create a soft, dreamy feeling.

How does Nilda feel about this place?

Literature Model

The sun came through the leaves, stems, and petals, streaming down like rows of bright ribbons landing on the dark green earth. . . . Nilda walked over to the flowers and touched them. Inhaling the sweet fragrance, she felt slightly dizzy, almost reeling. She sat down on the dark earth and felt the sun on her face, slipping down her body and over to the shrubs covered with roses. The bright sash of warm sunlight enveloped her and the flowers; she was part of them; they were part of her.

Nicholasa Mohr, *Nilda*

Reading Mohr's description, you might have thought about the warm sun. You might have thought about being dizzy or happy. When you read something, there's no right or wrong way to feel. The same piece of writing can bring out different responses in different people.

Teacher's Classroom Resources

The following resources can be used for planning, instruction, practice, reinforcement, assessment, reteaching, enrichment, or evaluation.

Teaching Tools
Lesson Plans

Transparencies
Fine Art Transparencies, 11–15
Writing Process Transparencies, 11–13B

Respond to a Description

One way to respond to a place description is with a creative project of your own. To begin, you might choose a place that the description makes you think of.

Once you've chosen your place, you might take some photos of it. With photos you can focus on details that create the feeling of your place. Here two students show photos from their trip to Bandelier National Monument in New Mexico.

Another way to describe your place is by making a map of it and drawing in the details. Below, the students show Bandelier National Monument in a homemade map.

Jenny and Katie Bresee,
George Washington Carver School,
San Francisco, California

Journal Writing

List the most memorable details in the model on page 118. What did they make you think or feel? Write your response in your journal.

TEACH

Guided Practice

L2 Using the Model

If students have trouble thinking of a place in response to the literature model, let them work with partners so they can first talk about the place. A listener might be able to ask questions that will help the student think of more descriptive details. Then when the student has talked about the place, he or she will find it easier to describe.

L1 Making a Diagram

Students may benefit by making a diagram of a familiar, current place before tackling a remembered one. Tell students to make a map of the classroom. They can construct the map as if they were looking down on it or looking into it, as from a doorway. They should sketch and label objects (furniture and people) as well as structural elements (windows and doors).

Two-Minute Skill Drill

Write these names on the board. Have students write them, capitalizing them correctly.

new jersey	belgium
eiffel tower	el salvador
lake erie	salt lake city

Journal Writing Tip

Picturing It Encourage students to think about a place or an experience they have had that the Literature Model reminded them of. Tell students that it is easier to write about thoughts and feelings if they have a place in mind that they can picture.

Blackline Masters

Thinking and Study Skills, pp. 9, 12, 22
Writing Across the Curriculum, pp. 4–5, 7–8
Cooperative Learning Activities, pp. 13–18
Composition Practice, p. 25
Composition Reteaching, p. 25
Composition Enrichment, p. 25

Assessment

Teacher's Guide to Writing Assessment

TEACH

Guided Practice

L3 Interviewing

If students are creating a brochure about a local place, encourage them to interview people who live or work there, or other students who may have visited it. That way they can get more information, or different impressions, which will make their brochure more interesting.

Independent Practice

- For further stimuli for descriptive writing, see *Fine Art Transparencies* 11–15.
- *Writing Process Transparencies,* 11–13B
- *Writing Across the Curriculum,* pp. 4–5, 7–8
- *Cooperative Learning Activities,* pp. 13–18

Skills Practice

- *Thinking and Study Skills,* pp. 9, 12, 22
- *Composition Practice,* p. 25

Grammar
Editing Tip

Names of places are proper nouns and always start with capital letters. For more information about proper nouns, see Lesson 9.1, page 284.

Do a Double Take

You can create a travel brochure by adding captions to your photos and map. Travel brochures describe places that people might like to visit. To create your own brochure, concentrate on the details of your place. Which ones might interest other people? Here is Jenny and Katie's travel brochure for Bandelier National Monument.

Jenny and Katie Bresee, George Washington Carver School, San Francisco, California

travel brochure

When you enter Bandelier National Monument it's a whole other world. It's like going back in time. There are cliff dwellings, ruins, rivers, streams, and even a bat cave.

When early humans came to Bandelier, they found that the small caves that dotted the cliff face made excellent homes. Inside the caves, the air is musty and cool like air conditioning.

The creek that runs through Bandelier is the Rito de los Frijoles. Lots of plants and animals depend on the water from the creek. You can see skunks, rabbits, mice, birds, bats, deer, coyotes and mountain lions come to drink at the Rito de los Frijoles.

Enabling Strategies

LEP Writing Names of Places

For their travel brochures, students may want to choose a place from their country of origin to describe. Point out that sometimes places and names do not have English translations. Have students write their descriptions without worrying about the translations. When they have finished writing, have them circle the words or phrases they are not sure of and look them up in a dictionary or atlas.

3.6 Writing Activities

Write a Travel Brochure

Create your own travel brochure in response to the literature selection on page 118. The purpose of a brochure is to get people to visit the place it describes. Plan to include at least two photos, drawings, or maps in your brochure. Then describe your place in writing.

- Freewrite to help you think of a place to write about.
- List details that tell what is special about your place.
- List your own feelings about the place.
- Choose facts that you think readers will respond to.

PURPOSE To create a travel brochure
AUDIENCE Vacationers
LENGTH 3–4 paragraphs

COMPUTER OPTION

Some word-processing programs offer a page-layout option. Using this option can help make your travel brochure look like the real thing. With page layout, you can design and view your brochure on screen. You can decide where to put text and captions and where to leave space for photos and maps. Then, after you print, you can put the photos and maps in the blank spaces.

Grammar Link

Capitalize proper nouns.

The names of specific people and places are proper nouns, which always begin with a capital letter. Note the proper nouns Jenny and Katie Bresee used in their travel brochure on page 120.

Write the sentences below. Then revise them, adding capital letters as necessary.

1. The island of puerto rico is near Florida.
2. The island's capital city is san juan.
3. The island is part of a group called the west indies.
4. Puerto rico is bounded on the north by the atlantic ocean.
5. To the south lies the caribbean sea.
6. The island is just east of the dominican republic.
7. A mountain named el yunque gets 200 inches of rain a year.
8. One early European visitor was christopher columbus.
9. The explorer ponce de leon began the first European settlement.
10. The first elected governor of Puerto rico was luis muñoz marin.

See Lesson 9.1, page 284.

ASSESS

Writing Activities Evaluation Guidelines

Write a Travel Brochure

Use these criteria to evaluate your students' writing.

- uses descriptive details to interest others
- arranges graphic material in an eye-catching way
- encourages people to travel to the site

See also the *Teacher's Guide to Writing Assessment.*

Grammar Link

(See Using the Grammar Link below.)

Reteaching

Composition Reteaching, p. 25

Enrichment

Composition Enrichment, p. 25

Use *Fine Art Transparencies* 11–15 for enrichment activities also.

CLOSE

Discuss how descriptive writing can bring about an emotional response in readers. Have students exchange travel brochures and write a response to the descriptive writing.

Using the Grammar Link

Grammar Link Answers

1. Puerto Rico
2. San Juan
3. West Indies
4. Puerto Rico, Atlantic Ocean
5. Caribbean Sea
6. Dominican Republic
7. El Yunque
8. Christopher Columbus
9. Ponce de Leon
10. Puerto Rico, Luis Muñoz Marin

Proper Nouns Have each student make a list of common nouns that refer to places, such as *river, stadium,* and *canyon.* Students can then switch papers and next to each common noun write a proper noun such as *Hudson River, Astrodome,* and *Grand Canyon.*

Setting the Purpose

Students now have the opportunity to apply what they have learned about descriptive writing to an independent writing project. They will use the stages of the writing process to create and present a finished piece.

FOCUS

Lesson Overview

Objective: To write a description of a memorable experience detailed enough for an artist to paint

Skills: using the five stages of the writing process: prewriting, drafting, revising, editing, and presenting

Critical Thinking: recalling; choosing sensory details; visualizing

Speaking and Listening: discussing

Bellringer

When students enter the classroom, have this assignment on the board: *Think back to your earliest possible memory. What do you remember? Write several sentences and include specific details.*

Grammar Link to the Bellringer

Have students underline the descriptive words they used in the Bellringer activity. Could they replace any of them with more vivid words?

Motivating Activity

Ask students what helps people remember one particular experience. (Students may suggest the emotions connected with the experience, such as winning a tight game, a family vacation, and so on.) What sensory images help people remember specific details of their experiences? (Maybe the reverberation of cheering at the game could be felt as well as heard.) Ask students what sensory images they most often remember from an experience.

UNIT 3

WRITING PROCESS IN ACTION

DESCRIPTIVE WRITING

In the preceding lessons, you've learned how to paint pictures with words. You've also had the chance to use details as you wrote descriptions of places, animals, and things. Now it's time to put together what you learned. In this lesson, you will describe something memorable in your life.

• Assignment •

Context	*An artist friend wants you to write a description of something memorable in your life. Afterward, your friend plans to paint a detailed picture based on your description.*
Purpose	*To inspire an artist with a memorable description*
Audience	*An artist*
Length	*1 page*

The following pages can help you plan and write your description. Read through them. Then refer to them as you need to, but don't be tied down by them. Remember that you're in charge of your own writing process.

Teacher's Classroom Resources

The following resources can be used for planning, instruction, practice, reinforcement, assessment, reteaching, enrichment, or evaluation.

Teaching Tools
Lesson Plans

Transparencies
Writing Process Transparencies, 11–13B

REVIEW

Reflecting on the Unit
You may have students respond to Reflecting on the Unit in writing or through discussion.

Writing Across the Curriculum
Remind students that making notes of first impressions and observing carefully help in gathering details. Point out that adding sensory details makes descriptive writing more interesting.

Adding to Your Portfolio
Encourage students to keep the checklist from this page to use whenever they complete descriptive writing activities. Tell them they can apply the checklist to previously written works in order to improve them. Finally, encourage students to have friends or relatives read their descriptive pieces to see whether there is anything still unclear about the descriptions.

Portfolio Evaluation
If you grade the individual portfolio selections, you may want to award two marks—one each for content and form. Explain your assessment criteria before students make their selections. Commend
- experimentation with creative prewriting techniques
- clear, concise writing in which the main idea, audience, and purpose are evident
- successful revisions
- work that shows a flair for language

Unit 3 Review

Reflecting on the Unit

Summarize what you learned in this unit by answering the following questions.

- What are some strategies for observing and noting details before you write?
- What kinds of details can help give the reader a vivid picture?
- How can you organize the details of your writing so that they have a clear order?
- How can you draw readers in and help them share your experiences and feelings?

Adding to Your Portfolio

Choose a selection for your portfolio. Look over the descriptive writing you did for this unit. Choose one completed piece for your portfolio. The piece you choose should show some or all of the following:

- a general impression, followed by details that create that impression
- descriptive details gathered by using all the senses
- a logical way of ordering of details that is clear to the reader
- transitions that are used to connect details

Reflect on your choice. Attach a note to the piece you chose, explaining briefly why you chose it and what you learned from writing it.

Set goals. How can you improve your writing? What skill will you focus on the next time you write?

Writing Across the Curriculum

Make an art connection. Find a photograph of an outdoor scene in the country, and compare it with the painting on page 113. Study details such as light and shadow, shapes, and color. Then describe both the painting and the photograph, and tell how each one makes you feel.

Teacher's Classroom Resources

The following resources can be used for assessment or evaluation.

Unit Assessment

Tests with Answer Key
Unit 3 Choice A Test, p. 9
Unit 3 Choice B Test, p. 10
Unit 3 Composition Objective Test, pp. 11–12

Test Generator
Unit 3 Choice A Test
Unit 3 Choice B Test
Unit 3 Composition Objective Test

You may wish to administer one of these tests as a mastery test.

Linking Writing and Literature

Readers Respond to the Model

What makes Michael Dorris's descriptive writing work?

Explore Michael Dorris's descriptions by answering these questions. Then read what other students recalled most clearly about Dorris's descriptions.

1. Morning Girl asks if her face is "round as a coconut." What other comparisons are part of the descriptions in the selection? What information do these details give you about the world that Morning Girl lives in?
2. How did you feel when you read how Morning Girl explored her face with her hand? What caused this feeling?
3. Choose a passage from the selection that you particularly like. Tell what specific words or images make it memorable.
4. How might reading this selection influence your descriptive writing? What specific ideas does it give you?

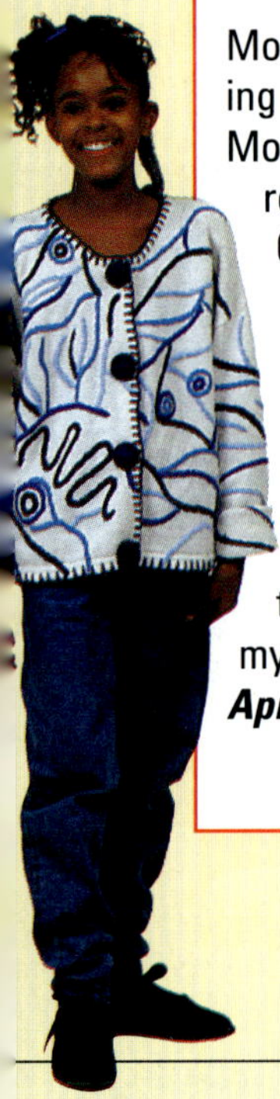

The description in the selection—the way Morning Girl's reflection in the water "broke into shining pieces"—made me think of how desperately Morning Girl wanted to see what she looked like. I remember most clearly the scene where Morning Girl was tracing the lines of her face and discovered what she thought she looked like. Morning Girl wanted to know what others saw when they looked at her face.

My favorite character was Morning Girl's father. He was helpful and understanding. I would recommend this literature selection to a friend. It is full of thought, and my friends like thoughtful stories.

April Andry

The scene I remember most clearly is where Morning Girl and her mother were walking along the beach. Her mother told her to close her eyes and to put one hand on her face and one on her mother's face.

Socorro Ayala

Connections Across the Curriculum

History

The home of Morning Girl and Star Boy is the present-day island of San Salvador, the landing site of Columbus's first voyage. Morning Girl and her family are Arawak, a people who lived on many Caribbean islands and along the Amazon in South America. The Caribbean Arawaks were destroyed by disease and slavery after the exploration of the Americas. The only remaining Arawaks live in Brazil, along the Xingu River.

ASSESS

Evaluation Guidelines for Discussion

As your students discuss the selection, either in small groups or as a class, encourage them to begin with a personal response. The student responses on this page might be used as a starting point.

Look for evidence that students
- have read the selection
- can state some of the writer's ideas in their own words
- understand the writer's point of view
- have connected the content to their own knowledge and experiences
- understand the ideas and implications of the selection

Some possible responses to the discussion questions on this page:

1. Other comparisons include arms and a yam; teeth and crooked pine trees; cheeks and hills; ears and shells; chin and a starfish; eyebrows and clouds and canoes. These details tell us that Morning Girl lives in a warm climate near the sea.
2. I found myself exploring my face with my hand. The author presents this scene so vividly that he made me feel as if I was experiencing it.
3. I like the final scene when Morning Girl's father kneels down and she looks into "the dark brown circles," and as she sees her reflection "their mouths grew wide."
4. This selection will influence me to be more specific in my own writing and to choose my words carefully so that I can convey a vivid picture to the reader.

CLOSE

Have students write a brief physical description of a person, using some of the techniques used in *Morning Girl*. Ask volunteers to share their writing.

TEACH

L2 Guided Reading

- What interesting and thought-provoking question does Morning Girl pose to her father?
- What does Morning Girl's father mean when he says, "And they are always here when you need to find them"?

Independent Practice

For further stimuli for descriptive writing, see *Fine Art Transparencies* 11–15.

Skills Practice

Thinking and Study Skills, pp. 3, 5, 6, 12

shore and get stranded when the tide leaves. Sometimes I see one and I think it's you, buried in the sand up to your neck."

When I went outside, Father was sitting on a log fixing a shark's tooth to use as a hook at the end of his fishing lance.

"Who is this?" he asked the lance. "Who is this with my wife's ears stuck onto the side of her head?"

"You laugh at me, too," I said. "But why is it so strange to want to know what everyone else already knows? Why should my own face be a secret from me?"

"There *is* a way," Father said kindly, and motioned me to stand beside him. He knelt down so that we would be the same size. "Look into my eyes," he told me. "What do you see?"

I leaned forward, stared into the dark brown circles, and it was like diving into the deepest pools. Suddenly I saw two tiny girls looking back. Their faces were clear, their brows straight as canoes, and their chins as narrow and clean as lemons. As I watched, their mouths grew wide. They were pretty.

"Who are they?" I couldn't take my eyes off those strange new faces. "Who are these pretty girls who live inside your head?"

"They are the answer to your question," Father said. "And they are always here when you need to find them."

Cultural Diversity

Using Word Clues

The English words *tobacco* and *canoe* come from the Arawak language. Ask students what conclusions they can draw about Arawak life from these two words. (The Arawak were a people who fished and farmed.)

WRITING PROCESS IN ACTION

Prewriting

You know so many people, places, and things. How do you choose a subject to describe? You might try exploring the possibilities through prewriting. The chart on this page suggests several methods of prewriting. You can freewrite, as the writer has in the example here. You can also build a cluster of details or brainstorm a list of impressions. You can even try combining approaches.

As you explore through prewriting, remind yourself to use all five senses. Try to discover specific details for each sense. Think about the small details that make things special.

Now that you've chosen a subject think about what details an artist would need to paint it. What order of details would be easiest to follow? What impressions do you want to give your reader?

Remember that there's no right or wrong prewriting strategy to use. Stick with whatever works best for you.

Option A
Make a cluster of details.

Option B
Brainstorm for a list of impressions.

Option C
Freewrite for ideas.

Drafting

While you draft, think about turning your prewriting into a clear, detailed description. Don't worry about your grammar, spelling, and punctuation at this point. Just let your ideas flow in an order that makes sense to you now. Try to make your reader understand what it's like to be there, up close to your subject. In the following model, Michael Dorris vividly describes a young girl's sense of wonder as she discovers the details of her own face reflected in her father's eyes:

Drafting Tip

For more information about gathering and recording effective details, see Lessons 3.2–3.3, pages 102–108.

UNIT 3
Writing Process in Action

TEACH

Prewriting

L2 Developing Ideas for Descriptive Writing

Remind students to consider an ordinary event when looking for a memorable experience to write about, like the example of the grandmother's spaghetti sauce on the notebook on page 123. A memorable experience might take only a few minutes or might be part of a series of events. What is important is that the experience is vivid in the writer's mind, as if it occurred just yesterday.

L1 Choosing a Subject

If students have difficulty thinking of a memorable event, suggest they look through some family photos or memorabilia or at photos from magazines. Students can choose a photo they are in or one they imagine they are in. They should use all senses as they list the details. Then they can write descriptions using their lists.

Skills Practice

Thinking and Study Skills, pp. 3, 5, 12

Drafting

L2 Deciding What to Include

Students may have difficulty choosing what to emphasize and what to omit from their descriptions. Encourage them to focus on what made this experience memorable for them and how they can best describe it so that readers can experience it themselves.

Blackline Masters
Thinking and Study Skills, pp. 3, 5, 12
Composition Practice, p. 29
Composition Reteaching, p. 29
Composition Enrichment, p. 29

Grammar Workbook
Lessons 98–105

Assessment
Teacher's Guide to Writing Assessment

UNIT
4
Narrative Writing

Composition

Lessons

UNIT GOALS

The goal of Unit 4 is to help students, through example and instruction, to develop an understanding of and an ability to use narrative concepts and techniques. The lessons focus on developing a real-life story, organizing the sequence of events, and using dialogue. The Case Study features author Virginia Hamilton and illustrates how the biography she writes is influenced by events in her life.

Unit Assessment

Tests with Answer Key
Unit 4 Choice A Test, p.13
Unit 4 Choice B Test, p. 14
Unit 4 Composition Objective Test, pp. 15–16

Test Generator
Unit 4 Choice A Test
Unit 4 Choice B Test
Unit 4 Composition Objective Test

You may wish to administer either the Unit 4 Choice A Test or the Unit 4 Choice B Test as a pretest.

Key to Ability Levels

Enabling Strategies have been coded for varying learning styles and abilities.

L1 Level 1 activities are within the ability range of Learning Disabled students.

L2 Level 2 activities are basic-to-average activities and are within the ability range of average students.

L3 Level 3 activities are challenging activities and are within the ability range of above-average students.

LEP LEP activities are within the ability range of Limited English Proficiency students.

Setting the Purpose

In the Unit 4 Case Study students examine the use of narrative writing in a real-life situation (in this case, a biography). Students will explore and practice biographical narrative in the lessons that follow.

FOCUS

Lesson Overview

Objective: To explore how narrative writing can tell the story of a person's life

Skills: identifying details about a person; using quotations correctly

Critical Thinking: synthesizing; main idea; recalling; summarizing; making inferences; building background

Speaking and Listening: discussing; interviewing; questioning; note-taking

Bellringer

When students come into the classroom, have this assignment on the board: *List five to ten people you admire. (They can be people you know personally or only know about; they can be people who are living or historical figures.)*

Grammar Link to the Bellringer

Remind students that certain words are always capitalized—names, for example. Ask students what other words require capitalization. Point out that the first word in a complete quotation is capitalized.

Motivating Activity

With the students, compile a list of people they admire. Encourage each student to contribute a name. Then call on volunteers to state briefly why they admire the person they named. Try to get students to refer to specific details when describing what they admire about the person.

UNIT 4 PREVIEW

Case Study

Narrative Writing
in the Real World

Hamilton Narrates a Life

FOCUS: By writing a biography, a writer can come to understand another person's life.

Virginia Hamilton grew up with stories. Long before she wrote such award-winning novels as *M. C. Higgins the Great* and *Sweet Whispers, Brother Rush,* she won prizes for reading the most books in her grade school. Hamilton also listened to stories at home. She says, "People were always telling stories. That's what I remember most."

Hamilton's father often read stories aloud from a magazine called *The Crisis.* Many of the stories were written by Dr. W.E.B. Du Bois, a writer, thinker, civil rights activist, and political leader. Hamilton recalls, "I didn't know the significance of it at the time. I just knew that Du Bois was someone my father greatly admired."

Later, as a young woman, Hamilton heard Du Bois speak in her hometown of Yellow Springs, Ohio. Dr. Du Bois spoke in a way she had never heard before, and, dressed in an elegant suit, he looked like no other person she had seen before. Hamilton couldn't yet connect the words of this sophisticated figure to any of her

◄ *Author Virginia Hamilton*

Teacher's Classroom Resources

The following resources can be used for planning, instruction, practice, reinforcement, assessment, or evaluation.

Teaching Tools
Lesson Plans

Transparencies
Writing Process Transparencies, 14–16B

experiences in Yellow Springs. But Dr. Du Bois was certainly on her mind.

In 1972 Virginia Hamilton published *W.E.B. Du Bois: A Biography.* Researching and writing about the 95 active years of Du Bois's life took her about 5 years. Hamilton remembers, "The material itself began to speak to me for him."

Prewriting

BUILDING THE STORY

Writing a biography is a process of organizing information to bring out the story of a life. To begin the story, it's helpful to start with the most basic information—what Hamilton calls "the bare bones." She says, "You've got all this material, all these facts, when you do a biography. All the dates in the world! And you say, 'How am I going to do this?' Well, the way you do it is you start with the beginning. You start with, this man was born, or this man died, and you go from there."

By starting simply, the biographer can build the story around the most important information. As Hamilton explains, "Writing demands that you focus in on what you want to do. You get a picture of it, and you break the picture down. You write one sentence at a time."

▲ *Dr. W.E.B. Du Bois, 1868–1963*

> ***"A life is a story. We each have a story. What you have to do is . . . find the story."***
> —Virginia Hamilton

TEACH

Building Background

Warm-up:

Have students list occasions for using biographical narrative.

Biographical Narrative in Speaking:

Invite students to think of situations in which they use biographical narrative in their everyday speech. For example, have they ever talked about what another person did in the past? ("Coach Mazzio said that when she was training for the Olympic team, she would always . . .")

Biographical Narrative in Writing:

Ask students if they have ever read, for school or on their own, any of the following:

- a book about a famous person's life
- a history book
- the story of an ordinary person who lived through a difficult or special time
- a poem describing a person's life
- a profile in a magazine
- the back of a baseball card

Preview the Case Study

Have students preview the Case Study by reading the heads and subheads and examining the visual at the top of page 136. Point out that the heads talk about "the story" in reference to the facts of someone's life. How is a life like a story? Direct students to read the case study.

Blackline Masters

Thinking and Study Skills, p. 9
Case Studies: Writing in the Real World, pp. 13–16
Cooperative Learning Activities, pp. 19–24

Assessment

Teacher's Guide to Writing Assessment

TEACH

Discussion Prompts

- What kinds of things can an object tell us about a person?
- What object might someone use to describe you?

Writing a Biography

Prewriting	Drafting	Revising

Building the Story	Making It Real	Shaping the Story

Drafting

MAKING IT REAL

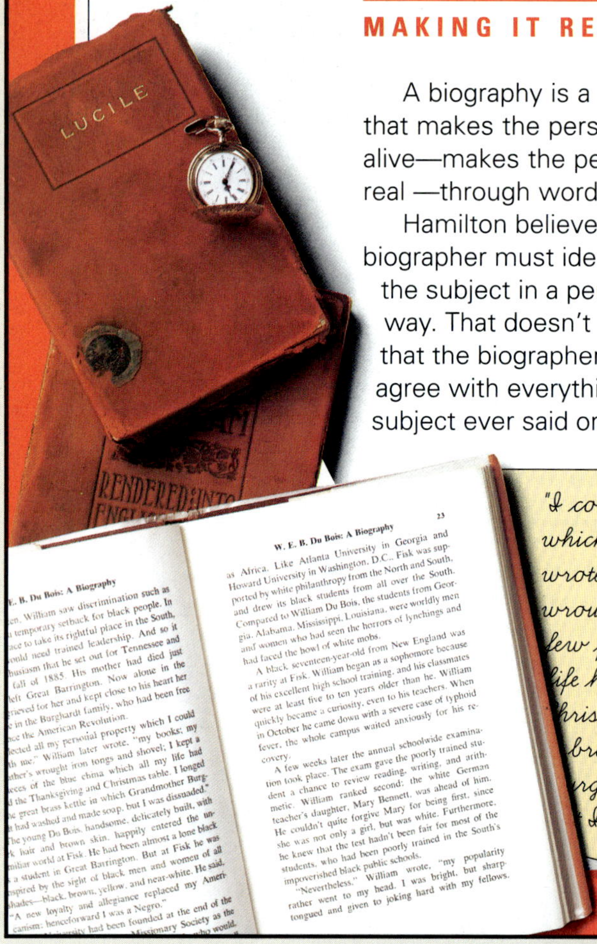

A biography is a story that makes the person come alive—makes the person real —through words.

Hamilton believes that the biographer must identify with the subject in a personal way. That doesn't mean that the biographer must agree with everything the subject ever said or did. "You must be involved with that person and sympathetic to him or her," Hamilton says.

One way to make the subject real in a biography is to use concrete details from the person's life. When Hamilton wrote about Du Bois's experience of going away to school, she brought the facts alive by relating it to

"I collected all my personal property which I could take with me," William later wrote, "my books; my grandfather's wrought iron tongs and shovel; I kept a few pieces of the blue china which all my life had graced the Thanksgiving and Christmas table. I longed for the great brass kettle in which Grandmother Burghardt had washed and made soap, but I was dissuaded."

Cultural Diversity

Understanding an Author's Motivation

Hamilton has written two biographies. The other was about singer and actor Paul Robeson (1891–1976), who sang opera as well as American spirituals. Hamilton's interest in Robeson, like her interest in Du Bois, grew out of her family circumstances. Her family was musical, and like Robeson, believed that people should stand up for their beliefs. Ask students to think of people their parents admire. Have students discuss what their parents admire about these people and whether students share their parents' feelings.

the details of her own experience of leaving home for school. "I took all my personal property, just like he did—my books and so forth, and a few things from my house," she remembers. The information she found about young Du Bois's packing for school seemed real to her. "It reminded me of how you have to dislocate yourself in order to proceed with your life, how you have to take something with you that will remind you of your past," she explains.

When we read a biography, we want to hear the person's own words. We want to have the experience, as much as possible, of hearing that person speak.

Hamilton believes strongly that biographers should quote their subjects' actual words, not put words into their subjects' mouths. "A lot of people like to, in a sense, create dialogue. I never liked doing that. It doesn't seem honest to me. So I use what the people say themselves," she explains.

▲ *To Hamilton, Dr. Du Bois's experience of leaving home was very moving. She made this experience real for the reader by using concrete details.*

TEACH

Discussion Prompts

- Do you think using made-up dialogue in a biography is a good idea? Why, or in what cases?
- How can a writer keep a biography interesting?

Connections Across the Curriculum

History

Point out that where and when people live has a huge effect on their lives. Technological, political, and social conditions are thus important factors in a biography. Du Bois, for example, lived at a time when equal rights for African Americans and other minorities were not guaranteed by law. Consequently, opportunities for people in those groups were limited. Ask students to consider how the stories of their own lives would differ had they lived fifty, a hundred, or five hundred years ago.

TEACH

Guided Practice

L2 Discussion

Stimulate a discussion of the Case Study. You may want to invite students to talk about

- starting points for biographies—at what point in Du Bois's life did Hamilton begin the narrative? Did her choice make the narrative more or less interesting? Why? How did Hamilton make the opening dramatic?
- the idea of a life as a story—if someone is still alive, how should the story end?
- what makes a life story worth reading about—is it more than events or achievements?

Independent Practice

Writing Process Transparencies, 14–16B

Case Studies: Writing in the Real World, pp. 13–16

Cooperative Learning Activities, pp. 19–24

Skills Practice

Thinking and Study Skills, p. 9

W.E.B. Du Bois died in Africa, far from the country where he had been born.

Of the Du Bois biography, Hamilton says, "It demanded I write it as simply as I could, and introduce to people this person whom they probably would have a hard time believing had existed."

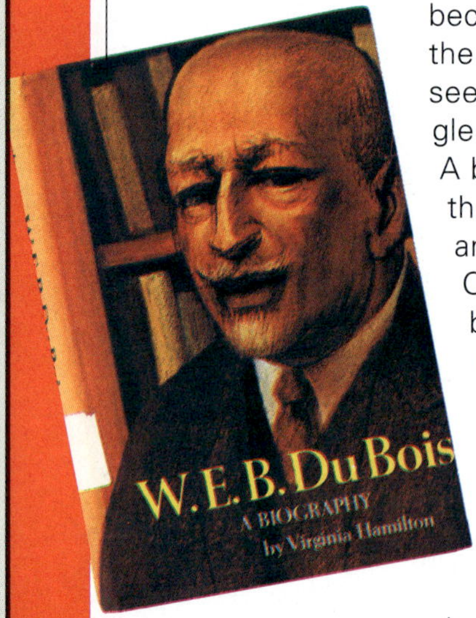

Revising

SHAPING THE STORY

Writing a biography can become complicated. All the facts and quotations can seem to take over and tangle the thread of the story. A biographer must shape the material into a clear and understandable story. Often parts will need to be cut or rearranged. As Hamilton explains, "All that information can't go into one, small biography. So you have to pick and choose."

To keep the story interesting, a biographer can present events in a way that creates suspense. For example, Hamilton began her Du Bois biography with his death in Africa. She wanted readers to wonder why Du Bois was dying far from his home, and why crowds were at a rally honoring him in Washington, D.C., the next day. Beginning with the end of her subject's life, Hamilton presented a dramatic moment in the very first sentence. In that first sentence readers can sense the impact of Du Bois's life on others.

Civic Literacy

Discussing *Crisis*

At Fisk University, W.E.B. Du Bois wrote that trained leadership was necessary if African Americans were to reach full equality with whites. Du Bois studied history and sociology. He earned an undergraduate degree at Fisk and advanced degrees at Harvard. His articles and editorials in *Crisis*, which he edited for 24 years, persuaded both African Americans and whites to work toward ending racial discrimination. Explain that *Crisis* was the publication of the NAACP. Why do students suppose that title was chosen?

Responding to the Case Study

1. Discussion

Discuss these questions about Virginia Hamilton's writing.

- How does Hamilton say the writer connects with the subject of the biography?
- What details did Hamilton include to make her subject real?
- Why do biographers often quote their subjects?
- What must the writer do with all the information she or he collects?

2. Narrative Writing

Write an opening to a biography. Choose a subject to write about—someone you know personally or someone you have studied. Looking at a photograph of your subject could help you get started. List several important events in this person's life. Find at least one quotation that shows the subject's ideas or personality. Then draft one or two paragraphs to introduce the person.

Grammar Link

Capitalize the beginnings of quotations.

If a direct quotation is a complete sentence, it begins with a capital letter. Write each sentence below, using capital letters as necessary.

1. "in 1888, Du Bois graduated from Fisk," said Cass.
2. Marley asked, "did you know he was the first African American to receive a Ph.D.?"
3. "he believed college-educated African Americans should lead the fight against discrimination," said Ms. Boston.
4. Kate pointed out, "the narrative begins by describing Du Bois's death."
5. Kwame added, "that is a very dramatic beginning."

See Lesson 18.1, page 438.

Using the Grammar Link

Grammar Link Answers

Capitalized words in each sentence are as follows:

1. "In . . .
2. "Did . . .
3. "He . . .
4. "The . . .
5. "That . . .

More Practice with Quotations Have pairs interview one another for five minutes, asking simple questions for a thumbnail biography and taking notes on their partner's answers. Have each student write a paragraph about the interview, including correctly punctuated quotations.

ASSESS

Responding to the Case Study

1. Discussion

- by identifying with the subject in a personal way
- mentions specific items Du Bois took when he left home
- so that readers can "hear" the subject speak
- organize it into a coherent story

2. Narrative Writing

Answers will vary. Students' paragraphs should include events from the subject's life and a quotation that reveals thoughts or personality.

See also the *Teacher's Guide to Writing Assessment.*

Grammar Link

(See Using the Grammar Link below.)

Reteaching

Ask students to write three questions about Du Bois that they would like answered in a biography.

Enrichment

Have students discuss ways in which a person's autobiography and biography might differ.

CLOSE

Invite students to write a brief biographical anecdote about an adult they know. Allow time to share stories in class.

Closing Note

Students may find inspiration in *Extraordinary Black Americans: From Colonial to Contemporary Times*, Susan Altman; *The First Women Who Spoke Out*, Nancy Smiler Levinson; or *Great Lives: Sports*, George Sullivan.

UNIT 4
Lesson 4.1

Setting the Purpose

In Lesson 4.1, students explore how to write a real-life narrative.

FOCUS

Lesson Overview

Objective: To create a narrative using real-life occurrences
Skills: capturing the reader's attention; finding the right idea
Critical Thinking: evaluating
Speaking and Listening: discussing

Bellringer

When students enter the classroom, have this assignment on the board: *Write down three events in your life, small or big, that you think would make interesting stories. Use complete sentences.*

Grammar Link to the Bellringer

Ask students to look at their responses to the Bellringer and identify the tense of each verb.

Motivating Activity

Students will be interested in hearing you tell a brief story about an incident in your own life. This could be anything: taking a trip, hosting an unusual house guest, or having some type of mishap. Humor often helps capture students' interest. After telling your story, invite students to share similar stories about their own lives.

LESSON **4.1**

Narrative Writing

Developing a Real-Life Story

A real-life story tells about actual events that happen to real people. A well-written real-life narrative, like good fiction, should hold the reader's attention by presenting interesting characters in a carefully thought-out setting and plot.

You can find stories in books, on television, and in films. What about the true stories in your own mind? You also have fascinating real-life stories to tell.

Stories can be as different as the people who tell them. No two storytellers have exactly the same background or outlook. Think of a hundred people having the same experience, such as attending a sporting event or watching a parade. Each of them would probably tell about the experience in a different way.

Teacher's Classroom Resources

The following resources can be used for planning, instruction, practice, reinforcement, assessment, reteaching, enrichment, or evaluation.

Teaching Tools
Lesson Plans

Transparencies
Fine Art Transparencies, 16–20
Writing Process Transparencies, 14–16b

Blackline Masters
Thinking and Study Skills, pp. 3, 5, 13, 22
Writing Across the Curriculum, pp. 4–8
Cooperative Learning Activities, pp. 19–24

Capture the Reader's Attention

A narrative is a story that answers the question *What happened?* Before you begin a narrative, decide why someone might read the story. Then think about *who* will read it.

Above all, a good narrative must capture a reader's attention from the very beginning. Strong opening paragraphs make the reader want to continue. Read the beginning of the story below.

Literature Model

"Owen! Time to go!"

I was spying down from behind the crest of the sand dune back of the house. Our car looked like an upside-down bug, a bug with spindly legs waving frantically in the air. Fishing rods were sticking out the back window, my bike was hanging off the rear, and the roof rack was piled with more junk than we had brought. It was the end of summer. Labor Day. Two o'clock in the afternoon. Time to go home.

But not me. I was going to stay.

"Owen! *Time to go!*"

My parents stood there, helpless, not knowing where to even begin to look for me.

Avi, *A Place Called Ugly*

How does the writer grab your attention and make you want to read on?

Grammar Editing Tip

When you edit your draft of a narrative, make sure that all verb tenses are used correctly. For more information, see Lessons 10.4–10.7, pages 304–311.

All well-written stories have the same elements. Good stories tell about characters who are involved in some sort of action in a certain place, presented in a clear order of events.

Journal Writing

You have stories to tell about experiences you've had. In your journal, jot down an idea for a story. Note the characters, place, and action for your story.

TEACH

Guided Practice

L2 Using the Model

Ask students to reread the passage from *A Place Called Ugly.* Remind them that this selection is taken from the very beginning of the book. Ask them to tell about the incident in their own words. What is the setting? Who is there? Why would they want to read on?

Two-Minute Skill Drill

Have students rewrite this opening sentence of a story, adding vivid words to make it more attention-getting:

Blanca was sitting on her porch one summer afternoon, waiting for the mail carrier.

Journal Writing Tip

Story Ideas If students have trouble generating ideas for a story, tell them to look back at their responses to the Bell-ringer assignment in this unit. They may be able to elaborate on one of their earlier ideas.

Speaking and Listening Activities, p. 23
Composition Practice, p. 29
Composition Reteaching, p. 29
Composition Enrichment, p. 29

Unit Assessment

Teacher's Guide to Writing Assessment

Tests with Answer Key
Unit 4 Choice A Test, p. 13
Unit 4 Choice B Test, p. 14

Test Generator
Unit 4 Choice A Test
Unit 4 Choice B Test

You may wish to administer either the Unit 4 Choice A Test or the Unit 4 Choice B Test as a pretest.

TEACH

Guided Practice

L2 Generating Ideas

On the board list the following approaches to generating ideas for narrative writing: brainstorming, listing, reading journal entries, and looking at pictures. Ask volunteers to explain how each approach works. Have students choose a technique they have not yet tried and use it to come up with a topic for a real-life narrative. Then call on volunteers to describe to the class how the activity helped them make a selection.

L1 Recalling Events

Ask students to imagine that a friend or relative who has been away for a long time will telephone soon. So that they will remember important events to tell this person, students will make notes in advance of the imaginary call. Then have students form pairs to share their notes and role-play their phone conversations.

Independent Practice

- For further stimuli for narrative writing, see *Fine Art Transparencies* 16–20.
- *Writing Process Transparencies,* 14–16b
- *Writing Across the Curriculum,* pp. 4–8
- *Cooperative Learning Activities,* pp. 19–24

Skills Practice

- *Thinking and Study Skills,* pp. 3, 5, 13, 22
- *Speaking and Listening Activities,* p. 23
- *Composition Practice,* p. 29

Find the Right Idea

Real-life stories may come from successes or failures in the lives of real people. They may come from accidents or struggles. Sometimes you'll find that ideas for real-life stories come easily. Other times you may find that you can't come up with an idea at all. When this happens, you may want to try a few different strategies. Reread some of your journal entries, or make a list of places, events, or people you know. Browse through a family scrapbook. Look at the ideas below.

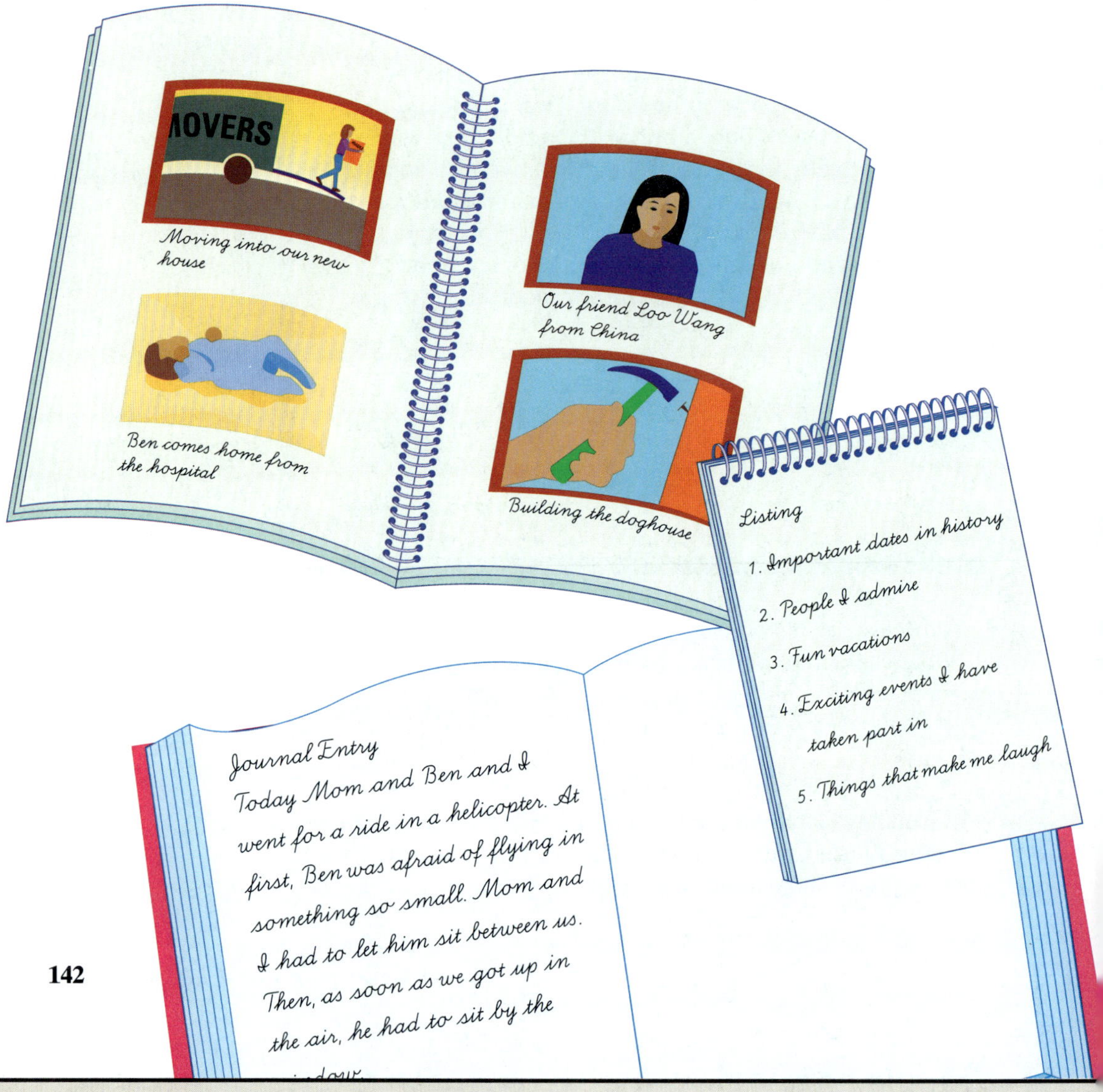

142

Enabling Strategies

LEP Choosing Words

If some students are unsure of what real-life event to write about, suggest that they write about their experiences learning a new language or living in a new place. Pairs of students can work together to come up with adjectives that describe their feelings and bring their narratives to life.

4.1 Writing Activities

Write About a Past Experience

Think of an important event in your life that you could describe to a friend. After you have chosen your event, think about what you want to tell about it, and how. To prepare for writing your description, make a list of sentences or phrases with beginnings such as *I saw, I remember, I felt,* and *I heard.*

- Use the list to help you compose your story.
- Present characters, a place, and action.
- Include interesting details about the characters and setting.
- Capture your reader's attention in the opening paragraph.

PURPOSE To record a real-life experience
AUDIENCE A friend
LENGTH 3–4 paragraphs

Cooperative Learning

Think of your favorite school experience from a past year. Write a brief narrative about this experience. Then, working in a small group, read your narratives to one another. Revise your own narrative based on what the group said was unclear or uninteresting. You could put all the narratives into a booklet.

Grammar Link

Use consistent verb tenses when you write.

Notice the consistent use of verb tense in this sentence from the model (all refer to a time in the past):

*Fishing rods **were sticking** out the back window, my bike **was hanging** off the rear and the roof rack **was piled** with more junk. . . .*

Rewrite each sentence below to make the verb tenses consistent.

1. On our vacation last year, my family and I visited Denver, and we see the capitol.
2. At camp I will learn to canoe; it was fun.
3. The game ended in a tie, and everyone in the stands will cheer for the teams.
4. My family move to San Diego at the end of the year, and my mom bought a business.
5. When I got home from school, my dog run happily and jumped with joy.

See Lessons 10.4–10.7, pages 304–311.

ASSESS

Writing Activities Evaluation Guidelines

Write About a Past Experience

Use these criteria when evaluating your students' writing:

- Does it use the list to help compose the story?
- Does it present characters, a place, and action?
- Does it include interesting details about the characters and setting?
- Does it capture the reader's attention in the opening paragraph?

See also the *Teacher's Guide to Writing Assessment.*

Cooperative Learning

Ask group members to evaluate each narrative. Do the narratives grab and hold the reader's attention? If students chose to collect their group's narratives in a booklet, does the final product reflect the combined efforts of all group members?

Grammar Link

(See Using the Grammar Link below.)

Reteaching

Composition Reteaching, p. 29

Enrichment

Composition Enrichment, p. 29

CLOSE

Ask students to name some of their favorite story plots from books, films, or television. What made these stories favorites? Draw students into a discussion of which plots or portions of plots could have come from real-life experiences.

Using the Grammar Link

Grammar Link Answers

1. Last year my family and I visited Denver, and we saw the capitol.
2. At camp I will learn to canoe; it will be fun.
3. The game ended in a tie, and everyone cheered for the teams.
4. My family plans to move to San Diego, and my mom is buying a business.
5. My dog ran happily and jumped with joy.

Using Consistent Tenses Ask students to check writing assignments from this unit for consistent verb tenses. Have them correct any errors they find.

Setting the Purpose

In Lesson 4.2, students learn how to use time order to organize a narrative about a real-life experience.

FOCUS

Lesson Overview

Objective: To organize, by selecting and sequencing events, a narrative about a real-life experience using time order

Skills: sorting through detail; putting events in order

Critical Thinking: evaluating; comparing

Speaking and Listening: discussing; informal speaking

Bellringer

When students enter the classroom, have this assignment on the board: *Imagine that you want to write a narrative about a surprise birthday party. Write down a detail that happens before the party, at the moment of surprise, and during the party.*

Grammar Link to the Bellringer

Have students rewrite one of their details using the comparative form of an adjective.

Motivating Activity

Ask students if they have ever watched a television program with the sound turned off. Have them discuss how they were able to follow the story without the benefit of words (background, sequence of events, facial expressions, clothing, etc.). Point out that creating a "wordless story" (for example, a dance, a painting, mime, or a picture book) can be a valid way of preparing for writing a narrative based on personal experience.

LESSON 4.2

Narrative Writing

Keeping a Story on Track

To tell a story that is clear, the events and details need to be arranged in a logical order. Many stories can even be told without words.

Glen Rabena, *Mosquito Mask* (in a Native American style), n.d.

Rhythmic drumbeats, beautifully dressed dancers, colorful masks, tall totem poles, carved house fronts—these are the props of the Kwakiutl storytellers. The Kwakiutl peoples of the northwestern coast of North America tell stories as a part of their everyday lives. They may use art, dancing, chanting, or the beating of drums. A new baby or a wedding may call for celebration with stories from nature. Often these storytellers use no words, yet the people understand their tales. The storyteller gives important details and events in an understandable order.

How would you tell a story without using words? Make a list of the ways you would try.

Edward S. Curtis, *Masked Kwakiutl Dancers,* c. 1915

Teacher's Classroom Resources

The following resources can be used for planning, instruction, practice, reinforcement, assessment, reteaching, enrichment, or evaluation.

Teaching Tools
Lesson Plans

Transparencies
Fine Art Transparencies, 16–20
Writing Process Transparencies, 14–16B

Sort Through the Details

When you write a story, you use words. Like the Kwakiutl storytellers, you should choose your details carefully. You also need to organize the details in a way that's clear to your readers.

When you begin to draft your narrative, you may find that you have too many details to tell. Choose only the details that are essential to your story. If you do this, your readers won't get confused by ideas that don't really matter. Sometimes you may have to cut out some details in order to keep the most important details clear. Look at the following notes, taken by a student preparing to write a short narrative. Which three notes do you think would be the strongest parts of a narrative called "My Paper Route"?

Revising Tip

When you are ready to revise, have a partner read your draft. Ask if you have left out any important details or if the order of the details is confusing.

My Paper Route

Journal Writing

Recall a day from last week. List the important events of that day. Highlight the events that were most important.

TEACH

Guided Practice

L1 Evaluating Details

To help students evaluate the notes on the student page, have volunteers read the notes aloud. Ask students what they think the main idea of the narrative is. After determining that the main idea is "My Paper Route," ask students to explain whether they think each note is strongly, somewhat, or not at all related to the main idea. If other students disagree with an evaluation, ask them to explain their reasoning.

Two-Minute Skill Drill

Write on the board this narrative about a trip to the dentist. Ask: *Which detail is the most important? Which is least important?*

I read a magazine in the waiting room. The dentist told me I needed braces. The office smelled like toothpaste.

Journal Writing Tip

Comparing To determine if an event on a given day was significant, students might ask themselves questions such as the following: Did the event change my mood? Did the event relate to one of my special interests? Did the event reveal some aspect of my personality? A yes answer probably means the idea would be a good one to include in students' writing.

Blackline Masters

Thinking and Study Skills, pp. 3, 5, 11, 34
Writing Across the Curriculum, pp. 4–8, 13
Cooperative Learning Activities, pp. 19–24
Speaking and Listening Activities, p. 23
Composition Practice, p. 30
Composition Reteaching, p. 30
Composition Enrichment, p. 30

Assessment

Teacher's Guide to Writing Assessment

TEACH

Guided Practice

L2 Using the Model

Ask students to select the time order words and phrases that help readers follow the story: *The first day, On the third day, Every morning, For the first few weeks, After a few weeks.* Also, point out to students that the story was probably not created directly from the five notes on page 145. Instead, the writer probably added and deleted notes before writing a first draft, then revised the draft one or more times.

L1 Using Time Order

For students who have difficulty with chronology, talk about and show some examples of time order, such as their daily school schedule, a calendar, or a bus schedule. Help students discuss their schedules, using words such as *first* or *next.* To help them organize their narratives, suggest they write each event in their narrative on a separate index card and then line up the cards in the correct order. Tell students to write transition words at the top of the cards to connect the events.

Independent Practice

For further stimuli for narrative writing, see *Fine Art Transparencies,* 16–20.

Writing Process Transparencies, 14–16B

Writing Across the Curriculum, pp. 4–8, 13

Cooperative Learning Activities, pp. 19–24

Skills Practice

Thinking and Study Skills, pp. 3, 5, 11, 34

Speaking and Listening Activities, p. 23

Composition Practice, p. 30

Put Events in Order

Drafting Tip

Write each part of the event as a separate sentence. You can decide later how you want to combine the details.

After you've chosen the important events for your narrative, you need to place them in some particular order. Time order is an effective way to organize your story. When using time order, you tell what happened first, second, and so on. You may use words like *then* or *next.* These words will help your readers follow your story.

The writer of the real-life story below uses three of the statements shown on page 145. Notice the other details the writer adds to fill out the story.

I began my paper route the day after my tenth birthday. The first day was the worst. A man from the newspaper office came with me. He and I walked more than 3 miles and delivered 423 papers. On the third day, I went out all by myself.

Every morning I got up at five o'clock. Then I rode my bike down to the drop-off point to pick up my papers. For the first few weeks, I didn't think I would ever finish. I felt so tired, and my feet hurt. My route, you see, was more than 3 miles long. After a few weeks, though, it didn't seem so bad. Sometimes, especially on nice mornings, I actually liked it.

Enabling Strategies

LEP Using Images to Organize

Students who have difficulty with time order words might benefit from first organizing their personal narrative as a series of drawings. After representing each event and detail in order, they can write appropriate time order words in their first language and then in English next to the images. The pictures and vocabulary reminders can serve as an outline when students write their narratives.

4.2 Writing Activities

Write a Narrative Paragraph

Study the painting below. Think about the action that is taking place. Make a list of details. Use your list to write a paragraph about the picture.

- Choose the details that are important to understanding the picture.
- Put the details in an order that makes sense.

PURPOSE To order details in a narrative
AUDIENCE Your teacher
LENGTH 5 sentences or more

Cross-Curricular: Music

As you listen to a piece of music, make notes for story ideas you get from the music. Draft a paragraph entitled "The Story in the Music."

Grammar Link

Use the comparative forms of *bad* correctly.

When you compare two things, use *worse.* Use *worst* to compare three or more things.

The first day was the **worst.**

Complete each sentence below with the correct form of *bad.*

1. Is Janice's cold ______ than Bill's?
2. Of all the suggestions, that one is the ______ .
3. Was the accident a ______ one?
4. That is the ______ idea of all.
5. My handwriting is ______ than yours.

See Lesson 12.4, page 350.

Taiso Yoshitoshi, *Fujiwara no Yasumasa Playing the Flute by Moonlight,* 1883

ASSESS

Writing Activities Evaluation Guidelines

Write a Narrative Paragraph

Use these criteria when evaluating your students' writing.
- The writer chooses details that are important to understanding the picture.
- The writer puts the details in an order that makes sense.

See also the *Teacher's Guide to Writing Assessment.*

Cross-Curricular: Music

The story should
- reflect the variations in the music used and students' individual interpretations
- follow some clear sequence

Grammar Link

(See Using the Grammar Link below.)

Reteaching

Composition Reteaching, p. 30

Enrichment

Composition Enrichment, p. 30

Use *Fine Art Transparencies* 16–20 for enrichment activities also.

CLOSE

An exercise in nonverbal storytelling may be a great way to bring together LEP, L1, L2, and L3 students. Give individual students instructions for pantomiming a simple story or concept. Ask the other students to guess what this individual is trying to convey without words. It may be an opportunity for students to share their first languages while engaged in the common struggle to understand and to be understood.

Using the Grammar Link

Grammar Link Answers

1. worse
2. worst
3. bad
4. worst
5. worse

About the Art

Taiso Yoshitoshi, *Fujiwara no Yasumasa Playing the Flute by Moonlight,* 1883
Three wood block prints, each 13 ½ by 9 inches, make up this triptych by Japanese artist Tsukioka (Taiso) Yoshitoshi. This work is now in the Takahashi Collection in Japan.

UNIT 4
Lesson 4.3

Setting the Purpose

Lesson 4.3 teaches students to use dialogue to enhance a narrative and to punctuate dialogue correctly.

FOCUS

Lesson Overview

Objective: To use dialogue to enhance a narrative
Skills: identifying the speaker; writing a dialogue; listening
Critical Thinking: organizing; clarifying; evaluating writing
Speaking and Listening: listening to conversations; tape-recording a story

Bellringer

When students enter the classroom, have this assignment on the board: *Write down three things you said this morning.*

Grammar Link to the Bellringer

Ask students if they used quotation marks when writing what they said. Have volunteers write their sentences, using quotation marks, on the board.

Motivating Activity

Challenge students to recall a short conversation they had recently. Invite volunteers to relate their dialogues. Remind them to say the exact words of both speakers as they remember them and to speak with the appropriate feelings. Point out that people often use fragments, slang, and shortened words in their everyday speech. Suggest students consider including dialogue in their narratives to make them more realistic and interesting.

LESSON 4.3

Narrative Writing
Writing Dialogue

Dialogue is the words spoken by the characters in a story. Well-written dialogue can help bring characters and events to life. What characters say, and how they say it, tells a lot about them.

Dialogue can help make a story lifelike and exciting. Read the passage below. Think about the message the dialogue gives about the characters.

The writer tells about Uncle Nachum in the first paragraph. In the dialogue he shows the character in action.

You don't have to use a short phrase to identify speakers each time they speak if the identity of the speaker is clear.

Literature Model

Uncle Nachum had a joke or witty remark for every occasion, telling them in his hoarse voice and enjoying what he said with a hearty laugh. . . . As I watched him at his tricks, he would throw me one of his clever questions, such as, "How many ends does a stick have?"

"Two!" I answered.

"And half a stick?"

"One!" I loudly declared.

And then Uncle Nachum would rock with great, thundering laughter. How did that short body come by such a tremendous laugh? When he laughed it seemed the walls laughed too.

Benjamin Tene, *In the Shade of the Chestnut Tree*

Teacher's Classroom Resources

The following resources can be used for planning, instruction, practice, reinforcement, assessment, reteaching, enrichment, or evaluation.

Teaching Tools
Lesson Plans

Transparencies
Fine Art Transparencies, 16–20
Writing Process Transparencies, 14–16B

Identify the Speaker

When you write a dialogue, you need to help your readers keep track of who is speaking. Show which words a character speaks by putting quotation marks around the words. Also, tell who is speaking by using a phrase such as *she said*. When a different character begins to speak, start a new paragraph.

Now look at how this conversation can be written as dialogue.

"Tommy told a funny story at school today. I almost died!" said Calvin.
"Tell it to me," said Hobbes.
"Well, actually the story itself wasn't so funny. It was the *way* he told it."
"How did he tell it?" asked Hobbes.
"He was drinking milk and when he laughed, it came up his nose!"

Tips for Writing Dialogue

Here's How	Here's Why
Use quotation marks before and after the speaker's exact words.	To show which words the character actually spoke
Use phrases with a word such as *said*.	To let the reader know who is speaking
Start a new paragraph each time a different character speaks.	To make the dialogue easier to follow

Journal Writing

Recall a recent conversation you had with a friend. Practice dialogue by recording the conversation in your journal. Be careful to make clear who is saying what.

TEACH

Guided Practice

L2 Using the Model

Point out that the use of dialogue helps give Uncle Nachum's questions more impact and makes the passage more interesting. To demonstrate, first read the passage without the dialogue, rewording it slightly. Then have a student read aloud the dialogue as written. Ask students why they think dialogue makes the passage better.

L1 Understanding Dialogue

Select a short narrative with a lot of dialogue. Have students take turns reading the narrator's part and the character's parts. Then ask students what difficulties they had, such as keeping the characters straight or distinguishing narration from dialogue. Ask them what they learned from listening to one another read.

Two-Minute Skill Drill

Write these phrases on the board. Have students choose an appropriate adverb to complete each phrase.

she said ________
he shouted ________
Tina asked ________
she remarked ________

Journal Writing Tip

Using Vivid Words Ask students to name some synonyms for the word *said*, such as *whispered*, *yelled*, or *mumbled*. Point out that using these vivid words can help give additional information about a speaker's mood and personality.

Blackline Masters

Thinking and Study Skills, pp. 3, 5, 34
Writing Across the Curriculum, pp. 4–8
Cooperative Learning Activities, pp. 19–24
Speaking and Listening Activities, p. 23
Composition Practice, p. 31
Composition Reteaching, p. 31
Composition Enrichment, p. 31

Assessment

Teacher's Guide to Writing Assessment

UNIT 4
Lesson 4.3

TEACH

Guided Practice

L2 Using the Model

Point out that the narrative on the left describes Ralph as "just a little kid." Guide students to see that the narrative on the right shows that Ralph is young by letting the reader in on what Ralph thinks and feels through what he says and how he says it. Next, direct students' attention back to the narrative on the left. How does it describe Meg? How does the narrative on the right describe her?

L3 Applying and Extending

Invite students to find passages of dialogue from a book or a magazine article. Have students meet in small groups to read their passages aloud. Before reading, students should describe the setting and action. Afterwards, have the students who are listening describe what they have learned about the characters from the dialogue.

Independent Practice

For further stimuli for writing dialogue, see *Fine Art Transparencies* 16–20.

Writing Process Transparencies, 14–16B

Writing Across the Curriculum, pp. 4–8

Cooperative Learning Activities, pp. 19–24

Skills Practice

Thinking and Study Skills, pp. 3, 5, 34

Speaking and Listening Activities, p. 23

Composition Practice, p. 31

Listen Carefully

Presenting Tip

After you write a story with dialogue, tape-record the story with different people reading the words of the characters.

Paying attention to conversations is one of the best ways to get to know people. In your narrative writing, the words your characters say can help readers get to know them, too.

Two short narratives are shown below. The first one does not use dialogue; the second one does. See how dialogue shows the personalities of the two characters in the second narrative. What is one example of how dialogue helps you get to know Meg and Ralph?

Vocabulary

Drafting Tip

When you draft dialogue, you can use adverbs in your identifying phrases to tell how a person is speaking. For more information about adverbs, see Lessons 13.1 and 13.2, pages 360–363.

The writer uses the adverbs "softly" and "excitedly" in these identifying phrases.

Enabling Strategies

LEP Choosing Words

Students learning English may need extra help in writing and identifying descriptive phrases in dialogue. First, write the following line on the board: *"Go home, Spot!" she said.* Ask students to name vivid verbs they could use instead of *said*. Then provide students with a picture of two people talking. Have students work in pairs to write dialogue for the two characters. Encourage them to use different verbs to show how the characters are speaking. Have them use a thesaurus if appropriate. Encourage students to read their dialogues aloud.

4.3 Writing Activities

Write a Dialogue

Write a conversation between two characters of different ages, backgrounds, or personalities.

- Create the dialogue to show what each person is like.
- Include identifying phrases to show who is speaking.
- Use quotation marks and other punctuation correctly.
- Begin a new line to show a change in speaker.

PURPOSE To use dialogue for characterization
AUDIENCE Your class
LENGTH At least 8 lines of dialogue

Edvard Munch, *Women on a Bridge,* c. 1903

Grammar Link

Use quotation marks before and after a direct quotation.

To make dialogue clear, use quotation marks around the words a character says.

"It may rain," Sue said.

Write the following sentences, adding quotation marks to mark the beginning and end of dialogue.

1. Maria said, It's pouring. Where did this rain come from?
2. Let's run under that awning! yelled Kiko.
3. Maria yelled back, We may have to swim there!
4. I'm not moving, said Seth as he sat in a puddle.
5. Oh no, said Maria, Seth is soaked to the bone!

See Lesson 19.6, page 464.

Cross-Curricular: Art

Study the painting. What might these women be saying? Describe the painting by writing a short narrative that includes dialogue.

ASSESS

Writing Activities Evaluation Guidelines

Write a Dialogue

Use these criteria when evaluating your students' writing:

- Does it show what each person is like?
- Does it include identifying phrases to show who is speaking?
- Does it use quotation marks and other punctuation correctly?
- Does it include line breaks to show changes in speakers?

See also the *Teacher's Guide to Writing Assessment.*

Cross-Curricular: Art

Evaluate the narrative based on the following:

- clarity in showing who says what
- variety in the verbs and adverbs used to describe how the characters are speaking
- creativity in imagining what the women might be saying

Grammar Link

(See Using the Grammar Link below.)

Reteaching

Composition Reteaching, p. 31

Enrichment

Composition Enrichment, p. 31

Use *Fine Art Transparencies* 16–20 for enrichment activities also.

CLOSE

Have students work in pairs, reading their dialogues aloud to each other. Partners can tell whether the dialogues clearly showed who said what. They can then discuss what each character seems like and why.

Using the Grammar Link

Grammar Link Answers

1. Maria said, "It's pouring. Where did this rain come from?"
2. "Let's run under that awning," yelled Kiko.
3. Maria yelled back, "We may have to swim there!"
4. "I'm not moving," said Seth as he sat in a puddle.
5. "Oh no," said Maria, "Seth is soaked to the bone!"

About the Art

Edvard Munch, *Women on a Bridge*, c. 1903

This oil-on-canvas painting, from the Munch Museum in Oslo, Norway, is not typical of Edvard Munch's work. The Norwegian painter and printmaker (1863–1944) usually chose more somber themes of love and death.

Setting the Purpose

Lesson 4.4 teaches students how to select details, describe feelings and events, and come to a conclusion when writing a personal narrative.

FOCUS

Lesson Overview

Objective: To consider purpose and audience when composing or revising personal narrative
Skills: setting a purpose; choosing important details; writing a conclusion
Critical Thinking: recalling an event; evaluating information; drawing a conclusion
Speaking and Listening: telling a story

Bellringer

When students enter the classroom, have this assignment on the board: *List three interesting or important events from your life.*

Grammar Link to the Bellringer

Ask students to write one sentence to describe each event, using a conjunction (*and*, *or*, or *but*) in each sentence.

Motivating Activity

Ask students to recall an encounter with an animal other than a pet. They might think of animals in the wild, at a park, at a zoo, or on a farm. Let them freewrite for five minutes about the incident. Then guide them in a discussion of what they wrote, encouraging them to explain what made the encounter interesting or unusual and how they felt at the time. Tell students that such an experience might be turned into an interesting narrative.

LESSON **4.4**

Narrative Writing

Writing About an Event

Real-life narratives often grow out of special experiences in a writer's life. The writer usually finds a way to tell readers how the experience was special.

Here's how one student wrote about a camping trip. Look for the ways she tells that this was a special event, and notice how she brings her story to a conclusion.

The writer begins her story by telling you that this was a real experience.

Student Model

It was during our most recent camping trip, in Yellowstone, that I had my first real bear experience. We'd finished dinner so we hung our leftover roast beef in a tree out of reach of any hungry bears, played three rounds of Boggle, and went to sleep.

In the middle of the night I woke up with an urgent need for the bathroom. I had just popped my head out of the tent when I saw someone reaching for our roast beef . . . He looked a little larger than my father, but who else could it be? I looked back into our tent and there was my father peacefully snoring. . . . I realized what it was—a bear!!! I zipped up the tent flap very, very slowly (all needs for the bathroom instantly cured) and crawled back into my sleeping bag.

Rebecca Bardach, Berkeley, California
First appeared in *Cricket*

Teacher's Classroom Resources

The following resources can be used for planning, instruction, practice, reinforcement, assessment, reteaching, enrichment, or evaluation.

Teaching Tools
Lesson Plans

Transparencies
Fine Art Transparencies, p. 16–20
Writing Process Transparencies, p. 14–16B

Make the Most of an Idea

Rebecca Bardach told her story because it was her first experience with a live bear. She gave some details about the camping trip to set the scene for her readers. Also, she let readers know she was frightened and unfamiliar with bears.

When you write about a real-life experience, think of the specific things that made it special to you. Make some notes about information you have that your audience may not have; these notes will help you realize what background you may need to give your readers. As you plan your story, use the three questions below to help you.

Prewriting Tip

To get started, imagine that you are telling your story to a friend on the telephone. Make a list of things you would tell your friend.

Making the Most of an Idea

1. Why do I want to tell this story?
2. What information does my audience need to understand the story?
3. How can my writing let my audience know who I am?

Journal Writing

Write a journal entry about a family event. What made this event special?

Blackline Masters

Thinking and Study Skills, pp. 3, 5, 11
Writing Across the Curriculum, pp. 4–8
Cooperative Learning Activities, pp. 19–24
Speaking and Listening Activities, p. 23
Composition Practice, p. 32
Composition Reteaching, p. 32
Composition Enrichment, p. 32

Assessment

Teacher's Guide to Writing Assessment

TEACH

Guided Practice

L2 Using the Model

Point out that the first sentence in the model tells why the experience was important to the writer. Students may not be sure how to start their own drafts. Once students have chosen events to write about, ask them the following questions: *What made this event special to you? What made it memorable?* Suggest they use their answers to write the opening sentence of their draft.

L3 Writing with Feeling

Rebecca uses three exclamation points to show her incredible surprise at discovering a wild bear. Tell students that there are other ways for writers to show amazement. Experienced writers carefully choose and arrange their words to convey the idea of surprise, instead of relying on exclamation points. Write the following line from the model, and ask students to rewrite it in a way that shows surprise without using exclamation points. *I realized what it was—a bear!!!*

Two-Minute Skill Drill

List these nouns on the board and have students write an adjective for each to make it more specific.

bear	air	sky
day	house	water

Journal Writing Tip

Setting the Scene Point out that vivid details of sight, sound, and smell can help readers visualize a scene.

TEACH

Guided Practice

L2 Using the Model

Copy the model text on the board, including revisions. Elicit students' comments and suggestions for further—or better—changes. When you and your students have finished, ask them to compare the version on the board to the original text from this page. Do they like the new version better? Why or why not?

L1 Discussing Conclusions

Ask students to suggest reasons why a good conclusion is important to a narrative. Tell students that sometimes it's hard to figure out how to conclude a narrative. Guide students to suggest different ways to conclude a real-life narrative, such as telling what they did, what they felt, what they learned, or what someone else did.

Independent Practice

- For further stimuli for narrative writing, see *Fine Art Transparencies* 16–20.
- *Writing Process Transparencies*, 14–16B
- *Writing Across the Curriculum*, pp. 4–8
- *Cooperative Learning Activities*, pp. 19–24

Skills Practice

- *Thinking and Study Skills*, pp. 3, 5, 11
- *Speaking and Listening Activities*, p. 23
- *Composition Practice*, p. 32

Finish the Job

Grammar Editing Tip

Proofread your narrative for spelling and punctuation. For information about punctuation of dialogue, see Lesson 19.6, page 464.

Every well-written narrative has a conclusion. One type of conclusion sums up the story and reflects on what happened.

The conclusion should give your audience the feeling that the story is complete. You might conclude with phrases like these: *I learned that . . .* or *From then on, I knew . . .* or *Ever since this experience, I have felt . . .*

Read this draft of a young writer's story. Notice how the writer revised the draft using the questions on page 153.

I am really excited about the ways that a computer has changed my life. It even helped me find a lost pet's owner.

When the kitten first showed up at our back door, I wanted to keep it. I knew, though, that it belonged to someone else.

Then I got an idea. I could use the computer at school to find the kitten's owner. I typed up an announcement with a description of the kitten and my address and phone number. Then I added a graphic of a cat at the top. ^ *I printed thirty copies of the announcement on orange paper.*

After school I put a copy of the announcement on the porch of every house on my street. At 7:30 that night, I was petting the kitten when the phone rang. "Yes, she's right here, and she's fine," I told the voice on the phone. ^ *When I hung up the phone, I had a good feeling inside.*

The writer left out an important detail. Readers need to know that she made many copies of the announcement.

To complete the story, the writer needs to tell how she felt about finding the kitten's owner.

Enabling Strategies

LEP Communicating Experience

Ask students from different countries to write about an experience they had while in their native country, while coming to the United States, or after they had arrived in the United States. Encourage students to work with an English-proficient partner or to use a thesaurus or a dictionary if necessary. Invite students to share their stories with the rest of the class.

4.4 Writing Activities

Write a Narrative About Learning a Skill

Learning a skill often takes hard work. Draft a narrative about a skill, such as swimming or riding a bike, you had difficulty learning. Write your narrative for a younger person who is having trouble mastering the skill.

As you plan your draft, list details about what helped you learn and what you learned about yourself from the experience.

- Include information that your readers will need.
- Let your audience know exactly how you were feeling.
- Write a conclusion that makes clear to your reader that the story is over.

PURPOSE To share a real-life experience
AUDIENCE A younger person
LENGTH 3–4 paragraphs

COMPUTER OPTION

The line-spacing function on your word processor can help when you plan to have a peer review your work. Double-space your draft to make it easier to read. Also, leave wide margins around your text. These changes will give your partner plenty of room to write comments.

Grammar Link

Avoid run-on sentences in your writing.

A run-on sentence is two or more sentences incorrectly written as one sentence.

Correct each run-on below. To do so, you may write separate sentences. You may also combine the sentences with a comma and a conjunction (*and, or,* or *but*) or with a semicolon.

1. Helen Keller's life is an inspiration she worked tirelessly for the visually impaired and the hearing-visually impaired.
2. John F. Kennedy was president in the 1960s, he started the Peace Corps.
3. Martin Delany was a journalist, physician, and social reformer in the nineteenth century he served in the Union Army.
4. Harriet Tubman was born a slave she escaped and led 300 other enslaved people out of slavery.
5. I didn't think I'd ever be able to do it I finally learned to ski last month.

See Lessons 7.2 and 8.6, pages 244 and 272.

ASSESS

Writing Activities Evaluation Guidelines

Write a Narrative About Learning a Skill

Use these criteria when evaluating your students' writing.

- reflects the personality and feelings of the writer
- presents a story about perseverance
- has a conclusion
- includes important details
- uses conjunctions correctly

See also the *Teacher's Guide to Writing Assessment.*

Computer Option

Students should have double-spaced their drafts and left wide margins.

Grammar Link

(See Using the Grammar Link below.)

Reteaching

Composition Reteaching, p. 32

Enrichment

Composition Enrichment, p. 32

CLOSE

Have pairs of students read each other's narratives. Then have them offer each other suggestions and feedback on the following points:

- Was there enough information in the narrative?
- Did the writer let the audience know how he or she was feeling?
- Was the conclusion strong?

Using the Grammar Link

Grammar Link Answers

Answers will vary. One suggeston is given below.

1. Helen … inspiration; she … impaired.

Correcting Run-on Sentences After students have corrected their sentences, write them on the board. Ask volunteers to write their corrections underneath. Then ask whether anyone corrected the sentences differently. Have volunteers write their corrections under the first ones.

Setting the Purpose

Lesson 4.5 teaches students various ways to respond in writing to a biography.

FOCUS

Lesson Overview

Objective: To respond to a biography in writing
Skills: writing in a journal; writing a biographical article
Critical Thinking: summarizing; analyzing
Speaking and Listening: role-playing an interview

Bellringer

When students enter the classroom, have this assignment on the board: *Think of a person you would like to learn more about. If you could meet this person, what questions would you ask him or her?*

Grammar Link to the Bellringer

Have students underline the verbs in the questions they wrote. Discuss verb tense, with the focus on the past tense.

Motivating Activity

Ask students to think of people whose biographies they have read. Do they enjoy stories about real people? Point out that most biographies do more than give information about a person's accomplishments. They often tell about making difficult decisions, adjusting to changes, and overcoming hardships. Point out that these stories often inspire readers and give them ideas they can use in their own lives.

LESSON **4.5**

Writing About Literature

Responding to a Biography

Reading biographies lets you learn about other people. In addition, your personal response to a biography may lead to other discoveries—about yourself and the world around you.

Rosa Parks is often called the mother of the civil rights movement in America. Her years of brave work began on a bus in Montgomery, Alabama. The following passage about the beginning of her 50-year struggle is from *Rosa Parks: The Movement Organizes* by Kai Friese.

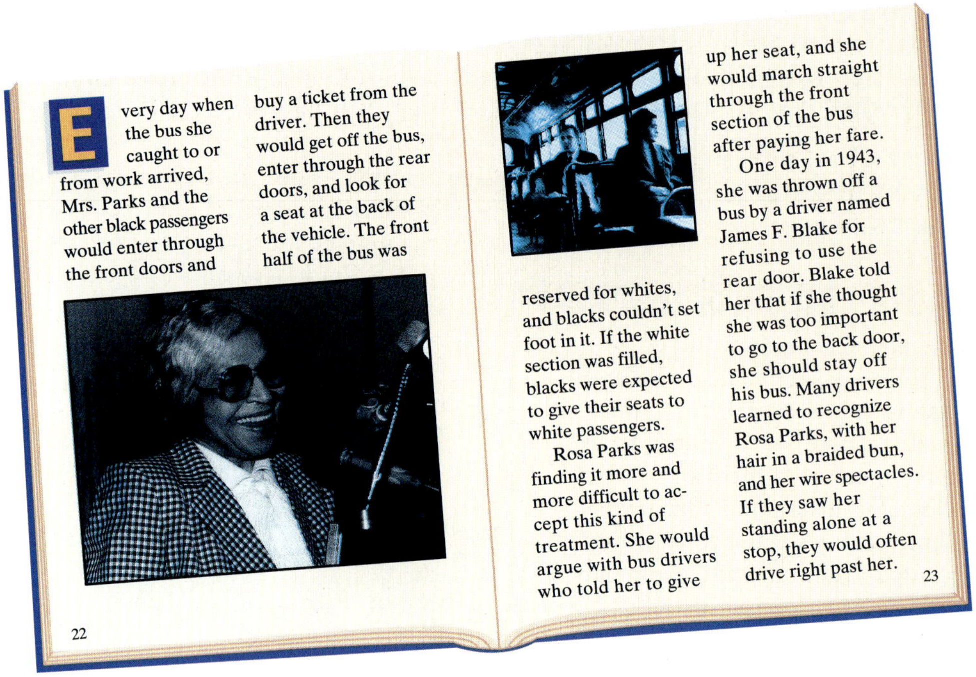

Every day when the bus she caught to or from work arrived, Mrs. Parks and the other black passengers would enter through the front doors and buy a ticket from the driver. Then they would get off the bus, enter through the rear doors, and look for a seat at the back of the vehicle. The front half of the bus was reserved for whites, and blacks couldn't set foot in it. If the white section was filled, blacks were expected to give their seats to white passengers.

Rosa Parks was finding it more and more difficult to accept this kind of treatment. She would argue with bus drivers who told her to give up her seat, and she would march straight through the front section of the bus after paying her fare.

One day in 1943, she was thrown off a bus by a driver named James F. Blake for refusing to use the rear door. Blake told her that if she thought she was too important to go to the back door, she should stay off his bus. Many drivers learned to recognize Rosa Parks, with her hair in a braided bun, and her wire spectacles. If they saw her standing alone at a stop, they would often drive right past her.

22 23

Teacher's Classroom Resources

The following resources can be used for planning, instruction, practice, reinforcement, assessment, reteaching, enrichment, or evaluation.

Teaching Tools
Lesson Plans

Transparencies
Fine Art Transparencies, 16–20
Writing Process Transparencies, 14–16B

Learn About Others

A biography is one kind of real-life narrative. It's the story of a person's life, written by someone else. The person being written about is the subject of the biography.

When you read a biography, you learn about a person's life and accomplishments. You learn about the events that affected the person's life. You may also learn, as in the story of Rosa Parks, how the subject of a biography affected history. Look at what the student writer of the model below learned from reading *Rosa Parks: The Movement Organizes.*

Prewriting Tip

To help you recall information as you read a biography, jot down notes about the details that impress you.

Student Model

Rosa Parks was a brave black woman who believed in herself. When she saw how unfairly blacks were treated by white people in Montgomery, she decided to fight back. She didn't fight with violence but with the "weapon of protest." One day she refused to give up her seat on a bus to a white person, so she was arrested. She had always obeyed this rule before, but this time she was tired of being pushed around.

Even though her arrest was a small matter, it started a big movement. First came the boycott of buses and businesses. Then came the protests and sit-ins. Then came the civil rights movement. Rosa Parks showed everyone how much power you can have if you believe in yourself.

Timmy Baltz, Hufford School, Joliet, Illinois

Journal Writing

Recall a biography you have read in a book, magazine, or newspaper, or one you have seen on film. Write in your journal what you thought about this biography.

TEACH

Guided Practice

L2 Changing Point of View

Invite students to project themselves into the situation described in the passage on page 156. Have them write about the event from the point of view of Rosa Parks. As they board the bus or wait at the bus stop, what do they see? What are they thinking? Remind students to use the pronoun *I* when they write from the point of view of the subject.

L2 Using the Model

Ask students to think about how they might feel if people started to avoid them or make their lives difficult because they had taken a stand on an issue that was important to them. Ask students to share current examples of people being treated in this manner.

Two-Minute Skill Drill

List these verbs on the board. Have students write the past tense of each verb and then orally provide examples of them in sentences.

talk	walk	dance
learn	collect	visit

Journal Writing Tip

Recording Thoughts About a Biography Encourage students to focus on what they learned from the biography. Did the person have to overcome difficulties? How do the students feel about what the person accomplished?

Blackline Masters

Thinking and Study Skills, pp. 9, 23–24, 35, 37
Writing Across the Curriculum, pp. 4–8
Cooperative Learning Activities, pp. 19–24
Speaking and Listening Activities, p. 23
Composition Practice, p. 33
Composition Reteaching, p. 33
Composition Enrichment, p. 33

Assessment

Teacher's Guide to Writing Assessment

TEACH

Guided Practice

L2 Comparing Biographies

Small groups of students might be interested in discussing different biographies of the same person. Suggest that everyone in the group read about the same incident or period in the subject's life. Each person should then share what he or she learned about the subject along with his or her personal feelings and thoughts about the subject. Encourage students to see that biographies can present the same information differently.

L3 Writing a Letter

Have students write a letter to the author of a biography they particularly enjoyed. What did they like most about the biography? What did they learn by reading it? Do they have any questions to ask the author?

Independent Practice

For further stimuli for narrative writing, see *Fine Art Transparencies*, 16–20.

Writing Process Transparencies, 14–16B

Writing Across the Curriculum, pp. 4–8

Cooperative Learning Activities, pp. 19–24

Skills Practice

Thinking and Study Skills, pp. 9, 23–24, 35, 37

Composition Practice, p. 33

Speaking and Listening Activities, p. 23

Respond in Different Ways

When you read a biography, you may be surprised. You may laugh. You may even cry. Probably more than anything else, you'll learn things you never expected to learn.

A good biography may prompt you to respond. You might tell a friend about it. You may respond in writing. The list below tells different ways you can respond to a biography.

Grammar
Revising Tip

As you revise your writing, make sure not to shift your verb tenses without a reason. For help with verb tenses, see Lessons 10.4–10.7, pages 304–311.

Ways to Respond to a Biography

1. Write an account of an event as if the subject of the biography is describing it.
2. Write a journal entry for one day in the person's life.
3. Compare the way the person reacted to an event to the way you would have reacted to the same event.
4. Write an imaginary interview with the person, using questions similar to those below.

An Interview with Rosa Parks

Why did you decide not to give up your seat that day?

Do you mean that you had stood up for your rights before this time?

Were you afraid of what might happen to you?

Mashi Fisher, Evanston, Illinois

Enabling Strategies

LEP Understanding Special Words

Students with limited English vocabulary may not be familiar with the words *boycott*, *sit-in*, and *protest*. Define these terms with the class, giving examples.

If students are very new to the United States, you may also want to provide a brief background on the civil rights movement.

4.5 Writing Activities

Write a Brief Biography

Read a biography or a short biographical article about an athlete, musician, or movie star. Then imagine that you have spent a day with the person. Write an account of what you did with this person. Tell where you went and what you talked about.

- Use information you learned from your reading.
- Relate that information to your own experience.

PURPOSE To respond to a biography
AUDIENCE Yourself
LENGTH 3–4 paragraphs

Cooperative Learning

With three or more classmates, choose a biography from a magazine. After reading the biography, each person should write questions he or she would like to ask the subject. In your group, take turns role-playing the subject while the others ask questions. When you are being questioned, use the information from the biography to help you answer. Record your questions and answers as a group response to the biography.

Grammar Link

Don't overuse the present tense of verbs in your writing.

To tell about an action that happened in the past, use the past tense or a helping verb with the past participle: *walked, have walked.* Forms of the helping verb *have* are often used with the past participle of a main verb.

Write the correct form of the verb in parentheses to complete each sentence.

1. Rosa Parks's life has (inspire) many young African Americans.
2. When Parks (refuse) to give up her seat, she made history.
3. I have (learn) how to play the clarinet this year.
4. I (practice) every day.
5. Our top player (pitch) a perfect game last night.
6. He had (pitch) another perfect game earlier this season.
7. It (snow) last night.
8. It has (snow) twice this winter.
9. Last year, it had (snow) more by this date.
10. I have (like) snow since I was a little kid.

See Lessons 10.4 and 10.5, pages 304–307.

ASSESS

Writing Activities Evaluation Guidelines

Write a Brief Biography

Use these criteria when evaluating your students' writing. Verify that the student's biography

- reflects an understanding of the biography's subject and his or her accomplishments or contributions
- expresses the student's thoughts about the subject
- reveals a personal response to something the subject has said or done

See also the *Teacher's Guide to Writing Assessment.*

Cooperative Learning

Encourage students to ask questions that go beyond the content of the biography. The responses to the questions should reflect an understanding of how the biography's subject might respond based on information provided in the biography.

Grammar Link

(See Using the Grammar Link below.)

Reteaching

Composition Reteaching, p. 33

Enrichment

Composition Enrichment, p. 33

Use *Fine Art Transparencies* 16–20 for enrichment activities also.

CLOSE

Initiate a discussion about other ways students might respond in writing to the biography of Rosa Parks. They might write a play, compose a protest song, or write a letter about civil rights and send it to a government leader.

Using the Grammar Link

Grammar Link Answers

1. inspired
2. refused
3. learned
4. practiced *OR* practice
5. pitched
6. pitched
7. snowed
8. snowed
9. snowed
10. liked

Using the Past Tense Have students write sentences about a biographical subject of their choice. Their sentences should include past tense verbs, either alone or with the helping verb *has, have,* or *had.*

UNIT 4
Writing Process in Action

Setting the Purpose

Students now have the opportunity to apply what they have learned about narrative writing to an independent writing project. They will use the stages of the writing process to create and present a finished piece.

FOCUS

Lesson Overview

Objective: To develop a narrative about an important real-life experience

Skills: using the five stages of the writing process: prewriting, drafting, revising, editing, and presenting; using a cluster diagram; writing dialogue

Critical Thinking: recalling; analyzing; evaluating; synthesizing

Speaking and Listening: discussing; reading aloud; telling a story

Bellringer

When students enter the classroom, have this assignment on the board: *List your three favorite pieces of clothing. After each one, write a sentence that tells why you like it.*

Grammar Link to the Bellringer

Ask students to rewrite the sentences they wrote for the Bellringer as dialogue. Put this example on the board: *"This coat is the most colorful coat I've ever seen," I said.* Remind students to use quotation marks and speaker words.

Motivating Activity

Have students describe how they feel when they wear one of the articles of clothing described in the Bellringer. What special significance does it have for them? Then ask students to describe a time when their clothing made them embarrassed or unhappy.

UNIT 4

WRITING PROCESS IN ACTION

NARRATIVE WRITING

In the preceding lessons, you've learned about turning real-life experiences into good stories. You've practiced using details in time order and writing dialogue that shows what characters are like. You've also had the chance to learn how to write a brief biography. Now it's time to put together everything you've learned. In this lesson, you will tell the story of how a piece of clothing affected your life.

• Assignment •

Context	You want to submit a real-life narrative to a make-believe publication called Wore Stories. Your story will focus on how a piece of clothing affected your life.
Purpose	To retell a past experience using narrative
Audience	Student readers of Wore Stories
Length	1 page

The next few pages can help you plan and write your story. Read through them and then refer to them as you need to. Don't be tied down by them, however. Remember, you're in charge of your own writing process.

Teacher's Classroom Resources

The following resources can be used for planning, instruction, practice, reinforcement, assessment, reteaching, enrichment, or evaluation.

Teaching Tools
Lesson Plans

Transparencies
Writing Process Transparencies, 14-16B

Prewriting

Prewrite to explore your thoughts about an old piece of clothing. How did you get it? How did you feel about wearing it? What happened to you while wearing it? The graphic below offers options to help you recall your thoughts and feelings.

Pages 10–13 offer more tips on freewriting. Your goal is to gather details and experiences to use in your real-life narrative.

Option A
Use a cluster diagram.

Option B
Review your journal.

Option C
Freewrite about a topic.

Drafting

As you look over the prewriting notes you made, think about how you want to begin your real-life narrative. The opening paragraph should capture and hold readers' attention from the very beginning. For example, notice how Gary Soto begins his narrative.

Literature Model

> My clothes have failed me. I remember the green coat that I wore in fifth and sixth grades when you either danced like a champ or pressed yourself against a greasy wall, bitter as a penny toward the happy couples.
>
> Gary Soto, "The Jacket"

Drafting Tip
For help with developing your opening, see Lesson 4.1, pages 140–142.

Soto begins by telling the reader that his clothes have let him down. Then he introduces a specific piece of clothing (his

TEACH

Prewriting

L2 Using a Cluster Diagram

Students may benefit from using a cluster diagram to help them gather details about their story idea. Suggest they freewrite first and then use details from what they have written to begin building the diagram. Encourage them to add more details, listing whatever comes to mind that relates to the main idea. Remind them that in the process they may uncover other writing ideas they will want to make note of for future use.

L1 Developing Ideas

Some students may feel more comfortable tape-recording their ideas. Have students think about a piece of clothing that is important to them, then talk about it to a friend while tape-recording the conversation. Tell students to ask each other questions about what they don't understand or want to know more about. When students are done, have them listen to their tapes and write down any interesting ideas.

Drafting

L2 Getting Started

Tell students that if they get stuck and can't think of a strong opening paragraph, they can start in the middle of their narrative—or even at the end! After they have some of their ideas on paper, it might be easier to think of a good beginning. Remind students to describe the setting and any characters in their narratives.

Blackline Masters
Thinking and Study Skills, pp. 15, 19
Composition Practice, p. 36
Composition Reteaching, p. 36
Composition Enrichment, p. 36

Grammar Workbook
Lesson 78

Assessment
Teacher's Guide to Writing Assessment

TEACH

Revising

L2 Peer Editing

Students can work in writing conferences with peer editors before they revise their writing. You may want to duplicate the Peer Response forms in the *Teacher's Guide to Writing Assessment.* Suggest that peer editors respond to the following questions: What effect did the clothing have on the writer's life? What details are the most effective?

Editing

L2 Peer Editing

After students have edited their own work, have them edit another student's writing. Remind them to refer to the Editing Checklist on the student page.

Presenting

Before students present their narrative writing, discuss how to prepare their papers for publication. Emphasize the importance of the final draft and that it must be neatly done.

Independent Practice

Writing Process Transparencies, 14-16B

Skills Practice

Thinking and Study Skills, pp. 15, 19

Composition Practice, p. 36

Grammar Workbook, Lesson 78

Journal Writing Tip

Remembering Details Tell students that one important, but sometimes difficult, aspect of writing a narrative is remembering details. Ask students what the writing of their narratives helped them to remember.

Grammar
Revising Tip

If you need help revising dialogue, see Lesson 4.3, pages 148–150.

jacket) that he wore during a certain period of time (fifth and sixth grade).

How will you begin your narrative? Perhaps you'll start by describing the piece of clothing. The choice is up to you.

Revising

To begin revising, read over your draft to make sure that what you have written fits your purpose and your audience. Then have a **writing conference**. Read your draft to a partner or a small group. Use your audience's reactions to help you evaluate your work so far. The following questions can help you and your listeners.

Question A
Does my first sentence grab readers' attention?

Question B
Have I included all the important information?

Question C
Are the events in an order that makes sense?

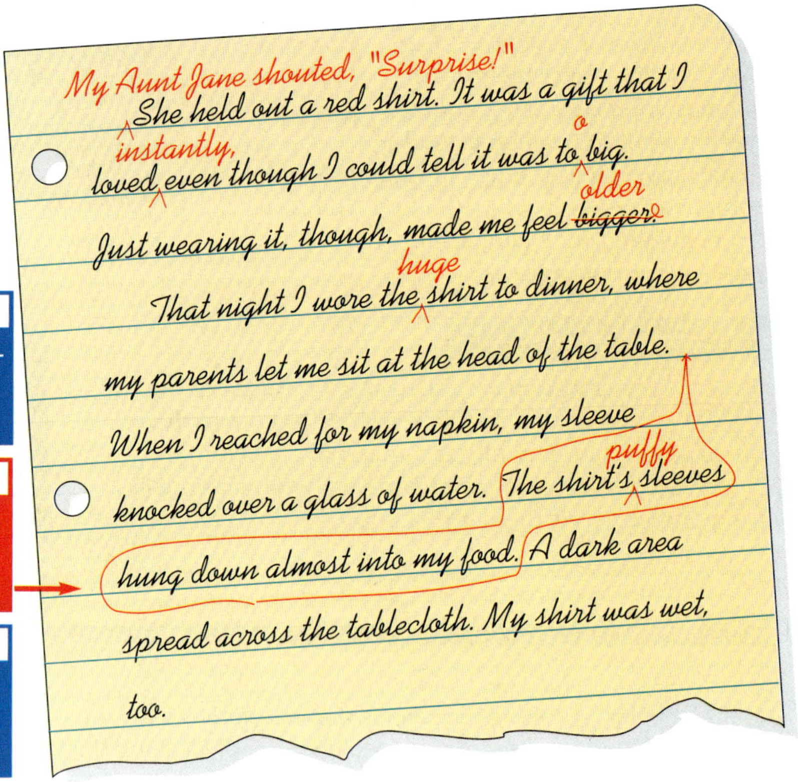

Enrichment and Extension

Follow-up Ideas

- Encourage students to illustrate their narratives, either with drawings or with photographs. Bind students' finished work into a class book.
- Have a story circle in which students take turns telling their stories.

Extending Narrative Writing

- Explore opportunities for extending narrative writing beyond the classroom, such as creating a newsletter for teenagers in which they share real-life narratives about important or interesting experiences.

Editing

You've worked hard to write your real-life narrative. You want your readers to focus on what you've written. You don't want to distract them with any mistakes. Pay attention to capitalization, punctuation, and spelling. You can find more specific **proofreading** help on pages 72–74.

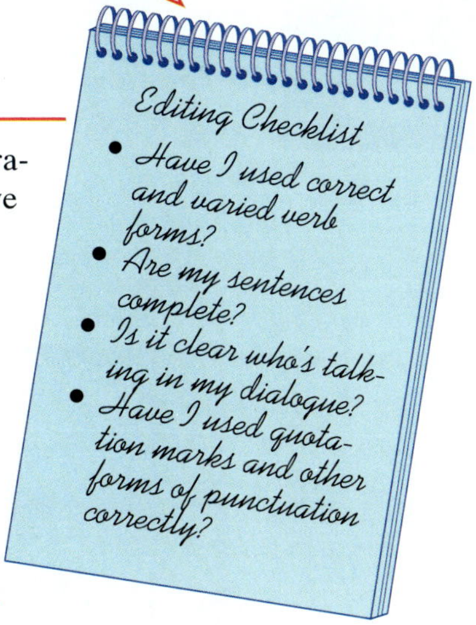

Presenting

Before writing your final copy, you may want to have a family member or friend read your narrative. She or he may have some suggestions that will help. Maybe you'd rather not share your story with anyone except your teacher.

You could include a photograph or a drawing of yourself wearing the piece of clothing. That would help your reader picture the events in your narrative even more clearly.

Proofreading

For proofreading symbols, see page 74.

Journal Writing

Reflect on your writing process experience. Answer these questions in your journal. What do you like best about your narrative? What was the hardest part of writing it? What did you learn from your writing conference? What new thing have you learned as a writer?

ASSESS

Evaluation Guidelines

Use the following questions to evaluate students' finished writing.

- Does the opening of the narrative draw the reader into the story?
- Does the narrative include important details and information?
- Are events in an order that makes sense?
- Is dialogue used effectively? Is it clear who's talking?
- Are verbs used correctly?
- Are the sentences complete?
- Have quotation marks been used correctly?
- Has the edited narrative been checked for grammar, usage, and mechanics?

Refer to the *Teacher's Guide to Writing Assessment* for further help with evaluating student writing.

Reteaching

Composition Reteaching, p. 36

Enrichment

Composition Enrichment, p. 36

CLOSE

Ask students what they enjoyed most about writing a real-life narrative. Did they like writing about an article of clothing? Why or why not? Ask students for other ideas, such as: a scary moment, a memorable meal, or a family vacation. Write students' suggestions on the board. Tell them to remember these ideas the next time they want to write a real-life narrative.

Cultural Diversity

Discussing Clothing

Point out that people sometimes wear clothing that reflects their ethnic background. Ask students to give some examples (yarmulkes, turbans, saris, kimonos, kilts, dashikis, and so on). If students are personally familiar with such clothing, ask them to explain its significance and whether it is worn on special occasions or every day. Tell students they may wish to consider clothing items related to their cultural background as they generate ideas for their narrative.

Setting the Purpose

In the Unit 4 Literature Model, students read a literature selection that illustrates in a very real way effective narrative writing. Such readings serve as models for students as they create their own narrative writing.

About the Author

Gary Soto (1952–) teaches English and Chicano Studies at the University of California at Berkeley. Primarily a poet, Soto has also published essays. The selection is from *Living up the Street* (1985), his award-winning memoirs about growing up in a working-class family in Fresno.

FOCUS

Lesson Overview

Objective: To understand how writing a story about a personal experience can lead to self-discovery
Skills: reading comprehension
Critical Thinking: analyzing
Speaking and Listening: discussing; oral reporting

Bellringer

When students enter the classroom, have this assignment on the board: *Have you ever had a piece of clothing that made you feel a certain way when you wore it? Tell about it in a paragraph.*

Motivating Activity

Tell students that in "The Jacket" Gary Soto describes part of his childhood during which he felt that nothing good would ever happen. Ask students if they have ever felt this way. Encourage them to write about this experience in their journals. Point out that even unhappy times offer an opportunity for self knowledge.

UNIT 4

Narrative Writing
Literature Model

Gary Soto

THE JACKET

In this narrative, Gary Soto writes about a time when he felt the shame and anger of an outsider. He blames his experiences on an ugly jacket he had to wear. As you read the story, note how Soto uses descriptive details to help the reader understand the importance of this real-life experience. Then try the activities in Linking Writing and Literature on page 169.

My clothes have failed me. I remember the green coat that I wore in fifth and sixth grades when you either danced like a champ or pressed yourself against a greasy wall, bitter as a penny toward the happy couples.

When I needed a new jacket and my mother asked what kind I wanted, I described something like bikers wear: black leather and silver studs with enough belts to hold down a small town. We were in the kitchen, steam on the windows

Teacher's Classroom Resources

The following resources can be used for planning, instruction, or practice.

Teaching Tools
Lesson Plans

Transparencies
Fine Art Transparencies, 16–20

Blackline Masters
Speaking and Listening Activities, p. 23
Thinking and Study Skills, p. 9

Assessment

Teacher's Guide to Writing Assessment

from her cooking. She listened so long while stirring dinner that I thought she understood for sure the kind I wanted. The next day when I got home from school, I discovered draped on my bedpost a jacket the color of day-old guacamole. I threw my books on the bed and approached the jacket slowly, as if it were a stranger whose hand I had to shake. I touched the vinyl sleeve, the collar, and peeked at the mustard-colored lining.

Augustín Lazo, *Head*, 1940

From the kitchen mother yelled that my jacket was in the closet. I closed the door to her voice and pulled at the rack of clothes in the closet, hoping the jacket on the bedpost wasn't for me but my mean brother. No luck. I gave up. From my bed, I stared at the jacket. I wanted to cry because it was so ugly and so big that I knew I'd have to wear it a long time. I was a small kid, thin as a young tree, and it would be years before I'd have a new one. I stared at the jacket, like an enemy, thinking bad things before I took off my old jacket whose sleeves climbed halfway to my elbow.

I put the big jacket on. I zipped it up and down several times, and rolled the cuffs up so they didn't cover my hands. I put my hands in the pockets and flapped the jacket like a bird's wings. I stood in front of the mirror, full face, then profile, and then looked over my shoulder as if someone had called me. I sat on the bed, stood against the bed, and combed my hair to see what I would look like doing something natural. I looked ugly. I threw it on my brother's bed and looked at it for a long time before I slipped it on and went out to the backyard, smiling a "thank you" to my mom as I passed her in the kitchen. With my hands in my pockets I kicked a ball against the fence, and then climbed it to sit looking into the alley. I hurled orange peels at the mouth of an open garbage can and when the peels were gone I watched the white puffs of my breath thin to nothing.

TEACH

L2 Guided Reading

- What is it about the jacket that bothers the narrator so much?
- What does wearing the jacket reveal about the writer of the story?
- What does the expression, "bitter as a penny" in the first paragraph mean? Do you think "bitter as a penny" is a good way to describe how a lonely sixth-grade student might feel?

About the Art

Augustín Lazo, *Head*, 1940
Cabeza—the title of the piece in Spanish—was painted with oil on celotex by Augustín Lazo (1896–1971) in 1940. It measures 19 by 15 ½ inches, and hangs in the collection of La Secretaría de Hacienda y Crédito Público, Mexico.

UNIT 4
Literature Model

TEACH

L2 Guided Reading

- How does a person's choice of clothes express who that person is? Think about personal taste, ethnic background, family income, and the desire to be part of a group.
- What happens to the narrator on the first day he wears the jacket to school?
- The narrator feels that his classmates and teachers are looking at him and talking about him. Do you think this is true? Why or why not?

Carmen Lomas Garza, *Cakewalk*, 1987

I jumped down, hands in my pockets, and in the backyard on my knees I teased my dog, Brownie, by swooping my arms while making bird calls. He jumped at me and missed. He jumped again and again, until a tooth sunk deep, ripping an L-shaped tear on my left sleeve. I pushed Brownie away to study the tear as I would a cut on my arm. There was no blood, only a few loose pieces of fuzz. [That] dog, I thought, and pushed him away hard when he tried to bite again. I got up from my knees and went to my bedroom to sit with my jacket on my lap, with the lights out.

That was the first afternoon with my new jacket. The next day I wore it to sixth grade and got a D on a math quiz. During the morning recess Frankie T., the playground terrorist, pushed me to the ground and told me to stay there until recess was over. My best friend, Steve Negrete, ate an apple while looking at me, and the girls turned away to whisper on the monkey bars. The teachers were no help: they looked my way and talked about how foolish I looked in my new jacket. I saw their heads bob with laughter, their hands half-covering their mouths.

About the Art

Carmen Lomas Garza, *Cakewalk*, 1987
Garza says, "I wanted to depict in fine art form all the things of our culture that are important or beautiful or meaningful." *Cakewalk*, a 36-by-48-inch acrylic-on-canvas painting represents a small town festival.

Genre and Style

Engaging the Reader

Living up the Street consists of sketches about meaningful incidents in the writer's life. Soto's prose is generally plain, yet his arresting images and comparisons give his essays a poetic flavor. His work draws the reader into the mind and heart of his younger self.

Even though it was cold, I took off the jacket during lunch and played kickball in a thin shirt, my arms feeling like braille from goose bumps. But when I returned to class I slipped the jacket on and shivered until I was warm. I sat on my hands, heating them up, while my teeth chattered like a cup of crooked dice. Finally warm, I slid out of the jacket but a few minutes later put it back on when the fire bell rang. We paraded out into the yard where we, the sixth graders, walked past all the other grades to stand against the back fence. Everybody saw me. Although they didn't say out loud, "Man, that's ugly," I heard a buzz-buzz of gossip and even laughter that I knew was meant for me.

And so I went, in my guacamole jacket. So embarrassed, so hurt, I couldn't even do my homework. I received Cs on quizzes, and forgot the state capitals and the rivers of South America, our friendly neighbor. Even the girls who had been friendly blew away like loose flowers to follow the boys in neat jackets.

I wore that thing for three years until the sleeves grew short and my forearms stuck out like the necks of turtles. All during that time no love came to me—no little dark girl in a Sunday dress she wore on Monday. At lunchtime I stayed with the ugly boys who leaned against the chainlink fence and looked around with propellers of grass spinning in our mouths. We saw girls walk by alone, saw couples, hand in hand, their heads like bookends pressing air together. We saw them and spun our propellers so fast our faces were blurs.

I blame that jacket for those bad years. I blame my mother for her bad taste and her cheap ways. It was a sad time for the heart. With a friend I spent my sixth-grade year in a tree in the alley waiting for something good to happen to me in that jacket, which had become the ugly brother who tagged along wherever I went. And it was about that time that I began to grow. My chest puffed up with muscle and, strangely, a few more ribs. Even my hands, those fleshly hammers, showed bravely through the cuffs, the fingers already hardening for the coming fights. But that L-shaped rip on the left sleeve got bigger; bits of stuffing coughed out from its wound after a hard day of play. I finally taped it closed, but in rain or

TEACH

L2 Guided Reading

- How does the author organize his narrative? How can you tell?
- Why does the narrator call his jacket "the ugly brother who tagged along wherever I went"?
- Soto's comparison of the jacket to an ugly brother is a metaphor. What other metaphors and similes does Soto use?

Writers and Writing

Writing Without Dialogue

Gary Soto chose to tell his story without using dialogue. Point out that including conversation would make the other characters more "visible" but might distract the reader. By not including conversation, Soto ensures that the reader stays inside the thoughts of the storyteller and gets to know the main character well. The absence of dialogue also emphasizes how isolated the narrator is.

UNIT 4

Literature Model

TEACH

L2 Guided Reading

- Why do you think the narrator picks the jacket up again after he throws it over the fence?
- Reread the ending of the story. Is it a strong ending, or does it leave you wondering what else happened?

Independent Practice

Fine Art Transparencies, 16–20

Skills Practice

Speaking and Listening Activities, p. 23

Thinking and Study Skills, p. 9

cold weather the tape peeled off like a scab and more stuffing fell out until that sleeve shriveled into a palsied arm. That winter the elbows began to crack and whole chunks of green began to fall off. I showed the cracks to my mother, who always seemed to be at the stove with steamed-up glasses, and she said that there were children in Mexico who would love that jacket. I told her that this was America and yelled that Debbie, my sister, didn't have a jacket like mine. I ran outside, ready to cry, and climbed the tree by the alley to think bad thoughts and watch my breath puff white and disappear.

But whole pieces still casually flew off my jacket when I played hard, read quietly, or took vicious spelling tests at school. When it became so spotted that my brother began to call me "camouflage," I flung it over the fence into the alley. Later, however, I swiped the jacket off the ground and went inside to drape it across my lap and mope.

I was called to dinner: steam silvered my mother's glasses as she said grace; my brother and sister with their heads bowed made ugly faces at their glasses of powdered milk. I gagged too, but eagerly ate big rips of buttered tortilla that held scooped up beans. Finished, I went outside with my jacket across my arm. It was a cold sky. The faces of clouds were piled up, hurting. I climbed the fence, jumping down with a grunt. I started up the alley and soon slipped into my jacket, that green ugly brother who breathed over my shoulder that day and ever since.

Cultural Diversity

Using Details

Invite students to list details in the story that, taken together, tell the reader about Gary Soto's Mexican background. (the recurring reference to guacamole, a Mexican food; a reference to wishing a "dark girl" would pay attention to him; his mother's reference to poor children in Mexico; the fact that the family eats tortillas and beans at dinner)

Linking Writing and Literature

Readers Respond to the Model

How does Gary Soto make his story appealing to young people?

Explore Gary Soto's narrative by answering these questions. Then read what other students liked about Soto's story.

1. Do you think that the jacket caused the narrator's problems? How was the jacket a symbol of his feelings? Explain your answer.
2. How do Soto's descriptions help the reader know what the narrator is thinking and feeling? Choose one paragraph as a good example.
3. Why might Soto's story hold interest for a young person today? Can you find a connection with your own life?
4. Why do you think Gary Soto chose not to use dialogue in his story?

My favorite character was the boy who had to wear the jacket he didn't like. He actually wore the jacket and didn't refuse. I liked him because I knew how he felt.

I would recommend this story to a friend because it was funny and you're not sure what's going to happen. I also like it because it's about someone my age who has the same problems that other boys do. They think that clothes are important and everyone will judge them by their clothes.

Matt Cassel

The selection is about a boy who ruins a year in school over a jacket that he can't stand the sight of. It seems to ruin his reputation and he blames his lack of happiness on the jacket.

I would recommend this selection to avid readers who like to read stories about people.

Chip Mulaney

ASSESS

Evaluation Guidelines for Discussion

As your students discuss the selection, either in small groups or as a class, encourage them to begin with a personal response. The student responses on this page might be used as a starting point.

Look for evidence that students
- have read the selection
- can state some of the writer's ideas in their own words
- understand the writer's point of view
- have connected the content to their own knowledge and experiences
- understand the ideas and implications of the selection

Some possible responses to the discussion questions on this page:
1. No, the narrator caused his own problems and blamed them on the jacket. The jacket was a symbol of how he didn't fit in.
2. In the first full paragraph on p. 167, Soto's descriptions of how badly he does in school and how the girls are interested in other boys show the reader how powerless he feels.
3. All young people feel left out sometimes. They can relate to the narrator's feelings.
4. Without dialogue, you see how lonely the narrator is. It seems as if he never has the courage to speak to anyone and is trapped in his own thoughts.

CLOSE

Ask students to recall a time when they felt embarrassed and imagined that everyone was laughing or looking at them. Have students write briefly in their journals about the incident and how they felt.

REVIEW

Reflecting on the Unit

You may have students respond to Reflecting on the Unit in writing or through discussion.

Writing Across the Curriculum

Have students consider how clothing needs are different in various parts of the world. Encourage students to think about the other person's point of view.

Adding to Your Portfolio

To help students choose pieces for their portfolios, suggest that they review journal entries and biography responses as well as the real-life stories they have written. Since this unit emphasizes personal narratives, they may want one of the portfolio pieces they select to be about the experience or event that was most meaningful to them.

Portfolio Evaluation

If you grade the individual portfolio selections, you may want to award two marks—one each for content and form. Explain your assessment criteria before students make their selections. Commend

- experimentation with creative prewriting techniques
- clear, concise writing in which the main idea, audience, and purpose are evident
- successful revisions
- work that shows a flair for language

Unit 4 Review

Reflecting on the Unit

Summarize what you learned in this unit by answering the following questions.

- What are the characteristics of a well-written real-life story?
- How can you keep a story clearly on track?
- What are the important things to remember when you write dialogue?
- How can you help your readers understand what was special about an event?
- In what ways might you learn from and respond to a biography?

Adding to Your Portfolio

Choose a selection for your portfolio. Look over the narrative writing you did during this unit. Select a completed piece of writing to put into your portfolio. The piece you choose should show some or all of the following:

- a beginning that makes the reader want to continue reading
- believable characters in a specific place, involved in clearly explained action
- realistic dialogue that gives details about the characters
- an order that helps the reader follow the action
- a conclusion that winds up the story

Reflect on your choice. Attach a note to the piece you chose, explaining briefly why you chose it and what you learned from writing it.

Set goals. How can you improve your writing? What skill will you focus on the next time you write?

Writing Across the Curriculum

Make a social studies connection. Think about how someone from another culture or part of the world might react to your narrative about a piece of clothing. How might you meet this person? What questions might he or she ask? How might you need to change or add to your narrative?

Teacher's Classroom Resources

The following resources can be used for assessment or evaluation.

Unit Assessment

Tests with Answer Key
Unit 4 Choice A Test, p. 13
Unit 4 Choice B Test, p. 14
Unit 4 Composition Objective Test, pp. 15–16

Test Generator
Unit 4 Choice A Test
Unit 4 Choice B Test
Unit 4 Composition Objective Test

You may wish to administer one of these tests as a mastery test.

UNIT

5 Expository Writing

Composition | Lessons

UNIT GOALS

The goal of Unit 5 is to help students, through example and instruction, to develop an understanding of the many uses of expository writing. The lessons focus on writing to inform, explaining through giving directions, writing research reports, and writing book reports. The Case Study details the process of creating a newspaper graphic that explains Michael Jordan's jumping ability.

Unit Assessment

Tests with Answer Key

Unit 5 Choice A Test, p. 17
Unit 5 Choice B Test, p. 18
Unit 5 Composition Objective Test, pp. 19–20

Test Generator

Unit 5 Choice A Test
Unit 5 Choice B Test
Unit 5 Composition Objective Test

You may wish to administer either the Unit 5 Choice A Test or the Unit 5 Choice B Test as a pretest.

Key to Ability Levels

Enabling Strategies have been coded for varying learning styles and abilities.

L1 Level 1 activities are within the ability range of Learning Disabled students.

L2 Level 2 activities are basic-to-average activities and are within the ability range of average students.

L3 Level 3 activities are challenging activities and are within the ability range of above-average students.

LEP LEP activities are within the ability range of Limited English Proficiency students.

Setting the Purpose

In the Unit 5 Case Study students examine the use of expository writing in an illustrated newspaper article. Students will explore and practice expository writing in the lessons that follow.

FOCUS

Lesson Overview

Objective: To use graphics in the creation of a piece of informative writing
Skills: researching; designing pages; writing explanations
Critical Thinking: thinking creatively; visualizing; using graphics; synthesizing
Speaking and Listening: discussing

Bellringer

When students enter the classroom, have this assignment on the board: *List four subjects for magazine or newspaper articles that you think should be illustrated for best effect.*

Grammar Link to the Bellringer

Ask students what is wrong with the following sentence: *An illustrated article is more better than one that is all writing.* Remind them that *better* is the only comparative needed.

Motivating Activity

Encourage students to skim through a current newspaper or magazine until a story catches their eye. Then ask them to discuss what it was about the story that grabbed their attention. (A headline, an illustration, a graphic, or a photograph may have piqued their interest.) Volunteers may wish to explain to the class why they found a particular headline or visual compelling.

UNIT 5 PREVIEW

Case Study

Expository Writing
in the Real World

Tribune Explores Hang Time

FOCUS: Good expository writing often combines words and drawings to explain something better than either could alone.

Steve Cvengros was leafing through *USA Today* when a headline caught his eye. "It only seems [Michael] Jordan floats longer. There's no such thing as defying gravity," the story said. As *Chicago Tribune* graphics editor, Cvengros knew he'd found a good idea. His team—writer Julie Sheer and artist Dennis Odom—agreed. They would do the story as a graphic—drawings and words combined—using a full sports page to explain Michael Jordan's flight.

◄ Chicago Tribune *team Cvengros, Sheer, and Odom*

Teacher's Classroom Resources

The following resources can be used for planning, instruction, practice, reinforcement, assessment, or evaluation.

Teaching Tools
Lesson Plans

Transparencies
Writing Process Transparencies, 17–19B

> ***"You have to constantly focus on what you're trying to get across, what you're trying to explain."***
>
> —Julie Sheer

Prewriting

BECOMING EXPERTS

Late in 1989 Sheer and Odom got to work. Sheer went after answers to all kinds of questions: Why is Chicago Bulls star Michael Jordan able to jump so high? Can he really hang in the air? How does gravity affect his flight?

She found some answers in reference books such as *Sport Science* and in books on Jordan. She got more information by interviewing coaches and scientists on the phone.

Sheer and Odom also interviewed Jordan before a Bulls game. "We wanted to get his point of view," Sheer said. "How does he do it?"

"At first Jordan kind of chuckled at our questions and the idea that we were going to do a graphic," Odom recalled. "How were we going to do it? He doesn't know how long he stays in the air. He thinks it appears he stays in the air longer because he can do acrobatics when he's up there."

Little by little, though, Odom and Sheer started to get the picture. They learned that Jordan's takeoffs are explosive. Part of the reason for this is that Jordan has a great number of fast-twitch fibers in his leg muscles. These fibers act as springs to rocket him off the ground. In flight, Jordan's arm and leg movements make it look as if he's floating.

▲ *Ideas can come from different sources. A headline in* USA Today *was the inspiration behind Cvengros's idea.*

TEACH

Building Background

Warm-up:
Have students make a brief list of occasions when they think illustrations might be used to complement expository writing.

Exposition in Speaking:
Remind students that exposition with illustration may be used in everyday conversation, as when someone sketches a map to go with spoken directions. On more formal occasions, a teacher or student might use transparencies to accompany a lesson or an oral report.

Invite students to describe other times when they have used graphics to support an explanation.

Exposition in Writing:
Discuss any expository writing with graphics that students have read. Use prompts such as the following:

- Have you ever read a description of a fish or other creature that included a labeled diagram?
- Have you ever read an illustrated explanation of a process such as how blood circulates or how a video game is played?

Preview the Case Study

Have students preview the title and focus of the case study. Point out that although the illustrations greatly enhance the newspaper article, the written explanation is essential to the meaning. Have students read the case study.

Blackline Masters
Cooperative Learning Activities, pp. 25–30
Thinking and Study Skills, pp. 8, 22, 39–40
Case Studies: Writing in the Real World, pp. 17–20

Assessment
Teacher's Guide to Writing Assessment

TEACH

Discussion Prompts

- At what tasks did the writer-illustrator team of Sheer and Odom work in the early stages of the project? (research, outlining)
- How much collaboration is necessary at the beginning of a shared project? Should the team members work separately at first?

Creating a Graphic

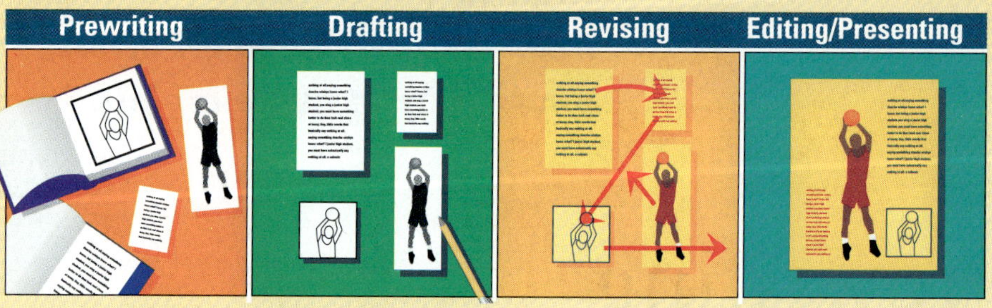

Becoming Experts | Illustrating and Writing | Designing the Page | Finishing the Page

Drafting

ILLUSTRATING AND WRITING

Gathering as much information as possible during the research stage will help when you're drafting.

Before starting to draw and write, the team agreed on a headline: "How Does Michael Fly?" They also agreed that they wanted a big painting of Jordan on the page.

Odom's first challenge was to do the painting. To find just the right pose, he studied thousands of photographs of Jordan in action. He looked for a shot of Jordan headed for a dunk.

Meanwhile, Sheer and Cvengros were zeroing in on the key ideas. As they chose topics, Sheer reviewed them with Odom. Then Odom went to work on the smaller illustrations while Sheer began to write. "I sat down at a computer and typed up some headlines," she said. These were subheads, which broke down the topic of "flight" into "the muscle behind the magic" and "stages of a vertical jump."

Cultural Diversity

Adapting Games

Tell students that although basketball was first popularized in the United States, by the latter half of the twentieth century it had become an international sport and an Olympic spectacle. When adopted by other countries, games such as basketball may be altered to suit the new playing community. Ask students if they know how any sports have been adapted to suit younger and smaller players. Do they know of sports that began elsewhere and are now popular in the United States? (Soccer is one example.) How have these sports changed?

"Then," Sheer said, "I started looking through the copies from scientists, plus books and magazine articles. I jotted notes under each headline about the subject."

The writing job was tough, Sheer said. "I had to pick out what was most important and boil it down so I understood it. Then I had to explain it so a reader could understand."

When Sheer finished her copy, she gave it to Cvengros. "I try not to read the raw copy until these guys think it's ready," Cvengros said. "That allows me to be a first reader." What did Cvengros look for? He looked for words used too often, facts without sources, writing that had become so technical that it lost its fun.

When putting together words and pictures, as in a graphic, a rough draft helps you to visualize the final page.

Revising

DESIGNING THE PAGE

After several weeks of work, the team had all the pieces. Now it was time to design the page.

Odom drew the outline of the finished page on a clean sheet of paper. Then he photocopied the painting of Jordan and pasted it in the center. He put the headline above Jordan. A quote from Jordan went below. Now the team was ready to fit the other pieces. It was like putting together a jigsaw puzzle.

How did the team organize the information to explain Jordan's skill? After several tries they decided on two long columns. The left column would explain the science of "hang time." The column on the right would explain the special features of Jordan's body.

UNIT 5
Case Study

TEACH

Discussion Prompts

- What should you be looking for as you prepare to revise a first draft of expository writing? What did the editor, Cvengros, look for as he read Sheer's first draft?
- What special problems might come up as you prepare to revise an illustrated explanation? How did the writer-illustrator team organize the information about Michael Jordan?

Civic Literacy

Using Newspaper Graphics

Newspapers often combine graphics with text to educate local readers about a particular danger and what might be done to avoid it. For example, before a solar eclipse, many newspapers present a diagram showing how to make a safe viewing screen for the event. As flu season opens, newspapers often print charts showing symptoms, treatments, and danger signs. Ask students to find and explain additional examples from their own local papers.

TEACH

Guided Practice

L2 Discussion

Stimulate a discussion of the case study. You may want to invite students to talk about

- how they would go about becoming an expert on the subject of their illustrated explanation
- whether they would plan the pictures or the text first
- how they would design their pages without wasted effort

Independent Practice

Writing Process Transparencies, 17–19B

Cooperative Learning Activities, pp. 25–30

Case Studies: Writing in the Real World, pp. 17–20

Skills Practice

Thinking and Study Skills, pp. 8, 22, 39–40

As the page took shape, Sheer trimmed her writing to fit the space. Then she ran copies to put on the page. Odom photocopied his drawings at many different sizes. He tried one size, then another, with Sheer's words. Slowly the team ruled out all designs but one.

When they settled on a design, Odom made copies for review. The team read the headlines and subheads. Were they clear? Fun? They studied the colors. They also read the copy and looked at the art. They saw that some ideas needed more space. Others had to be cut.

The final graphic contained many explanations of Jordan's "hang time" and physical features. The enlarged segment below explains Jordan's center of gravity.

Editing/Presenting

FINISHING THE PAGE

After everyone suggested changes, the team fine-tuned the page. Then Odom pasted it up again.

Team members read the page one last time. They made sure that the facts were correct. They read for misspelled words and mistakes in grammar. Copy editors proofread for errors. The sports editor reviewed the final page, too. "He's a real basketball nut, so he read every word," Sheer said. The page went to press February 27, 1990. The basketball season was going strong, and Jordan was on everyone's mind.

According to Cvengros, the big, colorful graphic was a huge success. Even Jordan liked the page. "We had a special copy made for Michael," Cvengros said.

Have body, will fly

At 6-6, Jordan's center of gravity is higher than that of the average person and his aerial acrobatics cause it to rise even higher during a jump. The terrific force he exerts on the floor gives him a quick takeoff and longer time in the air. Biomechanical researchers have concluded that a good jumper produces an average force of about two to three times his weight pushing off the ground.

Author's Craft

Editing to Fit the Space

Students may have difficulty trimming their own writing to fit a space, a necessary skill when making up pages with illustrations. Suggest that they practice this skill by taking a piece already in print and trying to shorten it by one or more lines without changing its meaning. To accomplish this, a student must read carefully to get a sense of what information is most important. Later, this sense can help students make their own writing concise and clear.

Responding to the Case Study

1. Discussion

Discuss these questions about the *Chicago Tribune*'s graphic story.

- How did writer Julie Sheer and artist Dennis Odom gather information for their story?
- Why did Sheer find writing the story difficult?
- How did the team work together to design and review the page?
- What did the team members check before sending the page to press?

2. Expository Writing

Write a paragraph explaining how to create a graphic story. Choose a person or topic of interest to you. Explain how the four students in the photograph might work together as a team to create a graphic story on your topic. List the steps they could follow to research, write, and produce the final page. Sketch or describe the illustrations they might use.

Grammar Link

Avoid double comparisons when you write.

Never use *more* or *most* with adjectives or adverbs ending in *-er* or *-est.* Note the comparative form of the adverb *long* in the case study.
[Jordan] stays in the air ***longer.*** . . .

Revise the sentences below, correcting the double comparisons.

1. Michael Jordan jumped more better than any other player.
2. On the court, Jordan was an even more greater performer than Julius Erving.
3. His center of gravity is more higher than that of most people.
4. Jordan had the most longest "hang time" of the Chicago Bulls.
5. Jordan is one of the most greatest players ever.

See Lesson 12.3, page 348, and Lesson 13.3, page 364.

ASSESS

Responding to the Case Study

1. Discussion

- from reference and other books; from interviews with coaches, scientists, and Jordan himself
- because she had to pick out what was important, understand it, and then explain it
- by fitting pieces together, trimming text, and resizing art
- facts, spelling, grammar

2. Expository Writing

Answers will vary, but some suggestions follow.

- Students should choose a manageable topic.
- The students in the photograph might function as researcher, writer, illustrator, and editor.
- Steps should relate to the steps of the writing process.
- Sketches should be part of the explanation, not decorations.

Grammar Link

(See Using the Grammar Link below.)

Reteaching

Remind students that when they create a graphic, the words and artwork should reinforce each other.

Enrichment

Visually oriented students might first conceive of an expository piece as a series of pictures. Then they can write a caption for each image as a first step toward completing a draft.

CLOSE

Have students discuss examples of expository writing with graphics they find in their textbooks.

Using the Grammar Link

Grammar Link Answers

1. Michael Jordan jumped better than any other player.
2. On the court, Jordan was an even greater performer than Julius Erving.
3. His center of gravity is higher than that of most people.
4. Jordan had the longest "hang time" of the Chicago Bulls.
5. Jordan is one of the greatest players ever.

Using *Most* for *Almost* Tell students that using *most* for *almost* is incorrect: *The bus is almost* (not *most*) *always on time.*

Setting the Purpose

Lesson 5.1 teaches students to recognize different kinds of expository writing and to write an explanation of a game.

FOCUS

Lesson Overview

Objective: To write a clear and concise explanation
Skills: recognizing ways to inform and explain; writing an explanation
Critical Thinking: identifying; defining and clarifying
Speaking and Listening: discussing; explaining a process

Bellringer

When students enter the classroom, have this assignment on the board: *Write three sentences explaining how to light a candle. Label your sentences* Step 1, Step 2, *and* Step 3.

Grammar Link to the Bellringer

Ask students to underline any pronouns in their Bellringer sentences. Is the referent of each pronoun clear?

Motivating Activity

To help students realize that they are already familiar with expository writing, encourage them to recall and discuss information they have learned through reading.

TEACH

Guided Practice

L2 Using the Model

Point out that the writer uses time references to help explain the development of the oil lamp. These references place the invention in a time frame readers can understand.

LESSON 5.1

Expository Writing

Writing to Help Others Understand

Expository writing is writing that shares knowledge. It informs or explains, sometimes by defining, classifying, or giving directions.

Literature Model

Some 20,000 years ago, people realized that they could get light by burning oil, and the first lamps appeared. These lamps were hollowed-out rocks full of animal fat. Lamps with wicks of vegetable fibers were first made in about 1000 B.C. They had a simple channel to hold the wick; later, the wick was held in a spout.

Lionel Bender, *Invention*

You may never have used an oil lamp. Having read this explanation, though, you know how and when lamps were invented. Bender has shared some knowledge on a subject you might not have known about.

Teacher's Classroom Resources

The following resources can be used for planning, instruction, practice, reinforcement, assessment, reteaching, enrichment, or evaluation.

Teaching Tools
Lesson Plans

Transparencies
Fine Art Transparencies, 21–25
Writing Process Transparencies, 17–19B

Blackline Masters
Thinking and Study Skills, pp. 6–9, 12–13, 17–18, 20
Writing Across the Curriculum, pp. 11–13, 15, 20–21
Cooperative Learning Activities, pp. 26–30
Speaking and Listening Activities, pp. 12–13, 21, 24

Learn from Expository Writing

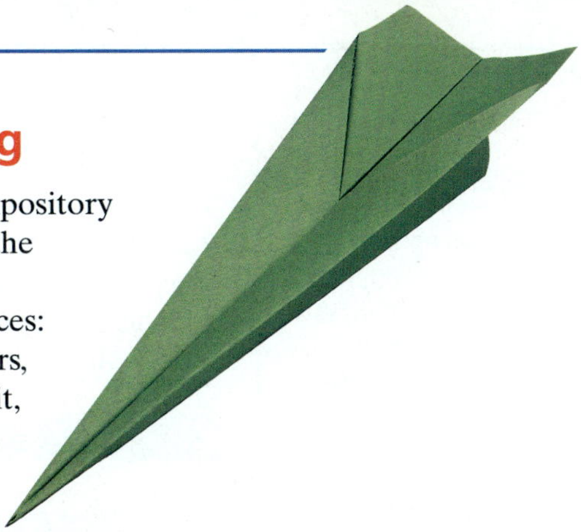

Bender's paragraph is a good example of expository writing. It informs. It helps people learn about the world around them.

You can find expository writing in many places: textbooks, cookbooks, encyclopedias, newspapers, instruction manuals. No matter where you find it, expository writing is always meant to help people learn.

If you've ever jotted down directions for someone, you have already done some expository writing. You've helped someone learn how to get somewhere. Look at the following directions. How does the writer share knowledge with the reader?

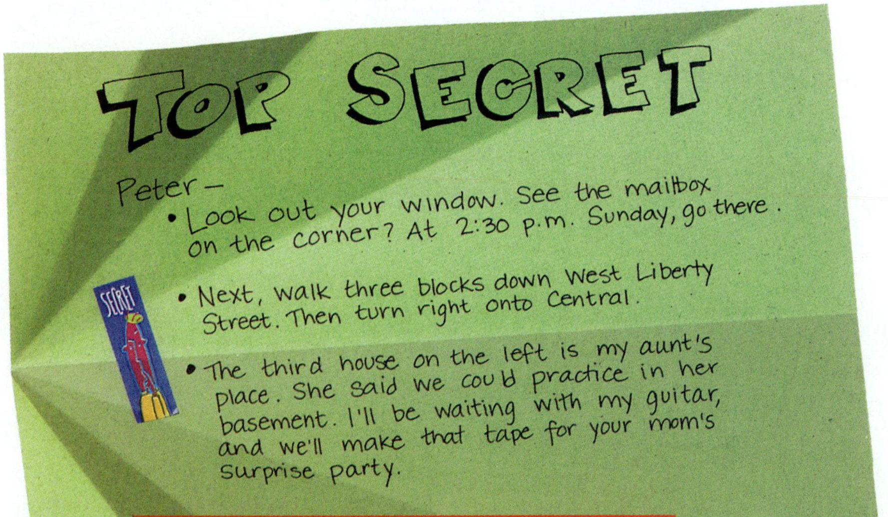

Journal Writing

List some topics that you could explain to others. Choose one idea and write down three pieces of information about it.

TEACH

Guided Practice

L2 Using the Model

In the example on the previous page, the writer gives step-by-step directions with clear and specific details. Point out that directions can become unclear when steps are missing, out of order, or incomplete. Call attention to the arrangement of these directions in short, easy-to-follow steps and the writer's use of visual details such as the mailbox, and the street name, which help orient the reader.

L1 Making Inferences

Ask students to think about how new inventions often arise from people's specific needs. What specific need led to the invention of the oil lamp? (the need to have light after sunset) Point out that one invention is often made obsolete by another. What invention made the oil lamp obsolete in many parts of the world? (the electric lightbulb)

Two-Minute Skill Drill

Have students write a clear, concise sentence to explain each of the following to someone who has never seen them.

a grape a ladybug

Journal Writing Tip

Classifying Ask students to examine their lists and try to group their topics into general categories—for instance, fun activities, chores, or places to go. This can help students get a sense of the types of topics they know most about and can explain best.

Sentence Combining Practice, pp. 30–32
Research Paper and Report Writing, pp. 32–38
Composition Practice, p. 37
Composition Reteaching, p. 37
Composition Enrichment, p. 37

Unit Assessment

Teacher's Guide to Writing Assessment

Tests with Answer Key
Unit 5 Choice A Test, p. 17
Unit 5 Choice B Test, p. 18

Test Generator
Unit 5 Choice A Test
Unit 5 Choice B Test

You may wish to administer either the Unit 5 Choice A Test or the Unit 5 Choice B Test as a pretest.

TEACH

Guided Practice

L2 Promoting Discussion

Discuss how a broad topic can be explored in a variety of ways. For the topic of astronomy, for instance, a student might define a star, explain the process by which the solar system formed, give instructions for focusing a telescope, compare two planets, or classify the different kinds of eclipses. Encourage students to identify how each topic is expository.

L3 Rewriting for Clarity

Ask students if they have ever been frustrated by poorly written instructions. Suggest that they try rewriting such instructions to make them easier to follow. Remind students that sometimes a difficult step can be made easier by dividing it into smaller steps.

Independent Practice

For further stimuli for expository writing, see *Fine Art Transparencies* 21–25.

Writing Process Transparencies, 17–19B

Writing Across the Curriculum, pp. 11–13, 15, 20–21

Cooperative Learning Activities, pp. 26–30

Skills Practice

Thinking and Study Skills, pp. 6–9, 12–13, 17–18, 20

Speaking and Listening Activities, pp. 12–13, 21, 24

Sentence Combining Practice, pp. 30–32

Research Paper and Report Writing, pp. 32–38

Composition Practice, p. 37

Vocabulary

Editing Tip

When editing, check your spelling. Many foreign words such as *mbria* have unusual spellings. For more information on words borrowed from other languages, see Lesson 22.1, page 506.

Inform and Explain in Different Ways

Directions, such as those on page 179, are one kind of expository writing. Other kinds of expository writing explain a process, provide a definition, compare and contrast two things, or divide things into groups. Read the two kinds of expository writing shown below.

Different Ways to Inform and Explain

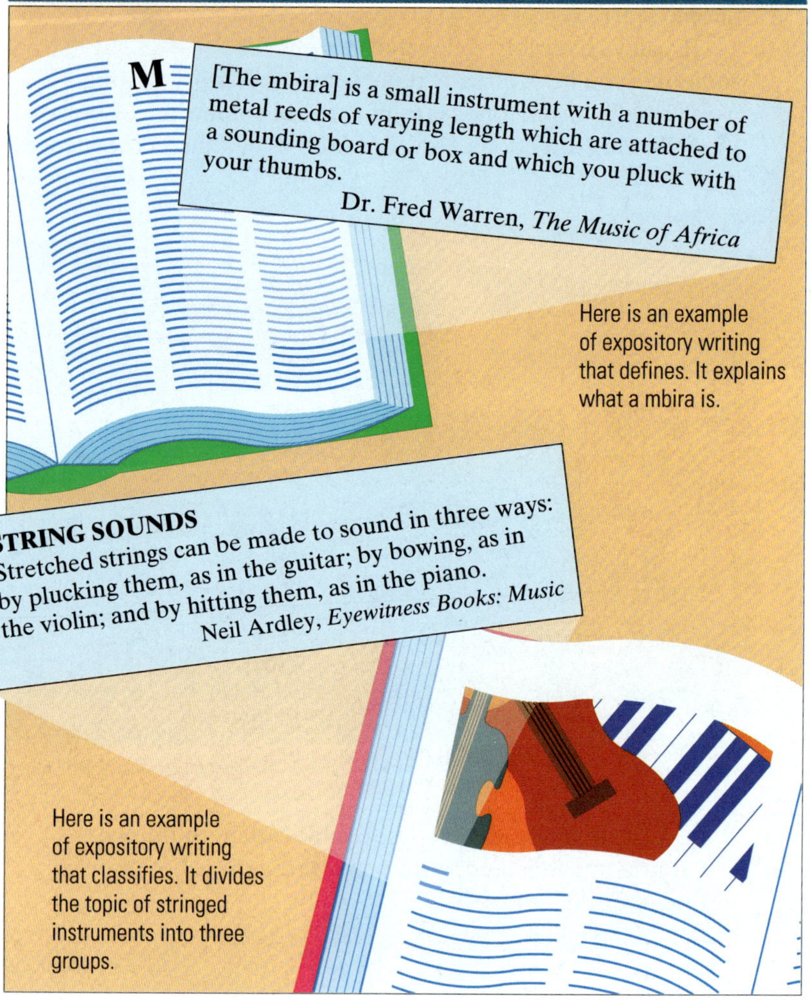

Enabling Strategies

LEP Understanding Directions

Invite students to discuss strategies for comprehending directions written in English. What strategies have been helpful to them in the past? Encourage students to discuss using photographs or other graphics, using a dictionary or context clues to define unfamiliar words, and breaking directions into smaller steps. You might wish to guide students through a complete set of directions using these strategies.

5.1 Writing Activities

Write an Explanation of a Game

Think about how to play snap-the-whip, the game pictured in the painting. List the rules for playing. Then write an explanation of the game for a younger student who has never played it.

- Define the game and its goal.
- Explain the steps in the game, in order from first to last.

PURPOSE To teach a new game
AUDIENCE A younger student
LENGTH 1–2 paragraphs

Cross-Curricular: History

In a history book, find a paragraph that explains something, such as how the Constitution was adopted. Read the paragraph at least twice. Then, in your own words, write what the paragraph is about.

Grammar Link

Make a pronoun clearly refer to its antecedent.

*. . . **people** realized that **they** could get light . . .*

Rewrite each sentence to make the meaning clear.

1. People have always invented things, and they have helped them learn more about the world.
2. Telescopes help us learn about the stars; they bring them into focus.
3. The inventor has a brother, and he helps him with his experiments.
4. They have many books about inventions in the school library.

See Lesson 11.3, page 330.

Winslow Homer, *Snap the Whip*, 1872

ASSESS

Writing Activities Evaluation Guidelines

Write an Explanation of a Game

Use these criteria when evaluating your students' writing.

- Did the student include a definition of the game and its goal?
- Did the student provide an explanation of the steps in order from first to last?

See also the *Teacher's Guide to Writing Assessment.*

Cross-curricular: History

Use the following questions to assess each student's paragraph:

- Did the student explain the paragraph's main idea?
- Did the student write the explanation in his or her own words?

Grammar Link

(*See Using the Grammar Link below.*)

Reteaching

Composition Reteaching, p. 37

Enrichment

Composition Enrichment, p. 37

Use *Fine Art Transparencies* 21–25 for enrichment activities also.

CLOSE

Ask students to take their journal entry from page 179 and expand it into a paragraph. Have them identify their paragraph as a definition, directions, classification, comparison, explanation of a process, or whatever type of expository writing it is.

Using the Grammar Link

Grammar Link Answers

Answers may vary. Suggestions follow:

1. . . . and these things have helped them . . .
2. . . . because they bring the stars into focus.
3. . . . and his brother helps him with his experiments.
4. There are many books . . .

About the Art

Winslow Homer, *Snap the Whip*, 1872

Winslow Homer (1836–1910) was first known for his lithographs of the Civil War. This 22-by-36-inch oil painting, an example of Homer's commitment to capturing everyday moments, is in the Butler Institute of American Art, Youngstown, Ohio.

Setting the Purpose

Lesson 5.2 teaches students to compare and contrast two things and to use a Venn diagram.

FOCUS

Lesson Overview

Objective: To note similarities and differences between two things and to write comparison-contrast pieces
Skills: organizing details; making a Venn diagram
Critical Thinking: analyzing; comparing; contrasting
Speaking and Listening: discussing; questioning; evaluating

Bellringer

When students enter the classroom, have this assignment on the board: *List four ways cats and dogs are alike and four ways they are different.*

Grammar Link to the Bellringer

Ask students to pick the correct verb for this sentence: *Neither my cat nor the dogs next door (has, have) any use for squirrels.* Tell them that *have* is correct and that they will be practicing the rule that explains this.

Motivating Activity

Encourage students to discuss two subjects that have meaning for them—two events (movies, holidays), two objects (video games, articles of clothing), or two people—comparing and contrasting by telling what they like and dislike about each subject.

LESSON 5.2

Expository Writing

Comparing and Contrasting Two Things

Comparison-contrast is one kind of expository writing. When you compare two things, you explain how they are similar. When you contrast them, you explain how they differ.

VS.

Superman and Batman are two of the best-known comic book superheroes. They are alike is some ways but different in other ways. Which crime fighter has which powers? How are the superheroes' personal histories similar and different? To answer these questions, you might write a comparison-contrast piece.

Teacher's Classroom Resources

The following resources can be used for planning, instruction, practice, reinforcement, assessment, reteaching, enrichment, or evaluation.

Teaching Tools
Lesson Plans

Transparencies
Fine Art Transparencies, 21–25
Writing Process Transparencies, 17–19B

Organize the Details

To compare and contrast in writing, you'll need to keep your details organized. The following methods can help you do that.

Examine Your Subjects A good way to begin your comparison-contrast piece is with a careful examination. First think about one subject, and list descriptive details that go with that subject. For example, you might note that Batman travels by car and wears a mask and a cape. Then make a list of the same kinds of details for Superman. How does he get around? What does he wear?

Sort What You See Once you've listed some details, you can sort them for comparison and contrast. At this point, some writers use a Venn diagram like the one below. A Venn diagram is made of two ovals. Each oval contains the details of one of the subjects. Details that the two subjects have in common go where the ovals overlap.

Grammar Drafting Tip

When comparing and contrasting two people, use the comparative form of an adjective. When comparing and contrasting two actions, use the comparative form of an adverb. For more about comparative adjectives and adverbs, see Lessons 12.3 and 12.4, pages 348–350, and Lesson 13.3, page 364.

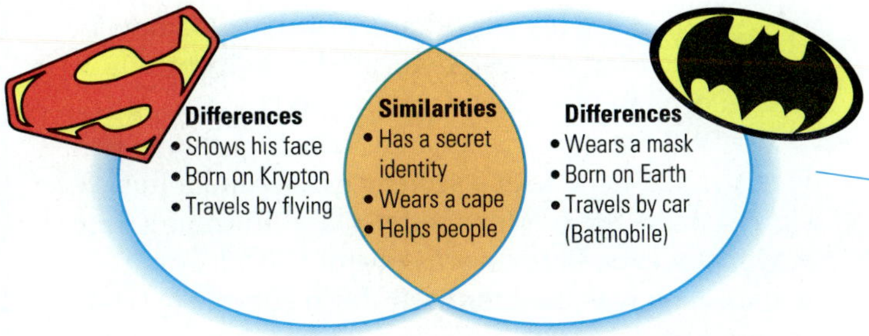

Notice how the details for each superhero come from a look at the same points of concern: costume, method of travel, birthplace, mission, and identity.

Journal Writing

Pick your two favorite activities. List the details of each activity. Then put the details into a Venn diagram. What is similar and different about the two activities?

TEACH

Guided Practice

L2 Making a Venn Diagram
When making a Venn diagram, some students may find it helpful to work with a partner. Suggest that each partner select a favorite activity. Students can then discuss the similarities and differences between the two activities, each noting the details of his or her activity in an oval—one half of a Venn diagram. Finally, partners can combine their individual ovals into a Venn diagram that contains details about both activities.

L1 Using Visual Cues
Point out to students that they can begin to compare and contrast Superman and Batman just by examining the artwork. How are the two superheroes similar? (Both wear costumes with capes; both are muscular.) How are they different? (Batman wears a mask, Superman does not; Batman's symbol is a bat, Superman's symbol is a large red *S*; Batman wears gloves, Superman does not.)

Two-Minute Skill Drill

Have students write one term of comparison and one term of contrast for each of the following:

happy	dark clouds
boots	courage

Journal Writing Tip

Analyzing Information Suggest that students delete all but the five or six most important details from their Venn diagrams. This can help make the diagrams manageable and readable.

Blackline Masters
Thinking and Study Skills, pp. 6, 8–9, 11, 15
Writing Across the Curriculum, pp. 11, 13, 15, 17, 19–21
Cooperative Learning Activities, pp. 26–30
Sentence Combining Practice, pp. 30–32
Speaking and Listening Activities, pp. 12–13, 21, 24
Research Paper and Report Writing, pp. 32–38
Composition Practice, p. 38
Composition Reteaching, p. 38
Composition Enrichment, p. 38

Assessment
Teacher's Guide to Writing Assessment

TEACH

Guided Practice

L2 Using the Model

Point out that the writer uses a separate paragraph for each subject. Words such as *like* and phrases such as *in some ways, however,* act as clues indicating the presence of a similarity or difference. Students may wish to refer to the Venn diagram to find the similarities and differences referred to in the model.

L3 Making Connections

Point out that cultural icons often arise from distinct historical periods. The image of the coonskin-capped pioneer hero dates back to early westward expansion. Likewise, the Star Trek characters arose when outer space became "the final frontier."

Students might discuss other fictional or legendary figures and try to identify by world affairs, cultural movements, or any other historical reference points the specific historical period out of which they came.

Independent Practice

For further stimuli for comparison-contrast writing, see *Fine Art Transparencies* pp. 21–25.

Writing Process Transparencies, 17–19B

Writing Across the Curriculum, pp. 11, 13, 15, 17, 19–21

Cooperative Learning Activities, pp. 26–30

Research Paper and Report Writing, pp. 32–38

Skills Practice

Thinking and Study Skills, pp. 6, 8–9, 11, 15

Sentence Combining Practice, pp. 30–32

Speaking and Listening Activities, pp. 12–13, 21, 24

Composition Practice, p. 38

Revising Tip

When revising a comparison-contrast piece, try making a separate paragraph for each subject you discuss. This will make the piece easier for your readers to follow. For more information about revising paragraphs, see Lesson 2.6, pages 64–66.

Write the First Draft

Now that you've made a Venn diagram, you're ready to write your draft. Details you pull from the middle of the Venn diagram are similarities. Details pulled from the outsides are differences. As you think about the order of presenting information, pull details from your diagram.

Notice how the following comparison-contrast piece is organized. First it tells about Superman. Then it tells about Batman. This kind of organization is called subject by subject. It's a way of showing clearly the similarities and differences between two subjects. It helps readers picture the subjects side by side.

Model

The Great Depression was in its final years. World War II waited across the ocean in Europe. Out of this time came two of our earliest comic-book superheroes.

Superman appeared in 1938. When fighting crime, he flew through the air, wearing a caped costume to disguise his true identity. Today we know him as The Man of Steel, dedicated to helping others, an orphan from the planet Krypton.

In 1939 Batman was created. Like Superman, he was a caped hero with a secret identity and a mission to make the world a better place. In some ways, however, Batman was one of a kind. For instance, he was the first Earth-born superhero. He covered his face with a mask. And to get around, he drove a one-of-a-kind car called the Batmobile.

Now, more than fifty years later, the world is a different place with many different problems. Although times have changed, many of our superheroes have stayed with us. With luck there will always be superheroes to call on whenever we need one.

Take a look at the similarities and differences covered in this selection. Notice that they are the same ones shown in the Venn diagram on page 183.

Enabling Strategies

LEP Choosing Words

Students who are not native English speakers may have difficulty choosing characteristics to use in a Venn diagram. Suggest that these students work with a partner and follow the Batman-Superman model on page 183. You might suggest that students compare and contrast themselves and their partner. Have them label the overlapping oval *Friends* and the individual ovals with each person's name. Next, have each student enter her or his birthplace, goals, favorite outfits, preferred mode of travel, and so on.

5.2 Writing Activities

Write a Comparison-Contrast Piece

Write to a good friend who has moved away. In your letter compare and contrast two things of interest to you both. For example, you might compare two soccer players or a movie and a book.

- List details about each subject.
- Create a Venn diagram.
- Organize your details subject by subject.
- Draft your letter.

PURPOSE To share information by comparing and contrasting
AUDIENCE A friend
LENGTH 2–3 paragraphs

Keith Haring, *Red Dog*, 1987

Cooperative Learning

In a small group, study and talk about the two dogs in the photograph. Each group member should add details to a Venn diagram comparing and contrasting the real dog and sculpture. Each should use the diagram to draft a short comparison-contrast piece.

Grammar Link

Be sure verbs agree with compound subjects.

When two or more subject words are linked by *or* or *nor,* the verb agrees with the subject that is closer to it.

Complete each sentence below by writing the correct form of the verb in parentheses.

1. Neither the superheroes' costumes nor their mission (has, have) changed in fifty years.
2. Either powers or weaknesses (is, are) more important.
3. The Power Rangers or Batman (is, are) the most popular today.
4. Neither Superman nor the Power Rangers (drives, drive) an amazing car.
5. (Is, Are) superheroes or a real-life hero more important to you?

See Lesson 15.3, page 408.

ASSESS

Writing Activities Evaluation Guidelines

Write a Comparison-Contrast Piece

Use these criteria when evaluating your students' writing. The assignment should show

- a Venn diagram with similarities and differences labeled
- a letter, organized subject by subject

See also the *Teacher's Guide to Writing Assessment.*

Cooperative Learning

Does each comparison-contrast piece accurately reflect details from the group's Venn diagram?

Grammar Link

(See Using the Grammar Link below.)

Reteaching

Composition Reteaching, p. 38

Enrichment

Composition Enrichment, p. 38

Use *Fine Art Transparencies* 21–25 for enrichment activities also.

CLOSE

To reinforce the concept of diagramming, challenge the class to suggest images for Venn diagrams of any two subjects they have been comparing and contrasting. For example, a Venn diagram that compares and contrasts two novels might appear as the outline of two overlapping books.

Using the Grammar Link

Grammar Link Answers

1. has
2. are
3. is
4. drive
5. Are

About the Art

Keith Haring, *Red Dog*, 1987
The art of Keith Haring (1958–1990) first drew public attention in 1980. He favored simply drawn or sculpted cartoon-like figures. He was committed to popular art and often collaborated with young street artists. *Red Dog*, a lacquered steel sculpture in a private collection, measures 6 by 6 1/2 by 7 feet.

Setting the Purpose

Lesson 5.3 teaches students to order the steps in a process and to explain those steps in writing, using clear transitions.

FOCUS

Lesson Overview

Objective: To write an explanation of how to do something

Skills: breaking a process into steps; linking the steps clearly; writing an explanation

Critical Thinking: analyzing; relating steps; clarifying

Speaking and Listening: informal speaking; listening critically

Bellringer

When students enter the classroom, have this assignment on the board: *Write a brief paragraph that explains how to take a photograph.*

Grammar Link to the Bellringer

Ask students to underline the verbs in their Bellringer paragraph. Have they used action verbs such as *pose* and *click,* or only vague verbs such as *do*?

Motivating Activity

Ask students to imagine that for some reason they can no longer use a camera. How would they direct an assistant to take pictures for them? How would they explain the process?

You might also try an activity in which students try to explain to each other a simple task (for example, how to whistle or how to tie a bow).

LESSON 5.3

Expository Writing

Explaining How to Do Something

Expository writing is used to explain a process, step by step. Transition words help make the order of the steps clear for the reader.

Pictured above is French painter Henri Matisse (1869–1954), an important artist of modern times. His painting was known for its bright colors and unusual shapes. Late in his life, Matisse became physically unable to paint as he once had. He then took up a new form—the collage. With the help of an assistant, he pinned paper shapes together to create pictures.

Teacher's Classroom Resources

The following resources can be used for planning, instruction, practice, reinforcement, assessment, reteaching, enrichment, or evaluation.

Teaching Tools
Lesson Plans

Transparencies
Fine Art Transparencies, 21–25
Writing Process Transparencies, 17–19B

If you were Matisse explaining your method to a new assistant, how would you make your instructions clear? Where would you start?

Drafting Tip

When writing an explanation of a process, try picturing it slowly in your mind. This will help you include all the steps.

Break the Process into Steps

If you've ever used a recipe or built a model, you've probably followed a process step by step. Almost any job is easier if you approach it one step at a time.

Explaining how to make a collage is no exception. If you explain the process in steps, your reader will have an easier time understanding it. Be sure to include every step and to present steps in the right order. Explain with extra care any steps that might be confusing.

Making a Collage

Journal Writing

Think of a process you go through every day. List all the steps in the process. Circle any steps that you think are hard to understand. Make notes about ways to explain these steps.

TEACH

Guided Practice

L2 Focusing on the Steps

Students may benefit by focusing on the imperative verbs in the directions for making a collage on this page. The verbs break the process into a series of actions. If students were to describe the steps in mounting a photograph, for example, they might make a list such as this one: (1) *Assemble* photograph, cardboard, glue, scissors; (2) *Cut* cardboard to size; (3) *Apply* glue to back of photograph; (4) *Press* photograph to cardboard until dry.

L1 Trying It Out

After students have written a process explanation, encourage them to try following their own directions, doing *only* the steps they have written down. Were they able to complete the process successfully?

Two-Minute Skill Drill

Have students reorder the following steps, adding transitions and a "How to" title.

Throw the skin in the garbage. Strip the rest of the skin off and finish eating. Break off the hard stem at the top. Peel back the skin in strips part way down and eat the top part of the fruit.

Journal Writing Tip

Defining and Clarifying Encourage students to check their explanations for steps that may be hard to follow. These steps may contain information better handled in two steps; they may be out of order or contain vague verbs such as *put* instead of exact verbs such as *pin* or *paste.*

Blackline Masters

Thinking and Study Skills, pp. 1, 8–9, 11, 17
Writing Across the Curriculum, pp. 9–10, 14
Cooperative Learning Activities, pp. 26–30
Sentence Combining Practice, pp. 30–32
Speaking and Listening Activities, pp. 12–13, 21, 24
Research Paper and Report Writing, pp. 32–38
Composition Practice, p. 39
Composition Reteaching, p. 39
Composition Enrichment, p. 39

Assessment

Teacher's Guide to Writing Assessment

TEACH

Guided Practice

L2 Using the Model
Discuss with students how the writer makes the explanation clear by dividing it into ordered steps, linked with transitions. Ask students how the writer might have marked the order of the steps other than with transition words. (with numbers)

L3 Explaining Another Process
Some students may wish to explain another artistic process, for instance, the making of a mobile or a woodblock print. Students might do research and then prepare a poster that shows the artistic process in steps.

Independent Practice
For further stimuli for expository writing, see *Fine Art Transparencies* 21–25.

Writing Process Transparencies, 17–19B

Writing Across the Curriculum, pp. 9–10, 14

Cooperative Learning Activities, pp. 26–30

Research Paper and Report Writing, pp. 32–38

Skills Practice
Thinking and Study Skills, pp. 1, 8–9, 11, 17

Speaking and Listening Activities, pp. 12–13, 21, 24

Sentence Combining Practice, pp. 30–32

Composition Practice, p. 39

Link the Steps

Once you've broken a process into steps, you're ready to write a draft. As you write, you might want to combine some steps. You might decide to explain others further. Think especially about the transitions between steps. What words will help link one step to another? The chart below shows some transition words that link the steps in making scrambled eggs.

How to Make Scrambled Eggs	
Transitions	
First	gather eggs, butter, a frying pan, a fork, a spoon, and a bowl.
Then	break the eggs into the bowl, and beat them with the fork.
After	beating the eggs, warm some butter in the frying pan on the stove.
Next	pour the eggs into the frying pan, and stir them with the spoon.
Finally	stir the eggs over a medium flame until they're ready to eat.

Now notice, in the passage below, the transition words that help link steps in Matisse's collage-making process.

"Then" is a transition word linking steps in the process.

What does the writer do to make this explanation clear and simple?

If you had never created a collage before, could you use this explanation to make one?

Literature Model

In order to do his paper cut-outs, Matisse had assistants paint sheets of paper with gouaches [water colors]; then he had a piece of unpainted white paper pinned to the wall of his studio. . . . Then he cut the painted papers into the shapes he wanted and pinned them, or, usually, directed an assistant to pin them, into the desired composition.

Jack Cowart, *Henri Matisse: Paper Cut-Outs*

By completing the process explained above, Matisse and his assistants were able to create beautiful collages. Look at the next page and see for yourself.

Enabling Strategies

LEP Picturing the Process
Students may benefit from first creating drawings or cutting pictures from magazines to outline their explanation. They can show each step and the materials it requires. For instance, to explain the steps involved in bathing a dog, students can include sketches of a dog, a tub or hose, soap, towels, and so forth. Students can then make notes with key English vocabulary next to the pictures. As they write the explanation of their chosen process, they can refer to the pictures and notes they made earlier.

5.3 Writing Activities

Write a "How to" Explanation

Pretend you will create a collage like the one shown below. You can use paper, ribbons, buttons, or other small objects. Make a rough sketch of your collage. Then write an explanation of how to create such a collage.

- Break the process into steps.
- Present each step in proper order.
- Use transitions to link the steps.

PURPOSE To explain how to make a collage
AUDIENCE Students in your art class
LENGTH 1–2 paragraphs

Henri Matisse, *Madame de Pompadour*, 1951

Grammar Link

Use action verbs to make your explanations clear.

In the diagram on page 187, the steps in making a collage are explained with exact action verbs: *gather, paint, cut, pin,* and *paste.*

Complete the steps in the recipe below by adding a different action verb to each.

How to Make a Milkshake

1. ______ 8 ounces of milk into a blender.
2. ______ 1–2 scoops of ice cream into the milk.
3. ______ 2 teaspoons of syrup for extra flavor.
4. ______ together the ingredients in the blender for 30 seconds.
5. For a smoother milkshake, ______ the blender on for another 30 seconds.

See Lesson 10.1, page 298.

Cross-Curricular: Math

Scan your math textbook and choose a word problem. Write a paragraph explaining the steps in solving the problem.

ASSESS

Writing Activities Evaluation Guidelines

Write a "How to" Explanation

Use these criteria when evaluating your students' writing.

- Has the student broken the process into steps?
- Are the steps presented in order with appropriate transitions?

See also the *Teacher's Guide to Writing Assessment.*

Cross-Curricular: Math

Paragraphs should explain the steps in logical order and should have clear transitions.

Grammar Link

(See Using the Grammar Link below.)

Reteaching

Composition Reteaching, p. 39

Enrichment

Composition Enrichment, p. 39

Use *Fine Art Transparencies* 21–25 for enrichment activities also.

CLOSE

To emphasize the necessity for completeness in giving directions, call on a volunteer to explain—without demonstrating—a simple process, such as tying a shoe or making a paper airplane, while another student follows the directions to the letter.

Using the Grammar Link

Grammar Link Answers

Answers will vary, but some suggestions are given below.

1. Pour . . .
2. Drop . . .
3. Add . . .
4. Mix (or Blend) . . .
5. . . . turn . . .

About the Art

Henri Matisse, *Madame de Pompadour*, 1951

Matisse's *Madame de Pompadour*, in the Los Angeles County Museum of Art, is a 31 1/2- by 23 1/4-inch lithograph of a paper-cutout collage. Matisse often sketched the collage forms on a wall before making cutouts.

Setting the Purpose

Lesson 5.4 teaches students to decide on a topic, gather information, and draft a report. They then write a short report on some aspect of the public library in their community.

FOCUS

Lesson Overview

Objective: To write a report according to specific rules
Skills: choosing a topic; asking questions; gathering information; writing a report
Critical Thinking: generating new information; summarizing; making inferences
Speaking and Listening: analyzing; questioning; discussing; evaluating

Bellringer

When students enter the classroom, have this assignment on the board: *Write possible titles for reports on three ocean-related topics.*

Grammar Link to the Bellringer

Ask students to underline the capital letters in their Bellringer titles. Did they remember to capitalize first and last words and all other important words?

Motivating Activity

Ask students to decide which of their Bellringer titles identifies a topic that would be the right size for a one-page report. Introduce the idea that finding something that is the right size is as crucial to good report writing as it is to buying shoes.

LESSON 5.4

Expository Writing
Writing a Report

To write a report, choose a topic that interests you. Gather information from a variety of sources. Organize what you learn and present it in your own words to inform your readers.

As the diagram below illustrates, you need to choose a topic that is the right size. A topic that is too broad will have too much information for a short report. A narrow topic will not give you enough about which to write.

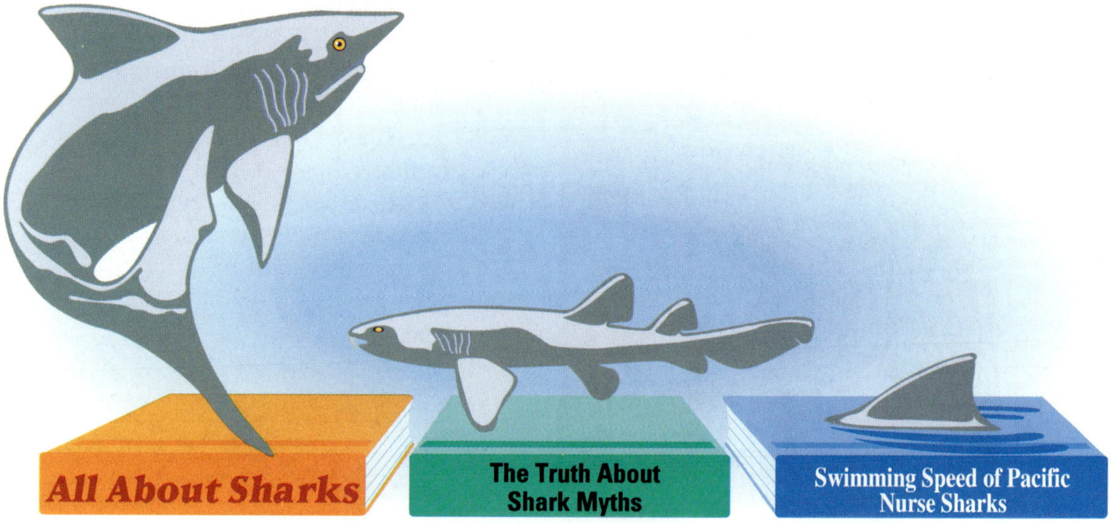

Gather Information

Reports are built on information—facts, statistics, examples—so you'll need to do some research. A good place to begin looking is the library. There you can find encyclopedias and other reference books to get you started. These materials

Teacher's Classroom Resources

The following resources can be used for planning, instruction, practice, reinforcement, assessment, reteaching, enrichment, or evaluation.

Teaching Tools
Lesson Plans

Transparencies
Fine Art Transparencies, 21–25
Writing Process Transparencies, 17–19B

can help you focus your search for information. They can also help you to ask questions about your topic and lead you to other resources. You may find books, magazine articles, pamphlets, and videos about your topic. Once you've found some sources, you can start to gather information.

As you read, think about what is important and worth remembering. Take notes, being sure to jot down the title and author of each source. Do not just copy information word for word. Think about what you're reading and write your notes in your own words.

Look at the source below. Then look at the handwritten notes, and see the difference. Notice how the writer includes the source's title and the author's name on the note card.

Editing Tip

Don't throw away your notes before your report is finished. As you edit, if you need to check a fact, you can look back at your notes.

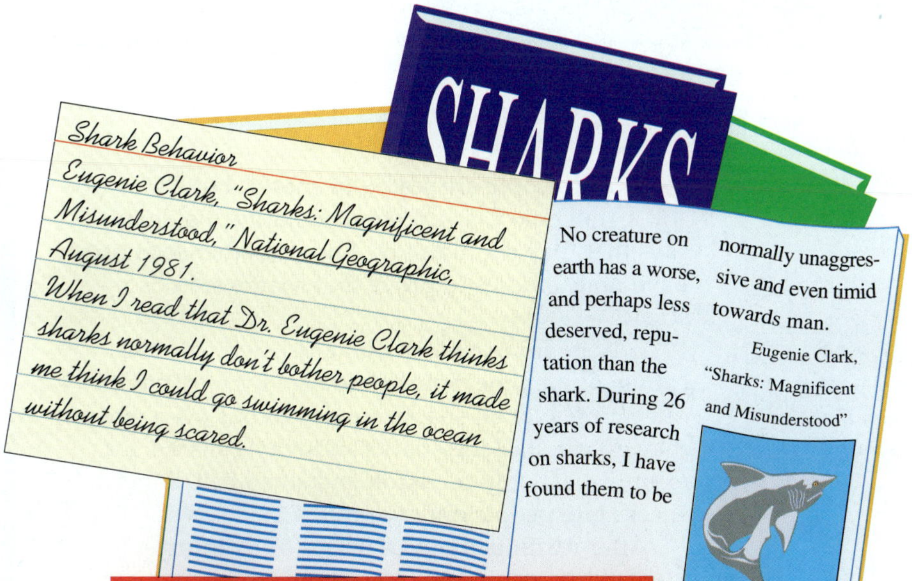

Journal Writing

Look back through your journal to find a few topics that you are interested in learning more about. Circle a topic you think that you'd want to write a report about. Then jot down a few ideas about where you might begin to research.

TEACH

Guided Practice

L2 Using the Model

Discuss with students the importance of documenting their sources when they conduct research. The note card includes both the title and author of the source. Without such attributions, students deprive authors and publishers of the recognition they deserve. Students who use an author's words without citing their source may also be guilty of plagiarism.

L1 Narrowing a Topic

Students having difficulty narrowing a topic may find the library's computer index helpful. You could point out that a student looking under a topic such as *Moon* might discover several subheads (narrower topics), including *charts, exploration, folklore,* and *influence on weather.* Mention that, on the computer screen, the main topic is usually highlighted and subheads appear below the main topic in alphabetical order.

Two-Minute Skill Drill

Suppose you had decided on *Tides* as a general topic for a research report. To help direct your research, list as many questions as you can about tides.

Journal Writing Tip

Acquiring Information Check to see if students have cited any nonprint sources of information. For instance, tape recordings, videos, movies, and the reference librarian can all be helpful sources when trying to find out more about a topic.

Blackline Masters

Thinking and Study Skills, pp. 2, 4, 11, 13, 23–24, 35
Writing Across the Curriculum, pp. 6, 19
Cooperative Learning Activities, pp. 26–30
Sentence Combining Practice, pp. 30–32
Speaking and Listening Activities, pp. 12–13, 21, 24
Research Paper and Report Writing, pp. 32–38
Composition Practice, p. 40
Composition Reteaching, p. 40
Composition Enrichment, p. 40

Assessment

Teacher's Guide to Writing Assessment

TEACH

Guided Practice

L2 Using the Model

Discuss with students how the introduction serves its purpose—stating the topic of the report and engaging the reader's attention.Then discuss how the conclusion shows what the writer has discovered—that people still have a lot to learn about sharks. Ask students whether the report makes them curious to learn more about sharks. Is the topic narrow enough for a three-paragraph report?

L3 Applying and Extending

Point out that research skills are used in many different professions. Invite students to discuss how detectives, lawyers, teachers, architects, doctors, artists, writers, and actors all may find that doing research can help them in their work. Can students think of other occupations in which research skills would be useful? Stress that good research skills can be used in and out of school and in all walks of life.

Independent Practice

For further stimuli for report writing, see *Fine Art Transparencies* 21–25.

Writing Process Transparencies, 17–19B

Writing Across the Curriculum, pp., 6, 19

Cooperative Learning Activities, pp. 26–30

Research Paper and Report Writing, pp. 32–38

Composition Practice, p. 40

Skills Practice

Thinking and Study Skills, pp. 2, 4, 11, 13, 23–24, 35

Speaking and Listening Activities, pp. 12–13, 21, 24

Sentence Combining Practice, pp. 30–32

Write About What You've Learned

After taking notes, organize them so that you can write. You might begin by asking yourself, "What's the report about?" Your answer can become the introduction to your report. As you write the body of your draft, answer this question: "What did I discover?" Finally, as you tie your paper together in the conclusion, think about what you learned. A good conclusion can leave both you and your readers with a better understanding of your topic. Read the model below and notice the three main parts.

In what way does the introduction do what it should do?

The body of the report shows what information the writer discovered.

What does the conclusion say about what the writer learned?

Model

Most people are scared of sharks, but Dr. Eugenie Clark, a famous marine biologist, says that they shouldn't be. She and other scientists have done studies to prove that sharks aren't so scary.

For one thing, sharks don't just swim around, eating all the time. Some sharks go for weeks without eating. Not all sharks are dangerous even when they do eat. Basking sharks and whale sharks, for example, eat only plankton and small fish. Other sharks bite people only to protect themselves.

After reading about Dr. Clark's adventures, I learned that people still have much to learn about sharks. It's good to learn more, though, because the new information lets us understand what's really true about sharks. Now I can swim without being scared.

Enabling Strategies

LEP Peer Reviewing Strategies

Students who are learning English should review each other's drafts and identify the introduction, the body, and the conclusion. If the locations of these parts are unclear, students should revise their drafts. Thoughtful reviewers whose first language is English should then read the drafts of the students learning English and give constructive comments. The reviewers might read passages aloud so that the writers can hear inaccuracies in the language and make revisions.

5.4 Writing Activities

Write a Report

The library can be a mysterious place for people who rarely go there. Write a report to help such people learn more about the public library in your community. You may explain the different sections of the library, tell how to find references, or choose a library topic of your own.

- Locate sources of information.
- Take notes on what you find.
- Organize the information into an introduction, a body, and a conclusion.

PURPOSE To present information about the public library
AUDIENCE People in the community who are unfamiliar with the library
LENGTH 3–4 paragraphs

COMPUTER OPTION

Desktop publishing software can give your report a professional look. Using desktop publishing, you can put text into columns and make a cover page. You can even provide space for pictures or diagrams to be scanned in or pasted on after printing.

Grammar Link

When you take notes, capitalize the names of authors; also capitalize the first and last words and all other important words in a title.

Note how the writer of the report on sharks wrote the title and author of the source: *Eugenie Clark, "Sharks: Magnificent and Misunderstood."*

Write each name or title below, using capital letters as needed.

1. virginia morrell
2. "The really secret life of plants"
3. william a. degregorio
4. *Presidential curiosities: The complete book of U.S. presidents*
5. francis parkman
6. *the oregon trail*
7. "antarctica, the last continent"
8. michael parfit
9. *Paul revere and the World he lived in*
10. esther forbes

See Lesson 18.2, page 440, and Lesson 18.4, page 444.

ASSESS

Writing Activities Evaluation Guidelines

Write a Report

Use these criteria when evaluating your students' writing.

- Have students presented a manageable topic?
- Have students included a clear introduction, body, and conclusion?
- Do students describe one or more library resources?

See also the *Teacher's Guide to Writing Assessment.*

Grammar Link

(See Using the Grammar Link below.)

Reteaching

Composition Reteaching, p. 40

Enrichment

Composition Enrichment, p. 40

CLOSE

Invite one or two volunteers to read their library reports aloud. The class can offer comments on the choice of a topic, the organization of the piece, and the usefulness of the information.

Using the Grammar Link

Grammar Link Answers

1. Virginia Morrell
2. "The Really Secret Life of Plants"
3. William A. DeGregorio
4. *Presidential Curiosities: The Complete Book of U.S. Presidents*
5. Francis Parkman
6. *The Oregon Trail*
7. "Antarctica, the Last Continent"
8. Michael Parfit
9. *Paul Revere and the World He Lived In*
10. Esther Forbes

Capitalizing Other Words Remind students also to capitalize proper adjectives and geographic areas: the Roosevelt era; the Far East.

Setting the Purpose

Lesson 5.5 teaches students to summarize and evaluate a book. They will then write a book report following a standard format.

FOCUS

Lesson Overview

Objective: To respond to a book by writing a book report
Skills: understanding the parts of a book report; expressing reactions; cooperating on an oral report
Critical Thinking: recalling; summarizing; evaluating
Speaking and Listening: discussing; oral reporting

Bellringer

When students enter the classroom, have this assignment on the board: *Write three sentences comparing two characters from a book or story you have read.*

Grammar Link to the Bellringer

Ask students to underline the subjects and verbs in their Bellringer sentences. Do any of the sentences have plural subjects? Do the verbs and subjects agree?

Motivating Activity

Initiate a discussion about books—what makes them memorable (good characters, exciting or intriguing plots, novel ideas or perspectives, humor) or forgettable (one-dimensional characters, predictable plotting, dull writing). Ask students to recall their favorite book or story. What did they like best about it? How would they explain it to a friend?

LESSON 5.5

Writing About Literature
Writing a Book Report

Reading is a ticket to adventure. By reading, you can travel to exciting places, meet interesting people, and learn about things you never knew existed. When you want to share reading experiences with others, write a book report.

Maybe the next book you read will be Mildred Taylor's *Roll of Thunder, Hear My Cry.* In this book you will meet the Logans, an African American family living in Mississippi. The year is 1933, and Cassie Logan and her brothers experience racial prejudice almost every day. When her parents challenge this prejudice, Cassie faces more danger than ever before.

Teacher's Classroom Resources

The following resources can be used for planning, instruction, practice, reinforcement, assessment, reteaching, enrichment, or evaluation.

Teaching Tools
Lesson Plans

Transparencies
Fine Art Transparencies, 21–25
Writing Process Transparencies, 17–19B

Include Information About the Book

A book report provides readers with information about a book. The report can also include your feelings about the book. The chart below explains the parts of a typical book report.

Parts of a Book Report

Title	Include the title of the book. Be sure to look at the book cover to make certain that you have spelled and punctuated correctly.
Author	Include the name of the author. Again, you want to give the author all the credit he or she deserves, so double-check the spelling of the name.
Main Characters	Give the names of the main characters and a few words about who they are. That way, people will know whom the book is about.
Setting	Tell about the setting. It includes when and where the story takes place. Telling about the setting helps people imagine the story.
Summary	Briefly explain what happens in the book. Just a few sentences to summarize should do it. But be sure not to give away any surprises.
What I Thought	At the end of a book report, write down how you feel about the book and why. This part of the report gives you a chance to express yourself.

Vocabulary
Prewriting Tip

In prewriting, try listing some words that express how the book made you feel. The list makes a good starting point for thinking about your book.

Presenting Tip

Assemble copies of class members' final book reports into a class book. Display the book in class, or donate it to the school library.

Journal Writing

Make a list of three or four books you've read. Pick the book you liked most or the book you liked least. Write a few sentences that explain why you feel that way.

TEACH

Guided Practice

L2 Interviewing About Books

Let students form pairs for a book interview. Each member of a pair should interview the other about a favorite or least favorite book. Each interviewer is allowed only four questions, so he or she must ask questions designed to elicit key information. One question should focus on the reader's feelings about the book. After the interviews, each pair can report to the class what they have learned.

L1 Simplifying the Task

Students overwhelmed by the prospect of writing an entire book report may find encouragement in completing the briefer sections of the report first (Title, Author, Main Characters, Setting). Then they can tackle the more extensive Summary and What I Thought sections, cheered by the knowledge that they've already completed two-thirds of their report.

Two-Minute Skill Drill

Have students name the last work of fiction they read. Have them list the main characters, along with a phrase or two describing each of them.

Journal Writing Tip

Comparing Encourage students to begin by comparing various aspects of the books on their lists. Ask them to consider these questions: Did the plots interest you? Were the characterizations realistic? Were the settings described in detail? Was the writing imaginative?

Blackline Masters

Writing Across the Curriculum, pp. 19–20
Thinking and Study Skills, pp. 7, 13, 18, 20
Cooperative Learning Activities, pp. 26–30
Speaking and Listening Activities, pp. 12–13, 21, 24
Composition Practice, p. 41
Composition Reteaching, p. 41
Composition Enrichment, p. 41
Sentence Combining Practice, pp. 30–32
Research Paper and Report Writing, pp. 32–38

Assessment

Teacher's Guide to Writing Assessment

TEACH

Guided Practice

L2 Using the Model

Remind students that a well-written book report can entice others to read the book. A report can suggest questions that only reading the book can answer. For example, after having read in the report on this page that Cassie and Little Man refused to use the ripped-up books, students might wonder: Do Cassie and her brother ever get good books? Does Mrs. Crocker realize she was wrong to punish the children? What other examples of racism do the children encounter?

L3 Comparing Books

Some students may wish to compare the book they have chosen to review with another they have read. In this way they can combine the book report format with a comparison-contrast piece. They also might draw some conclusions about different genres. For example, having read two mystery books, a student might conclude that most mysteries contain a plot twist.

Independent Practice

- For further stimuli for expository writing, see *Fine Art Transparencies* 21–25.
- *Writing Process Transparencies,* 17–19B
- *Writing Across the Curriculum,* pp. 19–20
- *Cooperative Learning Activities,* pp. 26–30
- *Research Paper and Report Writing,* pp. 32–38

Skills Practice

- *Thinking and Study Skills,* pp. 7, 13, 18, 20
- *Speaking and Listening Activities,* pp. 12–13, 21, 24
- *Sentence Combining Practice,* pp. 30–32
- *Composition Practice,* p. 41

Tell Your Feelings

One of the most useful parts of a book report is your feelings about the book. Here's how one student felt after reading *Roll of Thunder, Hear My Cry.*

In this report, the writer gives the title of the book right at the beginning. Why do you think she gives it again near the end?

At the end Natalie gives her opinion of the book—a definite thumbs-up.

Title: *Roll of Thunder, Hear My Cry*

Author: Mildred D. Taylor

Main Characters: The main characters are a black family called the Logans. Cassie is the only girl. Stacey is the older boy. Little Man is the younger boy.

Setting: Rural Mississippi in 1933

Summary: The novel is about the prejudiced way blacks were still being treated after the end of slavery. One example is the first day of school, when Cassie's and Little Man's teacher, Mrs. Crocker, tells them that this year they will have the privilege of using books. Cassie and Little Man are overjoyed—until they receive the tattered books and find out they received them only because they were too ripped up for the white children. When Cassie and Little Man refuse to use the books, they get punished by Mrs. Crocker. Much to Mrs. Crocker's surprise, though, Cassie and Little Man's mother think they did the right thing.

What I Thought: *Roll of Thunder, Hear My Cry* really shows you the unfair way blacks were treated back then, and it's a funny story in some parts and sad in others. It makes you think of the book's title, which comes from a song that slaves once sang. The song tells people not to be defeated by their enemies. That's mostly what the book's about, and I would definitely recommend reading it.

Natalie Bogira, Chute Middle School, Evanston, Illinois

Enabling Strategies

LEP Understanding the Parts of a Book Report

Have students who are still learning English pair with students who are fluent English speakers to review their book report drafts. Using the Parts of a Book Report graphic on page 195 as a checklist, the English-speaking students can model finding and labeling each part of their book reports. They should then assist their partners in identifying the required parts in their own reports. Have students prompt their partners to fill in any missing pieces.

5.5 Writing Activities

Write a Book Report

Look back at the books you listed in your journal. Choose one of the books, and write a short report about it for your school newspaper. Begin by jotting down your feelings and thoughts about the book. List scenes or other details that made you feel this way. Then write the first draft of your report.

- Include the title and author of the book.
- Identify the main characters and the setting.
- Summarize the story.
- Explain your personal reaction to the book.

PURPOSE To share your ideas about a book with others
AUDIENCE Readers of the school newspaper
LENGTH 3–4 paragraphs

Cooperative Learning

Work in a small group to prepare an oral book report. Choose a book that all the group members have read. Note the book's title, author, characters, and setting. Agree on a summary of the plot. Then discuss different feelings group members may have about the book. Include the different opinions in your oral report.

Grammar Link

Make subjects and verbs agree.

When two or more subjects are joined by *and*, the verb is usually plural. Note the subject-verb agreement in this sentence.

Cassie Logan and her brother experience *racial prejudice.*

For each sentence write the correct form of the verb in parentheses.

1. Courage and pride (are, is) what the Logan family possesses.
2. Both Cassie's mother and father (understand, understands) the importance of the land.
3. Farming fields and a vast forest (cover, covers) their 400 acres.
4. Big Ma and Mama also (own, owns) part of the land.
5. The taxes and mortgage on the land (have, has) not been paid.
6. Papa and other farmers (leave, leaves) home looking for work.
7. Big Ma, who is in her sixties, and Mama (run, runs) the farm.
8. Stacey and Little Man (set, sets) off for school in threadbare clothes.
9. First-graders and fourth-graders (share, shares) a classroom.
10. Where (are, is) Miss Crocker and Miss Davis?

See Lesson 15.3, page 408.

ASSESS

Writing Activities Evaluation Guidelines

Write a Book Report

Use these criteria when evaluating your students' writing.

- Does the report include the title and the author of the book?
- Does the report identify the main characters and setting?
- Does the report summarize the story?
- Does the report express the student's feelings about the book and support them with specific examples?
- Does the report contain enough information to familiarize someone with the book without giving away any surprises?

See also the *Teacher's Guide to Writing Assessment.*

Cooperative Learning

Each group's oral report should

- reflect input from all members of the group
- show that the book was discussed and that more than one opinion was considered

Grammar Link

(See Using the Grammar Link below.)

Reteaching

Composition Reteaching, p. 41

Enrichment

Composition Enrichment, p. 41

CLOSE

Ask a volunteer to read aloud a report on a favorite book that is not well known to the class. Encourage the class to make constructive comments afterward. Would they now be interested in reading this book?

Using the Grammar Link

Grammar Link Answers

1. are
2. understand
3. cover
4. own
5. have
6. leave
7. run
8. set
9. share
10. are

Using *There is* and *There are* Tell students that when a sentence begins with the introductory word *There,* the verb must agree with the subject that follows. Examples:

1. There *is* lively and engaging *action* in this novel.
2. There *are* thirty *students* in this class.

Setting the Purpose

Students now have the opportunity to apply what they have learned in Unit 5 about expository writing to an independent writing project. They will use the stages of the writing process to create and present a finished piece.

FOCUS

Lesson Overview

Objective: To write a step-by-step explanation of a process
Skills: using the five stages of the writing process: prewriting, drafting, revising, editing, and presenting
Critical Thinking: analyzing; synthesizing; generating new information
Speaking and Listening: discussing in small groups and as a class

Bellringer

When students enter the classroom, have this assignment on the board: *List three things that you can do that your classmates or younger students might not be able to do.*

Grammar Link to the Bellringer

Ask students who "you" and "them" are in the following sentence: "I bet I'm the only student who knows how to make a birdhouse, but you can make them quite easily." Remind students to use pronouns that are consistent and precise in meaning.

Motivating Activity

Ask students to share their responses to the Bellringer activity. Ask students whether they have ever tried to teach one of the skills on their list to a friend. What happened? What kinds of questions did they have to answer? Mention that explaining a process in writing requires the writer to anticipate readers' questions.

UNIT 5

WRITING PROCESS IN ACTION

EXPOSITORY WRITING

In preceding lessons you learned about ways to share knowledge with others through expository writing. You also had a chance to do your own expository writing—to compare and contrast, give directions, and write a report. Now it is time for you to put together what you know. In this lesson you are invited to write a "how-to" explanation of a process.

• Assignment •

Context	*The editors at How To, a magazine written by and for students wanting to share something they know, want you to write about a step-by-step process.*
Purpose	*To write an explanation of something you've learned to do*
Audience	*Student readers of How To*
Length	*1 page*

The following pages can help you plan and write your explanation. Read through them and then refer to them as you need to. Don't feel limited by them. Remember that you're in charge of your own writing process.

Teacher's Classroom Resources

The following resources can be used for planning, instruction, practice, reinforcement, assessment, reteaching, enrichment, or evaluation.

Teaching Tools
Lesson Plans

Transparencies
Writing Process Transparencies, 17–19B

Prewriting

Whether telling how to bathe an elephant or how to make a sandwich, you need to explain one step at a time. Explaining a process in steps makes it easier for a reader to follow along. The options here can help you explore ways to begin your explanation.

If you're having trouble focusing on your subject, you might visit the library to find more information. Remember to make notes about what you discover. If you're still stuck, try reviewing pages 190–192 for more ideas about research.

Option A
Try clustering to discover what steps go together.

Option B
Try drawing a picture of each step.

Option C
List everything you can recall about the process.

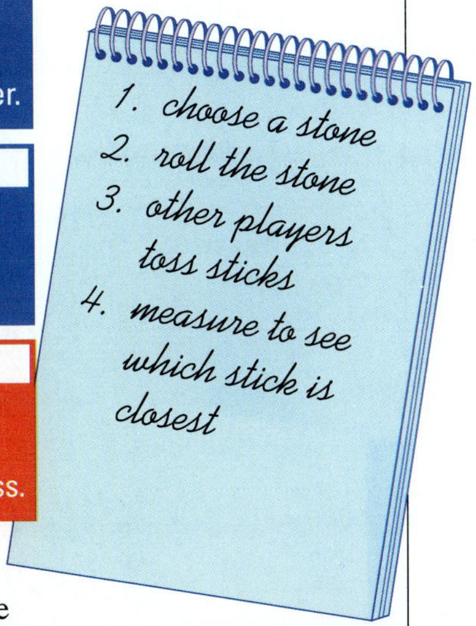

Drafting

Taking your reader through the steps in a process can be tricky. In your draft, try to include as much information as you can. Don't leave out anything your reader might need to know.

While you draft, think about ways to link the steps you listed in the prewriting stage. You might consider combining or expanding steps. Note how much detail Peggy Thomson includes as she explains one step in the process of bathing elephants at the zoo.

Vocabulary
Drafting Tip
For a list of transition words you can use to link steps in a process, see Lesson 5.3, page 188.

Literature Model

At this point Kathy pours out green oil soap from a bottle, letting it spread across the great gray expanses of skin and foaming it up with streamers from her hose. Now, with her ankus propped against the railings and her hose lying on the floor, she lights into a two-handed scrub job.

Peggy Thomson, *Keepers and Creatures at the National Zoo*

TEACH

Prewriting

L2 Developing Ideas for Expository Writing

Help students determine which information is vital to include in a step-by-step explanation of a process. Suggest that students focus on the process's end result. They should include anything they need to reach that result and can discard anything they do not need. As a test, students should consider each step in the process and imagine what would happen if it were left out. Could readers still complete the process?

L2 Sharing a Culture

Encourage students of different cultural backgrounds to explain processes familiar to them but not to students of other cultural backgrounds. Students might consider explaining how to play a traditional game, make or play a simple musical instrument, or create a special holiday dish.

Drafting

L1 Organizing Ideas

Help students to organize information and to prepare for revising as they draft. Suggest they do the following:

- Number each step of the process.
- Use the word *because* to explain something about each step: it will remind them to anticipate readers' questions of "why."
- Use a new paragraph for each step.
- Leave several line spaces between each paragraph so that later additions and corrections to the draft can be made more easily.

Blackline Masters
Thinking and Study Skills, pp. 4, 11, 14
Sentence Combining Practice, pp. 30–32
Composition Practice, p. 44
Composition Reteaching, p. 44
Composition Enrichment, p. 44

Grammar Workbook
Lessons 98–105

Assessment
Teacher's Guide to Writing Assessment

TEACH

Revising

L2 Peer Editing

Students can work in writing conferences with peer editors before they revise their writing. You may want to duplicate the Peer Response forms in the *Teacher's Guide to Writing Assessment.* Suggest that peer editors respond to the following questions: *Is any information missing? Which steps need more explanation? Are the steps in order?*

Editing

L2 Peer Editing

After students have edited their own work, have them edit another student's writing. Remind them to refer to the Editing Checklist on the student page.

Presenting

Before students present their expository writing, discuss how to prepare their papers for publication. Emphasize the importance of the final draft and that it must be neatly done.

Independent Practice

Writing Process Transparencies, 17–19B

Skills Practice

- *Thinking and Study Skills,* pp. 4, 11, 14
- *Sentence Combining Practice,* pp. 30–32
- *Composition Practice,* p. 44

Grammar Workbook, Lessons 98–105

Journal Writing Tip

Understanding Audience Ask students to decide whether their explanation was suited to their audience's interests, knowledge, and ability.

Some steps can be explained simply. Others may be so complicated that a diagram or picture will give the clearest explanation. As you draft, try whatever method seems best.

Revising Tip

When revising a "how-to" explanation, ask another person to follow your explanation. This will help you identify steps that are unclear or missing. For more help see Lesson 5.3, page 186.

Revising

To begin revising, read over your draft to make sure that what you have written fits the assignment, especially your purpose and your audience. Then have a **writing conference**. Read your draft to a partner or small group. Use your audience's reactions to help you evaluate your work so far. The questions below can help you and your listeners.

Question A
Have I included every step in the proper order?

Question B
Is each step stated clearly?

Question C
Have I linked my steps with transitions?

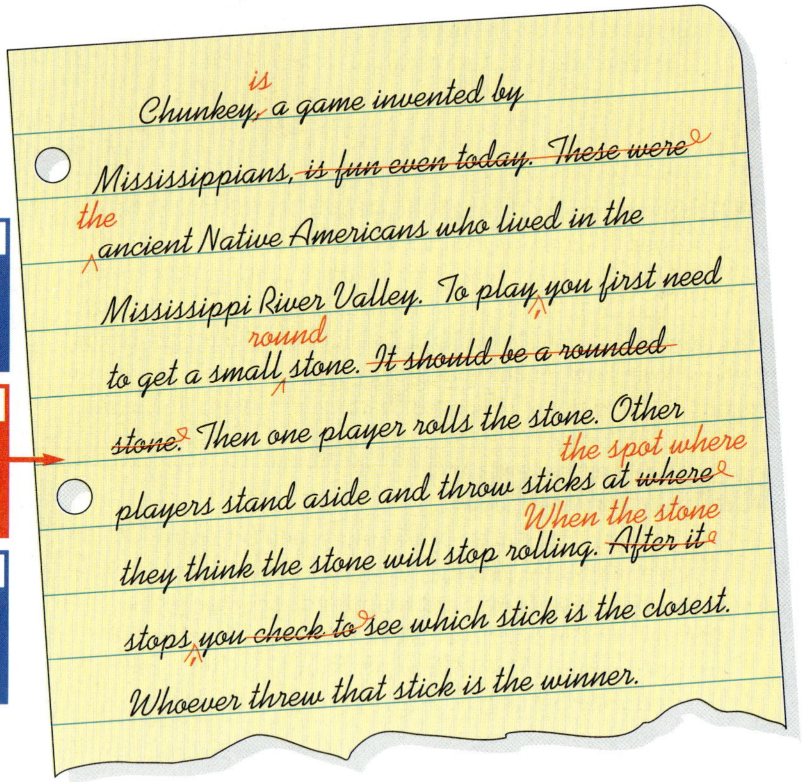

Enrichment and Extensions

Follow-up Ideas

- Suggest that students illustrate their process with photographs, drawings, or computer-generated art.
- Encourage students to contribute their writing to a "How to" anthology that can be kept in the school library.

Extending Exposition

Explore opportunities for extending expository writing beyond the classroom. Suggest that the entire class work together to write a guide for students transferring to their school or a "How to Cope" booklet for babysitters.

Editing

Following the steps of a process takes concentration. For that reason you'll want to **proofread** your draft for spelling, grammar, and punctuation errors. Such small mistakes might distract your audience.

The questions on the notepad can be your starting point. You also might share your draft with a friend or family member. Another person can often discover mistakes you have overlooked.

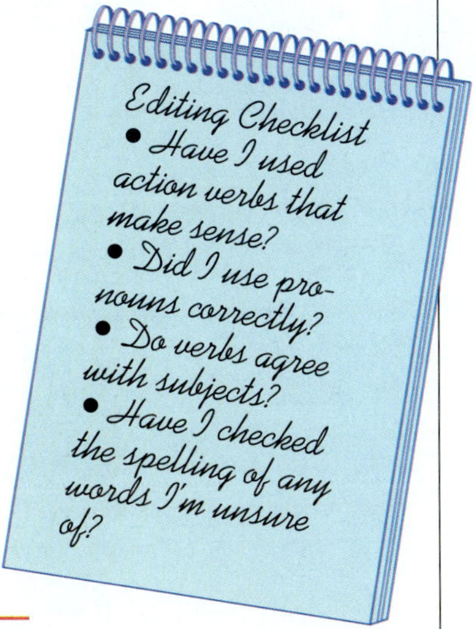

Presenting

Before presenting your explanation, ask yourself if *How To* readers could complete the process, following only your steps. If the answer is yes, then you're ready to present your paper. The final copy may include diagrams or pictures that would make your explanation even easier to understand.

Proofreading

For proofreading symbols, see page 74.

Grammar
Editing Tip

When editing your report, check that you have used pronouns correctly. If you need help with pronouns, refer to Lessons 11.1–11.5, pages 326–335.

Journal Writing

Reflect on your writing process experience. Answer these questions in your journal: What do you like best about your explanation? What was the hardest part of writing it? What did you learn in your writing conference? What new things have you learned as a writer?

ASSESS

Evaluation Guidelines

Use the following questions to evaluate students' finished writing.

- Are all necessary steps in the process included?
- Is each step clearly stated?
- Are the steps appropriately ordered and linked with transitions?
- Does the explanation include pictures or diagrams to clarify difficult steps?
- Does the explanation include cautions that will prevent readers from making mistakes or being injured?
- Does the explanation provide readers with enough information to complete the process from start to finish?
- Is the writing correct in grammar, usage, and mechanics?

Refer to the *Teacher's Guide to Writing Assessment* for further help with evaluating student writing.

Reteaching

Composition Reteaching, p. 44

Enrichment

Composition Enrichment, p. 44

CLOSE

Ask students to discuss the step-by-step explanations or processes that are easiest—and most difficult—for them to follow. Lead them to discuss what makes some instructions unsuccessful: The process is hard to visualize and is unsupported by pictures; the writer doesn't understand the reader's needs; the writer doesn't understand the process. Encourage students to add to the criteria for good instructions listed in this lesson.

Visual Thinking

Illustrating a Process

Some students may find it helpful to use illustrations to demonstrate the steps in their process. In describing how to use in-line skates, for instance, students might sketch the skates, the sidewalk or other skating area, correct movements for the skates, and so forth. Afterward, these illustrations could be cut out, ordered, and given captions. Captions could then be linked with transitions as a first step toward drafting or, in some cases, fleshed out so they can serve as the instructions.

Setting the Purpose

In the Unit 5 Literature Model students read a literature selection that illustrates in a very real way effective expository writing. Such readings serve as models for students as they create their own expository writing.

About the Author

Peggy Thomson is a journalist who lives close to the National Zoo in Washington, D.C. Her book is the result of months of work watching and talking to zookeepers.

FOCUS

Lesson Overview

Objective: To read a selection to examine and appreciate how a professional writer uses descriptive language, dialogue, and transition words to explain a step-by-step process
Skills: reading comprehension; identifying sensory details
Critical Thinking: analyzing; evaluating; identifying
Speaking and Listening: discussing

Bellringer

When students enter the classroom, have this assignment on the board: *List in order five things you do when washing a dog.*

Motivating Activity

Ask students to name some of the responsibilities of a pet owner. Next, mention that some people, such as veterinarians, zoo keepers, and animal trainers, have jobs that consist entirely of caring for animals. Have students write a short paragraph about which of these jobs they think they might enjoy, and why.

UNIT 5

Expository Writing
Literature Model

Peggy Thomson

BATHING ELEPHANTS

In Keepers and Creatures at the National Zoo, *Peggy Thomson explains how zookeepers go about their everyday tasks as well as how they relate to the animals. Giving elephants a daily bath is one way keeper Kathy Wallace has earned the elephants' trust and respect. As you read this chapter from the book, try picturing each step in the bathing process Thomson describes. Then complete the activities in Linking Writing and Literature on page 207.*

"Okay, Biki! Okay, Shant! Wiggle your ears!" Kathy commands. "And keep them wiggling." During this wash-behind-the-ears time, the keeper runs her fingers over the thin skin at the back of the ears and pricks a bit at the stick-out veins with the point of her ankus,[1] hoping to

1 **ankus** (ang' kəs) a pointed stick with a hook, used for leading an elephant

Teacher's Classroom Resources

The following resources can be used for planning, instruction, or practice.

Teaching Tools
Lesson Plans

Transparencies
Fine Art Transparencies, 21–25

prepare the animals for occasional needle pricks during check-ups by a veterinarian.

Now she wants her animals down. Lying down is a vulnerable[2] position for them. It's only because of feeling safe with her that Ambika and Shanthi obey. They go to their knees. At commands of "Down!" they flop to one side. And here the scrub up of this pair begins.

Elephants are cursed with dry, old skin on their backs. It builds up in a way that's unsightly and probably itchy. The skin cracks and harbors infections down inside, so keepers have to scrub away day in, day out, to lift the dead stuff off. Today Kathy uses a scrub brush on Ambika and, because of her blisters, a sponge on Shanthi. For Nancy's worse case of dead skin on the back she has tools of a rougher sort—a cement block with a handle and the kind of scraper used to remove rust from car bodies.

At this point Kathy pours out green oil soap from a bottle, letting it spread across the great gray expanses of skin and foaming it up with streamers from her hose. Now, with her ankus propped against the railings and her hose lying on the floor, she lights into a two-handed scrub job. Steam rises all about, shifted by whuffling puffs of air from the elephants' trunks. The keeper works hard, talking to Ambika: "This place is beginning to smell like a beauty parlor," and to Shanthi: "All right, I see you squinching[3] up your eyes. It stings on your blisters, I bet it does." Whatever the discomfort, the young elephant lies still, her feet crossed, her trunk up, quietly feeling about her forehead, her ears, her back and on beyond to touch "Auntie" and twine briefly with "Auntie's" trunk.

Midway through the bath, keeper Kathy masterminds the shift of the two large bodies, the rocking back up onto the knees and the flop down again from left to right side. Along the way various scraped patches of skin receive smeary dabs of yellow salve. (Elephant keepers say they never order lemon meringue

2 **vulnerable** (vul′ nər ə bəl) subject to physical injury
3 **squinching** (skwinch′ ing) looking with the eyes partly closed

TEACH

L2 Guided Reading

- Tell students that a good writer can create interest in even the most mundane of daily tasks. Ask students what techniques might make this possible. Ask them to pay attention to the parts of Thomson's explanation they find intriguing, and to notice the specific techniques the author uses to create interest. (Students might notice places where Thomson uses dialogue, specific and specialized vocabulary, detailed description, or the present tense, which puts readers more immediately in the scene.)
- Have students find the transition words and phrases that help order the steps in the bathing process. In the first two pages of the selection are these examples: "During this . . . time," "Now," "At this point," "Midway through the bath," "Along the way." Suggest that students find each transition and jot down briefly what is occurring at that point in the process.

Blackline Masters
Speaking and Listening Activities, pp. 21, 24

Assessment
Teacher's Guide to Writing Assessment

UNIT 5
Literature Model

TEACH

L2 Guided Reading

- Point out that although the selection is written in the expository mode, it still contains descriptive sensory details. You might ask that students locate examples of sensory details (for example, "Steam rises all about, shifted by whuffling puffs of air from the elephants' trunks").
- Tell students that a good writer can make a scene seem so real that the reader can almost see it. Mention that one way to do this is to use vivid adjectives and adverbs. Ask students to watch for vivid modifiers as they read the selection. Ask what words they found that helped them "see" the scene.

pie at restaurants. They've lost their appetite for it.) Sometimes, though not today, there's also an oiling for the wiry black bristles at the end of the tail.

Footwork, which comes last, is the most difficult part of the bath and the most crucial,[4] for feet must be sound to support an elephant's great weight. With the two bathers standing again, admired, praised, patted, hugged about the knees, Kathy asks for a "Foot up! Way up! Thank you!" A foot is presented, and she begins her careful look through all the cracks and fissures[5] of its pad for the presence of pebbles and other foreign matter.

Over the microphone the narrator describes the foot, how its callousy pads wear down in the wild with the long hikes each day in search of food, but how in a zoo the pads, which grow quickly, need to be rasped[6] down or even carved away in slices; and how keepers then check the fresh, smooth surface for tiny holes, which tell them a pebble has entered and may be working its way upward with each step, to cripple the elephant painfully once it touches bone.

Watchers from the railing can't see the foot up close. They see the probings with the pick or with the point of the ankus. They see Kathy using both hands on a drawknife[7] to cut away a slice of leathery, rubbery pad and then another. (It doesn't hurt the elephant.) And they hear the thunk of the slice into her bucket.

This morning Kathy does only one of Shanthi's front feet. At that, it takes almost half an hour, for she has to work around tender bruises and to wind up with a nicely rounded shape to the pad. Her knife will need a sharpening before she next uses it on the other feet, this afternoon and tomorrow. She must also rasp down the nails, which get too little scuffing in zoo life to wear down properly.

Bath and foot-care time now flows into demonstration time directed by the keeper team of Kathy and Morna out in the yard.

4 **crucial** (kro͞o′ shəl) very important
5 **fissures** (fish′ ərz) long, narrow, deep cracks
6 **rasped** (raspt) scraped or rubbed
7 **drawknife** (drô′ nīf) a knife with a handle at each end, used to shave surfaces

Genre and Style

Reading Expository Writing

This example of expository writing describes a step-by-step process. It explains a keeper's job in such a way that the reader learns about elephants, keepers, and the relationship between them. The selection also contains elements of biography and natural history.

About the Art

Andy Warhol, *Endangered Species: African Elephant*, 1983

Andy Warhol (1929–1987) was a leading figure in the pop art movement. This picture is a 38-by-38-inch silkscreen. It is currently housed at the Ronald Feldman Gallery in New York City.

Here people clap to see the elephants maneuver[8] on command, present a foot, balance on tiny stools, and move huge logs with their trunks. By the time Ambika and Shanthi take their bows, the keepers are beginning to wilt. There's an element of tension in the playful-looking baths they give and in the training shows—in just dealing with animals who could so easily pulverize[9] them if they chose to.

In the office, keepers Kathy and Morna speak of the awe they feel in the animals' trust of them and in the animals' forbearance,[10] *not* to hurt the keepers. They also speak of a kind of

8 **maneuver** (mə no͞o' vər) to move or proceed skillfully toward a desired goal
9 **pulverize** (pul' və rīz') to break down or crush completely
10 **forbearance** (fôr ber' əns) patience

Andy Warhol, *Endangered Species: African Elephant,* 1983

TEACH

L2 Guided Reading

- Tell students that good writing often makes the reader want to know more about a subject. Direct students to look for parts of the selection that made them want to know more. Ask them to explain what aroused their curiosity.
- Ask students to look for details that show how the keepers feel about the elephants. Which details in particular caught students' attention. How do they think the keepers feel? Does knowing how the keepers feel make the passage more interesting? Why or why not?

Writers and Writing

Combining Elements

Thomson combines different elements in a single paragraph. For example, in the third paragraph on page 203, she describes the washing process, the zoo keeper's words to the elephants, and the elephants' responses to being bathed. By combining these events in the same block of text, Thomson suggests that they are all happening simultaneously in a flurry of motion and sound.

TEACH

L2 Guided Reading

- Writers often use dialogue to add interest or to draw attention to something. Ask students: *For what purpose does Thomson use dialogue?* (Thomson uses dialogue to draw attention to the caring relationship between the keepers and the elephants.) Direct students' attention to the last page of the selection, and point out that it ends with dialogue. Why do they think the author used dialogue at such an important point in the writing?
- Thomson uses the present tense a great deal in this selection. Ask students how the use of the present tense makes them feel as they read. Point out that the present tense gives a feeling of immediacy. Ask them to try mentally rewriting a paragraph in the past tense. How does a tense change affect the way they respond to the writing?

Independent Practice

Fine Art Transparencies, 21–25

Skills Practice

Speaking and Listening Activities, pp. 21, 24

communication that goes on among the elephants, sometimes during bath time, more often first thing in the morning. "We're aware of it when we enter the building," says Morna. "We feel something. We feel it before we hear it, a kind of vibrating in the air, like a cat's purring, only just beyond our hearing. Sometimes that rumbling seems to be a message to us. Like: It's good to see you. We're glad you're here."

Nancy Schutt, *The Great Ones,* 1987

About the Art

Nancy Schutt, *The Great Ones*, 1987
Nancy Schutt (1953–) often depicts in her work the interaction of humans and animals. This oil painting, *The Great Ones*, measures 48 inches by 54 inches and is in a private collection in Seattle.

Linking Writing and Literature

Readers Respond to the Model

How does Peggy Thomson make the process of bathing elephants engaging and easy to understand?

Explore Peggy Thomson's expository writing by answering these questions. Then read what other students liked about her writing.

1. In what order does Peggy Thomson present the steps in bathing the elephants?
2. How does Peggy Thomson link the steps in the bathing process?
3. In addition to the bathing, what other topics does Thomson cover?
4. Why do you think Thomson uses dialogue in this chapter?
5. Would you recommend Thomson's book to a friend? Why?

I liked how the writer told how the elephants got complimented because they deserved it. The part about the vet's visit was so interesting.

I would describe the feeling between the keeper and the elephants if I had written the selection.

I didn't like the foot part because I thought, "Ouch!" (But I read the part about how it doesn't hurt the elephants.) Elephants always held my attention. I would recommend this to a friend. Ms. Thomson wrote a great piece of work.

Rose Vales

The writer kept my attention by showing step-by-step the trainers bathing the elephant.

I would recommend this to a friend who likes animals.

Magaly Fernandez

Cultural Diversity

Protecting Endangered Species

Sometimes an animal that is protected in one country is hunted and killed in another. Different nations rely on different animals for food and resources. Japan and Norway, for example, have ancient whaling traditions and have continued to hunt whales even after much of the world stopped whaling in the late twentieth century. The nations of the world continue to negotiate for the uniform protection of endangered animals around the globe.

ASSESS

Evaluation Guidelines for Discussion

As your students discuss the selection, either in small groups or as a class, encourage them to begin with a personal response. The student responses on this page might be used as a starting point.

Look for evidence that students

- have read the selection
- can state some of the writer's ideas in their own words
- understand the writer's point of view
- have connected the content to their own knowledge and experiences
- understand the ideas and implications of the selection

Some possible responses to the discussion questions of this page:

1. The author presents the steps in the order in which they occurred.
2. She uses transition words such as *now* and *at this point* that show how the steps relate in time.
3. She covers the relationship between the elephants and the keepers and some differences between life in the zoo and life in the wild.
4. Dialogue is a good way to demonstrate how the keepers feel about the elephants.

CLOSE

Point out that although many people think zoos are a means of preserving endangered animals, others believe zoos are cruel and exploitive places. Encourage students to discuss some of the pros and cons of taking animals out of their natural environment in order to protect them. Students might find it helpful to imagine themselves a zoo animal and then argue both sides.

REVIEW

Reflecting on the Unit

You may have students respond to Reflecting on the Unit in writing or through discussion.

Writing Across the Curriculum

Students may find it helpful to work with a partner as they complete their Venn diagrams. Remind students that creating a separate paragraph for each main idea makes their work easier to read.

Adding to Your Portfolio

Suggest that students work in pairs to select portfolio samples. Acting as peer reviewers, students can help their partners make their portfolio selections.

Portfolio Evaluation

If you grade the portfolio selections, you may want to award two marks—one each for content and form. Explain your assessment criteria before students make their selections. Commend

- experimentation with creative prewriting techniques
- clear, concise writing in which the main idea, audience, and purpose are evident
- successful revisions
- work that shows a flair for language

Unit 5 Review

Reflecting on the Unit

Summarize what you learned in this unit by answering the following questions.

- What are some different kinds of expository writing and the purpose of each?
- What prewriting methods can you use to organize information for a comparison-contrast essay?
- What strategies can help you write a clear explanation of a process?
- How do you gather information for a research report?
- What are the six main parts of a book report?

Adding to Your Portfolio

Choose a selection for your portfolio. Look over the expository writing you did for this unit. Choose a completed piece for your portfolio. The piece you select should show some or all of the following:

- for a comparison-contrast essay, details organized from a prewriting list, chart, drawings, or Venn diagram
- for a process explanation, steps presented in a clear order and with transitions to link them
- for a report, information gathered through research
- a clear introduction, body, and conclusion

Reflect on your choice. Attach a note to the piece you chose, explaining briefly why you chose it and what you learned from writing it.

Set goals. How can you improve your writing? What skill will you focus on the next time you write?

Writing Across the Curriculum

Make a history connection. Scan your history textbook and identify two people to compare and contrast—perhaps two political leaders or two explorers. List details about each person and create a Venn diagram showing the similarities and differences. Organize your findings, and then draft a short comparison-contrast essay.

Teacher's Classroom Resources

The following resources can be used for planning, assessment, or evaluation.

Unit Assessment

Tests with Answer Key
Unit 5 Choice A Test, p. 17
Unit 5 Choice B Test, p. 18
Unit 5 Composition Objective Test, pp. 19–20

Test Generator
Unit 5 Choice A Test
Unit 5 Choice B Test
Unit 5 Composition Objective Test

You may wish to administer one of these tests as a mastery test.

UNIT 6

Persuasive Writing

Composition

Lessons

UNIT GOALS

The goal of Unit 6 is to help students, through example and instruction, to develop an understanding of and ability to use persuasive writing concepts and techniques. The lessons focus on taking a position, making a statement, and using facts and opinions to support a position. The Case Study concerns a Children's Television Workshop program about sharing the world's resources.

Unit Assessment

Tests with Answer Key
Unit 6 Choice A Test, p. 21
Unit 6 Choice B Test, p. 22
Unit 6 Composition Objective Test, pp. 23–24

Test Generator
Unit 6 Choice A Test
Unit 6 Choice B Test
Unit 6 Composition Objective Test

You may wish to administer either the Unit 6 Choice A Test or the Unit 6 Choice B Test as a pretest.

Key to Ability Levels

Enabling Strategies have been coded for varying learning styles and abilities.

L1 Level 1 activities are within the ability range of Learning Disabled students.

L2 Level 2 activities are basic-to-average activities and are within the ability range of average students.

L3 Level 3 activities are challenging activities and are within the ability range of above-average students.

LEP LEP activities are within the ability range of Limited English Proficiency students.

Setting the Purpose

In the Unit 6 Case Study, students examine the use of persuasive writing in creating a script for a television program. Students will explore and practice persuasive writing in the lessons that follow.

FOCUS

Lesson Overview

Objective: To observe the process of creating an effective persuasive script and to identify the attributes of persuasive writing in a television script
Skills: researching; outlining and writing a script; planning a one-minute TV message
Critical Thinking: using prior knowledge; solving problems
Speaking and Listening: discussing

Bellringer

When students come into the classroom, have this assignment on the board: *Write an imaginary conversation between friends in which one tries to persuade the other to recycle paper.*

Grammar Link to the Bellringer
Have students check what they write for correct uses of commas with quotations.

Motivating Activity

Ask students what they know about how television programs are produced. When television producers, or others, have an idea for a program, how do they go about creating it? (Possible steps include research, planning, writing a script, choosing the visuals, filming, and so on.)

UNIT 6 PREVIEW
Case Study

Persuasive Writing
in the Real World

Anderson Fights for the Planet

F O C U S: A strong position based on solid research and vivid writing—these are the ingredients of powerful persuasion.

Television Script Writer Douglas Anderson

As the 1980s slipped into the 1990s, more and more people worried about planet Earth. Almost daily, news stories pointed out problems: acid rain, water pollution, global warming.

The producers at Children's Television Workshop (CTW) decided to begin work on a series of programs about threats to the earth. They planned to look at what may be the biggest problem of all: the way millions of people use resources. CTW asked television writer Douglas Anderson to produce a script describing the situation and persuading viewers to think about their actions.

Teacher's Classroom Resources

The following resources can be used for planning, instruction, practice, reinforcement, assessment, or evaluation.

Teaching Tools
Lesson Plans

Transparencies
Writing Process Transparencies, 20–22B

Writing a Television Program

Prewriting	Drafting	Revising/Presenting

Researching and Outlining	Writing the Script	Rewriting the Script

"Rule number one in persuasive writing is that you have to know what you're talking about. . . . Number two, telling people what to think doesn't work. Very often the most persuasive thing you can do is to set out the facts and let people develop their own ideas."

—Doug Anderson

Conservation of resources is a topic that concerns everyone. During the research stage, the CTW staff read about and discussed this issue.

Prewriting

RESEARCHING AND OUTLINING

Work on the series began with careful research. As Anderson said, "You don't necessarily know your position on an issue before you start researching."

CTW staff helped Anderson learn more about people and resources. Researcher Vivian Trakinski received information from the National Science Foundation. Scientist Edward Atkins suggested books and articles on resources for Anderson to read.

TEACH

Building Background

Warm-up:
Have students list as many occasions as they can where persuasive writing might be used.

Persuasion in Speaking:
Remind students that to be persuasive they must state their point and persuade others to agree. First, they must build up a case using examples and logical thinking; then they must back it up with facts or expert opinion. Tell students that they use persuasion every day, such as when they persuade a reluctant friend to go to the movies or talk someone into recycling a soft drink can instead of throwing it out.

Invite students to talk about times when they have stated an opinion or used persuasion to change someone's mind.

Persuasion in Writing:
Discuss any persuasive writing students have read. Use prompts such as the following:

- Have you ever seen an advertisement in a newspaper or magazine that made you want to go out and buy the product? What kind of words did the writers use?
- What issues have you seen written about in newspaper letters to the editor? How did the writers make their points convincing?

Preview the Case Study

Have students preview the title and focus of the Case Study. Discuss with them how television programs are able to influence people's opinions. Have students read the case study.

Blackline Masters

Cooperative Learning Activities, pp. 31–36
Thinking and Study Skills, pp. 3, 5, 22, 38
Research Paper and Report Writing, p. 33
Vocabulary and Spelling Practice, p. 6
Case Studies: Writing in the Real World, pp. 21–24

Assessment

Teacher's Guide to Writing Assessment

TEACH

Discussion Prompts

- Why is research important? How does research help to develop ideas for the program? Why does Anderson say, "All the neat ideas for the show come out of this [research] work?"
- Why might it be important to state a position before starting to write a persuasive piece? How does Anderson organize ideas, facts, and examples to back up his position?

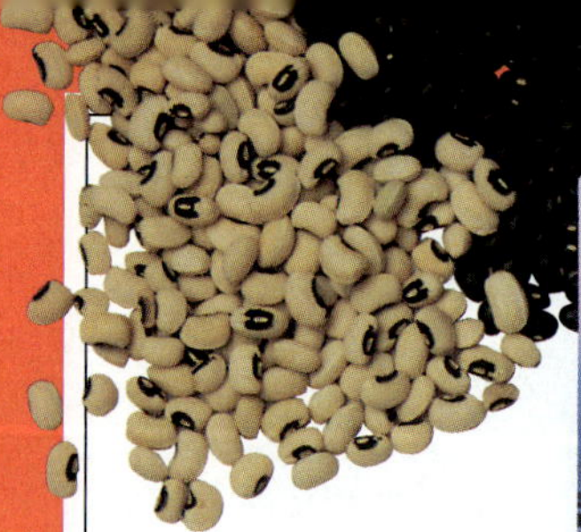

In the outline Anderson wanted to make clear the connection between conservation and resources.

Anderson and the CTW staff learned that the human population has reached five billion and that it is using vital resources at an alarming rate. Researching was important to Anderson. "In any kind of writing you have a responsibility to get the facts right. All the neat ideas for the show come out of this work."

Their research completed, the group then stated the program's position: To avoid running out of resources, people need to conserve and share.

Using this position and the facts uncovered in research, Anderson drafted an outline for the program. "This is where you define the ideas you want to convey and the order in which you want to say them," he said. He shared the outline with Trakinski, Atkins, and the producer.

The group discussed points in the script. Finally, they agreed on a two-page outline for "A Popular Little Planet," as the show would be called. The program would make three points: First, five billion people now live on the planet. Second, people gobble up resources. Sometimes they fight over resources because there aren't enough to go around. Third, there are ways people can help solve this problem. By sharing and conserving resources, people can make sure there is enough for everyone.

Cultural Diversity

Creating a Shared Culture

Because it reaches millions of viewers daily, television has become a powerful persuasive tool. Recent surveys show that United States households watch an average of seven hours of television a day. Discuss with students the role television plays in creating a shared culture.

Remind students of the television coverage of a recent crisis during which people across the nation shared information and experienced many of the same emotional responses. This is one way television creates a shared culture.

Drafting

WRITING THE SCRIPT

Anderson now had to figure out how to use the resources of television to make his points. He said, "I knew I could use everything from music to cartoons and graphics."

To write the program's script, Anderson had to think of ways to dramatize each point. How, for example, could he show the alarming amount of resources people use? Anderson wrote a scene in which Z, one of the actors, lists the things that belong to just one person. Z says, "The average American, over a lifetime, is going to use resources like 100 million gallons of water, 300 bushels of apples, oil, underwear, paper, and 147 pairs of shoelaces. . . . And that's just for one person. . . . Do we have enough stuff?"

To answer that question, Anderson wrote a scene in which Z and his partner, Stephanie, decide to make cookies and brownies. The problem? They each have only half the ingredients they need.

In the scene Stephanie and Z fight over the ingredients. "Then," Anderson said, "they realize that by sharing resources each person can have what he wants."

Anderson ended the segment with a real-life example of people and resources. He showed a film about water shortages in California, where 30 million people live. The point was clear: People must conserve water so that everyone will have enough.

◄ By listing the items that each person uses in a lifetime, Anderson brought a large problem into dramatic perspective. This was one method Anderson used in writing the program.

TEACH

Discussion Prompts

- What kind of facts did Anderson use to explain his point? Were they effective? Did they make you stop and think?
- Why did Anderson try to use fun examples to make his point? Do you think a show like his would be entertaining?

Connections Across the Curriculum

Social Studies

Relate the topic of the Case Study to local problems in the use of resources. Encourage students to find out what the local problems are, why they exist, what the community is doing about them, and how students and their families can help. Some students might wish to formulate a main-idea statement for a piece of persuasive writing.

TEACH

Guided Practice

L2 Discussion
Stimulate a discussion of the Case Study. You may also want to invite students to talk about

- how the writing process for creating a persuasive television program is the process they have used for other modes of writing
- how the television program was able to make the persuasive points dramatic
- how the revising stage was important in preparing the final script

Independent Practice

Writing Process Transparencies, 20–22B
Cooperative Learning Activities, pp. 31–36
Case Studies: Writing in the Real World, pp. 21–24

Skills Practice

Thinking and Study Skills, pp. 3, 5, 22, 38
Research Paper and Report Writing, p. 33
Vocabulary and Spelling Practice, p. 6

Anderson thinks these scenes were persuasive for several reasons. First, they were energetic and entertaining. Just as important, ideas were organized to draw viewers in step by step. "Using fun examples, we built up to the point we wanted to make," he said.

Revising/Presenting

REWRITING THE SCRIPT

When revising, Anderson had to make certain the program was energetic and entertaining. He says, "If viewers get bored and turn off the show, all the good facts in the world don't mean a thing."

Anderson's draft went through many reviews and revisions at CTW. First, the producer checked to be sure the show would entertain and persuade. Then the science adviser checked it for accuracy. CTW executives and students also reviewed the script. Anderson used everyone's comments to write a second draft, and after that he prepared a third version. Finally, several months later, after taping and editing were complete, "A Popular Little Planet" went on the air.

Did the program persuade people to use resources more carefully? "There's no way of knowing for sure whether people started behaving differently," Anderson said. "But we did get a lot of mail, and the mail was wonderful."

Civic Literacy

Shaping Opinions
Persuasive writing is one way of contributing to the informed discussion of issues that is part of democratic decision-making. Because so many people rely on television for information, persuasive television programs play an important role in shaping public debate. You might use an issue currently in the news, such as an election campaign or a job shortage, as an example of how television informs people and helps to shape their opinions.

Responding to the Case Study

1. Discussion

Discuss these questions about Doug Anderson's writing.

- What was the main goal of Anderson's script?
- What kinds of work did Anderson and his co-workers do before he wrote the script for the program?
- After Anderson drafted the script, what kinds of review and revision did it go through?
- How does Anderson describe the public's response to the finished program?

2. Persuasive Writing

Plan a one-minute TV message to persuade people to create less trash.

Brainstorm some ideas for the opening. You might use the photograph on this page as your starting place. Remember that you can use interviews, pictures, and music to help get your message across. Choose your most persuasive idea. Write a few lines of narrative or dialogue, and describe the images viewers will see.

Grammar Link

Use commas to set off direct quotations.

"Then," Anderson said, "they realize that by sharing resources each person can have what he wants."

Write the following sentences, adding commas to set off the quotations.

1. "Our trash disposal is a big problem" said the mayor.
2. "We hope" she continued "that the recycling program will help."
3. A reporter asked "Will the recycling include magazines?"
4. "Not until next year" a council member answered.
5. "For details" the mayor added "read the brochure we are mailing to each home."

See Lesson 19.4, page 460.

ASSESS

Responding to the Case Study

1. Discussion

- to inform and persuade people to save resources
- researched books and articles, stated their position, outlined the program
- reviewed by the producer, the science adviser, and the CTW executives and students
- received lots of mail

2. Persuasive Writing

Answers will vary but should include a position statement backed up with facts and examples.

See also the *Teacher's Guide to Writing Assessment.*

Grammar Link

(See Using the Grammar Link below.)

Reteaching

Review Anderson's words on page 211. Stress the importance of giving people the facts they need to make judgments.

Enrichment

Encourage students to suggest ways of dramatizing global warming or other environmental issues, such as the preservation of rain forests.

CLOSE

Ask students how Anderson dramatized the need to share resources. Then ask them to think of another way to dramatize the same point.

Closing Note

For more information on conservation, refer students to publications such as *Audubon, Garbage,* or *Worldwatch.*

Using the Grammar Link

Grammar Link Answers

1. ". . . big problem," said the mayor.
2. "We hope," she continued, "that . . ."
3. A reporter asked, "Will the . . . "
4. "Not until next year," a council . . .
5. "For details," the mayor added, "read the brochure we are mailing . . . "

Using Commas Have students check the dialogue they wrote for the one-minute TV message for correct use of commas to set off direct quotations.

Setting the Purpose

Lesson 6.1 teaches students how to write persuasively by stating a position and supporting it with appropriate evidence.

FOCUS

Lesson Overview

Objective: To write a position statement with two support statements
Skills: stating a goal; selecting support evidence; avoiding sentence fragments
Critical Thinking: analyzing; evaluating; using criteria
Speaking and Listening: discussing

Bellringer

When students enter the classroom, have this assignment on the board: *Write five sentences trying to persuade your parents to let you have a pet (or another pet).*

Grammar Link to the Bellringer

Have students check the sentences they have written for sentence fragments. Ask them to complete all sentence fragments.

Motivating Activity

Ask students if they have ever approached a cat or a dog that they did not know. What did they do? How did the animal react? Discuss whether it is okay to pet a strange dog or cat. Have students jot down their ideas in a brief paragraph.

LESSON 6.1

Persuasive Writing
Taking a Stand

One purpose of persuasive writing is to make readers think or feel a certain way about an idea or a product. Another purpose is to make readers take action. Sometimes it does both. What is the writer's goal in the model below?

Literature Model

Most dogs are very friendly once they get to know you. But, like people, dogs don't always want to be friends right away. They need time to get acquainted and decide that you're okay.

Don't make the mistake of trying to pet or hug a strange dog. You wouldn't like it if someone you didn't know ran up and hugged you. Most dogs don't like it either.

Dr. Ann Squire,
101 Questions and Answers About Pets and People

What does the writer tell you that might lead you to approach dogs carefully?

Teacher's Classroom Resources

The following resources can be used for planning, instruction, practice, reinforcement, assessment, reteaching, enrichment, or evaluation.

Teaching Tools
Lesson Plans, p. 4[illegible]

Transparencies
Fine Art Transparencies, 26–30
Writing Process Transparencies, 20–22B

Blackline Masters
Thinking and Study Skills, pp. 5–7, 9, 20
Writing Across the Curriculum, pp. 21–22
Cooperative Learning Activities, pp. 31–36

What Does It Take to Convince You?

Often persuasive writing begins by stating the writer's goal. Then evidence—information to support that goal—follows. Some support statements will make you think ("The rain forest is disappearing at the rate of . . ."). Some support statements will make you feel a certain way ("You won't fit in unless you wear . . ."). Finally, there is usually a reminder of what the writer wants you to think or do.

As a reader, you need to think carefully about the support presented in persuasive writing. After all, the writer is trying to change your thoughts or actions. Based on the excerpt on page 216, do you agree with the support statement in the chart below?

Drafting Tip

When drafting, make sure your main idea, or position, comes across in a sharp, clear statement. A single sentence usually works best.

Goal	Support
Do not hug or pet a strange dog.	Dogs don't always want to be friends right away.

Journal Writing

List in your journal three examples of persuasive writing you have read recently. Have any persuaded you to change your thoughts or actions? Write a brief paragraph explaining why or why not.

TEACH

Guided Practice

L2 Using the Model

Ask students to identify the sentence that states the writer's main point. ("Don't make the mistake of trying to pet or hug a strange dog.") Ask what the writer says that might affect the way the students approach dogs. (The writer compares dogs to people in that neither necessarily want to be friendly right away.)

L1 Identifying Persuasion

Ask students to identify examples of persuasive writing they come across every day (advertisements, billboards, posters, letters to the editor, editorial cartoons, reviews of movies or TV shows, political campaign speeches). Stress that the purpose of persuasive writing is to bring about change. Ask what kind of change the writer of each example hopes to bring about. (Students should identify changes in both thoughts and actions.)

Two-Minute Skill Drill

List these sentences on the board and have students choose the more persuasive sentence and explain why.

Wear Spikes air pump sneakers and you will fly to the basket.

Buy Spikes sneakers if you want to play basketball.

Journal Writing Tip

Evaluating Ideas Encourage students to cite persuasive appeals that actually did persuade them. What made these appeals effective? Some students might also describe unsuccessful appeals, explaining why these didn't work.

Assessment

Speaking and Listening Activities, pp. 22, 28
Composition Practice, p. 45
Composition Reteaching, p. 45
Composition Enrichment, p. 45

Teacher's Guide to Writing Assessment
Tests with Answer Key
Unit 6 Choice A Test, p. 21
Unit 6 Choice B Test, p. 22

Test Generator
Unit 6 Choice A Test
Unit 6 Choice B Test

You may wish to administer either the Unit 6 Choice A Test or the Unit 6 Choice B Test as a pretest.

TEACH

Guided Practice

L2 Comparing and Contrasting

To highlight some persuasive appeals used in advertising, you might ask students to pick ads for two brands of the same type of product and compare and contrast the effectiveness of each, based on the students' own responses. Another useful comparison might be how the same product or kind of product is advertised in a magazine with a teen-age audience and in a magazine with an adult audience.

L3 Changing the Audience

Challenge students to identify ways in which the letter on this page might be rewritten to appeal to a different audience, such as the girl's grandmother. Discuss changes they might make in the choice of arguments or language. Encourage students to mention a few specific details they'd include to persuade their own grandmother, or another adult, to visit.

Independent Practice

- For further stimuli for persuasive writing, see *Fine Art Transparencies,* 26–30.
- *Writing Process Transparencies,* 20–22B
- *Writing Across the Curriculum,* pp. 21–22
- *Cooperative Learning Activities,* pp. 31–36

Skills Practice

- *Thinking and Study Skills,* pp. 5–7, 9, 20
- *Composition Practice,* p. 45
- *Speaking and Listening Activities,* pp. 22, 28

How Often Do You Persuade?

Persuasive writing can take many forms, from a 500-page book to a few words on a billboard. It can even exist in friendly letters or cards.

Suppose that you want to persuade a friend who lives out of town to visit you during the summer. You might make up a package including posters, brochures, and articles about the attractions of your home town. You could present your best persuasive ideas in a letter like the one at the left. Read it to see where Rachel put her main idea and her support.

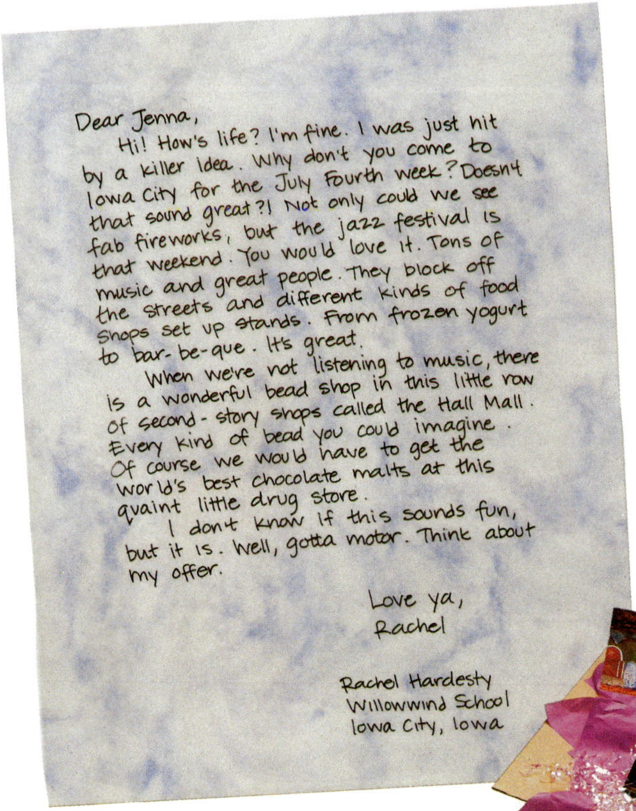
Dear Jenna,

Hi! How's life? I'm fine. I was just hit by a killer idea. Why don't you come to Iowa City for the July Fourth week? Doesn't that sound great?! Not only could we see fab fireworks, but the jazz festival is that weekend. You would love it. Tons of music and great people. They block off the streets and different kinds of food shops set up stands. From frozen yogurt to bar-be-que. It's great.

When we're not listening to music, there is a wonderful bead shop in this little row of second-story shops called the Hall Mall. Every kind of bead you could imagine. Of course we would have to get the world's best chocolate malts at this quaint little drug store.

I don't know if this sounds fun, but it is. Well, gotta motor. Think about my offer.

Love ya,
Rachel

Rachel Hardesty
Willowwind School
Iowa City, Iowa

Enabling Strategies

LEP Getting the Message

Students will benefit from seeing visual examples of persuasive writing. Bring in magazine and newspaper ads, editorials, brochures, and other materials to display and discuss. Ask volunteers to bring in their own examples. Work with students to identify the main persuasive messages in each example and the thoughts or actions they aim to change. Point out the evidence used in each example.

6.1 Writing Activities

Create a Persuasive Poster

Make a poster to convince students to wear safety equipment when biking or skateboarding. Use photos or drawings to reinforce your words.

- State clearly your main goal.
- Give at least two support statements.
- End with a reminder of what you want people to think or do.

PURPOSE To persuade others to use safety equipment
AUDIENCE Other students
LENGTH 1 page

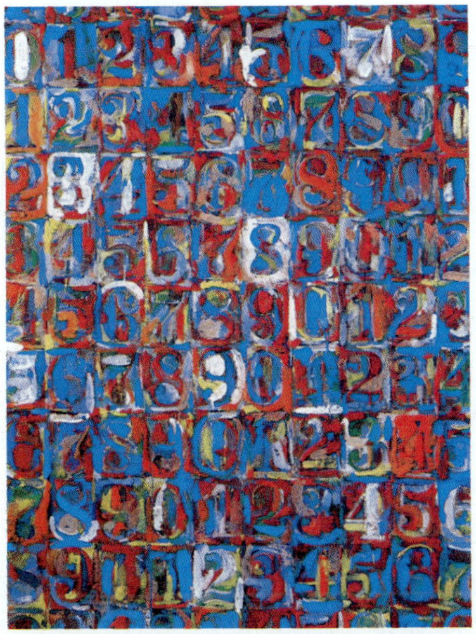

Jasper Johns, *Numbers in Color*, 1958–1959

Cross-Curricular: Art

Study the reproduction of *Numbers in Color* on this page, and then state your opinion of it. Supply at least two support statements to back up your opinion. Be persuasive!

Grammar Link

Avoid sentence fragments in your writing.

A *fragment* is a group of words that does not present a complete thought and may lack a subject, a predicate, or both. In formal writing, fragments can be confusing.

Revise each sentence fragment below to make a complete sentence.

1. Tons of music and great people.
2. From frozen yogurt to barbeque.
3. Every kind of bead you could imagine.
4. Not only fireworks but the jazz festival.
5. The best chocolate malts at this little drug store.

See Lesson 8.2, page 264.

Using the Grammar Link

Grammar Link Answers

Answers will vary, but some suggestions are given.

1. The party had tons of music . . .
2. The buffet had everything from . . .
3. . . . could imagine was in the store.
4. . . . jazz festival takes place.
5. I've had the best chocolate . . .

About the Art

Jasper Johns, *Numbers in Color*, 1958–1959
Johns's patterns, brushstrokes, and colors allow viewers to see familiar objects in new and exciting ways. *Numbers in Color*, 66 1/2 by 49 1/2 inches, Albright Knox Art Gallery, Buffalo, New York.

ASSESS

Writing Activities Evaluation Guidelines

Create a Persuasive Poster

Use these criteria when evaluating your students' writing.

- A position statement is clearly stated.
- Support statements are based on facts or logical examples.
- The poster reflects the interests of the targeted audience (other students).

See also the *Teacher's Guide to Writing Assessment.*

Cross-curricular: Art

Students' opinions may be positive or negative but should be supported with appropriate facts and examples.

Grammar Link

(See Using the Grammar Link below.)

Reteaching

Composition Reteaching, p. 45

Enrichment

Composition Enrichment, p. 45

Use *Fine Art Transparencies* 26–30 for enrichment activities also.

CLOSE

Have students write a persuasive letter based on an issue in their own lives, such as asking a parent for permission to attend an event or trying to persuade a teacher that video games can be educational. Encourage students to work with a peer reviewer. Students may wish to send off their letters to see if they really work!

Setting the Purpose

Lesson 6.2 teaches students the importance of adapting their persuasive writing to the target audience.

FOCUS

Lesson Overview

Objective: To present a position with a main-idea statement and supporting evidence that will appeal to its particular audience
Skills: writing a letter; capitalizing proper nouns and adjectives
Critical Thinking: evaluating; defining problems; identifying main ideas; using criteria
Speaking and Listening: discussing; speaking persuasively

Bellringer

When students enter the classroom, have this assignment on the board: *Think of an item you would like to sell. Write a brief paragraph telling how you would advertise it.*

Grammar Link to the Bellringer

Have students check their sentences for proper capitalization.

Motivating Activity

Have students write three persuasive slogans that could be used as advertisements for the items they wrote about in the Bellringer. Tell students to keep their audience in mind as they write the slogans. Ask students how the slogans might be changed if a different audience were targeted.

LESSON 6.2

Persuasive Writing
Stating a Position

Do I know enough about this topic?

When you have a goal you really care about, the challenge is winning over your audience.

As you choose a goal for your persuasive piece, answer the questions in the chart below. If you can answer *yes* to each question, you've found a good topic.

Finding a Persuasive Writing Topic

- Do I know enough about this topic?
- Do I care about this topic?
- Do people disagree about this topic?

The students at one school have several ideas for projects. Some want to put in a juice machine to raise money for new computers. Some want to start a garden to grow vegetables for a food pantry. Some want to organize an ethnic festival to celebrate different cultures. If you were the student council representative to the school board, it would be your job to persuade the school board to adopt one of the ideas.

Do I care about this topic?

Do people disagree on this topic?

Teacher's Classroom Resources

The following resources can be used for planning, instruction, practice, reinforcement, assessment, reteaching, enrichment, or evaluation.

Teaching Tools
Lesson Plans

Transparencies
Fine Art Transparencies, 26–30
Writing Process Transparencies, 20–22B

Give Reasons

Why should people adopt your ideas? You need to provide convincing reasons.

The proposal written by last year's representative to the school board appears below. Notice the clear organization and persuasive sound of the letter.

Grammar
Editing Tip

When you write a letter that speaks for a group or an organization, be sure to use the right pronouns. For more information on pronouns, see Lessons 11.1–11.5, pages 326–335.

Model

Dear Ms. Perez and the school board:

For this year's student project, we would like to set up paper-recycling bins at key places around the school. This project will benefit the school in several ways. It will give students a chance to improve the environment by cutting down on waste. It will encourage students from all grades to work together to set up and run the recycling project. It will also help raise money we can use for future projects.

We would like to put a recycling bin in each classroom. A group of students will be chosen each week to collect the bins and set them out for pickup. A permanent group will oversee the project with Mr. Hansen, the science teacher. With your support, this project will be a success.

Note that the first sentence is a statement of the main goal.

What reasons does the student provide in support of the proposal?

Journal Writing

Take two minutes to list as many persuasive-writing topics as you can. Circle those topics to which you can answer *yes* for all three of the questions on page 220. Why are some topics not circled? Change these enough so that you can circle them. Keep these topics for use in future projects.

TEACH

Guided Practice

L2 Using the Model

Ask students to identify the main purpose of each paragraph. (The first paragraph states the main idea and presents three benefits of the project. The second paragraph explains how the project would work.) Ask students how this letter might change if it were being written to the students instead of to the school board.

L1 Using a Visual

A visual might help students understand how evidence is used to support a main idea. Draw a triangular "roof" on the chalkboard, and write *Main Idea* on it. Below the roof, draw three supporting "pillars," writing *Evidence* on each one. Next, draw the same diagram on the board, without words, and invite volunteers to write the model's main idea and supporting details on its roof and pillars. Point out that just as pillars support a roof, pieces of evidence work together to support an opinion.

Two-Minute Skill Drill

Write this topic on the board and have students list three pieces of supporting evidence:

Support Paper Recycling!

Blackline Masters

Thinking and Study Skills, pp. 1–2, 4–5, 13, 20
Writing Across the Curriculum, pp. 21–22
Cooperative Learning Activities, pp. 31–36
Speaking and Listening Activities, pp. 22, 28
Composition Practice, p. 46
Composition Reteaching, p. 46
Composition Enrichment, p. 46

Assessment

Teacher's Guide to Writing Assessment

Journal Writing Tip

Evaluating Ideas You might suggest that students use a prewriting technique, such as clustering or listing. This will help them to determine whether they know enough about a topic and to revise some of their topics for later use.

TEACH

Guided Practice

L2 Using a Thesaurus

Ask students what special projects they'd like to have the school or the sixth-grade class undertake. Then have students explain how they'd go about trying to persuade the school board or principal to adopt their projects. (Include benefits to the school, to the community, and to students.) Ask the class to tell what reasons would be effective or ineffective, helping them identify those that might be especially appealing to their targeted audience.

L3 Choosing Words

Ask small groups of students to choose a school policy they would like to see changed. Ask them to propose a change, such as giving students a say in planning the lunch menus. Each group should identify the types of people they might need to persuade (parents, teachers, school board members, fellow students) and discuss what points would appeal to each audience. Then each team member should choose one of these audiences and write a letter proposing the policy change.

Independent Practice

For further stimuli for persuasive writing, see *Fine Art Transparencies* 26–30.

Writing Process Transparencies, 20–22B

Writing Across the Curriculum, pp. 21–22

Cooperative Learning Activities, pp. 31–36

Skills Practice

Thinking and Study Skills, pp. 1–2, 4–5, 13, 20

Speaking and Listening Activities, pp. 22, 28

Composition Practice, p. 46

Presenting Tip

Choose the form that best presents your argument. Will you send a letter or face your audience in person? The form of presentation may affect how you state your ideas.

Consider Your Audience

Whenever you try to convince someone of something, you need to keep your audience in mind. For example, imagine that you're trying to get your family to plan a day of activities in the city. You might spark your sister's interest by telling her about the great restaurants. Your mom might take more interest in the museums. The street performers might appeal more to your brother.

Different people have different interests and different levels of knowledge. Choose reasons that appeal to your audience. One student's goal was to argue for the ethnic festival. She sent a letter to the school board and another letter to the students. Her goal was the same, but at least one of her reasons was different. Why?

An ethnic festival will build pride and help students understand cultures different from their own.

The reason for the school board focuses on what the festival will teach students. The reason statement for students focuses on how much fun the festival will be.

An ethnic festival will give us a chance to enjoy sharing many different foods and customs.

Enabling Strategies

LEP Examining Advertisements

Supply students with a stack of magazines. Have students search through the magazines to find examples of persuasive writing in the advertisements. Work with students to find the main idea or position statement and identify the supporting evidence. Point out that sometimes ads rely on visual information rather than writing. Ask students how the illustrations can be persuasive.

6.2 Writing Activities

Write a Persuasive Proposal

Choose a project that your sixth-grade class might do in the school or in the community. Explain your idea in a written proposal to your teacher or the school principal.

- State your goal clearly.
- Follow it with supporting reasons that will appeal to your audience.

PURPOSE To practice persuading an adult audience
AUDIENCE Your teacher or principal
LENGTH 2–4 paragraphs

Grammar Link

Capitalize proper nouns and adjectives.

Capitalize the names of languages, countries, and nationalities in the list. You will need to capitalize 10 words.

1. haitian, chinese, and italian food
2. art from mexico
3. tapes of irish, israeli, and russian music
4. jewelry from india and greece
5. a cuban band

See Lesson 18.4, page 444.

Cooperative Learning

The principal of the school in the painting has decided to admit boys to the school next year. In a small group, brainstorm ideas for how you might persuade the girls' parents to accept boys in the school. First decide on a goal statement. Then list the arguments, or reasons, that might be most persuasive. Role-play possibilities with the group.

Allan Rohan Crite, *School's Out*, 1936

ASSESS

Writing Activities Evaluation Guidelines

Write a Persuasive Proposal

Use these criteria when evaluating your students' writing:

- Is the main idea or position presented clearly?
- Do the supporting reasons reflect an awareness of the needs and interests of the stated audience (teacher or principal)?

See also the *Teacher's Guide to Writing Assessment.*

Cooperative Learning

Students should collaborate in determining the goal statement. The reasons presented should indicate an awareness of the audience.

Grammar Link

(See Using the Grammar Link below.)

Reteaching

Composition Reteaching, p. 46

Enrichment

Composition Enrichment, p. 46

Use *Fine Art Transparencies* 26–30 for enrichment activities also.

CLOSE

Discuss how ordinary citizens might use persuasive writing to make changes in their communities. (They might write letters to the editor and to their legislators, write pamphlets or fliers to distribute to neighbors, or create posters to display.)

Using the Grammar Link

Grammar Link Answers

1. Haitian, Chinese, Italian
2. Mexico
3. Irish, Israeli, Russian
4. India, Greece
5. Cuban

About the Art

Allan Rohan Crite, *School's Out*, 1936
This 30 1/4-by-36 1/8-inch oil presents an after-school scene. Use this lively picture to spark comments about the benefits and drawbacks of all-girl, all-boy, and co-ed schools. This oil is in the National Museum of American Art in Washington, D.C.

Setting the Purpose

In Lesson 6.3, students are taught to differentiate between facts and opinions as supporting evidence for persuasive writing.

FOCUS

Lesson Overview

Objective: To use facts and opinions to support a position in a piece of persuasive writing
Skills: gathering evidence; organizing facts and opinions
Critical Thinking: classifying facts and opinions; ordering
Speaking and Listening: discussing

Bellringer

When students enter the classroom, have this assignment on the board: *Write a sentence that lists at least three animals that would make unusual pets.*

Grammar Link to the Bellringer

Remind students that items in a series must have commas to separate them. Have students check the sentences they wrote for commas within a series.

Motivating Activity

Ask students: *Have you ever had a pet snake or any other unusual pet? Would you recommend that pet to a friend? Why or why not?* Then have students jot down their ideas for possible class pets. Discuss their ideas, including the reasons students give. You might make a chart, writing each suggestion as a heading near the top of the chalkboard and listing pieces of supporting evidence under each heading.

LESSON **6.3**

Persuasive Writing
Using Facts and Opinions

What kinds of evidence will you use to support your goal and your reasons?

Each year Mrs. Van's class chooses a class pet. Her students write persuasive papers, arguing for their choice. What pet would you argue for? What evidence could you present to prove your point?

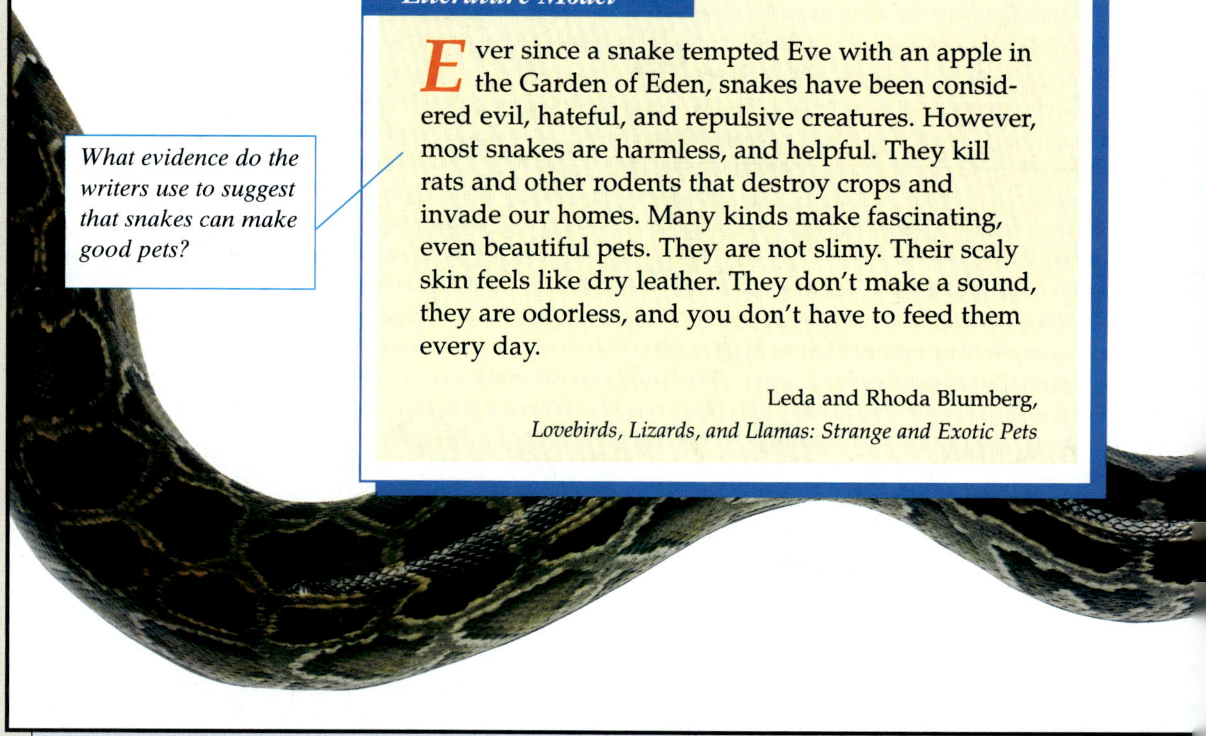

What evidence do the writers use to suggest that snakes can make good pets?

Literature Model

Ever since a snake tempted Eve with an apple in the Garden of Eden, snakes have been considered evil, hateful, and repulsive creatures. However, most snakes are harmless, and helpful. They kill rats and other rodents that destroy crops and invade our homes. Many kinds make fascinating, even beautiful pets. They are not slimy. Their scaly skin feels like dry leather. They don't make a sound, they are odorless, and you don't have to feed them every day.

Leda and Rhoda Blumberg,
Lovebirds, Lizards, and Llamas: Strange and Exotic Pets

Teacher's Classroom Resources

The following resources can be used for planning, instruction, practice, reinforcement, assessment, reteaching, enrichment, or evaluation

Teaching Tools
Lesson Plans

Transparencies
Fine Art Transparencies, 26–30
Writing Process Transparencies, 20–22B

Gather the Evidence

You believe that a snake would be the perfect class pet. How can you persuade your classmates and your teacher? Persuading people to change their attitudes or to take action requires evidence. Evidence comes in two forms: facts and opinions.

Facts Facts are statements that can be proved. For example, the statement "They are not slimy" is a fact. You could prove it by touching a snake or by reading about snakes.

Opinions An opinion is a personal belief or feeling. It can't be proved. The authors of the excerpt on page 224 think that snakes make fascinating pets. Because the authors are experts, you would probably believe them. The opinions of experts can be powerful evidence. Personal experience can also be good evidence. A person who has a lot of experience is often considered an expert.

Journal Writing

Select a persuasive article from a newspaper or magazine, and identify the goal. Save the article in your journal. Make notes in your journal about how facts and opinions support the goal.

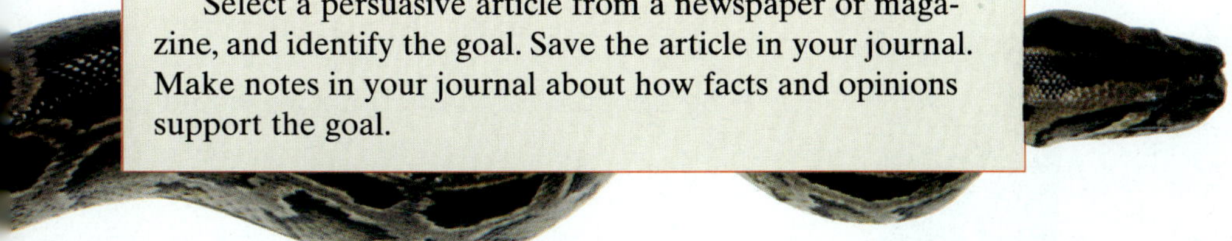

Prewriting Tip

As you gather evidence, write down the source of each fact or opinion you intend to use.

TEACH

Guided Practice

L2 Using the Model

Have students explain what evidence the writer uses to prove that snakes make good pets. (Most snakes are harmless, and they don't make noise, don't smell, and don't need to be fed every day.) Invite students to add any other reasons they think of. (the educational value of observing a snake closely)

L2 Comparing Results

Use the following Partners activity. Students form teams of four, each working with a partner. Each team creates a main idea statement about a pet they'd like to have in the classroom. Each partner pair makes a list of evidence supporting the main-idea statement. Encourage students to think of examples for each type of evidence shown in the chart on this page. Have students compare their results with those of the other partner pair in their team.

Two-Minute Skill Drill

Write the following on the board and ask students to write whether each is a fact or an opinion:

Some snakes are 30 feet long.
Snakes are fun to watch.

Journal Writing Tip

Evaluating ideas Encourage students to assess the effectiveness of each fact and opinion they find in their article. Suggest that they list evidence in order, from most convincing to least convincing.

Blackline Masters

Thinking and Study Skills, pp. 3, 10, 13, 14, 17–19
Writing Across the Curriculum, pp. 21–22
Cooperative Learning Activities, pp. 31–36
Speaking and Listening Activities, pp. 22, 28
Composition Practice, p. 47
Composition Reteaching, p. 47
Composition Enrichment, p. 47

Assessment

Teacher's Guide to Writing Assessment

TEACH

Guided Practice

L1 Identifying Fact and Opinion
Put the headings *Fact* and *Opinion* on the board. Read through the model and point out each piece of evidence to students. Work with them to decide if it is a fact (snakes are quiet, clean, do not cause allergies, eat worms, and are inexpensive to feed) or an opinion (snakes are fascinating, easy to feed, and more educational than a common pet).

L3 Changing the Audience
Ask students to revise the model as if they were trying to convince fellow students rather than the teacher. What order might be most effective for the pieces of evidence? (They might draw readers in by talking about how unusual and intriguing certain snakes are.) What other persuasive statements could they make? (They might give interesting information about snakes, such as their great variety; about 2,700 kinds exist.)

Independent Practice

For further stimuli for persuasive writing, see *Fine Art Transparencies* 26–30.

Writing Process Transparencies, 20–22B

Writing Across the Curriculum, pp. 21–22

Cooperative Learning Activities, pp. 31–36

Skills Practice

Thinking and Study Skills, pp. 3, 10, 13, 14, 17–19

Speaking and Listening Activities, pp. 22, 28

Composition Practice, p. 47

Organize Your Argument

Revising Tip
If you use others' opinions in persuasive writing, check while revising to make sure you say whose opinions they are.

After you gather your evidence, review it piece by piece. Which evidence is the strongest or most convincing? Sometimes you might want to put the strongest piece of evidence first in your paper. Other times you might want to save it until the end. Decide which order of evidence best supports your goal.

Make a list of your evidence in the order that seems most persuasive. Use this list to draft your persuasive argument. Of course, you may change the order of the evidence during revision. Notice the revisions of this draft about pet snakes.

What pieces of evidence does the writer use to support the goal statement?

Because this was written for Ms. Van, the writer thought it would be more persuasive to start with what the students would learn from a snake.

In choosing a class pet, we could pick no ~~better~~ finer animal than a snake. Experts point out that snakes are quiet, clean, and easy to care for. They aren't slimy, and they make fascinating pets.

The smaller kinds, which we are most likely to get, ~~feed on~~ eat worms. So they would be easy and inexpensive to feed. Also, people don't have allergies to snakes as they do to dogs, cats, and birds.

Snakes behave very differently from more common pets. We would learn more about the animal world by adopting a snake than we would by choosing a pet we know well.

Enabling Strategies

LEP Expressing Opinions
To help students distinguish between facts and opinions, tell them that opinions are usually based on what people think and feel. Opinions often begin with words such as, *I think, I believe,* or I *feel.* Show students some pictures of snakes. Have students make up sentences telling what they think, believe, or feel about snakes. Explain that facts are information that can be found in books or from observing. Facts can be proven; you know they are true.

6.3 Writing Activities

Write a Persuasive Letter

Television shows are canceled all the time. Sometimes even a popular TV show goes off the air. If many people write or call the network, sometimes the show returns. What if your favorite show had just been canceled? Write a letter to the president of the network to persuade him or her to bring back the show.

- Make your point clear in a goal statement.
- Use facts or opinions as evidence.
- Organize your evidence to appeal to your audience.

PURPOSE To keep your favorite TV program from being canceled
AUDIENCE A network executive
LENGTH 2–3 paragraphs

Cooperative Learning

In a small group, plan a campaign to persuade fellow students to support a community project. For example, you could suggest setting up donation boxes for homeless people or forming an after-school club to work on community environmental issues. Agree on the goal you wish to pursue. List evidence—facts and opinions—to support your position. Have two people plan ways to present your proposal while others think of slogans and attention-getting phrases that present your evidence.

Grammar Link

Use commas to separate three or more items in a series.

Note the use of commas in this description of snakes in the Literature Model.

Snakes have been considered evil, hateful, and repulsive.

Add commas as needed in the sentences below.

1. A good project for the fourth fifth and sixth graders would be to beautify the school grounds.
2. We could plant flowers shrubs and trees around the front and side of the building.
3. Students could sweep rake and trim on a regular schedule.
4. Some classes might also want to set off a small space where they could raise flowers food or herbs for sale.
5. People who might help us with the planning include the science teacher the building custodian and someone from the Parent-Teacher Association.

See Lesson 19.2, page 456.

ASSESS

Writing Activities Evaluation Guidelines

Write a Persuasive Letter

Use these criteria when evaluating your students' writing:

- Does the letter begin by stating the main idea?
- Does the letter include both facts and opinions?
- Is evidence ordered in a way that reflects awareness of the audience?

See also the *Teacher's Guide to Writing Assessment.*

Grammar Link

(See Using the Grammar Link below.)

Reteaching

Composition Reteaching, p. 47

Enrichment

Composition Enrichment, p. 47

CLOSE

Discuss with students what makes the best evidence for a persuasive piece—fact or opinion. Encourage students to give examples of both that are strong. Help students realize that sometimes facts are more persuasive and sometimes opinions or personal experience are more effective.

Using the Grammar Link

Grammar Link Answers

1. fourth, fifth, and sixth graders
2. flowers, shrubs, and trees
3. sweep, rake, and trim
4. flowers, food, or herbs
5. science teacher, the building custodian, and someone from the Parent-Teacher Association

Separating Items in a Long Series Have students add one or two more items to each sentence. Remind students to be careful of where the conjunction is placed as they add the items and place the commas.

Setting the Purpose

Lesson 6.4 teaches students how to respond critically to a television program. Students will learn how to take notes while watching the program, then write a review of its strengths and weaknesses as well as their response to the program.

FOCUS

Lesson Overview

Objective: To respond to a television program by writing a review of it
Skills: note taking; writing to persuade
Critical Thinking: summarizing; evaluating; identifying main ideas
Speaking and Listening: discussing

Bellringer

When students enter the classroom, have this assignment on the board: *Briefly describe a television show you saw recently that you particularly enjoyed.*

Grammar Link to the Bellringer

Ask students if they used any possessive nouns in their descriptions. Write some examples of these on the board and focus on the placement of the apostrophe in each.

Motivating Activity

Engage students in a discussion of their television viewing habits. What programs do they watch regularly? What programs do they like or dislike, and why? Students may have heard opinions about this year's newest offerings. Ask what they've heard and whether they agree. Discuss whether they watch network television, public television, cable, videotapes, or a combination of these. Explain that one way to respond to a television program is to write a review of it.

LESSON 6.4

Writing About Literature
Writing a TV Review

Do you ever find yourself trying to convince a friend to watch a rerun of a TV show? Try writing a review and reaching a larger audience.

All week you have looked forward to the National Geographic television special about the North Pole. What's it like at the top of the world? What animals live there, and how do they survive? What would it be like there in the summer when the sun never sets?

The program not only answers your questions, but it does more. It tells you about brave explorers who faced many dangers as they mapped the frozen lands. It makes you feel as if you're taking part in a month-long dog-sled journey. The beautiful photography and the haunting music fascinate you. To share what you've learned from this show, you could write a review of the program and try to persuade people to watch it in a rerun or on videotape.

Teacher's Classroom Resources

The following resources can be used for planning, instruction, practice, reinforcement, assessment, reteaching, enrichment, or evaluation.

Teaching Tools
Lesson Plans

Transparencies
Fine Art Transparencies, 26–30
Writing Process Transparencies, 20–22B

Gather Information

The best way to gather information for a TV review is to take notes while you watch the program. Jot down notes about facts or images that grab your attention.

You can use other methods, too, to help you review a TV program. If you have a videocassette recorder, tape the program and watch it again. The tape can help you strengthen your ideas about the program and add to your notes. You might watch the show with a friend. Afterward, discuss what each of you thought of the show. You can also make a chart like the one below to collect and organize information about a TV program.

Gathering Information for a TV Review	
Name of show and network	*National Geographic Explorer*, "North to the Pole," WTBS
Subject of the show	Dog-sled expedition to the North Pole
Characters (if appropriate)	Six-member team that takes part in the expedition
Strengths	Fast-paced, exciting
Weaknesses	Not enough information on the history of such expeditions
My responses	Makes me want to travel north and learn about winter camping

Journal Writing

Make a chart like the one above, and fill it in as you watch a television program. How does the chart help you gather information about the program? What questions could you add to make the chart a better prewriting tool? How else could you improve it?

TEACH

Guided Practice

L1 Taking Notes

Taking notes while watching a television show is difficult for many students. Remind them to jot down key words rather than writing whole sentences. They should not get so absorbed in note taking that they can't enjoy the show. They should also review their notes as soon as the show is over so they can complete them while the show is still fresh in their memory.

L3 Making Comparisons

Students might enjoy the challenge of comparing two programs that are similar in content. Help them devise a list of criteria that they will use to assess and evaluate the programs.

Two-Minute Skill Drill

Write this description on the board. Have volunteers underline the facts that they would write down if they were taking notes on an oral presentation of the description. What abbreviations could they use to save time?

Bits and Bytes is a weekly show presented from 8 to 9 on Tuesday nights on the educational channel. It not only explains the latest software programs available, but also responds to questions viewers have about their computers. You might be interested even if you don't have a computer!

Journal Writing Tip

Sharing Ideas Encourage students to share their revised charts with the rest of the class so that other students can select the chart that works best for them.

Blackline Masters

Thinking and Study Skills, pp. 17, 19
Writing Across the Curriculum, pp. 19–20
Cooperative Learning Activities, pp. 31–36
Speaking and Listening Activities, pp. 22, 28
Composition Practice, p. 48
Composition Reteaching, p. 48
Composition Enrichment, p. 48

Assessment

Teacher's Guide to Writing Assessment

TEACH

Guided Practice

L2 Using the Model

Discuss the order of information presented in the student model. Point out that each paragraph has a different purpose. Then ask students to identify the purpose of each paragraph. (The first paragraph identifies the program and briefly describes its content. In the second paragraph, the reviewer presents the program's strengths and weaknesses. The final paragraph sums up the reviewer's opinion of the program and gives his personal response.)

L3 Designing a Promotional Piece

Have students work in pairs to design a promotional poster or a script for a radio or television commercial promoting a favorite television show. Students should watch the program, take notes, and then discuss their opinions. The finished piece should include a descriptive paragraph summarizing the program and quotes from student reviewers reflecting what they liked best about it. The results can be posted in the classroom or presented to the rest of the class.

Independent Practice

For further stimuli for persuasive writing, see *Fine Art Transparencies* 26–30.

Writing Process Transparencies, 20–22B

Writing Across the Curriculum, pp. 19–20

Cooperative Learning Activities, pp. 31–36

Skills Practice

Thinking and Study Skills, pp. 17, 19

Speaking and Listening Activities, pp. 22, 28

Composition Practice, p. 48

Drafting the Review

Grammar Editing Tip

When you edit a review, make sure you've used tenses correctly. Most reviews discuss programs in present tense. For more information see Lesson 10.4, page 304.

Writing a review of a TV program is fairly straightforward. The best way to persuade people to watch a television show is to tell them what you like most about the program. Your enthusiasm can persuade your friends, teachers, parents, and anyone else who reads your review to give the show a try.

In the model below, Jack Costello's excitement about an episode of *The New Explorers* comes through in his review. How might his thumbs-up review make you want to watch the program?

Student Model

The name of the program I watched is *The New Explorers* and it is on WTTW. The subject of the program is computer art and how it is used in entertainment and medicine.

The program's strengths are that it is educational and fun to watch. I like the examples of computer graphics like *Tin Toy*. *Tin Toy* is an award-winning short cartoon about a toy soldier that comes to life. It is both funny and realistic. The weakness of this show is that it mentions only a few of the many people involved in making computer graphics.

Overall, I feel that the show is cool and really taught me a lot. Computer graphics can be used just about everywhere, including TV, movies, and commercials. It can also be used to help surgeons in the operating room. I think I might want to do something like this when I grow up.

Jack Costello, St. James School,
Arlington Heights, Illinois

Enabling Strategies

LEP Working Cooperatively on Reviews

Have students work on their reviews in pairs. Let each partner discuss the program first and ask his or her partner questions before beginning to write. Encourage partners to go beyond general observations ("It was a great program") to more specific ones ("I enjoyed learning about what it was like for a young soldier during the Civil War"). Any student who prefers can dictate his or her review to another student who is more experienced with written English.

6.4 Writing Activities

Write a TV Review

Imagine that the most popular segments of your favorite television program have just come out on videotape. Write a two- or three-paragraph review of the videotape that will appear on the package or on posters. The review, aimed at people who have never seen the program, should encourage them to buy the videotape.

- Tell what you like about the program.
- Give reasons that other people would enjoy it.
- Indicate why someone would want to own a copy of the tape.

PURPOSE To persuade someone to buy a videotape
AUDIENCE Customers of a video store
LENGTH 2–3 paragraphs

COMPUTER OPTION

Some computer programs allow the user to create charts. You can choose the number of columns and rows. You can even put a special border around your chart or shade certain areas. Create your own chart for reviewing TV programs. Use the chart on page 229 as a guide. Add any sections you think would be useful.

Grammar Link

Use apostrophes to form possessive nouns.

Note how Jack Costello used an apostrophe and an -*s* to form the possessive of a singular noun in his TV review.

*the **program's** strengths*

Where you place the apostrophe in a plural noun depends upon whether or not the plural ends in -*s*:

people's adults'

Write the sentences below, adding apostrophes to show possession.

1. The TV news show was about our towns plan to build a new bike path.
2. The council members want to get peoples ideas before they make final plans.
3. The shows purpose was to include the opinions of people from all age groups.
4. I especially liked one boys suggestions.
5. Some of the peoples opinions and ideas were not carefully thought through.

See Lesson 19.7, page 466.

ASSESS

Writing Activities Evaluation Guidelines

Write a Review

Use these criteria when evaluating your students' writing.

- Does the review include a brief summary of the program's content?
- Are specific details from the program given?
- Does the review include a main-idea urging readers to buy the videotape?
- Has the student listed reasons for liking the program?
- Has the student used carefully chosen descriptive words?

See also the *Teacher's Guide to Writing Assessment.*

Computer Option

Students will enjoy the option of being able to keep the chart structure while simply changing the content to match the show. Encourage them to be creative in their chart creations.

Grammar Link

(See Using the Grammar Link below.)

Reteaching

Composition Reteaching, p. 48

Enrichment

Composition Enrichment, p. 48

CLOSE

Engage students in a discussion of what they have learned about reviewing a television program. What techniques seem to have the most persuasive effect? Could these same techniques be applied to reviewing a movie?

Using the Grammar Link

Grammar Link Answers

1. town's **4.** boy's
2. people's **5.** people's
3. show's

Possessive Nouns After students have checked their sentences for correct placement of apostrophes, have them rewrite the sentences, changing each possessive from singular to plural or from plural to singular. In the first sentence, for example, students might change *our town's plans* to *several towns' plans*. Have students discuss their sentence changes and changes in the placement of the apostrophe.

Setting the Purpose

Students now have the opportunity to apply what they have learned about persuasive writing to an independent writing project. They will use the stages of the writing process to create and present a persuasive newspaper article.

FOCUS

Lesson Overview

Objective: To use persuasive writing techniques in writing a short article

Skills: using the five stages of the writing process: prewriting, drafting, revising, editing, and presenting

Critical Thinking: recalling; synthesizing; structuring information

Speaking and Listening: discussing; listening to a persuasive article

Bellringer

When students enter the classroom, have this assignment on the board: *What section of the newspaper would you go to if you wanted to read about someone's opinions rather than about facts in the news? Do you always agree with the opinions stated here?*

Grammar Link to the Bellringer

Have volunteers read their responses to the Bellringer activity. Have other volunteers identify the subjects and verbs in the sentences read. Do the subjects and verbs agree?

Motivating Activity

Ask students if they have ever felt strongly about an issue and tried to persuade others to agree with them. Did the students succeed? Ask students to consider the relative effectiveness of facts, opinions, and appeals to feelings to strengthen their appeals.

UNIT 6

WRITING PROCESS IN ACTION

PERSUASIVE WRITING

In preceding lessons you've learned about persuasive writing—about the importance of strong reasons, about using facts and opinions as evidence, about appealing to your audience. You've had the opportunity to do some persuasive writing, including a TV review. Now it's time to put together all that you've learned. In this lesson you're invited to write a persuasive newspaper article. You will try to convince your readers to take some action on an environmental issue.

• Assignment •

Context	Write an article for a local newspaper to persuade readers to make (or support) some change that will protect the environment.
Purpose	To convince people to think about or take action on an environmental issue
Audience	Readers of all types and ages
Length	1 page

The following pages can help you plan and write your newspaper article. Read through them and then refer to them as you need to. Don't be limited by them. You are in charge of your own writing process.

Teacher's Classroom Resources

The following resources can be used for planning, instruction, practice, reinforcement, assessment, reteaching, enrichment, or evaluation.

Teaching Tools
Lesson Plans

Transparencies
Writing Process Transparencies, 20–22B

Prewriting

What environmental issue do you think is especially important? Saving rain forests? Cleaning up air and water pollution? What issues have had a direct effect on your community?

Once you've selected a topic, explore your ideas by listing, clustering, or freewriting. Then use one of the options at the right, or an idea of your own, to select supporting evidence.

Before you draft, write your goal statement. Then list reasons that will persuade your audience.

Option A
Read a daily newspaper for new information.

Option B
Check a library magazine index for helpful articles.

Option C
Read other materials on your topic at the library.

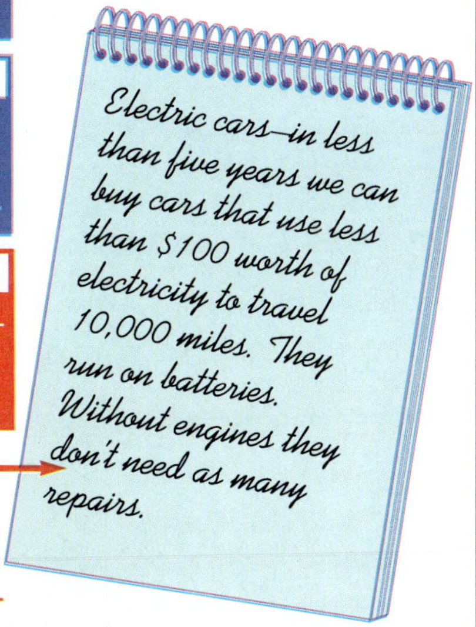

Drafting

As you draft, keep your audience constantly in mind, and use language that will persuade. Joseph Bruchac tells how a Native American named Swift Eagle persuaded some boys to change their behavior. Read Swift Eagle's words:

Literature Model

> "You know, our Creator gave the gift of life to everything that is alive. Life is a very sacred thing. But our Creator knows that we have to eat to stay alive. That is why it is permitted to hunt to feed ourselves and our people. So I understand that you boys must have been very, very hungry to kill those little birds."
>
> Joseph Bruchac, "Thanking the Birds"

TEACH

Prewriting

L2 Developing Ideas for Persuasive Writing

To underscore the importance of considering the audience's needs in persuasive writing, ask how students might interest a local audience in a global issue such as water pollution.

L1 Exploring Ideas with a Partner

Encourage students to spend extra time on prewriting. You might suggest that pairs of students discuss their prewriting ideas and ask each other questions to explore their topics fully before they begin drafting. You might also pair students with others who are already capable researchers.

Drafting

L2 Defending Opinions

Remind students that they might first write an opinion statement and then support or defend their opinion with specific facts. Students should avoid misleading statements or statements that exaggerate the truth. Remind them that, in order to be persuaded, readers must be convinced that what they are reading is true.

Blackline Masters
Thinking and Study Skills, p. 4, 11
Composition Practice, p. 51
Composition Reteaching, p. 51
Composition Enrichment, p. 51

Grammar Workbook
Lesson 48

Assessment

Teacher's Guide to Writing Assessment

UNIT 6
Writing Process in Action

TEACH

Revising

L2 Peer Editing

Students can work in writing conferences with peer editors before they revise their writing. You may want to duplicate the Peer Response forms in the *Teacher's Guide to Writing Assessment.* Suggest that peer editors respond to the following questions:

- Is the writer's opinion clearly stated?
- Is the opinion backed up by facts?
- Is the article convincing?

Editing

L2 Peer Editing

After students have edited their own work, have them edit another student's writing. Remind them to refer to the Editing Checklist on the student page.

Presenting

Before students present their persuasive writing, discuss how to prepare their papers for publication. Emphasize the importance of the final draft and that it must be neatly done.

Independent Practice

Writing Process Transparencies, 20–22B

Skills Practice

Thinking and Study Skills, pp. 4, 11

Composition Practice, p. 51

Grammar Workbook, Lesson 48

Journal Writing Tip

Analyzing Difficulties Help students find the reason for any difficulties experienced while writing.

Drafting Tip

For help with organizing your information, see Lesson 6.2, pages 220–222.

Do Swift Eagle's words persuade you? Do they help you feel responsibility for treating nature with respect?

Remember, in the drafting stage you need to express your ideas in sentences and paragraphs. Don't worry about grammar and spelling now. You can make changes later. This is the time to get your ideas on paper.

Revising

Revising Tip

For ideas about reviewing and improving your draft, see Lesson 6.3, page 226.

To begin revising, read over your draft to make sure that what you've written fits your purpose and audience. Then have a **writing conference**. Read your draft to a partner or small group. Use your audience's reactions to help you evaluate your work. The following questions can help you and your listeners.

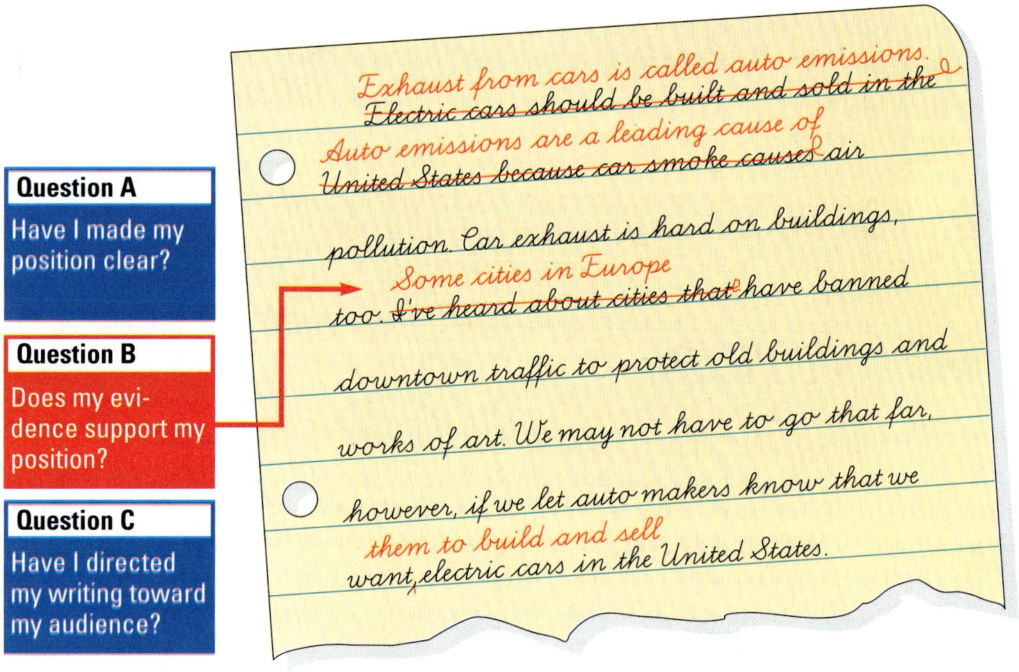

Enrichment and Extension

Follow-up Ideas

- If students are interested in an issue of local importance, they might write persuasive letters to local officials.
- Students might write letters to the editor of the local paper asking for a regular feature for student writers.

Extending Persuasion

Brainstorm with students ways they can use their expertise in persuasive writing in other subject areas. For example, in social studies, they might try to convince others that a certain group of people has been treated unjustly.

Editing

As you prepare your article, **proofread** it to eliminate distracting errors. A newspaper editor is more likely to publish your writing if it is free of mistakes in spelling, grammar, and usage.

The checklist at the right will help you catch errors you might otherwise overlook. Read and reread your work with care. Use a dictionary and the Grammar, Usage, and Mechanics section of this book to help you.

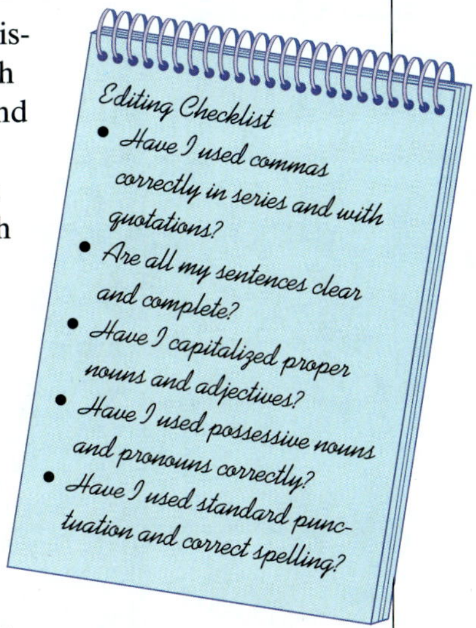

Presenting

Make sure your article is neatly written or typed on clean white paper before you submit it to your local newspaper. You might want to include a photo or drawing that illustrates the environmental issue you're writing about. Also, include any visual aids such as charts or graphs that make the evidence easier to understand.

Another way to present your writing is for you and your classmates to produce a school newsletter. The purpose of the newsletter would be to keep students up to date on issues that affect the environment.

For proofreading symbols, see page 74.

Journal Writing

Reflect on your writing process experience. Answer these questions in your journal: What do you like best about your article? What was the hardest part of writing it? What did you learn in your writing conference? What new thing have you learned as a writer?

ASSESS

Evaluation Guidelines

Use the following questions to evaluate students' finished writing:

- Does the article focus on an environmental topic?
- Does it clearly state a position or opinion?
- Is the position supported with strong, relevant evidence?
- Is the article neatly written or typed?
- Does it reflect careful editing for spelling, grammar, and punctuation?

Refer to the *Teacher's Guide to Writing Assessment* for further help with evaluating student writing.

Reteaching

Composition Reteaching, p. 51

Enrichment

Composition Enrichment, p. 51

CLOSE

Ask students to discuss what is required in persuading someone to agree with them. How can understanding how other people feel about an issue help students prepare their arguments?

Enabling Strategies

LEP Using the Writing Process to Persuade

Stress with students the fact that their thoughts and ideas matter. Encourage them to spend a great deal of time in the prewriting stage—making lists, jotting down ideas. Be sure that they write about something they know well. When students find an idea they care about, ask them whom they want to persuade. Point out that drafts need not be perfect. Students can work with peer editors who are fluent English speakers to help them with revising and editing their drafts.

Setting the Purpose

Students read a literature selection that illustrates in a very real way effective persuasive writing. Such readings serve as models for students as they create their own persuasive writing.

About the Author

Joseph Bruchac has written over twenty books of poetry and fiction reflecting his Abenaki ancestry. He says, "My writing is informed by several key sources. One of these is nature, another is the Native American experience." He teaches and writes because "it gives me a chance to share my insights into the beautiful and all too fragile world of human life and living things we have been granted."

FOCUS

Lesson Overview

Objective: To examine the way in which a professional writer uses a story to change his readers' relationship with the natural world
Skills: reading comprehension
Critical Thinking: decision-making
Speaking and Listening: discussing

Bellringer

When students enter the classroom, have this assignment on the board: *What does the next sentence mean?*

The art of persuasion can be a powerful tool.

Motivating Activity

Ask students what action they would take if they saw other people doing something they didn't approve of. How would students try to convince others to change? What methods seem to work best in convincing people to change their behavior?

UNIT 6

Persuasive Writing
Literature Model

Joseph Bruchac
from
THANKING THE BIRDS

The following essay is taken from Keepers of the Earth, *a book created to help people understand the delicate relationship between humans and the natural world. Joseph Bruchac is an award-winning novelist and poet who was born in the Adirondack Mountain region. As you read, pay special attention to the ways he tries to change people's attitudes and behaviors. Then try the activities in Linking Writing and Literature on page 239.*

One day 30 years ago, Swift Eagle, an Apache man, visited some friends on the Onondaga Indian Reservation in central New York. While he was out walking, he heard sounds of boys playing in the bushes.

"There's another one. Shoot it!" said one of the boys.

Teacher's Classroom Resources

The following resources can be used for planning, instruction, or practice.

Teaching Tools
Lesson Plans

Transparencies
Fine Art Transparencies, 26–30

Blackline Masters
Speaking and Listening Activities, pp. 8, 24
Thinking and Study Skills, pp. 13, 19
Vocabulary and Spelling Practice, p. 12

When he pushed through the brush to see what was happening, he found that they had been shooting small birds with a BB gun. They had already killed a chickadee, a robin, and several blackbirds. The boys looked up at him, uncertain what he was going to do or say.

There are several things that a non-Indian bird lover might have done: given a stern lecture on the evil of killing birds; threatened to tell the boys' parents on them for doing something they had been told not to do; or even spanked them. Swift Eagle, however, did something else.

"Ah," he said, "I see you have been hunting. Pick up your game and come with me."

He led the boys to a place where they could make a fire and cook the birds. He made sure they said a 'thank you' to the spirits of the birds before eating them, and as they ate he told stories. It was important, he said, to be thankful to the birds for the gifts of their songs, their feathers, and their bodies as food. The last thing he said to them they never forgot—for it was one of those boys who told me this story many years later: "You know, our Creator gave the gift of life to everything that is alive. Life is a very sacred thing. But our Creator knows that we have to eat to stay alive. That is why it is permitted to hunt to feed ourselves and our people. So I understand that you boys must have been very, very hungry to kill those little birds."

Amy Cordova, *The Red Dress,* 1989

TEACH

L2 Guided Reading

- How does Swift Eagle want to change the boys' ideas and actions?
- What techniques does he use to do so?

Assessment

Teacher's Guide to Writing Assessment

About the Art

Amy Cordova, *The Red Dress,* 1989
Amy Cordova's paintings reflect her Hispanic and Native American heritage as well as the quilt-making artistry of Amish neighbors. Cordova's subjects grow out of the experiences of everyday life and her dreams and imagination.

TEACH

L2 Guided Reading

- If you had been one of the boys caught shooting the birds, what would you have said to Swift Eagle? How would you feel about having to cook and eat the birds?
- How has the selection affected the way you feel about your surroundings? How can you "thank the birds" in your own environment?

Independent Practice

For further stimuli for persuasive writing, see *Fine Art Transparencies* 26–30.

Skills Practice

Speaking and Listening Activities, pp. 8, 24
Thinking and Study Skills, pp. 13, 19
Vocabulary and Spelling Practice, p. 12

Similarities Among Native People

I have always liked that story, for it illustrates several things. Although there was a wide range of customs, lifeways and languages—in pre-Columbian[1] times more than 400 different languages were spoken on the North American continent—many close similarities existed between virtually all of the Native American peoples. Thus ideas held by an Apache from the Southwest fitted into the lives and traditions of Onondagas in the Northeast.

One of these ideas, expressed in Swift Eagle's words to the boys, was the continent-wide belief that mankind depended on the natural world for survival, on the one hand, and had to respect it and remain in right relationship with it, on the other. . . .

As the anecdote[2] about Swift Eagle also shows, the children were taught the values of their cultures through example and stories. Instead of scolding or lecturing them, Swift Eagle showed the boys how to build a fire and cook the game they had shot, giving the songbirds the same respect he would have given a rabbit or deer. He told stories that pointed out the value of those birds as living beings. The ritual[3] activity of making the fire, thanking the spirit of the birds, hearing the stories, and then eating the game they had killed taught the boys more than a hundred stern lectures would have done, and the lesson stayed with them all their lives.

1 **pre-Columbian** before Columbus's arrival in 1492
2 **anecdote** (an'ik dōt') a very short story
3 **ritual** (rich'o͞o əl) a system of special ceremonies

Genre and Style

Reading a Persuasive Essay

"Thanking the Birds" uses an anecdote to support its main point, that humans need to respect the natural world. Its purpose is to change readers' ideas and actions toward the natural world by causing them to reflect on the anecdote's lesson.

Linking Writing and Literature

Readers Respond to the Model

What made Swift Eagle's approach so persuasive and memorable?

Explore Joseph Bruchac's writing by answering these questions. Then read how other students reacted to Bruchac's essay.

1. How did Bruchac learn the story he tells in his essay?
2. How does Bruchac combine facts and opinions in presenting his story?
3. How did Swift Eagle instruct and persuade the boys? How does his story affect the reader?

The literature selection was about an Indian who teaches some boys how to value life, food, and change their ways. He makes them realize killing birds and not eating them is senseless.

I liked best that the man taught the boys and did not yell at them. Instead of telling them they were wrong, he showed them how to be right.

I would recommend this selection because some kids are environmentalists and I am sure they would like the "respecting nature" idea.

Chip Mulaney

[An Apache] man found some boys having fun and shooting birds. He knew that they were doing it for fun and not for food, but he pretended that he thought they were hungry. I thought it was funny when he said, "So I understand that you boys must have been very, very hungry to kill those little birds."

John Moore

ASSESS

Evaluation Guidelines for Discussion

As your students discuss the passage either in small groups or as a class, encourage them to begin with a personal response. The student responses on this page might be used as a starting point.

Look for evidence that students
- have read the passage
- can state some of the writer's ideas in their own words
- understand the writer's point of view
- have connected the content to their own knowledge and experiences
- understand the ideas and implications of the passage

Some possible responses to the discussion questions on this page:

1. One of the boys in the story told Bruchac the story many years after it happened.
2. Bruchac intertwines facts and opinions in his story. He also uses facts to support his opinions.
3. Swift Eagle used examples and stories to instruct and persuade the boys. His story makes the reader want to protect and preserve the natural world.

CLOSE

Initiate a discussion about how Swift Eagle might react to some of the efforts being made today to protect the environment. To which environmental issues would he relate strongly?

Cultural Diversity

Understanding Common Beliefs

The story Bruchac tells reflects the values of many Native American cultures. In fact, Bruchac says that the attitude Swift Eagle teaches the boys results from "continent-wide" beliefs held by "virtually all of the Native American peoples," who are sometimes vastly different in their customs and languages.

REVIEW

Reflecting on the Unit

You may have students respond to Reflecting on the Unit in writing or through discussion.

Writing Across the Curriculum

Remind students to state their goal or main idea and to back it up with supporting evidence.

Adding to Your Portfolio

Students should choose pieces for their portfolios that include the basic elements of persuasive writing: a strong opinion statement and supporting evidence presented in the most persuasive order. Encourage students to consider choosing those pieces that peer reviewers and others found the most persuasive.

Portfolio Evaluation

If you grade the portfolio selections, you might want to award two marks—one each for content and form. Explain your assessment criteria before students make their selections. Commend

- experimentation with creative prewriting techniques
- clear, concise writing in which the main idea, audience, and purpose are evident
- successful revisions
- work that shows a flair for language

Unit 6 Review

Reflecting on the Unit

Summarize what you learned in this unit by answering the following questions.

- When you write to persuade, why is it important to keep your audience in mind?
- What are some good ways to use opinions as supporting evidence?
- How can you use the revising stage to improve a piece of persuasive writing?
- What techniques can help you gather information to review a television program?

Adding to Your Portfolio

Choose a selection for your portfolio. Look over the persuasive writing you did during this unit. Select a completed piece of writing to put into your portfolio. The writing you choose should show some or all of the following:

- an attempt to get readers to believe or do something
- a clear goal statement
- reasons that support the goal statement
- evidence ordered in a way that is persuasive to the intended audience

Reflect on your choice. Attach a note to the piece you chose, explaining briefly why you chose it and what you learned from writing it.

Set goals. How can you improve your writing? What skill will you focus on the next time you write?

Writing Across the Curriculum

Make a geography connection. Think about a weather condition or natural phenomenon that might threaten your community (a tornado, flood, electrical storm, or earthquake). Write a persuasive argument to convince people to protect themselves or their property. Put your argument in any form you wish—perhaps a newspaper article, poster, or radio announcement.

Teacher's Classroom Resources

The following resources can be used for assessment or evaluation.

Unit Assessment

Tests with Answer Key
Unit 6 Choice A Test, p. 21
Unit 6 Choice B Test, p. 22
Unit 6 Composition Objective Test, pp. 23–24

Test Generator
Unit 6 Choice A Test
Unit 6 Choice B Test
Unit 6 Composition Objective Test

You may wish to administer one of these tests as a mastery test.

UNIT 7

Troubleshooter

Composition | Lessons

Use Troubleshooter to help you correct common errors that you might make in your writing. You can indicate the errors on your paper using the handwritten codes in the left-hand column. Then the Table of Contents below will help you locate solutions to correct errors.

INTRODUCING
Unit 7

UNIT GOALS

The goal of **Troubleshooter** is to help students become more independent and competent writers and language users.

About the Troubleshooter

Teachers know that they mark some grammar, usage, and mechanics errors more often than others. Current research corroborates this experience. The Writer's Choice Troubleshooter, Grades 9–12, was prepared by Glencoe editors after they consulted one such study by Robert J. Connors and Andrea Lunsford, reported in "Frequency of Formal Errors in Current College Writing, or Ma and Pa Kettle Do Research" (College Composition and Communication, Vol. 39, No. 4, December, 1988), but neither Connors nor Lunsford participated in Writer's Choice. For the Grades 6–8 Troubleshooter, Glencoe editors selected pertinent errors and added errors common to middle school students.

Setting the Purpose

Lesson 7.1 teaches students how to avoid using sentence fragments in their writing.

FOCUS

Lesson Overview

Objective: To recognize the most common types of sentence fragments: a fragment lacking a subject, a fragment lacking a predicate, and a fragment lacking both a subject and a predicate

Bellringer

When students enter the classroom, have this assignment on the board: *Copy down the following sentences, then rewrite them correctly:*

Ellen and Sarah went to the aquarium. Saw seals. And the dolphins. Then they had lunch. At one o'clock.

Motivating Activity

Discuss with students why the sentences in the Bellringer were confusing. Explain that using sentence fragments can make writing hard to understand. This lesson will teach students how to avoid using sentence fragments in their writing.

TEACH

Cross-reference: Usage

For instruction and practice of the material in Lesson 7.1, refer students to Lesson 8.2, p. 264.

7.1 Sentence Fragment

PROBLEM 1

Fragment that lacks a subject

frag Tess left town. Went to Maine.

frag The horse trotted home. Ate some hay.

frag Hasina teaches school. Teaches English literature.

SOLUTION

Tess left town. She went to Maine.

The horse trotted home. It ate some hay.

Hasina teaches school. She teaches English literature.

Add a subject to the fragment to make a complete sentence.

PROBLEM 2

Fragment that lacks a predicate

frag A woman was singing. The beautiful song.

frag A noise woke me up. The dog next door again.

frag Joyce bought a skirt. That blue linen skirt.

Teacher's Classroom Resources

The following resources can be used for planning, instruction, practice, or reinforcement.

Teaching Tools
Lesson Plans

Grammar Workbook
Lesson 6

SOLUTION

The woman was singing. The song was beautiful.

A noise woke me up. The dog next door was barking again.

Joyce bought a skirt. That skirt was blue linen.

Add a predicate to make the sentence complete.

PROBLEM 3

Fragment that lacks both a subject and a predicate

frag Miriam left work late. With her friend.

frag The store closed. At two o'clock.

SOLUTION

Miriam left work late with her friend.

The store closed at two o'clock.

Combine the fragment with another sentence.

Need More Help?

If you need more help avoiding sentence fragments, see Lesson 8.2, page 264.

TEACH

Two-Minute Skill Drill

Write these sentence fragments on the board and have students rewrite them as complete sentences:

Walked three miles.
The bus driver.
At the gym.

Independent Practice

Skills Practice

Grammar Workbook, Lesson 6

CLOSE

Have students explain in their own words the three kinds of sentence fragments. Ask them to check their current writing assignments and rewrite any sentence fragments as complete sentences.

Setting the Purpose

Lesson 7.2 teaches students how to avoid run-on sentences in their writing.

FOCUS

Lesson Overview

Objective: To recognize and avoid using the different kinds of run-on sentences: a comma splice, two main clauses with no punctuation between them, and two main clauses with no comma before a coordinating conjunction

Bellringer

When students enter the classroom, have this assignment on the board: *Tell why the following sentences are difficult to read. Then write them correctly.*

I play basketball at the park, Jimmy plays baseball.
The dog barked it growled, too.
I went to the theater and I watched a movie.

Motivating Activity

Invite students to discuss why they found the sentences difficult to read. If necessary, help them to rewrite the sentences correctly. Explain that run-on sentences can be hard to read and understand. This lesson will teach students how to avoid run-on sentences in their writing.

TEACH

Cross-reference: Usage

For instruction and practice of the material in Lesson 7.2, refer students to Lesson 8.6, pp. 272–273.

7.2 Run-on Sentence

PROBLEM 1

Two main clauses separated only by a comma

run-on I like to play volleyball, Luis prefers hockey.

SOLUTION A

I like to play volleyball. Luis prefers hockey.

Replace the comma with a period or other end mark. Begin the new sentence with a capital letter.

SOLUTION B

I like to play volleyball; Luis prefers hockey.

Replace the comma with a semicolon.

SOLUTION C

I like to play volleyball, but Luis prefers hockey.

Add a coordinating conjunction after the comma.

PROBLEM 2

Two main clauses with no punctuation between them

run-on Ada writes poetry she dances, too.

Teacher's Classroom Resources

The following resources can be used for planning, instruction, practice, or reinforcement.

Teaching Tools
Lesson Plans

Grammar Workbook
Lesson 7

SOLUTION A

Ada writes poetry. She dances, too.

Separate the clauses with a period or other end mark.

SOLUTION B

Ada writes poetry; she dances, too.

Place a semicolon between the main clauses.

SOLUTION C

Ada writes poetry, and she dances, too.

Add a comma and a conjunction between the main clauses.

PROBLEM 3

Two main clauses with no comma before the coordinating conjunction

run-on I climbed the mountains and I explored the forests.

SOLUTION

I climbed the mountains, and I explored the forests.

Add a comma before the coordinating conjunction.

Need More Help?

If you need more help avoiding run-on sentences, see Lesson 8.6, page 272.

TEACH

Two-Minute Skill Drill

Write these run-on sentences on the board and have students rewrite them correctly:

The clown juggled oranges, she sang a song.

We swim at the beach we also go fishing.

Joan did her math problems and she painted her model airplane.

Independent Practice

Skills Practice

Grammar Workbook, Lesson 7

CLOSE

Invite students to explain in their own words the three different kinds of run–on sentences presented in this Troubleshooter. Ask them to check their current writing assignment for similar situations and correct any run–on sentences.

Setting the Purpose

Lesson 7.3 teaches students how to avoid lack of subject-verb agreement in their writing.

FOCUS

Lesson Overview

Objective: To recognize the constructions that commonly lead to lack of subject-verb agreement and to avoid or correct the misuse of these types of constructions

Bellringer

When students enter the classroom, have this assignment on the board: *Tell what is confusing about the following sentences and then write them correctly.*

One of his answers are wrong.
Here is two slices of pizza.
Shauna and John is going to the dance.

Motivating Activity

Discuss with students why the sentences in the Bellringer are wrong. Explain that this lesson will teach students to avoid and correct subject-verb disagreement in their writing.

TEACH

Cross-reference: Usage

For instruction and practice of the material in Problems 1 and 2, refer students to Lesson 15.2, pp. 406–407.

7.3 Lack of Subject-Verb Agreement

PROBLEM 1

A subject that is separated from the verb by an intervening prepositional phrase

agr One of the jars are broken.

SOLUTION

One of the jars is broken.

Ignore a prepositional phrase that comes between a subject and a verb. Make sure that the verb agrees with the subject of the sentence. The subject is never the object of the preposition.

PROBLEM 2

A sentence that begins with **here** ***or*** **there**

agr There is private beaches all over that tropical island.

SOLUTION

There are private beaches all over that tropical island.

The subject is never *here* or *there.* The subject comes after the verb. The verb must agree with this subject.

Teacher's Classroom Resources

The following resources can be used for planning, instruction, practice, or reinforcement.

Teaching Tools
Lesson Plans

Blackline Masters
Sentence Combining Practice, pp. 19–20

Grammar Workbook
Lesson 48

PROBLEM 3

A compound subject that is joined by and

agr Music and dance is taught at school.

SOLUTION

Music and dance are taught at school.

If the parts of the compound subjects refer to different people or things, use a plural verb.

PROBLEM 4

A compound subject that is joined by or *or* nor

agr Neither the bat nor the mitts belongs to me.

agr Either cookies or ice cream are a good dessert.

SOLUTION

Neither the bat nor the mitts belong to me.

Either cookies or ice cream is a good dessert.

Make the verb agree with the subject that is closer to it.

Need More Help?

If you need more help with subject-verb agreement, see Lessons 15.1 through 15.3, pages 404–409.

TEACH

Cross-reference: Usage

For instruction and practice of the material in Problems 3 and 4, refer students to Lesson 15.3, pp. 408–409.

Two-Minute Skill Drill

Write the following sentence on the board:

Either Lupe or her brothers is going to babysit for Mrs. Garcia.

Have students rewrite the sentence so the subject and verb agree.

Independent Practice

Skills Practice

Sentence Combining Practice, pp. 19–20

Grammar Workbook, Lesson 48

CLOSE

Have students explain in their own words the four kinds of subject-verb disagreement presented in this Troubleshooter. Ask them to check their current writing assignments for similar situations and fix any subject-verb agreement errors.

Setting the Purpose

Lesson 7.4 teaches students how to avoid or correct errors in verb tense and form.

FOCUS

Lesson Overview

Objective: To learn to recognize the most common kinds of errors in verb tense or form and to avoid or correct these errors

Bellringer

When students enter the classroom, have this assignment on the board: *Decide what is wrong with the following sentences, and then write them correctly:*

Ricky is sing in the school musical.
We runned to meet Mom when she came home.
Rhonda has drank her orange juice.

Motivating Activity

Discuss with students why the sentences in the Bellringer activity are wrong. Explain that this lesson will teach students how to use the correct tense and form of verbs.

TEACH

Cross-reference: Grammar

For instruction and practice of the material in Problem 1, refer students to Lesson 10.5, pp. 306–307.

7.4 Incorrect Verb Tense or Form

PROBLEM 1

An incorrect or missing verb ending

tense I have (learn) how to play the violin in the past year.

SOLUTION

I have learned how to play the violin in the past year.

Add *-ed* to a regular verb to form the past tense and the past participle.

PROBLEM 2

An improperly formed irregular verb

tense Jan (builded) a greenhouse in the yard.

The past and past participle forms of irregular verbs vary. Memorize these forms, or look them up.

SOLUTION

Jan built a greenhouse in the yard.

Use the correct past or past participle form of an irregular verb.

Teacher's Classroom Resources

The following resources can be used for planning, instruction, practice, or reinforcement.

Teaching Tools
Lesson Plans

Grammar Workbook
Lesson 16

PROBLEM 3

Confusion between the past form and the past participle

tense Carlos has began to play the guitar.

SOLUTION

Carlos has begun to play the guitar.

Use the past participle form of an irregular verb, not the past form, when you use the auxiliary verb *have.*

PROBLEM 4

Improper use of the past participle

tense I seen two plays this month.

SOLUTION

I have seen two plays this month.

Add the auxiliary verb *have* to the past participle of an irregular verb to form a complete verb.

Need More Help?

If you need more help with correct verb forms, see Lessons 10.3 through 10.9, pages 302–315.

TEACH

Two-Minute Skill Drill

Write this sentence on the board:

Joel and Marie been looking forward to going in-line skating.

Have students rewrite the sentence so that the verb form is correct.

Independent Practice

Skills Practice

Grammar Workbook, Lesson 16

CLOSE

Have students explain in their own words the four kinds of verb tense and form problems discussed in this Troubleshooter. Ask them to check their current writing assignments for similar situations and fix any verb tense or form errors.

Setting the Purpose

Lesson 7.5 teaches students about pronouns and their antecedents and the correct use of subject and object pronouns.

FOCUS

Lesson Overview

Objective: To recognize the constructions that give rise to incorrect pronoun use

Bellringer

When students enter the classroom, have this assignment on the board: *Tell what is confusing about the following sentence, and then write it correctly:*

Sharon and Tina went to the movies, but she didn't like it.

Motivating Activity

Discuss with students why the sentence in the Bellringer is confusing. Have volunteers write their corrected sentences on the board. If students come up with more than one solution, have them explain why each sentence is correct.

TEACH

Cross-reference: Grammar

For instruction and practice of the material in Problem 1, refer students to Lesson 11.3, pp. 330–331.

Cross-reference: Grammar

For instruction and practice of the material in Problem 2, refer students to Lesson 11.1, pp. 326–327.

7.5 Incorrect Use of Pronouns

PROBLEM 1

A pronoun that can refer to more than one antecedent

pro Carla went to the concert with Ana, but she didn't stay long.

pro When the neighbors accused my brothers, they were angry.

SOLUTION

Carla went to the concert with Ana, but Carla didn't stay long.

When the neighbors accused my brothers, my brothers were angry.

Rewrite the sentence, substituting a noun for the pronoun.

PROBLEM 2

Object pronouns as subjects

pro Kyoko and me left for summer camp.

pro Her and Satchel had an argument today.

pro Nita and them are in the school play.

Teacher's Classroom Resources

The following resources can be used for planning, instruction, practice, or reinforcement.

Teaching Tools
Lesson Plans

Grammar Workbook
Lessons 25–27

SOLUTION

Kyoko and I left for summer camp.

She and Satchel had an argument today.

Nita and they are in the school play.

Use a subject pronoun as the subject part of a sentence.

PROBLEM 3

Subject pronouns as objects

pro Please help Amos and I with the groceries.

pro Sonia left her books with Alan and I.

pro Megan bought a ticket for she and Ian.

SOLUTION

Please help Amos and me with the groceries.

Sonia left her books with Alan and me.

Megan bought a ticket for her and Ian.

Use an object pronoun as the object of a verb or a preposition.

Need More Help?

If you need more help with the correct use of pronouns, see Lessons 11.1 through 11.5, pages 326–335.

TEACH

Cross-reference: Usage

For instruction and practice of the material in Problem 3, refer students to Lesson 11.1, pp. 326–327.

Two-Minute Skill Drill

Write this sentence on the board and have students rewrite it so the pronouns are used correctly:

Hoang and me rode the train and Melissa waved goodbye to him and I.

Independent Practice

Skills Practice

Grammar Workbook
Lessons 25–27

CLOSE

Discuss with students how recognizing the incorrect use of pronouns can help their writing. Have them check their current writing assignments for incorrect pronouns and fix any unclear pronoun references.

Setting the Purpose

Lesson 7.6 teaches students how to avoid incorrect use of comparative and superlative adjectives.

FOCUS

Lesson Overview

Objective: To recognize and avoid the incorrect use of regular and irregular comparative and superlative adjectives

Bellringer

When students enter the classroom, have this assignment on the board: *Tell what is incorrect about the following sentence, and then write it correctly:*

Helena's orange is more bigger than Alberto's.

Motivating Activity

Discuss with students that comparative adjectives such as *bigger* do not use the word *more.* Have students create sentences with comparative and superlative adjectives, adding *-er* or *-est* as appropriate.

TEACH

Cross-reference: Grammar

For instruction and practice of the material in Lesson 7.6, refer students to Lessons 12.3 and 12.4, pp. 348–351 .

7.6 Incorrect Use of Adjectives

PROBLEM 1

Incorrect use of good, better, best

adj Selma felt more good after her nap.

adj Harry is the most good artist in the class.

adj Vinnie is a more better writer than Jenny.

SOLUTION

Selma felt better after her nap.

Harry is the best artist in the class.

Vinnie is a better writer than Jenny.

The comparative and superlative forms of *good* are *better* and *best.* Do not use *more* or *most* before irregular forms of comparative and superlative adjectives.

PROBLEM 2

Incorrect use of bad, worse, worst

adj This painting is more bad than the one in the den.

adj This is the baddest book I've ever read.

adj That was the most worst speech of the day.

Teacher's Classroom Resources

The following resources can be used for planning, instruction, practice, or reinforcement.

Teaching Tools
Lesson Plans

Grammar Workbook
Lessons 32–33

SOLUTION

This painting is worse than the one in the den.

This is the worst book I've ever read.

That was the worst speech of the day.

The comparative and superlative forms of *bad* are *worse* and *worst.* Do not use *more* or *most* before irregular forms of comparative and superlative adjectives.

PROBLEM 3

Incorrect use of comparative and superlative adjectives

adj Greta is more younger than her sister.

adj Samuel drove the most fast car in the race.

SOLUTION

Greta is younger than her sister.

Samuel drove the fastest car in the race.

Do not use both *-er* and *more* or *-est* and *most* at the same time.

Need More Help?

If you need more help with the correct use of adjectives, see Lessons 12.3 and 12.4, pages 348–351.

TEACH

Two-Minute Skill Drill

Write this sentence on the board and have students rewrite it to correct the comparative and superlative adjectives:

Sonia is more wiser than Renata, but Johanna is most wiser of all.

Independent Practice

Skills Practice

Grammar Workbook
Lessons 32–33

CLOSE

Have students use comparative and superlative adjectives to compare their favorite sports, types of music, or movie personalities.

Setting the Purpose

Lesson 7.7 teaches students how to avoid the incorrect use of commas in their writing.

FOCUS

Lesson Overview

Objective: To recognize and use commas to separate items in a series of words, phrases, or clauses, and to set off direct quotations

Bellringer

When students enter the classroom, have this assignment on the board: *Tell what is missing from the following sentence and write the sentence correctly.*

In my garden I grow cauliflower cantaloupe brussels sprouts and eggplant.

Motivating Activity

Have a volunteer add the missing commas to the sentence on the board. Discuss with students why the sentence is not clear without the commas.

TEACH

Cross-reference: Mechanics

For instruction and practice of the material in Problem 1, refer students to Lesson 19.2, pp. 456–457.

7.7 Incorrect Use of Commas

PROBLEM 1

Missing commas in a series of three or more items

com Today we studied history science and mathematics.

com Orson Welles wrote directed and starred in many classic films.

SOLUTION

Today we studied history, science, and mathematics.

Orson Welles wrote, directed, and starred in many classic films.

Use commas to separate three or more items in a series..

PROBLEM 2

Missing commas with direct quotations

com "This movie" Marcia said "is really exciting."

com "I want to leave" Dorie said "before the storm begins."

Teacher's Classroom Resources

The following resources can be used for planning, instruction, practice, or reinforcement.

Teaching Tools
Lesson Plans

Grammar Workbook
Lesson 72

SOLUTION

"This movie," Marcia said, "is really exciting."

"I want to leave," Dorie said, "before the storm begins."

The first part of an interrupted quotation ends with a comma followed by quotation marks. The interrupting words are also followed by a comma.

Need More Help?

If you need more help with commas, see Lessons 19.2 through 19.4, pages 456–461.

TEACH

Cross-reference: Mechanics

For instruction and practice of the material in Problem 2, refer students to Lesson 19.6, pp. 464–465.

Two-Minute Skill Drill

Write this sentence on the board and have students rewrite it, adding commas in the correct places:

"This story" said Tory "has adventure mystery action and comedy."

Independent Practice

Skills Practice

Grammar Workbook, Lesson 72

CLOSE

Spark a discussion about why using commas correctly helps make writing clear and understandable. Have students explain in their own words the rules for the correct use of commas that are presented in this Troubleshooter.

Setting the Purpose

Lesson 7.8 teaches students how to avoid incorrect use of the possessive apostrophe.

FOCUS

Lesson Overview

Objective: To use possessive apostrophes correctly and to recognize the most common instances in which possessive apostrophes are missing or misused: after singular nouns, after plural nouns ending in *-s*, after plural nouns not ending in *-s*, and with possessive pronouns

Bellringer

When students enter the classroom, have this assignment on the board: *Circle and correct the punctuation errors in the following sentences:*

Billys sneakers' have red stars on them.
Ten peoples cars were towed away.
The ice skates are her's.

Motivating Activity

If necessary, help students as they correct the use of apostrophes in the Bellringer. Ask students to talk about difficulties they have had in deciding how to use apostrophes. Explain that this lesson will help them learn to use apostrophes correctly.

TEACH

Cross-reference: Usage
For instruction and practice of the material in Problems 1 and 2, refer students to Lesson 19.7, pp. 466–467.

7.8 Incorrect Use of Apostrophes

PROBLEM 1

Singular possessive nouns

apos We found James calculator lying on Martas desk.

SOLUTION

We found James's calculator lying on Marta's desk.

Use an apostrophe and an *-s* to form the possessive of a singular noun, even one that ends in *-s*.

PROBLEM 2

Plural possessive nouns ending in -s

apos The acrobats stunts thrilled their audience.
apos The horses bridles are in the stable.

SOLUTION

The acrobats' stunts thrilled their audience.

The horses' bridles are in the stable.

Use an apostrophe alone to form the possessive of a plural noun that ends in *-s*.

256 *Troubleshooter*

Teacher's Classroom Resources

The following resources can be used for planning, instruction, practice, or reinforcement.

Teaching Tools
Lesson Plans

Grammar Workbook
Lesson 80

PROBLEM 3

Plural possessive nouns not ending in -s.

apos The childrens paints are on the table.

SOLUTION

The children's paints are on the table.

Use an apostrophe and an *-s* to form the possessive of a plural noun that does not end in *-s.*

PROBLEM 4

Possessive personal pronouns

apos This seat is her's, and the one over there is your's.

SOLUTION

This seat is hers, and the one over there is yours.

Do not use an apostrophe with any of the possessive personal pronouns.

Need More Help?

If you need more help with apostrophes, see Lesson 19.7, page 466.

TEACH

Cross-reference: Usage

For instruction and practice of the material in Problems 3 and 4, refer students to Lesson 19.7, pp. 466–467.

Two-Minute Skill Drill

Write these sentences on the board and have students correct all apostrophe errors:

Marias cousins visited her last Tuesday. They brought her two books' for her birthday. The childrens parents joined in the birthday party.

Independent Practice

Skills Practice

Grammar Workbook, Lesson 80

CLOSE

Invite students to prepare a pamphlet explaining the proper use of the possessive apostrophe. They could keep their pamphlet for reference or distribute it as a guide for other student writers.

Setting the Purpose

Lesson 7.9 teaches students how to avoid the incorrect use of capitalization in their writing.

FOCUS

Lesson Overview

Objective: To recognize and correct errors in the use of capitalization when referring to nationalities, languages, and ethnic groups, and in the first word of direct quotations

Bellringer

When students enter the classroom, have this assignment on the board: *Find the error in each of the following sentences, and then write them correctly:*

A russian diplomat wrote a letter to the newspaper.
Janelle wants to travel in Mexico, so she is studying spanish.
Dad said, "help your brother with his homework."

TEACH

Cross-reference: Mechanics

For instruction and practice of the material in Problem 1, refer students to Lesson 18.4, pp. 444–445.

Cross-reference: Mechanics

For instruction and practice of the material in Problem 2, refer students to Lesson 18.1, pp. 438–439.

Independent Practice

Skills Practice

Grammar Workbook
Lessons 63–70

7.9 Incorrect Capitalization

PROBLEM 1

Words referring to ethnic groups, nationalities, and languages

cap A brazilian student is studying french.

SOLUTION

A Brazilian student is studying French.

Capitalize proper nouns and adjectives that refer to ethnic groups, nationalities, and languages.

PROBLEM 2

The first word of a direct quotation

cap Duane said, "school will begin soon."

SOLUTION

Duane said, "School will begin soon."

Capitalize the first word in a direct quotation.

Need More Help? *If you need more help with capitalization, see Lessons 18.1 through 18.4, pages 438–445.*

CLOSE

Have students imagine they are exchange students in a foreign country. Ask them to write a paragraph or two about the country and the people they meet there. Have them include at least two lines of dialogue. Remind students to watch out for the capitalization errors addressed in this Troubleshooter.

Teacher's Classroom Resources

The following resources can be used for planning, instruction, practice, or reinforcement.

Teaching Tools *Lesson Plans*

Grammar Workbook, Lessons 63–70

Part 2

Grammar, Usage, and Mechanics

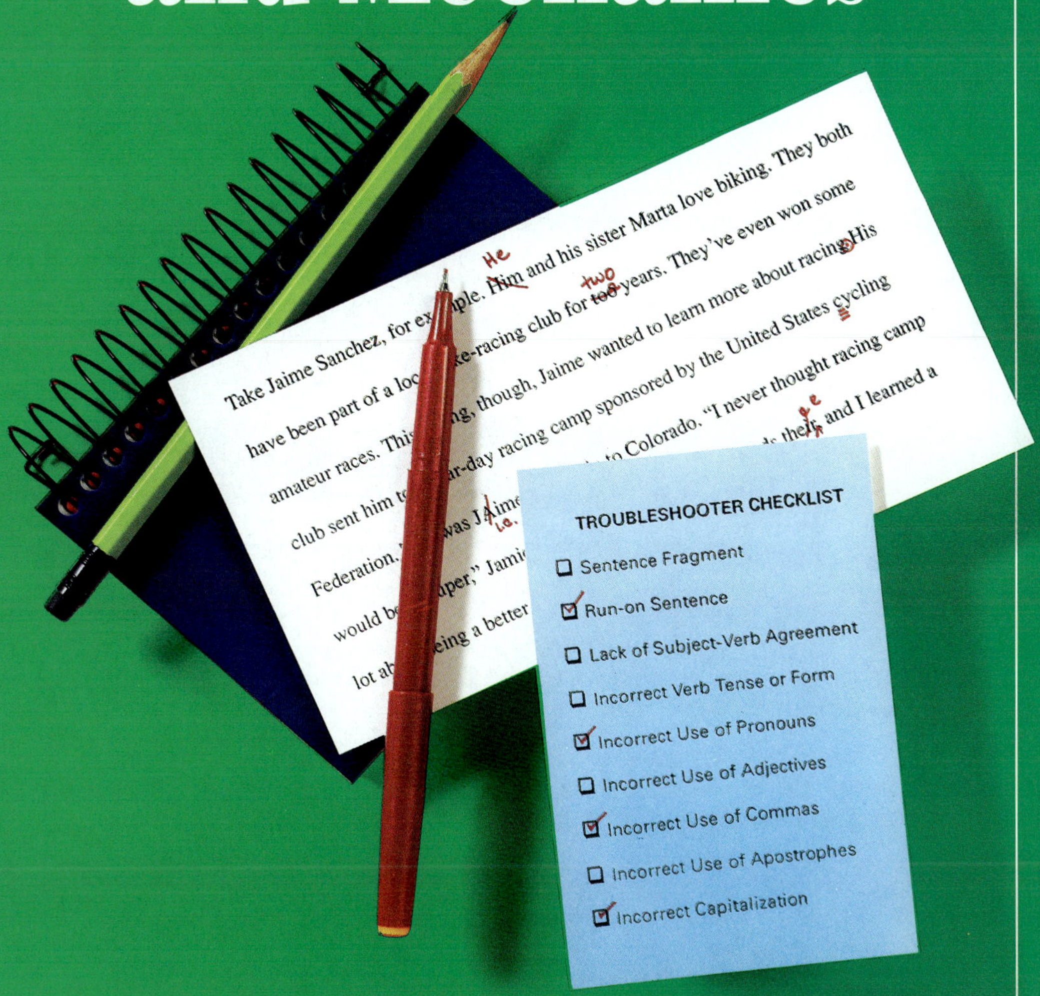

Part 2 Grammar, Usage, and Mechanics

UNIT
8 Subjects, Predicates, and Sentences

Grammar | Lessons

UNIT GOALS

The goal of Unit 8 is to help students, through example and instruction, to develop an understanding of and an ability to use complete sentences. The lessons teach students to identify the four kinds of sentences, to recognize sentence fragments, and to recognize the subjects and predicates of simple and compound sentences.

Unit Assessment

Tests with Answer Key
Unit 8 Pretest, pp. 29–30
Unit 8 Mastery Test, pp. 31–32

Test Generator
Unit 8 Pretest
Unit 8 Mastery Test

You may wish to administer the Unit 8 Pretest at this point.

Key to Ability Levels

Enabling Strategies have been coded for varying learning styles and abilities.

L1 Level 1 activities are within the ability range of Learning Disabled students.

L2 Level 2 activities are basic-to-average activities and are within the ability range of average students.

L3 Level 3 activities are challenging activities and are within the ability range of above-average students.

LEP LEP activities are within the ability range of Limited English Proficiency students.

Setting the Purpose

Lesson 8.1 teaches students to identify the four kinds of sentences—declarative, interrogative, exclamatory, and imperative—and to punctuate them correctly.

FOCUS

Lesson Overview

Objective: To identify the four kinds of sentences and punctuate them correctly

Bellringer

When students enter the classroom, have this assignment on the board: *Rewrite these sentences as questions:*

The dog catches the ball.
The dog is happy!
Throw the ball again.

Motivating Activity

Discuss with students what they needed to change or add to the sentences in the Bellringer to make them into questions. Point out any changes in word order, and note the different punctuation marks.

TEACH

Speaking and Listening

Encourage students to listen for the four kinds of sentences in normal conversation. The intonation people use indicates the kind of sentence being spoken. Use students' own speech or recorded dialogue to help students recognize the correspondence between oral intonation and written punctuation.

8.1 Kinds of Sentences

A **sentence** is a group of words that expresses a complete thought.

Different kinds of sentences have different purposes. A sentence can make a statement, ask a question, give a command, or express strong feeling. All sentences begin with a capital letter and end with a punctuation mark.

A **declarative sentence** makes a statement or tells something. It ends with a period.

James M. Barrie lived in England.

An **interrogative sentence** asks something. It ends with a question mark.

Have you read the book *Peter Pan*?

An **exclamatory sentence** shows strong feeling. It ends with an exclamation point.

What fun Peter had!

An **imperative sentence** commands someone to do something. It usually ends with a period.

Tell me about the movie.

The movie *Hook* was based on the book *Peter Pan*.

Have you seen the movie yet?

Describe Captain Hook.

What amazing special effects the movie has!

Teacher's Classroom Resources

The following resources can be used for planning, instruction, practice, reinforcement, assessment, reteaching, enrichment, or evaluation.

Teaching Tools
Lesson Plans

Blackline Masters
Grammar Practice, p. 1
Grammar Reteaching, p. 1
Grammar Enrichment, p. 1

Grammar Workbook
Lessons 1–2

Unit Assessment
Tests with Answer Key
Unit 8 Pretest, pp. 29–30

Test Generator
Unit 8 Pretest

You may wish to administer the Unit 8 Pretest at this point.

Exercise 1 Identifying Kinds of Sentences

Write *declarative, interrogative, exclamatory,* or *imperative* to identify each sentence.

1. Peter Pan protected a group of young orphans.
2. Did he protect them?
3. How mean Captain Hook and his pirates were!
4. Watch carefully for pirate ships on the horizon.
5. How did Peter Pan learn to fly?

Exercise 2 Punctuating Different Kinds of Sentences

Write the following sentences, beginning and ending each correctly.

1. my favorite character in the story is Tinker Bell
2. how I love fantasy stories
3. why did Peter hide outside the window
4. peter lost his shadow in Wendy's home
5. please sew my shadow back onto my feet
6. come to Never-Never Land with me
7. how excited Wendy must have been
8. the pirates kidnapped Wendy and the children
9. what will the wicked pirates do to the poor children
10. explain how Peter rescued his friends
11. who walked off the end of the plank
12. the story has been a play on Broadway, a television show, and an animated movie
13. do you know when the play was first produced
14. believe it or not, it was about one hundred years ago
15. a woman played the role of Peter in the Broadway play
16. how excited audiences were to see her fly through the air
17. the fairy Tinker Bell helps Peter
18. tell me the story again
19. do you think adults believe in Tinker Bell
20. what a great story this is

Enabling Strategies

LEP Forming Questions

Tell students that English forms yes-no questions in a variety of ways. One way is to insert a form of the word *do* in front of the subject: Do the pirates capture Wendy? Explain that forming yes-no questions by inserting *do* is an unusual feature of English. Most languages form yes-no questions by reordering the words or by changing the intonation. Have students practice forming questions using the correct form of *do* (*do, does,* or *did*).

PRACTICE AND ASSESS

Answers: Exercise 1

1. declarative
2. interrogative
3. exclamatory
4. imperative
5. interrogative

Answers: Exercise 2

1. My favorite . . . Tinker Bell.
2. How I love fantasy stories!
3. Why did Peter . . . the window?
4. Peter lost . . . home.
5. Please sew . . . onto my feet.
6. Come to . . . with me.
7. How excited . . . must have been!
8. The pirates . . . and the children.
9. What will . . . children?
10. Explain how . . . his friends.
11. Who walked . . . the plank?
12. The story . . . an animated movie.
13. Do you know . . . produced?
14. Believe it . . . years ago! (*or* .)
15. A woman . . . Broadway play.
16. How excited . . . through the air!
17. The fairy Tinker Bell helps Peter.
18. Tell me the story again.
19. Do you think adults believe in Tinker Bell?
20. What a great story this is!

Independent Practice

Skills Practice

Grammar Practice, p. 1
Grammar Reteaching, p. 1
Grammar Enrichment, p. 1

Grammar Workbook, *Lessons 1–2*

CLOSE

Have students check some of their recent writing for correct punctuation of the four kinds of sentences.

Setting the Purpose

In Lesson 8.2 students learn to identify the two sentence parts—subject and predicate—as well as to identify and correct sentence fragments.

FOCUS

Lesson Overview

Objective: To use complete sentences and avoid or correct sentence fragments

Bellringer

When students enter the classroom, have this assignment on the board: *Put the following phrases in the correct order to make a complete sentence:*

walk through green forests
Jared, Jean, and Jonah
and colorful meadows

Motivating Activity

Ask students how they knew which phrase would come first in the sentence. Are any of the phrases by themselves complete sentences? Why or why not?

TEACH

Teaching Tip

Point out to students that sentences follow certain patterns and that each pattern must include a subject and a predicate. Compare a sentence to a dinner plate, and a fragment to a piece of a broken plate. The piece (fragment) may contain the subject, the predicate, or another part of the sentence—but a whole plate (sentence) must contain at least a subject and a predicate.

8.2 Sentences and Sentence Fragments

Every sentence has two parts: a subject and a predicate.

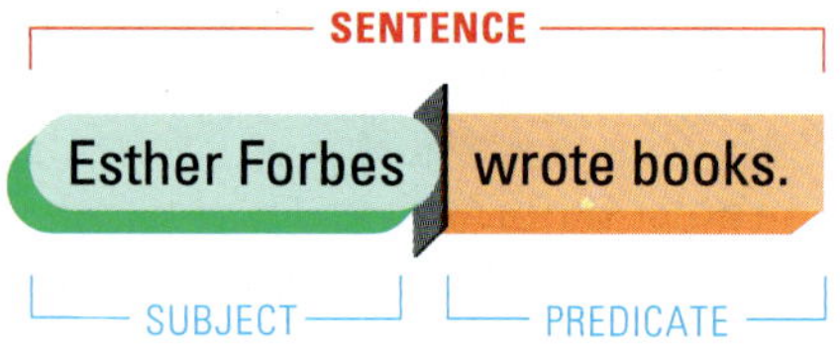

The **subject part** of a sentence names whom or what the sentence is about.

The **predicate part** of the sentence tells what the subject does or has. It can also describe what the subject is or is like.

A sentence must have both a subject and a predicate. It must also express a complete thought.

A **sentence fragment** does not express a complete thought. It may also be missing a subject, a predicate, or both.

You often use sentence fragments when you speak. You should avoid using them when you write, however.

Correcting Sentence Fragments		
Fragment	**Problem**	**Sentence**
Paul Revere.	The fragment lacks a predicate. *What did Paul Revere do?*	Paul Revere warned the people.
Worked for Paul Revere.	The fragment lacks a subject. *Who worked for Paul Revere?*	Johnny Tremain worked for Paul Revere.
About history.	The fragment lacks both a subject and a predicate.	Esther Forbes wrote books about history.

Teacher's Classroom Resources

The following resources can be used for planning, instruction, practice, reinforcement, reteaching, or enrichment.

Teaching Tools
Lesson Plans

Blackline Masters
Grammar Practice, p. 1
Grammar Reteaching, p. 2
Grammar Enrichment, p. 1

Grammar Workbook
Lesson 6

Exercise 3 **Identifying Sentences and Fragments**

Write *sentence* or *fragment* for each item. If an item is a fragment, explain what is missing.

1. The book *Johnny Tremain* is historical fiction.
2. A Newbery Medal winner.
3. Esther Forbes's nonfiction book on Paul Revere won a Pulitzer Prize.
4. The silversmith Paul Revere.
5. Offered Johnny a job.
6. Johnny liked his work.
7. Made things of silver.
8. Johnny burned his hand.
9. A terrible accident.
10. An operation made his hand well again.

Exercise 4 **Identifying Subjects and Predicates**

Write each sentence, underlining each subject part once and each predicate part twice. If the item is not a complete sentence, write *fragment.*

1. The setting is the American Revolution.
2. Sam Adams, John Hancock, and Paul Revere.
3. Real historical characters fill the book.
4. Americans wanted independence from England.
5. Fought for freedom of speech and other rights.
6. Johnny participated in the Boston Tea Party.
7. The Americans disliked the British tax on tea.
8. The townspeople disguised themselves.
9. As Mohawk Indians.
10. The Sons of Liberty planned the Boston Tea Party.
11. The rebels threw the tea into the harbor waters.
12. British officials decided to close Boston harbor.
13. Starved into submission.
14. The other colonies came to Boston's rescue.
15. Johnny's injured hand prevented him from being a soldier.

PRACTICE AND ASSESS

Answers: Exercise 3

1. sentence
2. fragment; missing predicate
3. sentence
4. fragment; missing predicate
5. fragment; missing subject
6. sentence
7. fragment; missing subject
8. sentence
9. fragment; missing predicate
10. sentence

Answers: Exercise 4

1. The setting is the American Revolution.
2. fragment
3. Real historical characters fill the book.
4. Americans wanted independence from England.
5. fragment
6. Johnny participated in the Boston Tea Party.
7. The Americans disliked the British tax on tea.
8. The townspeople disguised themselves.
9. fragment
10. The Sons of Liberty planned the Boston Tea Party.
11. The rebels threw the tea into the harbor waters.
12. British officials decided to close Boston Harbor.
13. fragment
14. The other colonies came to Boston's rescue.
15. Johnny's injured hand prevented him from being a soldier.

Independent Practice

Skills Practice

- *Grammar Practice,* p. 1
- *Grammar Reteaching,* p. 2
- *Grammar Enrichment,* p. 1
- ***Grammar Workbook,*** Lesson 6

Enabling Strategies

LEP Exploring Fragments

Students may become confused when discussing sentence fragments, because in conversational English it is common to use fragments in response to questions. Have pairs of students practice asking questions and responding in complete sentences.

CLOSE

Have students explain in their own words how they know when a sentence is complete and when it is a fragment.

Setting the Purpose

Lesson 8.3 teaches students to identify the simple subject or predicate within the complete subject or predicate.

FOCUS

Lesson Overview

Objective: To identify and use simple and complete subjects and predicates

Bellringer

When students enter the classroom, have this assignment on the board: *Write a complete sentence using as few words as possible.*

Motivating Activity

Call on volunteers to write their sentences on the board. Work with students to determine the shortest complete sentence. Have students identify the subject and predicate in each short sentence they wrote.

TEACH

Teaching Tip

A good way to teach the difference between simple and complete subjects and predicates is to give students a pronoun as a simple subject and a single verb as the predicate and then have the students add words to create a long sentence. For example, starting with *She reads,* they could expand this to *The little girl next door always reads my magazines in her treehouse.*

8.3 Subjects and Predicates

A sentence consists of a subject and a predicate, which together express a complete thought. Both a subject and a predicate may consist of more than one word.

Complete Subject	Complete Predicate
The main character	is Kit Tyler.
Kit	travels from the tropics to Connecticut.

The complete subject includes all of the words in the subject of a sentence.

The complete predicate includes all of the words in the predicate of a sentence.

Not all of the words in the subject or the predicate are of equal importance.

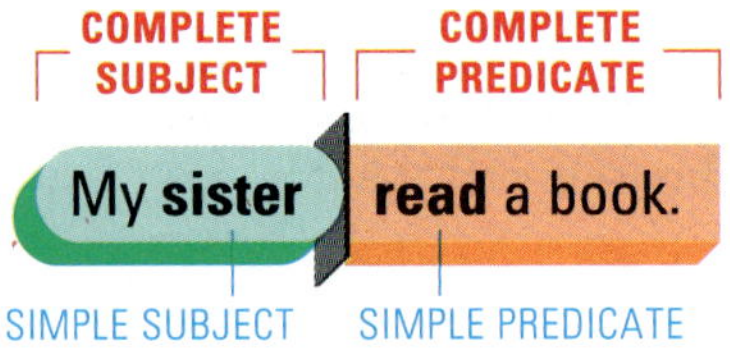

The simple subject is the main word or group of words in the complete subject.

The simple subject is usually a noun or a pronoun. A **noun** is a word that names a person, a place, a thing, or an idea. A **pronoun** is a word that takes the place of one or more nouns.

The simple predicate is the main word or group of words in the complete predicate.

The simple predicate is always a verb. A **verb** is a word that expresses an action or a state of being.

Sometimes the simple subject is also the complete subject. Similarly, the simple predicate may also be the complete predicate.

Teacher's Classroom Resources

The following resources can be used for planning, instruction, practice, reinforcement, reteaching, or enrichment.

Teaching Tools
Lesson Plans

Blackline Masters
Grammar Practice, p. 2
Grammar Reteaching, p. 3
Grammar Enrichment, p. 2

Grammar Workbook
Lesson 3

Exercise 5 Identifying Complete Subjects and Predicates

Write each sentence. Underline each complete subject once and each complete predicate twice.

1. My sister read *The Witch of Blackbird Pond.*
2. The book was written by Elizabeth George Speare.
3. It describes island life in the 1680s.
4. A young girl is the main character.
5. Kit lived a life of luxury.
6. She loved the island life.
7. This girl of the islands enjoyed the sun and the sea.
8. Her grandfather gave many parties.
9. Many friends attended her festive dance parties.
10. Kit's happiness ended with her grandfather's death.
11. Young Kit lost all her money.
12. Her life of luxury was over.
13. Kit had no family left in the islands.
14. Her aunt lived in the Connecticut Colony in America.
15. Kit went there to live.
16. She traveled to America by ship.
17. She was very lonely aboard ship.
18. A storm blew Kit's ship about for four days.
19. The ship approached land after many days.
20. The Connecticut Colony shore looked gray and bleak.

Exercise 6 Identifying Simple Subjects and Simple Predicates

Write the simple subject and simple predicate from each sentence.

1. Kit traveled far to meet her new family.
2. They were very different from Kit.
3. Kit's new family worked very hard.
4. The colonists wore plain clothing.
5. Kit's bright, colorful dresses shocked them.
6. These serious people discouraged parties.
7. Kit's strange island customs made her unpopular.
8. Snow was a surprise for Kit.
9. Kit's past winters were balmy.
10. Kit longed for her island home.

PRACTICE AND ASSESS

Answers: Exercise 5

1. My sister read *The Witch of Blackbird Pond.*
2. The book was written by Elizabeth George Speare.
3. It describes island life in the 1680s.
4. A young girl is the main character.
5. Kit lived a life of luxury.
6. She loved the island life.
7. This girl of the islands enjoyed the sun and the sea.
8. Her grandfather gave many parties.
9. Many friends attended her festive dance parties.
10. Kit's happiness ended with her grandfather's death.
11. Young Kit lost all her money.
12. Her life of luxury was over.
13. Kit had no family left in the islands.
14. Her aunt lived in the Connecticut Colony in America.
15. Kit went there to live.
16. She traveled to America by ship.
17. She was very lonely aboard ship.
18. A storm blew Kit's ship about for four days.
19. The ship approached land after many days.
20. The Connecticut Colony shore looked gray and bleak.

Answers: Exercise 6

1. subj. *Kit;* pred. *traveled*
2. subj. *They;* pred. *were*
3. subj. *family;* pred. *worked*
4. subj. *colonists;* pred. *wore*
5. subj. *dresses;* pred. *shocked*
6. subj. *people;* pred. *discouraged*
7. subj. *customs;* pred. *made*
8. subj. *Snow;* pred. *was*
9. subj. *winters;* pred. *were*
10. subj. *Kit;* pred. *longed*

CLOSE

Have students refer to a text in another subject area and identify the simple subjects and simple predicates in sentences.

Enabling Strategies

LEP Finding Simple Subjects and Simple Predicates

Explain to students that when people learn a language, they often speak telegraphically using just nouns and verbs to communicate. Have students make a chart with nouns or pronouns in one column and verbs in another. Have them pair words to make simple subjects and predicates. Students can check that their "sentence" makes sense in this simple form. Extend the activity by having students embellish each sentence; then go back to find the subject and predicate.

Setting the Purpose

Lesson 8.4 teaches students to use varied and appropriate sentence structures by identifying subjects in inverted sentences and understood subjects.

FOCUS

Lesson Overview

Objective: To rewrite questions as statements and identify the normal subject-predicate word order of sentences

Bellringer

When students enter the classroom, have this assignment on the board: *Write examples of a statement, a question, and a command.*

Motivating Activity

Have volunteers write their sentences from the Bellringer on the board. Ask students to find the subject and predicate in each. If students need help, have them note which type of sentence gives them difficulty.

TEACH

Critical Thinking

On the board, write the sentence *Robinson sometimes wrote in a diary while stranded on the island.* Tell students that when sentences follow normal word order, the subject comes before the predicate. Then have students move a word or phrase from the predicate to the beginning of the sentence: *Sometimes Robinson wrote ...;* or *While stranded on the island, Robinson sometimes wrote...*

8.4 Finding Subjects

Most statements begin with the subject.

SUBJECT: Daniel Defoe | PREDICATE: wrote *Robinson Crusoe.*

Other kinds of sentences, such as questions, may begin with part or all of the predicate. The subject comes next, followed by the rest of the predicate.

PREDICATE: Did | SUBJECT: Defoe | PREDICATE: write the book?

To locate the subject of a question, rearrange the words to form a statement.

Predicate	Subject	Predicate
Have	all of the students	finished reading the book?
	All of the students	have finished reading the book.

Sometimes statements may have inverted word order. In these sentences the predicate comes before the subject.

PREDICATE: Across the beach walked | SUBJECT: Robinson.

In requests and commands, the subject is usually not stated. The word *you* is understood to be the subject.

UNDERSTOOD SUBJECT: (You) | PREDICATE: read a chapter tonight

Teacher's Classroom Resources

The following resources can be used for planning, instruction, practice, reinforcement, reteaching, or enrichment.

Teaching Tools
Lesson Plans

Blackline Masters
Grammar Practice, p. 3
Grammar Reteaching, p. 4
Grammar Enrichment, p. 3

Grammar Workbook
Lesson 4

Exercise 7 Rewriting Questions as Statements

Rewrite each question as a statement. Underline each complete subject.

1. Did Robinson build a house?
2. Did the goats on the island provide fresh milk?
3. Did Robinson plant corn on the island?
4. Did the stranded man carve a canoe out of a tree?
5. Was the weather favorable?

Exercise 8 Finding Subjects

Write each sentence. Underline each subject. Write *(You)* before any sentence with an understood subject.

1. Did a parrot learn English from Robinson?
2. Many years passed before Robinson's rescue.
3. Did the time pass slowly without a clock?
4. Robinson explored every part of the island.
5. Read the last chapter for homework.
6. Do animal skins make good clothing?
7. He sent smoke signals from the top of a hill.
8. On the beach sat a man.
9. Tell me the ending of the story.
10. On the island waited the unfortunate man.
11. Describe how Robinson returns to London.
12. Did Robinson find his own footprint in the sand?
13. Defoe wrote the adventure almost 300 years ago.
14. He based his story on a real person, Alexander Selkirk.
15. Selkirk survived four years on a deserted island.
16. Imagine having to survive by your wits.
17. Was Robinson Crusoe on the island 24 years?
18. England changed greatly in that time.
19. Defoe wrote his book for adults.
20. Many young people like the book, too!

Enabling Strategies

LEP Forming Questions with *Do*

English uses *do* to form questions (***Did** I see it?*) and for emphasis (*I **did** see it*). The *do* that makes questions is different from the *do* that indicates emphasis. When we turn a question that begins with *do* back into a statement, the *do* can disappear because there is no real need for it. For example, *Did I see it?* corresponds to two statements: *I saw it* and *I did see it*. Either is acceptable, but many writers would use the *did* version primarily where greater emphasis was required.

PRACTICE AND ASSESS

Answers: Exercise 7

1. Robinson built a house.
2. The goats on the island provided fresh milk.
3. Robinson planted corn on the island.
4. The stranded man carved a canoe out of a tree.
5. The weather was favorable.

Answers: Exercise 8

1. subj.: a parrot
2. subj.: Many years
3. subj.: the time
4. subj.: Robinson
5. subj.: You
6. subj.: animal skins
7. subj.: He
8. subj.: a man
9. subj.: You
10. subj.: the unfortunate man
11. subj.: You
12. subj.: Robinson
13. subj.: Defoe
14. subj.: He
15. subj.: Selkirk
16. subj.: You
17. subj.: Robinson Crusoe
18. subj.: England
19. subj.: Defoe
20. subj.: Many young people

Independent Practice

Skills Practice

- *Grammar Practice*, p. 3
- *Grammar Reteaching*, p. 4
- *Grammar Enrichment*, p. 3
- ***Grammar Workbook***, Lesson 4

CLOSE

Have each student create a sentence with inverted word order, either a question or a statement. They can then exchange papers and rewrite the sentences in normal word order.

Setting the Purpose

Lesson 8.5 teaches students how to use compound subjects and compound predicates in sentences.

FOCUS

Lesson Overview

Objective: To identify compound subjects and compound predicates

Bellringer

When students enter the classroom, have this assignment on the board: *Write two sentences that both start with "The artist drew . . ."*

Motivating Activity

Have volunteers write their sentences on the board. Have students combine the two sentences to make one complete sentence. Ask students if it is necessary to repeat the words *"The artist drew"* in the combined sentence.

TEACH

Cooperative Learning

Sentences with compound subjects and compound predicates can be broken down into smaller component sentences. Have one student make up a compound subject. Another can add to that a compound predicate. Have students write the completed sentence and then work as a group to figure out how many smaller sentences can be made from the parts of the larger compound sentence. (Eight new sentences can be made.)

8.5 Compound Subjects and Compound Predicates

Some sentences have more than one simple subject.

A **compound subject** has two or more simple subjects that have the same predicate. The simple subjects are joined by *and*, *or*, or *but*.

COMPOUND SUBJECT

Many **painters** and **sculptors** | lead colorful lives.

Other sentences have more than one simple predicate.

A **compound predicate** has two or more simple predicates, or verbs, that have the same subject. The verbs are joined by *and, or,* or *but.*

COMPOUND PREDICATE

Juan | **lived** in Spain and **studied** painting.

Some sentences have both a compound subject and a compound predicate.

COMPOUND SUBJECT — COMPOUND PREDICATE

Juan and his **family** | **were** poor but **worked** hard.

When a sentence has three or more simple subjects or three simple predicates, the word that joins them usually comes before only the last simple subject or predicate. Notice the position of *and* in the sentence below.

Velázquez, El Greco, and **Picasso** are three famous Spanish painters.

Teacher's Classroom Resources

The following resources can be used for planning, instruction, practice, reinforcement, reteaching, or enrichment.

Teaching Tools
Lesson Plans

Blackline Masters
Grammar Practice, p. 4
Grammar Reteaching, p. 5
Grammar Enrichment, p. 4

Grammar Workbook
Lesson 4

Exercise 9 **Identifying Compound Subjects and Predicates**

Write the compound subject and compound predicate in the sentences below. Underline the compound subjects and circle the compound predicates.

1. Many authors and artists have varied interests.
2. Elizabeth Borton de Treviño researched and wrote the book *I, Juan de Pareja.*
3. She studied violin and worked at a newspaper.
4. She and Juan knew and valued hard work.
5. Illness and poverty made Juan very weak.
6. A monk and a dog nursed him back to health.
7. Young Juan and his father loved art but lacked money for art supplies.
8. Brushes, canvas, and paint were available but cost too much money for the family.
9. Juan left his hometown and looked for a job.
10. He missed his home but longed to be an artist.
11. A baker hired him but paid him very little.
12. Did Juan work in the bakery and sleep there, too?
13. The boy left the bakery and traveled to Madrid.
14. Juan met an artist in Madrid and worked for him.
15. The king or his family often posed for the artist.
16. The painter and his helper worked well together.
17. Juan cured the king's sick dog and won a reward.
18. Juan and Velázquez traveled and studied together.
19. Have you read this book or heard about it?
20. King Philip IV of Spain liked Velázquez and made him the official court painter.
21. Velázquez painted people skillfully and showed the dignity and worth of each subject.
22. Sensitive portraits of ordinary people and a great portrait of Pope Innocent X are among Velázquez's well-known works.
23. The Infanta Margarita, her two maids, and the artist appear in Velázquez's famous painting *Las Meninas.*
24. The painting's subject, its composition, and its size were unique for the time.
25. Most paintings at that time showed people in formal poses and depicted important events.

Enabling Strategies

LEP Building Compounds

Students learning English may understand sentences with compound predicates more clearly if you write the component simple sentences on the board: *Juan lived in Spain. Juan studied painting.* Have a volunteer read the sentences while the others listen for the subject that is the same. Ask the group to tell you how to make these two sentences into one with a compound predicate.

PRACTICE AND ASSESS

Answers: Exercise 9

1. comp. subj.: authors, artists
2. comp. pred.: researched, wrote
3. comp. pred.: studied, worked
4. comp. subj.: She, Juan; comp. pred.: knew, valued
5. comp. subj.: Illness, poverty
6. comp. subj.: monk, dog
7. comp. subj.: Juan, father; comp. pred.: loved, lacked
8. comp. subj.: Brushes, canvas, paint, comp. pred.: were, cost
9. comp. pred.: left, looked
10. comp. pred.: missed, longed
11. comp. pred.: hired, paid
12. comp. pred.: work, sleep
13. comp. pred.: left, traveled
14. comp. pred.: met, worked
15. comp. subj.: king, family
16. comp. subj.: painter, helper
17. comp. pred.: cured, won
18. comp. subj.: Juan, Velázquez; comp. pred.: traveled, studied
19. comp. pred.: have read, heard
20. comp. pred.: liked, made
21. comp. pred.: painted, showed
22. comp. subj.: portraits, portrait
23. comp. subj.: Infanta Margarita, maids, artist
24. comp. subj.: subject, composition, size
25. comp. pred.: showed, depicted

Independent Practice

Skills Practice

Grammar Practice, p. 4
Grammar Reteaching, p. 5
Grammar Enrichment, p. 4

Grammar Workbook, Lesson 4

CLOSE

Discuss with students why writers use compound subjects and compound predicates (to avoid repetitive sentences and make writing more interesting).

Setting the Purpose

Lesson 8.6 teaches students how to identify and use simple and compound sentences and how to correct run-on sentences.

FOCUS

Lesson Overview

Objective: To identify simple, compound, and run-on sentences

Bellringer

When students enter the classroom, have this assignment on the board: *Write down five different compound words.*

Motivating Activity

Students might deepen their understanding by considering the meaning of *compound* in different contexts. A compound eye (the kind many insects have) is composed of many simple eyes. Ask students to explain what a compound word is (words, such as *hotline, ice cream,* or *cross-reference,* that are composed of two or more words). Similarly, a compound sentence is made up of two or more sentences.

TEACH

Critical Thinking

Ask students to identify the two simple sentences contained in the compound sentence below:

> Clyde's report card was on the kitchen table, and we all sat around it like it was some kind of a big important document.
>
> —Walter Dean Myers, *Fast Sam, Cool Clyde, and Stuff*

8.6 Simple and Compound Sentences

A **simple sentence** has one subject and one predicate.

SIMPLE SENTENCE

The book *Carry On, Mr. Bowditch* | tells Nat's story.

A **compound sentence** is a sentence that contains two or more simple sentences joined by *and, but,* or *or.*

COMPOUND SENTENCE

Nat | boarded the ship, (and) the crowd | waved.

SIMPLE SENTENCE — SIMPLE SENTENCE

Remember that a simple sentence may have a compound subject, a compound predicate, or both. A compound sentence, however, contains two simple sentences.

Compound Subjects, Predicates, and Sentences	
Compound subject	**Nat** and the **captain** talked.
Compound predicate	The crew **worked** and **sang.**
Compound sentence	**Nat talked,** and **the crew worked.**

A **run-on sentence** is two or more sentences incorrectly written as one sentence. To correct a run-on, write separate sentences, or combine the sentences. If you combine the sentences, use either a semicolon alone or a comma with *and, or,* or *but.*

Correcting Run-on Sentences	
Run-on Sentences	**Corrected Sentences**
Nat boarded the ship the crowd waved. Nat boarded the ship, the crowd waved.	Nat boarded the ship**. T**he crowd waved. Nat boarded the ship**;** the crowd waved. Nat boarded the ship**, and** the crowd waved.

Teacher's Classroom Resources

The following resources can be used for planning, instruction, practice, reinforcement, reteaching, or enrichment.

Teaching Tools
Lesson Plans

Blackline Masters
Grammar Practice, p. 5
Grammar Reteaching, p. 6
Grammar Enrichment, p. 5

Grammar Workbook
Lesson 5

Exercise 10 Identifying Simple and Compound Sentences

Write whether each of the following sentences is *simple* or *compound*.

1. Nat and his family valued a good education.
2. His family had little money; he frequently worried about them.
3. The boy found a job and worked in a supply store for a while.
4. Nat read about sailing, or he studied mathematics.
5. Will Nat read about the stars, study navigation, and go to sea?
6. No teacher taught him, but Nat learned Spanish.
7. The boy sailed on a ship and worked as a navigator.
8. Sailors used charts of the stars, but Nat found errors in some of the measurements.
9. Nat taught the sailors mathematics, and the crew learned quickly.
10. He gathered information and wrote a book about navigation.

Exercise 11 Identifying Simple, Compound, and Run-on Sentences

Write whether each of the following sentences is *simple, compound,* or *run-on*. If it is a run-on sentence, rewrite it correctly.

1. Another ship adventure is *The True Confessions of Charlotte Doyle*.
2. Charlotte was brought up as a proper young lady she attended boarding school in England.
3. She returned to America her voyage to her home would not be an easy one.
4. Crew members wanted revenge on Captain Jaggery, the captain drove his crew hard, he treated them cruelly.
5. Charlotte told him the crew was about to mutiny.
6. Charlotte took responsibility and offered to help the crew.
7. The ship pitched and rolled in an awful storm, and the captain sent Charlotte aloft to fix a sail.
8. The captain killed his first mate and accused Charlotte of the murder.
9. The crew thought Charlotte was guilty; they didn't lift a finger to save her.
10. How did Charlotte escape being hanged, and what did she do when she reached America?

PRACTICE AND ASSESS

Answers: Exercise 10

1. simple	6. compound
2. compound	7. simple
3. simple	8. compound
4. compound	9. compound
5 simple	10. simple

Answers: Exercise 11

1. simple
2. run-on; . . . young lady. She . . .
3. run-on; . . . America. Her . . .
4. run-on; . . . Jaggery. The captain drove his crew hard and treated them cruelly.

5 simple	8. simple
6. simple	9. compound
7. compound	10. compound

Two-Minute Skill Drill

Have students change the following sentences into one sentence:

The captain steered the ship.

The crew worked hard.

Independent Practice

Skills Practice

- *Grammar Practice,* p. 5
- *Grammar Reteaching,* p. 6
- *Grammar Enrichment,* p. 5
- ***Grammar Workbook,*** Lesson 5

CLOSE

Have students look at the sentences in Exercise 10 and count the number of subjects and predicates in each one. Ask students what patterns they notice. (Compound sentences have two subjects and two predicates.)

Enabling Strategies

LEP Recognizing Compound Sentences

Students for whom English is a second language may need help in understanding the difference between a compound sentence and a run-on sentence. Write the following on the board: *Nat boarded the ship the crowd waved. Nat boarded the ship, and the crowd waved.* Point out that each sentence is really two sentences in one. Adding the comma and the word *and* makes one sentence—a compound sentence. Explain how the punctuation has changed. (*Nat boarded the ship and waved to the crowd.* The comma is deleted because it no longer joins two simple sentences.)

TEACH

About the Literature

Explain that the review contains a passage from Betty Smith's *A Tree Grows in Brooklyn.* After students have finished reading, use the passage to reinforce their understanding of simple subjects, complete subjects, simple predicates, and complete predicates. The exercises that follow are based on this passage and related topics.

Linking Grammar and Literature

Grammar Tip

Some students may notice that the author violates some of the rules covered in this unit: the first sentence lacks a comma before the conjunction; one sentence lacks a verb in the part following the semicolon. Emphasize that writers of fiction sometimes violate grammar rules in order to serve some other purpose in their writing.

Critical Thinking

Ask students to think about what kind of person Francie is as you reread the passage aloud. (She likes to read. She is interested in many different subjects. She is determined, organized, and systematic. She plans ahead. She hasn't seen libraries outside her neighborhood.)

UNIT 8

Unit Review

Grammar Review

Subjects, Predicates, and Sentences

In this passage from *A Tree Grows in Brooklyn,* it is 1912, and 11-year-old Francie Nolan plans to read every book in her local library. The passage has been annotated to show some of the sentence elements and sentence structures covered in this unit.

Literature Model

from A TREE GROWS IN BROOKLYN

by Betty Smith

Francie [Simple subject] thought that all the books in the world were in that library and she had a plan about reading all the books in the world. She was reading a book a day in alphabetical order and not skipping [Compound predicate] the dry ones. She remembered that the first author had been Abbott. She had been reading a book a day for a long time now and she was still in the B's. Already she had read about bees and buffaloes, Bermuda vacations and Byzantine architecture. For all of her enthusiasm, she had to admit that some of the B's had been hard going. But Francie was [Simple predicate] a reader. She read everything she could find: trash, classics, time tables and the grocer's price list. Some of the reading [Complete subject] had been wonderful; the Louisa Alcott books for example. She planned to read all the books over again when she had finished with the Z's.

Saturdays were different. [Simple sentence] She treated herself by reading a book not in the alphabetical sequence [Complete predicate]. On that day she asked the librarian to recommend a book.

Teacher's Classroom Resources

The following resources can be used for planning, instruction, practice, reinforcement, assessment, reteaching, or evaluation.

Teaching Tools
Lesson Plan

Grammar Workbook
Lessons 1–7
Unit 1 Review

Unit Assessment

Tests with Answer Key
Unit 8 Mastery Test, pp. 31–32

Test Generator
Unit 8 Mastery Test

Exercise 1

Writing Sentences from Fragments The following sentences and sentence fragments are based on the passage from *A Tree Grows in Brooklyn* on the preceding page. Rewrite each fragment as a complete sentence.

SAMPLE Francie loved to read. Planned to read all the books in the world.
ANSWER She planned to read all the books in the world.

1. She hoped to read a book a day. The first author.
2. Some of the books interested Francie more than others. Those by Louisa Alcott.
3. Francie read the books in alphabetical order. Was working her way through the B's.
4. One day a week she allowed herself a treat. Were special.
5. Francie asked the librarian to recommend a book. Didn't have to be in alphabetical order.

Exercise 2

Identifying Subjects and Predicates in Questions Rewrite each question to form a statement. Then underline each complete subject once and each complete predicate twice.

SAMPLE Does the librarian recommend a book?
ANSWER The librarian does recommend a book.

1. Has Francie read the book before?
2. Do Francie and the librarian like the book?
3. Does the girl choose a book for Sunday?
4. Can Francie read the book quickly?
5. Have the girl's parents encouraged her?
6. Can Francie read more than one book a day?
7. Does Francie read many books a day?
8. Are those books the most interesting?
9. Does Francie prefer adventure?
10. Is she in the library this afternoon?

PRACTICE AND ASSESS

Answers: Exercise 1

Answers will vary, but some suggestions are given below.

1. The first author was Abbott.
2. Those by Louisa Alcott were wonderful.
3. She was working her way through the B's.
4. Saturdays were special.
5. Her Saturday book didn't have to be in alphabetical order.

Answers: Exercise 2

1. Francie has read the book before.
2. Francie and the librarian like the book.
3. The girl chooses a book for Sunday.
4. Francie can read the book quickly.
5. The girl's parents have encouraged her.
6. Francie can read more than one book a day.
7. Francie reads many books a day.
8. Those books are the most interesting.
9. Francie prefers adventure.
10. She is in the library this afternoon.

Answers: Exercise 3

1. interrogative
2. declarative
3. declarative
4. declarative
5. exclamatory
6. declarative
7. interrogative
8. declarative
9. declarative
10. imperative

Answers: Exercise 4

1. Avi
2. great-grandparents
3. Avi
4. disability
5. teachers
6. Avi
7. book
8. Avi
9. writing
10. You

Exercise 3

Identifying Kinds of Sentences The following paragraph gives some information about the author Avi, who wrote *The True Confessions of Charlotte Doyle*. Write whether each sentence is *declarative*, *interrogative*, *exclamatory*, or *imperative*.

SAMPLE Learn more about the writer Avi.
ANSWER imperative

[1]Why do parents, teachers, and students all praise Avi's novels? [2]As Avi himself said, "Most of all I want them to enjoy a good read." [3]His notably readable, award-winning novels include mystery, adventure, historical, and comic novels. [4]Imaginative, fast-paced plots capture the reader quickly. [5]How exciting the books are! [6]Readers would be misled, however, if that is all they expected. [7]What are Avi's other goals as a writer for young people? [8]Avi writes about complex issues that are full of contradiction and irony. [9]He wants readers to think about these issues. [10]Check out an Avi book today.

Exercise 4

Identifying the Subject of a Sentence Write the simple subject from each sentence. Write *(You)* for any sentence with the subject understood.

SAMPLE A vivid imagination is one of Avi's gifts.
ANSWER imagination

1. Avi was born in Manhattan in 1937.
2. His great-grandparents were writers.
3. In school Avi had difficulty with writing.
4. A learning disability caused him to misspell many words.
5. His teachers thought he was sloppy and inattentive.
6. In spite of constant criticism, Avi succeeded.
7. Was Avi's first published book a collection of short stories for very young readers?
8. Avi based the book on his stories for his young sons.
9. Avi's writing for his growing sons became more sophisticated.
10. Read Avi's Newbery Honor books, *The True Confessions of Charlotte Doyle* and *Nothing But the Truth*.

Exercise 5

Rewriting Sentence Fragments Turn the following sentence fragments into complete sentences by adding a complete subject or a complete predicate. Include at least two examples of each sentence type: declarative, interrogative, imperative, and exclamatory.

SAMPLE My favorite books
ANSWER My favorite books have lots of action.

1. Adventure books for young readers.
2. Faces great danger.
3. Life on the high seas.
4. Climbs the rigging.
5. Tells of strange lands.
6. The courageous captain.
7. Loved ships and the sea.
8. Explored the harbor.
9. Listened to the storytellers.
10. Spent her childhood near the water.
11. Some of the best adventure stories.
12. The whole plot.
13. Portrays fires and shipwrecks.
14. Another author of adventure stories.
15. Ran away to live on a mountain.
16. Have been made into movies and plays.
17. A buried treasure.
18. Floated down the river on a raft.
19. An adventure on the river.
20. Survived in the wilderness.
21. Almost drowned in the rapids.
22. Saved the boy's life.
23. A leaky boat.
24. My two favorite heroes.
25. Held the captain hostage.
26. Followed the map's directions.
27. An action-packed movie.
28. Bobbed down the Delaware in an inner tube.
29. Always finds a good solution.
30. My next adventure story.

Answers: Exercise 5

Answers will vary, but some suggestions are given below.

1. Read adventure books for young readers.
2. Does he face great danger?
3. What an exciting life we'll have on the high seas!
4. The crew climbs the rigging.

Answers: Exercise 6

1. Louisa May Alcott's (father) (ran) schools unlike most others of their time.
2. (Mr. Alcott) (used) his liberal ideas in teaching his four daughters.
3. (Louisa May Alcott) (wrote) "rubbishy novels" under the name A. N. Barnard.
4. (She) (published) her famous novel *Little Women* in 1869.
5. (Alcott) (based) the story of the March girls on her own family.

Answers: Exercise 7

1. Painters in Paris in the late nineteenth century experimented with color and developed new techniques.
2. Rapid brushstrokes and dabs of color created the style of painting called Impressionism.
3. Light and color give Impressionist paintings their brilliance.
4. Impressionist artists escaped from the studio and captured the life of the streets and open air.
5. Monet, Degas, Pissarro, and Renoir were all important Impressionist painters.

Exercise 6

Identifying Simple and Complete Subjects and Predicates The following sentences tell about the author Louisa May Alcott. Write each sentence. Underline the complete subject once and the complete predicate twice. Then circle the simple subject and the simple predicate.

SAMPLE Alcott's family influenced her writing.
ANSWER Alcott's (family) (influenced) her writing.

1. Louisa May Alcott's father ran schools unlike most others of their time.
2. Mr. Alcott used his liberal ideas in teaching his four daughters.
3. Louisa May Alcott wrote "rubbishy novels" under the name A. N. Barnard.
4. She published her famous novel *Little Women* in 1869.
5. Alcott based the story of the March girls on her own family.

Exercise 7

Identifying Compound Subjects and Predicates Write each sentence. If the sentence has a compound subject, draw a line under each simple subject. If the sentence has a compound predicate, draw two lines under each simple predicate.

SAMPLE France and Impressionism are closely identified.
ANSWER France and Impressionism are closely identified.

1. Painters in Paris in the late nineteenth century experimented with color and developed new techniques.
2. Rapid brushstrokes and dabs of color created the style of painting called Impressionism.
3. Light and color give Impressionist paintings their brilliance.
4. Impressionist artists escaped from the studio and captured the life of the streets and open air.
5. Monet, Degas, Pissarro, and Renoir were all important Impressionist painters.

Exercise 8

Writing Compound Sentences The following pairs of related simple sentences are about Francie and her family in *A Tree Grows in Brooklyn.* Combine each pair to form a compound sentence using *and*, *but*, or *or*.

SAMPLE Francie buys bread for her family. Her brother Neeley helps her carry it home.

ANSWER Francie buys bread for her family, and her brother Neeley helps her carry it home.

1. Francie's father works as a singing waiter. He can't always find work.
2. Her mother cleans houses for a living. She also cooks the family's meals.
3. On Saturdays the family eats a big dinner. They even have dessert.
4. Francie's parents don't have very much money. They work very hard to provide for their children.
5. The family must save every spare penny. They won't have enough money for their daily food.

Exercise 9

Correcting Run-on Sentences Correct the following run-on sentences by rewriting them as separate sentences or combining them, using a comma, a semicolon, or the words *and*, *or*, or *but.*

SAMPLE Writing for children of any age is not an easy task writing for very young children is the most difficult.

ANSWER Writing for children of any age is not an easy task, but writing for very young children is the most difficult.

1. Beatrix Potter wrote in the early 1900s, her books for young children are now considered classics.
2. She spent her summers in the country, she spent winters in London.
3. Potter's summer experiences sparked her imagination she found life in the country exciting and vital.
4. *The Tale of Peter Rabbit* was originally written as a letter to a child who was ill Potter added to the letter and sent it to a publisher.
5. The Beatrix Potter books are strong because of their common sense and humor they are exciting because of their action and adventure.

Answers: Exercise 8

1. Francie's ... waiter, but he ...
2. Her mother ... living, and she ...
3. On Saturdays... dinner, and they...
4. Francie's ... money, but they ...
5. The family ... penny, or they ...

Answers: Exercise 9

Answers may vary, but some suggestions are given below.

1. ... early 1900s. Her books ...
2. ... country, but she spent ...
3. ... imagination. She found ...
4. ... ill; Potter ...
5. ... and humor. They are ...

UNIT 8
Review

Answers: Exercise 10

Proofreading

This proofreading activity provides editing practice with (1) the current or previous units' skills, (2) the **Trouble-shooter** errors, and (3) spelling errors. Students should be able to complete the exercise by referring to the units, the **Troubleshooter**, and a dictionary. (Note: A run-on sentence counts as one error.)

	Error (Type of Error)
1.	• French (proper adjective)
	• painter. (end punctuation)
2.	• time. (end punctuation)
3.	• outdoors so (sentence fragment)
	• their (spelling)
4.	• outdoors. Women *or* outdoors; *or* outdoors, and (run-on sentence)
5.	• read (subject-verb agreement)
6.	• shows (subject-verb agreement)
	• child's (singluar possessive)
7.	• picture? (end punctuation)

Exercise 10 **Proofreading**

The following passage is about the artist Pierre-Auguste Renoir, whose work appears on this page. Rewrite the passage, correcting errors in spelling, capitalization, grammar, and usage. Add any missing punctuation. There are 10 errors.

Pierre-Auguste Renoir

1 Best known for his cheerful scenes of everyday life, french artist Pierre-Auguste Renoir (1841–1919) was an Impressionist painter 2 The ➡

Pierre-Auguste Renoir, *The Reading*, 1892

About the Art

Pierre-Auguste Renoir,
***The Reading*, 1892**

This painting titled *The Reading* is not Renoir's only painting about reading. He also painted a scene of two small girls sitting on a sofa looking at books, titled *Girls Reading*, as well as a picture of an older girl named Margot as she sat and read, titled *Girl Reading*. *The Reading* is a 21 1/2 by 25 3/4 inch oil on canvas, located in the Musée d'Orsay, Paris, France.

Impressionists tried to represent what they saw at one particular moment in time. [3]They preferred to paint outdoors there subjects could sit in natural light. [4]Renoir frequently painted people outdoors, women and children were his favorite subjects. [5]In *The Reading,* for example, two young girls reads a book in a pretty, sunlit setting. [6]Like the passage from *A Tree Grows in Brooklyn*, the painting show a childs' love of reading. [7]Can you imagine yourself in this picture

Exercise 11 **Mixed Review**

Revise each example, following the directions in parentheses.

1. Monet spent the summer of 1869 at Bougival. Renoir spent that summer at Bougival, also. (Write one simple sentence with a compound subject.)
2. Did Renoir and Monet develop the broken-color technique that became known as Impressionism? (Rewrite the sentence as a declarative sentence.)
3. Renoir traveled to Italy in 1880. He studied Renaissance painters there. (Write one simple sentence with a compound predicate.)
4. Concentrated on drawing for several years after this trip. (Make the fragment into a sentence.)
5. He studied at Charles Gleyre's studio. He was influenced by Edouard Manet. (Rewrite the pair as a compound sentence using *and*, *but*, or *or*.)
6. Light color and atmospheric effects are important elements of Impressionist paintings (Punctuate the sentence.)
7. Monet used muted colors to paint landscapes Renoir was more interested in painting figures and using rich color. (Correct the run-on sentence.)
8. Painters before the Impressionists painted in studios and used north light. The Impressionists painted outdoors and used natural light. (Rewrite the pair as a compound sentence.)
9. Who were some important Impressionist painters (Punctuate the sentence.)
10. What a marvelous sense of color and form Renoir had (Punctuate the sentence.)

Answers: Exercise 11

Mixed Review

1. Monet and Renoir spent the summer of 1869 at Bougival.
2. Renoir and Monet developed the broken-color technique that became known as Impressionism.
3. Renoir traveled to Italy in 1880 and studied Renaissance painters there.
4. Renoir concentrated on drawing for several years after this trip.
5. He studied at Charles Gleyre's studio, but he was influenced by Edouard Manet.
6. Light, color, and atmospheric effects are important elements of Impressionist paintings.
7. Monet used muted colors to paint landscapes. Renoir was more interested in painting figures and using rich color.
8. Painters before the Impressionists painted in studios and used north light, but the Impressionists painted outdoors and used natural light.
9. Who were some important Impressionist painters?
10. What a marvelous sense of color and form Renoir had!

CLOSE

Invite students to write a paragraph of fiction. Then have them underline each complete subject once and each complete predicate twice. Encourage them to correct any sentence fragments and run-on sentences they find.

Compound Predicates and Compound Sentences in Writing

Have students read the passage silently. Discuss the sentences that have compound predicates and the sentence that is a compound sentence in relation to the Techniques with Sentences below.

Techniques with Sentences

Discuss the techniques and have students examine recent writing projects and revise them using the techniques they have learned.

Practice

The answers to this challenging and enriching activity will vary. Refer to Techniques with Sentences as you evaluate student choices.

Writing Application

Compound Predicates and Compound Sentences in Writing To give her writing interest and texture, Nicholasa Mohr varies her sentences in this passage from *Nilda*. Some sentences have compound predicates. The last sentence is a compound sentence. As you read the passage, focus on the italicized parts.

> The sun came through the leaves, stems, and petals, streaming down like rows of bright ribbons landing on the dark green earth. . . . Nilda *walked* over to the flowers and *touched* them. Inhaling the sweet fragrance, she felt slightly dizzy, almost reeling. She *sat* down on the dark earth and *felt* the sun on her face, slipping down her body and over to the shrubs covered with roses. *The bright sash of warm sunlight enveloped her and the flowers; she was part of them; they were part of her.*

Techniques with Sentences Try to apply Nicholasa Mohr's writing techniques when you write and revise your own work.

1. Use a compound predicate to make two simple sentences into one.

Two sentences Nilda *walked* over to the flowers. She *touched* them.
Mohr's version Nilda *walked* over to the flowers and *touched* them.

2. Combine simple sentences into compound sentences.

Separate sentences The bright sash of warm sunlight enveloped her and the flowers. She was part of them. They were part of her.
Mohr's version The bright sash of warm sunlight enveloped her and the flowers; she was part of them; they were part of her.

Practice Practice these techniques by revising the following passage on a separate sheet of paper. Use compound predicates and compound sentences.

Children's Book Week has a long history. In the early 1900s, Frederic Melcher headed the American Booksellers Association. Melcher wanted children to read more good books. He suggested that a medal be given for outstanding children's books. He organized a special committee. The committee decided to celebrate Children's Book Week each year. The first Children's Book Week was held in 1919. The idea was a success. The event still occurs each year. It attracts people from all over.

Teacher's Classroom Resources

The following resources can be used for assessment or evaluation.

Unit Assessment

Tests with Answer Key
Unit 8 Mastery Test, pp. 31–32

Test Generator
Unit 8 Mastery Test

You may wish to administer the Unit 8 Mastery Test at this point.

UNIT 9

Nouns

Grammar

Lessons

UNIT GOALS

The goal of Unit 9 is to help students, through example and instruction, to develop an understanding of and an ability to use nouns effectively. The lessons teach students to identify nouns and the major categories and forms of nouns: common and proper nouns, collective nouns, singular and plural forms, and possessive nouns.

Unit Assessment

Tests with Answer Key
Unit 9 Pretest, pp. 33–34
Unit 9 Mastery Test, pp. 35–36

Test Generator
Unit 9 Pretest
Unit 9 Mastery Test

You may wish to administer the Unit 9 Pretest at this point.

Key to Ability Levels

Enabling Strategies have been coded for varying learning styles and abilities.

L1 Level 1 activities are within the ability range of Learning Disabled students.

L2 Level 2 activities are basic-to-average activities and are within the ability range of average students.

L3 Level 3 activities are challenging activities and are within the ability range of above-average students.

LEP LEP activities are within the ability range of Limited English Proficiency students.

Setting the Purpose

Lesson 9.1 teaches students to identify common and proper nouns and to use them effectively in their writing.

FOCUS

Lesson Overview

Objective: To identify common and proper nouns and to use them effectively

Bellringer

When students enter the classroom, have this assignment on the board: *Name all of the nouns in the first paragraph of the passage from* Black Star, Bright Dawn *by Scott O'Dell, found on page 290.*

Motivating Activity

Ask students to write the nouns in the first paragraph of the passage by Scott O'Dell. Point out that all of the nouns are common. Have students choose five of the nouns and change them into proper nouns.

TEACH

Teaching Tip

Remind students that nouns usually follow the articles *a, an,* or *the* and that they can be either singular or plural. Tell them also that if the noun is not capitalized, it is most likely a common noun.

Cross-reference: Capitalizing

For instruction and practice in capitalizing proper nouns, refer students to Lessons 18.2–18.4, pp. 440–445.

9.1 Common and Proper Nouns

A **noun** is a word that names a person, place, thing, or idea.

Nouns	
Persons	brother, judge, athlete, teacher, mother-in-law
Places	neighborhood, county, city
Things	book, shoe, flower, pencil
Ideas	pride, skill, truth, democracy, success

There are two basic kinds of nouns: common nouns and proper nouns.

A **common noun** is a noun that names *any* person, place, thing, or idea.

A **proper noun** is a noun that names a *specific* person, place, thing, or idea.

A proper noun may consist of one or more words. You should always begin a proper noun with a capital letter. For proper nouns of more than one word, capitalize the first word and all other important words. Some examples of proper nouns are listed below.

	Common Noun	Proper Noun
People	actor singer athlete	Emilio Estevez Phil Collins Jackie Joyner-Kersee
Places	building city river	Tower of London Tucson Nile
Things	book movie song	*Johnny Tremain* *Peter Pan* "This Land Is Your Land"

Teacher's Classroom Resources

The following resources can be used for planning, instruction, practice, reinforcement, assessment, reteaching, enrichment, or evaluation.

Teaching Tools
Lesson Plans

Blackline Masters
Grammar Practice, p. 6
Grammar Reteaching, p. 7
Grammar Enrichment, p. 6

Grammar Workbook
Lesson 9

Unit Assessment

Tests with Answer Key
Unit 9 Pretest, pp. 33–34

Test Generator
Unit 9 Pretest

You may wish to administer the Unit 9 Pretest at this point.

Exercise 4 Identifying Plural Noun Forms

Write the correct form of the noun in parentheses.

1. My father loves to tell funny baseball (stories, storys).
2. He said that at one game the first four (benchs, benches) in the stadium collapsed.
3. The (spectatores, spectators) crashed to the ground and were covered with mud; but no one was hurt!
4. The umpires were the (heros, heroes) at that game.
5. They interrupted the game so that the fans could clean (themselves, themselfs) off.

Exercise 5 Forming Plural Nouns

Write the plural form of each singular noun.

1. radish
2. box
3. cherry
4. watch
5. country
6. ant
7. banana
8. horseshoe
9. loaf
10. valley
11. bush
12. bus
13. baby
14. piano
15. echo
16. volcano
17. radio
18. self
19. mosquito
20. knife

Exercise 6 Identifying Collective Nouns

Write each collective noun and label it *S* for *singular* or *P* for *plural.* Pay close attention to the verb.

1. The volleyball club meets after school.
2. Each volleyball team has six players.
3. The group take their individual positions.
4. The committee discuss their reactions.
5. Our class watches the volleyball match.
6. The school band plays at every game.
7. Our family sit separately in the stadium.
8. The crowd is always friendly at the games.
9. The team share their feelings about each game at the end.
10. The coaching staff also meet after each game to discuss strategy.

PRACTICE AND ASSESS

Answers: Exercise 4

1. stories
2. benches
3. spectators
4. heroes
5. themselves

Answers: Exercise 5

1. radishes
2. boxes
3. cherries
4. watches
5. countries
6. ants
7. bananas
8. horseshoes
9. loaves
10. valleys
11. bushes
12. buses *or* busses
13. babies
14. pianos
15. echoes
16. volcanoes
17. radios
18. selves
19. mosquitoes
20. knives

Answers: Exercise 6

1. club, S
2. team, S
3. group, P
4. committee, P
5. class, S
6. band, S
7. family, P
8. crowd, S
9. team, P
10. staff, P

Independent Practice

Skills Practice

Grammar Practice, p. 7
Grammar Reteaching, p. 8
Grammar Enrichment, p. 7

Grammar Workbook
Lessons 9–10

CLOSE

Have students write a paragraph describing the sport they like best. Ask them to use some plural nouns and collective nouns. Remind them to think about whether each collective noun they use should be treated as singular or plural.

Enabling Strategies

LEP Nouns That Are Always Singular

Some students may have difficulty with the surprisingly large class of nouns in English that cannot be made plural. The names of some baking ingredients cannot be made plural: *flour, salt,* and *sugar*. We say or write *flour* and *salt,* for example, but not usually *flours* and *salts.* Explain to the students that units of measure such as *cups* and *tablespoons* can be used with these nouns to show a specific quantity: ***cups** of flour,* and ***tablespoons** of salt.*

Setting the Purpose

Lesson 9.3 teaches students to use possessive nouns in both the singular and plural forms effectively in writing.

FOCUS

Lesson Overview

Objective: To identify possessive nouns, and to form singular and plural possessives correctly

Bellringer

When students enter the classroom, have this assignment on the board: *Add any needed apostrophes to the following sentence: Harrys sisters dogs tail is always wagging.*

Motivating Activity

Have students added the three apostrophes needed in the Bellringer sentence? If necessary, remind them that the tail belongs to the dog, the dog belongs to the sister, and the sister belongs to Harry.

TEACH

Teaching Tip

Since the plural and the possessive sound exactly alike, most students who write phonetically have great difficulty distinguishing between the plural and possessive *-s* in writing. When students first begin to use the apostrophe for possessive nouns, they often overgeneralize and use it with plural nouns and sometimes with possessive pronouns as well. Remind them that possessive pronouns, including *its,* are written without an apostrophe.

9.3 Possessive Nouns

A noun can show ownership or possession. This kind of noun is called a **possessive noun.** Possessive nouns, like all nouns, can be singular or plural.

A **possessive noun** names who or what has something.

Notice the possessive nouns in the following sentences.

The World Cup is the amateur **skiers'** competition.
A prize is awarded for the outstanding **man's** achievement.
The **women's** division also awards a prize.

The following chart shows how to form possessives from singular and plural nouns.

Forming Possessive Nouns

Nouns	To Form Possessive	Examples
Most singular nouns	Add an apostrophe and *-s* (**'s**).	Karen has new skis. Karen**'s** skis are new.
Singular nouns ending in *-s*	Add an apostrophe and *-s* (**'s**).	Chris got new skis last year. Chris**'s** skis are in the attic.
Plural nouns ending in *-s*	Add an apostrophe (').	Many skiers wear goggles. The skiers' goggles are sturdy.
Plural nouns not ending in *-s*	Add an apostrophe and *-s* (**'s**).	The men have warm sweaters. The men**'s** sweaters are warm.

When you are writing, remember that possessive nouns always contain apostrophes. Ordinary plural nouns do not.

Distinguishing Between Possessive Nouns and Plural Nouns

Singular possessive noun	Where is the **athlete's** school?
Plural possessive noun	Where is the **athletes'** school?
Plural noun	Where are the **athletes**?

Teacher's Classroom Resources

The following resources can be used for planning, instruction, practice, reinforcement, reteaching, or enrichment.

Teaching Tools
Lesson Plans

Blackline Masters
Grammar Practice, p. 8
Grammar Reteaching, p. 9
Grammar Enrichment, p. 8

Grammar Workbook
Lesson 11

Exercise 7 Identifying Possessive Nouns

Write each possessive noun and label it *S* for *singular* or *P* for *plural.*

1. The *Fédération Internationale du Ski* is an amateur's organization.
2. The World Ski Championships are a skier's goal.
3. A committee reviews all entrants' applications.
4. It considers skiers' qualifications for the races.
5. The committee's guidelines for amateur status are very strict.

Exercise 8 Using Singular and Plural Possessives

Write the possessive form of the noun in parentheses.

1. The (sport) history began thousands of years ago.
2. Each (person) skis were made of animal bone.
3. Leather straps held the (skier) boots to the skis.
4. Many (skiers) toe straps came loose.
5. One (historian) discoveries include skis from Sweden.
6. The (skis) ages ranged from 2,500 to 5,000 years.
7. In Norway a (soldier) means of travel was skiing.
8. A (Norwegian) skis were for both cross-country and downhill skiing.
9. The (men) cross-country speed record was broken by Bill Koch.
10. (Koch) average speed was 15.57 miles per hour.

Exercise 9 Forming Possessive Nouns

Copy and complete the chart, adding the possessive forms.

Singular Noun	Singular Possessive	Plural Noun	Plural Possessive
1. woman		women	
2. Ms. Smith		the Smiths	
3. child		children	
4. senior		seniors	
5. family		families	

PRACTICE AND ASSESS

Answers: Exercise 7

1. amateur's, S
2. skier's, S
3. entrants', P
4. skiers', P
5. committee's, S

Answers: Exercise 8

1. sport's
2. person's
3. skier's
4. skiers'
5. historian's
6. skis'
7. soldier's
8. Norwegian's
9. men's
10. Koch's

Answers: Exercise 9

1. woman's, women's
2. Ms. Smith's, the Smiths'
3. child's, children's
4. senior's, seniors'
5. family's, families'

Independent Practice

Skills Practice

- *Grammar Practice,* p. 8
- *Grammar Reteaching,* p. 9
- *Grammar Enrichment,* p. 8
- ***Grammar Workbook,*** Lesson 11

CLOSE

Ask students to imagine that they are watching a skiing exhibition. Have them write a paragraph describing the skiing events. Remind them to include possessive nouns, both singular and plural.

Enabling Strategies

LEP Identifying Possessive Nouns

Students whose first language is not English may be used to forming possessives in other ways. (In Spanish, possessives can be expressed by *de*, meaning *of*, plus a proper noun.) A good way for students to check whether a noun is possessive is to try using it in a *whose* question. For example, in the sentence ***Karen's** boots are new*, *Karen's* is possessive because we can ask *whose* boots are new and receive the possessive noun answer, *Karen's*. Only possessive nouns can be used in *whose* questions.

TEACH

About the Literature

Explain that the review contains a passage followed by exercises on related topics. After students have read the passage, discuss the author's use of nouns. Ask: *How do specific nouns, such as* headwind *for* wind *or* parka *for* coat *help the reader picture the scene?*

In his book, *Black Star, Bright Dawn,* writer Scott O'Dell succeeded in making the reader aware of both the ecstasy and the pain this teen-ager experiences as she races her dog team across a brutal land.

Linking Grammar and Literature

Teaching Tip

Point out to students that most nouns in the passage are common nouns because they name a person, place, thing, or idea (exception: the name *Oteg*). Ask students to read each noun and tell whether it names a person, a place, a thing, or an idea.

Critical Thinking

Students can compare and contrast Scott O'Dell's writing with that of another author. Suggest that they find a passage from a magazine or newspaper article. Tell them to circle all the common and proper nouns. Ask: *Are the nouns specific? Do they help create a picture in the reader's mind?*

UNIT 9 Unit Review

Grammar Review

Nouns

Black Star, Bright Dawn by Scott O'Dell is about a young Inuit woman named Bright Dawn who enters the Iditarod, a dog-sled race. The race covers more than a thousand snow-covered miles between Anchorage and Nome, Alaska. In the following excerpt, Bright Dawn battles sleep as she guides the team led by her dog Black Star. The passage has been annotated to show some of the kinds of nouns covered in this unit.

Literature Model

from BLACK STAR, BRIGHT DAWN

by Scott O'Dell

Common noun — forest
Singular noun — parka
Plural noun — hills

We left the forest and were now in open country, with far-off hills on the horizon and a moon. A strong headwind was blowing, but the temperature was well above zero. I took off my parka and gloves and opened my sweater. Still I was warm.

The slick runners made whispering sounds. The dogs ran together in long, loping strides. They made scarcely a sound in the snow. They were tired. I didn't push them. The moon and the hills became a hazy blur.

I began to nod once more. I was drifting down a broad river filled with salmon. Their golden scales glittered in the moonlight. They were leaping out of the water. They were trying to tell me something—one word over and over.

The dream suddenly faded. Again I was on a sled, moving through the night. I glanced over my ➡

Teacher's Classroom Resources

The following resources can be used for planning, instruction, practice, reinforcement, assessment, or evaluation.

Teaching Tools
Lesson Plans

Grammar Workbook
Lessons 8–11
Unit 2 Review
Cumulative Review: Units 1–2

Unit Assessment
Tests with Answer Key
Unit 9 Mastery Test, pp. 35–36

Test Generator
Unit 9 Mastery Test

shoulder. A team had slipped up behind me. The musher's lamp sent out a blinking glare. It was Oteg.

"Trail!" he shouted. "Trail!"

I pulled my dogs over and let him pass.

Collective noun (team)
Possessive noun (musher's)
Proper noun (Oteg)

Exercise 1

Using Common and Proper Nouns Rewrite each sentence, correcting the capitalization of common and proper nouns.

SAMPLE Bright Dawn chose black star to lead her Team of dogs in the iditarod.

ANSWER Bright Dawn chose Black Star to lead her team of dogs in the Iditarod.

1. The team raced from anchorage on the gulf of alaska to nome on the bering sea.
2. The temperature rose as the inuit mushed across alaska's lonely, open Wilderness.
3. As bright dawn raced over the moonlit Landscape, she became sleepy.
4. Bright Dawn dreamed of golden Salmon leaping from a broad River.
5. A Racer named oteg, who had befriended the young woman, woke her.

Exercise 2

Using Proper Nouns Replace the underlined words with proper nouns. Use the information and the literature model on page 290 to help you.

SAMPLE <u>An author</u> wrote *Black Star, Bright Dawn.*

ANSWER Scott O'Dell wrote *Black Star, Bright Dawn.*

1. <u>The state</u> is cold for much of the year.
2. The race was between Anchorage and <u>another city</u>.
3. The <u>race</u> is one of the most dangerous races in the world.
4. <u>The girl</u> was in danger of freezing to death.
5. <u>Her dog</u> led the team.

PRACTICE AND ASSESS

Answers: Exercise 1

1. Anchorage ... Gulf ... Alaska ... Nome ... Bering Sea
2. Inuit ... Alaska's ... wilderness
3. Bright Dawn ... landscape
4. salmon ... river
5. racer ... Oteg

Answers: Exercise 2

1. Alaska
2. Nome
3. Iditarod
4. Bright Dawn
5. Black Star

UNIT 9 Review

Answers: Exercise 3

1. Huskies
2. lives
3. reflexes
4. valleys
5. photos

Answers: Exercise 4

1. perform
2. studies
3. helps
4. scatter
5. does
6. are
7. was
8. struggles
9. pulls
10. was

Exercise 3

Forming Plural Nouns Write the plural form of the noun in parentheses.

SAMPLE The real (hero) of the Iditarod are the dogs.
ANSWER The real heroes of the Iditarod are the dogs.

1. (Husky) are the dogs most often used to pull sleds.
2. The (life) of these animals are devoted to the sport.
3. Their (reflex) are quick, and their strength is amazing.
4. They usually race over flat ground rather than hills or (valley).
5. During the Iditarod, newspapers run many (photo) of these dogs and the sleds they pull.

Exercise 4

Using Collective Nouns Write the correct form of the verb in parentheses.

SAMPLE Bright Dawn's family (lives, live) in its home in the small village of Womengo.
ANSWER lives

1. Her family (perform, performs) their daily activities.
2. At school Bright Dawn's class (studies, study) its English lesson.
3. A team of dogs (helps, help) its owner, Bright Dawn's father, hunt for food.
4. The team (scatters, scatter) in different directions when he drifts toward the sea on an ice floe.
5. A group of men (does, do) its best to save him.
6. Bright Dawn's family (are, is) supportive of one another.
7. Because of the difficult journey, the team (was, were) tired.
8. The team of dogs (struggle, struggles) on listening for Bright Dawn's words of support.
9. Another group (pull, pulls) its sled in front of Bright Dawn.
10. The crowd (was, were) surprised when it saw the winner was Bright Dawn.

Exercise 5

Forming Possessive Nouns Write each possessive noun correctly.

SAMPLE Bright Dawns father encouraged her to enter the race.
ANSWER Bright Dawn's

1. The mens faces looked doubtful when the young woman announced she would compete.
2. Bright Dawn depended on her one lead dogs guidance.
3. Otegs advice also helped her during the race.
4. The young womans lead was erased when she stopped to help other mushers.
5. Her parents eyes teared when Bright Dawn won.

Exercise 6

Using Singular and Plural Possessive Nouns Write a sentence using each of the following nouns in the possessive form shown in parentheses.

SAMPLE team (singular possessive)
ANSWER The team's owner is Bright Dawn.

1. dog (singular possessive)
2. woman (plural possessive)
3. class (singular possessive)
4. group (plural possessive)
5. man (singular possessive)
6. skier (plural possessive)
7. snow (singular possessive)
8. crowd (singular possessive)
9. team (plural possessive)
10. sled (plural possessive)
11. Alaska (singular possessive)
12. winner (plural possessive)
13. sport (singular possessive)
14. wilderness (singular possesive)
15. race (singular possesive)
16. bear (singular possesive)
17. village (singular possesive)
18. doctor (plural possesive)
19. family (plural possesive)
20. journey (singular possesive)
21. newspaper (plural possesive)
22. river (singular possesive)
23. hill (plural possesive)
24. moonlight (singular possesive)
25. wolf (plural possesive)

Answers: Exercise 5

1. men's
2. dog's
3. Oteg's
4. woman's
5. parents'

Answers: Exercise 6

Sentences will vary, but the correct possessive forms are given below.

1. dog's
2. women's
3. class's
4. groups'
5. man's
6. skiers'
7. snow's
8. crowd's
9. teams'
10. sleds'
11. Alaska's
12. winners'
13. sport's
14. wilderness's
15. race's
16. bear's
17. village's
18. doctors'
19. families'
20. journey's
21. newspapers'
22. river's
23. hills'
24. moonlight's
25. wolves'

Answers: Exercise 7

Proofreading

This proofreading activity provides editing practice with (1) the current or previous units' skills, (2) the **Troubleshooter** errors, and (3) spelling errors. Students should be able to complete the exercise by referring to the units, the **Troubleshooter,** and a dictionary.

	Error (Type of Error)
1.	• American (proper adjective)
2.	• depict (subject-verb agreement)
	• sea, (commas in a series)
	• coastlines, (plural noun)
3.	• people's (plural possessive)
	• loneliness (spelling)
4.	• Alaska (proper noun)
5.	• Kent's (singular possessive)
6.	• dogs (spelling of plural noun)
7.	• lives (spelling of plural noun)

Exercise 7 **Proofreading**

The following passage is about artist Rockwell Kent, whose work appears on this page. Rewrite the passage, correcting the errors in spelling, capitalization, grammar, and usage. Add any missing punctuation. There are 10 errors.

Rockwell Kent

[1]Rockwell Kent (1882–1971) was an important american book illustrator and landscape painter. [2]Many of his paintings depicts the open sea rugged mountains, and coastlines'. [3]Kent used these scenes to convey peoples lonelyness. ➡

Rockwell Kent, *The Expedition,* 1940–1960

About the Art

Rockwell Kent, *The Expedition,* 1940–1968

Rockwell Kent (1892–1971) was first paid for doing fanciful letters and decorative borders at age 15. He was also a writer. He wrote this about his year in Alaska with his son: "The steel-sharp, bitter nights, the vast and heartless depths of space that they revealed, enhanced the warmth and comfort of our cabin. There we would sit, we two, the only living beings, so it seemed, in all the universe." Kent is known for his illustrations of such books as *Candid*, *Moby-Dick*, and the complete works of Shakespeare.

[4]The artist visited alaska in 1918 and was inspired by the vast spaces near the Arctic Circle. [5]Kents' experiences resulted in *The Expedition.* [6]The painting, which depicts figures guiding their dogs' and sleds, could be an illustration for *Black Star, Bright Dawn.* [7]It's easy to imagine the lifes of these people.

Exercise 8 **Mixed Review**

Write all the underlined nouns. Label each one *common* or *proper, singular* or *plural,* and *possessive* if it shows ownership.

SAMPLE Hikers respect natural resources.
ANSWER Hikers – common, plural

1. People hike on paths and trails across America.
2. The Appalachian Trail goes through fourteen states.
3. The campers' gear must be light enough to be carried on their backs.
4. Storms are the camper's worst fear.
5. My family hikes in the Berkshire Mountains in Massachusetts.
6. Sleeping bags help provide a good night's sleep for a camper.
7. Many camping stores' supplies are limited.
8. Tents protect campers from rain and wind.
9. A tent's usefulness depends on many factors.
10. Next year my class is going on a trip to the Rocky Mountains.
11. We plan to travel by bus across the Midwest.
12. The seventh grade will go, too.
13. The buses' seats will be filled with suitcases.
14. The classes are looking forward to the trip.
15. To raise money we have established West Middle School's Dog and Car Wash.

UNIT 9 Review

Answers: Exercise 8

Mixed Review

1. people—common, plural
2. Appalachian Trail—proper, singular
3. campers'—common, plural, possessive
4. camper's—common, singular, possessive
5. Berkshire Mountains—proper, plural
6. night's—common, singular, possessive
7. stores'—common, plural, possessive
8. Tents—common, plural
9. tent's—common, singular, possessive
10. class—common, singular
11. Midwest—proper, singular
12. grade—common, singular
13. buses'—common, plural, possessive
14. classes—common, plural
15. West Middle School's—proper, singular, possessive

CLOSE

Ask students to write three sentences describing a recent sports event. Then have them underline all the common and proper nouns. Remind students to use specific nouns in their writing.

Nouns in Writing

Have students read the passage from *Keepers and Creatures at the National Zoo* silently. Then go back and discuss with them the underlined noun choices. Discuss these choices in relation to Techniques with Nouns below.

Techniques with Nouns

Discuss Peggy Thomson's use of precise, concrete nouns. Then ask students to look at sentence 4 in the proofreading practice on page 295. As an example of expanding common nouns, point out the writer's use of the expression *vast spaces near the Arctic Circle* instead of *scenery*.

Practice

The answers to this challenging and enriching activity will vary. Refer to Techniques with Nouns as you evaluate student choices.

Writing Application

Nouns in Writing In her book *Keepers and Creatures at the National Zoo,* Peggy Thomson describes zookeeper Kathy Wallace's daily routine. In the passage below, the author tells details of caring for an elephant's feet. Examine the passage, paying special attention to the italicized nouns.

> *Watchers* from the *railing* can't see the foot up close. They see the *probings* with the *pick* or with the point of the *ankus.* They see *Kathy* using both *hands* on a *drawknife* to cut away a *slice* of leathery, rubbery pad and then another. (It doesn't hurt the elephant.) And they hear the *thunk* of the slice into her *bucket.*

Techniques with Nouns When you write and revise your own work, try to use nouns in some of the ways Peggy Thomson does.

1. Whenever possible, replace general words with precise concrete nouns.

General words thing, tool
Thomson's version pick, ankus, drawknife

2. To identify people clearly in your writing, use proper nouns or specific common nouns.

General words woman, people
Thomson's version Kathy, watchers

3. Whenever possible, expand single common nouns into longer word groups that create images of details.

Single nouns noise, sound
Thomson's version the thunk of the slice into her bucket

Practice Practice these techniques by revising the following passage. Use a separate sheet of paper. Pay particular attention to the underlined words.

On one day, our teacher took our class to a zoo. We took our school things and our food. The purpose of the visit was to study and compare the eating habits of different animals. A person from the place first led us to the monkey place. A man fed the animals. They peeled the food and ate as they swayed from one place to another. Then we went to observe the big cats. Lunchtime in their place was quite different. They were serious as they tore apart their food. These animals were not thinking about play. Later we ate our own food.

Teacher's Classroom Resources

The following resources can be used for assessment or evaluation.

Unit Assessment

Tests with Answer Key
Unit 9 Mastery Test, pp. 35–36

Test Generator
Unit 9 Mastery Test

You may wish to administer the Unit 9 Mastery Test at this point.

UNIT
10 Verbs

Grammar | **Lessons**

UNIT GOALS

The goal of Unit 10 is to help students, through example and instruction, to develop an understanding of and an ability to use action verbs, linking verbs, and helping verbs in sentences. The lessons teach students the different types and tenses of verbs as well as direct and indirect objects, predicate nouns and predicate adjectives that complete the action of verbs in sentences.

Unit Assessment

Tests with Answer Key
Unit 10 Pretest, pp. 37–38
Unit 10 Mastery Test, pp. 39–40

Test Generator
Unit 10 Pretest
Unit 10 Mastery Test

You may wish to administer the Unit 10 Pretest at this point.

Key to Ability Levels

Enabling Strategies have been coded for varying learning styles and abilities.

L1 Level 1 activities are within the ability range of Learning Disabled students.

L2 Level 2 activities are basic-to-average activities and are within the ability range of average students.

L3 Level 3 activities are challenging activities and are within the ability range of above-average students.

LEP LEP activities are within the ability range of Limited English Proficiency students.

Setting the Purpose

Lesson 10.1 teaches students to recognize action verbs and direct objects and to use them appropriately in writing.

FOCUS

Lesson Overview

Objective: To identify action verbs and direct objects and to distinguish between transitive and intransitive verbs

Bellringer

When students enter the classroom, have this assignment on the board: *Supply a verb that names an action for each of the following sentences:*

1. The hikers _______ the river to reach the other bank.

2. The waiting lions _______ the hikers as they came ashore.

Motivating Activity

Discuss the verbs that students used in the Bellringer sentences, and ask what nouns receive the action of the verbs. Do students recall that such nouns are called direct objects?

TEACH

Teaching Tip

Explain to students that most verbs in English are action verbs. The term *action* is used in its broadest sense. In the following sentence, for example, the verb expresses mental action: *Sam forgot the meeting.* In this sentence the direct object of *forgot*—the noun that receives the action of the verb—is *meeting.*

10.1 Action Verbs and Direct Objects

ACTION VERB

There are two kinds of verbs: action verbs and linking verbs. Action verbs tell what the subject does.

An **action verb** names an action. It may contain more than one word.

Jay **has visited** Africa.

ACTION VERB

An action verb is often followed by a noun that receives the action of the verb. This noun is called the direct object. In the sentence above, the noun *Africa* is the direct object of the verb *has visited.*

A **direct object** receives the action of a verb. It answers the question *whom?* or *what?* after an action verb.

what?

Sightseers paid the **fees.**

DIRECT OBJECT

Not all action verbs take direct objects.

A **transitive** verb has a direct object.

An **intransitive** verb does not have a direct object.

You must examine how an action verb is used in a sentence to determine whether it is transitive or intransitive. Some verbs can be used both ways.

Sheila **read** a book about Africa. [transitive]
Sheila **read** in a great hurry. [intransitive]

Teacher's Classroom Resources

The following resources can be used for planning, instruction, practice, reinforcement, assessment, reteaching, enrichment, or evaluation.

Teaching Tools
Lesson Plans

Blackline Masters
Grammar Practice, p. 9
Grammar Reteaching, p. 10
Grammar Enrichment, p. 9

Grammar Workbook
Lesson 12

Unit Assessment

Tests with Answer Key,
Unit 10 Pretest, pp. 37–38

Test Generator
Unit 10 Pretest

You may wish to administer the Unit 10 Pretest at this point.

Exercise 1 Identifying Action Verbs and Direct Objects

For the sentences below, write each action verb. If the verb has a direct object, write it and underline it.

1. The equator divides Africa in two.
2. Streams and wells create oases in the desert.
3. Camels can travel in the desert for days without water.
4. Not even cars cross the sand dunes.
5. In the eastern Sahara, the sun shines for 4,300 hours every year.
6. Boats transport goods down the Nile River.
7. In flat regions the Nile River flows slowly.
8. Many people build their homes in the Nile Valley.
9. Grasslands border the Sahara on the south.
10. Bushes and small trees grow in the grasslands.
11. Wild animals roam the grasslands of Central Africa.
12. Large herds of cattle graze on the grasslands.
13. Herders tend the cattle.
14. African farmers grow coffee.
15. Much rain falls in the tropical forests.
16. Many tourists visit the jungles.
17. Europeans established colonies in Africa.
18. Explorers crossed the Mediterranean Sea for riches.
19. Others hunted elephants for their ivory tusks.
20. Miners sought gold under the ground.
21. Scientists study gorillas in remote forests.
22. Many Africans have won independence.
23. Anthropologists explore for evidence of early peoples.
24. Game parks protect wildlife.
25. Many Africans raise livestock.

Exercise 2 Writing Action Verbs

Write five brief sentences about yourself. Use an action verb in each sentence. Underline the action verb. If the verb has a direct object, circle the direct object.

SAMPLE ANSWER I eat a big (breakfast)

Enabling Strategies

LEP Identifying Transitive Verbs

To help students learning English determine whether a verb has a direct object, have them identify the simple subject and simple predicate in sentences. Have students use these parts with *what* and *whom* to form questions. If they can answer the questions, then there is a direct object and the verb is transitive. For example, *Camels travel across deserts. Camels travel what?* (can't answer) *Camels travel whom?* (can't answer) The verb is intransitive. *Many tourists visit the desert. Tourists visit what?* (the desert) This verb is transitive.

PRACTICE AND ASSESS

Answers: Exercise 1

1. divides, Africa
2. create, oases
3. can travel
4. cross, dunes
5. shines
6. transport, goods
7. flows
8. build, homes
9. border, Sahara
10. grow
11. roam, grasslands
12. graze
13. tend, cattle
14. grow, coffee
15. falls
16. visit, jungles
17. established, colonies
18. crossed, Mediterranean Sea
19. hunted, elephants
20. sought, gold
21. study, gorillas
22. have won, independence
23. explore
24. protect, wildlife
25. raise, livestock

Answers: Exercise 2

Answers will vary. A sample is given:
I told my (story) to the class.

Independent Practice

Skills Practice

- *Grammar Practice,* p. 9
- *Grammar Reteaching,* p. 10
- *Grammar Enrichment,* p. 9
- ***Grammar Workbook,*** Lesson 12

CLOSE

Discuss the sentences students wrote for Exercise 2. Ask students to identify the transitive and intransitive verbs in their sentences as well as any direct objects.

Setting the Purpose

Lesson 10.2 teaches students to recognize direct and indirect objects and to use them appropriately in writing.

FOCUS

Lesson Overview

Objective: To identify and distinguish between direct and indirect objects

Bellringer

When students enter the classroom, have this assignment on the board: *Complete each sentence with a word that tells to whom the action was done:*

His aunt sent ______ a birthday gift.
He wrote ______ a thank-you note.

Motivating Activity

Discuss the Bellringer sentences. Explain that the words students have filled in are indirect objects, and the words that end the sentences are direct objects.

TEACH

Teaching Tips

Explain that indirect objects are often used with verbs of telling, asking, and giving. Indirect objects name the receiver of the message, question, or gift.

Although all but two of the examples of direct and indirect objects in the exercises in this lesson are nouns, students should remember that pronouns can also function as objects.

Cross-reference: Grammar

For instruction and practice with object pronouns, refer students to Lesson 11.2, pp. 328–329.

10.2 Indirect Objects

A direct object answers the question *whom?* or *what?* after an action verb. In the sentence below, the direct object is *Egypt. Egypt* answers the question *what?* after the action verb *visited.*

Rachel visited **Egypt** last year.

An action verb may also have an indirect object.

An **indirect object** answers the question *to whom?* or *for whom?* the action was done.

The direct object in the sentence above is *fees.* It answers the question *what?* after the action verb *paid.* The indirect object is *guides. Guides* answers the question *to whom?* after the action verb.

Indirect objects appear only in sentences that have a direct object. Two clues will help you identify indirect objects. First, the indirect object always comes before the direct object. Second, if you add the word *to* or *for* in front of the indirect object, the sentence still makes sense.

Teacher's Classroom Resources

The following resources can be used for planning, instruction, practice, reinforcement, reteaching, or enrichment.

Teaching Tools
Lesson Plans

Blackline Masters
Grammar Practice, p. 10
Grammar Reteaching, p. 11
Grammar Enrichment, p. 10

Grammar Workbook
Lesson 13

Exercise 3 Distinguishing Between Direct and Indirect Objects

Write whether the underlined word is a *direct object* or an *indirect object.*

1. Egypt gives tourists lessons in history.
2. The pyramids show visitors life in the past.
3. Sculptors produced statues for tombs and temples.
4. Artists made decorative objects of pottery.
5. Archaeologists study the ancient tombs.
6. The tombs contain valuable historic scrolls.
7. The guide read the tourists scrolls' messages.
8. Send us a map of Egypt.
9. We gave my parents a cruise on the Nile.
10. Artists gave the pharaohs beautiful golden objects.
11. The ruins offer historians facts about a culture of long ago.
12. Ancient Egyptians built pyramids for their pharaohs.
13. Government leaders gave the people guidance.
14. Instructors taught students mathematics.
15. Scribes taught composition skills to the boys.
16. Festivals gave Egyptians relaxation from work.
17. Musicians offered the families entertainment.
18. Governors sent the pharaoh taxes.
19. The people gave the priests their obedience.
20. Cleopatra sailed her barge down the Nile.

Exercise 4 Identifying Direct and Indirect Objects

For each sentence write the direct object. Then write and underline each indirect object.

1. The floodwaters of the Nile gave farmers rich soil.
2. Wealthy Egyptians built themselves beautiful homes.
3. Parents fed their children bread.
4. Some Egyptians wrote relatives letters.
5. Gardens and rivers gave the Egyptians food.

PRACTICE AND ASSESS

Answers: Exercise 3

1. IO	11. IO
2. IO	12. DO
3. DO	13. IO
4. DO	14. DO
5. DO	15. DO
6. DO	16. IO
7. IO	17. IO
8. IO	18. DO
9. DO	19. DO
10. IO	20. DO

Answers: Exercise 4

1. soil, farmers
2. homes, themselves
3. bread, children
4. letters, relatives
5. food, Egyptians

Independent Practice

Skills Practice

Grammar Practice, p. 10
Grammar Reteaching, p. 11
Grammar Enrichment, p. 10

Grammar Workbook, Lesson 13

CLOSE

Students have learned to identify indirect objects by changing them into prepositional phrases. Make sure they understand this relationship by having them reverse the process, changing prepositional phrases into indirect objects in sentences such as these: *The coach told her funniest story to the team. The principal gave his usual speech for the visitors.*

Enabling Strategies

LEP Telling Direct Objects from Indirect Objects

Students learning English may have difficulty distinguishing between direct and indirect objects. Remind them that the indirect object always comes before the direct object. Providing practice with paraphrasing indirect objects as phrases that begin with *to* or *for* will help students to recognize indirect objects confidently.

Setting the Purpose

Lesson 10.3 teaches students to recognize linking verbs and to use predicate nouns and adjectives appropriately in writing.

FOCUS

Lesson Overview

Objective: To distinguish between action verbs and linking verbs and to identify predicate nouns and adjectives

Bellringer

When students enter the classroom, have this assignment on the board: *Write two short sentences that begin with the words* I am. *The first sentence should tell who or what you are. The second should tell what you are like.*

Motivating Activity

Discuss the Bellringer sentences. Explain that the first sentence should contain a predicate noun, and the second sentence should contain a predicate adjective.

TEACH

Teaching Tip

A good way to test for a linking verb is to see whether a form of the verb *to be* can be substituted for it in a sentence. Take this sentence, for example: *The farmer* grows *tired.* If *is* is substituted for *grows,* the sentence still makes sense: *The farmer is tired.* Therefore, *grows* is a linking verb in this sentence.

10.3 Linking Verbs and Predicate Words

LINKING VERB

A **linking verb** connects the subject of a sentence with a noun or adjective in the predicate.

Africa **is** a continent.
LINKING VERB

In the sentence above, the linking verb *is* connects *Africa,* the subject, with *continent,* a noun in the predicate. *Continent* is called a *predicate noun.*

A **predicate noun** is a noun that follows a linking verb and tells what the subject is.

A **predicate adjective** is an adjective that follows a linking verb and tells what the subject is like.

Predicate Nouns and Adjectives	
Predicate Noun	Zambia is a **country.**
Predicate Adjective	Zambia is **scenic.**

In the first sentence above, the predicate noun *country* renames the subject. In the second sentence, the predicate adjective *scenic* describes the same subject. Predicate nouns and adjectives follow only linking verbs.

Common Linking Verbs			
be	seem	feel	grow
become	appear	taste	look

Some linking verbs can also be used as action verbs.

The farmer **grows** tired. [linking verb]
The farmer **grows** corn. [action verb]

Teacher's Classroom Resources

The following resources can be used for planning, instruction, practice, reinforcement, reteaching, or enrichment.

Teaching Tools
Lesson Plans

Blackline Masters
Grammar Enrichment, pp. 9, 11

Grammar Workbook
Lesson 15

Exercise 5 Identifying Action and Linking Verbs and Predicate Words

For each sentence write the verb. Then write whether it is an *action* verb or a *linking* verb. If it is a linking verb, write whether it is followed by a *predicate noun* or a *predicate adjective.*

1. Village life changes slowly in Zambia.
2. Many people live in grass-roofed houses.
3. Villagers raise food crops on the land.
4. Some farmers appear content with their lives.
5. Other people move to the mining towns.
6. The country is rich in copper.
7. The copper industry grows successful.
8. A common food in Zambia is corn porridge.
9. Many Zambians respect the old customs.
10. They seem happy with their traditions.
11. Zambia is a land of farmers and miners.
12. Each family group developed its own culture.
13. Traditions became important for each group.
14. No individual owned land.
15. The family group was responsible for its members.
16. Most Zambians speak a native Bantu language.
17. Sometimes communication between groups is a problem.
18. The English language is common among businesspeople.
19. Some languages seem unfamiliar to a nearby group.
20. Zambia's population grows quickly.

Exercise 6 Using Predicate Nouns and Adjectives

To complete each sentence, write a predicate noun or predicate adjective as indicated in parentheses. You may need to write more than one word.

1. I feel *(predicate adjective).*
2. My family is *(predicate adjective).*
3. I am *(predicate noun).*
4. My favorite food is *(predicate noun).*
5. I think basketball is *(predicate adjective).*

Enabling Strategies

LEP Understanding Linking Verbs

To help students understand linking verbs, focus on the verb *be*. Point out that the verb links or joins the subject with a noun, pronoun, or adjective following the verb. Give examples showing that a subject and a predicate noun are equal and that a predicate adjective tells about the subject. *Maria* is my *cousin. She* is my *cousin. Maria* is *intelligent. She* is *intelligent.* When you feel that students understand *be* as a linking verb, give examples of other linking verbs. Show students that *be* can be substituted for other linking verbs, as in *Maria* seems *happy*.

PRACTICE AND ASSESS

Answers: Exercise 5

1. changes, action v.
2. live, action v.
3. raise, action v.
4. appear, linking v., pred. adj.
5. move, action v.
6. is, linking v., pred. adj.
7. grows, linking v., pred. adj.
8. is, linking v., pred. n.
9. respect, action v.
10. seem, linking v., pred. adj.
11. is, linking v., pred. n.
12. developed, action v.
13. became, linking v., pred. adj.
14. owned, action v.
15. was, linking v., pred. adj.
16. speak, action v.
17. is, linking v., pred. n.
18. is, linking v., pred. adj.
19. seem, linking v., pred. adj.
20. grows, action v.

Answers: Exercise 6

Answers will vary, but some suggestions are given below.

1. I feel sleepy.
2. My family is Puerto Rican.
3. I am a student.
4. My favorite food is pizza.
5. I think basketball is exciting.

Independent Practice

Skills Practice

Grammar Enrichment, pp. 9, 11

Grammar Workbook, Lesson 15

CLOSE

Have students write a paragraph about their favorite foods, using both action verbs and linking verbs. They should also use at least one predicate noun and one predicate adjective.

Setting the Purpose

Lesson 10.4 teaches students to recognize present, past, and future tenses and to use them appropriately in writing.

FOCUS

Lesson Overview

Objective: To distinguish between present, past, and future verb tenses

Bellringer

When students enter the classroom, have this assignment on the board: *Write three sentences that tell about (1) something you do regularly, (2) something you used to do, and (3) something you will do in the future.*

Motivating Activity

Using two or more representative sets of students' Bellringer sentences, point out the three verb forms in each.

TEACH

Cooperative Learning

Students may use the adverbs *today, yesterday,* and *tomorrow* to indicate present, past, and future tenses. When they need to identify a verb tense in a sentence, let them add the adverb they think sounds right.

Have students pair off for a Pairs Check activity. Ask each pair to write three sentences, using present, past, and future tenses. Have pairs exchange sentences and write the verb, along with the appropriate adverb—*today, yesterday,* or *tomorrow*—beside each sentence. Pairs should then check each other's answers.

10.4 Present, Past, and Future Tenses

A verb changes its form to show tense and to agree with its subject. The **tense** of a verb tells when an action takes place.

The **present tense** of a verb names an action that happens regularly. It can also express a general truth.

The present tense is the base form of the verb. When the subject is a singular noun or *he, she,* or *it,* you usually add ***-s*** to the verb. The chart below shows the present tense forms of the verb *visit.*

Present-Tense Forms	
Singular	**Plural**
I **visit.** You **visit.** He, she, *or* it **visits.**	We **visit.** You **visit.** They **visit.**

The present tense of the verb *be* differs from the base form: *am, are, is.*

Present Tense
Thousands of tourists **visit** the pyramids each year.

The **past tense** of a verb names an action that already happened.

Form the past tense of most verbs by adding *-ed* to the base form of the verb.

The **future tense** of a verb names an action that will take place in the future.

Form the future tense by adding the helping verb *will* or *shall* to the base form of the verb.

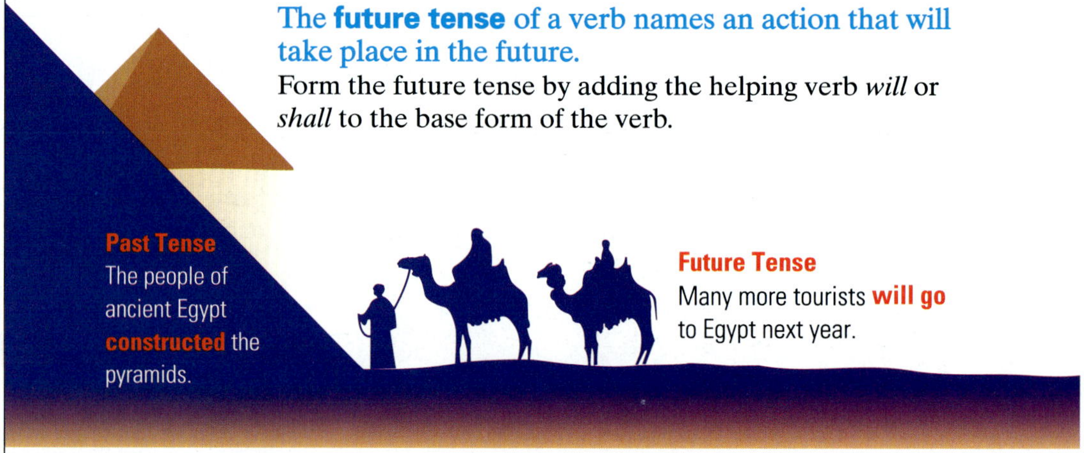

304 *Verbs*

Teacher's Classroom Resources

The following resources can be used for planning, instruction, practice, reinforcement, reteaching, or enrichment.

Teaching Tools
Lesson Plans

Blackline Masters
Grammar Practice, p. 11
Grammar Reteaching, p. 13
Grammar Enrichment, p. 12

Grammar Workbook
Lesson 16

Exercise 7 Distinguishing Present, Past, and Future Tenses

For each sentence write the verb. Then write whether it is in the *present, past,* or *future* tense.

1. Larry learns about archaeology in the library.
2. Someday he and his parents will travel to Egypt.
3. Larry and his friend Ann watched a film about the Sahara.
4. This vast desert extends into Egypt.
5. The survival of the ancient Egyptians depended on the Nile River.
6. The Nile still provides the country's water.
7. Silt from the Nile fertilized farmland.
8. The Nile flows into the Mediterranean Sea.
9. Silt protected land near the Mediterranean from erosion.
10. The Aswan High Dam harnesses the water of the Nile.
11. Water from the dam will increase Egypt's agricultural production.
12. The dam traps the silt from floodwaters in Lake Nasser.
13. Instead of silt, farmers will use chemical fertilizers.
14. The dam will damage the environment.
15. A Greek historian called Egypt the "gift of the Nile."
16. Like other ancient civilizations, Egypt developed on fertile land near a river.
17. Egyptian monuments will puzzle people far into the future.
18. The Nile's floods begin in June.
19. Farmlands cover less than 4 percent of the land of Egypt.
20. Today Egypt exports cotton.

Exercise 8 Using Present, Past, and Future Tenses

For each sentence write the present, past, and future forms of the verb in parentheses.

1. The capital, Cairo, (prosper) near the base of the Nile delta.
2. This part of the country (collect) the most rain.
3. The Western Desert (contain) few oases.
4. Oases (support) small villages and farms.
5. The sands of the Eastern Desert (extend) from the Nile River almost to the Red Sea.

Enabling Strategies

LEP Verb Tenses

Students learning English may have experience forming past forms of verbs in other ways. Have students explain how past, present, and future tenses are expressed in their first language. Encourage them to set up a chart in their journals like the one on page 304 with heads for past, present, and future verb tenses. Have students look at previous assignments, noting troublesome verbs or verb forms. Have them use a dictionary to fill in their charts. Encourage students to write context sentences to help them understand the use of each verb tense.

PRACTICE AND ASSESS

Answers: Exercise 7

1. learns, present
2. will travel, future
3. watched, past
4. extends, present
5. depended, past
6. provides, present
7. fertilized, past
8. flows, present
9. protected, past
10. harnesses, present
11. will increase, future
12. traps, present
13. will use, future
14. will damage, future
15. called, past
16. developed, past
17. will puzzle, future
18. begin, present
19. cover, present
20. exports, present

Answers: Exercise 8

1. prospers, prospered, will prosper
2. collects, collected, will collect
3. contains, contained, will contain
4. support, supported, will support
5. extend, extended, will extend

Independent Practice

Skills Practice

- *Grammar Practice,* p. 11
- *Grammar Reteaching,* p. 13
- *Grammar Enrichment,* p. 12
- ***Grammar Workbook,*** Lesson 16

CLOSE

Ask students to imagine that they are archaeologists in Egypt. Have them write a paragraph describing what they find in the ruins and what they expect to find. Remind them to use present, past, and future tenses.

Setting the Purpose

Lesson 10.5 teaches students to recognize main verbs and helping verbs and to use them correctly. It also teaches them to recognize present participles and past participles.

FOCUS

Lesson Overview

Objective: To distinguish between main verbs and helping verbs and to identify the present participles and past participles

Bellringer

When students enter the classroom, have this assignment on the board: *Identify the main verb in each of the following sentences:* I am going. She will go. He had gone. They should have gone.

Motivating Activity

Discuss the Bellringer sentences, and see whether students recognize that a form of the verb *go* is the main verb in each sentence. Tell them that the main verb is always the last word in a verb phrase.

TEACH

Teaching Tip

The term *participle* can be confusing for students. First, the past and past participle forms of regular verbs are identical. Second, a participle is a verb form that may be used as a noun, an adjective, or an adverb in a sentence. To help students distinguish between these two uses of participles, remind them that helping verbs are used with participles that are part of verb phrases, such as, *is learning; have learned.*

10.5 Main Verbs and Helping Verbs

Verbs have four principal parts. The chart below shows the principal parts of the verb *learn.*

Principal Parts of the Verb *Learn*			
Base Form	**Present Participle**	**Past Form**	**Past Participle**
learn	learning	learned	learned

The principal parts of a verb can be combined with helping verbs to form verb phrases.

A **helping verb** is a verb that helps the main verb tell about an action or make a statement.

A **verb phrase** consists of one or more helping verbs followed by a main verb.

The most common helping verbs are *be* and *have.* The helping verb *be* makes a verb phrase with the present participle of a main verb, as in the following chart.

Be and the Present Participle			
Present		**Past**	
Singular	**Plural**	**Singular**	**Plural**
I **am** learning. You **are** learning. She **is** learning.	We **are** learning. You **are** learning. They **are** learning.	I **was** learning. You **were** learning. He **was** learning.	We **were** learning. You **were** learning. They **were** learning.

The helping verb *have* makes a verb phrase with the past participle of a main verb.

Have and the Past Participle			
Present		**Past**	
Singular	**Plural**	**Singular**	**Plural**
I **have** learned. You **have** learned. She **has** learned.	We **have** learned. You **have** learned. They **have** learned.	I **had** learned. You **had** learned. He **had** learned.	We **had** learned. You **had** learned. They **had** learned.

Teacher's Classroom Resources

The following resources can be used for planning, instruction, practice, reinforcement, reteaching, or enrichment.

Teaching Tools
Lesson Plans

Blackline Masters
Grammar Practice, p. 12
Grammar Reteaching, p. 14
Grammar Enrichment, p. 13

Grammar Workbook
Lessons 17–18

Exercise 9 Identifying Helping Verbs in Verb Phrases

Write each verb phrase. Then underline the helping verb.

1. Some African societies have changed greatly.
2. The people of Malawi were living in family groups.
3. They had looked to chiefs for leadership.
4. They have formed one nation from many different family groups.
5. Many children in Malawi are working at jobs.
6. Malawi workers have produced beautiful items for export.
7. The country's name has changed along with its society.
8. Today it has become Malawi, "land of flame."
9. Before 1964 people had called the country Nyasaland.
10. For almost thirty years Hastings Banda had ruled the country.

Exercise 10 Identifying Past and Present Participles

Write each verb phrase, and label its main verb as a *present participle* or *past participle.*

1. Malawi had acquired independence in 1964.
2. Bakili Muluzi has now assumed leadership.
3. The people have named Mr. Muluzi president.
4. The president has appointed a cabinet.
5. The cabinet is helping the president.
6. Malawi is developing into a stable nation.
7. The government has improved agriculture.
8. Malawi's economy has strengthened.
9. Young people are training for leadership roles.
10. The people of Malawi have learned valuable skills.
11. Farmers are tending cattle, goats, and sheep.
12. Malawi is depending on other nations for access to the sea.
13. Men with jobs in cities have mailed money home.
14. Most farmers are growing enough food for themselves and their families.
15. Half of the people in Malawi are living in small villages.
16. In Malawi women historically have raised the crops.
17. The economy is based on agriculture.
18. Malawi has received money from the United States for its schools.
19. Europeans have planted tea in the highlands.
20. The Bantu people had arrived in the region of Malawi in the 1500s.

PRACTICE AND ASSESS

Answers: Exercise 9

1. have changed
2. were living
3. had looked
4. have formed
5. are working
6. have produced
7. has changed
8. has become
9. had called
10. had ruled

Answers: Exercise 10

1. had acquired, past participle
2. has assumed, past participle
3. have named, past participle
4. has appointed, past participle
5. is helping, present participle
6. is developing, present participle
7. has improved, past participle
8. has strengthened, past participle
9. are training, present participle
10. have learned, past participle
11. are tending, present participle
12. is depending, present participle
13. have mailed, past participle
14. are growing, present participle
15. are living, present participle
16. have raised, past participle
17. is based, past participle
18. has received, past participle
19. have planted, past participle
20. had arrived, past participle

Independent Practice

Skills Practice

Grammar Practice, p. 12
Grammar Reteaching, p. 14
Grammar Enrichment, p. 13

Grammar Workbook, Lessons 17–18

CLOSE

Ask students to write a paragraph describing some differences between life in Malawi and life in their own community. Have them underline any helping verbs and all past and present participles.

Enabling Strategies

LEP Tenses in Other Languages

Concepts of present, past, and future are reflected differently in the grammar of different languages. Chinese, for example, does not change a verb to show the time of an action, but instead adds an adverb: *I want to go* ***now****; I want to go* ***tomorrow***. Some students may find it confusing that present tense in English does not usually indicate "present time." Present tense indicates "timeless" habitual actions or general truths. Explain the difference between present and present progressive tense.

Setting the Purpose

Lesson 10.6 teaches students to recognize present and past progressive forms and to use them appropriately in writing.

FOCUS

Lesson Overview

Objective: To identify and use the present and past progressive tenses

Bellringer

When students enter the classroom, have this assignment on the board: *Write a sentence that tells what you are doing at this moment. Write another sentence that tells what you were doing at this time yesterday.*

Motivating Activity

Discuss students' Bellringer sentences, and point out that their first sentences use the present progressive tense, and their second sentences use the past progressive.

TEACH

Teaching Tip

Tell students that if the main verb in a verb phrase ends in *-ing,* then the verb is in the progressive form. The present progressive generally refers to an action taking place at the present time: *The children **are feeding** the chicks.* The past progressive refers to an action in progress at some specific moment in the past: *The chicks **were chirping** for food.*

10.6 Present and Past Progressive Forms

The present tense of a verb names an action that occurs regularly. To describe an action that is continuing, use the present progressive form of the verb.

The **present progressive form** of a verb tells about an action that is continuing right now.

The children **are listening** to a story.

The present progressive form of a verb consists of the present participle of the main verb and the helping verb *am, are,* or *is.*

Present Progressive Form	
Singular	**Plural**
I **am singing.**	We **are singing.**
You **are singing.**	You **are singing.**
He, she, *or* it **is singing.**	They **are singing.**

The past tense describes an action that was started and completed in the past. To describe an action that was continuing, use the past progressive form.

The **past progressive form** of a verb tells about an action that was continuing at an earlier time.

The women **were singing** a folk song.

The past progressive form of a verb consists of the present participle and the helping verb *was* or *were.*

Past Progressive Form	
Singular	**Plural**
I **was singing.**	We **were singing.**
You **were singing.**	You **were singing.**
He, she, *or* it **was singing.**	They **were singing.**

Teacher's Classroom Resources

The following resources can be used for planning, instruction, practice, reinforcement, reteaching, or enrichment.

Teaching Tools
Lesson Plans

Blackline Masters
Grammar Practice, p. 13
Grammar Reteaching, p. 15
Grammar Enrichment, p. 14

Grammar Workbook
Lesson 19

Exercise 13 Review: Identifying Tenses

For each sentence write the verb. Then write whether the verb is in the *present, past, present perfect,* or *past perfect* tense.

1. Moroccan ships pass through the Strait of Gibraltar.
2. Morocco has exported fish and minerals.
3. In the year 711, Moroccans invaded Spain.
4. For some time they ruled most of Spain.
5. The Moroccans had left many influences in Spain.
6. Most Moroccans speak Arabic.
7. Farmers had raised dates, olives, and citrus fruit.
8. Artisans have handed down their skills.
9. Artisans have learned their skills from earlier generations.
10. Tourists value Moroccan leather.

Exercise 14 Using the Perfect Tenses

For each sentence write the perfect tense of the verb. If the verb is in the present tense, change it to the present perfect tense. If the verb is in the past tense, change it to the past perfect tense.

1. Before modern times Moroccan artisans created intricate silver jewelry.
2. They pounded metal sheets into delicate shapes.
3. In the recent past craftspeople constructed products from leather.
4. They also work on carpets for export.
5. Farmers raise barley, wheat, fruits, and vegetables.
6. Shepherds tend their flocks in green meadows.
7. Morocco trades with many other countries.
8. Long ago ships from many countries docked in Casablanca.
9. Tourists visited the old section of the city.
10. Merchants crowded the narrow streets.
11. Marrakesh's hospitality charmed many travelers in the nineteenth century.
12. Fat bears dance in the public square.
13. Visitors watch talented jugglers and acrobats.
14. The Berbers lived in the mountains for centuries.
15. Centuries ago the Moroccan Berbers helped the Arabs conquer Spain.

PRACTICE AND ASSESS

Answers: Exercise 13

1. pass, present
2. has exported, present perfect
3. invaded, past
4. ruled, past
5. had left, past perfect
6. speak, present
7. had raised, past perfect
8. have handed, present perfect
9. have learned, present perfect
10. value, present

Answers: Exercise 14

1. had created
2. had pounded
3. have constructed
4. have worked
5. have raised
6. have tended
7. has traded
8. had docked
9. had visited
10. had crowded
11. had charmed
12. have danced
13. have watched
14. have lived
15. had helped

Independent Practice

Skills Practice

- *Grammar Practice,* p. 14
- *Grammar Reteaching,* p. 16
- *Grammar Enrichment,* p. 15
- ***Grammar Workbook,*** Lesson 20

CLOSE

Have students write a paragraph describing an event from American history. Ask them to use present perfect and past perfect tenses in at least one sentence each. If they have trouble using the present perfect tense, suggest that they think of one thing about the event that happened in the

Enabling Strategies

LEP Using *Have*

In American English, we form questions differently when *have* is a main verb than when *have* is a helping verb. Write on the board these examples of *have* as a main verb: *You* have *a friend.* Do *you* have *a friend?* Then write these sentences and point out to students the helping verb *have*: *You* have seen *my coat.* Have *you* seen *my coat?* Tell students that in British English, questions are formed in the same way whether *have* is used as a main verb or as a helping verb: Have *you a friend?* Have *you* seen *my coat?*

Setting the Purpose

Lesson 10.8 teaches students to recognize and use the correct past and past participle forms of some irregular verbs.

FOCUS

Lesson Overview

Objective: To learn the past and past participle forms of some irregular verbs

Bellringer

When students enter the classroom, have this assignment on the board: *Correct any incorrect verbs in the following sentence: As I set down and swang on the old swing, I sung a little song about the day I brang my toad to school and catched another one to keep it company.*

Motivating Activity

Discuss students' corrections of the Bellringer sentence. If they have missed any of the five errors, refer them to the chart on page 312.

TEACH

Teaching Tip

Ask students to look at the past and past participle forms of the irregular verbs on page 312, particularly those in the bottom part of the chart. Remind them that the past participle should follow the helping verb *have.*

Cross-reference: Troubleshooter

For instruction and practice with irregular verbs, refer students to Lesson 7.4, pp. 248–249.

10.8 Irregular Verbs

Irregular verbs do not form their past and past participle by adding the ending *-ed.* The irregular verbs below are grouped according to how their past and past participle are formed.

Irregular Verbs

Pattern	Base Form	Past Form	Past Participle
One vowel changes to form the past and the past participle.	begin	began	begun
	drink	drank	drunk
	ring	rang	rung
	shrink	shrank *or* shrunk	shrunk
	sing	sang	sung
	spring	sprang *or* sprung	sprung
	swim	swam	swum
The past form and the past participle are the same.	bring	brought	brought
	buy	bought	bought
	catch	caught	caught
	feel	felt	felt
	get	got	got *or* gotten
	keep	kept	kept
	lay	laid	laid
	lead	led	led
	leave	left	left
	lend	lent	lent
	lose	lost	lost
	make	made	made
	pay	paid	paid
	say	said	said
	seek	sought	sought
	sell	sold	sold
	sit	sat	sat
	sleep	slept	slept
	swing	swung	swung
	teach	taught	taught
	think	thought	thought
	win	won	won

Teacher's Classroom Resources

The following resources can be used for planning, instruction, practice, reinforcement, reteaching, or enrichment.

Teaching Tools
Lesson Plans

Blackline Masters
Grammar Practice, p. 15
Grammar Reteaching, p. 17
Grammar Enrichment, p. 16

Grammar Workbook
Lessons 21–24

Exercise 15 **Using the Past Tense of Irregular Verbs**

For each sentence write the past tense form of the verb in parentheses.

1. African merchants (begin) work before dawn.
2. Peddlers (bring) their goods to market.
3. They (lay) out their wares in attractive displays.
4. The sun (feel) hot in the open marketplace.
5. Children (seek) the shade of date trees.
6. Infants (sleep) in spite of the chaos.
7. People (make) requests about animals for sale.
8. Some traders (sing) songs about their goods.
9. Some people (buy) gourds of all sizes.
10. A tailor (win) some new customers.

Exercise 16 **Using the Past Participle of Irregular Verbs**

For each sentence write the past participle of the verb in parentheses.

1. Some women have (sell) bracelets and necklaces.
2. Traders had (bring) gorgeous robes and veils.
3. The material has not (shrink).
4. Herders have (leave) cattle in the stalls.
5. Herders had (lead) livestock to market.
6. The herder has (catch) the stray.
7. Some people have (keep) pots of stew warm.
8. Artisans have (teach) their children their craft.
9. Some merchants have (sleep) in the sun.
10. The market has (lose) business to other villages.
11. The merchants had (think) competition might be good.
12. One merchant has (say) the market needs competition.
13. People have (pay) by trading.
14. How much fruit have people (buy)?
15. A mother has (lend) her child money to buy a trinket.
16. The child had (get) some candy.
17. The candy had (begin) to stick to the child's fingers.
18. Merchants have (sit) on beautiful rugs.
19. By evening a cool breeze has (spring) up.
20. Wind chimes have (ring) in the breeze.

Two-Minute Skill Drill

List these verbs on the board and have students supply the past and past participle forms.

lend	swim
seek	say

PRACTICE AND ASSESS

Answers: Exercise 15

1. began	**6.** slept
2. brought	**7.** made
3. laid	**8.** sang
4. felt	**9.** bought
5. sought	**10.** won

Answers: Exercise 16

1. sold	**11.** thought
2. brought	**12.** said
3. shrunk	**13.** paid
4. left	**14.** bought
5. led	**15.** lent
6. caught	**16.** got *or* gotten
7. kept	**17.** begun
8. taught	**18.** sat
9. slept	**19.** sprung
10. lost	**20.** rung

Independent Practice

Skills Practice

Grammar Practice, p. 15
Grammar Reteaching, p. 17
Grammar Enrichment, p. 16

Grammar Workbook,
Lessons 21–24

Enabling Strategies

LEP Irregular Verbs

Show students that each verb in the first part of the chart changes *i* to *a* in the past and *i* to *u* in the past participle. Go on to the second part of the chart, being certain that students realize that the past and the past participle are identical.

CLOSE

Have students write a paragraph describing some places where they have shopped. Ask them to use several irregular verbs in the past or present perfect tense. If they use irregular verbs that are not in the chart on page 312, encourage them to look up the words in a dictionary.

Setting the Purpose

Lesson 10.9 teaches students to recognize and use the correct past and past participle forms of some irregular verbs.

FOCUS

Lesson Overview

Objective: To learn the past and past participle forms of some irregular verbs

Bellringer

When students enter the classroom, have this assignment on the board: *Correct any incorrect verbs in the following sentences: I seen how he run off after he had broke the window. Before he come back, he had rode his bike all over town.*

Motivating Activity

If students have missed any of the five errors in the Bellringer sentences, refer them to the chart on page 314.

TEACH

Teaching Tip

An effective way of learning irregular verb forms is constant exposure to the forms and occasional correction when the learner makes a mistake. Ask students to make personal dictionaries of troublesome irregular forms, including such verbs as *go, run, have,* and *see.*

Vocabulary Link

Spanish, too, has irregular verbs. The third person singular of the verb *ir,* which means "to go," is *va* in the present tense and *fue* in the past tense.

10.9 More Irregular Verbs

Irregular Verbs

Pattern	Base Form	Past Form	Past Participle
The base form and the past participle are the same.	become	became	become
	come	came	come
	run	ran	run
The past form ends in *-ew,* and the past participle ends in *-wn.*	blow	blew	blown
	draw	drew	drawn
	fly	flew	flown
	grow	grew	grown
	know	knew	known
	throw	threw	thrown
The past participle ends in *-en.*	bite	bit	bitten *or* bit
	break	broke	broken
	choose	chose	chosen
	drive	drove	driven
	eat	ate	eaten
	fall	fell	fallen
	give	gave	given
	ride	rode	ridden
	rise	rose	risen
	see	saw	seen
	speak	spoke	spoken
	steal	stole	stolen
	take	took	taken
	write	wrote	written
The past form and the past participle do not follow any pattern.	am, are, is	was, were	been
	do	did	done
	go	went	gone
	tear	tore	torn
	wear	wore	worn
The base form, past form, and past participle are all the same.	burst	burst	burst
	cut	cut	cut
	let	let	let
	put	put	put

Teacher's Classroom Resources

The following resources can be used for planning, instruction, practice, reinforcement, reteaching, or enrichment.

Teaching Tools
Lesson Plans

Blackline Masters
Grammar Practice, p. 15
Grammar Reteaching, p. 17
Grammar Enrichment, p. 16

Grammar Workbook
Lessons 21–24

Exercise 17 Using the Past Tense of Irregular Verbs

For each sentence write the past tense form of the verb in parentheses.

1. Crystal (do) research for her project.
2. She (go) to the library for books about Nigeria.
3. Some of her information (come) from magazines.
4. Fulani people (eat) well in the rainy season.
5. Children (ride) on cattle from camp to camp.
6. Their camps (are) temporary homes.
7. The Hausa (become) skilled potters and weavers.
8. CThe men (wear) long robes and loose-fitting trousers.
9. Teachers (run) schools for Nigerian children.
10. In 1954 the government (take) control of all the schools.

Exercise 18 Using the Past Participle of Irregular Verbs

For each sentence write the past participle of the verb in parentheses.

1. In Kenya's dry season no rain had (fall).
2. A dry wind has (blow) over the land.
3. The families had (eat) beans and potatoes.
4. By March the farmers had (go) to the fields.
5. People have (do) the farm work by hand.
6. Pumps had (draw) water from wells.
7. Farmers had (grow) gardens close to the house.
8. By noon the sun had (rise) high in the sky.
9. Travelers have (go) to Kenya for years.
10. Tourists have (see) herders with cattle sticks.
11. The herders had (choose) each new camp carefully.
12. A fire had (drive) away mosquitoes and flies.
13. Kenyans have (grow) tea and coffee in the highlands.
14. Tourists have (fly) over Kenya's Tsavo National Park.
15. They have (ride) in trucks deep into the countryside.
16. Have you (speak) to any of them?
17. My parents had (take) many pictures on a photo safari.
18. One camera had (break).
19. They had (know) the tour guide.
20. The tour guide has not (let) tourists off the paths.

Enabling Strategies

LEP Mastering Irregular Verbs

Show students the chart on page 308. Call their attention to the Pattern column as an aid to seeing similarities and differences in the formation of the past and the past participle. Suggest that they can also look up a troublesome main verb in a dictionary. Tell students that a dictionary lists the past tense and the past participle of all verbs.

PRACTICE AND ASSESS

Answers: Exercise 17

1. did
2. went
3. came
4. ate
5. rode
6. were
7. became
8. wore
9. ran
10. took

Answers: Exercise 18

1. fallen
2. blown
3. eaten
4. gone
5. done
6. drawn
7. grown
8. risen
9. gone
10. seen
11. chosen
12. driven
13. grown
14. flown
15. ridden
16. spoken
17. taken
18. broken
19. known
20. let

Independent Practice

Skills Practice

Grammar Practice, p. 15
Grammar Reteaching, p. 17
Grammar Enrichment, p. 16

Grammar Workbook, Lessons 21–24

CLOSE

Ask students to imagine that they are magazine reporters. Have them write a paragraph describing their most interesting assignment. Ask them to use several irregular verbs in the past or present perfect tense. If they use irregular verbs that are not in the chart on page 314, encourage them to look up the words in a dictionary.

TEACH

About the Literature

Direct students to read the passage from "All Stories Are Anansi's," an Ashanti folktale retold by Harold Courlander. Then initiate a discussion about the characters, the setting, and the mood of the passage. Ask students to focus on the highlighted verbs in the passage. Do the shifts in verb tense and form add to or detract from the story? Would the action in the story flow as well if only past tense were used?

Linking Grammar and Literature

Teaching Tip

Explain to students that the animal-trickster story told in the passage reflects a common theme in African folktales. The tricksters in tales from different regions of Africa include the hare, the spider, and the tortoise. Anansi, the spider-trickster, is the opponent of the Sky God. Tales about Anansi tell how he steals the Sky God's stories or tricks the Sky God into allowing disease to enter the world.

Critical Thinking

Students can use prior knowledge to discuss other folktales they know and to compare and contrast these with the passage. Ask them to name one characteristic of Anansi that they can identify from the passage. (He is confident.)

Speaking and Listening

Invite a volunteer to read the passage aloud. Can students follow the shifts in tense? Do they recognize that the narration is in the past tense but the dialogue is in the present?

UNIT 10
Unit Review

Grammar Review

Verbs

The excerpt below is from a traditional Ashanti folktale. The Ashanti are the largest and most powerful ethnic group in the West African country of Ghana. The passage has been annotated to show some of the kinds of verbs covered in this unit.

Literature Model

from ALL STORIES ARE ANANSI'S

an Ashanti folktale by Harold Courlander

In the beginning, all tales and stories belonged to Nyame, the Sky God. But Kwaku Anansi, the spider, yearned to be the owner of all the stories known in the world, and he went to Nyame and offered to buy them. [Past tense]

The Sky God said: "I am willing to sell the stories, but the price is high. Many people have come to me offering to buy, but the price was too high for them. Rich and powerful families have not been able to pay. Do you think you can do it?" [Present perfect tense]

Anansi replied to the Sky God: "I can do it. What is the price?"

"My price is three things," the Sky God said. "I must first have Mmoboro, the hornets. I must then have Onini, the great python. I must then have Osebo, the leopard. For these things I will sell you the right to tell all stories." [Linking verb followed by a predicate noun]

Anansi said: "I will bring them." [Action verb followed by a direct object]

Teacher's Classroom Resources

The following resources can be used for planning, instruction, practice, reinforcement, assessment, reteaching, or evaluation.

Teaching Tools
Lesson Plans

Grammar Workbook
Lessons 58–62
Unit 3 Review
Cumulative Review: Units 1–3

Unit Assessment
Tests with Answer Key
Unit 10 Mastery Test, pp. 39–40
Test Generator
Unit 10 Mastery Test

Exercise 1

Identifying Action Verbs and Direct Objects For the sentences below, write each action verb and direct object. Underline the direct objects. If a sentence has no direct object, write *none.*

1. We boarded the ship for Africa.
2. Our ship entered the harbor after a long wait.
3. We photographed the animals.
4. We visited several African plateaus.
5. Boaters rode the river rapids.
6. Hikers walked through the jungles.
7. Our guide traveled with us.
8. She selected the best places for overnight camps.
9. We traced our trip on a large map.
10. The tourists gave the guide a generous tip.

Exercise 2

Identifying Direct and Indirect Objects For each sentence write the verb plus any direct object and indirect object. Then circle the verb, underline each *direct object* once and each *indirect object* twice. (Not all sentences will have both kinds of object. One sentence has neither.)

SAMPLE Storytellers tell children fascinating stories.
ANSWER (tell) children stories

1. Joel Chandler Harris adapted African American folk legends.
2. He collected the stories in the book *Uncle Remus, His Songs and Sayings.*
3. Uncle Remus tells a boy stories about a fox, a rabbit, and a bear.
4. Brer Rabbit is the American version of the African character Zomo.
5. Brer Rabbit told Brer Fox his terms.
6. Harris used humor in his stories.
7. The *Atlanta Constitution* published the stories.
8. As a boy, Harris visited a plantation near his home.
9. African Americans told Harris stories.
10. Brer Fox took Brer Bear some honey.

PRACTICE AND ASSESS

Answers: Exercise 1

1. boarded, ship
2. entered, harbor
3. photographed, animals
4. visited, plateaus
5. rode, rapids
6. walked, none
7. traveled, none
8. selected, places
9. traced, trip
10. gave, tip

Answers: Exercise 2

1. (adapted) legends
2. (collected) stories
3. (tells) stories, boy
4. (is)
5. (told) terms, Brer Fox
6. (used) humor
7. (published) stories
8. (visited) plantation
9. (told) stories, Harris
10. (took) honey, Brer Bear

UNIT 10 Review

Answers: Exercise 3

1. is, linking verb, predicate noun
2. flows, action verb
3. seem, linking verb, predicate adjective
4. is, linking verb, predicate noun
5. appear, linking verb, predicate adjective
6. graze, action verb
7. is, linking verb, predicate adjective
8. looks, linking verb, predicate adjective
9. are, linking verb, predicate noun
10. gathers, action verb

Answers: Exercise 4

Answers will vary. Samples follow.

1. The Sky God was the owner of stories.
2. Nyname was the Sky God.
3. Anansi was bold.
4. Anansi is a spider.
5. Onini is the great python.
6. Hornets are Mmoboro.
7. Anansi stories are folktales.
8. The python is great.
9. All children are storytellers.
10. The price of the stories is high.

Exercise 3

Distinguishing Linking Verbs and Action Verbs For each sentence write the verb and whether it is an *action verb* or a *linking verb*. If it is a linking verb, write whether it is followed by a *predicate noun* or a *predicate adjective*.

1. The Nile River is the world's longest river.
2. The Nile flows from Lake Victoria.
3. Bright blue and orange birds seem exotic.
4. Africa is a land of geographical wonders.
5. Its plateaus appear flat.
6. Wild animals graze on the plains.
7. The weather in the high plateaus and mountains is mild.
8. The mountain looks beautiful.
9. Community ceremonies are an important rural tradition.
10. Everyone gathers for celebrations of births and marriages.

Exercise 4

Writing Predicate Nouns and Predicate Adjectives Write a predicate noun or a predicate adjective as indicated to complete each sentence below. You may need to add other words. (Use the Literature Model on page 316 to help you.)

1. The Sky God was _______________. (predicate noun)
2. Nyame was _______________. (predicate noun)
3. Anansi was _______________. (predicate adjective)
4. Anansi is a _______________. (predicate noun)
5. Onini is a _______________. (predicate noun)
6. Hornets are _______________. (predicate noun)
7. Anansi stories are _______________. (predicate noun)
8. The python is _______________. (predicate adjective)
9. All children are _______________. (predicate noun)
10. The price of the stories is _______________. (predicate adjective)

Exercise 5

Using Present, Past, and Future Tenses For each sentence write the verb form indicated in parentheses.

1. Folklorists (present tense of *collect*) stories from all parts of Africa.
2. Many stories (future tense of *tell*) about the past.
3. Animals (present tense of *act*) like humans in some stories.
4. Folklorists (past tense of *record*) many "Why" stories.
5. One story (present tense of *explain*) why there are rainbows.
6. Many stories' endings (past tense of *surprise*) listeners.
7. Children (present tense of *enjoy*) the surprises.
8. Folklorists (past tense of *discover*) versions of an Ethiopian tale in Turkey.
9. A Congolese fable (future tense of *teach*) children that families stick together.
10. These stories (future tense of *help*) children understand other cultures.

Exercise 6

Using Present, Past, and Progressive Forms For each sentence write the verb form indicated in parentheses.

SAMPLE Most Ashanti people (present progressive form of *live*) in Ghana.
ANSWER are living

1. Desert (present tense of *cover*) most of northern Africa.
2. In parts of western Africa, rain (present tense of *fall*) all year long.
3. Nomads (past progressive form of *travel*) to grazing areas.
4. Animals (present progressive form of *roam*) the lands by the lake.
5. Berber families (past progressive form of *end*) their meal with tea and pastries.
6. The Ashanti (present tense of *remain*) a very powerful ethnic group.
7. Many Ashanti people (present progressive form of *work*) as farmers.
8. For years the Ashanti (past tense of *speak*) English as a second language.
9. The British (past tense of *rule*) several colonies in West Africa.
10. In the 1950s the Ashanti and other African peoples (past progressive form of *struggle*) for their independence.

UNIT 10
Review

Answers: Exercise 5

1. collect
2. will tell
3. act
4. recorded
5. explains
6. surprised
7. enjoy
8. discovered
9. will teach
10. will help

Answers: Exercise 6

1. covers
2. falls
3. were traveling
4. are roaming
5. were ending
6. remain
7. are working
8. spoke
9. ruled
10. were struggling

Answers: Exercise 7

1. had planted
2. had raised
3. have migrated
4. had lived
5. had stayed
6. had used
7. have tried
8. had reflected
9. have rented
10. have opened

Answers: Exercise 8

1. sought
2. drew
3. come
4. made
5. known
6. grown
7. sang
8. sung
9. written
10. wrote

Exercise 7

Using Present Perfect and Past Perfect Tenses For each sentence write the verb form indicated in parentheses.

SAMPLE Young people (present perfect tense of *learn*) crafts from their elders.
ANSWER have learned

1. Many people (past perfect tense of *plant*) crops.
2. Others (past perfect tense of *raise*) livestock.
3. Some people (present perfect tense of *migrate*) to the cities.
4. Many rural families (past perfect tense of *live*) in mud houses.
5. Village life (past perfect tense of *stay*) the same for generations.
6. Some farmers (past perfect tense of *use*) the same methods as their ancestors did.
7. Some people (present perfect tense of *try*) new methods.
8. The architecture in cities (past perfect tense of *reflect*) traditional styles.
9. Some city families (present perfect tense of *rent*) modern apartments.
10. Outdoor markets (present perfect tense of *open*) on city streets.

Exercise 8

Using Past and Past Participle Forms of Irregular Verbs For each sentence write the past or past participle form of the verb in parentheses. Be sure your sentences make sense.

1. Explorers (seek) prehistoric paintings in the Sahara.
2. Early peoples (draw) pictures of animals.
3. Figures and masks of wood have (come) from many African sculptors.
4. Some early Africans (make) bronze or ivory sculptures.
5. Until the 1900s few people outside Africa had (know) about African arts.
6. Western art has (grow) from the influence of African sculpture.
7. African Americans (sing) songs incorporating African musical rhythms.
8. Africans have (sing) complicated rhythms.
9. Only in a few areas had Africans (write) their stories down.
10. A small minority of people in Ethiopia (write) in Coptic script.

Exercise 9

Writing Present Perfect and Past Perfect Tenses of Irregular Verbs

Write each sentence, using the verb and tense indicated in the parentheses.

SAMPLE Some Africans (present perfect tense of *leave*) their rural homes.
ANSWER Some Africans have left their rural homes.

1. Many African cities (present perfect tense of *become*) prosperous.
2. Many people (past perfect tense of *grow*) corn or maize.
3. City attractions (present perfect tense of *lead*) rural people to move.
4. Africa (past perfect tense of *make*) some progress in agriculture.
5. Periods of drought (present perfect tense of *be*) a problem.
6. Many Africans (present perfect tense of *speak*) Arabic, Swahili, or Hausa.
7. More and more women (present perfect tense of *take*) advantage of new career opportunities.
8. Elders (past perfect tense of *teach*) traditional skills and values.
9. Many African peoples (present perfect tense of *win*) their independence.
10. Black South Africans (past perfect tense of *seek*) the right to vote.

Exercise 10

Write the italicized verbs in the following sentences. For each verb write whether it is in the *present*, *past*, *future*, *present perfect*, or *past perfect* tense. Underline all the verbs that are in the progressive form.

[1]I *am leaving* next week on a trip to Africa. [2]I *have saved* my money for two years. [3]My whole family *is going*. [4]We *have gotten* all the tourist brochures. [5]The travel agent *helped* us plan our route. [6]We *will go* to Morocco, Egypt, and Kenya. [7]I *had hoped* for a stop in Ghana, too. [8]My parents *chose* a different tour. [9]We *were studying* the maps last night. [10]The trip *looks* terrific!

UNIT 10 Review

Answers: Exercise 9

1. have become
2. had grown
3. have led
4. had made
5. have been
6. had taught
7. had paid
8. had given
9. have won
10. have sought

Answers: Exercise 10

1. am leaving—present prog
2. have saved—present perfect
3. is going—present prog
4. have gotten—present perfect
5. helped—past
6. will go—future
7. had hoped—past perfect
8. chose—past
9. were studying—past prog
10. looks—present

UNIT 10 Review

Answers: Exercise 11

Proofreading

This proofreading activity provides editing practice with (1) the current or previous units' skills, (2) the **Troubleshooter** errors, and (3) spelling errors. Students should be able to complete the exercise by referring to the units, the **Troubleshooter,** and a dictionary. (Note: A run-on sentence counts as one error.)

	Error (Type of Error)
1.	• taken (verb form) • painting. The *or* painting; *or* painting, and (run-on sentence) • chosen (verb form)
2.	• given (verb form) • fierce (spelling)
3.	• save (verb form)
4.	• addresses *or* addressed *or* is addressing (verb form)
5.	• Schutt's (singular possessive) • deal (subject-verb agreement) • humans, (commas in a series)

Exercise 11 **Proofreading**

The following passage is about Nancy Schutt's painting *Vanishing,* which appears on this page. Rewrite the passage, correcting the errors in spelling, capitalization, grammar, and usage. Add any missing punctuation. There are ten errors.

Nancy Schutt

1 The artist has took an endangered species as the subject for this painting, the animal she has chose is the leopard. 2 The size and strength of these cats have gave them a feirce reputation. 3 Will their reputation saved them from

Nancy Schutt, *Vanishing*, 1992

About the Art

Nancy Schutt, *Vanishing*, 1992

Nancy Schutt's acrylic-on-canvas painting *Vanishing* is held in the collection of the artist and measures 40 by 42 inches. The artist has earned degrees in printmaking at Colorado State University and the University of Oregon. She has professional experience as a teacher, an artist-in-residence, and as a courtroom artist. Schutt's work has appeared in many books and magazines. It has been exhibited in the U.S. and Canada and has won numerous awards.

extinction? [4]That is the question Nancy Schutt addressing in her painting *Vanishing*. [5]Many of Schutts' paintings deals with the theme of interaction among humans animals, and the natural world.

Exercise 12

Mixed Review

For each sentence write the verb and tell whether it is an *action verb* or a *linking verb*. Then write and label any *direct object*, *indirect object*, *predicate noun*, or *predicate adjective*.

SAMPLE We left home last month for our trip.
ANSWER left, action verb; home, direct object

1. We boarded the ship for Africa.
2. The ship seemed large and modern.
3. It was a freighter.
4. We photographed the animals.
5. We sent our friends pictures.

For each sentence write the form of the verb indicated in parentheses.

6. Herds of elephants (past perfect tense of *live*) on many parts of the African continent.
7. People (present perfect tense of *cause*) animals' habitats to shrink.
8. The white rhinoceros and gorilla (present progressive form of *become*) extinct.
9. Animal parks (future tense of *protect*) some endangered species.
10. Governments (present progressive form of *outlaw*) hunters in these areas.

Answers: Exercise 12

Mixed Review

1. boarded, action verb; ship: direct object
2. seemed, linking verb; large and modern: predicate adjectives
3. was, linking verb; freighter: predicate noun
4. photographed, action verb; animals: direct object
5. sent, action verb; pictures: direct object; friends: indirect object
6. had lived
7. have caused
8. are becoming
9. will protect
10. are outlawing

CLOSE

Ask students to return to the passage and circle all the verbs. Then have them label the verbs: *A* for action and *L* for linking. Remind students that action verbs make writing vivid and exciting. Encourage them to use specific action verbs in their own writing.

Action Verbs in Writing

Ask students to read the passage from *Julie of the Wolves* silently and then to consider the verbs, including those in italics. Suppose the author had used the verb *changed* twice in the last sentence, instead of *softened* and *hardened.* Would the sentence have been as effective?

Techniques with Action Verbs

Discuss the two techniques and ask how students would apply them to the second sentence in the practice paragraph: *Her two cubs played nearby.* How might they make the verb more specific? How might they expand it, using more than one specific verb?

Practice

The answers to this challenging and enriching activity will vary. Refer to Techniques with Action Verbs as you evaluate student choices. Some suggestions are given below.

The lioness stretched lazily in the hot sun. Her two cubs frolicked nearby. She occasionally lifted her head to look around her.

Writing Application

Action Verbs in Writing Jean Craighead George uses precise action verbs in this passage from *Julie of the Wolves* to make her writing lively and vivid. Examine the passage, focusing especially on the italicized verbs.

> Amaroq [one of the wolves] *glanced* at his paw and slowly *turned* his head her way without *lifting* his eyes. He *licked* his shoulder. A few matted hairs *sprang* apart and *twinkled* individually. Then his eyes *sped* to each of the three adult wolves that made up his pack and finally to the five pups who were sleeping in a fuzzy mass near the den entrance. The great wolf's eyes *softened* at the sight of the little wolves, then quickly *hardened* into brittle yellow jewels as he *scanned* the flat tundra [ground].

Techniques with Action Verbs Try to apply some of Jean Craighead George's writing techniques when you write and revise your own work.

1. Whenever possible, replace general words with precise verbs. Compare the following:

General word looked
George's version glanced, scanned

2. Expand a single verb into longer groups of words with more than one specific verb:

Single verb A few matted hairs *separated.*
George's version A few matted hairs *sprang* apart and *twinkled* individually.

Practice Practice these techniques by revising the following passage. Use a separate sheet of paper.

The lioness lay lazily in the hot sun. Her two cubs played nearby. She occasionally moved her head to look around her. She was suddenly alert. A herd of zebra was nearby. The lioness watched her prey. Partially hidden in the tall grass, she moved close to the zebra herd. She suddenly came out of the grass. The zebras walked away, but one was small and weak. The huntress moved again and caught the zebra. She brought the dead zebra back to the cubs. They all ate their fill. Afterward they cleaned themselves, and then they rested.

Teacher's Classroom Resources

The following resources can be used for assessment or evaluation.

Unit Assessment

Tests with Answer Key
Unit 10 Mastery Test, pp. 39–40

Test Generator
Unit 10 Mastery Test

You may wish to administer the Unit 10 Mastery Test at this point.

UNIT

11 Pronouns

Grammar | **Lessons**

UNIT GOALS

The goal of Unit 11 is to help students, through example and instruction, to develop an understanding of and an ability to identify personal pronouns that function as subjects or objects or that indicate possession. The lessons teach students to use personal, possessive, and indefinite pronouns that agree with their antecedents.

Unit Assessment

Tests with Answer Key
Unit 11 Pretest, pp. 41–42
Unit 11 Mastery Test, pp. 43–44

Test Generator
Unit 11 Pretest
Unit 11 Mastery Test

You may wish to administer the Unit 11 Pretest at this point.

Key to Ability Levels

Enabling Strategies have been coded for varying learning styles and abilities.

L1 Level 1 activities are within the ability range of Learning Disabled students.

L2 Level 2 activities are basic-to-average activities and are within the ability range of average students.

L3 Level 3 activities are challenging activities and are within the ability range of above-average students.

LEP LEP activities are within the ability range of Limited English Proficiency students.

Setting the Purpose

Lesson 11.1 teaches students about personal pronouns and how to replace nouns with subject pronouns and object pronouns.

FOCUS

Lesson Overview

Objective: To identify personal pronouns used as subject pronouns and object pronouns

Bellringer

When students enter the classroom, have this assignment on the board: *Tell what is wrong with the following sentence and write it correctly:*

Jaime walked to Jaime's school, but Jaime forgot Jaime's books.

Motivating Activity

Write the corrected sentence from the Bellringer on the board. Ask students what was changed in the sentence to make it correct. (pronouns) How did they decide which pronoun to use? Which sentence sounds better? Why?

TEACH

Vocabulary Link

The prefix *pro-* in *pronoun* means "substituting for or taking the place of." A pronoun takes the place of a noun.

11.1 Personal Pronouns

A **pronoun** is a word that takes the place of one or more nouns and the words that describe those nouns.

The most frequently used pronouns are called personal pronouns. The words *she* and *it* in the sentence below are personal pronouns.

Dana has a favorite folktale, and **she** tells **it** often.

Pronouns that are used to refer to people or things are called **personal pronouns.**

Personal pronouns perform different functions in sentences. Some personal pronouns are used as the simple subject. Others are used as the direct or indirect object of a verb. In the example above, the pronoun *she* replaces the noun *Dana* as the subject. The pronoun *it* replaces *a favorite folktale* as the direct object of the verb *tells.*

A **subject pronoun** is a personal pronoun that is used as the subject of a sentence or a part of a sentence.

An **object pronoun** is a personal pronoun that is used as the direct or indirect object of a verb.

I will read that fable. [subject pronoun]
Jesse told **me** about the story. [object pronoun]

Personal Pronouns	Singular	Plural
Used as Subjects	I you he, she, it	we you they
Used as Objects	me you him, her, it	us you them

Teacher's Classroom Resources

The following resources can be used for planning, instruction, practice, reinforcement, assessment, reteaching, enrichment, or evaluation.

Teaching Tools
Lesson Plans

Blackline Masters
Grammar Practice
Grammar Reteaching, p. 18
Grammar Enrichment, p. 17

Grammar Workbook
Lesson 25

Unit Assessment

Tests with Answer Key
Unit 11 Pretest, pp. 41–42

Test Generator
Unit 11 Pretest

You may wish to administer the Unit 11 Pretest at this point.

Exercise 1 Identifying Personal Pronouns

Write each pronoun, and label it *subject* or *object*.

1. I read "The Bundle of Sticks," a fable by Aesop.
2. It taught me the value of cooperation.
3. A man had four sons, and they always fought.
4. They started an argument in the morning and continued it all day.
5. He became impatient and scolded them.
6. They ignored him and continued to argue.
7. He decided to teach the sons a lesson.
8. They needed it.
9. The father was sure this plan would help them.
10. Now I will tell you the end of the fable.

Exercise 2 Using Subject and Object Pronouns

Write a personal pronoun to replace the underlined words.

1. <u>The father</u> asked <u>the sons</u> for a bundle of sticks.
2. <u>The father</u> tied <u>the bundle</u> up with string.
3. <u>The father</u> gave <u>the bundle</u> to the sons.
4. <u>The father</u> said, "Break <u>the bundle</u>."
5. The boys tried, but <u>the boys</u> were too weak to break <u>the bundle</u>.
6. Then the father untied <u>the bundle</u>.
7. <u>The brothers</u> easily broke <u>the sticks</u> one by one.
8. United, <u>the brothers</u> were strong.
9. The father said, "<u>This lesson</u> has taught <u>my sons</u>."
10. <u>The sons</u> also realized the importance of cooperation.

Exercise 3 Using Subject and Object Pronouns

For each numbered item, write the correct pronoun in parentheses.

[1]George and Maria love stories. (They, Them) especially like fables. [2]Maria wanted to go to the library with George. Could (he, him) go after school?

[3]"We can borrow some books of stories by Aesop," (she, her) said.

[4]George said, "Our library may not have (they, them). [5](We, Us) should go to the county library instead."

PRACTICE AND ASSESS

Answers: Exercise 1

1. I—subject
2. It—subject; me—object
3. they—subject
4. They—subject; it—object
5. He—subject; them—object
6. They—subject; him—object
7. He—subject
8. They—subject; it—object
9. them—object
10. I—subject; you—object

Answers: Exercise 2

1. He; them
2. He; it
3. He; it
4. He; it
5. they; it
6. it
7. They; them
8. they
9. It; them
10. They

Answers: Exercise 3

1. They
2. he
3. she
4. them
5. We

Independent Practice

Skills Practice

Grammar Reteaching, p. 18
Grammar Enrichment, p. 17
Grammar Workbook, Lesson 25

CLOSE

Discuss why writers use pronouns in place of nouns.

Enabling Strategies

LEP Practicing Pronouns

Personal pronouns are used in all languages. The form that these pronouns take frequently differs, however. For example, some languages use a single form for both subject and object pronouns. Others use the same pronoun to refer to men and women. Have students work in groups of three or more. As they pass an object around, one student announces the action. For example: *I pass the book to you. You pass it to him. He passes it to her.*

Setting the Purpose

Lesson 11.2 teaches students to use a subject pronoun as the subject of a sentence and an object pronoun as the object of a verb.

FOCUS

Lesson Overview

Objective: To identify subject and object pronouns

Bellringer

When students enter the classroom, have this assignment on the board: *Write this sentence with nouns in place of the pronouns:*
She and he brought it to him and her.

Motivating Activity

Tell students that a fable usually has a moral or teaches a lesson. Have them read the following moral from "The Crow and the Pitcher." Ask them which pronoun in parentheses correctly completes the first line (*us*) and whether the pronoun is a subject pronoun or an object pronoun (object).

So wisdom informs (*us*, *we*) in
this little rhyme,
That little by little will work
every time.

—"The Crow and the Pitcher,"
retold by Tom Paxton

TEACH

Grammar Tip

To see whether a pronoun in a compound subject or object is correct, replace the compound with the correct plural pronoun: *Lia and I go. We go.*

11.2 Using Pronouns Correctly

People sometimes confuse subject pronouns and object pronouns. They write or say *me* when they should use *I*. They use *we* when they should use *us*. Remember to use a subject pronoun as the subject. Use an object pronoun as the object of a verb.

She owns a collection of fables. [subject]
He told **her** an amusing fable. [indirect object]
The fable entertained **us.** [direct object]

Be sure to use a subject pronoun in a compound subject and an object pronoun in a compound object.

Richard and **I** recited the fable. [not *Richard and me*]
Jennifer helped Richard and **me**. [not *Richard and I*]

In the first sentence above, *Richard and I* is the subject. In the second *Richard and me* is the object of the verb *helped.*

If you're having trouble deciding which form of the pronoun to use in a compound subject or compound object, try saying the sentence without the noun. *Me recited the fable* does not sound correct. *I recited the fable* sounds—and is—correct.

Whenever the pronoun *I* or *me* is joined with a noun or another pronoun to form a compound subject or object, *I* or *me* should come last.

Jennifer and **I** enjoy folktales. [not *I and Jennifer*]

In formal writing and speaking always use a subject pronoun—not an object pronoun—after a linking verb. If the sentence sounds awkward, rearrange the words.

The winner is **she**. [not *The winner is her.*]
She is the winner.

Richard and **I** visited a storyteller.

She told Richard and **me** a fascinating story.

Teacher's Classroom Resources

The following resources can be used for planning, instruction, practice, reinforcement, reteaching, or enrichment.

Teaching Tools
Lesson Plans

Blackline Masters
Grammar Practice, p. 16
Grammar Reteaching, p. 19
Grammar Enrichment, p. 17

Grammar Workbook
Lesson 26

Exercise 4 Using Subject and Object Pronouns

Read the following dialogue between the North Wind and the Sun. Write the correct pronoun for each item.

1. North Wind: (I, me) am the strongest power.
2. Sun: How will you show (I, me)?
3. North Wind: You and (I, me) will have a contest.
4. Sun: A traveler is approaching (we, us).
5. North Wind: I see his dog and (he, him).
6. Sun: You or (I, me) must steal his cloak from him.
7. North Wind: The winner will be you or (I, me).
8. Sun: No, (I, me) cannot lose this contest.
9. North Wind: Watch (I, me) closely as I blow the cloak from the traveler.
10. Sun: I will watch (him, he), but I know you will fail.

Exercise 5 Using Pronouns Correctly

Write a personal pronoun to replace each underlined group of words. Label each pronoun *subject* or *object.*

1. The North Wind blew fiercely. (He, Him)
2. The traveler resisted the North Wind. (he, him)
3. The North Wind watched the Sun work. (she, her)
4. The man felt the rays of the Sun on his back. (they, them)
5. Before long the man was glad to remove the cloak. (he, him)
6. "Now North Wind and the Sun know who's more powerful," said the Sun. (you and I, you and me)
7. The North Wind could not overpower the Sun. (He, Him)
8. However, the Sun and North Wind realized that they both had powers. (she and he, her and him)
9. "This world needs both North Wind and the Sun," said the Sun. (you and me, you and I)
10. From that point on, the world respected the Sun and North Wind equally. (they, them)

Exercise 6 Writing with Personal Pronouns

Write five sentences. Use at least one of these pronouns in each sentence: *I, she, he, we, they, me, her, him, us, them*. Use both subject and object pronouns.

PRACTICE AND ASSESS

Answers: Exercise 4

1. I	6. I
2. me	7. I
3. I	8. I
4. us	9. me
5. him	10. him

Answers: Exercise 5

1. He—subj.	6. you and I—subj.
2. him—obj.	7. He—subj.
3. her—obj.	8. she and he—subj.
4. them—obj.	9. you and me—obj.
5. he—subj.	10. them—obj.

Answers: Exercise 6

Answers will vary, but some suggestions are given below.

She and I ran after them.
They gave the box to him and me.

Two-Minute Skill Drill

List these pronouns on the board. Have students tell whether they are subject or object pronouns.

they	him
she	us
me	them

Independent Practice

Skills Practice

- *Grammar Practice,* p. 16
- *Grammar Reteaching,* p. 19
- *Grammar Enrichment,* p. 17
- ***Grammar Workbook,*** Lesson 26

CLOSE

Have students read a paragraph in a book, write down the pronouns , and identify them as subjects or objects.

Enabling Strategies

LEP Testing for Compounds

Tell students that they can see whether they are using the correct pronoun in a compound subject or object by replacing the compound with a plural pronoun, such as *they* or *them.* If *they* can be used to replace the compound, then a subject pronoun should be used in the compound. *(Diana and I are reading a book.)* If them can replace the compound, then an object pronoun should be used. *(Darna lent the book to Diana and me.)*

Setting the Purpose

Lesson 11.3 teaches students to use personal pronouns and their antecedents correctly so that there is agreement in number and gender.

FOCUS

Lesson Overview

Objective: To identify correct agreement in number and gender between pronouns and their antecedents

Bellringer

When students enter the classroom, have this assignment on the board: *Write five sentences with at least one pronoun in each.*

Motivating Activity

Have volunteers write sentences from the Bellringer on the board. Ask them to circle the pronoun and draw an arrow back to the noun it refers to. If the noun is not within the sentence, have them state the noun to which the pronoun refers.

TEACH

Cooperative Learning

Divide the class into small groups for a roundtable activity. Provide each group with a pencil and paper. Then ask the groups to create their own folktale, fable, or fairy tale. Members of each group should take turns writing a sentence of the story as the pencil and paper are passed around. Each student can write a sentence that builds on the developing story. Remind students to make sure that the pronouns they use agree with the antecedents used by other members of the group.

11.3 Pronouns and Antecedents

The noun that a pronoun refers to is called its **antecedent.**

Albert read "Sleeping Beauty." **He** found **it** exciting.

Here, the noun *Albert* is the antecedent of the pronoun *He. "Sleeping Beauty"* is the antecedent of the pronoun *it.*

The pronoun must agree with its antecedent in number (singular or plural) and gender. The gender of a noun may be masculine (male), feminine (female), or neuter (referring to things).

The king and queen were proud of the baby girl, and **they** loved **her** dearly.

In the sentence above, the pronoun *they* agrees with its antecedent, *The king and queen.* The pronoun *her* agrees with its antecedent, *the baby girl.*

The antecedent for a pronoun should be clear.

The parents showed the baby to friends. **They** admired **her.**

In the second sentence above, does the pronoun *they* refer to *parents* or *friends*? If the antecedent is not clear, it is best to avoid using a pronoun altogether.

The friends admired the baby.

Be especially careful when you use the pronoun *they.*

They have several collections of folktales at the library. [unclear]
The library has many books of folktales. [clear]

Teacher's Classroom Resources

The following resources can be used for planning, instruction, practice, reinforcement, reteaching, or enrichment.

Teaching Tools
Lesson Plans

Blackline Masters
Grammar Practice, p. 17
Grammar Reteaching, p. 20
Grammar Enrichment, p. 18

Grammar Workbook
Lesson 27

Exercise 7 Identifying Antecedents

The sentences below are about "The White Bear," a Russian folktale. Write the antecedent of each underlined pronoun.

1. A man lived in the forest. He was very poor.
2. He had many children. He could not feed them.
3. One night the wind blew hard. It shook the walls.
4. The house stood firm. It was well built.
5. The children heard a noise outside. They were afraid.
6. A white bear appeared. The man approached it.
7. The bear asked the man, "Will you give me your youngest daughter?"
8. This was a strange request. The man had never heard anything like it.
9. His daughter was dear to the man. What could he tell her?
10. The man listened to the bear. He wanted to learn what it would offer.

Exercise 8 Using Personal Pronouns

Write the correct pronoun to complete each sentence below. Then write and circle its antecedent.

1. The bear made a promise. ______ promised the family great wealth.
2. The man spoke with his children. He told ______ about the bear's request.
3. The youngest daughter became worried. The bear's request frightened ______.
4. The girl listened to her family. They said, "If ______ go, the bear promises ______ will be rich."
5. Finally the girl told her father and her brothers and sisters, " ______ will go because I love ______."

Exercise 9 Writing with Personal Pronouns

Read each sentence. Write a new second sentence, replacing the underlined antecedent with a personal pronoun.

1. Many stories have a wolf as a main character.
2. In one story three pigs outsmart a wolf.
3. Little Red Riding Hood meets a wolf in another story.
4. Instead of a wolf, Goldilocks meets three bears.
5. Goldilocks ate the porridge before the bears returned.

Enabling Strategies

LEP Checking Pronoun Agreement

Point out that when the antecedent of a pronoun is another pronoun, the two pronouns should agree. Explain that a common mistake is shifting from *they* to *you* or from *I* to *you* within the same sentence; for example, *They often go to the library, where you can read folktales from all over the world* or *I like this story because you can really relate to it.* You might suggest that students try reading their own sentences aloud to make sure the pronouns agree.

PRACTICE AND ASSESS

Answers: Exercise 7

1. man
2. children
3. wind
4. house
5. children
6. bear
7. bear
8. request
9. daughter
10. man

Answers: Exercise 8

1. It—bear
2. them—children
3. her—daughter
4. you—girl; we—family
5. I—girl; you—father, brothers, sisters

Answers: Exercise 9

Answers will vary, but some suggestions are given below.

1. They have a wolf as a main character.
2. In one story they outsmart a wolf.
3. She meets a wolf in another story.
4. Instead of a wolf, she meets three bears.
5. Goldilocks ate it before the bears returned.

Independent Practice

Skills Practice

- *Grammar Practice*, p. 17
- *Grammar Reteaching*, p. 20
- *Grammar Enrichment*, p. 18
- ***Grammar Workbook***, Lesson 27

CLOSE

Have students give examples of pronouns that agree in number and pronouns that agree in gender.

Setting the Purpose

Lesson 11.4 teaches students to use the two different kinds of possessive pronouns in their singular and plural forms.

FOCUS

Lesson Overview

Objective: To identify possessive pronouns that are used before a noun or that stand alone in a sentence

Bellringer

When students enter the classroom, have this assignment on the board: *What's wrong with this sentence? Write it correctly.*

Jacob took Jacob's homework to Jacob's teacher and asked, "Is Jacob's answer correct?"

Motivating Activity

Write the sentence from the Bellringer on the board, inserting possessive pronouns as appropriate. Point out the repetition in the original sentence. Ask students why the corrected sentence sounds better than the original.

TEACH

Grammar Tip

Tell students that to see if *its* is a contraction, they should replace *its* with *it is*. If the result makes sense, then they can write *it's*.

11.4 Possessive Pronouns

Some personal pronouns indicate ownership or possession. These pronouns are called possessive pronouns, and they replace the possessive forms of nouns.

A **possessive pronoun** is a pronoun that names a person or thing that has something.

Some possessive pronouns are used before nouns. They replace the name of the person or thing that has something.

> **Aesop's** fables are famous. **His** fables are famous.
> **A fable** is a brief tale. **Its** characters are often animals.

Other possessive pronouns stand alone in a sentence.

> This book is **yours.**
> **Aesop's Fables** is a favorite of **mine.**

The chart below shows the singular and plural forms of the two different kinds of possessive pronouns.

Possessive Pronouns	Singular	Plural
Used Before Nouns	my your her, his, its	our your their
Used Alone	mine yours hers, his, its	ours yours theirs

This is my mug
It's handle is broken

The house was his and hers.

The prize is ours not yours or theirs

Possessive pronouns do not contain an apostrophe. Do not confuse the possessive pronoun *its* with the word *it's*. *It's* is a contraction, or shortened form, of the words *it is*: *It's a humorous tale.*

Teacher's Classroom Resources

The following resources can be used for planning, instruction, practice, reinforcement, reteaching, or enrichment.

Teaching Tools
Lesson Plans

Blackline Masters
Grammar Practice, p. 18
Grammar Reteaching, p. 21
Grammar Enrichment, p. 19

Grammar Workbook
Lesson 28

Exercise 10 Identifying Kinds of Possessive Pronouns

The sentences below are about a fable. Write each possessive pronoun, and write whether it *stands alone* or is used *before a noun.*

1. A miller, his son, and a mule walked to market.
2. "Ride on its back," a stranger suggested.
3. The boy got on, and his father walked.
4. A man they knew saw them and said, "You will spoil that son of yours."
5. The man said, "Will you follow a stranger's advice or mine?"

Exercise 11 Using Possessive Pronouns

Write a possessive pronoun to replace each underlined word or phrase.

1. The miller talked to a friend and followed <u>the friend's</u> advice.
2. The boy walked beside the mule; the man rode on <u>the mule's</u> back.
3. Next a woman gave <u>the woman's</u> opinion, and they followed that advice and rode together.
4. <u>The man and the boy's</u> weight was too great.
5. The mule collapsed, and the man and boy worried about <u>the mule's</u> health.
6. They carried the mule on <u>the man's and the boy's</u> shoulders.
7. The man's shoulders were tired. He asked the boy, "How do <u>your shoulders</u> feel?"
8. "<u>My shoulders</u> are tired as well," the boy answered.
9. The man saw that only fools think other people's opinions are better than <u>the fools'</u> own.
10. If the miller had followed <u>the miller's</u> own instincts, the mule would not have collapsed.

Exercise 12 Writing Sentences with Possessive Pronouns

Write a pair of sentences using each phrase. In one sentence of each pair, replace part of the phrase with a possessive pronoun.

SAMPLE the boy's bike
ANSWER The boy's bike was new. His bike was new.

1. the woman's idea
2. the friends' words
3. the mule's back
4. a girl's opinion
5. people's thoughts

Enabling Strategies

LEP Using Possessive Pronouns

To help students acquiring English with the use of possessive pronouns, pair them with students who are proficient in English. Provide pairs with pictures from magazines, and have them write a phrase describing something in the picture (the man's camera) and a related phrase using a possessive pronoun (his camera). Have them list as many of these paired phrases as they can think of.

PRACTICE AND ASSESS

Answers: Exercise 10

1. his—before a noun
2. its—before a noun
3. his—before a noun
4. yours—stands alone
5. mine—stands alone

Answers: Exercise 11

1. his or her
2. its
3. her
4. Their
5. its
6. their
7. yours
8. Mine
9. their
10. his

Answers: Exercise 12

Answers will vary, but some suggestions are given below.

1. The woman's idea was powerful. Her idea was powerful.
2. The friends' words were kind. Their words were kind.
3. The mule's back was sturdy. Its back was sturdy.
4. A girl's opinion was important. Her opinion was important.
5. People's thoughts were with her. Their thoughts were with her.

Independent Practice

Skills Practice

- *Grammar Practice,* p. 18
- *Grammar Reteaching,* p. 21
- *Grammar Enrichment,* p. 19
- ***Grammar Workbook,*** Lesson 28

CLOSE

Have students create sentences using possessive pronouns before nouns and possessive pronouns that stand alone.

Setting the Purpose

Lesson 11.5 teaches students to use indefinite pronouns with verbs that agree in number.

FOCUS

Lesson Overview

Objective: To identify indefinite pronouns as singular or plural

Bellringer

When students enter the classroom, have this assignment on the board: *Write four sentences, each beginning with one of the following words:*

Everyone	*Both*
Most	*Somebody*

Motivating Activity

Have volunteers write their sentences from the Bellringer on the board. Have students underline the verb and circle the pronoun in each sentence. Tell students that the sentence starter words are indefinite pronouns and that the verb in each sentence must agree with the pronoun in number.

TEACH

Teaching Tip

Many writers try to avoid the phrase *his or her* by using a plural indefinite pronoun. Compare the following sentences: *Each of the students has his or her opinion about the moral of the fairy tale. All of the students have their own opinions about the moral of the fairy tale.* As an alternative, a writer may use the indefinite article *a* or *an*: *Each student has an interesting opinion about the moral of the fairy tale.*

11.5 Indefinite Pronouns

An **indefinite pronoun** is a pronoun that does not refer to a particular person, place, or thing.

Like possessive pronouns, indefinite pronouns can be used alone or with nouns.

> Has **any of the students** read this Native American folktale?
> Have **any** students read "The Voice of the River"?

When used alone, indefinite pronouns are singular or plural.

Indefinite Pronouns			
Always Singular			Always Plural
another	everybody	no one	both
anybody	everyone	nothing	few
anyone	everything	one	many
anything	much	somebody	others
each	neither	someone	several
either	nobody	something	

When an indefinite pronoun is used as the subject of a sentence, it may be singular or plural, depending on the noun that follows. Indefinite pronouns that change their number include *all, any, most, none,* and *some.*

> **Some** people **are** familiar with this folktale. [plural]
> **Most** of this tale **takes** place in Africa. [singular]
> **Most** of the characters **are** animals. [plural]

Possessive pronouns often have indefinite pronouns as their antecedents. In such cases, the pronouns must agree in number.

> **Many** are happy to share **their** folktales. [plural]
> **Each** must be willing to wait **his** or **her** turn. [singular]

Teacher's Classroom Resources

The following resources can be used for planning, instruction, practice, reinforcement, reteaching, or enrichment.

Teaching Tools
Lesson Plans

Blackline Masters
Grammar Practice, p. 19
Grammar Enrichment, p. 20

Grammar Workbook
Lesson 29

Exercise 13 Using Indefinite Pronouns

For each sentence, write the correct singular or plural indefinite pronoun in parentheses.

1. (Everyone, Many) likes to read an exciting myth.
2. (Each, Many) are originally from Greece.
3. (One, Others) from Greece is about a father and son.
4. (Anyone, Few) were able to guess the myth's ending.
5. (All, Anybody) enjoy the myth of Daedalus and Icarus.
6. (Both, One) mythical characters live on the island of Crete.
7. Daedalus has artistic talents; (none, nobody) can deny that.
8. (Few, Somebody) match Daedalus's skill in design.
9. (Some, Each) of these students model their work on his art.
10. (Each, Both) of the characters is interesting.

Exercise 14 Using Indefinite Pronouns

Write the word or words in parentheses that correctly complete each sentence.

1. Most of the people (praises, praise) Daedalus's ideas for the huge palace.
2. Few know (his, their) craft as well as Daedalus.
3. No one (is, are) more pleased than King Minos.
4. Although many try, no one (escapes, escape) the king's maze.
5. Everything (changes, change) when Daedalus tells the secret.
6. At last someone finds (his or her, their) way out.
7. Some of the readers (knows, know) the rest of the story: the king forbids Daedalus to leave.
8. Something (takes, take) shape in Daedalus's skilled hands—wax wings for himself and Icarus.
9. Both (plans, plan) an escape across the sea.
10. Each puts on (his, their) pair of waxy wings.
11. At first everything (goes, go) well for the pair.
12. Several (sees, see) them flying in the sky.
13. One (flies, fly) too close to the sun; the wax melts, and he plunges to his death.
14. Which one (lands, land) safely in Sicily?
15. When someone tries to do the impossible, disaster can strike (him or her, them).

Enabling Strategies

LEP Using the Pronoun Chart

Encourage students to copy into their journals the chart of singular and plural indefinite pronouns on page 334. Then they can refer to the chart when they write.

L2 Using Indefinite Pronouns

Many students have difficulty determining whether *everyone* and *everybody* are singular or plural. Tell students that all indefinite pronouns that end in *-one*, *-body*, or *-thing* are singular.

Two-Minute Skill Drill

List these indefinite pronouns on the board. Have students choose a verb that agrees with each pronoun in number.

everybody	few
anyone	something
each	both

PRACTICE AND ASSESS

Answers: Exercise 13

1. Everyone
2. Many
3. One
4. Few
5. All
6. Both
7. none, nobody
8. Few
9. Some
10. Each

Answers: Exercise 14

1. praise
2. their
3. is
4. know
5. takes
6. plan
7. his
8. see
9. flies
10. him or her

Independent Practice

Skills Practice

Grammar Practice, p. 19
Grammar Enrichment, p. 20
Grammar Workbook, Lesson 29

CLOSE

Ask students to write several sentences describing a conversation among three friends without using any of the friends' names. Have them circle the indefinite pronouns they use.

TEACH

About the Literature

After students have read the passage from "The Wise Old Woman," discuss the highlighted pronouns. Encourage students to determine what noun—and its modifiers, if appropriate—could be substituted for each pronoun.

The passage reproduced in the student book appears at the end of "The Wise Old Woman," after the old woman has solved two of Lord Higa's riddles. Yoshiko Uchida often wrote about Japanese culture and the Japanese American experience.

Linking Grammar and Literature

Teaching Tip

In informal speech, people tend to use pronouns carelessly, often ignoring a pronoun's antecedent. For example, many speakers use the second-person pronoun *you* to refer to a third-person antecedent: *Carlos went to the festival, where you could see a performance of* Cinderella. Explain that replacing *you* with a specific word will make the meaning of the sentence clearer: *Carlos went to the festival, where the public could see a performance of* Cinderella.

Speaking and Listening

Read the passage from "The Wise Old Woman" aloud to the class, replacing each pronoun with an appropriate noun. Then ask students to discuss how the substitutions affect the passage. Does the abundance of nouns make the writing seem repetitious and boring? Now read the passage again, but this time substitute a pronoun for each noun. Discuss the effect. Does the absence of nouns make the writing hard to understand?

UNIT 11 Unit Review

Grammar Review

Pronouns

In "The Wise Old Woman," a Japanese folktale, a young lord banishes everyone over 71 years of age from his village. A farmer disobeys the ruler and hides his mother. In the following passage, the ruler discovers that the old woman has saved the village. The passage has been annotated to show some of the pronouns covered in this unit.

Literature Model

from THE WISE OLD WOMAN

Japanese Folktale

Retold by Yoshiko Uchida

The young farmer was amazed at his mother's wisdom. "You are far wiser than any of the wise men of the village," he said. He hurried to tell the young lord how to complete Lord Higa's third task. [Possessive pronoun: *his*]

When the lord heard the answer, he was greatly impressed. "Surely a young man like you cannot be wiser than all my wise men," he said. "Tell me honestly, who has helped you solve all these difficult problems?" [Object pronoun agrees with its antecedent, *the lord*: *me*]

The young farmer could not lie. "My lord," he began slowly, "for the past two years I have broken the law of the land. I have kept my aged mother hidden beneath the floor of my house. It is she who solved each of your problems and saved the village from Lord Higa." [Indefinite pronoun: *each*]

He trembled as he spoke, for he feared the lord's displeasure and rage. Surely now the soldiers would be called to throw him into the dark dungeon. ➡

Teacher's Classroom Resources

The following resources can be used for planning, instruction, practice, reinforcement, assessment, reteaching, enrichment, or evaluation.

Teaching Tools
Lesson Plans

Grammar Workbook
Lessons 25–29
Unit 4 Review
Cumulative Review: Units 1–4

Unit Assessment
Tests with Answer Key
Unit 11 Mastery Test, pp. 43–44
Test Generator
Unit 11 Mastery Test

But when he glanced fearfully at the lord, he saw that the young ruler was not angry at all. Instead, the lord was silent and thoughtful. At last he realized how much wisdom and knowledge old people possess.

Subject pronoun agrees with its antecedent, *the lord*

Exercise 1

Using Personal Pronouns as Subjects and Objects Read the following dialogue. For each item write the correct pronoun.

1. The Ruler: (I, Me) declare that all old people are useless.
2. Farmer: The other villagers and (I, me) do not agree with you.
3. The Ruler: What can you tell (I, me) to change my mind?
4. Farmer: It is my old mother who saved this village. You do not know (she, her), but (her, she) is wise.
5. The Ruler: Perhaps I was wrong. Let it be known to all old people. (Me, I) declare (they, them) are welcome in the land.

Exercise 2

Making Pronouns and Antecedents Agree Write the correct pronoun to complete the second sentence in each pair.

SAMPLE The young farmer's mother was not troubled by Lord Higa's tasks. _______ knew how to complete them.
ANSWER She

1. The wise men couldn't solve the problems. _______ were bewildered.
2. The farmer told the lord that he had hidden his mother. "It is _______ who saved the village," he said.
3. The young farmer was frightened. He thought the soldiers would throw _______ into the dungeon.
4. The young lord looked thoughtful. He said, "_______ have been wrong."
5. The ruler had thought that old people were useless. At last _______ realized that they should be honored.

UNIT 11
Review

PRACTICE AND ASSESS

Answers: Exercise 1

1. I
2. I
3. me
4. her; she
5. I; they

Answers: Exercise 2

1. They
2. she
3. him
4. I
5. he

Answers: Exercise 3

1. He—subject
2. He—subject
3. him—object
4. me—object
5. I—subject; her—object
6. She—subject
7. them—object
8. them—object
9. We—subject
10. You—subject

Answers: Exercise 4

1. She; he
2. them
3. She
4. She; he
5. We
6. her
7. us
8. He; she
9. them
10. him

Exercise 3

Identifying Personal Pronouns as Subjects or Objects Write each pronoun and label it *subject* or *object.*

1. Aesop is famous. He wrote many fables.
2. He was a Greek writer and lived in the sixth century B.C.
3. People admire him.
4. A girl told me that Aesop's fables are fun to read.
5. I asked her to name a favorite fable.
6. She named "The Fox and the Mouse."
7. Because Aesop's stories are often about animals, children especially enjoy them.
8. Roman and medieval writers collected them.
9. We read Aesop's fables that were collected by Phaedrus.
10. You can find them in many anthologies.

Exercise 4

Using Personal Pronouns as Compound Subjects and Objects Write pronouns to replace the underlined words.

SAMPLE Kate and Martin read the story.
ANSWER She and he
SAMPLE Kate and Martin liked it.
ANSWER They

1. Amy and John wrote a fable.
2. They read Mr. Jackson and Ms. Diaz their tale.
3. Gina and I saw Amy and John after school.
4. Amy and John asked us to watch them act out their fable.
5. Gina and I applauded Amy and John after their great performance.
6. Amy and John thanked Gina and me.
7. They told Gina and me that they appreciated our applause.
8. Mr. Jackson and Ms. Diaz applauded too.
9. Ms. Diaz gave Amy and John a flower.
10. Mr. Jackson saluted Amy and John.

Exercise 5

Using Possessive Pronouns with Nouns The following sentences are based on passages in "The Wise Old Woman" that do not appear in this textbook. Write a possessive pronoun to replace the underlined words in each sentence.

SAMPLE The villagers' leader issued a cruel decree.
ANSWER Their

1. The ruler wanted all of the ruler's people to be young and strong.
2. The lord said, "I have no use for old people in the lord's village."
3. No one guessed that the woman was hiding in the young farmer's house.
4. The ruler was amazed by the old woman's wisdom.
5. The farmer told the ruler, "It was the farmer's aged mother who solved the ruler's problems."
6. The villagers were no longer forced to abandon the villagers' parents in the mountains.
7. Lord Higa left the village alone, declaring that the village's people be allowed to live in peace.
8. The young farmer now had the farmer's worry lifted from the farmer's mind.
9. The ruler's new understanding would allow the villagers to live full lives.
10. The people would always remember how the farmer's courage had saved the people's village.

Exercise 6

Writing Sentences with Indefinite Pronouns Write a sentence for each item below. Use the pronoun as the subject and the correct word from each pair as the verb.

1. Someone	listens, listen	4. Everybody	plays, play
2. All	makes, make	5. Many	enjoys, enjoy
3. Several	talks, talk		

UNIT 11 Review

Answers: Exercise 5
1. his
2. my
3. his
4. her
5. my; your
6. their
7. its
8. his; his
9. His
10. their

Answers: Exercise 6
Answers will vary, but some suggestions are provided below.
1. Someone listens to a story.
2. All make a loud noise.
   All of this pie makes a huge serving.
3. Several talk to their friends.
4. Everybody plays the game.
5. Many enjoy the game.

UNIT 11 Review

Answers: Exercise 7

Proofreading

This proofreading activity provides editing practice with (1) the current or previous units' skills, (2) the **Troubleshooter** errors, and (3) spelling errors. Students should be able to complete the exercise by referring to the units, the **Troubleshooter**, and a dictionary.

	Error (Type of Error)
1.	• grew (subject-verb agreement)
2.	• him (object pronoun)
3.	• teens, and (compound sentence)
	• he (subject pronoun)
4.	• his (possessive pronoun)
5.	• portray (subject-verb agreement)
6.	• find (subject-verb agreement)
	• appealing (spelling)
7.	• his (pronoun-antecedent agreement)
8.	• learns (subject-verb agreement)

Exercise 7 **Proofreading**

The following passage is about African American artist Jacob Lawrence. Rewrite the passage, correcting the errors in spelling, capitalization, grammar, and usage. Add any missing punctuation. There are 10 errors.

Jacob Lawrence

[1]Jacob Lawrence, who was born in 1917, growed up in Harlem. [2]This thriving artistic center influenced he. [3]Lawrence chose to become a painter in his teens and him was encouraged by artists in his community. [4]Lawrence was twenty-four years old when his' work was exhibited in a New York art gallery. ➡

Jacob Lawrence, *Men Exist for the Sake of One Another*, 1958

About the Art

Jacob Lawrence, *Men Exist for the Sake of One Another*, 1958

Jacob Lawrence's paintings celebrate people and the universality of human experience. In *Men Exist for the Sake of One Another* (1958), for example, the artist presents the universal image of children learning at an adult's knee.

[5]Lawrence's paintings portrays the lives and struggles of African Americans. [6]Most people finds his work apealing. [7]In their painting on the previous page, Lawrence shows a man talking to some children. [8]The painting reminds us that everyone learn from others.

Mixed Review

Exercise 8

Number a sheet of paper from 1 to 20. Then choose a pronoun from the box below to fill in each blank. You will not need to use all the pronouns, but you may need to use some pronouns more than once.

our	she	my
him	they	it
them	mine	its
nobody	us	I
me	her	we
everyone	yours	his

[1]_____ class read a fable written by Aesop. [2]_____ was the story of a very hungry fox. Some grapes tempted [3]_____. However, [4]_____ were out of [5]_____ reach. The fox knew other animals could probably reach the grapes. The fox thought of a way to reach [6]_____, too. If you want to know how this story ends, you will have to read [7]_____.

Almost [8]_____ enjoys a good folktale. Our teacher told [9]_____ class a story based on a Native American folktale. Mae and I found [10]_____ wise. The story taught [11]_____ about life in a village. It amused and surprised both her and [12]_____. Later Mae read the tale again to [13]_____ sister, Ann.

Yesterday my brother and [14]_____ went to the library. [15]_____ were both looking for a book of fables. [16]_____ brother found a book of Aesop's fables. [17]_____ is better known for fables than Aesop. The book is now a favorite of [18]_____. There is a story in [19]_____ about a vixen. In it, she talks about [20]_____ cubs.

Answers: Exercise 8

Mixed Review

1. Our; My
2. It
3. her; him
4. they
5. her; his
6. them
7. it
8. everyone
9. our; my
10. it
11. us
12. me
13. her
14. I
15. We
16. My
17. Nobody
18. his; mine
19. it
20. her

CLOSE

Ask students to summarize in a few sentences what is happening in Jacob Lawrence's painting *Men Exist for the Sake of One Another* on page 340. Then ask them to circle the pronouns they used in their summaries. Remind them to be sure their pronouns and antecedents agree.

Pronouns in Writing

Have students read the passage silently. Then go back and discuss the italicized pronoun choices. Discuss these choices in relation to the Techniques with Pronouns.

Techniques with Pronouns

Discuss the techniques described and have students examine how they are used. Students can look for examples in other books or stories.

Practice

The answers to this challenging and enriching activity will vary. Refer to Techniques with Pronouns as you evaluate student choices.

Writing Application

Pronouns in Writing Michael Dorris uses pronouns in this passage from *Morning Girl* to make his writing clear and concise. Read the passage, paying particular attention to the pronouns that are italicized.

> *I* knew *my* hands very well. *I* study *them* when *I* trim *my* nails with the rough edge of a broken shell, making *them* smooth and flat. *I* could spread *my* fingers and press *them* into wet sand to see the shape *they* leave. Once *I* tried to do that with *my* head, but *all* I got was a big shallow hole and dirty hair.
>
> *I* knew the front of *my* body, the bottoms of *my* feet. *I* knew the color of *my* arms—tan as the inside of a yam after the air has dried *it*—and if *I* stretched *my* tongue *I* could see *its* pink tip.

Techniques with Pronouns Try to use pronouns in some of the ways that Michael Dorris does when you write and revise your own work.

1. Always check that a pronoun agrees with its antecedent.

Incorrect use I knew my *hands* very well. I study *it* . . .
Dorris's version I knew my *hands* very well. I study *them* . . .

2. To make your writing smooth, replace repeated nouns with pronouns.

Repeated words I asked *Mother* one day when *Mother* and I were walking . . .
Dorris's version I asked Mother one day when *we* were walking . . .

Practice Practice these techniques by revising the following passage on a separate sheet of paper.

Morning Girl spends every day with Morning Girl's brother Star Boy. Morning Girl and Star Boy go to the beach. The brother and sister walk along the shore. Star Boy finds smooth pebbles. Star Boy finds unbroken shells and gives them to Morning Girl. The boy and girl wade in the shallow water and find tiny crabs and starfish. Morning Girl and Star Boy take Morning Girl's and Star Boy's treasures home. They put their treasures in a shaded pool next to the house where they live with their parents. Morning Girl and Star Boy will watch the crabs and starfish for several hours. Then the children will return the live creatures to the sea.

Teacher's Classroom Resources

The following resources can be used for assessment or evaluation.

Unit Assessment

Tests with Answer Key
Unit 11 Mastery Test, pp. 43–44

Test Generator
Unit 11 Mastery Test

You may wish to administer the Unit 11 Mastery Test at this point.

UNIT
12 Adjectives

Grammar | Lessons

UNIT GOALS

The goal of Unit 12 is to help students, through example and instruction, to develop an understanding of and an ability to identify and use proper adjectives, articles, and adjectives that compare.

Unit Assessment

Tests with Answer Key
Unit 12 Pretest, pp. 45–46
Unit 12 Mastery Test, pp. 47–48

Test Generator
Unit 12 Pretest
Unit 12 Mastery Test

You may wish to administer the Unit 12 Pretest at this point.

Key to Ability Levels

Enabling Strategies have been coded for varying learning styles and abilities.

L1 Level 1 activities are within the ability range of Learning Disabled students.

L2 Level 2 activities are basic-to-average activities and are within the ability range of average students.

L3 Level 3 activities are challenging activities and are within the ability range of above-average students.

LEP LEP activities are within the ability range of Limited English Proficiency students.

Setting the Purpose

Lesson 12.1 helps students to identify adjectives. It explains how adjectives describe nouns and teaches students to capitalize proper adjectives.

FOCUS

Lesson Overview

Objective: To identify adjectives and proper adjectives and to capitalize proper adjectives

Bellringer

When students enter the classroom, have this assignment on the board: *Circle the words that describe (adjectives) in these two sentences:*

1. *The shiny green car was parked beside the Korean restaurant.*
2. *The rest of the huge parking lot was empty.*

TEACH

Teaching Tip

If students are unsure about how to identify predicate adjectives, tell them the following: 1. A predicate adjective answers the question *What kind?* about the subject; 2. The word *very* can be inserted before a predicate adjective; 3. A predicate adjective can be converted to a comparative or superlative form.

Cross-reference: Adjectives

For instruction and practice with adjectives, refer students to Lesson 3.1, pp. 98–101 and Lesson 3.3, pp. 106–109.

12.1 Adjectives and Proper Adjectives

The words that we use to describe people, places, and things are called adjectives.

An **adjective** is a word that describes a noun or a pronoun.

Adjectives describe, or modify, nouns in three ways.

How Adjectives Describe Nouns	
What kind?	We studied **modern** history.
How many?	I read **four** volumes.
Which one?	**That** invention changed the world.

Most adjectives come before the nouns they modify. Sometimes adjectives follow linking verbs and modify the subject, as in the example below. These adjectives are called **predicate adjectives.**

These inventions are **important.**

Some adjectives are formed from proper nouns and begin with a capital letter. These are called proper adjectives.

Proper adjectives are adjectives formed from proper nouns.

Proper adjectives often have the same form as the noun. Others are formed by adding an ending to the noun form.

Forming Proper Adjectives	
Proper Noun	**Proper Adjective**
Oranges from **Florida**	**Florida** oranges
A symphony by **Mozart**	A **Mozart** symphony
Food from **Italy**	**Italian** food

Teacher's Classroom Resources

The following resources can be used for planning, instruction, practice, reinforcement, assessment, reteaching, enrichment, or evaluation.

Teaching Tools
Lesson Plans

Blackline Masters
Grammar Practice, p. 22
Grammar Reteaching, p. 20
Grammar Enrichment, p. 21

Grammar Workbook
Lesson 30

Unit Assessment

Tests with Answer Key
Unit 12 Pretest, pp. 45–46

Test Generator
Unit 12 Pretest

You may wish to administer the Unit 12 Pretest at this point.

Exercise 1 Identifying Adjectives

Write each adjective. Beside it write the noun or pronoun it describes. If it is a predicate adjective, label it *P.A.*

1. Young Gandhi studied at a small school in India.
2. He later lived for a while in busy London.
3. Sometimes Gandhi was homesick.
4. Gandhi heard the truth of an inner voice.
5. He was courageous and purposeful.
6. Gandhi often fasted for many days.
7. After fasting, Gandhi grew weak, but he remained brave.
8. The mature Gandhi returned to India and led the nationalist movement.
9. He used nonviolent resistance as a protest against foreign rule.
10. He spent seven years in prison for that resistance.
11. The long struggle against foreign rule ended in 1947.
12. Two separate nations—India and Pakistan—were formed.
13. Most Hindus remained in independent India.
14. Large numbers of Muslims settled in Pakistan.
15. In 1971 the eastern portion of Pakistan became the new nation of Bangladesh.

Exercise 2 Identifying Proper Adjectives

Write each adjective. Beside it write the noun it describes. Capitalize each proper adjective.

1. Victoria was a famous ruler in english history.
2. She was the energetic granddaughter of George III.
3. Victoria was the english queen from 1837 to 1901.
4. Victoria was also the queen of the scottish and welsh people.
5. During that time Britain built a colonial empire.
6. The vast empire included indian plantations.
7. Victoria established asian and african colonies.
8. The colonial empire made Britain a rich country.
9. Victoria was wise and capable.
10. She became the symbol of british greatness.
11. The diamond jubilee was celebrated by immense crowds.
12. The Royal Princess Victoria married a german prince.
13. Prince Edward was crowned the next british monarch.
14. Students of english history are knowledgeable about the victorian era.
15. The elizabethan and edwardian eras are famous, too.

Enabling Strategies

LEP Learning Proper Adjectives

In some languages, proper adjectives derived from place names are identical to the proper noun. Students who speak these languages might say such things as, a Japan pear or an Italy sweater. Encourage these students to learn a group of proper adjectives in English with each of the following endings: *-ese (Chinese, Japanese, Sudanese); -i (Israeli, Pakistani); -an (Nigerian, Italian, Korean, Texan); -ish (Danish, English, Spanish).*

PRACTICE AND ASSESS

Answers: Exercise 1

1. Young—Gandhi; small—school
2. busy—London
3. homesick—Gandhi, P.A.
4. inner—voice
5. courageous—He, P.A.; purposeful—He, P.A.
6. many—days
7. weak—Gandhi, P.A.; brave—he, P.A.
8. mature—Gandhi; nationalist—movement
9. nonviolent—resistance; foreign—rule
10. seven—years; that—resistance
11. long—struggle; foreign—rule
12. Two—nations; separate—nations
13. Most—Hindus; independent—India
14. large—numbers
15. eastern—portion; new—nation

Answers: Exercise 2

1. famous—ruler; English—history
2. energetic—granddaughter
3. English—queen
4. Scottish—people; Welsh—people
5. colonial—empire
6. vast—empire; Indian—plantations
7. Asian—colonies; African—colonies
8. colonial—empire; rich—country
9. wise—Victoria; capable—Victoria
10. British—greatness
11. diamond—jubilee; immense—crowds
12. Royal—Princess Victoria; German—prince
13. British—monarch
14. English—history; knowledgeable—students; Victorian—era
15. Elizabethan—eras; Edwardian—eras; famous—eras

Independent Practice

Skills Practice

Grammar Practice, p. 22
Grammar Reteaching, p. 20
Grammar Enrichment, p. 21

Grammar Workbook, Lesson 30

CLOSE

Have students look through previous writing assignments to identify adjectives and to check for capitalization of proper adjectives. Ask them to consider how adjectives can make their writing more vivid.

Setting the Purpose

Lesson 12.2 helps students to understand the usage rules for articles and demonstrative adjectives and pronouns.

FOCUS

Lesson Overview

Objective: To identify and correctly use articles and demonstrative adjectives and distinguish demonstrative adjectives from demonstrative pronouns

Bellringer

When students enter the classroom, have this assignment on the board: *Explain why the following sentences are confusing, and write them correctly.*

I ate a egg and an sandwich for breakfast.

I sat at the table in a kitchen of our house.

Motivating Activity

Encourage students to talk about the difficulties they have with using articles correctly. Explain that this lesson will help them use articles more effectively.

TEACH

Teaching Tip

The use of *a/an* and *the* is extraordinarily complex. A noun naming a specific item is preceded by the definite article *the. A/an* (the indefinite article) is used the first time that a nonspecific item is mentioned. When the noun is mentioned again, it is no longer nonspecific. Since it now refers to the specific item already mentioned, *the* is used. For example, *I looked at a new car yesterday, but the car costs more than I can afford.*

12.2 Articles and Demonstratives

The words *a, an,* and *the* are special kinds of adjectives. They are called **articles.**

The points to a specific item or items. *A* and *an* refer to any one item of a group. Use *a* before words that begin with a consonant sound. Use *an* before words that begin with a vowel sound.

> William Shakespeare is **the** most famous English playwright.
> Getting **a** lead role in **a** Shakespeare play is **an** honor.

The words *this, that, these,* and *those* are called **demonstrative adjectives.** They are used to point out something.

> Take **this** umbrella with you. **That** store is closed.
> Take **these** boots also. **Those** clouds are lovely.

Use *this* and *that* with singular nouns. Use *these* and *those* with plural nouns. Use *this* and *these* to point out something that is close to you. Use *that* and *those* to point out something that is far from you.

Demonstratives		
	Singular	**Plural**
Near	this	these
Far	that	those

Demonstratives can be used with nouns or without them. When used alone, they are called **demonstrative pronouns.**

> **This** is mine. **These** are for you.

Teacher's Classroom Resources

The following resources can be used for planning, instruction, practice, reinforcement, reteaching, or enrichment.

Teaching Tools
Lesson Plans

Blackline Masters
Grammar Practice, p. 21

Grammar Workbook
Lesson 31

Exercise 3 Using Articles

For each sentence write the correct article.

1. William Shakespeare was (an, the) English playwright.
2. Was he (a, the) greatest writer of all time?
3. (A, The) town of Stratford-on-Avon was his birthplace.
4. Shakespeare was (a, an) country boy.
5. He was (a, an) poet and (a, an) actor.
6. His plays caused (a, an) sensation in London.
7. Shakespeare had one of (a, the) largest vocabularies of any English writer.
8. Many of his plays were performed at (a, the) Globe Theatre.
9. *Romeo and Juliet* is (a, an) popular play.
10. (A, The) main celebration of Shakespeare's birth takes place on April 23.

Exercise 4 Using Demonstratives

For each sentence write the correct demonstrative word.

1. (This, That) biography I'm holding is about Florence Nightingale.
2. (This, These) woman dreamed of being a nurse.
3. Her friends encouraged (that, those) dream.
4. (That, Those) sick soldiers lacked expert care.
5. (This, These) injustice created great concern.
6. (This, These) concern brought about reforms.
7. Florence Nightingale led (that, those) nurses.
8. Nightingale could organize and take care of details, and (that, those) abilities made her successful.
9. (This, These) behavior was unusual for a rich woman of her time.
10. Florence Nightingale's achievements remain famous to (this, that) day.

Exercise 5 Writing Sentences with Demonstratives

Write a pair of sentences for each of these words: *this*, *that*, *these*, and *those*. In one sentence of each pair, use the word as a demonstrative adjective. In the other, use it as a demonstrative pronoun.

SAMPLE ANSWER These boots are too small. (demonstrative adjective)
These will fit you. (demonstrative pronoun)

Enabling Strategies

LEP Provide Usage Rules for Articles

When making generalizations about a noun, use no article if the noun is plural (cats are smart). Use an article if the noun is singular (a dog is a good pet). Use *the* when the noun is unique (I saw the moon), is a specific one of a category (the car runs), or when the listener knows what is being said (we won the game).

TEACH

Teaching Tip

To help students get used to using *a* and *an*, have them choose a newspaper article and read through it, circling the articles *a* and *an* and indicating whether the word that follows begins with a consonant or a vowel sound. If students are confused by when to use *an* as an article with words such as *hour,* remind them to listen for the beginning sound.

PRACTICE AND ASSESS

Answers: Exercise 3

1. an	6. a
2. the	7. the
3. The	8. the
4. a	9. a
5. a, an	10. The

Answers: Exercise 4

1. This	6. This
2. This	7. those
3. that	8. those
4. Those	9. This
5. This	10. this

Answers: Exercise 5

Answers will vary but should include the demonstratives labeled as indicated.

Independent Practice

Skills Practice

Grammar Practice, p. 21

Grammar Workbook, Lesson 31

CLOSE

Invite students to explain in their own words the rules for using articles, demonstrative adjectives, and demonstrative pronouns. Have them support their interpretations with written examples.

Setting the Purpose

Lesson 12.3 teaches students to identify the comparative and superlative forms of adjectives and to avoid common usage errors.

FOCUS

Lesson Overview

Objective: To identify and correctly use the comparative and superlative forms of adjectives

Bellringer

When students enter the classroom, have this assignment on the board: *Find and correct the errors in the following sentences.*

It was the interestingest art show I have seen. The gallery was more smaller than the other one I visited. I think Ms. Johnson's paintings were beautifuller than any of the others.

Motivating Activity

Have students rewrite the sentences from the Bellringer correctly. Ask them to discuss how they were able to spot the errors. What makes using *more, most, -er,* and *-est* correctly so difficult?

TEACH

Cross-reference

Students will use comparative adjectives in expository paragraphs that compare and contrast. For instruction and practice on this writing strategy, refer students to Lesson 5.2, Comparing and Contrasting Two Things, pp. 182–184.

12.3 Adjectives That Compare

You can use adjectives to compare two or more nouns.

The **comparative form** of an adjective compares two things or people.

For most adjectives of one syllable, form the comparative by adding *-er*. For most adjectives of two or more syllables, form the comparative by using *more* before the adjective.

Is Venezuela **larger** than Peru?
Is Argentina **more beautiful** than Ecuador?

The **superlative form** of an adjective compares more than two things or people.

For most adjectives of one syllable, form the superlative by adding *-est*. For most adjectives of two or more syllables, form the superlative by using *most* before the adjective.

Is Brazil the **richest** country in South America?
Simón Bolívar was one of South America's **most successful** generals.

Do not use *more* or *most* before adjectives that already are in the comparative or superlative form.

Comparative and Superlative Forms

Adjective	Comparative	Superlative
small	small**er**	small**est**
dark	dark**er**	dark**est**
active	**more** active	**most** active
intelligent	**more** intelligent	**most** intelligent

Teacher's Classroom Resources

The following resources can be used for planning, instruction, practice, reinforcement, assessment, reteaching, enrichment, or evaluation.

Teaching Tools
Lesson Plans

Blackline Masters
Grammar Practice, p. 23
Grammar Reteaching, p. 22
Grammar Enrichment, p. 23

Grammar Workbook
Lesson 32

Exercise 6 Using the Comparative and Superlative Forms

Write the correct comparative or superlative form of the adjective in parentheses.

1. Simón Bolívar was one of the (great) heroes of South America.
2. He was (successful) as an older man than as a younger man.
3. The general was (wise) than before about the struggle.
4. Simón Bolívar was the (loyal) of patriots.
5. The general cherished the (important) dream of all.
6. He is (famous) in Europe than in the United States.
7. Maria Tallchief was one of the (noted) dancers in the world.
8. The Canadian tour was the (challenging) of all the tours.
9. Away from home Tallchief was (homesick) this time than ever before.
10. Maria received the (marvelous) opportunity of all.
11. The Russian composer Igor Stravinsky thought she was the (suitable) dancer for some of his ballets.
12. The Firebird was perhaps Tallchief's (memorable) role.
13. George Balanchine gave her the (prominent) roles of all.
14. George Balanchine may be the (famous) ballet choreographer of this century.
15. Some of his ballets are (inventive) than others.
16. Balanchine choreographed ballets to (romantic) music than Stravinsky's music.
17. Dancing requires (hard) work than some other professions.
18. Only the (dedicated) dancers make it as professionals.
19. Although ballets have music, scenery, and costumes, the (important) part is the dancing.
20. American ballet is often (energetic) than Russian ballet.

Exercise 7 Writing Sentences to Show Comparison

Write five sentences that make comparisons. After each sentence, write whether the comparison is in the *comparative* or *superlative* form.

SAMPLE ANSWER The dancers needed longer rehearsals. (comparative)

TEACH

Teaching Tip

Invite students to create written advertisements that compare one or more real or imaginary products. Encourage them to take the position that one product is clearly superior. Help them to include comparative and superlative adjectives in their advertisements. Students may wish to look at how comparative and superlative adjectives are used in existing advertisements.

PRACTICE AND ASSESS

Answers: Exercise 6

1. greatest	**11.** most
2. more	**12.** most
3. wiser	**13.** most
4. most	**14.** most
5. most	**15.** more
6. more	**16.** more
7. most	**17.** harder
8. most	**18.** most
9. more	**19.** most
10. most	**20.** more

Answers: Exercise 7

Answers will vary, but should include the comparative or superlative adjective form as indicated.

Independent Practice

Skills Practice

- *Grammar Practice,* p. 23
- *Grammar Reteaching,* p. 22
- *Grammar Enrichment,* p. 23
- ***Grammar Workbook,*** Lesson 32

Enabling Strategies

LEP Writing Adjectives that Compare

Provide students with objects or photos of objects which are similar: three cars or two books. Ask students to write comparisons of the objects. When students have finished, have them check their work for proper usage of comparative and superlative adjectives.

CLOSE

Ask students to create posters illustrating rules for using comparative and superlative forms of adjectives. Students might wish to include examples of common usage errors along with corrections and the rules which cover each example.

Setting the Purpose

Lesson 12.4 teaches students to identify adjectives with irregular comparative and superlative forms and to use them correctly.

FOCUS

Lesson Overview

Objective: To identify and correctly use irregular comparative and superlative forms of adjectives

Bellringer

When students enter the classroom, have this assignment on the board: *Complete the following sentences with the correct form of* good.

1. *Sara had a ____ vacation at her grandmother's farm.*
2. *Who do you think is the ____ singer of all?*
3. *Of the two plays, which do you think is ____?*

Motivating Activity

Have students discuss difficulties they had providing comparatives and superlatives for the Bellringer sentences. What is unusual about comparative and superlative forms of this adjective?

TEACH

Teaching Tip

Point out to students that the comparative and superlative forms of the adjective *good* are *better* and *best*. The comparative and superlative forms of the adverb *well* (as in *He behaved well*) are also *better* and *best*.

12.4 Special Adjectives That Compare

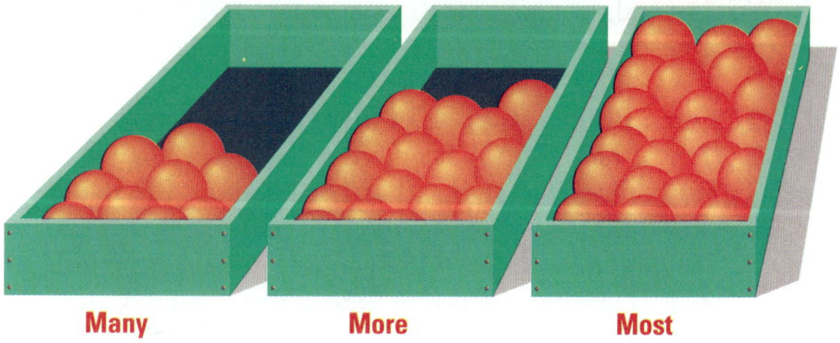

The comparative and superlative forms of some adjectives are not formed in the regular manner.

Harriet Tubman believed in a **good** cause.
She knew that freedom was **better** than slavery.
The Underground Railroad was the **best** route to freedom.

In the sentences above, *better* is the comparative form of the adjective *good*. *Best* is the superlative form of *good*.

Irregular Comparative and Superlative Forms

Adjective	Comparative	Superlative
good	better	best
bad	worse	worst
much, many	more	most
little	less	least

Do not use *more* or *most* before irregular adjectives that are already in the comparative or superlative form.

Tubman felt **better** at the end of the day. [not *more better*]

Teacher's Classroom Resources

The following resources can be used for planning, instruction, practice, reinforcement, assessment, reteaching, enrichment, or evaluation.

Teaching Tools
Lesson Plans

Blackline Masters
Grammar Practice, p. 24
Grammar Reteaching, p. 22
Grammar Enrichment, p. 24

Grammar Workbook
Lesson 33

Exercise 8 Identifying the Comparative and Superlative Forms

Write whether each underlined adjective is in the *comparative* or *superlative* form. Then write the adjective from which it was formed.

1. Martin Luther King Jr. wanted a better life for all Americans.
2. His best speeches inspired people.
3. He worked hard on his better speeches.
4. There were more people in his audience near the end of his life than there had been at the beginning.
5. King paid less attention to his critics than to his supporters.
6. King believed that nonviolent protest was the best way to achieve equality for everyone.
7. Other people believed in the use of more force.
8. Some of the worst conditions in housing were located in northern cities rather than in the South.
9. Many hoped for a better education for their children.
10. Most listeners were inspired by King's "I Have a Dream" speech.

Exercise 9 Using the Comparative and Superlative Forms

Write the correct comparative or superlative form of the adjectives in parentheses.

1. After her husband's death, Eleanor Roosevelt did even (much) work than before.
2. Mrs. Roosevelt's newspaper column was (good) than many other newspaper columns.
3. She gave her (good) efforts to the United Nations.
4. Perhaps she did her (good) work of all in the cause of peace.
5. Which of her speeches is the (good)?
6. She had (many) projects than previous first ladies.
7. She may have been the (good) writer of them all.
8. When Franklin was alive, Eleanor made (many) trips than he did.
9. Being crippled by polio was one of the (bad) personal problems Franklin faced.
10. Eleanor worked to help people who had (little) power and influence than she had.

PRACTICE AND ASSESS

Answers: Exercise 8

1. comparative—good
2. superlative—good
3. comparative—good
4. comparative—many
5. comparative—little
6. superlative—good
7. comparative—much
8. superlative—bad
9. comparative—good
10. superlative—many

Answers: Exercise 9

1. more
2. better
3. best
4. best
5. best
6. more
7. best
8. more
9. worst
10. less

Independent Practice

Skills Practice

Grammar Practice, p. 24
Grammar Reteaching, p. 22
Grammar Enrichment, p. 24

Grammar Workbook, Lesson 33

CLOSE

Have students check the advertisements they created in Lesson 12.3 or other previous writing assignments to make sure that any irregular comparative or superlative adjectives were used correctly.

Enabling Strategies

LEP Special Adjectives

Students who have difficulty with Exercise 9 may find it helpful to break the exercise into parts. Encourage these students to use the boxed list of Irregular Comparative and Superlative Forms on page 348. Suggest that as students write each sentence they hold their papers next to the box, trying each form of the appropriate adjective in the blank. Having these choices in front of them may make it easier for students to select the correct form.

TEACH

About the Literature

Explain that the review contains a passage taken from Studs Terkel's *Giants of Jazz.*

Before he became a writer, Studs Terkel worked as an actor, a disc jockey, a radio commentator, and a television host. He is known for capturing the details of human experience as is evidenced in this passage. He traveled extensively to interview people from all walks of life for his books, *Working, Giants of Jazz,* and the Pulitzer-Prize-winning *The Good War: an Oral History of World War Two.*

Have students read the passage and identify the adjectives. Then ask them to discuss the ways in which these adjectives provide useful information and clarity.

Linking Grammar and Literature

Critical Thinking

Invite students to consider situations in which adjectives are necessary for accurate communication. Examples of such situations might be giving travel directions, building a birdhouse, and fixing a car.

Cooperative Learning

Invite students to work together in small groups to write a version of the passage in which all adjectives have been removed. Then ask one volunteer to read to his or her group the passage with the adjectives and another volunteer to read the passage without the adjectives. Students can then discuss the differences. Which passage was more interesting? Which provided more information? Why?

UNIT 12
Unit Review

Grammar Review

Adjectives

In the following selection, Chicago writer Studs Terkel looks at the early years of famed jazz musician Louis Armstrong. The passage has been annotated to show some of the kinds of adjectives covered in this unit.

Literature Model

from GIANTS OF JAZZ

by Studs Terkel

Kid Ory's Band was the most popular one in New Orleans. They played just about everywhere, for fancy parties as well as for rough-and-tumble get-togethers. Louis was the most sought-after jazzman. He had no days off. When the Ory group was resting, he'd be playing at some dance or funeral. Often he blew second cornet with the Papa Celestin's Tuxedo Brass Band. In later years he recalled, "I thought I was in heaven, playing with that band. They had funeral marches that would touch your heart, they were so beautiful."

One day he was approached by a red-headed band leader. It was Fate Marable, the riverboat king. Excellent jazz was being played on the excursion boats that glided up and down the Mississippi. Easily the best of these boat bands was Marable's, of the steamer *Sydney.* His repertoire was far more varied than that of any New Orleans band. His men could *read* music!

"Come on, Louis," urged Fate. "Join us and see what the rest of the country looks like." Armstrong, eager for new adventures and new learning, readily accepted.

Annotations:
- Superlative form of *popular* — most popular
- Demonstrative adjective — that
- Predicate adjective — beautiful
- Comparative form of *varied* — more varied
- Proper adjective — New Orleans
- Article — the

Teacher's Classroom Resources

The following resources can be used for planning, instruction, practice, reinforcement, assessment, reteaching, or evaluation.

Teaching Tools
Lesson Plans

Grammar Workbook
Lessons 30–33
Unit 5 Review
Cumulative Review: Units 1–5

Unit Assessment
Tests with Answer Key
Unit 12 Mastery Test, pp. 47–48
Test Generator
Unit 12 Mastery Test

Exercise 1

Using Articles Write the correct article for each blank.

SAMPLE Jazz is truly _______ American style of music.
ANSWER an

1. While it is impossible to say when and where jazz was first played, many people call New Orleans _______ one and only "cradle of jazz."
2. Improvisation and syncopation made jazz _______ unusual form of folk music.
3. In the late 1800s, creative musicians combined _______ rhythms of West Africa with European harmony and American folk music.
4. Jazz historians say that before _______ turn of _______ century this type of music was not as popular as it is today.
5. In the South many bands played _______ new music in street parades and funeral processions.

Exercise 2

Identifying Adjectives and Proper Adjectives The following sentences are about jazz. Write each adjective. (Do not include articles.) Beside it write the noun it describes. Capitalize any proper adjectives you find.

SAMPLE Jazz is an american style of music.
ANSWER American style

1. The rhythm section of a jazz band usually includes a piano and drums.
2. Scott Joplin was a good pianist and a noted composer of ragtime music.
3. Joplin received a Pulitzer citation in 1976.
4. The popular Gene Krupa drew attention for skill on the drums.
5. The famous drummer started a new band.
6. The mournful sound of "blues" characterized early jazz.
7. Bessie Smith was a blues singer.
8. The legendary Buddy Boldon was a new orleans musician.
9. Musicians on mississippi riverboats brought the new sound to Chicago.
10. Benny Goodman, a clarinet player, started a dance band in Chicago.

PRACTICE AND ASSESS

Answers: Exercise 1

1. the
2. an
3. the
4. the, the
5. the

Answers: Exercise 2

1. rhythm—section; jazz—band
2. good—pianist; noted—composer; ragtime—music
3. Pulitzer—citation
4. popular—Gene Krupa
5. famous—drummer; new—band
6. mournful—sound; early—jazz
7. blues—singer
8. legendary—Buddy Boldon; New Orleans—musician
9. Mississippi—riverboats; new—sound
10. clarinet—player; dance—band

Answers: Exercise 3

1. proper adjective
2. predicate adjective
3. demonstrative adjective
4. article
5. article

Answers: Exercise 4

1. This
2. those
3. those
4. these
5. those
6. those
7. that
8. this
9. that
10. these

Exercise 3

Distinguishing Kinds of Adjectives Number your paper from 1 to 5. Identify each underlined word as a *proper adjective,* a *predicate adjective,* an *article,* or a *demonstrative adjective.*

[1]American musicians often serve as good-will ambassadors to other countries. [2]Jazz is popular all over the world. [3]Audiences everywhere respond enthusiastically to this music. [4]A musician may be as well known overseas as at home. [5]Music seems to be an international language.

Exercise 4

Using Demonstratives Write the best demonstrative—*that, this, those,* or *these*—for each sentence.

SAMPLE A truly unique style of music is _______ music called jazz.
ANSWER this

1. Many people living in New Orleans have said, "_______ city is the cradle of jazz."
2. When players make up some of the music they are playing, _______ players are improvising.
3. In syncopation, _______ beats that are normally unaccented are accented.
4. Improvisation and syncopation—_______ give jazz its unusual form.
5. Louis Armstrong was one of _______ early jazz musicians who became famous throughout the United States.
6. Armstrong also traveled to many foreign countries; he was very popular with fans in _______ countries.
7. In 1955 Armstrong toured Western Europe; _______ trip was a smashing success.
8. Armstrong was the first to use scat; in _______ kind of singing, meaningless syllables replace words.
9. Many other jazz singers have copied _______ style.
10. Armstrong's great trumpet playing and his famous scratchy singing voice are still admired _______ days.

Exercise 5

Identifying Comparative and Superlative Forms Write whether each underlined adjective is in the *comparative* or *superlative* form. Then write the adjective from which it is formed.

SAMPLE Some of the liveliest jazz was once played on a cornet.
ANSWER superlative, lively

1. The cornet and the trumpet are very similar brass instruments, but the cornet is the shorter of the two.
2. Duke Ellington had some of the greatest musical ideas of his time.
3. Many people think Ellington's band was the finest band of the swing era.
4. Was Benny Goodman a better clarinet player than any other clarinet player of his time?
5. Bebop was perhaps the best jazz style developed in the decade of the 1940s.

Exercise 6

Using Adjectives That Compare Write the correct comparative or superlative form of the adjective in parentheses.

SAMPLE Louis Armstrong received his (early) formal music instruction at a children's home in New Orleans.
ANSWER earliest

1. Being (persistent) than other teenage spectators, Armstrong borrowed clothes and went to the jazz clubs almost every evening.
2. Fate Marable's group had the (great) repertoire of any New Orleans band.
3. Was Joe "King" Oliver the (good) cornet player in Kid Ory's orchestra?
4. Many critics feel that of these two great musicians, Armstrong was the (talented).
5. Armstrong ranks high among the world's (popular) jazz musicians of all time.

Answers: Exercise 5

1. comparative—short
2. superlative—great
3. superlative—fine
4. comparative—good
5. superlative—good

Answers: Exercise 6

1. more persistent
2. greatest
3. best
4. more talented
5. most popular

UNIT 12
Review

Answers: Exercise 7
Proofreading
This proofreading activity provides editing practice with (1) the current or previous units' skills, (2) the **Trouble-shooter** errors, and (3) spelling errors. Students should be able to complete the exercise by referring to the units, the **Troubleshooter**, and a dictionary. (Note: A run-on sentence counts as one error.)

	Error (Type of Error)
1.	• an age (article before a vowel sound)
	• Egypt's (singular possessive)
	• art, (commas in a series)
2.	• light, (compound sentence)
3.	• most prominent (superlative adjective form)
4.	• studied (spelling)
	• Boston (proper adjective)
5.	• went (verb form)
	• American (proper adjective)
	• painting. She *or* painting; she (run-on sentence)

Exercise 7 **Proofreading**

The following passage discusses the art of Lois Mailou Jones, an African American artist, whose work appears below. Rewrite the passage, correcting the errors in spelling, capitalization, grammar, and usage. Add any missing punctuation. There are 10 errors in all.

Lois Mailou Jones

[1]This painting by Lois Mailou Jones combines images from a age of Egypts greatness with images from African American art drama, and music. [2]The climbing figures are bathed in golden light and gold is used again

Lois Mailou Jones, *The Ascent of Ethiopia*, 1932

About the Art

Lois Mailou Jones, *The Ascent of Ethiopia*, 1932
Lois Mailou Jones was born in 1905 in Boston and studied at the Boston Normal Art School; the School of the Museum of Fine Arts in Boston; Columbia University Teachers College in New York; Howard University in Washington, D.C.; and the Académie Julien and the École des Beaux Arts in Paris. Jones painted *The Ascent of Ethiopia* (oil on canvas, measuring 23 1/2 by 17 1/4 inches) in 1932. The painting is in the artist's own collection.

on the pyramids and the circle that represents music. [3]The entire painting consists of shades of gold, green, blue, and violet; blue is the more prominent color of all, however.

[4]The artist was born in Boston and studyed at two boston art schools. [5]Later she gone to other american cities and to Paris to learn more about painting, she has won many awards for her work.

Mixed Review

Exercise 8

For each sentence write the correct choices from the words in parentheses. When you find a proper adjective that is not capitalized, write it with the correct capitalization.

1. Boogie-woogie was (a, an) popular jazz style that used eight beats to a bar instead of (a, the) usual four beats to a bar.
2. Boogie-woogie, which developed in (a, the) 1930s, was (more intense, most intense) than other jazz styles.
3. Two of the (more important, most important) boogie-woogie artists of all were Pinetop Smith and Meade Lux Lewis.
4. Cool jazz emphasized (a, an) lagging beat and (more unusual, unusualler) orchestrations.
5. A belgian guitarist and (a, an) english pianist influenced american jazz artists.
6. The newport festival, first held in 1954, and other (big, biggest) jazz festivals introduced the new music to ever (larger, largest) audiences.
7. Since the 1950s small combos have become (more prominent, most prominent) than before.
8. Jazz musicians continue to incorporate influences from (many, most) sources; the (better, best) among them constantly try new sounds and new combinations of instruments.
9. The american jazz musicians of the modern era that are (better, best) known include guitarist George Benson, trumpeter Wynton Marsalis, and pianist Herbie Hancock.
10. Wynton Marsalis, known for his excellent tone and flawless technique, was perhaps the (better, best) new jazz musician of the 1980s.

Answers: Exercise 8

Mixed Review

1. a, the
2. the, more intense
3. most important
4. a, more unusual
5. Belgian, an, English, American
6. Newport Festival, big, larger
7. more prominent
8. many, best
9. American, best
10. best

CLOSE

Encourage students to write a descriptive passage about a place or an object of their choice, using adjectives to make their writing vivid and interesting.

Adjectives in Writing

Have students read the passage from *The Invisible Thread* silently. Then have them discuss how Yoshiko Uchida has used adjectives and specific words to make this passage interesting, informative, and enjoyable to read. Ask: *How does the writer use words to make a vivid picture in the reader's mind?*

Techniques with Adjectives

Ask students to look at another piece of writing that they have enjoyed. Then ask them to discuss how the writer of the piece used adjectives and specific words to make a vivid picture. Ask: *How was the writer's technique similar to Yoshiko Uchida's? How was it different?*

Practice

The answers to this challenging and enriching activity will vary. Refer to Techniques with Adjectives as you evaluate student choices.

Writing Application

Adjectives in Writing Yoshika Uchida uses specific words and adjectives in this passage from *The Invisible Thread* to convey her feelings about a visit to the country. Examine the passage, focusing especially on the italicized adjectives.

> They [the stars] seemed *brighter* and *closer* than they were in Berkeley. It was as though the *entire* sky had dropped closer to earth to spread out its *full* glory right there in front of me.
>
> I listened to the *slow* clop-clop of the mules as they plodded through the fields, probably wondering why they were pulling a wagonload of people in the dark, instead of hauling boxes of grapes to the shed under the *hot, dry* sun.

Techniques with Adjectives Try to apply some of Yoshiko Uchida's writing techniques when you write and revise your own work.

1. Whenever possible, use specific adjectives to make your descriptions more precise.

Without adjectives under the sun

Uchida's version under the *hot, dry* sun

2. Use comparisons for clarity and brevity.

Without comparisons [the stars] seemed bright and close

Uchida's version They seemed *brighter* and *closer* than they were in Berkeley.

Practice Practice these techniques by revising the following passage, using a separate sheet of paper. Add adjectives to enhance the description. Use comparisons where appropriate.

At dusk we were one of the groups of people enjoying a picnic on the grass. We were clustered on blankets on the hill in front of the band shell. The smells of foods floated in the air around us. The dark descended as the musicians gathered on stage and tuned their instruments. They began the concert with several jazz standards. Some people in the audience stood and began to sway to the music. Soloists took turns showing their skills. Soon everyone was standing, moving, and swaying.

Teacher's Classroom Resources

The following resources can be used for assessment or evaluation.

Unit Assessment

Tests with Answer Key
Unit 12 Mastery Test, pp. 47–48

Test Generator
Unit 12 Mastery Test

You may wish to administer the Unit 12 Mastery Test at this point.

UNIT

13 Adverbs

Grammar | **Lessons**

UNIT GOALS

The goal of Unit 13 is to help students, through example and instruction, to develop an understanding of and an ability to identify adverbs, including comparative and superlative adverbs. The lessons in this unit teach students to distinguish between adjectives and adverbs and to avoid double negatives.

Unit Assessment

Tests with Answer Key
Unit 13 Pretest, pp. 49–50
Unit 13 Mastery Test, pp. 51–52

Test Generator
Unit 13 Pretest
Unit 13 Mastery Test

You may wish to administer the Unit 13 Pretest at this point.

Key to Ability Levels

Enabling Strategies have been coded for varying learning styles and abilities.

L1 Level 1 activities are within the ability range of Learning Disabled students.

L2 Level 2 activities are basic-to-average activities and are within the ability range of average students.

L3 Level 3 activities are challenging activities and are within the ability range of above-average students.

LEP LEP activities are within the ability range of Limited English Proficiency students.

Setting the Purpose

Lesson 13.1 teaches students to identify adverbs that modify verbs and to recognize the different positions that these adverbs can occupy in a sentence.

FOCUS

Lesson Overview

Objective: To identify and use adverbs that modify verbs and to vary the position of these adverbs in a sentence

Bellringer

When students enter the classroom, have this assignment on the board: *Circle the verbs and underline the adverbs in the following sentences:*

Alan ran quickly to the window. He had never seen anyone famous. Finally the president's motorcade arrived. Alan hoped he might see the president if he looked carefully.

Motivating Activity

Invite students to think of ways to change the position of the adverbs in the Bellringer sentences without changing the meaning of the sentences.

TEACH

Cross-reference: Spelling Rules

When *-ly* is added to an adjective to form an adverb, the spelling of the word sometimes changes. For instruction and practice in spelling rules, refer students to Lessons 22.6–22.7, pp. 520–526.

13.1 Adverbs Modifying Verbs

Adjectives are words that modify, or describe, nouns and pronouns. Adverbs are another type of modifier. They modify verbs, adjectives, and other adverbs.

An **adverb** is a word that describes a verb, an adjective, or another adverb.

In the example below, the adverb *grandly* describes the action verb *entertained.*

Thomas Jefferson entertained **grandly** at the White House.

An adverb supplies one of three types of information.

Ways Adverbs Modify Verbs	
Adverbs Tell	**Examples**
How	grandly, royally, quickly
When	rarely, later, immediately, often, usually
Where	downstairs, below, here

When modifying an adjective or another adverb, an adverb usually comes before the word. When modifying a verb, an adverb can occupy different positions in a sentence.

Positioning of Adverbs	
Position	**Examples**
Before the Verb	Guests **often** dined in the State Dining Room.
After the Verb	Guests dined **often** in the State Dining Room.
At the Beginning	**Often** guests dined in the State Dining Room.
At the End	Guests dined in the State Dining Room **often.**

Most adverbs are formed by adding *-ly* to an adjective, as in *actively, fondly,* and *quietly.* Some adverbs are exceptions, however. These include *after, often, now,* and *later.*

Teacher's Classroom Resources

The following resources can be used for planning, instruction, practice, reinforcement, assessment, reteaching, enrichment, or evaluation.

Teaching Tools
Lesson Plans

Blackline Masters
Grammar Practice, p. 23
Grammar Reteaching, p. 25
Grammar Enrichment, p. 25

Grammar Workbook
Lesson 34

Unit Assessment

Tests with Answer Key
Unit 13 Pretest, pp. 49–50

Test Generator
Unit 13 Pretest

You may wish to administer the Unit 13 Pretest at this point.

Exercise 1 Identifying Adverbs

On your paper write the adverb to complete each sentence.

1. The federal government looked ______ for an architect. (build, eager, everywhere, official)
2. A committee ______ chose James Hoban. (decide, finally, happy, enthusiastic)
3. Hoban's White House stood ______ on a large plot of land. (proud, sit, majestically, to)
4. The Adams family ______ moved into the unfinished house. (eagerly, quick, had, grand)
5. They ______ gave visitors tours of their new home. (glad, proudly, want, famous)

Exercise 2 Identifying Adverbs

Write each sentence. Underline the adverb, and draw an arrow to the word it describes.

1. Thomas Jefferson lived happily in the White House.
2. Jefferson quickly sought the aid of another architect.
3. Fire nearly destroyed the mansion during the War of 1812.
4. Theodore Roosevelt had it rebuilt completely.
5. Franklin Roosevelt further expanded it.
6. Workers built a swimming pool indoors.
7. One president thoughtfully added a bowling alley.
8. Eager tourists often come to the White House.
9. They proudly tour their nation's capital.
10. Our school always sends the seventh graders on a trip to Washington, D.C.

Exercise 3 Writing Adverbs to Complete Sentences

On your paper, write an adverb that describes the verb in each sentence.

1. Our class _____ goes to the White House when visiting Washington, D.C.
2. We _____ visit the other attractions.
3. We _____ travel by bus to our nation's capital.
4. Last year the seventh graders waited _____ in line to see Congress in session.
5. The tour guide spoke _____ to us.

TEACH

Teaching Tip

Tell students that they can use the *when, where,* or *how* test to identify adverbs that modify verbs. Words that answer these questions must be adverbs. For example, in the sentence *Guests often dined in the State Dining Room, often* is an adverb because it answers the question *when*: When did the guests dine? They dined often.

PRACTICE AND ASSESS

Answers: Exercise 1

1. everywhere
2. finally
3. majestically
4. eagerly
5. proudly

Answers: Exercise 2

1. happily—lived
2. quickly—sought
3. nearly—destroyed
4. completely—rebuilt
5. further—expanded
6. indoors—built
7. thoughtfully—added
8. often—come
9. proudly—tour
10. always—sends

Answers: Exercise 3

Answers will vary, but some suggestions are given below.

1. always
2. often
3. quickly
4. patiently
5. quietly

Independent Practice

Skills Practice

- *Grammar Practice,* p. 23
- *Grammar Reteaching,* p. 25
- *Grammar Enrichment,* p. 25
- ***Grammar Workbook***, Lesson 34

Enabling Strategies

LEP Identifying Adverbs

Invite students to read through a literature passage and write down all the words that end in *-ly*. Then help students to decide if the *–ly* words are adverbs by asking if the words answer the question *when*, *where*, or *how*.

CLOSE

Invite students to write five sentences that include adverbs modifying verbs. Then have them rewrite each sentence with the adverbs in as many different positions as possible.

Setting the Purpose

Lesson 13.2 teaches students the ways in which adverbs are used to modify adjectives and other adverbs.

FOCUS

Lesson Overview

Objective: To identify and use adverbs that modify adjectives and other adverbs

Bellringer

When students enter the classroom, have this assignment on the board: *Underline the adverbs in the following sentences:*

Yesterday the weather was extremely beautiful. Today the sky is partly cloudy. Rain is falling very softly.

Motivating Activity

Help students to decide which words are modified by each adverb in the Bellringer sentences.

TEACH

Speaking and Listening

Adverbs that modify adjectives and other adverbs can never be moved away from the words they modify. Invite students to test this by writing sentences with adverbs of this type. Ask students to read the sentences aloud, move the adverbs, and read them again. Do the sentences sound right? Why not?

13.2 Adverbs Modifying Adjectives and Adverbs

Adverbs are often used to modify adjectives and other adverbs. Notice how adverbs intensify the meaning of the adjectives in the following sentences. Most often they tell **how**.

> Harry Truman used **extremely** direct language.
>
> He became a **very** popular president.

In the first sentence, the adverb *extremely* modifies the adjective *direct.* The adverb tells how direct Truman's language was. In the second sentence, the adverb *very* modifies the adjective *popular.* The adverb tells how popular Truman was.

In the sentences below, adverbs modify other adverbs.

> Truman entered politics **unusually** late in life.
>
> He moved through the political ranks **quite** quickly.

In the first sentence above, the adverb *unusually* modifies the adverb *late. Unusually* tells how late Truman entered politics. In the second sentence the adverb *quite* describes the adverb *quickly. Quite* tells how quickly Truman moved through the ranks.

When modifying adjectives and other adverbs, adverbs almost always come directly before the word they describe. Below is a list of some adverbs that are often used to describe adjectives and other adverbs.

Adverbs Often Used to Describe Adjectives and Other Adverbs

very	really	rather	just
too	so	nearly	somewhat
almost	partly	barely	totally
quite	extremely	unusually	hardly

Teacher's Classroom Resources

The following resources can be used for planning, instruction, practice, reinforcement, reteaching, or enrichment.

Teaching Tools
Lesson Plans

Blackline Masters
Grammar Practice, p. 24
Grammar Reteaching, p. 26
Grammar Enrichment, p. 25

Grammar Workbook
Lesson 35

Exercise 4 **Identifying Adverbs**

Write each sentence. Underline each adverb, and draw an arrow to the word it modifies. Then write whether that word is a *verb,* an *adjective,* or an *adverb.*

1. Truman's career as vice president was unusually brief.
2. The extremely tragic death of Franklin D. Roosevelt left the presidency in Truman's hands.
3. Truman established a new procedure almost immediately.
4. He arose quite early each morning for a walk.
5. News reporters nearly always followed him.
6. Very important events took place during Truman's term.
7. World War II finally ended.
8. It ended almost immediately after Truman became president.
9. Truman very often played the piano for guests.
10. He found music particularly soothing.
11. Truman regularly spent his evenings at home.
12. Rather serious problems were discovered in the White House.
13. The Trumans moved somewhat abruptly into Blair House.
14. They felt reasonably secure in that place.
15. They lived in Blair House for nearly four years.
16. Dwight Eisenhower was elected president just after Harry Truman.
17. Eisenhower was greatly admired as a general during World War II.
18. His wife, Mamie, was quite popular throughout the country.
19. In the newspapers Dwight Eisenhower was most often referred to as Ike.
20. Ike's vice president, Richard Nixon, was eventually elected president.

Exercise 5 **Writing Adverbs to Modify Adjectives and Adverbs**

Choose an adverb from the box to modify each word below. On your paper write a sentence for each pair of words you form.

nearly	hardly	just	extremely	somewhat
very	unusually	too	rather	so

1. ________ ever
2. ________ enough
3. ________ quiet
4. ________ late
5. ________ popular
6. ________ hungry
7. ________ difficult
8. ________ quickly
9. ________ angrily
10. ________ finished

PRACTICE AND ASSESS

Answers: Exercise 4

1. unusually—brief (adj.) **2.** extremely—tragic (adj.) **3.** almost—immediately (adv.); immediately—established (v.) **4.** quite—early (adv.); early—arose (v.) **5.** nearly—always (adv.); always—followed (v.) **6.** Very—important (adj.) **7.** finally—ended (v.) **8.** almost—immediately (adv.); immediately—ended (v.) **9.** very—often (adv.); often—played (v.) **10.** particularly—soothing (adj.) **11.** regularly—spent (v.) **12.** Rather—serious (adj.) **13.** somewhat—abruptly (adv.); abruptly—moved (v.) **14.** reasonably—secure (adj.) **15.** nearly—four (adj.) **16.** just—was elected (v.) **17.** greatly—admired (adj.) **18.** quite—popular (adj.) **19.** most—often (adv.); often—was referred (v.) **20.** eventually—was elected (v.)

Answers: Exercise 5

Answers will vary. Some suggestions are given below.

1. We hardly ever go swimming.
2. Tom brought just enough food for lunch.
3. It was unusually quiet last evening.
4. We arrived so late that we missed the boat.
5. The band's new song is very popular.
6. Matt and I are rather hungry.
7. The job is too difficult for me.
8. I can run extremely quickly.
9. He responded somewhat angrily.
10. The painting is nearly finished.

Independent Practice

Skills Practice

Grammar Practice, p. 24
Grammar Reteaching, p. 26
Grammar Enrichment, p. 25
Grammar Workbook, Lesson 35

CLOSE

Ask students to explain in their own words how adverbs can be used to modify adjectives or other adverbs. Encourage them to illustrate their explanations with written examples.

Enabling Strategies

LEP Using Adverbs

Have students work in pairs to complete Exercise 4. Partners can take turns. One student can work on a sentence while the other student coaches.

After each pair completes two sentences, students should check their answers with another pair of students to make sure their answers are the same.

Setting the Purpose

Lesson 13.3 teaches students to identify comparative and superlative adverbs and to avoid common errors in usage.

FOCUS

Lesson Overview

Objective: To identify and use correctly the comparative and superlative forms of adverbs

Bellringer

When students enter the classroom, have this assignment on the board: *Circle the errors in the following sentences:*

We traveled quicklier by train than by car. We arrived more earlier than usual. Tom traveled farthest to get there than we did.

Motivating Activity

Invite students to discuss difficulties they have had using comparative and superlative adverbs. Why do students think it is so difficult to use comparative and superlative adverbs correctly? Explain that this lesson will provide students with rules for the correct use of these adverbs.

TEACH

Critical Thinking

If an adverb or adjective is comparative or superlative, do not add more *or* most. Invite students to test this statement by choosing comparative and superlative adverbs and adding *more* or *most*. Why is the addition of *more* or *most* unnecessary?

13.3 Adverbs That Compare

The **comparative** form of an adverb compares two actions or things. The **superlative** form of an adverb compares more than two actions or things.

For most adverbs of only one syllable, add *-er* to make the comparative form and *-est* to make the superlative form.

Comparing One-Syllable Adverbs	
Comparative	Ronald Reagan served **longer** as president than Jimmy Carter.
Superlative	Franklin Roosevelt served **longest** of any president.

For adverbs that end in *-ly* or that have more than one syllable, use the word *more* to form the comparative and *most* to form the superlative.

Comparing Two-Syllable Adverbs	
Comparative	Our class studied Roosevelt **more thoroughly** than Reagan.
Superlative	We studied Abraham Lincoln **most thoroughly** of all.

If an adverb already is comparative or superlative, do not add *more* or *most.* Never say, for example, *more harder* or *most hardest.*

Some adverbs do not form the comparative and superlative in the regular manner. Study the irregular forms below.

Irregular Comparative Forms

Adverb	Comparative	Superlative
well	better	best
badly	worse	worst
little (amount)	less	least
far (distance)	farther	farthest
far (degree)	further	furthest

Teacher's Classroom Resources

The following resources can be used for planning, instruction, practice, reinforcement, reteaching, or enrichment.

Teaching Tools
Lesson Plans

Blackline Masters
Grammar Practice, p. 25
Grammar Enrichment, p. 26

Grammar Workbook
Lessons 36–37

Exercise 6 Using the Comparative and Superlative Forms

For each sentence choose the correct form of the adverb in parentheses. Write the adverb on your paper.

1. Of all Theodore Roosevelt's nieces, Eleanor Roosevelt came (close, closest) to the presidency.
2. Many liked Mrs. Roosevelt (better, best) than they had liked any of the previous first ladies.
3. Mrs. Roosevelt worked (more actively, most actively) for human rights than for any other cause.
4. She fought (harder, hardest) of all for minorities.
5. She appeared at human-rights rallies (more frequently, most frequently) than her husband.

Exercise 7 Writing Comparative and Superlative Forms

Write each sentence. Use *-er, -est, more,* or *most* to make the needed form of the adverb in parentheses. Write the adverb on your paper.

1. Of all the first ladies, Eleanor Roosevelt gave (freely) of her time.
2. She traveled (readily) than any other president's wife to distant parts of the globe.
3. She journeyed (far) in her later years than in her youth.
4. She was (sympathetic) than many other people to the plight of the poor.
5. Eleanor Roosevelt lived (long) than her husband.
6. As Franklin Roosevelt became weaker, Eleanor took on some of his duties and worked (busily) than ever.
7. She (often) attended meetings in place of the president than many people realize.
8. Mrs. Roosevelt seemed to care (deeply) of all about the problems of ordinary people.
9. Eleanor Roosevelt was even (widely) recognized for her work with the UN than she had been for her devotion to duty as first lady.
10. Her humanitarian reputation surely will extend years (long) than her life.

TEACH

Cross-reference: Comparing and Contrasting

For instruction and practice in the comparative and superlative forms of adverbs, refer students to Lesson 5.2, pp. 182–185. Point out that comparing and contrasting two items often requires the correct use of the comparative and superlative forms of adverbs.

Two-Minute Skill Drill

List these comparative and superlative forms of adverbs on the board, and have students circle and correct those that have been used incorrectly.

more deeply	more carefully
badder	more honestly
most long	

PRACTICE AND ASSESS

Answers: Exercise 6

1. closest
2. better
3. more actively
4. hardest
5. more frequently

Answers: Exercise 7

1. most freely
2. more readily
3. farther
4. more sympathetic
5. longer
6. more busily
7. more often
8. most deeply
9. more widely
10. longer

Independent Practice

Skills Practice

Grammar Practice, p. 25
Grammar Enrichment, p. 26

Grammar Workbook
Lessons 36–37

Enabling Strategies

LEP Comparing with Adverbs

Invite students to sort a list of adverbs, writing the one-syllable adverbs in one column and the adverbs that have two syllables or end in *-ly* in another. Have them add *-er* or *-est* to the adverbs in the first column and *more* or *most* to the adverbs in the second column.

CLOSE

Invite students to create posters or pamphlets that show correct usage rules for comparative and superlative adverbs. They might consider illustrating common usage errors and how to avoid them.

Setting the Purpose

Lesson 13.4 teaches students how to tell adjectives and adverbs apart. Students will practice using adjectives and adverbs correctly.

FOCUS

Lesson Overview

Objective: To distinguish adjectives from adverbs and to use the correct forms of adjectives and adverbs

Bellringer

When students enter the classroom, have this assignment on the board: *Circle the adjectives (except for the articles) and underline the adverbs in the following sentences:*

The sketches look good. Susan displays real talent. She draws really well. The subjects seem almost real.

Motivating Activity

Invite students to discuss any strategies they have for telling whether a word in a sentence is an adjective or an adverb. Explain that this lesson offers strategies for telling adjectives from adverbs.

TEACH

Grammar Tip

Predicate adjectives describe the subject. Adverbs that modify the verb describe the action of the verb.

Cross-reference: Linking Verbs

For instruction and practice with linking verbs, refer students to Lesson 10.3, pp. 302–303.

13.4 Telling Adjectives and Adverbs Apart

It can be hard to tell whether a word in a sentence is an adjective or an adverb. Look carefully at how the word is used.

Martha Washington was **happy** at Mount Vernon.
Martha Washington lived **happily** at Mount Vernon.

In the first sentence, *happy* is a predicate adjective. It follows the linking verb *was* and modifies the subject. In the second sentence, *happily* is an adverb. It modifies the action verb *lived.*

People sometimes confuse the words *bad, badly, good,* and *well. Bad* and *good* are both adjectives. They are used after linking verbs. *Badly* and *well* are adverbs. They are used after action verbs. *Well* can also be used after linking verbs to describe a person's health or appearance. At these times *well* is an adjective—for example, *He looks well.*

Distinguishing Adjectives from Adverbs	
Adjective	**Adverb**
The sound is **bad.** The band sounds **good.**	The actor sang **badly.** The band played **well.**

Three pairs of modifiers often confuse people: *real, really; sure, surely;* and *most, almost. Real* and *sure* are adjectives. *Really, surely,* and *almost* are adverbs. *Most* can be an adjective or an adverb.

Distinguishing Adjectives from Adverbs	
Adjective	**Adverb**
Music is a **real** art. A pianist needs **sure** hands. **Most** pianos have 88 keys.	Music is **really** popular. Piano music is **surely** popular. Piano strings **almost** never break.

Teacher's Classroom Resources

The following resources can be used for planning, instruction, practice, reinforcement, reteaching, or enrichment.

Teaching Tools
Lesson Plans

Blackline Masters
Grammar Practice, p. 26
Grammar Reteaching, p. 27
Grammar Enrichment, p. 27

Grammar Workbook
Lesson 38

Exercise 8 Telling Adjectives and Adverbs Apart

On your paper write each sentence, using the correct adjective or adverb.

1. Martha Washington lived (courageous, courageously).
2. She managed the position of first lady (good, well).
3. She supported her husband (active, actively).
4. President Washington must have felt (good, well) about his wife's support.
5. (Sure, Surely) he was appreciative.
6. Martha Washington was known as a (real, really) gracious hostess.
7. During the war Mrs. Washington had (able, ably) organized a sewing circle.
8. The group was (quick, quickly) in mending clothes for the troops.
9. In those days it was important to be able to sew (good, well).
10. If a woman sewed (bad, badly), she would rip her work out.
11. People (most, almost) always took notice of Mrs. Washington's common sense and charm.
12. It is also said that she was (real, really) beautiful.
13. She and her husband lived (good, well).
14. Their life together at Mount Vernon remained (cheerful, cheerfully).
15. Martha Washington had been married (previous, previously) to Daniel Parke Custis.
16. After his death she became (popular, popularly) known as one of the richest widows in Virginia.
17. When she married George Washington, she added (substantial, substantially) to his property.
18. Martha was known as an (amiable, amiably) hostess at the many formal dinners Washington held as president.
19. She outlived her husband by a (short, shortly) time.
20. Two years after his death, Martha died (peaceful, peacefully) at Mount Vernon.

Exercise 9 Identifying and Using Adjectives and Adverbs

On your paper identify each word as an *adjective* or an *adverb*. Then write a sentence using the word correctly.

1. good
2. really
3. sure
4. almost
5. real
6. surely
7. well
8. badly
9. bad
10. most

PRACTICE AND ASSESS

Answers: Exercise 8

1. courageously
2. well
3. actively
4. good
5. Surely
6. really
7. ably
8. quick
9. well
10. badly
11. almost
12. really
13. well
14. cheerful
15. previously
16. popularly
17. substantially
18. amiable
19. short
20. peacefully

Answers: Exercise 9

1. adjective
2. adverb
3. adjective
4. adverb
5. adjective
6. adverb
7. adverb or adjective
8. adverb
9. adjective
10. adjective

Sentences will vary, but should include correctly used adjectives or adverbs. A sample sentence: 1. *Janet felt good about the grades she earned.*

Independent Practice

Skills Practice

- *Grammar Practice,* p. 26
- *Grammar Reteaching,* p. 27
- *Grammar Enrichment,* p. 27
- ***Grammar Workbook,*** Lesson 38

CLOSE

Have students read a literary passage containing adjectives and adverbs. As they read, they can make one list of the adjectives in the passage and another list of the adverbs.

Enabling Strategies

LEP Creating a Reference File

Students may find it helpful to keep a file of adjectives and adverbs that confuse them. The file should include sentences demonstrating the correct use of each adjective and adverb. Students can refer to the file when they need help with adjectives and adverbs.

L2 Using *Good* and *Well*

Predicate adjectives follow linking verbs; adverbs modify action verbs. The following sentence can help students remember that *good* is an adjective used with linking verbs and *well* is an adverb used with action verbs: *The car is good because it runs well.*

Setting the Purpose

Lesson 13.5 teaches students to recognize double negatives and to avoid using double negatives in their writing.

FOCUS

Lesson Overview

Objective: To identify double negatives and avoid using them

Bellringer

When students enter the classroom, have this assignment on the board: *What makes the following sentences difficult to understand?*

We didn't never hear the president speak. There was not no radio where we stayed. We never read none of the speech in the paper, either.

Motivating Activity

Invite students to give suggestions for making the sentences in the Bellringer easier to read and understand.

TEACH

Speaking and Listening

Prepare a group of sentences, some of which have double negatives and some of which have negative constructions used correctly. Read the sentences aloud. Encourage students to respond when they hear a double negative and to rewrite the sentence correctly.

Cross-reference: Writing Dialogue

For instruction and practice in writing dialogue, refer students to Lesson 4.3, pp. 148–151.

13.5 Avoiding Double Negatives

The adverb *not* is a **negative word**, expressing the idea of "no" in a sentence. The word *not* often appears in its shortened form, the contraction *-n't*.

Contractions with *Not*		
is not = isn't	cannot = can't	have not = haven't
was not = wasn't	could not = couldn't	had not = hadn't
were not = weren't	do not = don't	would not = wouldn't
will not = won't	did not = didn't	should not = shouldn't

Other words besides *not* may be used to express the negative. Each negative word has several opposites, or affirmative words, that show the idea of "yes." Study the following list of negative and affirmative words.

Negative and Affirmative Words

Negative	Affirmative
never	ever, always
nobody	anybody, somebody
none	one, all, some, any
no one	everyone, someone
nothing	something, anything
nowhere	somewhere, anywhere

People sometimes mistakenly use two negative words together as in the sentence *Lincoln hadn't never gone to college.* Avoid using a **double negative** such as this. You need only one negative word to express a negative idea.

You can correct a double negative by removing one of the negative words or by replacing it with an affirmative word, as in the following sentences.

> Lincoln had **never** gone to college.
> Lincoln had **not ever** gone to college.

Teacher's Classroom Resources

The following resources can be used for planning, instruction, practice, reinforcement, reteaching, or enrichment.

Teaching Tools
Lesson Plans

Blackline Masters
Grammar Practice, p. 27
Grammar Reteaching, p. 28
Grammar Enrichment, p. 28

Grammar Workbook
Lesson 40

Exercise 10 Expressing Negative Ideas

On your paper write each sentence so that it correctly expresses a negative idea.

1. Lincoln didn't (never, ever) have a speech writer.
2. Nothing (didn't make, made) him bitter during the war.
3. Lincoln wasn't dishonest with (no one, anyone).
4. The president didn't (never, ever) become discouraged.
5. A strong leader, Lincoln wasn't afraid of (nobody, anyone).
6. Honest Abe didn't (never, ever) try to trick the public.
7. He tried not to show favoritism to (anybody, nobody).
8. Nothing (meant, didn't mean) more to Lincoln than justice.
9. Nobody (ever, never) cared more about saving the Union than Lincoln.
10. There wasn't (nobody, anybody) more loyal to the cause of the Civil War.
11. I can't find Carl Sandburg's biography of Lincoln (nowhere, anywhere).
12. Some feared the country wouldn't (ever, never) get over the shock of Lincoln's death.
13. You can't tell me (nothing, anything) about Lincoln that I don't know.
14. I never met (nobody, anybody) who found Lincoln's life uninteresting.
15. Some people might think he didn't (never, ever) make a mistake.
16. A humble man, Lincoln wouldn't (ever, never) believe he was perfect.
17. You couldn't find a more concerned president (nowhere, anywhere).
18. The local library hasn't got (any, no) books about Lincoln's children.
19. As a volunteer in the Black Hawk War, Lincoln didn't see (any, no) fighting.
20. Except for George Washington, there aren't (no, any) other presidents that have a special holiday.

Exercise 11 Writing Sentences to Express Negative Ideas

On your paper write five sentences to express negative ideas. In each sentence, use the word from Column A and one of the words from Column B.

	Column A	Column B
1.	couldn't	ever, never
2.	has	anything, nothing
3.	doesn't	any, no
4.	can	anywhere, nowhere
5.	nothing	anybody, nobody

PRACTICE AND ASSESS

Answers: Exercise 10

1.	ever	11.	anywhere
2.	made	12.	ever
3.	anyone	13.	anything
4.	ever	14.	anybody
5.	anyone	15.	ever
6.	ever	16.	ever
7.	anybody	17.	anywhere
8.	meant	18.	any
9.	ever	19.	any
10.	anybody	20.	any

Answers: Exercise 11

Answers will vary, but none of the sentences should contain double negatives. A sample sentence:
1. Allen couldn't ever find anyone from his group.

Independent Practice

Skills Practice

- *Grammar Practice,* p. 27
- *Grammar Reteaching,* p. 28
- *Grammar Enrichment,* p. 28
- ***Grammar Workbook,*** Lesson 40

CLOSE

Invite students to write a paragraph or two explaining how to avoid using double negatives. It might be helpful for students to imagine they are writing their explanations for a person who knows none of the rules for using negatives in a sentence.

Enabling Strategies

LEP Expressing Negative Ideas

Many languages use two or more negative words to express a negative idea. As a result, students who speak these languages may have trouble avoiding double negatives in English. Encourage non-native speakers of English to read aloud sentences that express negative ideas to help them get used to the sound of the single negative word. Remind students that the contraction *-n't* also expresses "no" in a sentence. They may want to express contractions in two words so they can hear the word *not.*

TEACH

About the Literature

Explain that the review features a passage from Irene Hunt's historical novel about the Civil War, *Across Five Aprils*. This passage details one character's reaction to General Grant and his position as commander of the Union Army. *Across Five Aprils* is Irene Hunt's first book.

After students have read the passage, initiate a discussion of the characters, the setting, and the mood of the passage. Then ask students to focus on the highlighted adverbs. Invite them to decide which words are essential to the meaning of the passage and which are not. The exercises that follow are based on this passage and related topics.

Linking Grammar and Literature

Teaching Tip

To help students avoid confusing adjectives and adverbs, remind them that adverbs can modify only verbs, adjectives, or other adverbs.

Cooperative Learning

Invite students to work together to choose a literature passage that exemplifies an effective use of adverbs. Suggest that students start by looking for examples of adverb use in several books they enjoy. They can then give short presentations explaining how the effective use of adverbs contributes to the strength of the passage.

Speaking and Listening

Listening for adverbs can help students reinforce what they have learned. Encourage students to listen for adverbs in their daily speech. How often, for example, do they use adverbs such as very, always, or really? When they compare things, how often do they use adverbs?

UNIT 13 Unit Review

Grammar Review

Adverbs

The action in Irene Hunt's *Across Five Aprils* takes place during the Civil War, which began in April 1861 and ended in April 1865. The following excerpt from the book focuses on a letter sent by a character named Shadrach Yale to a younger boy named Jethro. The passage has been annotated to show some of the adverb uses covered in this unit.

Literature Model

from ACROSS FIVE APRILS

by Irene Hunt

Shadrach wrote that he and Jenny had seen the President and General Grant as they drove through the Washington streets together.

"... The President's face is deeply lined, and his cheeks are gaunt. I have seen so many soldiers whose cheeks have had that sunken look, even though they were young faces. . . . The President looks at least twenty years older than the pictures you and I used to study together in the early days of the war. But his face was full of light as the crowds cheered; I think he knew they were cheering Grant and that pleased him, for I'd guess that he, too, wanted to cheer the little man who sat beside him.

Grant does not have the appearance of a great general; he looks awkward, ill at ease, and carelessly dressed. But we have had enough of charm and polish; this commander who doesn't even walk like a military man is the one who will, I believe, restore the Union."

Adverb modifying the verb *drove* (together)

Adverb modifying the adjective *lined* (deeply)

Adverb modifying the adjective *many* (so)

Negative adverb modifying the verb *does have* (not)

Teacher's Classroom Resources

The following resources can be used for planning, instruction, practice, reinforcement, assessment, reteaching, enrichment, or evaluation.

Teaching Tools
Lesson Plans

Grammar Workbook
Lessons 34–40
Unit 6 Review
Cumulative Review: Units 1–6

Unit Assessment
Tests with Answer Key
Unit 13 Mastery Test, pp. 51–52
Test Generator
Unit 13 Mastery Test

Exercise 1

Writing Adverbs to Modify Verbs On your paper write an adverb to correctly complete each sentence.

SAMPLE Students _____ read *Across Five Aprils* in sixth grade.
ANSWER sometimes

1. Librarians ______ order new copies of *Across Five Aprils* because of the book's popularity.
2. ______ our teacher assigns a group book report to the class.
3. My friends and I ______ volunteered to write about *Across Five Aprils.*
4. I thought I left my copy of *Across Five Aprils* _____.
5. Irene Hunt was ______ honored when she received the Newbery Award for her book.

Exercise 2

Identifying Adverbs That Modify Verbs On your paper identify the adverb in each sentence, and write whether it tells *how, when,* or *where.*

SAMPLE I read the book quickly.
ANSWER quickly—how

1. Soon Shadrach would write to his friend Jethro.
2. He proudly described his experience.
3. War can age a president rapidly.
4. Shadrach saw President Lincoln there.
5. Grant was often criticized.
6. Sometimes Grant felt uncomfortable around people.
7. Lincoln privately admired Grant.
8. Lincoln sat outside with Grant.
9. They drove together through Washington, D.C.
10. Shadrach firmly believed in Grant's ability as a leader.

PRACTICE AND ASSESS

Answers: Exercise 1

Answer will vary, but some suggestions are given below.

1. always
2. Occasionally
3. once
4. here
5. quite

Answers: Exercise 2

1. Soon—when
2. proudly—how
3. rapidly—how
4. there—where
5. often—when
6. Sometimes—when
7. privately—how
8. outside—where
9. together—how
10. firmly—how

UNIT 13 Review

Answers: Exercise 3
1. carefully—placed (verb)
2. thoughtfully—wrote (verb)
3. loudly—cheered (verb)
4. very—pleased (adjective); enthusiastically—reacted (verb)
5. extremely—well (adverb); well—fought (verb)
6. Eventually—would be elected (verb)
7. quite—easily (adverb); easily—triumphed (verb)
8. carefully—organized (verb)
9. unanimously—was renominated (verb)
10. quite—widespread (adjective)

Answers: Exercise 4
Answers will vary, but some suggestions are given below.
1. very
2. extremely
3. finally
4. Eventually
5. long

Exercise 3

Identifying Adverbs and the Words They Modify On your paper write each sentence. Underline each adverb. Then write the word that the adverb describes, and write whether the word is a *verb, adjective,* or *adverb. (*Some sentences have more than one adverb.)

SAMPLE President Lincoln and General Grant rode through the streets together.

ANSWER President Lincoln and General Grant rode through the streets together. (rode—verb)

1. Jethro read the letter, and he placed it carefully in a big envelope.
2. Shadrach wrote thoughtfully; he described events in Washington.
3. The large crowd cheered loudly for the popular General Grant.
4. Lincoln was very pleased that the crowd reacted enthusiastically.
5. Union troops fought extremely well under General Grant.
6. Eventually Grant would be elected president.
7. He triumphed quite easily over his Democratic opponent.
8. Grant carefully organized his presidency like the army.
9. Grant was unanimously renominated by his party to run for a second term as president.
10. Scandals were quite widespread during his second term.

Exercise 4

Writing Adverbs in Sentences On your paper write each sentence, replacing the blank with an adverb that describes the underlined word.

SAMPLE Being a large-boned man, Lincoln was _____ suited for hard work.

ANSWER Being a large-boned man, Lincoln was **quite** suited for hard work.

1. As a boy, Lincoln was a _____ gifted speaker.
2. He worked ______ hard as a clerk in a store.
3. In 1832 Lincoln ______ bought a grocery store with a partner.
4. ______ the grocery store failed.
5. Even though his partner died, Lincoln paid off the ______ unpaid debts from the store.

Exercise 5

Using the Comparative and Superlative Forms On your paper rewrite each sentence, using the correct comparative or superlative form in parentheses.

SAMPLE The troops fought (harder, more harder) under General Grant.
ANSWER The troops fought harder under General Grant.

1. The crowd applauded (more loudly, loudlier) than they had for any other Union general.
2. The North fared (worse, worst) than the South until Grant took command.
3. Grant drove his armies (farther, farthest) into the South than they had gone before.
4. Grant commanded (better, best) than the other Union generals.
5. Crops in the North suffered (less, lesser) from the war than crops in the South did.
6. The divisions caused by the war lasted far (longer, more longer) than anyone expected.
7. Grant was (more careless, more carelessly) dressed than Shadrach expected.
8. President Lincoln's face was (more deeper, more deeply) lined than it was in the days of the war.
9. Of all his generals, Lincoln admired Grant (more, most).
10. The Civil War lasted years (longer, longest) than people had thought it would.

Exercise 6

Using Comparative and Superlative Adverbs On your paper write each sentence, using the comparative or superlative adverb form of the word in parentheses.

1. Which is the (frequently) visited building in the city?
2. Who entertained (grandly), Dolley Madison or Elizabeth Monroe?
3. Of the two, who guarded her privacy (carefully)?
4. Of all the presidents, who enjoyed the White House the (little)?
5. Who lived there (long) of all?

Answers: Exercise 5

1. more loudly
2. worse
3. farther
4. better
5. less
6. longer
7. more carelessly
8. more deeply
9. most
10. longer

Answers: Exercise 6

1. most frequently
2. more grandly
3. more carefully
4. least
5. longest

Answers: Exercise 7

1. lavish—adjective
2. well—adverb
3. proudly—adverb
4. greatly—adverb
5. almost—adverb
6. elegant—adjective
7. private—adjective
8. extravagantly—adverb
9. really—adverb
10. surprisingly—adverb

Answers: Exercise 8

Answers will vary, but some suggestions are given below.

1. a great—adjective
2. an easy—adjective
3. a difficult—adjective
4. Very—adverb
5. quite—adverb
6. easily—adverb
7. best—adjective
8. less—adverb
9. eventually—adverb
10. good—adjective

Exercise 7

Telling Adjectives and Adverbs Apart On your paper write the correct word from parentheses. Then write whether the word is an *adverb* or *adjective*.

1. Dolley Madison gave (lavish, lavishly) parties.
2. She entertained (good, well).
3. She (proud, proudly) wore rich silks.
4. She was (great, greatly) admired.
5. Her parties were (most, almost) always a success.
6. From 1801 to 1817 Dolley was an (elegant, elegantly) Washington hostess.
7. While the White House was being rebuilt, she lived with President Madison in a (private, privately) mansion.
8. Wherever she lived, Dolley entertained (extravagant, extravagantly).
9. She (real, really) enjoyed her role as hostess.
10. After her husband's death, Dolley (surprising, surprisingly) returned to live in Washington.

Exercise 8

Using Adverbs and Adjectives Correctly On your paper write the following paragraph. Choose an adjective or adverb from the list below to go in each blank. Write *adjective* or *adverb* to identify each word you add.

difficult	good	least	best
very	less	better	easily
easy	quite	great	eventually

Elizabeth Blackwell had a(n) [1]_____ desire for a medical education. Her goal was not a(n) [2]_____ one. She faced a(n) [3]_____ struggle to become a doctor. Blackwell began by writing letters to doctors all over the country. [4]_____ few answered her. Most people thought it was [5]_____ foolish for a woman to think of becoming a doctor, but Blackwell was not [6]_____ discouraged. She wrote to the [7]_____ medical schools in the country, hoping they would admit her. She then wrote to schools that were [8]_____ famous than the others. She was accepted by one school in Geneva, New York, and [9]_____ became the first American woman to receive a medical degree. Elizabeth Blackwell's example remains a [10]_____ model for young women today.

Exercise 9

Avoiding Double Negatives On your paper complete each sentence so that it correctly expresses a negative idea.

1. No one (ever, never) forgets our twenty-sixth president.
2. I can't find (anyone, no one) else in history like Theodore Roosevelt.
3. I didn't know (nothing, anything) about him until recently.
4. I wasn't (ever, never) expecting to be so impressed.
5. I didn't expect to find (any, no) books about Teddy Roosevelt at the library.
6. I couldn't have learned more about him (anywhere, nowhere) else.
7. You might think there isn't (nobody, anybody) else as interested in him as I am.
8. There wasn't (no, any) other president who worked harder.
9. It seemed he didn't do (anything, nothing) else.
10. There isn't (anyone, no one) I admire more.

Exercise 10

Expressing Negative Ideas On your paper rewrite each sentence to correctly express a negative idea. (There is more than one correct way to write most sentences.)

SAMPLE The Browns didn't never expect to visit Washington, D.C.
ANSWER The Browns didn't ever expect to visit Washington, D.C.

1. The Browns weren't never planning to go to the capital.
2. Margie Brown had never met no one who had been there.
3. They hadn't gone nowhere near Washington before last summer.
4. Little Billy hadn't known nothing about the surprise trip.
5. The family hadn't never seen nothing as impressive as the White House.
6. Nobody in their family had never seen the Cherry Blossom Festival.
7. They couldn't never have imagined the beauty of the mall in springtime.
8. They hadn't never before visited the Senate Office Building.
9. Never before hadn't they imagined the thrill of the Air and Space Museum.
10. They concluded that no one shouldn't turn down an opportunity to visit the nation's capital.

Answers: Exercise 9

1. ever
2. anyone
3. anything
4. ever
5. any
6. anywhere
7. anybody
8. any
9. anything
10. anyone

Answers: Exercise 10

Answers will vary, but some suggestions are given below.

1. weren't ever
2. never met anyone
3. anywhere near
4. had known nothing
5. had never seen anything
6. had ever seen
7. could never
8. hadn't ever
9. had they imagined
10. should turn down

UNIT 13
Review

Answers: Exercise 11

Proofreading

This proofreading activity provides editing practice with (1) the current or previous units' skills, (2) the **Troubleshooter** errors, and (3) spelling errors. Students should be able to complete the exercise by referring to these units, the **Troubleshooter,** and a dictionary.

	Error (Type of Error)
1.	• Brown is a (sentence fragment)
2.	• surely (adverb form)
3.	• developed (verb form)
4.	• clearly (adverb form)
5.	• immediately (adverb form)
6.	• It's nothing as, *or* It's not anything as (double negative)
7.	• against (spelling)
8.	• soldiers (plural noun)
9.	• entirely (adverb form)
10.	• really (adverb form)

Exercise 11 Proofreading

The following passage is about American artist Roger Brown, whose painting *Lost America* appears below. Rewrite the passage, correcting the errors in spelling, capitalization, grammar, and usage. Add any missing punctuation. There are 10 errors.

Roger Brown

[1]Born in 1941, Roger Brown a painter who lives in Chicago. [2]His works, such as *Lost America*, have sure made him influential in the art world. [3]Brown has develop a highly individual style over the past twenty years. [4]*Lost America* clear exhibits many of the characteristics of his work.

Roger Brown, *Lost America*, 1989

About the Art

Roger Brown, *Lost America,* 1989

In *Lost America* Abraham Lincoln contemplates his responsibilities as president of the United States at a time when the country indeed seemed lost. Ask students to identify some of the images in Roger Brown's painting that symbolize the Civil War and its effect on Lincoln. (The threatening clouds symbolize the storm of dissent in the nation. The rows of vegetation suggest lines of soldiers at the ready. Lincoln's face is purple, as if the war had physically bruised him.)

[5]The painting is immediate recognizable as a portrait of Abraham Lincoln. [6]It's not nothing as simple as that. [7]Lincoln is silhouetted agenst a sky full of threatening clouds lined up in tightly packed rows. [8]At the bottom of the painting is vegetation that resembles the kind of fence that soldiers' erect in battle.

[9]Except for the dark purple of his face, the figure of Lincoln is entire in black and white. [10]Lincoln appears real gloomy and thoughtful; perhaps, as the title *Lost America* suggests, he is thinking about the war and the possible division of the United States into two separate countries.

Exercise 12 — Mixed Review

Rewrite each sentence, replacing the underlined word with an adverb that makes sense. Underline your adverb.

SAMPLE An eccentric usual behaves in an unexpected way.
ANSWER An eccentric usually behaves in an unexpected way.

1. Claiming to be emperor of the United States would certain be considered eccentric behavior.
2. In the middle of the nineteenth century, Joshua Norton actual claimed to be Norton I, Emperor of the United States.
3. The people of San Francisco willing accepted his claim.
4. Emperor Norton took his job quite serious.
5. The best clothing store in the entire city made special clothing for him.
6. Their "emperor" was real loved by the people of San Francisco.
7. The people of San Francisco haven't never forgotten Norton.
8. Perhaps Norton's ideas were inspired part by Napoleon.
9. Napoleon conquered most all of Europe.
10. Norton sure would have heard about Napoleon.

UNIT 13 Review

Answers: Exercise 12

Mixed Review

1. certainly
2. actually
3. willingly
4. seriously
5. specially
6. really
7. ever
8. partly
9. almost
10. surely

CLOSE

Ask students to write a paragraph comparing two United States presidents whom they admire. Encourage them to use adjectives and adverbs correctly to make their comparisons more vivid.

Adverbs in Writing

Ask students to read silently this passage from Betsy Byars's novel *Coast to Coast.* Discuss with them how the author has used adverbs to make her writing more vivid and to enhance the mood and tone of the passage.

Techniques with Adverbs

Discuss with students the techniques for using adverbs that are outlined here. Then have them look at the proofreading passage on pages 376–377. Ask: *How has the writer used adverbs to make the piece more vivid or to enhance its mood and tone?*

Practice

The answers to this challenging and enriching activity will vary. Refer to Techniques with Adverbs as you evaluate student choices.

Writing Application

Adverbs in Writing In this excerpt from Betsy Byars's novel *Coast to Coast*, 13-year-old Birch tries to convince her grandfather to take her up in his 1940 airplane. As you read, pay special attention to the underlined words.

> "I really want to go!" As she said it, she realized it was true. She needed to get away from this world, and this was the way to do it. "What are we waiting for?"
>
> "I don't guess it would hurt to fly to the beach and back."
>
> "Then get in! Let's go!"
>
> "Don't get in too big a hurry." Her grandfather smiled. It was his first real smile of the afternoon.
>
> Birch followed him around the plane. "What are you doing?"
>
> "Well, right now, I'm doing a preflight inspection. I check the tires, the control surfaces, move them for freedom and cable looseness."

Examine the passage, focusing on the underlined words.

Techniques with Adverbs Try to apply some of Betsy Byars's writing techniques when you write and revise your own work.

1. To make your writing more vivid, add adverbs to tell exactly when the action is occurring. Compare the following:

General words Well, I'm doing a preflight inspection.
Byars's version Well, *right now* I'm doing a preflight inspection.

2. Use adverbs to reinforce the mood and tone of your writing.

Unspecified tone I want to go.
Byars's version I *really* want to go.

Practice Practice these techniques by revising the following passage on a separate sheet of paper. Remember that adverbs can modify verbs, adjectives, and other adverbs.

Many people read Betsy Byars's books. She is one of the popular young adult authors of our time. In her book *Coast to Coast,* Ms. Byars's love of flying comes across to her readers. Thirteen-year-old Birch does not want her grandfather to sell his plane. She is sure the plane can keep him young at heart. Birch talks grandfather into letting her get into the plane. He shows her how to operate it. He gets into the plane with her. Will they fly the old airplane? You'll have to read this exciting book to find out.

Teacher's Classroom Resources

The following resources can be used for assessment or evaluation.

Unit Assessment

Tests with Answer Key
Unit 13 Mastery Test, pp. 51–52

Test Generator
Unit 13 Mastery Test

You may wish to administer the Unit 13 Mastery Test at this point.

UNIT 14

Prepositions, Conjunctions, and Interjections

Grammar | Lessons

UNIT GOALS

The goal of Unit 14 is to help students, through example and instruction, to develop an understanding of and an ability to use prepositions, prepositional phrases, conjunctions, and interjections.

Unit Assessment

Tests with Answer Key
Unit 14 Pretest, pp. 53–54
Unit 14 Mastery Test, pp. 55–56

Test Generator
Unit 14 Pretest
Unit 14 Mastery Test

You may wish to administer the Unit 14 Pretest at this point.

Key to Ability Levels

Enabling Strategies have been coded for varying learning styles and abilities.

L1 Level 1 activities are within the ability range of Learning Disabled students.

L2 Level 2 activities are basic-to-average activities and are within the ability range of average students.

L3 Level 3 activities are challenging activities and are within the ability range of above-average students.

LEP LEP activities are within the ability range of Limited English Proficiency students.

Setting the Purpose

Lesson 14.1 teaches students to use a preposition to show the relationship of a noun or pronoun to some other word in a sentence.

FOCUS

Lesson Overview

Objective: To identify prepositions of one or more words

Bellringer

When students enter the classroom, have this assignment on the board: *Write a few sentences that explain how to find the closest public library.*

Motivating Activity

Explain that prepositions are words such as *down, to, under,* or *near* that show the relationship between a noun or pronoun and another word. Have each student exchange the Bellringer sentences with a partner and underline the prepositions. Encourage volunteers to share their sentences on the board.

TEACH

Teaching Tip

English usage allows the terminal preposition, as in *This is the new library I told you about.* Attempts to avoid the terminal preposition often result in strained, wooden sentences: *This is the new library about which I told you.* Perhaps the most famous sentence used to defend the terminal preposition is that attributed to Winston Churchill: *This is the kind of nonsense up with which I will not put.*

14.1 Prepositions

A **preposition** is a word that relates a noun or a pronoun to some other word in a sentence.

The dictionary **on** the desk was open.
An almanac was **under** the dictionary.
Meet me **at** three o'clock tomorrow.

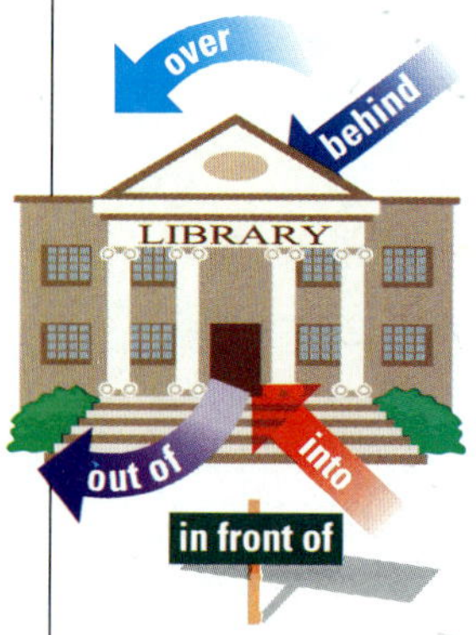

Commonly Used Prepositions				
aboard	as	despite	near	since
about	at	down	of	through
above	before	during	off	to
across	behind	except	on	toward
after	below	for	onto	under
against	beneath	from	opposite	until
along	beside	in	out	up
amid	between	inside	outside	upon
among	beyond	into	over	with
around	by	like	past	without

A preposition can consist of more than one word.

I borrowed the almanac **along with** some other reference books.

Prepositions of More Than One Word				
according to	along with	because of	in spite of	on top of
across from	aside from	in front of	instead of	out of

Read each sentence below. Any word that fits in the blank is a preposition.

Use the almanac that is ______ the table.
I took the atlas ______ your room.

Teacher's Classroom Resources

The following resources can be used for planning, instruction, practice, reinforcement, assessment, reteaching, enrichment, or evaluation.

Teaching Tools
Lesson Plans

Blackline Masters
Grammar Practice, p. 28
Grammar Reteaching, p. 29
Grammar Enrichment, p. 29

Grammar Workbook
Lesson 41

Unit Assessment
Tests with Answer Key
Unit 14 Pretest, pp. 53–54

Test Generator
Unit 14 Pretest

You may wish to administer the Unit 14 Pretest at this point.

Exercise 1 **Identifying Prepositions**

Write each preposition from the following sentences.

1. Many famous libraries around the world are tourist attractions.
2. The New York Public Library on Fifth Avenue serves the New York metropolitan community.
3. Two marble lions in front of the library greet visitors.
4. The library houses a large number of books on a vast range of topics.
5. The library also holds several exhibitions during the year.
6. Its branches hold millions of volumes.
7. The New York Public Library is one of the largest systems in the world.
8. The first public library in America was built in the year 1833.
9. Many important library developments occurred during the 1800s.
10. Melvil Dewey established a system for the classification of books.

Exercise 2 **Identifying Prepositions of More Than One Word**

Write the preposition or prepositions from each sentence. Circle each preposition of more than one word.

1. The classification number of a library book is found upon the spine of the book, usually below the title.
2. Along with the Dewey Decimal Classification system, Melvil Dewey also established the American Library Association and the *Library Journal*.
3. The Dewey system puts books into ten main categories.
4. The research library in front of the administration building uses a different system of classifying books.
5. The Library of Congress classification system categorizes books into twenty-one major areas of knowledge.
6. This system was developed in the early 1900s because of the large number of books in this library.
7. Aside from being one of the largest research libraries in the world, it has the largest collection of books printed before 1501.
8. Among the books in its collection is a perfect copy of the Gutenberg Bible.
9. According to the guide, the library provides reference assistance along with research for the United States Congress.
10. On the back of a book's title page, you will find cataloging data.

PRACTICE AND ASSESS

Answers: Exercise 1

1. around
2. on
3. in front of
4. of, on, of
5. during
6. of
7. of, in
8. in, in
9. during
10. for, of

Answers: Exercise 2

1. of, upon, of, below
2. (Along with)
3. into
4. (in front of,) of
5. of, into, of
6. in, (because of,) of, in
7. (Aside from,) of, in, of, before
8. among, in, of
9. (According to,) (along with,) for
10. On, of

Independent Practice

Skills Practice

Grammar Practice, p. 28
Grammar Reteaching, p. 29
Grammar Enrichment, p. 29

Grammar Workbook, Lesson 41

CLOSE

Ask students to write directions for getting from their classroom to the school library. Then have them circle all the prepositions they used.

Enabling Strategies

LEP Choosing Prepositions

Because many prepositions are part of idiomatic phrases, LEP students may have difficulty identifying which preposition to use. To give them practice in using prepositions correctly, write on slips of paper a few simple sentences that contain prepositions. (Examples: *The student stands behind the desk. She sits in front of the blackboard.*) Then ask student volunteers to act out the sentences. Have other students guess what each sentence is; then write the sentence on the board, underlining the preposition.

Setting the Purpose

Lesson 14.2 teaches students where to use prepositional phrases in a sentence and how to use them as a means to combine sentences.

FOCUS

Lesson Overview

Objective: To identify prepositional phrases and objects of prepositions

Bellringer

When students enter the classroom, have this assignment on the board: *Write a sentence or two that tells where and when you might read a book.*

Motivating Activity

Tell students that prepositional phrases are often the words that tell where and when something takes place. (Example: *We met in front of the library at noon. In front of the library* tells where and *at noon* tells when.) Have students exchange Bellringer sentences and circle the prepositional phrases that tell where and when.

TEACH

Teaching Tip

Write one of the sentences from the lesson on the board and draw an arrow from the preposition to its object. Then write several sentences on the board, and ask volunteers to supply the arrows.

Vocabulary Link

In grammar the term *phrase* refers to a group of related words that does not contain a subject and a verb and that acts as a single part of speech.

14.2 Prepositional Phrases

A prepositional phrase is a group of words that begins with a preposition and ends with a noun or pronoun that is called the object of the preposition.

Dr. Chin has an almanac **from the 1800s.**
The almanac has a special meaning **for him.**

A preposition can have a compound object.

Almanacs contain lists **of facts and figures.**
Grace showed one **to her sisters and her classmates.**

A sentence can have more than one prepositional phrase.

We left our notes **under the almanac on the shelf.**

A prepositional phrase can appear anywhere in a sentence—at the beginning, in the middle, or at the end.

At the library students examined the almanac.
Students **at the library** examined the almanac.
Students examined the almanac **at the library.**

Sometimes you can use a prepositional phrase to combine sentences.

Gary wrote a newspaper article.
He wrote about old almanacs.
Gary wrote a newspaper article **about old almanacs.**

In the second sentence above, the prepositional phrase *about old almanacs* tells more about the newspaper article. You can combine the sentences by adding the phrase to the first sentence.

Teacher's Classroom Resources

The following resources can be used for planning, instruction, practice, reinforcement, reteaching, or enrichment.

Teaching Tools
Lesson Plans

Blackline Masters
Grammar Practice, p. 28
Grammar Reteaching, p. 30
Grammar Enrichment, p. 29

Grammar Workbook
Lesson 42

Exercise 3 Identifying Prepositions and Their Objects

Write each prepositional phrase. Underline each object of the preposition. Some sentences have more than one prepositional phrase.

1. Calendars are often included in almanacs.
2. Many almanacs predict the weather through a certain year and give information on population.
3. Some newspapers and organizations publish almanacs with special information.
4. *Poor Richard's Almanac* is a well-known almanac from the American colonial period.
5. Benjamin Franklin published the book in 1733.
6. It is filled with facts and lists of various sorts.
7. Many other kinds of reference books are found in the library.
8. The library is open from nine o'clock in the morning to nine o'clock at night.
9. Encyclopedias are located in the reference section of most school and public libraries.
10. International cookbooks contain information about foods from various countries.
11. The pages of a dictionary list many different kinds of words.
12. Almanacs are useful for the study of many kinds of information.
13. An atlas can help you learn about the location of all the countries in the world.
14. In most libraries the reference material cannot be taken out of the building.
15. Many libraries today have collections of phonograph records, CDs, and videotapes.
16. Many large cities have branch libraries in various neighborhoods.
17. School libraries and public libraries are funded by taxes and contributions.
18. Because of the rising cost of material and equipment, library budgets have been under pressure.
19. One third of the public libraries in the United States are branch libraries.
20. A library should have a good collection of reference materials, current magazines, and technical reports.

PRACTICE AND ASSESS

Answers: Exercise 3

1. in <u>almanacs</u>
2. through a certain <u>year</u>; on <u>population</u>
3. with special <u>information</u>
4. from the American colonial <u>period</u>
5. in <u>1733</u>
6. with <u>facts</u> and <u>lists</u>; of various <u>sorts</u>
7. of reference <u>books</u>; in the <u>library</u>
8. from <u>nine</u> o'clock; in the <u>morning</u>; to <u>nine</u> o'clock; at <u>night</u>
9. in the reference <u>section</u>; of most school and public <u>libraries</u>
10. about <u>foods</u>; from various <u>countries</u>
11. of a <u>dictionary</u>; of <u>words</u>
12. for the <u>study</u>; of many <u>kinds</u>; of <u>information</u>
13. about the <u>location</u>; of all the <u>countries</u>; in the <u>world</u>
14. In most <u>libraries</u>; out of the <u>building</u>
15. of phonograph <u>records</u>, <u>CDs</u>, and <u>videotapes</u>
16. in various <u>neighborhoods</u>
17. by <u>taxes</u> and <u>contributions</u>
18. of the rising <u>cost</u>; of <u>material</u> and <u>equipment</u>; under <u>pressure</u>
19. of the public <u>libraries</u>; in the <u>United States</u>
20. of reference <u>materials</u>, current <u>magazines</u>, and technical <u>reports</u>

Independent Practice

Skills Practice

- *Grammar Practice,* p. 28
- *Grammar Reteaching,* p. 30
- *Grammar Enrichment,* p. 29
- ***Grammar Workbook,*** Lesson 42

CLOSE

Ask students how to identify the object of a preposition. (Find a preposition, look at the whole prepositional phrase, and then find the noun or pronoun that ends the phrase.)

Enabling Strategies

LEP Identifying Prepositions

Students learning English as a second language may have difficulty identifying prepositions. Explain that the prefix *pre-* means "before." A *pre*position, then, usually comes *before* a noun or a pronoun; it doesn't stand by itself.

Setting the Purpose

Lesson 14.3 teaches students to use an object pronoun when a pronoun is the object of a preposition.

FOCUS

Lesson Overview

Objective: To identify the correct object pronoun to follow a preposition

Bellringer

When students enter the classroom, have this assignment on the board: *Tell what is wrong with this sentence and write it correctly:*

Lisa's dog ran to Lisa, jumped on Lisa, and stole a cookie from Lisa.

Motivating Activity

Remind students that using pronouns helps writers to avoid repeating nouns over and over. Check that students have substituted pronouns for the noun *Lisa* in the Bellringer. Have them underline the prepositional phrases and circle the pronouns.

TEACH

Teaching Tip

Sometimes the compound object of a preposition consists of two pronouns. A sentence such as the following may confuse students: *Yuri gave the thesaurus to you and me.* When students want to use a compound object with two pronouns, suggest they say the sentence aloud with only one pronoun at a time following the preposition.

Cross-reference: Grammar

For instruction and practice in using object pronouns, refer students to Lesson 11.1, pp. 326–327.

14.3 Pronouns After Prepositions

When a pronoun is the object of a preposition, remember to use an object pronoun and not a subject pronoun.

Yoshi handed the dictionary to Akilah.
Yoshi handed the dictionary to **her.**

In the example above, the object pronoun *her* replaces *Akilah* as the object of the preposition *to.*

Sometimes a preposition will have a compound object consisting of a noun and pronoun. Remember to use an object pronoun in a compound object.

I borrowed the almanac from Jorge and Lisa.
I borrowed the almanac from Jorge and **her.**

An object pronoun is used in the sentence above. *Jorge and her* is the compound object of the preposition *from.*

If you are unsure about whether to use a subject pronoun or an object pronoun, try saying the sentence aloud with only the pronoun following the preposition.

The pronouns *who* and *whom* are often confused. *Who* is a subject pronoun, and *whom* is an object pronoun. Note how the pronouns are used in the following sentences.

Who told you about it?
To **whom** did you lend the almanac?

Teacher's Classroom Resources

The following resources can be used for planning, instruction, practice, reinforcement, reteaching, or enrichment.

Teaching Tools
Lesson Plans

Blackline Masters
Grammar Practice, p. 29
Grammar Reteaching, p. 31
Grammar Enrichment, p. 30

Grammar Workbook
Lesson 43

Exercise 4 **Choosing Pronouns After Prepositions**

For each sentence write the correct pronoun.

1. Jorge and Lisa told you about (who, whom)?
2. Vanessa spoke to Lisa and (he, him) at the game.
3. What did Vanessa show to (them, they)?
4. Mr. Valdes bumped into Vanessa and (she, her) in the corridor.
5. Lisa had still not given her homework assignment to (him, he).
6. He walked with Lisa and (her, she) to the door.
7. Who knows what he said to (they, them)?
8. After class they had lunch with Jorge and (he, him).
9. Lisa is going to the library with (he, him).
10. She picked a topic that would interest both of (they, them).

Exercise 5 **Using Pronouns After Prepositions**

In each item a proper noun is underlined. Replace the proper noun with the correct object pronoun.

1. Mr. Valdes handed an almanac to <u>Alice</u>.
2. Alice learned about Ukraine from <u>Mr. Valdes</u>.
3. Ukraine had been part of <u>the Soviet Union</u>.
4. Alice wanted information for <u>Aunt Greta</u>.
5. Aunt Greta often speaks of <u>Victor</u>, her brother.
6. Victor lives with <u>Tanya</u>, his wife.
7. Alice mailed Victor a package from <u>Aunt Greta</u>.
8. Faraway places are exciting to <u>Alice</u>.
9. Alice wants to learn much more about <u>Victor</u>.
10. She plans a visit to <u>Victor</u> next year.

Exercise 6 **Writing Sentences with Prepositions and Object Pronouns**

Write a sentence for each item. Use the pronouns listed as objects of a preposition. Underline the preposition and its object pronoun.

SAMPLE them
ANSWER We wrote a letter <u>to them</u>.

1. me
2. her
3. her and him
4. them
5. him

Enabling Strategies

LEP Practicing Object Pronouns
Some students may speak a language with a single form for subject and object pronouns. Have student pairs review the list of object pronouns in Lesson 11.1, p. 326. Let one answer questions 1–5 in Exercise 5, above, while the other checks the list.

L2 Using *Who* or *Whom*
Help students decide whether to use the subject pronoun *who* or the object pronoun *whom* in a question. Suggest they rewrite the question as a statement and substitute *he* or *she* or *him* or *her* for *who* or *whom*.

Two-Minute Skill Drill

List these prepositional phrases on the board. Have students write a sentence using each.

to her	*about whom*
with us	*with you and me*
from them	*from him and her*

PRACTICE AND ASSESS

Answers: Exercise 4

1. whom	6. her
2. him	7. them
3. them	8. him
4. her	9. him
5. him	10. them

Answers: Exercise 5

1. her	6. her
2. him	7. her
3. it	8. her
4. her	9. him
5. him	10. him

Answers: Exercise 6

Answers will vary, but some suggestions are given below.

1. She visited <u>with me</u>.
2. I went to dinner <u>with her</u>.
3. I borrowed the book <u>from them</u>.
4. I gave a magazine <u>to them</u>.
5. I wrote <u>about him</u>.

Independent Practice

Skills Practice

Grammar Practice, p. 29
Grammar Reteaching, p. 31
Grammar Enrichment, p. 30

Grammar Workbook, Lesson 43

CLOSE

Have students write sentences with object pronouns after prepositions.

Setting the Purpose

Lesson 14.4 teaches students to use an adjective phrase to describe a noun or a pronoun and to use an adverb phrase to describe a verb, an adjective, or another adverb.

FOCUS

Lesson Overview

Objective: To identify prepositional phrases as adjectives or adverbs

Bellringer

When students enter the classroom, have this assignment on the board: *Write five sentences with at least one prepositional phrase in each.*

Motivating Activity

Have students exchange papers and underline the prepositional phrase or phrases in each sentence. Later, after students have read about how prepositional phrases function as adjectives and adverbs, have them draw a line from each phrase to the word it describes.

TEACH

Teaching Tip

An adverb phrase that modifies a verb can usually be moved to another position in the sentence. For example, the sentence *A map of each state can be found in this atlas* can also be written *In this atlas a map of each state can be found.* An adjective phrase, however, cannot be separated from the noun it modifies. In the following sentence, for example, *of California* must follow *shores: The Pacific Ocean washes the shores of California.*

14.4 Prepositional Phrases as Adjectives and Adverbs

Prepositional phrases function as adjectives and adverbs in sentences.

A prepositional phrase functioning as an adjective describes a noun or a pronoun.

These phrases can describe subjects, direct and indirect objects, predicate nouns, or objects in other prepositional phrases. An adjective phrase usually comes directly after the noun or pronoun it describes.

Africa is a continent **with many natural resources.**

One **of the articles** describes Africa vividly.

The wildlife **of Africa** is varied and abundant.

A prepositional phrase functioning as an adverb describes a verb, an adjective, or another adverb.

Adverb Phrases	
Function	**Examples**
Describes a Verb	Wildlife abounds **in Africa.** Dry savannas extend **over many acres.**
Describes an Adjective	Birds are plentiful **in the rain forests.**
Describes an Adverb	The Nile River flows west **of Cairo.**

Teacher's Classroom Resources

The following resources can be used for planning, instruction, practice, reinforcement, reteaching, or enrichment.

Teaching Tools
Lesson Plans

Blackline Masters
Grammar Practice, p. 30
Grammar Enrichment, p. 31

Grammar Workbook
Lesson 44

Exercise 7 Identifying Adjective and Adverb Phrases

Write each prepositional phrase and whether it is used as an *adjective* or an *adverb*.

1. The Congo Basin lies on the equator.
2. The grass grows quickly near the rain forests.
3. The Red Sea borders Africa on the northeast.
4. What is the climate of Cairo?
5. There is little vegetation in the Sahara.
6. I read a brief article about new African nations.
7. The people of Somalia are suffering a great deal of hardship.
8. Burkina Faso is a small country that lies between Mali and Ghana.
9. The waters of the Atlantic Ocean wash the shores of the Ivory Coast.
10. Southern African nations have recently emerged from years of conflict.
11. Much of this kind of information can be found in an atlas.
12. Bill gave an atlas to Cheryl for her birthday.
13. Cheryl left it beside the globe.
14. An atlas tells about geography.
15. Facts and figures are shown on maps and in tables.
16. An index is an important part of an atlas.
17. It is the guide to the riches of an atlas.
18. Information in an atlas is useful for research.
19. Several governments publish national atlases about their countries.
20. Early atlases had maps that were hand-drawn by cartographers.

Exercise 8 Writing Adjective and Adverb Phrases

On your paper expand each sentence below by adding at least one adjective or adverb phrase to the sentence. Draw a line from each phrase to the word it describes.

1. An atlas gives information.
2. The birds are colorful.
3. The zebras gather.
4. The monkeys are calling.
5. The lion dozes.
6. The climate is humid.
7. The desert seems endless.
8. The plants bloom.
9. A traveler needs water.
10. The sunset glows.

PRACTICE AND ASSESS

Answers: Exercise 7

1. on the equator—adv.
2. near the rain forests—adv.
3. on the northeast—adv.
4. of Cairo—adj.
5. in the Sahara—adv.
6. about new African nations—adj.
7. of Somalia—adj.; of hardship—adj.
8. between Mali and Ghana—adv.
9. of the Atlantic Ocean—adj.; of the Ivory Coast—adj.
10. from years—adv.; of conflict—adj.
11. of this kind—adj.; of information—adj.; in an atlas—adv.
12. to Cheryl—adv.; for her birthday—adv.
13. beside the globe—adv.
14. about geography—adv.
15. on maps—adv.; in tables—adv.
16. of an atlas—adj.
17. to the riches—adj.; of an atlas—adj.
18. in an atlas—adj.; for research—adv.
19. about their countries—adj.
20. by cartographers—adv.

Answers: Exercise 8

Answers will vary. A sample sentence:

1. An atlas gives information about countries. (*about countries* modifies *information*)

Independent Practice

Skills Practice

Grammar Practice, p. 30
Grammar Enrichment, p. 31
Grammar Workbook, Lesson 44

CLOSE

Have students describe the difference between an adjective phrase and an adverb phrase.

Enabling Strategies

LEP Identifying Adjective and Adverb Phrases

Students might benefit from going step by step through the process of determining whether prepositional phrases are adjective or adverb phrases. Provide students with a passage containing prepositional phrases. Have students go through the sentences and circle all of the prepositional phrases. Then help the students to determine whether the phrases modify nouns or pronouns (adjective phrases), or verbs, adjectives, or adverbs (adverb phrases).

Setting the Purpose

Lesson 14.5 teaches students that some words can function as prepositions or as adverbs. The lesson explains the difference between prepositions and adverbs and shows students how to use them.

FOCUS

Lesson Overview

Objective: To distinguish between prepositions and adverbs

Bellringer

When students enter the classroom, have this assignment on the board: *Create four sentences using the following words:*

above inside over before

Motivating Activity

Have students look over the sentences they wrote in the Bellringer. For each sentence, write the word or words that answer the question *where?* or *when?* For example: *The clock is above the door. Where is the clock?* (above the door)

TEACH

Teaching Tip

To help students decide whether a word is used as a preposition or as an adverb, suggest they check to see whether the word is contained within a prepositional phrase. A prepositional phrase begins with a preposition and usually ends with a noun or pronoun—the object of the preposition. A word used as an adverb does not have an object and is not contained within a prepositional phrase.

14.5 Telling Prepositions and Adverbs Apart

We ate our lunch **outside.**

We ate our lunch **outside** the **library**.

Sometimes it is difficult to tell whether a word is a preposition or an adverb. Both types of words can answer the questions *where?* and *when?* In addition, some words can be used as either prepositions or adverbs.

Words That Can Be Used as Prepositions or Adverbs		
about	below	out
above	down	outside
around	in	over
before	inside	through
behind	near	up

If you're having trouble deciding whether a word is used as a preposition or as an adverb, look at the other words in the sentence. If the word is followed closely by a noun, the word is probably a preposition, and the noun is the object of the preposition.

We ate our lunch **outside** the **library.**

In the sentence above, the word *outside* is followed closely by the noun *library. Outside* is a preposition, and *library* is the object of the preposition.

If the word is not followed closely by a noun, then the word is probably an adverb.

We ate our lunch **outside.**

In this sentence the word *outside* answers the question *where?* but is not followed by a noun. In this sentence *outside* is an adverb.

Teacher's Classroom Resources

The following resources can be used for planning, instruction, practice, reinforcement, reteaching, or enrichment.

Teaching Tools
Lesson Plans

Blackline Masters
Grammar Practice, p. 31

Grammar Workbook
Lesson 45

Exercise 9 Distinguishing Between Adverbs and Prepositions

Write whether each underlined word is used as a *preposition* or as an *adverb.*

1. Who left this book of quotations behind?
2. Gene found the book behind the lockers.
3. We searched through the biographical dictionary.
4. I had read the same article before.
5. I will report on the article before Friday.
6. Please look inside the almanac.
7. Jeff will bring the encyclopedia inside.
8. Kim pointed to the important notes below.
9. My note cards lie below the top shelf.
10. Did you read the article about Gandhi?
11. It was about his early life.
12. Outside class I shall have a chance to read the article through.
13. I can think my impressions over while taking a walk outside.
14. I enjoy a walk in the park.
15. Kim carried the atlas around.
16. She walked hastily around the library.
17. Lee carried his article up the stairs but came down without it.
18. Bob's dictionary was found near his desk.
19. Kim reads down the pages of the almanac.
20. Her conversation goes over my head.
21. A map of the United States hangs near the front door.
22. A portrait of the president hangs above.
23. Mr. Cleese brought in an overdue video about India.
24. Did I leave my card in that book?
25. Grandma checked out a videotape.

Exercise 10 Using Words as Prepositions or Adverbs

Write each word below in a sentence. If you use the word as a preposition, underline the prepositional phrase.

1. above
2. in
3. around
4. near
5. up
6. out
7. through
8. before
9. over
10. down

PRACTICE AND ASSESS

Answers: Exercise 9

1. adverb
2. preposition
3. preposition
4. adverb
5. preposition
6. preposition
7. adverb
8. adverb
9. preposition
10. preposition
11. preposition
12. preposition; adverb
13. adverb; adverb
14. preposition
15. adverb
16. preposition
17. preposition; adverb
18. preposition
19. preposition
20. preposition
21. preposition
22. adverb
23. adverb
24. preposition
25. adverb

Answers: Exercise 10

Answers will vary, but some suggestions are given below.

1. The shelf is above my head. **2.** The book is in the bag. **3.** Cookbooks are around the corner. **4.** Travel books are near the window. **5.** To see the sign, look up. **6.** The student walked out the door. **7.** Read through the introduction. **8.** I read that book before. **9.** Study time is over. **10.** The librarian put the book down.

Independent Practice

Skills Practice

Grammar Practice, p. 31

Grammar Workbook, Lesson 45

CLOSE

Ask students to use the words from the list on page 388 to write sentences. Have them exchange papers and tell whether each word was used as a preposition or as an adverb.

Enabling Strategies

LEP Using the Photographs

Use the pictures on page 370 to help students find the preposition in the sentence *We ate our lunch outside the library.* Ask: Which word answers the question *outside what?* (the library). Point out that this noun is represented in the larger picture. In the sentence *We ate our lunch outside,* there is no answer to the question *outside what?* In this sentence *outside* is an adverb. Suggest students work with partners to practice with their own pairs of sentences. Ask the students to label prepositions and adverbs.

Setting the Purpose

Lesson 14.6 teaches students to show the relationship between ideas by using the most appropriate coordinating or correlative conjunctions.

FOCUS

Lesson Overview

Objective: To identify and distinguish between coordinating and correlative conjunctions

Bellringer

When students enter the classroom, have this assignment on the board: *Write four sentences using each of the following conjunctions:*

and	*but*
or	*either, or*

Motivating Activity

Invite volunteers to write their sentences from the Bellringer on the board. Work with students to figure out whether their sentences have compound subjects or compound predicates, or whether they are compound sentences.

TEACH

Teaching Tip

Conjunctions join words or groups of words that have equal grammatical weight in a sentence: subjects, predicates, phrases, and independent clauses. Point out that correlative conjunctions make the relationship between words or groups of words a little clearer than do coordinating conjunctions.

14.6 Conjunctions

A **conjunction** is a word that joins words or groups of words in a sentence.

The most common conjunctions are *and, but,* and *or.* They are called **coordinating conjunctions.** *And* and *or* are used to form compound subjects. *And, but,* and *or* are used to form compound predicates and compound sentences.

Using Conjunctions to Form Compounds	
Compound Subject	Mexico **and** Canada are both on a map of North America.
Compound Predicate	Students can check the map **or** use the globe.
Compound Sentence	I would lend you my atlas, **but** Felicia already borrowed it.

A comma should be placed before the conjunction in a compound sentence. Do not, however, place a comma between the two parts of a compound subject and a compound predicate.

Although the conjunctions are used in a similar fashion, they are not interchangeable. Each has a different meaning.

Coordinating Conjunctions

Conjunction	Meaning	Example
And	Introduces an additional idea	The map **and** the globe are in the classroom.
But	Introduces a contrasting idea	The map is old, **but** the globe is new.
Or	Introduces a choice or second possibility	Students check the map **or** use the globe.

Pairs of conjunctions such as *either, or; neither, nor;* and *both, and* are called **correlative conjunctions**. They join the same kinds of words as do the conjunctions *and, but,* and *or.*

Either Lucy **or** I will use the atlas.

Teacher's Classroom Resources

The following resources can be used for planning, instruction, practice, reinforcement, reteaching, or enrichment.

Teaching Tools
Lesson Plans

Blackline Masters
Grammar Practice, p. 32
Grammar Reteaching, p. 32
Grammar Enrichment, p. 32

Grammar Workbook
Lesson 46

Exercise 11 Identifying Conjunctions and Compounds

Write each conjunction. Then write whether it forms a *compound subject, compound predicate,* or *compound sentence*.

1. Ramón and Sal are using the class atlas.
2. They are studying rivers and comparing figures.
3. The Mississippi River flows southward and increases in width along the way.
4. The Amazon is long, but it is not the longest river.
5. Who has studied or visited mountains in Europe?
6. The Chaco and the Serengeti are vast plains.
7. Sal has been to Argentina, or he is planning to go there.
8. Either the Himalayas or the Urals are the world's highest mountains.
9. Bolivia contains some of the highest mountains in South America but also has some very hot, humid lowlands.
10. Denver is called the mile-high city, but Leadville is at an even higher altitude.

Exercise 12 Using Conjunctions

Write the conjunctions that best fit in the sentences.

1. Judy wrote a report ______ drew a map of the Himalayas.
2. Tibet ______ Nepal lie north of India.
3. Is the Upper Nile in north ______ south Egypt?
4. Australia ______ New Zealand is easy to reach from North America.
5. Is Mount Everest in Asia, ______ is it in Europe?
6. I have a map of India, ______ I do not have one of Japan.
7. ______ Tokyo ______ Hiroshima are in Japan.
8. Her ambition was to climb the highest mountain on each continent, ___________ she planned to start with Mt. McKinley in Alaska.
9. Mt. Everest is the highest at 29,028 feet, ___________ two other Himalayan peaks are more than 28,000 feet high.
10. ___________ Mt. Fuji in Japan ___________ Mt. Etna in Italy is nearly as high.

Enabling Strategies

LEP Joining with Conjunctions

Tell students that conjunctions are like a glue that joins similar things. Write sentences with conjunctions on the board. Discuss why the pairs go together. Ask students to make up their own sentences and identify the compound parts in each.

L3 Correlative Conjunctions

Tell students that when the correlative conjunction *not only ... but also* joins clauses, the verb in the first clause precedes the subject. For example: *Not only have I studied Japan's history, but I have also studied its language.* Ask students to create sentences using this conjunction.

PRACTICE AND ASSESS

Answers: Exercise 11

1. and—compound subject
2. and —compound predicate
3. and—compound predicate
4. but—compound sentence
5. or—compound predicate
6. and—compound subject
7. or—compound sentence
8. Either, or—compound subject
9. but—compound predicate
10. but—compound sentence

Answers: Exercise 12

1. and
2. and
3. or
4. or
5. or
6. but
7. Both, and
8. and
9. but *or* and
10. Neither, nor

Independent Practice

Skills Practice

Grammar Practice, p. 32
Grammar Reteaching, p. 32
Grammar Enrichment, p. 32

Grammar Workbook, Lesson 46

CLOSE

Ask students to explain, in their own words, the differences between the coordinating conjunctions *and, or,* and *but.* Then have them tell what a correlative conjunction is.

Setting the Purpose

Lesson 14.7 teaches students to express strong feelings in writing by using interjections. They learn that interjections can stand alone or be written as part of a sentence.

FOCUS

Lesson Overview

Objective: To identify and punctuate interjections correctly and to use interjections effectively for expressing strong feelings

Bellringer

When students enter the classroom, have this assignment on the board: *Write three sentences, each of which expresses strong feelings about something.*

Motivating Activity

Invite volunteers to share their sentences with the class. Then ask students to look at the list of common interjections on page 392. Have them add one of the interjections to their sentences. Discuss how the tone of the sentence may have changed when the interjection was added.

TEACH

Teaching Tip

Students often confuse interjections with imperative sentences. Interjections are sentence fragments when they stand alone. An imperative sentence only appears to be a fragment; its subject is always understood to be *you,* and it always contains a verb.

14.7 Interjections

An **interjection** is a word or group of words that expresses strong feeling.

Common Interjections			
aha	great	oh	phew
awesome	ha	oh, no	well
come on	hey	oops	wow
gee	hooray	ouch	yes

An interjection that expresses a very strong feeling may stand alone, either before or after a sentence. Such interjections are followed by an exclamation mark.

Oh, no! I wrote *horse* instead of *hoarse.*

When an interjection expresses a milder feeling, it appears as part of the sentence. In that case it is separated from the rest of the sentence by a comma.

Oh, I thought I knew the definition of that word.

Use interjections sparingly. Overuse ruins the effect.

Teacher's Classroom Resources

The following resources can be used for planning, instruction, practice, reinforcement, reteaching, or enrichment.

Teaching Tools
Lesson Plans

Blackline Masters
Grammar Practice, p. 32
Grammar Reteaching, p. 33
Grammar Enrichment, p. 32

Grammar Workbook
Lesson 47

Exercise 13 Identifying Interjections

Write each interjection. Include any punctuation mark that goes with it.

1. Phew, this dictionary is heavy.
2. Jack will carry it for me. Hooray!
3. Great! I made no mistakes on my spelling test.
4. Oh, no! I forgot the double *b* in *hobble*.
5. Oops, I think I forgot to sign my name.
6. Hey! Studying the English language is fun!
7. Simon has the answer to our problem. Aha!
8. Gee, I would like to know more about Old English.
9. Ouch! Spelling rules can be complicated.
10. Wow, I am going to the state spelling bee. Yes!
11. Mr. Robinson just showed me the unabridged dictionary. Awesome!
12. Oh, no! Do I need that to prepare for the spelling bee? Come on!
13. So this is Middle English. Well!
14. Ha! I recognize a few words.
15. Oh, I didn't hear you, Mr. Lyons.
16. Oops, I lost my English book.
17. Mr. Lyons found it on the floor. Great!
18. Aha! I dropped it in the reference room.
19. Gee, Mr. Lyons, you saved the day. Phew!
20. Ouch, it's time to get back to that dictionary.
21. Hey, spellers! Watch out for me. Yes!
22. Oh, no! I think I spelled *accommodate* with one *m* and two *d*'s.
23. Hey, do you know how to spell *embarrass*?
24. Come on, if *alto* is from an Italian word meaning "high," why does it refer to low female singing voices?
25. I had no idea so many common expressions were originally written by Shakespeare. Wow!

Exercise 14 Writing Sentences with Interjections

Write 10 sentences, using a different interjection in each. Take care to punctuate each sentence correctly.

PRACTICE AND ASSESS

Answers: Exercise 13

1. Phew,
2. Hooray!
3. Great!
4. Oh, no!
5. Oops,
6. Hey!
7. Aha!
8. Gee,
9. Ouch!
10. Wow, Yes!
11. Awesome!
12. Oh, no! Come on!
13. Well!
14. Ha!
15. Oh,
16. Oops,
17. Great!
18. Aha!
19. Gee, Phew!
20. Ouch,
21. Hey, Yes!
22. Oh, no!
23. Hey,
24. Come on,
25. Wow!

Answers: Exercise 14

Answers will vary. Make sure that an interjection expressing strong feeling is followed by an exclamation mark. An interjection expressing milder feeling should be separated from the rest of the sentence by a comma.

Independent Practice

Skills Practice

- *Grammar Practice,* p. 32
- *Grammar Reteaching,* p. 33
- *Grammar Enrichment,* p. 32
- ***Grammar Workbook,*** Lesson 47

CLOSE

Have volunteers say aloud a sentence with an interjection. The rest of the students can write the sentence they hear. Check that punctuation of the interjection is appropriate.

Enabling Strategies

LEP Recognizing Interjections

Students whose second language is English may not readily recognize the situations in which some interjections are used. Pair these students with native English speakers and have the partners go over the sentences in Exercise 13. The more fluent student should explain why the interjection in each sentence is appropriate, and both students should suggest other interjections that could be substituted. If a student doesn't understand a particular interjection, encourage the partner to explain it—perhaps by acting it out.

TEACH

About the Literature

After students have read the passage by Eudora Welty, initiate a discussion of the characters and the mood of the excerpt. Then ask students to focus on the highlighted words in the passage. Have them identify the prepositional phrases that are not highlighted and determine whether each functions as an adjective or adverb.

The passage from *One Writer's Beginnings* tells about Eudora Welty's early love of books. The book is composed of a series of lectures the author delivered at Harvard University in 1983.

Linking Grammar and Literature

Teaching Tip

Ask students to make up sentences based on their reaction to the passage from *One Writer's Beginnings*. Tell students they may explain their own relationship to books, imagine a dialogue between themselves and the young Eudora Welty, or respond in some other way to the passage. Each sentence should contain a preposition, a conjunction, or an interjection. After the students have completed the assignment, invite them to share their sentences with the rest of the class.

Speaking and Listening

Interjections are often used in writing dialogue. Invite students to imagine a short dialogue between Eudora Welty and Mrs. Calloway, the librarian. Have them use interjections as appropriate. Suggest students work in pairs and share their dialogues with a partner. Can students hear and identify the interjection?

UNIT 14

Unit Review

Grammar Review

Prepositions, Conjunctions, and Interjections

Eudora Welty is an American short-story author and novelist who writes about small-town life in the South. In her book *One Writer's Beginnings,* published in 1984, she describes the influence of her family and surroundings on her writing. The following passage has been annotated to show some uses of prepositions and conjunctions.

Literature Model

from ONE WRITER'S BEGINNINGS

by Eudora Welty

Mrs. Calloway made her own rules about books. You could not take back a book to the Library on the same day you'd taken it out; it made no difference to her that you'd read every word in it and needed another to start. You could take out two books at a time and two only; this applied as long as you were a child and also for the rest of your life, to my mother as severely as to me. So two by two, I read library books as fast as I could go, rushing them home in the basket of my bicycle. From the minute I reached our house, I started to read. Every book I seized on, from *Bunny Brown and His Sister Sue at Camp Rest-a-While* to *Twenty Thousand Leagues Under the Sea,* stood for the devouring wish to read being instantly granted. I knew this was bliss, knew it at the time. Taste isn't nearly so important; it comes in its own time. I wanted to read *immediately.* The only fear was that of books coming to an end.

Annotations:
- Preposition (about)
- Pronoun as object of the preposition (her)
- Conjunction connecting compound predicate (and)
- Noun as object of the preposition (life)
- Prepositional phrase (adjective phrase) (of my bicycle)
- Prepositional phrase (adverb phrase) (at the time)

Teacher's Classroom Resources

The following resources can be used for planning, instruction, practice, reinforcement, assessment, reteaching, enrichment, or evaluation.

Teaching Tools
Lesson Plans

Grammar Workbook
Lessons 41–47
Unit 14 Review
Cumulative Review: Units 1–13

Unit Assessment
Tests with Answer Key
Unit 14 Mastery Test, pp. 55–56
Test Generator
Unit 14 Mastery Test

Exercise 1

Identifying Prepositions Write each preposition in the sentences below.

SAMPLE Eudora Welty writes about the beginning of her love for books.
ANSWER about, of, for

1. Mrs. Calloway was an important part of Welty's early reading life.
2. The rules made by Mrs. Calloway seemed ridiculous to a young reader.
3. The library's rules were the same for all.
4. The important thing for Eudora Welty was having books available.
5. Welty read books by any author about any topic.

Exercise 2

Using Prepositions Write an appropriate preposition to replace each blank. Try to use a different preposition in each sentence.

SAMPLE Libraries ______ very large communities often have several branches.
ANSWER in

1. People ______ library cards can take home any of the books on the shelves.
2. All ______ the branches are available to anyone with a library card in the city.
3. There are library rules ______ children and adults.
4. A librarian is usually available to help you find your way ______ the library.
5. Short story collections are ______ the fiction section.
6. ______ this library is a wonderful section of young adult fiction.
7. The section is ______ the back wall.
8. You can find it ______ the librarian's desk.
9. The librarian's desk is ______ the reference section.
10. The reference section is ______ the rare book room and the fiction section.

UNIT 14 Review

Answers: Exercise 1

1. of
2. by; to
3. for
4. for
5. by; about

Answers: Exercise 2

Answers will vary, but some suggestions are provided below.

1. with
2. of
3. for
4. through; around
5. in
6. Within
7. at; along
8. on; behind
9. near
10. between

UNIT 14
Review

Answers: Exercise 3

1. about fine arts or early printed books; to the Morgan Library; in New York City
2. Near the Capitol; in Washington, D.C.
3. Opposite the Folger; across the street; of Congress
4. at Yale University; inside a six-story glass enclosure; on campus
5. because of the excellent collections; within these libraries; along with you and me

Answers: Exercise 4

1. them
2. whom
3. them
4. them
5. her
6. her
7. him
8. me
9. us
10. them

Exercise 3

Identifying Prepositional Phrases and Their Objects Write the prepositional phrases from each sentence. Underline the object of each preposition.

SAMPLE Scholars often go to specialized libraries for information.
ANSWER to specialized libraries for information

1. Researchers needing information about fine arts or early printed books may go to the Morgan Library in New York City.
2. Near the Capitol in Washington, D.C., is the Folger Shakespeare Library.
3. Opposite the Folger, across the street, sits the huge Library of Congress.
4. The Beinecke Rare Book and Manuscript Library at Yale University is housed inside a six-story glass enclosure on campus.
5. Because of the excellent collections within these libraries, scholars can study any subject along with you and me.

Exercise 4

Choosing Object Pronouns Write the correct pronoun for each sentence.

1. Books were Mrs. Calloway's subject, and she made rules about (they, them).
2. To (who, whom) did Mrs. Calloway's rules apply?
3. The rules applied equally to the two of (they, them), Eudora and her mother.
4. Eudora read so many books that she seemed to race through (they, them).
5. According to (she, her), she started to read as soon as she returned from the library.
6. Although Eudora may not have liked Mrs. Calloway, despite (she, her), the girl certainly enjoyed reading.
7. Although Eudora does not mention her father in this passage, her love of books may have been influenced by (he, him).
8. I, too, have always loved having books around (I, me).
9. My family and I always keep stacks of unread books near (we, us).
10. Without (they, them) we feel lost.

Exercise 5

Telling Prepositions from Adverbs The following sentences are about Eudora Welty's life. Identify each underlined word as a *preposition* or an *adverb*. If the word is a preposition, write its object or objects.

1. *One Writer's Beginnings* is Eudora Welty's book about her own life.
2. The book discusses how the effects of her early years in the South come through in her stories.
3. Eudora Welty is an important Southern writer known both for her short stories and her novels.
4. In a library drawer Welty's father kept musical instruments of all kinds.
5. Welty often looked inside to see the wonderful instruments.

Exercise 6

Identifying Adjective and Adverb Phrases Write each sentence. Underline each prepositional phrase and draw an arrow to the word it describes. Write whether the phrase functions as an *adjective* or an *adverb*.

SAMPLE Eudora Welty writes about her love of books.

ANSWER Eudora Welty writes about her love of books.
adverb phrase adjective phrase

1. Mrs. Calloway was an important part of Welty's early reading life.
2. Mrs. Calloway's rules were tiresome for an ardent reader.
3. Welty said everyone except her mother was afraid of Mrs. Calloway.
4. Mrs. Calloway asked everyone for silence.
5. The library's rules applied to adults and children.
6. Eudora rode her bike to the library.
7. Because of her love of books, she obeyed Mrs. Calloway's rules.
8. Eudora read books by any author.
9. A critic said parts of *One Writer's Beginnings* are a gift from Welty to her readers.
10. The Weltys had five encyclopedias in the bookcase in the living room.

Answers: Exercise 5

1. preposition—life
2. adverb
3. preposition—stories, novels
4. preposition—drawer
5. adverb

Answers: Exercise 6

1. of Welty's early reading life—part—adjective
2. for an ardent reader—tiresome—adverb
3. except her mother—everyone—adjective; of Mrs. Calloway—afraid—adverb
4. for silence—asked—adverb
5. to adults and children—applied—adverb
6. to the library—rode—adverb
7. Because of her love—obeyed—adverb; of books—love—adjective
8. by any author—books—adjective
9. of *One Writer's Beginnings*—parts—adjective; from Welty—gift—adjective; to her readers—gift—adjective
10. in the bookcase—had—adverb; in the living room—bookcase—adjective

Answers: Exercise 7

Answers will vary, but some suggestions are given below.

1. What do you think of your local library, and how do you use it?—compound sentence
2. Consider the function of the library, and also think about the ways in which it serves the community. —compound sentence
3. Our library and the town government are in a municipal building. —compound subject
4. Some libraries provide a place for community meetings or exist just for reading and research.—compound predicate
5. Small towns have limited funds for a library but may join with other nearby communities to form a regional library.—compound predicate
6. Large cities have more than one library, and each may house a specialized collection, such as business or health and medicine. —compound sentence
7. No library can contain all the books its users need, but interlibrary loans allow readers to borrow books from other libraries.—compound sentence
8. At the library people can either exchange community information and post notices, or they can pick up tax forms and other printed material.—compound sentence
9. Library exhibits highlight special events and seasonal activities, and they suggest reading related to the topic.—compound sentence
10. Many libraries have special collections of books for children, or they may provide story hours, films, and workshops for children.—compound sentence

Exercise 7

Using Conjunctions to Combine Sentences Combine each pair of sentences below by using the conjunction in parentheses to form a compound sentence, compound subject, or compound object. Write whether your sentence is a *compound sentence* or a sentence with a *compound subject* or a *compound predicate.*

SAMPLE Public libraries provide useful services. Budget problems are forcing some public libraries to cut back the services they provide. (but)

ANSWER Public libraries provide useful services, but budget problems are forcing some public libraries to cut back the services they provide. compound sentence

1. What do you think of your local library? How do you use your library? (and)
2. Consider the function of the library. Also think about the ways in which it serves the community. (both, and)
3. Our library is in a municipal building. The same building houses the town government. (and)
4. Some libraries provide a place for community meetings. Other libraries are just for reading and research. (or)
5. Small towns have limited funds for a library. Small towns may join with other nearby communities to form a regional library. (but)
6. Large cities have more than one library. Each of those libraries may house a specialized collection, such as business or health and medicine. (and)
7. No library can contain all the books its users need. Interlibrary loans allow readers to borrow books from other libraries. (but)
8. At the library people can exchange community information and post notices. People can pick up tax forms and other printed material. (either, or)
9. Library exhibits highlight special events and seasonal activities. The exhibits suggest reading related to the topic. (and)
10. Many libraries have special collections of books for children. They may provide story hours, films, and workshops for children. (or)

Exercise 8

Writing Sentences Write 15 sentences, following the directions given below.

SAMPLE Write a sentence that begins with an interjection and contains a compound predicate.
ANSWER Oh, I fell and skinned my knee!

1. Write a sentence with a compound subject.
2. Write a compound sentence joined by the conjunction *and*.
3. Write a sentence that begins with an interjection followed by a comma.
4. Write a sentence with a compound predicate.
5. Write a sentence that uses the conjunctions *either* and *or*.
6. Write a sentence that is preceded by an interjection followed by an exclamation mark.
7. Write a compound sentence joined by the conjunction *but*.
8. Write a sentence that includes a prepositional phrase with a compound object.
9. Write a sentence that uses the conjunctions *both* and *and*.
10. Write a compound sentence that is joined by the conjunction *or* and contains an interjection.
11. Write a sentence that begins with a prepositional phrase in which the object is a pronoun.
12. Write a sentence that ends with a prepositional phrase in which the object is made up of two pronouns.
13. Write a sentence in which one part of the compound object of a preposition is a pronoun.
14. Write a compound sentence that contains a preposition of more than one word.
15. Write a sentence that contains two prepositional phrases, one used as an adjective and one as an adverb.

Answers: Exercise 8

Answers will vary. Students' sentences should employ what they have learned in this unit.

UNIT 14 Review

Answers: Exercise 9

Proofreading

This proofreading activity provides editing practice with (1) the current or previous units' skills, (2) the **Troubleshooter** errors, and (3) spelling errors. Students should be able to complete the exercise by referring to the units, the **Troubleshooter**, and a dictionary.

	Error (Type of Error)
1.	• Fish's (singular possessive)
2.	• ambition (spelling)
3.	• sculptor, (run-on sentence)
4.	• printmaking, (comma in a series)
	• life's (singular possessive)
5.	• to her (object pronoun)
6.	• shows (subject-verb agreement)
7.	• influenced (verb form)
	• her training (possessive pronoun)
8.	• mirrors (subject-verb agreement)

Exercise 9 — Proofreading

The following passage is about Janet Fish, whose painting *Toby and Claire Reading* appears on this page. Rewrite the passage, correcting the errors in spelling, capitalization, grammar, and usage. Add any missing punctuation. There are 10 errors.

Janet Fish

[1]Janet Fish' early interest in art is similar to Eudora Welty's love of books. [2]Her ambiton from early childhood was to be a sculptor. [3]Fish's mother was a sculptor and her grandfather was a painter. [4]Fish studied sculpture, printmaking and abstract painting in college, but painting was to become her lifes work. [5]The effects of light on various surfaces are especially interesting to she. [6]The painting *Toby and Claire Reading* show the importance of light and color for her. [7]Although Fish's paintings are realistic, her art is strongly influence by she training in abstract painting. [8]The painting *Toby and Claire Reading* mirror Eudora Welty's early love of books.

Janet Fish, *Toby and Claire Reading*, 1984

About the Art

Janet Fish, *Toby and Claire Reading*, 1984

In *Toby and Claire Reading*, Janet Fish presents the effect of full summer sunlight on an outdoor scene. The light emphasizes some of the painting's details and blurs others. As a result, the painting has an almost photographic realism. The observer peers into the picture to try to read the comics and the titles of the books on the grass. This 1984 oil-on-canvas painting measures 50 by 100 inches and is held by the Robert Miller Gallery.

Exercise 10

Mixed Review

Rewrite each item, following the directions in parentheses.

SAMPLE The Maya wrote their history __________ stone monuments. (Add a preposition.)

ANSWER on

1. Information was written __________ clay tablets in Mesopotamia and on papyrus in Egypt. (Add a preposition. Write whether the prepositional phrase is used as an *adjective* or an *adverb*.)
2. Papyrus was a writing material made __________ the fibers of water reeds. (Add a preposition. Draw an arrow from the prepositional phrase to the word it describes.)
3. __________ the fragile nature of papyrus, many ancient writings have not survived. (Begin with a preposition of more than one word.)
4. Ptolemy I made the Alexandrian Library the greatest in the ancient world. Ptolemy II made the Alexandrian Library the greatest in the ancient world. (Use a conjunction to form one sentence with a compound subject.)
5. It is amazing that not a trace of such a great library has ever been found. (Add an interjection.)
6. In 1859 British archaeologists found thousands of clay tablets. Scholars have not been able to understand the writing on them. (Use a conjunction to form a compound sentence.)
7. To __________, the cuneiform script on the tablets has been an unbreakable code. (Add an object pronoun to replace the words *the archaeologists*.)
8. Monks in monasteries copied religious works such as the Bible. They preserved the works of ancient scholars. (Use a conjunction to write one sentence with a compound predicate.)
9. Paper made books easier to produce. Movable type made books easier to produce. (Use a pair of correlative conjunctions to write one sentence with a compound subject.)
10. __________ the invention of the printing press, it took many hours of hand-copying to produce a Bible. (Add a preposition.)

UNIT 14 Review

Answers: Exercise 10

Mixed Review

Answers will vary, but some suggestions are given below.

1. on—adverb
2. from the fibers—made
3. Because of
4. Ptolemy I and II made …
5. Wow!
6. … tablets, but scholars …
7. them
8. … Bible and preserved …
9. Both paper and movable type …
10. Before

CLOSE

Ask students how they like to spend a carefree summer's day. Do they like to read voraciously, like Eudora Welty? Or do they like to lie in the sun and do nothing? After the discussion, ask students to write sentences based on their responses. Each sentence should contain one or more of the following: a prepositional phrase (*We meet our friends at the pool.*), a conjunction (*We blow bubbles, and our dog chases them.*), or an interjection (*Gee! I wish it were summer right now!*).

Prepositions and Conjunctions in Writing

Have students read the passage silently to themselves. Then go back and discuss the italicized words. Discuss these choices in relation to the Techniques with Prepositions and Conjunctions section.

Techniques with Prepositions and Conjunctions

Discuss the examples of the use of prepositional phrases and conjunctions. Encourage students to find additional examples in books or stories, or they can examine a current writing project of their own to find places to apply the techniques.

Practice

The answers to this challenging and enriching activity will vary. Refer to Techniques with Prepositions and Conjunctions as you evaluate student choices.

Writing Application

Prepositions and Conjunctions in Writing Freeman Hubbard uses prepositions and conjunctions in this passage from *The Great Days of the Circus* to help him convey the excitement of the circus's arrival. Examine the passage, focusing especially on the italicized words.

> The street was alive *with noise* as the first four lovely ladies on horseback, trumpets lifted to their lips, came into sight. They were always lithe and lovely, *and* the plumes they wore danced as their horses pranced. Then came the band, *in red uniforms with gold braid*, riding *on a gilded band wagon* that was sometimes drawn by as many as forty horses. The band never stopped playing: the big bass drum thumped steadily, the trumpets *shrilled and blared*, the cymbals flashed *in the sun*. Behind the band came great floats.

Techniques with Prepositions and Conjunctions Try to apply some of Hubbard's writing techniques when you write and revise your own work.

1. Use prepositional phrases as adjectives and adverbs to add specific details to your writing.

Without Prepositional Phrases Then came the band.
Hubbard's Version Then came the band, in red uniforms with gold braid, riding on a gilded band wagon.

2. To vary your writing, use conjunctions to form compound subjects, predicates, and sentences.

Without Conjunctions The trumpets shrilled. The trumpets blared.
Hubbard's Version The trumpets shrilled and blared.

Practice Practice these techniques by revising the following passage on your own paper. Use prepositional phrases to add details and conjunctions to vary your sentences.

> Marty and Josh had some free time. They decided to go to the library. It was a favorite place. The reading corner was surrounded by shelves. There were chairs and a couch. Marty chose a best-seller. Josh picked out a magazine. They settled down for a good read. They had an hour before Josh's mother was to pick them up. The room was quiet. The light was soft. No one disturbed them. It was so restful that both boys forgot the time.

Teacher's Classroom Resources

The following resources can be used for assessment or evaluation.

Unit Assessment

Tests with Answer Key
Unit 14 Mastery Test, pp. 55–56

Test Generator
Unit 14 Mastery Test

You may wish to administer the Unit 14 Mastery Test at this point.

UNIT
15 Subject-Verb Agreement

Grammar

Lessons

UNIT GOALS

The goal of Unit 15 is to help students, through example and instruction, to develop an understanding of and an ability to use correct subject-verb agreement, to locate the subject, and to identify singular and plural verbs.

Unit Assessment

Tests with Answer Key
Unit 15 Pretest, pp. 57–58
Unit 15 Mastery Test, pp. 59–60

Test Generator
Unit 15 Pretest
Unit 15 Mastery Test

You may wish to administer the Unit 15 Pretest at this point.

Key to Ability Levels

Enabling Strategies have been coded for varying learning styles and abilities.

L1 Level 1 activities are within the ability range of Learning Disabled students.

L2 Level 2 activities are basic-to-average activities and are within the ability range of average students.

L3 Level 3 activities are challenging activities and are within the ability range of above-average students.

LEP LEP activities are within the ability range of Limited English Proficiency students.

UNIT 15

Lesson 15.1

Setting the Purpose

Lesson 15.1 teaches students to identify subjects and verbs and to use subject-verb agreement in their writing.

FOCUS

Lesson Overview

Objective: To identify subjects and verbs and to recognize the need for agreement between subject and verb

Bellringer

When students enter the classroom, have this assignment on the board: *Choose the correct verbs in the following sentences:*

Many tourists (visits, visit) Acadia National Park each year.

Acadia (features, feature) a rocky coastline.

Motivating Activity

Discuss the verbs that students chose in the Bellringer sentences. Ask them how the two verbs are different. Do they notice that one verb ends in *-s* and the other does not? Can they explain why?

TEACH

Teaching Tip

The following helping verbs do not change to show subject-verb agreement: *can, may, must, will,* and *shall.* Ask students to explain why the word *cans* in the following sentence is or is not an exception to this rule: *Every summer she cans tomatoes.*

Cross-reference: Grammar

For instruction and practice in using singular and plural subject pronouns, refer students to Lesson 11.1, pp. 326–327.

15.1 Making Subjects and Verbs Agree

A subject and its verb are the basic parts of a sentence. The subject and its verb must *agree in number.* A singular noun subject takes a singular form of the verb. A plural noun subject takes a plural form of the verb. In the present tense, the singular form of the verb usually ends in *-s* or *-es.*

Read the sentences in the chart below. You can see that the subjects and verbs agree in number.

Subject Noun and Verb Agreement

Singular	Plural
A **mountain rises** sharply to the sky. A **naturalist teaches** us about nature.	**Mountains rise** sharply to the sky. **Naturalists teach** us about nature.

Verbs and subject pronouns must also agree in number. In the present tense, the *-s* ending is used with the subject pronouns *it, he,* and *she.*

Subject Pronoun and Verb Agreement

Singular	Plural
He, she, or it **travels.** You **travel.** I **travel.**	We **travel.** You **travel.** They **travel.**

The irregular verbs *be, do,* and *have* can be main verbs or helping verbs. They must agree with the subject, regardless of whether they are main verbs or helping verbs.

I **am** fine. He **is** ready. [main verb]
They **are** questioning a ranger. [helping verb]

She **does** well. [main verb]
She **does** work hard. They **do** sing. [helping verb]

He **has** a boat. [main verb]
He **has** visited Utah. They **have** eaten. [helping verb]

Teacher's Classroom Resources

The following resources can be used for planning, instruction, practice, reinforcement, assessment, reteaching, enrichment, or evaluation.

Teaching Tools
Lesson Plans

Blackline Masters
Grammar Practice, p. 33
Grammar Reteaching, p. 34
Grammar Enrichment, p. 33

Grammar Workbook
Lesson 48

Unit Assessment

Tests with Answer Key
Unit 15 Pretest, pp. 57–58

Test Generator
Unit 15 Pretest

You may wish to administer the Unit 15 Pretest at this point.

Exercise 1 Using Subject and Verb Agreement

For each sentence write the correct form of the verb in parentheses.

1. Acadia National Park (lies, lie) along Maine's coast.
2. Several islands (is, are) in the park.
3. Acadia (features, feature) a rocky coastline.
4. Mount Desert Island (is, are) very beautiful.
5. Many people (travels, travel) to Acadia every year.
6. They (photographs, photograph) the wildlife.
7. Mammoth Cave (is, are) in Kentucky.
8. The passageways (winds, wind) for nearly two hundred miles.
9. An underground river (flows, flow) through the caves.
10. Tour guides (leads, lead) people through the chambers.
11. Many visitors (enjoys, enjoy) the sense of adventure.
12. For example, my mother (does, do).
13. Yellowstone National Park (has, have) some of the few existing grizzly bears.
14. Campers (does, do) enjoy the wilderness.
15. Large bears sometimes (approaches, approach).
16. Park visitors (does, do) require protection.
17. A camper (carries, carry) bedding and supplies.
18. Yellowstone (has, have) a beautiful waterfall.
19. Our national parks (contains, contain) natural wonders.
20. Wind Cave (has, have) unusual crystals.
21. Tiny white crystals (lines, line) the cave walls and ceiling.
22. Ancient animal fossils (lies, lie) in the Agate Fossil Beds.
23. The park (includes, include) the remains of two-horned rhinoceroses.
24. Unusual rock formations (fills, fill) Death Valley.
25. The National Park Service (protects, protect) Death Valley and other national monuments.

Exercise 2 Writing Sentences with Subject and Verb Agreement

Write ten original sentences. Use singular subjects in some sentences and plural subjects in others. Be sure each verb agrees with its subject. In each sentence, underline the subject once and the verb twice. Write whether the subject is *singular* or *plural*.

SAMPLE ANSWER: My friends are packing for a camping trip. (plural)

PRACTICE AND ASSESS

Answers: Exercise 1

1. lies
2. are
3. features
4. is
5. travel
6. photograph
7. is
8. wind
9. flows
10. lead
11. enjoy
12. does
13. has
14. do
15. approach
16. do
17. carries
18. has
19. contain
20. has
21. line
22. lie
23. includes
24. fill
25. protects

Answers: Exercise 2

Answers will vary, but some suggestions are given below.

My brothers love to go camping. (plural)

Ana often comes with us. (singular)

Independent Practice

Skills Practice

Grammar Practice, p. 33
Grammar Reteaching, p. 34
Grammar Enrichment, p. 33

Grammar Workbook, Lesson 48

CLOSE

Discuss the sentences students wrote for Exercise 2.

Enabling Strategies

LEP Learning About Agreement

Students whose first language is non-European often have great difficulty with subject-verb agreement in English. They cannot see what meaning subject-verb agreement adds to the sentence (as opposed, for example, to a past tense ending, which changes the time of the action, or a plural ending on a noun, which changes its number). You might point out to these students that English speakers often have a similar problem with adjective-noun gender agreement in other languages.

UNIT 15
Lesson 15.2

Setting the Purpose

Lesson 15.2 teaches students how to locate the subject when it is separated from the verb by a prepositional phrase or when a sentence begins with *here* or *there*.

FOCUS

Lesson Overview

Objective: To make the subject and the verb in a sentence agree when the subject is separated from the verb by a prepositional phrase or when the sentence begins with *here* or *there*

Bellringer

When students enter the classroom, have this assignment on the board: *Write these sentences. Then underline the subject and circle the verb in each.*

Here is a wilderness.
There are people in the city who are lonelier than I.

—Jean Craighead George, *My Side of the Mountain*

Motivating Activity

Ask students to rearrange each sentence from the Bellringer activity, placing the subject and verb in their more typical positions, with the subject first.

TEACH

Grammar Tip

By deleting a prepositional phrase that comes between the subject and the verb, students can more easily check for subject-verb agreement.

15.2 Problems with Locating the Subject

You know how to make a subject and a verb agree when the verb directly follows the subject. However, sometimes a prepositional phrase comes between the subject and the verb. When that happens, make sure that the verb agrees with the subject of the sentence and not with the object of the preposition.

A **park** in the islands **contains** a volcano.
The **parks** of Hawaii **contain** volcanoes.

In the first sentence, *in the islands* is a prepositional phrase. The singular verb *contains* agrees with the subject of the sentence, *park,* not with the plural noun *islands,* which is the object of the preposition.

In the second sentence, *of Hawaii* is a prepositional phrase. The plural verb *contain* agrees with the plural subject *parks,* not with the singular noun *Hawaii,* which is the object of the preposition.

Some sentences begin with *here* or *there. Here* or *there* is never the subject of a sentence. Look for the subject after the verb in this type of sentence.

There **is** a **park** on Maui.
Here in the park **are** tropical **forests**.

To make it easier to find the subject, try rearranging these sentences and placing the subject and verb in their usual positions. This rearrangement makes clear how the subject and the verb agree in number.

A **park is** there on Maui.
Tropical **forests are** here in the park.

Teacher's Classroom Resources

The following resources can be used for planning, instruction, practice, reinforcement, reteaching, or enrichment.

Teaching Tools
Lesson Plans

Blackline Masters
Grammar Practice, p. 34
Grammar Reteaching, p. 35
Grammar Enrichment, p. 34

Grammar Workbook
Lesson 50

Exercise 3 **Choosing the Correct Verb Form**

For each sentence write the correct form of the verb in parentheses.

1. The island of Oahu (has, have) a mild climate.
2. Islands of volcanic origin (rises, rise) in the Pacific.
3. Travelers to Haleakala (sees, see) a huge crater.
4. A hike along the cliffs (is, are) exciting.
5. There (is, are) lush, green trees everywhere.
6. Our trip to the islands (delights, delight) us.
7. A busload of tourists (arrives, arrive) in the park.
8. Parts of Kauai (has, have) served as movie locations.
9. The rain forests of Hawaii (needs, need) protection.
10. There (is, are) many visitors to the Hawaii Volcanoes National Park.

Exercise 4 **Making Subjects and Verbs Agree**

Write each sentence. Underline the subject once and its verb twice. If they agree, write *correct.* If they do not agree, correct the verb.

1. Protection of rare plants are vital.
2. Our system of parks include forests.
3. The islands of Hawaii contain two national parks.
4. A student of volcanoes prepare an exhibit.
5. Studies of plant life occurs in the parks.
6. Protectors of the environment works there.
7. There are many opportunities for research.
8. Here is a list of the national parks.
9. Our system of national parks have protected natural wonders.
10. The oldest park in the system is Yellowstone.
11. The National Park Service oversees our parks and monuments.
12. There are many activities throughout the park system.
13. Tour guides from the service describes points of interest to guests.
14. Visitors to the Appalachian National Scenic Trail hike from Maine to Georgia.
15. There is rafting adventures at the Delaware Scenic River Park.

Exercise 5 **Using Subject-Verb Agreement in Sentences**

Write five original sentences. Begin each sentence with *Here is*, *Here are*, *There is*, or *There are*. Underline the subject of each sentence.

PRACTICE AND ASSESS

Answers: Exercise 3

1. has	6. delights
2. rise	7. arrives
3. see	8. have
4. is	9. need
5. are	10. are

Answers: Exercise 4

1. Protection—subj.; is—verb
2. system—subj.; includes—verb
3. islands—subj.; contain—verb; correct
4. student—subj.; prepares—verb
5. Studies—subj.; occur—verb
6. Protectors—subj.; work—verb
7. opportunities—subj.; are—verb; correct
8. list—subj.; is—verb; correct
9. system—subj.; has protected—verb
10. park—subj.; is—verb; correct
11. National Park Service—subj.; oversees—verb; correct
12. activities—subj.; are—verb; correct
13. guides—subj.; describe—verb
14. Visitors—subj; hike—verb; correct
15. adventures—subj.; are—verb

Answers: Exercise 5

Answers will vary, but some suggestions are given below.

1. Here is my <u>house</u>.
2. Here are my <u>sisters</u>.
3. There are two <u>cats</u> in the yard.
4. There is a <u>bowl</u> of apples.
5. Here are my <u>books</u>.

Independent Practice

Skills Practice

- *Grammar Practice*, p. 34
- *Grammar Reteaching*, p. 35
- *Grammar Enrichment*, p. 34
- ***Grammar Workbook,*** Lesson 50

CLOSE

Have students work in small groups to discuss complicated sentences. Give students several complicated sentences, and have them identify and discard phrases that interrupt the subject and verb.

Enabling Strategies

LEP Recognizing Prepositions

Students acquiring English may have difficulty recognizing prepositional phrases, which may make it difficult to locate the subject of a sentence. Write the following list of prepositions on the board: *of, for, to, in, by, with.* Explain that these words often begin a prepositional phrase and that a prepositional phrase sometimes comes between a subject and a verb. Remind students that the noun in a prepositional phrase is never the subject of a sentence.

Setting the Purpose

Lesson 15.3 teaches students how to determine whether a compound subject takes a singular or a plural verb.

FOCUS

Lesson Overview

Objective: To recognize compound subjects and to use verbs that agree in number with compound subjects

Bellringer

When students enter the classroom, have this assignment on the board: *Write these sentences and underline the compound subject in each:*

1. *Tony and the dogs are out for a walk.*
2. *Neither Harry nor the twins eat cereal.*
3. *Dirt and rocks cover the road.*

Motivating Activity

Write the following sentence on the board: *Neither my parents nor my brother cook dinner.* Ask students whether they can figure out what is wrong with it.

TEACH

Teaching Tip

Many students see the parts of a compound subject as separate units. In a sentence such as *The salt and pepper are gone,* students may want to use a singular verb. Remind students that compound subjects connected by *and* are treated as plural.

15.3 Agreement with Compound Subjects

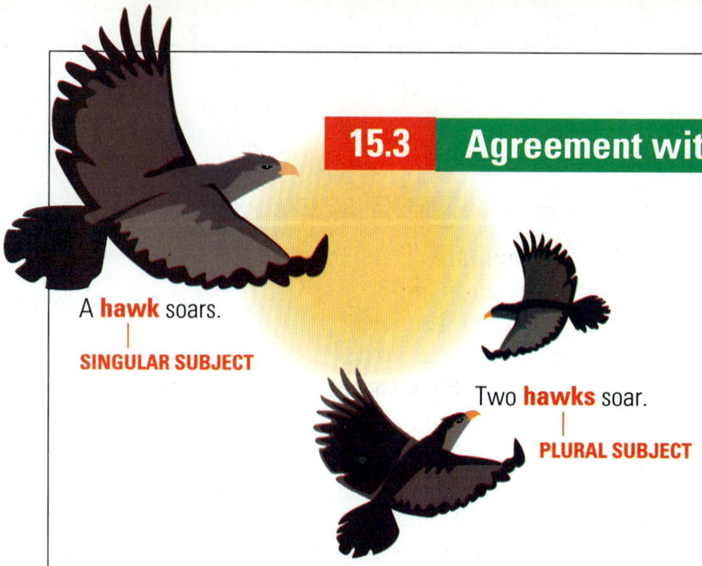

A subject and its verb must agree in number. A singular noun subject takes a singular form of the verb. A plural noun subject takes a plural form of the verb. In the present tense the singular form of the verb usually ends in *-s* or *-es.*

A **compound subject** contains two or more subjects that have the same verb. You can tell whether the compound subject takes a singular or a plural verb form by looking at the way the subjects are joined. When two or more subjects are joined by *and* or by *both . . . and*, the verb is plural.

Both a grizzly bear **and** a bobcat **live** near here.

This sentence refers to more than one thing, so the form of the verb is plural. When two or more subjects are joined by *or, nor,* or *either . . . or* or *neither . . . nor,* the verb must agree in number with the subject that is closest to it.

An eagle **or** a hawk **soars** in the sky.
Either the loon **or** its chicks **swim** nearby.
Neither the bears **nor** the bobcat **crosses** our path.

In the first sentence the verb *soars* agrees in number with *hawk,* which is the subject closer to it. The verb is singular in form because *hawk* is a singular subject. In the second sentence the verb *swim* agrees with *chicks,* which is the closer subject. The verb is plural in form because *chicks* is a plural subject. In the third sentence the verb *crosses* agrees with *bobcat,* which is the closer subject. The verb is singular in form because *bobcat* is a singular subject.

Teacher's Classroom Resources

The following resources can be used for planning, instruction, practice, reinforcement, reteaching, or enrichment.

Teaching Tools
Lesson Plans

Blackline Masters
Grammar Practice, p. 35
Grammar Reteaching, p. 36
Grammar Enrichment, p. 35

Grammar Workbook
Lesson 51

Exercise 6 Identifying the Correct Verb Form

For each sentence, write the correct form of the verb in parentheses.

1. A deer and a heron (wades, wade) in the lake.
2. Both a coyote and an antelope (outruns, outrun) a bear.
3. Neither hunting nor mining (is, are) allowed in protected areas.
4. An alligator and an egret (hunts, hunt) for food in the swamp.
5. Both Bryce Canyon Park and Yellowstone Park (has, have) wonderful hiking trails.
6. Birds and insect life (thrives, thrive) in the swamp.
7. Either experienced campers or the ranger (leads, lead) the evening talks.
8. Neither heat nor mosquitoes (disturbs, disturb) us.
9. Dams and pollution (is, are) destroying the swamp.
10. Newspapers and television (reports, report) on this problem.

Exercise 7 Making Verbs Agree with Compound Sentences

Write each sentence, correcting the verb if necessary. Underline the subject once and its verb twice. Remember to underline the complete compound subjects.

1. Either the factories or the swamp are in danger.
2. Both bears and frogs hibernate in winter.
3. Neither alligators nor crocodiles likes the cold.
4. The blue heron and the egret lives in the Everglades.
5. Our national seashores and parks are a great resource.
6. The grizzly bear and the polar bear is carnivorous.
7. Both Florida and Hawaii have underwater parks.
8. There is breeding sea lions and nesting birds at Channel Islands National Park in California.
9. A rare orchid or brilliantly colored birds attracts many photographers.
10. Wolves and a large moose herd roams the Isle Royale National Park.

Exercise 8 Using Compound Subjects in Sentences

Write five original sentences with compound subjects. Join the subjects in each sentence by using the word or words indicated.

1. and
2. or
3. both . . . and
4. either . . . or
5. neither . . . nor

Enabling Strategies

LEP Understanding Compounds

Students acquiring English may need extra practice in determining whether a subject takes a singular or plural verb. First, explain that a compound subject has more than one subject in it. Review with students the rules for using verbs with compound subjects, and give a few examples. Then show students a variety of pictures, each showing more than one person or thing. Have students work in pairs to write sentences about the pictures that contain compound subjects.

PRACTICE AND ASSESS

Answers: Exercise 6

1. wade
2. outrun
3. is
4. hunt
5. have
6. thrive
7. leads
8. disturb
9. are
10. report

Answers: Exercise 7

1. Either the factories or the swamp is in danger.
2. Both bears and frogs hibernate in winter.
3. Neither alligators nor crocodiles like the cold.
4. The blue heron and the egret live in the Everglades.
5. Our national seashores and parks are a great resource.
6. The grizzly bear and the polar bear are carnivorous.
7. Both Florida and Hawaii have underwater parks.
8. There are breeding sea lions and nesting birds at Channel Islands National Park in California.
9. A rare orchid or brilliantly colored birds attract many photographers.
10. Wolves and a large moose herd roam the Isle Royale National Park.

Answers: Exercise 8

Answers will vary, but some suggestions are given below.

1. Mary and Eva live here.
2. Cats or a dog sleeps in this bed.
3. Both you and I love ice cream.
4. Either Jodi or Leo is singing.
5. Neither a new bike nor a million dollars tempt me.

CLOSE

Have students write a short paragraph about their families, including pets. Ask students to include at least three sentences that have compound subjects.

TEACH

About the Literature

Explain that the review contains a passage from Eden Force's biography of John Muir followed by exercises on related topics. The passage describes some of the natural wonders of Yosemite Valley. Thanks in large part to Muir's efforts, the valley appears today much as it did when the conservationist first explored the area in 1868. Encourage students to read through the Literature Model for information and enjoyment, reminding them that regular reading is the best way to develop a feeling for standard usage. After students read the passage, discuss examples it contains of subject-verb agreement.

Linking Grammar and Literature

☑ Teaching Tip

Have students reread the passage and look for any phrases that separate subjects and verbs.

Speaking and Listening

Have students take turns reading aloud sentences from the passage. After each sentence, the students who are listening can write down the subject and the verb, and note whether each is singular or plural.

UNIT 15 Unit Review

Grammar Review

Subject-Verb Agreement

John Muir by Eden Force is a biography of the naturalist and explorer whose efforts influenced Congress to pass the Yosemite National Park Bill in 1890. The bill established both Yosemite and Sequoia national parks. Both of these parks are justly famous for their variety of breathtaking natural wonders. In the following excerpt from the book, the writer describes the beautiful scenery of Yosemite Valley, which Muir explored for six years. The passage has been annotated to show some examples of subject-verb agreement covered in this unit.

Literature Model

from JOHN MUIR

by Eden Force

Yosemite Valley includes some of the world's most awe-inspiring natural wonders. El Capitan, a block of stone more than 600 times Muir's height, faces Bridalveil Fall. Bridalveil tumbles 620 feet from high rocks into the valley. Farther up the Merced River is Yosemite Falls, rushing down in two sections to Yosemite Valley. North of the river is North Dome, a dome-shaped peak about as high as El Capitan. It towers above the landscape. South of North Dome and east of Tenaga Creek stands a strange peak even taller than North Dome. It is Half Dome. As the name suggests, Half Dome looks like a dome that a giant has sliced down the middle from top to bottom. Only one half of the rock dome remains.

Agreement between a singular noun subject and a singular verb

Agreement between a singular pronoun subject and a singular verb

Agreement between a singular subject and verb that have a prepositional phrase between them

Teacher's Classroom Resources

The following resources can be used for planning, instruction, practice, reinforcement, assessment, reteaching, or evaluation.

Teaching Tools
Lesson Plans

Grammar Workbook
Lessons 48–51
Unit 8 Review
Cumulative Review: Units 1–8

Unit Assessment
Tests with Answer Key
Unit 15 Mastery Test, pp. 59–60

Test Generator
Unit 15 Mastery Test

Exercise 1

Making Subjects and Verbs Agree Write the correct form of the verb in parentheses.

SAMPLE Merced River (forms, form) a white ribbon through the valley.
ANSWER forms

1. Sometimes a family of bears (stops, stop) to swim and play in the river.
2. El Capitan (rises, rise) high above Yosemite Valley.
3. In shape it (resembles, resemble) a boot.
4. Yosemite's natural wonders (is, are) awe-inspiring. P
5. They (attracts, attract) thousands of visitors. P
6. The visitors (hike, hikes) 700 miles of trails. P
7. The most spectacular scenery (is, are) in Yosemite Valley. S
8. The peaks of California's Sierra Nevada (is, are) millions of years old. P
9. Deep gorges (creates, create) beautiful views. P
10. The National Park Service (has, have) begun a public transportation system to reduce traffic in the park. S

3pts

Exercise 2

Making Subjects and Verbs Agree Write each sentence, correcting the verb if necessary. Write whether the subject is *singular* or *plural*.

1. Yosemite National Park lies in the mountains 200 miles east of San Francisco.
2. Giant sequoias graces three groves in the park.
3. The Grizzly Giant Tree measure thirty-four feet in diameter, more than most roads.
4. This huge tree stands in the famous Mariposa Grove.
5. The sequoias are some of the oldest living things on earth.
6. The wood of the sequoias resists fire.
7. Sequoia National Park feature some giant trees with the names of Civil War generals.
8. Redwoods are related to giant sequoias.
9. The redwood grow even taller than the giant sequoia.
10. These enormous trees grows from tiny seeds.

4 pts

UNIT 15 Review

PRACTICE AND ASSESS

Answers: Exercise 1

1. stops
2. rises
3. resembles
4. are
5. attract
6. hike
7. is
8. are
9. create
10. has

Answers: Exercise 2

1. correct, singular
2. grace, plural
3. measures, singular
4. correct, singular
5. correct, plural
6. correct, singular
7. features, singular
8. correct, plural
9. grows, singular
10. grow, plural

Exercise 1 example 1. family S stops
2. El Capitan S rises
3. it S resembles

Exercise 2 1. Yosemite National Park S lies correct
2. sequoias P graces grace
3. Grizzly Giant Tree S measure measures

UNIT 15 Review

Answers: Exercise 3

1. Sierra Club owes
2. campaign continues
3. forest is
4. forest honors
5. glacier bears
6. *The Yosemite* is
7. Copies are
8. Muir describes
9. governor declares
10. Admirers celebrate

Answers: Exercise 4

1. Merced River, correct
2. terrain, is
3. landscapes, are
4. effects, correct
5. book, correct

3pts each

Exercise 3

Identifying Subjects and Making Verbs Agree Write the correct form of the verb in parentheses.

SAMPLE There (is, are) books written by John Muir.
ANSWER are

1. The Sierra Club, with branches throughout the United States, (owes, owe) its existence to Muir. S
2. Muir's campaign for preserving forests (continues, continue) to inspire environmentalists. S
3. In California there (is, are) a redwood forest called Muir Woods. S
4. The forest near San Francisco (honors, honor) the achievements of John Muir. S
5. A glacier in Alaska also (bears, bear) his name. S
6. *The Yosemite* by John Muir (is, are) a classic. S
7. Copies (is, are) available at my local library. P
8. Muir, in his journals, (describes, describe) the natural wonders of Yosemite. S
9. The governor of California (declares, declare) each April 21 "John Muir Day." S
10. Admirers of Muir and his causes (celebrates, celebrate) at the John Muir National Historic Site. P

4pts each

Exercise 4

Locating Subjects and Making Verbs Agree Locate and write the subject of each sentence. If the verb in the sentence is correct, write *correct*. If the verb is not correct, rewrite the sentence, correcting the verb.

1. There is the Merced River in Yosemite Valley. S
2. There are rough terrain in some Yosemite wilderness areas. S
3. There is lovely landscapes in the valley. P
4. Here in Yosemite Valley are effects of volcanoes and glaciers. P
5. There is a book about Muir's glacial theory. S

Examples Ex. 3 1. Sierra Club S owes
2. campaign S continues
3. forest S is

Ex 4. 1. Merced River S is correct
2. terrain S are is

Exercise 5

Making Verbs Agree with Compound Subjects For each sentence, write the correct form of the verb in parentheses.

1. Both Glacier Point and Taft Point (provides, provide) a great view. P
2. Neither Half Dome nor El Capitan (is, are) the highest point in the valley. S
3. Both Vernal Falls and Nevada Falls (pours, pour) over giant rocks formed by glaciers. P
4. Neither cold weather nor drenching rains (discourages, discourage) backpackers. P
5. Bears or other animals sometimes (steals, steal) the backpackers' food. P
6. A student and a backpacker (walks, walk) toward the glacier. P
7. A van and a camper (waits, wait) at the entrance to the park. P
8. Snow or ice (lies, lie) in many of the ravines of the Sierra Nevada. S
9. Both a robin and a yellow warbler (sings, sing) near the campsite. P
10. Either a dome or spires (crowns, crown) the granite mountains forming the valley. P

3 pts each

Exercise 6

Writing the Correct Verb Form for Compound Sentences For each sentence, write the correct present-tense form of the verb in parentheses. Make sure your verb agrees with the subject of the sentence.

SAMPLE Parks and other areas (be) part of the National Park System.
ANSWER are

1. A noteworthy landscape or a historic site (form) the basis of most national parks. S
2. Both Indiana and Wisconsin (boast) national lakeshores. P
3. The Blue Ridge and the Natchez Trace (be) national parkways. P
4. National battlefields and a national scenic trail (be) part of the National Park System. P
5. Air and water pollution and overcrowding (pose) threats to the most popular parks. P

3 pts each

UNIT 15 Review

Answers: Exercise 5

1. provide
2. is
3. pour
4. discourage
5. steal
6. walk
7. wait
8. lies
9. sing
10. crown

Answers: Exercise 6

1. forms
2. boast
3. are
4. are
5. pose

Ex. 5 1. and P provide
2. El Capitan S is
3. and P pour

Ex 6. 1. site S forms
2. and P boast

UNIT 15 Review

Answers: Exercise 7

1. Geysers attract
2. We photograph
3. Yellowstone is
4. Pools bubble
5. Steam changes
6. Yellowstone Lake is
7. forests cover
8. feeding defies
9. regulations are
10. variety surprises
11. Memorials exist
12. Some become
13. junction forms
14. Potomac River meets
15. park is
16. Students visit
17. They learn
18. museum records
19. actions become
20. John Brown is

Exercise 7

Choosing Verbs Write the subject of each sentence and the correct present tense of the verb in parentheses.

1. Geysers (attract) visitors to Yellowstone National Park.
2. We (photograph) the geysers and hot springs at the park.
3. Yellowstone, in the northwest corner of Wyoming, (be) the oldest national park in the United States.
4. Pools of hot mud (bubble) in the Lower Geyser Basin section of the park.
5. Steam (change) the hard surrounding rock into soft clay.
6. Yellowstone Lake, with geysers and hot springs along its shores, (be) the largest high-altitude lake in North America.
7. Evergreen forests of firs, spruce, and pine (cover) much of the park.
8. The feeding of bears within the park's boundaries (defy) park regulations.
9. Park regulations about fishing in the lakes and rivers (be) also strict.
10. The variety of landscapes in the region (surprise) new visitors to the park.
11. Memorials to past events (exist) in every state.
12. Some of these memorials (become) national historical parks.
13. The junction of two rivers (form) one such park.
14. The Potomac River (meet) the Shenandoah River at Harpers Ferry, West Virginia.
15. The park by the rivers (be) Harpers Ferry National Historical Park.
16. Students of the Civil War (visit) this park.
17. They (learn) about John Brown's attack on the arsenal at Harpers Ferry in 1859.
18. A museum at the park (record) how John Brown worked for the end of slavery.
19. John Brown's actions at his trial for treason (become) an inspiration to some writers.
20. John Brown (be) the subject of an epic poem by Stephen Vincent Benét.

Exercise 8

Making Verbs Agree For each sentence, write the correct present-tense form of the verb in parentheses.

1. Acts of Congress (designate) areas as part of the National Park System.
2. Unique natural landscapes or historic sites (form) the basis of the majority of national parks.
3. The Edgar Allan Poe National Historic Site and the Georgia O'Keeffe National Historic Site (honor) famous Americans.
4. Prehistoric dwellings (be) preserved at a number of different sites.
5. Some people (be) surprised to learn that the White House is part of the National Park System.
6. The largest of the national parks (be) the Wrangell-St. Elias system in Alaska.
7. National parks (range) in area from 8 million acres to about 6 thousand acres.
8. The John F. Kennedy birthplace and some other national historic sites (occupy) less than an acre.
9. National battlefield parks and national battlefield sites (include) Civil War and Revolutionary War sites.
10. There (be) other areas primarily for recreational use.
11. There (be) national parklands along rivers in eleven states.
12. The Alganak Wild River Park and New River Gorge Park (have) exciting stretches of white water.
13. There (exist) national recreation areas in states across the country from New York to California.
14. Alaska or Texas (contain) most of the national preserves.
15. Blue Ridge and Natchez Trace (be) the only national parkways.
16. The John D. Rockefeller, Jr., Memorial Parkway (connect) two beautiful national parks, Yellowstone and Grand Teton.
17. The Appalachian National Scenic Trail (extend) for 2,000 miles from Maine to Georgia.
18. The Glen Canyon Dam and the Hoover Dam (create) the largest national recreation areas.
19. Sand dunes in both Colorado and Indiana (form) part of the National Park System.
20. Arizona (have) many national monuments and two national parks.

Answers: Exercise 8

1. designate
2. form
3. honor
4. are
5. are
6. is
7. range
8. occupy
9. include
10. are
11. are
12. have
13. exist
14. contains
15. are
16. connects
17. extends
18. create
19. form
20. has

Answers: Exercise 9

Proofreading

This proofreading activity provides editing practice with (1) the current or previous units' skills, (2) the **Troubleshooter** errors, and (3) spelling errors. Students should be able to complete the exercise by referring to the units, the **Troubleshooter**, and a dictionary.

	Error (Type of Error)
1.	• was (subject-verb agreement)
	• admired (spelling)
2.	• American (proper noun)
3.	• capture (subject-verb agreement)
4.	• shows (subject-verb agreement)
5.	• appear (subject-verb agreement)
6.	• bathes (subject-verb agreement)
7.	• tan, (commas in a series)
8.	• pause (subject-verb agreement)
	• nature's (singular possessive)

Exercise 9 **Proofreading**

Proofreading The following passage is about artist Thomas Moran, whose work appears below. Rewrite the passage, correcting the errors in spelling, capitalization, grammar, and usage. Add any missing punctuation. There are 10 errors.

Thomas Moran

[1]When he were an art student, Thomas Moran (1837–1926) admirred European landscape painters. [2]However, Moran wanted to "paint as an american." [3]His paintings, such as *Cliffs of the Upper Colorado River, Wyoming Territory,* captures the beauty of the American West. ➡

Thomas Moran, *Cliffs of the Upper Colorado River, Wyoming Territory*, 1882

About the Art

Thomas Moran, *Cliffs of the Upper Colorado River, Wyoming Territory*, 1882

In his life Moran returned often to the American West. He conveyed the scenery of the western landscape through paintings like this 16-by-24-inch oil-on-canvas.

[4]The painting at the bottom of page 416 show a scene in the West. [5]Two seperate rocks appears in the distance. [6]The sun bathe the rocks in light and shadow. [7]Tones of rust, brown, tan orange, and sand are used by the artist. The riders and horses pauses near the river to view natures majesty.

Exercise 10 **Mixed Review**

Mixed Review Rewrite each sentence, correcting the verb if necessary. Write whether the subject is *singular*, *plural*, or *compound*.

1. The sculptures and paintings of Frederic Remington records the changing West of the 1800s.
2. Action and drama characterizes the best of Remington's art.
3. Other recorders of the land and life of the Old West includes Albert Bierstadt, Charles M. Russell, and George Catlin.
4. Russell's experience as a cowboy and trapper show in his detailed artwork.
5. George Catlin's paintings records the life of Native Americans along the Missouri River and the Western Plains.
6. Catlin's portrait of a Blackfeet chief hangs in The Smithsonian Institution.
7. Albert Bierstadt is one of the great American Romantic landscape painters.
8. Drama and grandeur sometimes overtakes realism in his huge canvases.
9. Both Bierstadt and Thomas Moran has large paintings on display in the U.S. Capitol.
10. George Caleb Bingham are remembered for his scenes of frontier life.
11. The Metropolitan Museum of Art and the National Gallery house his colorful work.
12. Events from the Wild West springs to life through these works.
13. What forms of art depict today's events?
14. A great twentieth-century photographer of the American West is Ansel Adams.
15. The granite domes of Yosemite are the subjects of many of Adams's photos.

UNIT 15 Review

Answers: Exercise 10

Mixed Review

1. record, compound
2. characterize, compound
3. include, plural
4. shows, singular
5. record, plural
6. correct, singluar
7. correct, singular
8. overtake, compound
9. have, compound
10. is remembered, singluar
11. correct, compound
12. spring, plural
13. correct, plural
14. correct, singular
15. correct, plural

CLOSE

Suggest that students write a paragraph describing an ideal park. Have them check their writing for subject-verb agreement.

Subject-Verb Agreement in Writing

Ask students to read the passage from "Bathing Elephants." Ask them to point out examples of singular subjects, plural subjects, compound subjects, and subjects in sentences that begin with *here* or *there*. Have students name the verb for each of these subjects. Encourage them to discuss anything in the passage that they find confusing, such as why a particular subject takes a singular or plural verb.

Techniques with Subjects and Their Verbs

Remind students that using a variety of types of subjects helps make writing clearer and more interesting. Discuss the examples from "Bathing Elephants," and then have students look back to page 417 at the last paragraph from the proofreading passage. Have students find the subject and verb in each sentence and determine whether the subject is singular, plural, or compound.

Practice

The answers to this challenging and enriching activity will vary according to how much rewriting students do. Refer to Techniques with Subjects and Their Verbs as you evaluate students' choices. They should at least correct the verbs in sentences 1, 3, and 5, which should be *are, is,* and *rises,* respectively.

Writing Application

Subject-Verb Agreement in Writing Peggy Thomson uses singular, plural, and compound subjects in this passage from "Bathing Elephants." Examine the passage, noting how subjects and verbs agree in number.

> Bath and foot-care time now flows into demonstration time directed by the keeper team of Kathy and Morna out in the yard. Here people clap to see the elephants maneuver on command, present a foot, balance on tiny stools, and move huge logs with their trunks. By the time Ambika and Shanthi take their bows, the keepers are beginning to wilt. There's an element of tension in the playful-looking baths they give and in the training shows—in just dealing with animals who could so easily pulverize them if they chose to.

Techniques with Subjects and Their Verbs Try to use singular, plural, and compound subjects when you write and revise your own work. Be sure your subjects and their verbs agree in number. Look at these examples from "Bathing Elephants."

1. With a singular subject, be sure you use the singular form of the verb. With a plural subject, be sure you use the plural form of the verb.

Thomson's examples Bath and foot-care <u>time</u> now <u>flows</u>; <u>people</u> <u>clap</u>; <u>keepers</u> <u>are</u>

2. With a compound subject connected with *and*, be sure to use the plural form of the verb.

Thomson's examples <u>Kathy and Morna</u> <u>speak</u>; <u>Ambika and Shanthi</u> <u>take</u>

Practice Revise the following passage. Be sure all the subjects and their verbs agree in number.

> [1]My family and I am going on a car trip through Colorado and Wyoming this summer. [2]We plan stops at a number of different national parks and historic sites. [3]The first stop on our journey are Yellowstone, the oldest park in the national park system.[4]We have reservations at Old Faithful Inn. [5]The beautiful open lobby of the inn rise more than ninety feet.

Teacher's Classroom Resources

The following resources can be used for assessment or evaluation.

Unit Assessment

Tests with Answer Key
Unit 15 Mastery Test, pp. 59–60

Test Generator
Unit 15 Mastery Test

You may wish to administer the Unit 15 Mastery Test at this point.

UNIT

16 Glossary of Special Usage Problems

Grammar | **Lessons**

UNIT GOALS

The goal of Unit 16 is to help students, through example and instruction, to develop an understanding of and an ability to use correctly words and expressions that present usage problems. These words and expressions are commonly confused or misused because they sound alike or have similar meanings.

Unit Assessment

Tests with Answer Key
Unit 16 Pretest, pp. 61–62
Unit 16 Mastery Test, pp. 63–64

Test Generator
Unit 16 Pretest
Unit 16 Mastery Test

You may wish to administer the Unit 16 Pretest at this point.

Key to Ability Levels

Enabling Strategies have been coded for varying learning styles and abilities.

L1 Level 1 activities are within the ability range of Learning Disabled students.

L2 Level 2 activities are basic-to-average activities and are within the ability range of average students.

L3 Level 3 activities are challenging activities and are within the ability range of above-average students.

LEP LEP activities are within the ability range of Limited English Proficiency students.

Setting the Purpose

Lesson 16.1 teaches students to understand the difference between words that are often confused because they sound alike or have similar meanings.

FOCUS

Lesson Overview

Objective: To understand the meanings of and the differences between some commonly confused words

Bellringer

When students enter the classroom, have this assignment on the board: *Find two words in the following sentence that sound the same.* Except *for this part, I* accept *the plan. Now write two more sentences using these two words correctly.*

Motivating Activity

Invite volunteers to share their sentences from the Bellringer activity. Ask students to suggest other word pairs that they confuse. Explain that often the only way to remember which word or expression to use is to master both the meaning and spelling.

TEACH

Teaching Tip

The possessive pronoun *its* (*The cat chased* its *tail*) and the contraction *it's* (It's *the fastest train*) are often confused because the use of an apostrophe is associated with possessive nouns. Suggest to students that they try replacing *it's* or *its* with *it is* in a particular sentence. If the sentence still makes sense, then the contraction is correct. If the sentence does not make sense, then the possessive form (*its*) should be used.

16.1 Using Troublesome Words I

Like all languages, English contains a number of confusing words. The following glossary will help you understand some of the more troublesome ones.

Word	Meaning	Example
accept **except**	"to receive" "other than"	Ships **accept** most cargo. Ships move at a rapid speed **except** in storms.
all ready **already**	"completely prepared" "before" or "by this time"	The flight crew is **all ready**. The plane had **already** left when I arrived at the airport.
all together **altogether**	"in a group" "completely"	The wagons traveled **all together** for protection. Wagons are **altogether** too slow.
a lot	"very much" *A lot* is two words. Its meaning is vague; avoid using it.	Sailors travel **a lot**. [vague] Sailors travel frequently. [more precise]
beside **besides**	"next to" "in addition to"	Railroad tracks often run **beside** roads. **Besides** trains we ride buses.
between **among**	Use *between* when referring to two people or things. Use *among* when talking about groups of three or more.	Ships sail **between** ports. Trains are **among** the best ways to travel.
choose **chose**	"to select" "selected"	Many people **choose** a window seat when they fly. I **chose** an aisle seat the last time I flew to New York.
in **into**	"inside" indicates movement from outside to a point within	Freight is stored **in** cargo bays. The pilot guided the ship **into** port.
its **it's**	the possessive form of *it* the contraction of *it is*	The ship is moving to **its** pier. **It's** hard to dock a ship.

Teacher's Classroom Resources

The following resources can be used for planning, instruction, practice, reinforcement, assessment, reteaching, enrichment, or evaluation.

Teaching Tools
Lesson Plans

Blackline Masters
Grammar Practice, p. 36
Grammar Reteaching, p. 37
Grammar Enrichment, p. 36

Grammar Workbook
Lessons 58–60

Unit Assessment

Tests with Answer Key
Unit 16 Pretest, pp. 61–62

Test Generator
Unit 16 Pretest

You may wish to administer the Unit 16 Pretest at this point.

Exercise 1 Choosing the Correct Word

Write each sentence, choosing the correct word or words in parentheses.

1. We are traveling (altogether, all together).
2. The conductor will (accept, except) our tickets.
3. Every railroad car (accept, except) ours is going all the way to Chicago.
4. Did we (choose, chose) the wrong one?
5. (Its, It's) difficult to choose without checking the schedule.
6. The train that is (beside, besides) ours at the station is headed for Omaha.
7. The conductor says we are (all ready, already) to leave.
8. Before you know it, the train has (all ready, already) left the station.
9. We settle (in, into) our seats and look out the window.
10. This time I (choose, chose) the seat closest to the window.
11. The train is moving along (its, it's) track at a steady speed.
12. We talk (between, among) ourselves about the passing scenery.
13. There are many people on this train (besides, beside) my family.
14. Freight trains are (between, among) the busiest carriers.
15. Elevators load grain (in, into) railroad hoppers.

Exercise 2 Using the Correct Word

Write each sentence, using the correct word or words from the lesson as defined in parentheses.

1. Truckers stop _____ highways to rest. (next to)
2. Truckers can drive _____ the city. (from outside to a point within)
3. Heavy trucks can cause _____ too much damage to highways. (completely)
4. Our moving van is _____ . (completely prepared)
5. The circus trucks have _____ left. (by this time)
6. Of all the trucks on this lot, which one would you _______ to drive? (select)
7. Does this parkway _____ trucks? (receive)
8. This highway runs _____ Baltimore, Maryland, and Washington, D.C. (referring to two places)
9. _____ truck traffic, it gets much commuter traffic. (in addition to)
10. The highway is crowded _____ on weekends. (other than)

PRACTICE AND ASSESS

Answers: Exercise 1

1. all together
2. accept
3. except
4. choose
5. It's
6. beside
7. all ready
8. already
9. into
10. choose
11. its
12. among
13. besides
14. among
15. into

Answers: Exercise 2

1. beside
2. into
3. altogether
4. all ready
5. already
6. choose
7. accept
8. between
9. Besides
10. except

Independent Practice

Skills Practice

Grammar Practice, p. 36
Grammar Reteaching, p. 37
Grammar Enrichment, p. 36

Grammar Workbook, Lessons 58–60

CLOSE

Have students write two lines of dialogue, each line containing one word from the troublesome word pairs in the lesson. Invite volunteers to write their dialogue on the board, omitting the troublesome word or words. Have each volunteer choose a student to complete the sentences with the correct words. As an example, write the following on the board:

"Let's swim to the other side of the pond _____," Mr. Lopez suggested to the group. (all together)

Alex responded, "The water is _____ too cold for me!" (altogether)

Enabling Strategies

LEP Using Troublesome Words

Help students understand troublesome word pairs by describing situations in the classroom. Andy sits *between* Ramon and Claudia. Andy sits *among* many students. Celia put her notebook *into* her desk. Celia's notebook is *in* her desk. Invite students to present examples to the class.

L3 Using Descriptive Words

Challenge students to think of alternatives for the vague phrase *a lot.* Encourage them to use their word in a sentence. Provide examples: There was *a lot* of food at the picnic. There was an *abundance* of food at the picnic.

Setting the Purpose

Lesson 16.2 teaches students to understand the difference between words that are often confused because they sound alike or have similar meanings.

FOCUS

Lesson Overview

Objective: To understand the meanings of and the differences between some commonly confused words

Bellringer

When students enter the classroom, have this assignment on the board: *What does the following quote mean? Write your explanation.*

> Sometimes you can *learn* things people don't even know they're *teaching*.
>
> —Bette Greene, *Summer of My German Soldier*

Motivating Activity

Invite volunteers to share their explanation of the quote. Explain the distinction between the words *teach* and *learn.* Students might distinguish between the two words by remembering this sentence: If you want to be sure you learned something, try teaching it to someone else.

TEACH

☑ Grammar Tip

Help students distinguish between the pairs *lay* and *lie*, *raise* and *rise*, and *sit* and *set* by explaining that the first verb in each pair involves causing something to happen. For example, *to lay something down* is "to cause it to lie."

16.2 Using Troublesome Words II

Word	Meaning	Example
lay	"to put" or "to place"	Sailors **lay** the ropes in coils.
lie	"to recline" or "to be positioned"	Passengers **lie** in bunks.
learn	"to receive knowledge"	Crews **learn** rescue tactics.
teach	"to give knowledge"	Some pilots **teach** flying.
leave	"to go away"	Most buses **leave** on time.
let	"to allow"	**Let** the children board.
loose	"not firmly attached"	**Loose** cargo is dangerous.
lose	"to misplace" or "to fail to win"	You could **lose** your luggage.
raise	"to cause to move upward"	The sailors **raise** the anchors before the ships depart.
rise	"to move upward"	The anchors **rise** slowly.
set	"to place" or "to put"	Cranes **set** cargo in the hold.
sit	"to place oneself in a seated position"	I will **sit** by you.
than	*Than* introduces the second part of a comparison.	Ships are larger **than** boats.
then	"at that time" or "soon after"	Raise the anchor, and **then** sail.
their	*Their* is the possessive form of *they.*	We like **their** fast trains.
they're	*They're* is the contraction of *they are.*	**They're** designed for speed.
to	"in the direction of"	Trains carry coal **to** ports.
too	"in addition to" or "excessively"	Coal is **too** bulky for planes.
two	the number after one	The supertanker is as long as **two** football fields.
who's	*Who's* is the contraction of *who is.*	I have a friend **who's** a pilot.
whose	*Whose* is the possessive form of *who.*	**Whose** flight leaves first?

Teacher's Classroom Resources

The following resources can be used for planning, instruction, practice, reinforcement, reteaching, or enrichment.

Teaching Tools
Lesson Plans

Blackline Masters
Grammar Practice, p. 36
Grammar Reteaching, p. 37
Grammar Enrichment, p. 36

Grammar Workbook
Lessons 60–62

Exercise 3 **Choosing the Correct Word**

Write each sentence, choosing the correct word in parentheses.

1. (Who's, Whose) instructions will the pilot follow?
2. The pilot will (learn, teach) you to use radar.
3. The pilot will help you with math, (to, too).
4. The best pilots (set, sit) their planes down gently.
5. Planes are faster (than, then) trains.
6. Once in flight, passengers may (lay, lie) back in their seats.
7. Planes almost never (loose, lose) their way.
8. After taking off, planes (raise, rise) to a suitable flying height.
9. During this time, the plane's pilot (raises, rises) the landing gear.
10. After the plane reaches its cruising altitude, (than, then) the crew can relax more.
11. They may (set, sit) and chat.
12. They may study the navigational charts that (their, they're) using.
13. They understand (who's, whose) responsible for what duties.
14. (Their, They're) well trained, and all crew members know their jobs.
15. (Who's, Whose) job is flying the plane?
16. (Raise, Rise) your hand if you know the answer.
17. I sometimes wonder whether flying the plane is more difficult (than, then) tending the passengers.
18. Flight attendants see that all (loose, lose) luggage is safely secured.
19. (Their, They're) primary responsibility is the safety and comfort of the passengers.
20. They (leave, let) the flying to the pilot and copilot.

Exercise 4 **Using the Correct Word**

Write each sentence, using the correct word or words from the lesson as defined in parentheses.

1. ______ near the bow so we can see the harbor. (place yourself in a seated position)
2. Ships will not ______ port until high tide. (go away)
3. ______ me help you down the gangplank. (allow)
4. The crew saw the playful whale ______ from the water. (move upward)
5. Vessels ______ flags as signals. (cause to move upward)

PRACTICE AND ASSESS

Answers: Exercise 3

1. Whose	11. sit
2. teach	12. they're
3. too	13. who's
4. set	14. They're
5. than	15. Whose
6. lie	16. Raise
7. lose	17. than
8. rise	18. loose
9. raises	19. Their
10. then	20. leave

Answers: Exercise 4

1. Sit
2. leave
3. Let
4. rise
5. raise

Independent Practice

Skills Practice

Grammar Practice, p. 36
Grammar Reteaching, p. 37
Grammar Enrichment, p. 36

Grammar Workbook, Lessons 60–62

CLOSE

Ask students to write two questions. Have them include one of the troublesome words in each question. Then have them exchange papers with a partner. Each partner responds to the questions with an answer that includes the other troublesome word. Write the following on the board as an example.

Will you let me borrow your new tape tonight?

If you promise not to leave it at home tomorrow.

Enabling Strategies

LEP Practicing Pronunciation

Some students do not hear the difference between such word pairs as *accept, except; choose, chose; loose, lose;* and *set, sit.* Pair them with English speakers who can help them practice. Ask students to exaggerate the pronunciation to help their partners detect subtle differences in the words.

L2 Acting Out Words

To help students distinguish troublesome word pairs, have volunteers act out the words. For example, after a student puts a book on a desk, another student describes the action: *Anna is setting the book on the desk.* Have volunteers write the words on the board.

TEACH

About the Literature

Explain that the review features a passage from Robert D. Ballard's *Exploring the Titanic.* The passage recounts Ballard's impressions of the *Titanic* as he and his crew observed the ship from their submarine, and their efforts to explore the *Titanic* and the watery world that surrounds the sunken ship. The exercises that follow are based on this passage and related topics.

After students have read the passage, initiate a discussion about the author's description of the *Titanic.* Then ask students to focus on the highlighted words in the passage. Would the meaning of the passage be as clear if the writer had used these words incorrectly?

Linking Grammar and Literature

☑ Grammar Tip

Students may be confused by the use of the past tense of *lie* in the passage. Explain the distinction between *lay*, the past tense of *lie*, and present tense *lay*, meaning to put or place (something). Remind students that the verbs *lie* and *rise*, used in the past tense in the passage, never take an object.

☑ Teaching Tip

Students might point out that they were advised to avoid the use of the vague expression *a lot.* You might explain that because Robert Ballard's passage is so descriptive and visual, the use of *a lot* in this instance is acceptable. Invite students to think of alternative words that the author could have used.

UNIT 16

Unit Review

Grammar Review

Glossary of Special Usage Problems

In *Exploring the* Titanic, Robert D. Ballard writes about his explorations of the largest ship of its time, the *Titanic,* which sank after hitting an iceberg in the North Atlantic Ocean on April 15, 1912. More than 1,500 passengers and crew died; fewer than half that number survived.

Literature Model

from EXPLORING THE *TITANIC*

by Robert D. Ballard

It looked as though the metal hull was slowly melting away. What seemed like frozen rivers of rust covered the ship's side and spread out over the ocean bottom. It was almost as if the blood of the great ship lay in pools on the ocean floor.

Past tense of the verb *lie*, meaning "to be positioned"

As *Alvin* rose in slow motion up the ghostly side of the ship, I could see our lights reflecting off the still-unbroken glass of the *Titanic*'s portholes. They made me think of cats' eyes gleaming in the dark. In places the rust formations over the portholes looked like eyelashes with tears, as though the *Titanic* were crying. I could also see a lot of reddish-brown stalactites of rust over the wreck, like long icicles. I decided to call them "rusticles." This rust turned out to be very fragile. If touched by our sub, it disappeared like a cloud of smoke.

A lot spelled as two words

As we rose further and began to move across the mighty forward deck, I was amazed at the sheer ➡

Past tense of the verb *rise*, meaning "to move upward"

Teacher's Classroom Resources

The following resources can be used for planning, instruction, practice, reinforcement, assessment, reteaching, enrichment, or evaluation.

Teaching Tools
Lesson Plans

Grammar Workbook
Lessons 58–62
Unit 10 Review
Cumulative Review: Units 1–10

Unit Assessment
Tests with Answer Key
Unit 16 Mastery Test, pp. 63–64

Test Generator
Unit 16 Mastery Test

size of everything: giant bollards and shiny bronze capstans that were used for winding ropes and cables; the huge links of the anchor chains. When you were there on the spot, the ship was truly titanic.

Exercise 1

Making Usage Choices Write each sentence, choosing the correct word or words in parentheses.

SAMPLE The *Titanic* hit an iceberg (in, into) the North Atlantic.
ANSWER The *Titanic* hit an iceberg in the North Atlantic.

1. The *Titanic* was on its way (to, too, two) New York when it hit an iceberg.
2. Passengers hurriedly crowded (in, into) the lifeboats.
3. Crew members sat (between, among) the passengers in the crowded boats.
4. The *Titanic* had (all ready, already) sunk by the time other ships got to the area.
5. More passengers died (than, then) survived.

Exercise 2

Making Usage Choices Write each sentence, choosing the correct word or words in parentheses.

SAMPLE The explorers could see the *Titanic*'s (to, too, two) anchors.
ANSWER The explorers could see the *Titanic*'s two anchors.

1. The *Titanic* (lays, lies) on the ocean floor nearly two and a half miles below the surface.
2. The sub *Alvin* rose slowly (beside, besides) the ship.
3. By exploring the wreck up close, Ballard was able to (learn, teach) much about the *Titanic*.
4. The entire ship was visible (accept, except) for the bow.
5. The *Titanic*'s bow was (all together, altogether) buried in the mud.

PRACTICE AND ASSESS

Answers: Exercise 1

1. to
2. into
3. among
4. already
5. than

Answers: Exercise 2

1. lies
2. beside
3. learn
4. except
5. altogether

Answers: Exercise 3

Proofreading

This proofreading activity provides editing practice with (1) the current or previous units' skills, (2) the **Troubleshooter** errors, and (3) spelling errors. Students should be able to complete the exercise by referring to the units, the **Troubleshooter**, and a dictionary. (Note: A run-on sentence counts as one error.)

	Error (Type of Error)
1.	• 1941. He *or* 1941; he *or* 1941, and he (run-on sentence)
	• raised (troublesome word)
2.	• too (troublesome word)
	• Studio, (compound sentence)
3.	• Their (troublesome word)
4.	• battles, (commas in a series)

Exercise 3 **Proofreading**

The following passage is about American artist Richard Shaw, whose work appears on this page. Rewrite the passage, correcting the errors in spelling, capitalization, grammar, and usage. Add any missing punctuation. There are 10 errors.

Richard Shaw

[1]Richard Shaw was born in 1941 he was risen in Hollywood, California. [2]His father worked as a cartoonist for Walt Disney Studio and his mother was an artist, two. [3]They're friends were all artists, cartoonists, and writers. [4]Shaw remembers spending much time as a child drawing train wrecks, battles and maritime disasters. ➡

Richard Shaw, *Rough Seas,* 1991

About the Art

Richard Shaw, *Rough Seas,* 1991

Richard Shaw (1941–) began painting and making movies in high school. Shaw later studied at the San Francisco Art Institute, where he became interested in ceramic sculpture. He received his B.F.A. from the school in 1965 and has taught there since 1966. Although he lives and works primarily in California, Shaw's influence on younger ceramic artists extends throughout the country.

Rough Seas is made of porcelain, measures 8 1/2 by 12 inches, and is in the Franklin/Adams Gallery in New York.

[5] Beside his interest in painting, Shaw also became interested in filmmaking and ceramic sculpture. [6] In the work on the opposite page, he uses ceramic to show the immense power of the see. [7] The ocean liner sets precariously on the top of a huge wave. [8] The *Titanic,* of course, met it's fate in the form of an iceberg, not a wave.

Mixed Review

Exercise 4

The following sentences provide information about icebergs. For each sentence write the correct word in parentheses.

1. An iceberg is a large drifting piece of ice that has broken off (altogether, all together) from a freshwater glacier.
2. It is really a (loose, lose) piece of ice floating in the sea.
3. In the Northern Hemisphere the main source of icebergs (lays, lies) along the southwestern coast of Greenland.
4. In the south the glacial flow from Antarctica releases large icebergs, some of which (raise, rise) hundreds of feet into the air.
5. (A lot, Many) of these icebergs are dangerous to shipping, since only a small portion of each iceberg is visible above the water.
6. Most of the iceberg (lays, lies) under the water.
7. The biggest of the icebergs are (to, too) large to be easily recognized as icebergs.
8. They are much larger (than, then) the largest supertankers.
9. Sometimes (their, they're) over sixty miles long.
10. If you were on a big ship (beside, besides) one of these giant icebergs, you might think you were next to an island.
11. Would you (choose, chose) to live in such an icy place?
12. (Its, It's) hard to imagine, but some animals do!
13. Emperor penguins swim (between, among) ice and land.
14. Seals (set, sit) on the frigid surfaces.
15. (Leave, Let) me bask on a sunny, sand-filled beach!

UNIT 16 Review

Answers: Exercise 3

(continued from previous page)

	Error (Type of Error)
5.	• Besides (troublesome word)
6.	• sea (spelling)
7.	• sits (troublesome word)
8.	• its (troublesome word)

Answers: Exercise 4

Mixed Review

1. altogether
2. loose
3. lies
4. rise
5. Many
6. lies
7. too
8. than
9. they're
10. beside
11. choose
12. It's
13. between
14. sit
15. Let

CLOSE

Following a discussion of what it must have been like on board the *Titanic* on the night of April 15, 1912, have students write a paragraph from the point of view of one of the passengers or crew members. They should include in their paragraph some of the troublesome words discussed in this unit.

Usage of Glossary Words in Writing

Have students read the passage silently, paying particular attention to the italicized words. Discuss the italicized words in relation to the Techniques with Correct Usage.

Techniques with Correct Usage

Discuss the techniques used to determine correct usage. Then have students refer to the first paragraph of the passage on page 424. Ask why Robert Ballard said *lay in pools* and not *lay into pools*. Then have students refer to the first paragraph on page 428 and explain the use of *whose* in the first sentence.

Practice

Answers:

1. in
2. to
3. in
4. into
5. two
6. too
7. Whose
8. into
9. Who's
10. into

Writing Application

Usage of Glossary Words in Writing

In this passage from *The Jacket,* Gary Soto uses several of the words you have studied to describe the boy's reactions to his new jacket. As you read, concentrate on the italized words.

> "I threw my books on the bed and approached the jacket slowly, as if it were a stranger *whose* hand I had to shake. I touched the vinyl sleeve, the collar, and pecked at the mustard-colored lining.
>
> From the kitchen Mother yelled that my jacket was *in* the closet. I closed the door *to* her voice and pulled at the rack of clothes *in* the closet, hoping the jacket on the bedpost wasn't for me but my mean brother."

Techniques with Correct Usage

Gary Soto was careful to use the correct word of a pair that could easily be confused. When you draft and revise your writing, try to be as careful.

1. Remember the difference between the use of *who's* and *whose.*

Incorrect . . . as if it were a stranger *who's* hand I had to shake.
Correct . . . as if it were a stranger *whose* hand I had to shake.

2. Learn the difference between *in* and *into*.

Incorrect My jacket was *into* the closet.
Correct My jacket was *in* the closet.

3. Don't confuse *to, too,* and two.

Incorrect I closed the door *too* her voice . . .
Correct I closed the door *to* her voice . . .

Practice Practice these techniques by rewriting the following paragraph, making the correct choice from each word pair.

What was (in, into) the back of the closet? I tiptoed nervously (to, too) the closet door. Gingerly, I opened the door and reached (in, into). Slowly, I edged my hand further (in, into) the closet. My hand slid between (too, two) coats that seemed almost (to, too) silky to the touch. (Who's, Whose) could they be? A sudden screech sent me crashing sideways (in, into) the door. "(Who's, Whose) that?" I managed to whisper. The answer launched itself (in, into) me, knocking me backwards. My dog!

Teacher's Classroom Resources

The following resources can be used for assessment or evaluation.

Unit Assessment

Tests with Answer Key
Unit 16 Mastery Test, pp. 63–64

Test Generator
Unit 16 Mastery Test

You may wish to administer the Unit 16 Mastery Test at this point.

UNIT 17

Diagraming Sentences

Grammar | Lessons

UNIT GOALS

The goal of Unit 17 is to help students, through example and instruction, to develop an understanding of and an ability to identify parts of sentences: simple subjects, simple predicates, direct and indirect objects, adjectives and adverbs, predicate nouns and predicate adjectives, and prepositional phrases. Students also practice representing these parts in sentence diagrams.

Unit Assessment

Tests with Answer Key
Unit 17 Pretest, pp. 65–66
Unit 17 Mastery Test, pp. 67–68

Test Generator
Unit 17 Pretest
Unit 17 Mastery Test

You may wish to administer the Unit 17 Pretest at this point.

Key to Ability Levels

Enabling Strategies have been coded for varying learning styles and abilities.

L1 Level 1 activities are within the ability range of Learning Disabled students.

L2 Level 2 activities are basic-to-average activities and are within the ability range of average students.

L3 Level 3 activities are challenging activities and are within the ability range of above-average students.

LEP LEP activities are within the ability range of Limited English Proficiency students.

Setting the Purpose

Lesson 17.1 teaches students how simple subjects and simple predicates function as parts of a sentence.

FOCUS

Lesson Overview

Objective: To identify simple subjects and simple predicates, represent them in sentence diagrams, and see how they function as parts of a sentence

Bellringer

When students enter the classroom, have this assignment on the board: *Write three sentences and label the subject and predicate in each one.*

PRACTICE AND ASSESS

Answers: Exercise 1

1. Families | arrive
2. They | began
3. people | are swimming
4. child | has found
5. Gwen | has built

CLOSE

Ask students to contribute ideas for a paragraph about summer experiences. Write the sentences on the board and diagram them.

17.1 Diagraming Simple Subjects and Simple Predicates

Every sentence contains a subject and a predicate. To diagram a sentence, first draw a horizontal line. Then draw a vertical line that crosses the horizontal line.

To the left of the vertical line, write the simple subject. To the right of the vertical line, write the simple predicate. Use capital letters as they appear in the sentence, but do not use punctuation.

Waves crash.

Waves | crash

Be sure to write only the simple subject and the simple predicate in this part of the diagram. Remember that the simple predicate can include a helping verb.

The **breakers are pounding** the rocks.

breakers | are pounding

Exercise 1 Diagraming Simple Subjects and Simple Predicates

Diagram the simple subject and simple predicate of each sentence.

1. Families arrive.
2. They began the day early.
3. Some people are swimming.
4. A child has found a shell.
5. Gwen has built a sand castle.

Teacher's Classroom Resources

The following resources can be used for planning, instruction, practice, reinforcement, assessment, reteaching, enrichment, or evaluation.

Teaching Tools
Lesson Plans

Grammar Workbook
Lesson 52

Unit Assessment

Tests with Answer Key
Unit 17 Pretest, pp. 65–66

Test Generator
Unit 17 Pretest

You may wish to administer the Unit 17 Pretest at this point.

17.2 Diagraming the Four Kinds of Sentences

The simple subject and the simple predicate of four kinds of sentences are diagramed below. Notice that the location of the simple subject and the simple predicate in a sentence diagram is always the same, regardless of word order in the sentence.

DECLARATIVE
Fishers depend upon the sea.

Fishers | depend

INTERROGATIVE
Do you live near the ocean?

you | Do live

IMPERATIVE
Read this book about the sea.

(you) | Read

EXCLAMATORY
How majestic the **oceans are**!

oceans | are

In an interrogative sentence, the simple subject often comes between the two parts of a verb phrase. In an imperative sentence, the simple subject is the understood *you*.

Exercise 2 Diagraming Simple Subjects and Simple Predicates

Diagram the simple subject and simple predicate of each sentence.

1. Have you seen an ocean?
2. Oceans cover about 70 percent of the earth's surface.
3. Does our planet look like one large ocean?
4. Think about that.
5. How small the continents seem!
6. The largest ocean on earth is the Pacific Ocean.
7. Look at the map in this atlas.
8. Does the Pacific Ocean extend to Japan?
9. Is the Indian Ocean the smallest one?
10. Find it on the globe.

Setting the Purpose

Lesson 17.2 teaches students how simple subjects and simple predicates function in each of the four kinds of sentences.

FOCUS

Lesson Overview

Objective: To identify and diagram declarative, imperative, interrogative, and exclamatory sentences

Bellringer

When students enter the classroom, have this assignment on the board: *Write one declarative, one imperative, one interrogative, and one exclamatory sentence.*

PRACTICE AND ASSESS

Answers: Exercise 2

1. you | Have seen
2. Oceans | cover
3. planet | Does look
4. (you) | Think
5. continents | seem
6. ocean | is
7. (you) | Look
8. Pacific Ocean | Does extend
9. Indian Ocean | Is
10. (you) | Find

Teacher's Classroom Resources

The following resources can be used for planning, instruction, practice, reinforcement, reteaching, or enrichment.

Teaching Tools
Lesson Plans

Grammar Workbook
Lesson 53

CLOSE

Have students diagram the sentences they wrote for the Bellringer activity.

Setting the Purpose

Lesson 17.3 teaches students how direct and indirect objects function as parts of sentences.

FOCUS

Lesson Overview

Objective: To identify direct and indirect objects and to represent them in sentence diagrams

Bellringer

When students enter the classroom, have this assignment on the board: *Write three sentences that contain both direct objects and indirect objects. Circle the direct object and underline the indirect object in each.*

PRACTICE AND ASSESS

Answers: Exercise 3

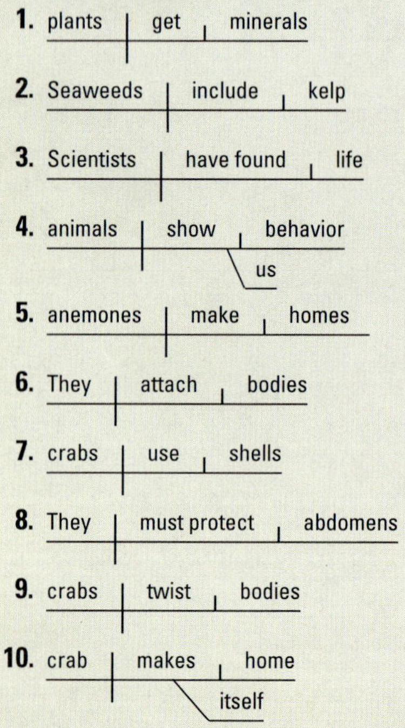

17.3 Diagraming Direct and Indirect Objects

You know that the predicate of a sentence often contains a direct object. In a sentence diagram, place the direct object to the right of the simple predicate, or verb. Draw a vertical line to separate the verb from the direct object. This vertical line, however, does *not* cross the horizontal line.

The sea contains many **creatures**.

In some sentences an indirect object comes between the verb and the direct object. In a sentence diagram, place the indirect object on a line below and to the right of the verb. Draw a slanted line to connect the indirect object to the verb.

Coral reefs give some **animals** a home.

Exercise 3 Diagraming Sentences

Diagram the simple subject, simple predicate, and direct object of each sentence. If the sentence contains an indirect object, diagram it, too.

1. Sea plants get minerals from the water.
2. Seaweeds include the long, thin kelp.
3. Scientists have found animal life at impressive depths.
4. Many sea animals show us their picturesque behavior.
5. Some anemones make homes in crab shells.
6. They attach their bodies to the shells of hermit crabs.
7. Hermit crabs use the shells of sea snails for homes.
8. They must protect their soft abdomens.
9. The crabs twist their bodies into the snail shells.
10. The Atlantic hermit crab makes itself a home in a whelk shell.

CLOSE

Have students diagram the sentences they wrote in the Bellringer activity.

Teacher's Classroom Resources

The following resources can be used for planning, instruction, practice, reinforcement, reteaching, or enrichment.

Teaching Tools
Lesson Plans

Grammar Workbook
Lesson 54

17.4 Diagraming Adjectives and Adverbs

An adjective modifies a noun or pronoun. In a diagram write the adjective on a slanted line beneath the noun or pronoun it modifies. Diagram possessive nouns and pronouns and the articles *a, an,* and *the* just as you would diagram other kinds of adjectives.

Our new boat encountered **a stormy** sea.

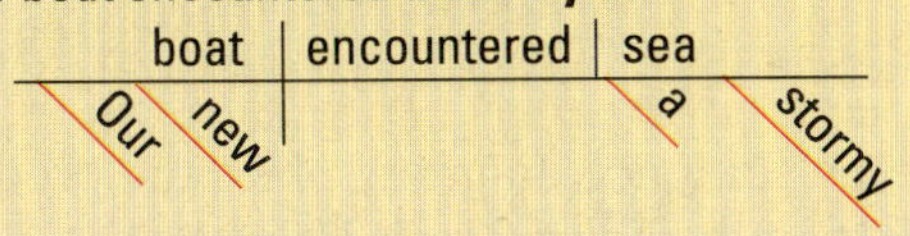

An adverb can modify a verb, an adjective, or another adverb. Notice how adverbs are diagramed.

We have **almost never** seen **such** violent weather.

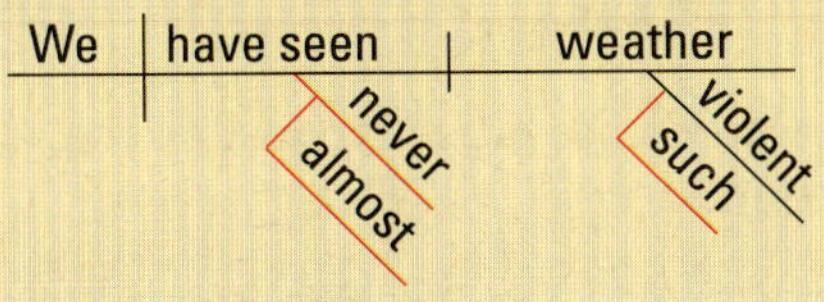

Exercise 4 Diagraming Sentences

Diagram each sentence.

1. Winds cause most waves.
2. Gravity causes the tides.
3. Earthquakes sometimes create dangerous waves.
4. Enormous waves move quite rapidly.
5. Ocean storms frequently cause coastal floods.
6. A very severe flood damaged a seaside town.
7. It rapidly leveled several wooden houses.
8. The inhabitants fortunately escaped.
9. Their supplies had been washed away.
10. Most people had never seen a worse flood.

Setting the Purpose

Lesson 17.4 teaches students how adjectives and adverbs function in simple sentences.

PRACTICE AND ASSESS

Answers: Exercise 4

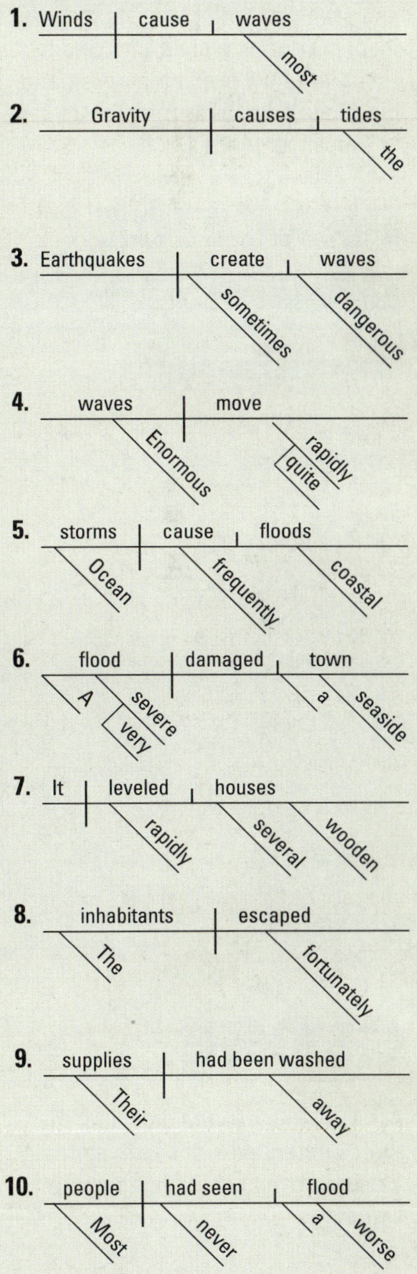

Teacher's Classroom Resources

The following resources can be used for planning, instruction, practice, reinforcement, reteaching, or enrichment.

Teaching Tools
Lesson Plans

Grammar Workbook
Lesson 55

CLOSE

Have students write and diagram four simple sentences that have a predicate adjective or predicate adverb.

UNIT 17
Lesson 17.5

Setting the Purpose

Lesson 17.5 teaches students how predicate nouns and predicate adjectives function as parts of simple sentences.

FOCUS

Lesson Overview

Objective: To identify predicate nouns and predicate adjectives, to represent them in sentence diagrams, and to recognize how predicate nouns and predicate adjectives function as parts of simple sentences

PRACTICE AND ASSESS

Answers: Exercise 5

1.
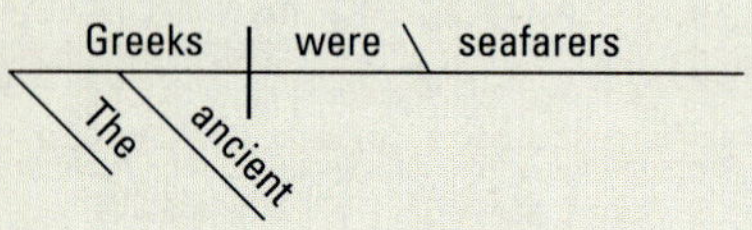

2.
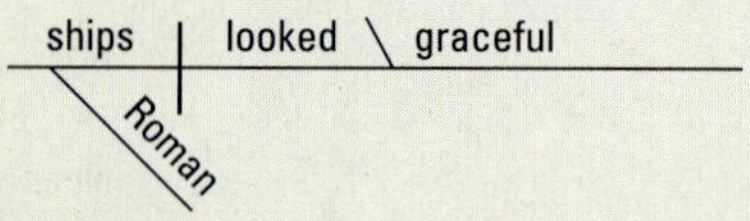

3.
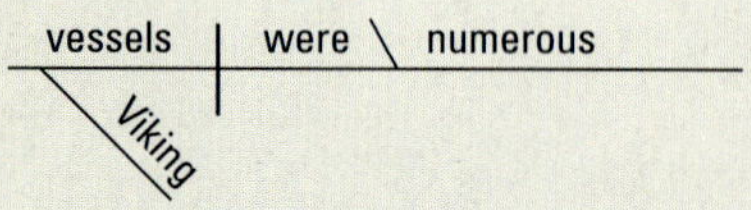

4.
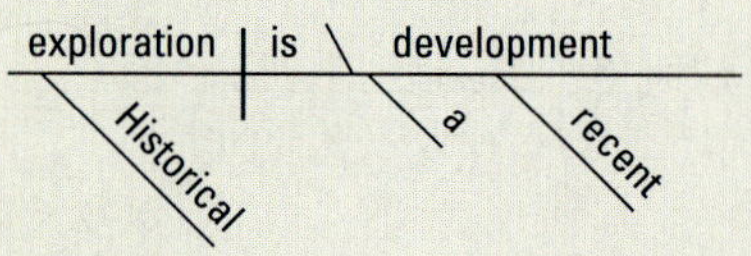

5.
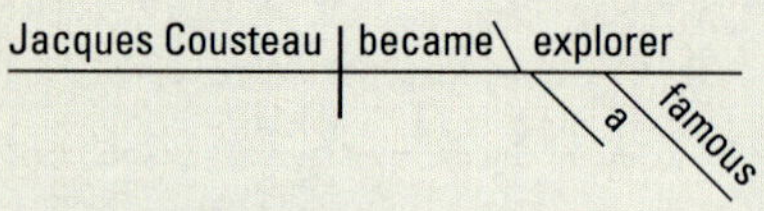

CLOSE

Ask students to write and diagram three sentences—one with a predicate noun and two with predicate adjectives.

17.5 Diagraming Predicate Nouns and Predicate Adjectives

In a sentence diagram, the direct object is placed to the right of a vertical line after the action verb.

Ancient peoples sailed the oceans.

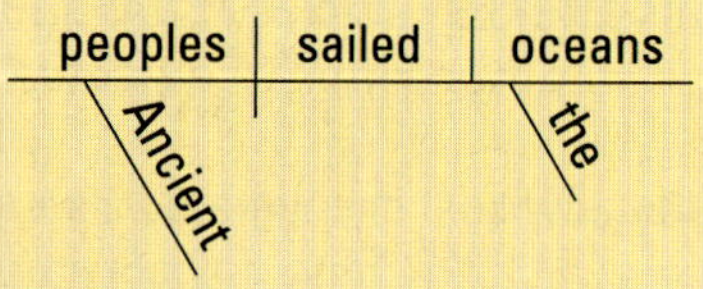

Similarly, in a sentence diagram, place the predicate noun to the right of the linking verb. Draw a slanted line to separate the verb from the predicate noun.

The Phoenicians were **explorers.**

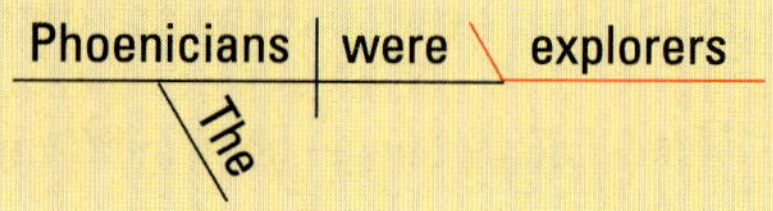

Diagram a predicate adjective just as you would diagram a predicate noun.

These ships were quite **seaworthy.**

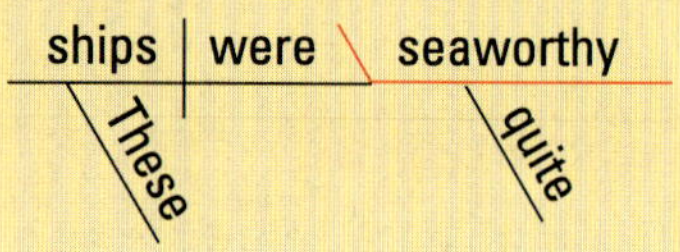

Exercise 5 Diagraming Sentences

Diagram each sentence.

1. The ancient Greeks were seafarers.
2. Roman ships looked graceful.
3. Viking vessels were numerous.
4. Historical exploration is a recent development.
5. Jacques Cousteau became a famous explorer.

Teacher's Classroom Resources

The following resources can be used for planning, instruction, practice, reinforcement, reteaching, or enrichment.

Teaching Tools
Lesson Plans

Grammar Workbook
Lesson 55

17.6 Diagraming Prepositional Phrases

Here is an example of a prepositional phrase used as an adjective.

The waves **along the rocky shore** crashed loudly.

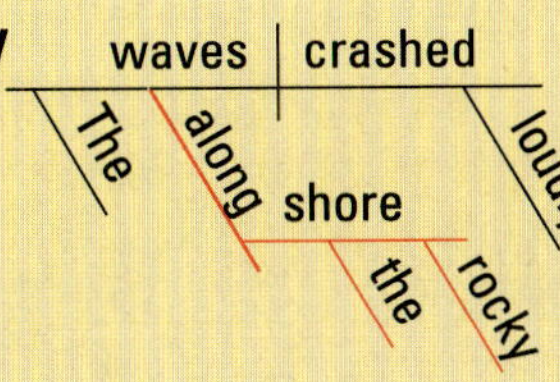

The prepositional phrase, *along the rocky shore,* is connected to the word that it modifies, the noun *waves.*

Here is an example of the same prepositional phrase used as an adverb.

Enormous waves crashed **along the rocky shore**.

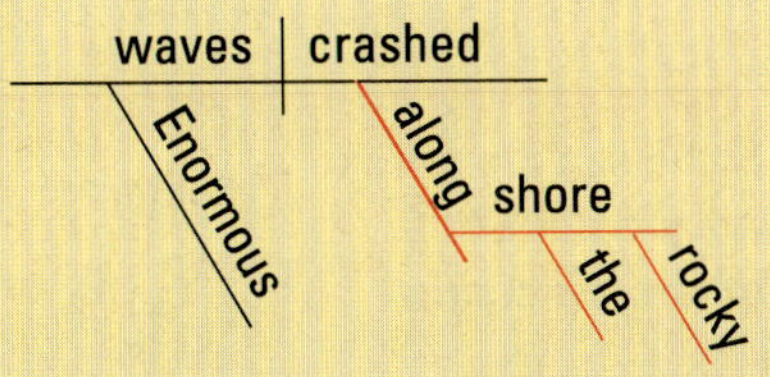

The prepositional phrase, *along the rocky shore,* is connected to the word that it modifies, the verb *crashed.*

Exercise 6 **Diagraming Sentences**

Diagram each sentence.

1. The floor of the ocean has remarkable features.
2. Many mountains exist beneath the surface.
3. These mountains below the waves include active volcanoes.
4. Many Pacific islands are really mountains on the ocean floor.
5. Deep trenches cut into the South Pacific floor.

Setting the Purpose

Lesson 17.6 teaches students how prepositional phrases function in simple sentences.

FOCUS

Lesson Overview

Objective: To identify prepositional phrases in sentences and to represent them in sentence diagrams

PRACTICE AND ASSESS

Answers: Exercise 6

1.
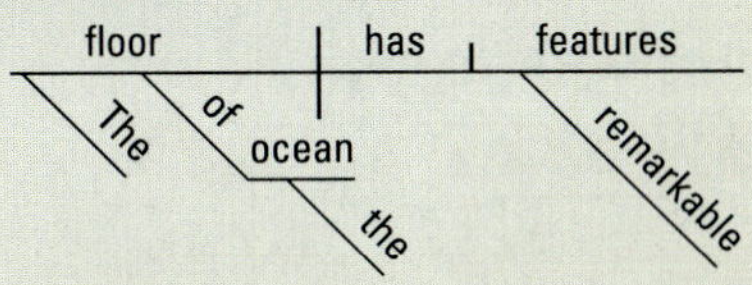

2.
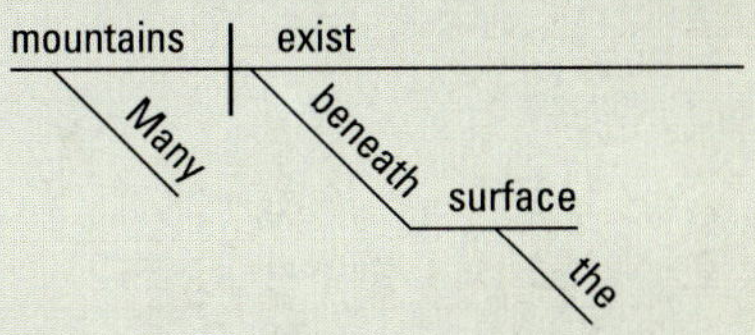

3.
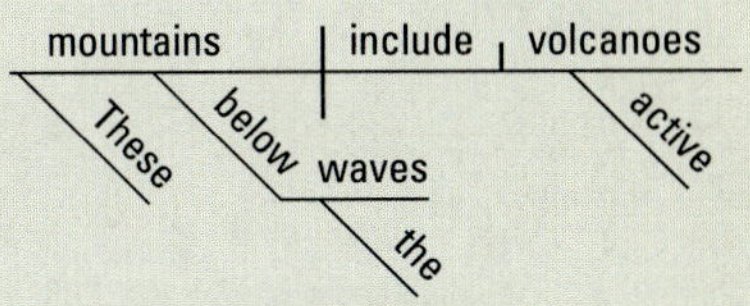

4.
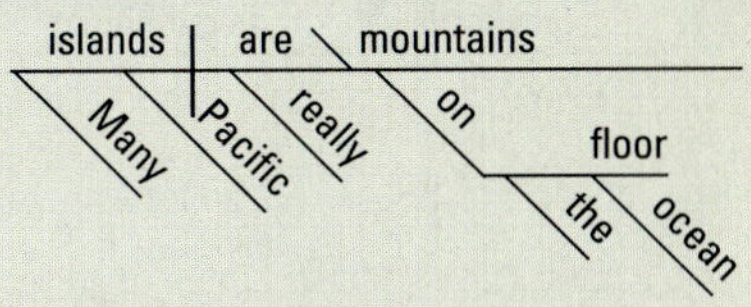

5.
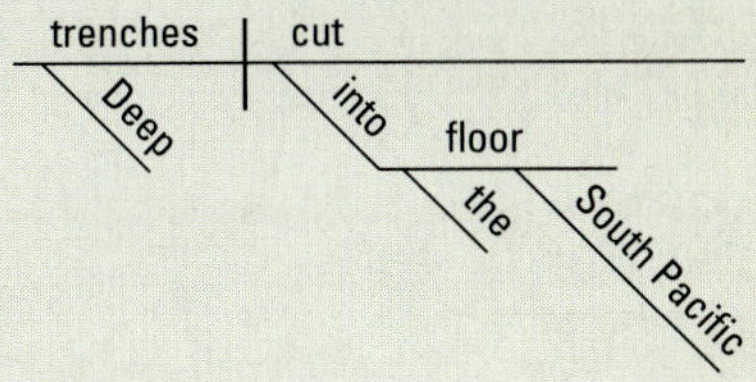

Teacher's Classroom Resources

The following resources can be used for planning, instruction, practice, reinforcement, reteaching, or enrichment.

Teaching Tools
Lesson Plans

Grammar Workbook
Lesson 56

CLOSE

Have students write and diagram three simple sentences, each having a prepositional phrase.

Setting the Purpose

Lesson 17.7 teaches students how compound sentence parts and compound sentences function.

FOCUS

Lesson Overview

Objective: To identify compound sentence parts and compound sentences and to represent them in sentence diagrams

PRACTICE AND ASSESS

Answers: Exercise 7

1.
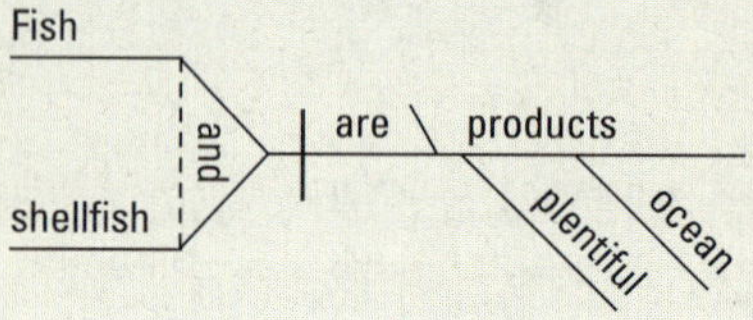

2.
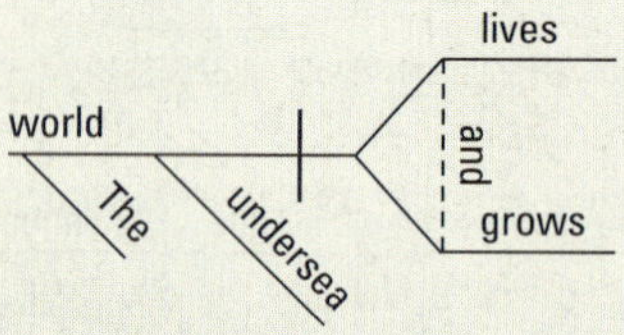

3.
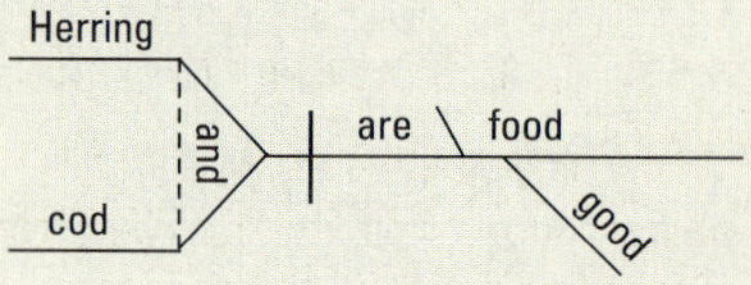

4.
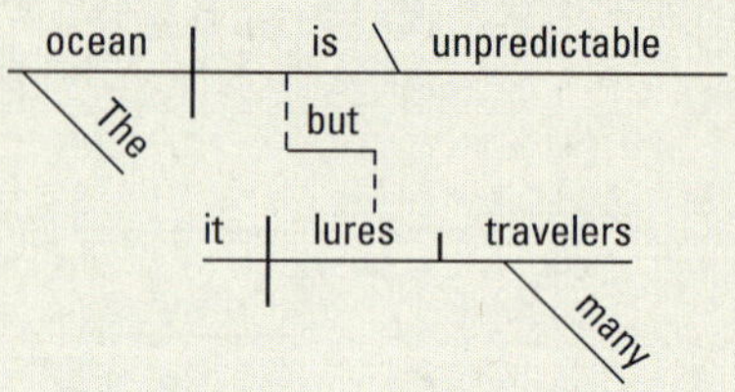

5.
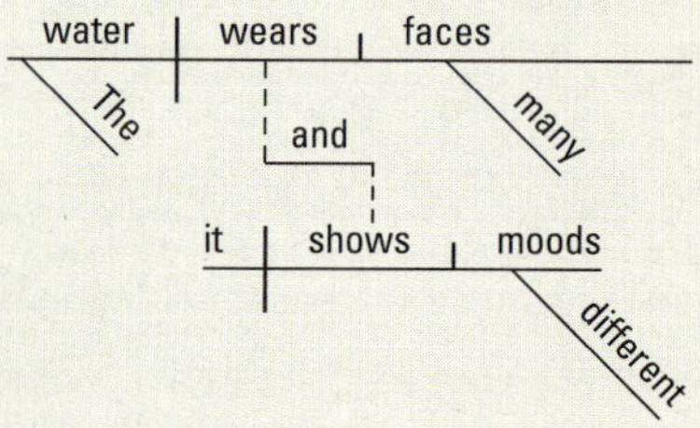

17.7 Diagraming Compound Sentence Parts

Conjunctions such as *and, but,* and *or* are used to join words, phrases, or sentences, creating compound constructions. When you diagram compound parts of a sentence, place the second part of the compound below the first.

Compound Subject
The sea and its products benefit people.

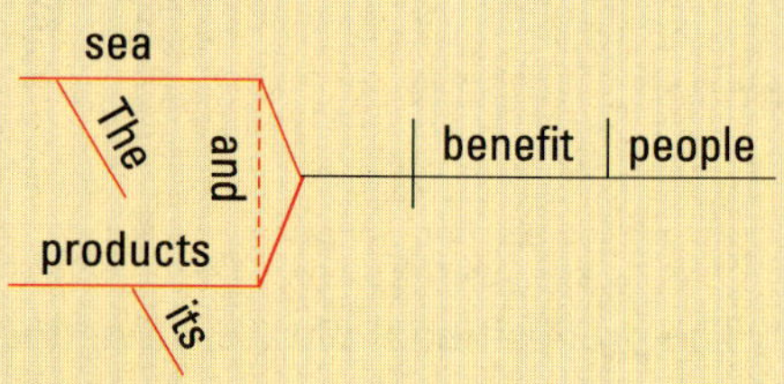

Compound Predicate
Sea creatures **eat and sleep.**

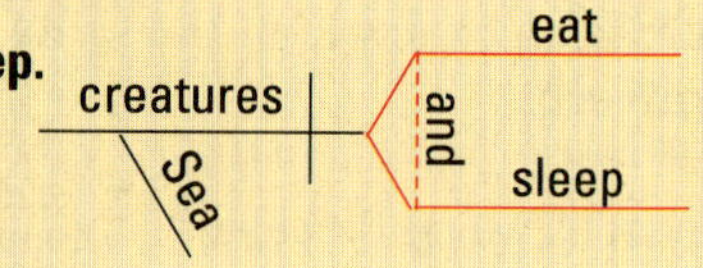

Compound Sentence
Some sea creatures are plentiful, but others are scarce.

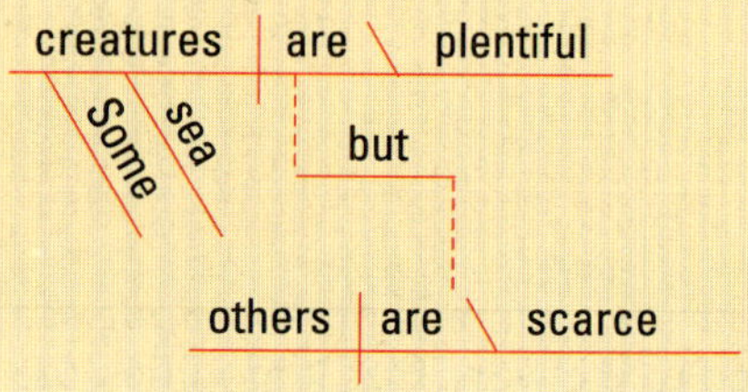

Exercise 7 Diagraming Sentences

Diagram each sentence.

1. Fish and shellfish are plentiful ocean products.
2. The undersea world lives and grows.
3. Herring and cod are good food.
4. The ocean is unpredictable, but it lures many travelers.
5. The water wears many faces, and it shows different moods.

Teacher's Classroom Resources

The following resources can be used for planning, instruction, practice, reinforcement, assessment, reteaching, enrichment, or evaluation.

Teaching Tools
Lesson Plans

Grammar Workbook
Lesson 57

Unit Assessment

Tests with Answer Key
Unit 17 Mastery Test, pp. 67–68

Test Generator
Unit 17 Mastery Test

You may wish to administer the Unit 17 Mastery Test at this point.

UNIT

18 Capitalization

Grammar

Lessons

UNIT GOALS

The goal of Unit 18 is to help students, through example and instruction, to develop an understanding of and an ability to use standard rules of capitalization for sentences, salutations, proper nouns, and adjectives.

Unit Assessment

Tests with Answer Key
Unit 18 Pretest, pp. 69–70
Unit 18 Mastery Test, pp. 71–72

Test Generator
Unit 18 Pretest
Unit 18 Mastery Test

You may wish to administer the Unit 18 Pretest at this point.

Key to Ability Levels

Enabling Strategies have been coded for varying learning styles and abilities.

L1 Level 1 activities are within the ability range of Learning Disabled students.

L2 Level 2 activities are basic-to-average activities and are within the ability range of average students.

L3 Level 3 activities are challenging activities and are within the ability range of above-average students.

LEP LEP activities are within the ability range of Limited English Proficiency students.

Setting the Purpose

Lesson 18.1 teaches students to capitalize words that begin sentences, direct quotations, and salutations.

FOCUS

Lesson Overview

Objective: To recognize and use correct capitalization of words that begin sentences, direct quotations, and salutations

Bellringer

When students enter the classroom, have this assignment on the board: *Capitalize and punctuate the following sentence correctly.*

"That's my point," she said "that's it exactly."

Motivating Activity

Do students realize that the second part of the quotation—"that's it exactly"—is a separate sentence that must be preceded by a period and must begin with a capital? If they are uncertain, refer them to Rule 3 on page 438.

TEACH

Teaching Tip

Many students have difficulty distinguishing between direct and indirect quotations. Suggest that students look for the word *that,* which is often (though not always) inserted after the verb in indirect quotations. The word *that* does not follow the verb in direct quotations. Indirect: *Lois said* that *Canada's largest city was Toronto.* Direct: *Lois said, "Canada's largest city is Toronto."*

18.1 Capitalizing Sentences, Quotations, and Salutations

A capital letter appears at the beginning of a sentence. A capital letter also marks the beginning of a direct quotation and the salutation and closing of a letter.

RULE 1: Capitalize the first word of every sentence.

The country of Canada extends across North America.

RULE 2: Capitalize the first word of a direct quotation that is a complete sentence. A direct quotation gives a speaker's exact words.

Duane said, "About twenty-nine million people live in Canada."
"Many Canadians live near the southern border," Regina said.

RULE 3: When a quoted sentence is interrupted by explanatory words, such as *she said,* do not begin the second part of the sentence with a capital letter.

"Most Canadians," said Minh, "live in cities or towns."
"Canada's largest city," Lois added, "is Toronto."

When the second part of a quotation is a new sentence, put a period after the interrupting expression, and begin the second part of the quotation with a capital letter.

"I've been to Toronto," said Paul. "My mother was born there."

RULE 4: Do not capitalize an indirect quotation. An indirect quotation does not repeat a person's exact words and does not appear in quotation marks. It is often introduced by the word *that.*

Paul said that his mother was born in Toronto.

RULE 5: Capitalize the first word in the salutation and closing of a letter. Capitalize the title and name of the person addressed.

Dear Mrs. Moulin,	Yours truly,
To whom it may concern,	Sincerely yours,

Teacher's Classroom Resources

The following resources can be used for planning, instruction, practice, reinforcement, assessment, reteaching, enrichment, or evaluation.

Teaching Tools
Lesson Plans

Grammar Workbook
Lessons 63–64

Unit Assessment

Tests with Answer Key
Unit 18 Pretest, pp. 69–70

Test Generator
Unit 18 Pretest

You may wish to administer the Unit 18 Pretest at this point.

Exercise 1 **Capitalizing Sentences, Quotations, and Salutations**

Write each sentence. Use capital letters where needed. If a sentence contains no errors, write *correct.*

1. we were talking about our summer vacations.
2. Renée said, "last summer I visited Canada."
3. "you were lucky," said Paul, "because you went in the summer."
4. "Canada has cold winters," Jim remarked.
5. Paul said that summer winds from the Gulf of Mexico often bring hot weather to Canada.
6. "does that mean that on some days it's as hot in Canada as it is in Mexico?" asked Jim.
7. Jim said that in the Northwest Territories the summers are very short.
8. "I'm not surprised," said Renée, "for the Northwest Territories reach up to the North Pole."
9. "anyway," she said, "we visited only Quebec."
10. Paul said that he'd go to Quebec next year.

Exercise 2 **Using Capitalization in a Letter**

Rewrite the letter using correct capitalization. The letter contains ten errors.

January 2, 1996

dear Jack,

my family and I are having a great vacation here in the New Hampshire mountains. Dad says that We may come back again next year. The snow is perfect, and we love the town where we are staying.

believe it or not, your cousin is also here on vacation. She told me today that you were not feeling well. "perhaps a letter," I said, "Will cheer him up." So I sat down after lunch and wrote you this letter. I hope You are feeling better. Next week I will be returning home. then I can visit you in person.

your good Friend,
Pete

PRACTICE AND ASSESS

Answers: Exercise 1

1. We were ...
2. Renée said, "Last ..."
3. "You were ..."
4. correct
5. correct
6. "Does that ..."
7. correct
8. correct
9. "Anyway, ..."
10. correct

Answers: Exercise 2

Dear Jack,

My family and I are having a great vacation here in the New Hampshire mountains. Dad says that **we** may come back again next year. The snow is perfect, and we love the town where we are staying.

Believe it or not, your cousin is also here on vacation. She told me today that you were not feeling well. "**P**erhaps a letter," I said, "**w**ill cheer him up." So I sat down after lunch and wrote you this letter. I hope **y**ou are feeling better. **N**ext week I will be returning home. **T**hen I can visit you in person.

Your good friend,
Pete

Independent Practice

Skills Practice

Grammar Workbook, Lessons 63–64

CLOSE

Ask students to imagine they are taking a trip to Canada. Have them write a letter to a friend describing the trip. Ask them to use at least one direct and one indirect quotation.

To refresh students' understanding of how to write friendly letters, refer them to Lesson 1.3, pp. 18–21.

Enabling Strategies

LEP Capitalizing Quotations

Some students may have difficulty determining when to begin a direct quotation with a capital letter. Remind them that the rule is the same as for any other sentence: If a group of words is a complete sentence, it should begin with a capital letter. Encourage pairs of students to work together on Exercise 1 so that they have the benefit of each other's reasoning.

Setting the Purpose

Lesson 18.2 teaches students to capitalize names and titles of people correctly.

FOCUS

Lesson Overview

Objective: To recognize people's names as proper nouns; to distinguish between titles used as proper nouns and titles used as common nouns

Bellringer

When students enter the classroom, have this assignment on the board: *Capitalize the following names correctly:*

billy the kid	*donald duck*
jabba the hut	*peggy o'neal*
mr. mcdonald	*catherine the great*

Motivating Activity

Discuss students' answers to the Bellringer assignment. Do they realize that nicknames, too, are capitalized? Do they know that certain types of names—such as names beginning with *O'*, *Mc*, or *La*—frequently have two capitals?

TEACH

Teaching Tip

Explain to students that when we refer to a person by his or her title only (usually after an article or a possessive noun or pronoun), the title is a common noun and is not capitalized. When we use a title to address someone directly, the title is a proper noun and, therefore, capitalized. Compare *This is the commander* (common noun) and *Good evening, Commander* (proper noun, direct address).

18.2 Capitalizing Names and Titles of People

A common noun is the general name of a person, place, or thing. A common noun is not capitalized. A proper noun names a particular person, place, or thing and is capitalized.

RULE 1: Capitalize the names of people and the initials that stand for their names.

Louis H. Lafontaine   S. D. Thompson   John Cabot

RULE 2: Capitalize a title or an abbreviation of a title when it comes before a person's name or when it is used in direct address.

General James Wolfe   Dr. Michelle Turner   Ms. Chavez

In 1610 Captain Hudson searched for a passage to Asia.
Later people asked him, "Did you find it, Captain?"

Do not capitalize a title that follows or stands for a person's name.

James Madison was president of the United States in 1812.

RULE 3: Capitalize the names and abbreviations of academic degrees that follow a person's name. Capitalize *Jr.* and *Sr.*

Tina Ibarra, Ph.D.   Linda Tsang, M.D.   David Melo, Jr.

RULE 4: Capitalize words that show family relationships when used as titles or as substitutes for a person's name.

Last year Father and Aunt Beth retraced Cartier's journey.

Do not capitalize words that show family relationships when they follow a possessive noun or pronoun.

Jody's uncle took photographs of the voyage.

RULE 5: Always capitalize the pronoun *I*.

Champlain is the explorer I admire most.

Teacher's Classroom Resources

The following resources can be used for planning, instruction, practice, reinforcement, reteaching, or enrichment.

Teaching Tools
Lesson Plans

Blackline Masters
Grammar Practice, p. 38
Grammar Reteaching, p. 39
Grammar Enrichment, p. 38

Grammar Workbook
Lessons 65–66

Exercise 3 Capitalizing Names and Titles

Write each item. Use capital letters where needed.

1. ms. lucy jojola
2. dr. claude c. islas
3. captain richards
4. aunt anna
5. richard bennett jr.
6. daniel roget, ph.d.
7. uncle louis
8. jeanette canales, m.d.
9. judge jean luc
10. w. r. mackenzie
11. president jefferson
12. sir james smith
13. mr. robert townsend sr.
14. queen victoria
15. madam marie curie
16. lord roy nesbett
17. warren g. malloy jr.
18. professor talmon
19. mr. and mrs. ortiz
20. general davidson

Exercise 4 Using Capital Letters in Names and Titles

Write each sentence. Use capital letters where needed for names and titles.

1. In 1497 king henry VII of England hired a navigator.
2. This navigator, john cabot, landed in what is now Canada.
3. The Italian navigator verrazano probably reached Canada in 1524.
4. In 1534 king francis I of France, i believe, sent jacques cartier to the New World.
5. In 1608 another French explorer, champlain, founded Quebec.
6. In 1673 joliet and marquette sailed down the Mississippi River.
7. Nine years later the explorer la salle claimed for France all the land drained by the Mississippi River.
8. In 1789 sir alexander mackenzie followed a river to the Arctic Ocean.
9. Last year dad and Uncle bill traveled down this river.
10. Pike's Peak was first sighted by mr. zebulon Pike in 1806.

The **d**octor will see you now.

This is **D**r. Gonzales.

PRACTICE AND ASSESS

Answers: Exercise 3

1. Ms. Lucy Jojola
2. Dr. Claude C. Islas
3. Captain Richards
4. Aunt Anna
5. Richard Bennett Jr.
6. Daniel Roget, Ph.D.
7. Uncle Louis
8. Jeanette Canales, M.D.
9. Judge Jean Luc
10. W. R. Mackenzie
11. President Jefferson
12. Sir James Smith
13. Mr. Robert Townsend Sr.
14. Queen Victoria
15. Madam Marie Curie
16. Lord Roy Nesbett
17. Warren G. Malloy Jr.
18. Professor Talmon
19. Mr. and Mrs. Ortiz
20. General Davidson

Answers: Exercise 4

1. King Henry VII
2. John Cabot
3. Verrazano
4. King Francis I; I; Jacques Cartier
5. Champlain
6. Joliet; Marquette
7. La Salle
8. Sir Alexander Mackenzie
9. Dad; Bill
10. Mr. Zebulon Pike

Independent Practice

Skills Practice

- *Grammar Practice*, p. 38
- *Grammar Reteaching*, p. 39
- *Grammar Enrichment*, p. 38

Grammar Workbook
Lessons 65–66

CLOSE

Ask students to imagine exploring North America in the 1600s. Have them write a journal entry about a day's events. The entry should include names and titles.

Enabling Strategies

LEP Capitalizing Words That Show Family Relationships

Some students may need practice in determining when to capitalize words that show family relationships. Have students write two sentences using the word *aunt*. Then have them work with a partner to determine in which sentences *aunt* should be capitalized. Remind students that when such a word is modified by a possessive word or article, the word is a common noun and should not be capitalized.

Setting the Purpose

Lesson 18.3 teaches students to capitalize the names of specific places correctly.

FOCUS

Lesson Overview

Objective: To recognize names of specific places as proper nouns that should be capitalized

Bellringer

When students enter the classroom, have this assignment on the board: *Add capital letters as needed in the following phrases:*

1. *along the Hudson river*
2. *the river known as the Rio Grande*
3. *born in the south*
4. *south of the border*

Motivating Activity

Discuss students' answers to the Bellringer assignment. The rules on page 442 will help them understand why *river* should be capitalized in the first phrase but not in the second, and *south* should be capitalized in the third phrase but not in the fourth.

TEACH

Teaching Tip

Explain to students that the popular names of regions are usually capitalized: Back Bay (Boston); the Channel (English Channel); Bay Area (San Francisco); the Badlands (South Dakota). The word *state* is capitalized if it follows the name of the state (Washington State), but it is not capitalized if it precedes the name of the state (the state of Washington).

18.3 Capitalizing Names of Places

The names of specific places are proper nouns and are capitalized. Do not, however, capitalize articles and prepositions that are part of geographical names.

RULE 1: Capitalize the names of cities, counties, states, countries, and continents.

Toronto	Mexico	Europe
New Hampshire	Cook County	Hong Kong

RULE 2: Capitalize the names of bodies of water and other geographical features.

Atlantic Ocean	Hudson Bay	Cape Cod
Mojave Desert	the Great Lakes	Monument Valley

RULE 3: Capitalize the names of sections of the country.

the Southwest	New England	Midwest

RULE 4: Capitalize compass points when they refer to a specific section of the country.

the East Coast	the South	the Northeast

Do not capitalize compass points when they are used to indicate direction.

Mexico is south of San Diego.

Do not capitalize adjectives formed from words showing direction.

northerly wind	eastern Texas

RULE 5: Capitalize the names of streets and highways.

Hyde Street	Hollywood Freeway

RULE 6: Capitalize the names of specific buildings, bridges, and monuments.

Washington Monument	Empire State Building

Teacher's Classroom Resources

The following resources can be used for planning, instruction, practice, reinforcement, reteaching, or enrichment.

Teaching Tools
Lesson Plans

Blackline Masters
Grammar Practice, p. 39
Grammar Reteaching, p. 40
Grammar Enrichment, p. 39

Grammar Workbook
Lessons 67–68

Exercise 5 Capitalizing Place Names

Write each word or group of words. Use capital letters where needed.

1. new mexico
2. acapulco
3. asia
4. peru
5. brooklyn bridge
6. yucatán peninsula
7. the pacific northwest
8. amarillo avenue
9. northern texas
10. san diego freeway
11. route 66
12. chrysler building
13. the southeast
14. indian ocean
15. alaska
16. portola valley
17. southern oregon
18. world trade center
19. rocky mountains
20. the united states

Exercise 6 Using Capital Letters for Place Names

Write each sentence. Use capital letters where needed for geographical names.

1. The country of mexico is south of the united states of america.
2. Mexico is the most northern country in latin america.
3. Its capital and largest city is mexico city.
4. This city of 19 million people has the largest population of any city in north america and south america.
5. The largest cities in mexico exist in the region known as the plateau of mexico.
6. The large peninsula located west of the gulf of california is known as baja california.
7. The sierra madre is part of the rockies.
8. The highest mountain in north america is mount mcKinley.
9. Mount mcKinley is in central alaska.
10. hawaii is surrounded by the pacific ocean, and puerto rico has the atlantic to the north and the caribbean sea to the south.

Exercise 7 Writing Place Names in a Paragraph

Write at least five sentences telling about the state you live in. Include the names of cities, rivers, and other specific places. Name the states that border your state.

PRACTICE AND ASSESS

Answers: Exercise 5

1. New Mexico
2. Acapulco
3. Asia
4. Peru
5. Brooklyn Bridge
6. Yucatán Peninsula
7. the Pacific Northwest
8. Amarillo Avenue
9. northern Texas
10. San Diego Freeway
11. Route 66
12. Chrysler Building
13. the Southeast
14. Indian Ocean
15. Alaska
16. Portola Valley
17. southern Oregon
18. World Trade Center
19. Rocky Mountains
20. the United States

Answers: Exercise 6

1. Mexico, United States of America
2. Latin America
3. Mexico City
4. North America, South America
5. Mexico, Plateau of Mexico
6. Gulf of California, Baja California
7. Sierra Madre, Rockies
8. North America, Mount McKinley
9. Mount McKinley, Alaska
10. Hawaii, Pacific Ocean, Puerto Rico, Atlantic, Caribbean Sea

Answers: Exercise 7

Answers will vary, but a sample is given below.

I live in the state of Michigan. It has two peninsulas, the Upper Peninsula and the Lower Peninsula. Four of the Great Lakes—Huron, Erie, Michigan, and Superior—almost surround my state. It borders the states of Ohio, Indiana, and Wisconsin, and also Canada on its eastern side. The capital of Michigan is Lansing, and the largest city is Detroit.

Independent Practice

Skills Practice

Grammar Practice, p. 39
Grammar Reteaching, p. 40
Grammar Enrichment, p. 39

Grammar Workbook
Lessons 67–68

Enabling Strategies

LEP Capitalizing Direction Words

When the definite article *the* is used with a direction word, the direction word is a proper noun and should be capitalized. For example, *far west* tells what direction and how far, but *the Far West* names a specific area.

CLOSE

Invite students to plan a trip to Mexico. Have them look at a map and choose an area they would like to visit. Ask them to write a paragraph about the area, including place names and direction words.

Setting the Purpose

Lesson 18.4 teaches students to capitalize proper nouns and proper adjectives correctly.

FOCUS

Lesson Overview

Objective: To identify adjectives made from proper nouns as proper adjectives

Bellringer

When students enter the classroom, have this assignment on the board: *What part of speech are the underlined words below? From what part of speech are they formed?*

Parisian fashion
Chinese food
Napoleonic Wars

Motivating Activity

Do students recognize that the underlined words in the Bellringer are adjectives; that they are formed from the proper nouns *Paris, China,* and *Napoleon;* and that they are called proper adjectives?

TEACH

Teaching Tip

Explain that the names of important historical events, time periods, documents, and organizations often include proper adjectives. Distribute a list such as the following: Iroquois League, American Revolution, Truman Doctrine, Jacksonian Era, Vietnam War. Ask students to identify the proper adjectives in the list and name the proper noun from which each was formed.

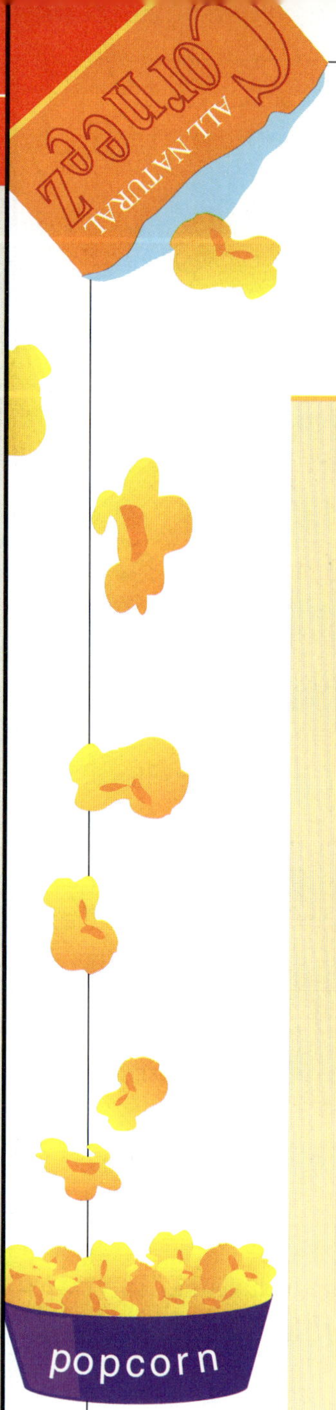

18.4 Capitalizing Other Proper Nouns and Adjectives

Many nouns besides the names of people and places are proper nouns and, therefore, always capitalized. The adjectives that are formed from proper nouns are called proper adjectives and are also always capitalized.

RULE 1: Capitalize all important words in the names of clubs, organizations, businesses, institutions, and political parties.

Fraternal Order of Police   Girl Scouts

RULE 2: Capitalize brand names but not the nouns following them.

Downhome cookies   Cruncho crackers

RULE 3: Capitalize all important words in the names of important historical events, periods of time, and documents.

War of 1812   Bronze Age   Constitution

RULE 4: Capitalize the names of days of the week, months of the year, and holidays. Do not capitalize names of the seasons.

Monday   August   New Year's Day   spring

RULE 5: Always capitalize the first and last words of the titles of literary works, songs, films, television series, magazines, and newspapers. Capitalize all other words except articles, coordinating conjunctions, and prepositions of fewer than five letters.

Julie of the Wolves   *Time* magazine

RULE 6: Capitalize the names of ethnic groups, nationalities, and languages.

Native American   Canadian   Italian

RULE 7: Capitalize all proper adjectives including those formed from names of ethnic groups and nationalities.

Native American crafts   Mexican art   Victorian era

Teacher's Classroom Resources

The following resources can be used for planning, instruction, practice, reinforcement, reteaching, or enrichment.

Teaching Tools
Lesson Plans

Blackline Masters
Grammar Practice, p. 40
Grammar Reteaching, p. 41
Grammar Enrichment, p. 40

Grammar Workbook
Lessons 69–70

Exercise 8 Capitalizing Proper Nouns and Adjectives

Write the following items. Use capital letters where needed.

1. madison school
2. december
3. world war I
4. native american poetry
5. "casey at the bat"
6. *oliver twist*
7. input corporation
8. mello yogurt
9. french
10. japanese
11. "we are the world"
12. *chicago tribune*
13. international workers union
14. "my life and difficult times"
15. african american stories
16. valentine's day
17. daughters of the american revolution
18. *popular mechanics* magazine
19. spanish dances
20. declaration of independence

Exercise 9 Using Capital Letters for Proper Nouns and Adjectives

Write each sentence. Use capital letters where needed for proper nouns and adjectives.

1. Mexico is a latin american country rich in art and tradition.
2. For centuries the arts have played a very important part in mexican life.
3. Long before Columbus discovered america, the maya and toltec peoples built beautiful temples.
4. The aztec people composed music and poetry.
5. The mexican revolution of 1910 changed the course of Mexico's art and literature.
6. Have you read the poem "wind and water and stone" by the famous mexican writer Octavio Paz?
7. In Mexico independence day is in september.
8. Holidays in mexico are colorfully celebrated.
9. We learned that mexico is the most southern part of the continent of north america.
10. The names of many cities in the southwestern united states originated from mexican and spanish words.

PRACTICE AND ASSESS

Answers: Exercise 8

1. Madison School
2. December
3. World War I
4. Native American poetry
5. "Casey at the Bat"
6. *Oliver Twist*
7. Input Corporation
8. Mello yogurt
9. French
10. Japanese
11. "We Are the World"
12. *Chicago Tribune*
13. International Workers Union
14. "My Life and Difficult Times"
15. African American stories
16. Valentine's Day
17. Daughters of the American Revolution
18. *Popular Mechanics* magazine
19. Spanish dances
20. Declaration of Independence

Answers: Exercise 9

1. Latin American
2. Mexican
3. America, Maya, Toltec
4. Aztec
5. Mexican Revolution
6. "Wind and Water and Stone," Mexican
7. Independence Day, September
8. Mexico
9. Mexico, North America
10. United States, Mexican, Spanish

Independent Practice

Skills Practice

- *Grammar Practice,* p. 40
- *Grammar Reteaching,* p. 41
- *Grammar Enrichment,* p. 40

Grammar Workbook
Lessons 69–70

CLOSE

Ask students to imagine they are starting their own country. Have them write a description of some holidays they would celebrate. Remind them to use proper nouns and adjectives.

Enabling Strategies

LEP Adjectives Made from Proper Nouns

Students with limited English proficiency may have difficulty identifying the adjectives made from proper nouns in Exercise 9. Pair these students with more proficient students who can act as coaches and help them identify the proper adjectives in Exercise 9.

TEACH

About the Literature

After students have read the passage from Quentin Reynolds's "A Secret for Two," ask them which words are or are not essential to the meaning of the passage, paying particular attention to the large number of capital letters in the passage. Go over the highlighted words with them. Ask students to identify other examples of capitalization in the text. The exercises that follow are based on this passage and related topics.

Linking Grammar and Literature

Cooperative Learning

Bring to class several newspapers and magazines. Have teams of three or four students find examples that demonstrate each rule of capitalization in this unit. Teams can then work together to create a chart of their findings.

Critical Thinking

Encourage students to consider the reasons for the rules they have learned about capitalization. Remind them that capital letters make it easier to understand the meaning of what we read. Call on students to explain how the capital letter in each of the highlighted words on page 446 helps them understand the sentences more quickly.

UNIT 18
Unit Review

Grammar Review

Capitalization

"A Secret for Two" by Quentin Reynolds tells the story of a visually impaired milk deliverer, Pierre Dupin, and Joseph, the horse that drew his wagon. The passage has been annotated to show some of the rules of capitalization covered in this unit.

Literature Model

from A SECRET FOR TWO

by Quentin Reynolds

Montreal is a very large city, but, like all large cities, it has some very small streets. Streets, for instance, like Prince Edward Street, which is only four blocks long, ending in a cul-de-sac. No one knew Prince Edward Street as well as did Pierre Dupin, for Pierre had delivered milk to the families on the street for thirty years now.

During the past fifteen years the horse which drew the milk wagon used by Pierre was a large white horse named Joseph. In Montreal, especially in that part of Montreal which is very French, the animals, like children, are often given the names of saints. When the big, white horse first came to the Provincale Milk Company, he didn't have a name. They told Pierre that he could use the white horse henceforth. Pierre stroked the softness of the horse's neck; he stroked the sheen of its splendid belly, and he looked into the eyes of the horse.

"That is a kind horse, a gentle and a faithful horse," Pierre said. . . .

Annotations:
- Name of a street (Prince Edward Street)
- Name of a person (Pierre Dupin)
- First word of a sentence (During)
- Name of a city (Montreal)
- Proper adjective (French)
- Name of a company (Provincale Milk Company)
- First word of a direct quotation (That)

Teacher's Classroom Resources

The following resources can be used for planning, instruction, practice, reinforcement, assessment, reteaching, enrichment or evaluation.

Teaching Tools
Lesson Plans

Grammar Workbook
Lessons 63–70
Unit 11 Review
Cumulative Review: Units 1–11

Unit Assessment
Tests with Answer Key
Unit 18 Mastery Test, pp. 71–72

Test Generator
Unit 18 Mastery Test

Exercise 1

Capitalizing Sentences and Quotations Rewrite each sentence, correcting any errors in capitalization. If a sentence has no errors, write *correct.*

SAMPLE Pierre Dupin said, "no one loves Joseph as much as I do."
ANSWER Pierre Dupin said, "No one loves Joseph as much as I do."

1. for most of his adult life, Pierre Dupin delivered milk to the families on Prince Edward Street.
2. after fifteen years of delivering milk, Pierre got his horse, Joseph.
3. the horse would lead his master to each house on the street.
4. Pierre thought, "what would I do without my loyal Friend, Joseph?"
5. Pierre and Joseph spent many years together in Montreal, Canada.
6. all the families on the street recognized Pierre and Joseph.
7. Pierre said, "fifteen years ago my supervisor gave me a horse to pull my milk wagon."
8. "Look into his eyes," said the supervisor. "this horse will be your faithful friend."
9. Pierre thought His new horse was kind and gentle.
10. "I think," said Pierre, "That I will name him Joseph."

Exercise 2

Using Capitalization in a Letter Rewrite the following letter, using correct capitalization. The letter contains ten errors.

March 19, 1996

dear Sara,

Today we read a story about a milk deliverer. My teacher said, "class, I know you will like this story. it is one of my favorites." I can see why my teacher says He likes the story so much.

last summer you said to me, "someday I hope I can have my own horse." you might like to read this story. It's called "A Secret for Two." tell me What you think of it.

your friend,
Chris

UNIT 18 Review

PRACTICE AND ASSESS

Answers: Exercise 1

1. For ...
2. After ...
3. The ...
4. ... "What ... friend ..."
5. correct
6. All ...
7. Pierre said, "Fifteen ... "
8. "This ..."
9. ... his ...
10. ... that ... "

Answers: Exercise 2

Dear Sara,

Today we read a story about a milk deliverer. My teacher said, "**C**lass, I know you will like this story. **I**t is one of my favorites." I can see why my teacher says **h**e likes the story so much.

Last summer you said to me, "**S**omeday I hope I can have my own horse." **Y**ou might like to read this story. It's called "A Secret for Two." **T**ell me **w**hat you think of it.

Your friend,
Chris

Answers: Exercise 3

1. Mr. Robert Chang
2. Uncle John
3. correct
4. Professor R. D. Diego
5. correct
6. Queen Elizabeth
7. Margaret Lee, M.D.
8. Lieutenant Juarez
9. correct
10. Ms. Evert
11. Governor Whitman
12. Dr. Chris Cross
13. President Lincoln
14. Emily Cox, Ph.D.
15. E. B. White
16. Mrs. Doubtfire
17. Sir Edmund Hillary
18. Aunt Maria and I
19. Ken Griffey Jr.
20. Lady Jane Grey

Answers: Exercise 4

1. Diego Rivera
2. Rivera; Mexico
3. Aunt Sharice; National Palace; Mexico City
4. Yucatán Peninsula
5. Gulf of Mexico; Caribbean Sea
6. Juan Perez, Ph.D.
7. Dr. Perez; General Santa Anna
8. Mexico
9. Anna; Texas; Mexico
10. San Jacinto River

Exercise 3

Capitalizing Names and Titles of People Rewrite the following names and titles using correct capitalization. If an item contains no errors, write *correct.*

1. mr. robert chang
2. uncle john
3. the club's president
4. professor r.d. diego
5. my aunt and uncle
6. queen elizabeth
7. margaret lee, m.d.
8. lieutenant juarez
9. the captain of the ship
10. ms. evert
11. governor whitman
12. dr. chris cross
13. president lincoln
14. emily cox, ph.d.
15. e.b. white
16. mrs. doubtfire
17. sir edmund hillary
18. aunt maria and i
19. ken griffey jr.
20. lady jane grey

Exercise 4

Capitalizing Titles and Names of People and Places Write each sentence. Use capital letters where needed.

SAMPLE Our art teacher, ms. whitney, showed us paintings from mexico.
ANSWER Our art teacher, Ms. Whitney, showed us paintings from Mexico.

1. The brilliant Mexican artist diego rivera painted murals.
2. Born in 1886, rivera became famous for his murals of mexico.
3. Last summer aunt sharice saw the murals in the national palace in mexico city.
4. My aunt then visited the yucatán peninsula.
5. That peninsula is surrounded by the gulf of mexico and the caribbean sea.
6. Her tour guide was juan perez, ph.d.
7. One evening dr. perez discussed general santa anna.
8. In 1833 the general became president of mexico.
9. Santa anna led the fight against the American colonists who wanted to take texas from mexico.
10. He was captured in a famous battle fought on the banks of the san jacinto river in 1836.

Exercise 5

Capitalizing Proper Nouns Rewrite each sentence, correcting any errors in capitalization.

SAMPLE Within a year joseph knew the milk route as well as Pierre.
ANSWER Within a year Joseph knew the milk route as well as Pierre.

1. Pierre began his work for the provincale milk company every morning at five o'clock.
2. Without any direction from pierre, Joseph stopped at each house on prince edward street.
3. Jacques, the Supervisor of the company, thought that Pierre should retire after thirty years of work.
4. Jacques didn't know that pierre was visually impaired.
5. Only Joseph, i believe, knew Pierre couldn't see.

Exercise 6

Capitalizing Proper Nouns and Proper Adjectives Rewrite each sentence, correcting any errors in capitalization.

SAMPLE Montreal is in the canadian province of quebec.
ANSWER Montreal is in the Canadian province of Quebec.

1. The city is located in Southern Quebec, the province's most fertile region.
2. In 1535 Jacques Cartier of france became the first european explorer to reach present-day montreal.
3. The British captured the city in 1760 during the french and indian war.
4. Today french is the official language of Montreal.
5. Montreal is the largest french-speaking city in the world after Paris.
6. In addition to french, english is spoken in Montreal.
7. The St. lawrence river runs Northeast through quebec, a province of Canada.
8. Two states in new england and some other canadian provinces border Quebec on the East.
9. Quebec shares its Southern border with New york and vermont.
10. The National capital of canada is ottawa.

UNIT 18 Review

Answers: Exercise 5

1. Provincale Milk Company
2. Pierre; Prince Edward Street
3. supervisor
4. Pierre
5. I

Answers: Exercise 6

1. southern
2. France; European; Montreal
3. French and Indian War
4. French
5. French-speaking
6. French; English
7. Lawrence River; northeast; Quebec
8. New England; Canadian; east
9. southern; York; Vermont
10. national; Canada; Ottawa

UNIT 18 Review

Answers: Exercise 7

Proofreading

This proofreading activity provides editing practice with (1) the current or previous units' skills, (2) the **Troubleshooter** errors, and (3) spelling errors. Students should be able to complete the exercise by referring to the units, the **Troubleshooter,** and a dictionary.

	Error (Type of Error)
1.	• Scotland (capitalization of place names)
2.	• art (capitalization; common noun)
3.	• artist (capitalization; common noun)
	• recognition (spelling)
4.	• Kane's (singluar possessive)
5.	• rise (verb form)
6.	• Two (capitalization of titles)
7.	• Like (capitalization of first word in a sentence)
	• are (subject-verb agreement)
	• city's (capitalization; common noun)

Exercise 7 Proofreading

The following passage is about the artist John Kane, whose work appears below. Rewrite the passage, correcting the errors in spelling, capitalization, grammar, and usage. Add any missing punctuation. There are 10 errors.

John Kane

[1]Born in scotland, John Kane (1860–1934) immigrated to Pennsylvania with his family when he was nineteen. [2]Kane began sketching as a youth, ➡

John Kane, *Across the Strip,* 1929

About the Art

John Kane, *Across the Strip,* 1929

John Kane's painting *Across the Strip* depicts details of urban life in Pittsburgh along with its steel mills, structures, and natural features. At one time Kane painted railroad cars for a living. During his lunch hours, he painted his landscapes on the sides of the railroad cars; when he returned to work, he painted them out. Kane's work was first exhibited in 1927 at Carnegie International Exhibition in Pittsburgh. At the age of 67, he became a celebrity. *Across the Strip*, an oil-on-canvas painting, measures 32 1/4 inches by 34 1/2 inches. It is now in the Phillips Collection in Washington, D.C.

but he couldn't afford to go to Art school. [3] The self-taught Artist finally achieved reckognition at the age of sixty-seven with the exhibition of one of his paintings in Pittsburgh.

[4] Many of Kanes' paintings present detailed images of everyday life in Pittsburgh, where the artist spent much of his life. [5] In *Across the Strip*, for example, mills and warehouses risen up behind apartment buildings, where clothes are hung out to dry. [6] A man in a horse-drawn wagon delivers bread on a route similar to that in "A Secret for two." [7] like Pierre and Joseph, the man and horse is a familiar part of their City's daily life.

Exercise 8

Mixed Review

Rewrite the following letter, capitalizing all necessary words. You will need to capitalize 25 letters.

april 21, 19—

dear lenny,

Since you were absent last week, I thought I would tell you what we did in our history class. we are learning about pyramids. ms. nelson said that great civilizations thrived in Mexico a thousand years ago.

Barry asked, "is it true that some native americans built pyramids?"

Anna answered, "at the town of teotihuacán, people built pyramids dedicated to the sun."

Our teacher added, "in the religious centers of southern Mexico, the mayan people built pyramids with temples on top. In addition," she continued, "there are other ancient pyramids."

Ms. Nelson then told us about the pyramids in egypt. The Great Pyramid stands near the nile river. It is believed to have been built around 2700 B.C. when pharaoh khufu reigned. some pyramids were actually the tombs of egyptian pharaohs.

Maybe we will still be studying pyramids when you return next week. All of us at west middle school miss you

your pal,
stan

UNIT 18 Review

Answers: Exercise 8

Mixed Review

April 21, 19—

Dear **L**enny,

Since you were absent last week, I thought I would tell you what we did in our history class. **W**e are learning about pyramids. **M**s. **N**elson said that great civilizations thrived in Mexico a thousand years ago.

Barry asked, "**I**s it true that some **N**ative **A**mericans built pyramids?"

Anna answered, "**A**t the town of **T**eotihuacán, people built pyramids dedicated to the sun."

Our teacher added, "**I**n the religious centers of southern Mexico, the **M**ayan people built pyramids with temples on top. In addition," she continued, "there are other ancient pyramids."

Ms. Nelson then told us about the pyramids in **E**gypt. The Great Pyramid stands near the **N**ile **R**iver. It is believed to have been built around 2700 B.C. when **P**haraoh **K**hufu reigned. **S**ome pyramids were actually the tombs of **E**gyptian pharaohs.

Maybe we will still be studying pyramids when you return next week. All of us at **W**est **M**iddle **S**chool miss you.

Your pal,
Stan

CLOSE

Ask students to write a paragraph describing the city or town they live in. Remind them to check their capitalization of place names and proper adjectives.

Capitalization in Writing

Encourage students to read the passage in their books silently. Then discuss the italicized words in relation to the Techniques with Capitalization.

Techniques with Capitalization

Discuss the techniques described and ask students to apply them to the letter in Exercise 8 on page 451. They will find examples of proper adjectives (Egyptian pharaohs), place names (Egypt), and direction or location words (southern Mexico).

Practice

The answers to this challenging activity may vary if students have made revisions in addition to correcting errors. Corrections are as follows:

Today ... Canada ... English ... However ... Quebec ... Canadians ... French ... Champlain ... Quebec ... English ... French and Indian War ... Quebec ... British ... British ... American

Writing Application

Capitalization in Writing Study the italicized examples of capitalization in this excerpt from Joseph Bruchac's essay, "Thanking the Birds." Think about why each is capitalized.

> *One* day 30 years ago, *Swift Eagle*, an *Apache* man, visited some friends on the *Onondaga Indian Reservation* in central *New York*. *While* he was out walking, he heard sounds of boys playing in the bushes.
>
> "*There's* another one. Shoot it!" said one of the boys.
>
> *When* he pushed through the brush to see what was happening, he found that they had been shooting small birds with a BB gun.

Techniques with Capitalization Try to apply the rules of capitalization in your own writing, just as Joseph Bruchac has done in his.

1. Capitalize adjectives that are formed from proper nouns.

Incorrect version an apache man
Bruchac's version an Apache man

2. Capitalize the names of specific geographical places.

Incorrect version the onondaga indian reservation
Bruchac's version the Onondaga Indian Reservation

3. Do not capitalize adjectives formed from words showing direction or location.

Incorrect version Central New York
Bruchac's version central New York

Practice Practice using correct capitalization by revising the following passage on a separate sheet of paper.

today the official languages of canada are english and French. however, most of the people of quebec are French-speaking canadians. Although it was the french explorer champlain who founded quebec, the english captured Quebec City during the french and indian war. They acquired quebec by the Treaty of Paris in 1783. Over the next few decades thousands of british colonists came to canada from the british Isles and the american colonies.

Teacher's Classroom Resources

The following resources can be used for assessment or evaluation.

Unit Assessment

Tests with Answer Key
Unit 18 Mastery Test, pp. 71–72

Test Generator
Unit 18 Mastery Test

You may wish to administer Unit 18 Mastery Test at this point.

UNIT

19 Punctuation

Grammar

Lessons

UNIT GOALS

The goal of Unit 19 is to help students, through example and instruction, to develop an understanding of and an ability to recognize the appropriate use of punctuation marks in sentences and in numbers.

Unit Assessment

Tests with Answer Key
Unit 19 Pretest, pp. 73–74
Unit 19 Mastery Test, pp. 75–76

Test Generator
Unit 19 Pretest
Unit 19 Mastery Test

You may wish to administer the Unit 19 Pretest at this point.

Key to Ability Levels

Enabling Strategies have been coded for varying learning styles and abilities.

L1 Level 1 activities are within the ability range of Learning Disabled students.

L2 Level 2 activities are basic-to-average activities and are within the ability range of average students.

L3 Level 3 activities are challenging activities and are within the ability range of above-average students.

LEP LEP activities are within the ability range of Limited English Proficiency students.

Setting the Purpose

Lesson 19.1 teaches students the use of the period, question mark, and exclamation mark. It also teaches them to distinguish between declarative, imperative, interrogative, and exclamatory sentences and to recognize interjections.

FOCUS

Lesson Overview

Objective: To recognize the correct use of three end punctuation marks

Bellringer

When students enter the classroom, have this assignment on the board: *Can you end the following sentence with three different punctuation marks? How does the meaning of the sentence change?*

You have a gift for me

Motivating Activity

Invite volunteers to read aloud their sentences from the Bellringer activity and tell which punctuation marks they used. Explain that, unlike oral language, written language depends on punctuation marks to convey the meaning.

TEACH

Teaching Tip

To reinforce how end marks can change the meaning of a sentence, write this sentence on the board: *She enjoyed that movie.* Ask students to identify the sentence type (declarative), and then have them change it into an interrogative sentence (*Did she enjoy that movie?*) and an exclamatory sentence (*She really enjoyed that movie!*).

19.1 Using the Period and Other End Marks

Different end marks are used with the different types of sentences. The period is used for declarative and imperative sentences. The question mark is used for interrogative sentences, and the exclamation point is used for exclamatory sentences.

RULE 1: Use a period at the end of a declarative sentence. A declarative sentence makes a statement.

The Wright brothers built the first successful airplane.
They built this pioneering machine at a cost of around $1,000.

RULE 2: Use a period at the end of an imperative sentence. An imperative sentence gives a command or makes a request.

Open your book to the chapter on airplanes. [command]
Please read about the first successful flight. [request]

RULE 3: Use a question mark at the end of an interrogative sentence. An interrogative sentence asks a question.

When did jet planes first begin flying?
Do most jet planes have space for more than 100 passengers?

RULE 4: Use an exclamation point at the end of an exclamatory sentence. An exclamatory sentence expresses strong feeling.

What a wonderful invention the jet engine was!
How fast jet planes fly!

RULE 5: Use an exclamation point at the end of an interjection. An interjection is a word or group of words that expresses strong emotion.

Wow!	Whew!
My goodness!	Ouch!

Teacher's Classroom Resources

The following resources can be used for planning, instruction, practice, reinforcement, assessment, reteaching, enrichment, or evaluation.

Teaching Tools
Lesson Plans

Blackline Masters
Grammar Practice, p. 41
Grammar Reteaching, p. 42
Grammar Enrichment, p. 41

Grammar Workbook
Lesson 71

Unit Assessment

Tests with Answer Key
Unit 19 Pretest, pp. 73–74

Test Generator
Unit 19 Pretest

You may wish to administer the Unit 19 Pretest at this point.

Exercise 1 Using End Marks

Write the correct end mark for each sentence. Then write whether the sentence is *declarative, imperative, interrogative,* or *exclamatory.*

1. Leonardo da Vinci drew a design of an airplane more than four hundred years ago
2. How imaginative da Vinci was
3. Did the Wright brothers make the first successful airplane flight
4. On December 17, 1903, Orville Wright made the first successful piloted flight in a power-driven airplane
5. What an important day in history it was
6. Please tell me the name of Orville's brother
7. On that day Wilbur Wright also made a successful flight
8. The Wright brothers did not believe airplanes would ever be able to fly at night
9. How wrong they were
10. The Wright brothers were from Dayton, Ohio
11. Why did the brothers begin flying
12. The Wright brothers read about the death of a glider pilot named Otto Lilienthal
13. How that man's work affected them
14. Why did they make their flights in Kitty Hawk, North Carolina
15. Did the Weather Bureau in Washington advise them
16. In 1900 they tested their own glider
17. Did that early glider have good lifting power
18. They received a patent on a glider they made in 1902
19. Describe that machine
20. Later the two brothers built a motor-powered airplane
21. They made experimental flights for several years
22. In 1905 they made 105 flights, totaling only forty-five minutes in the air
23. Imagine that
24. Newspapers began giving longer reports on their flights after that time
25. Don't forget the Wright brothers' important role in history

PRACTICE AND ASSESS

Answers: Exercise 1

1. . (declarative)
2. ! (exclamatory)
3. ? (interrogative)
4. . (declarative)
5. ! (exclamatory)
6. . (imperative)
7. . (declarative)
8. . (declarative)
9. ! (exclamatory)
10. . (declarative)
11. ? (interrogative)
12. . (declarative)
13. ! (exclamatory)
14. ? (interrogative)
15. ? (interrogative)
16. . (declarative)
17. ? (interrogative)
18. . (declarative)
19. . (imperative)
20. . (declarative)
21. . (declarative)
22. . (declarative)
23. ! (exclamatory)
24. . (declarative)
25. . (imperative)

Independent Practice

Skills Practice

- *Grammar Practice,* p. 41
- *Grammar Reteaching,* p. 42
- *Grammar Enrichment,* p. 41

Grammar Workbook, Lesson 71

CLOSE

Ask students to imagine how the Wright brothers would react to today's modern flying technology. Have them write five sentences about the brothers' reactions. The sentences should represent the interjection and the four types of sentences presented in the lesson.

Enabling Strategies

LEP Using Question Marks

Deciding when to use the question mark in standard English may be confusing for some nonnative speakers. For example, the question mark is not used with an indirect question: *He asked me if I was going out.* With a polite request or courtesy question in business letters, it is also usually left out: *Will you please send six boxes of computer paper.* Remind Hispanic students, who are accustomed to putting the question mark at both the beginning and end of the sentence, that it is used only at the end of a question in English.

Setting the Purpose

Lesson 19.2 teaches students to use a comma to signal a pause or a separation between sentence parts.

FOCUS

Lesson Overview

Objective: To recognize the correct use of commas in signaling a pause or separation between parts of a sentence

Bellringer

When students enter the classroom, have this assignment on the board: *Explain the difference between these two sentences:*

I will divide the pizza into equal pieces for Bobbie, Jo, Lou, Ann, and me.

I will divide the pizza into equal pieces for Bobbie, Jo, Lou Ann, and me.

Motivating Activity

Invite volunteers to describe the difference between the two sentences in the Bellringer activity. Students should understand that commas can make a difference in the meaning of a sentence.

TEACH

Teaching Tip

Ask students to write sentences modeled after the example sentences in the text. Assign the example sentences to individual students. Have the students write the sentences on the chalkboard along with an original sentence following the form of the model.

19.2 Using Commas I

Commas can make sentences easier to understand because they signal a pause or separation between sentence parts.

RULE 1: Use commas to separate three or more items in a series.

Mary McLeod Bethune served as a teacher, adviser, and administrator.
Bethune lived, studied, and worked in the South.

RULE 2: Use a comma to show a pause after an introductory word.

Yes, she became the first African American woman to head an agency in the United States government.
No, her family had very little money.

RULE 3: Use a comma after two or more prepositional phrases at the beginning of a sentence.

For a number of years, she served as director of the National Youth Administration's Division of Negro Affairs. [two prepositional phrases—*For a number* and *of years*]

You need not use a comma after a single prepositional phrase, but it is not incorrect to do so.

For years she served as President Roosevelt's special adviser on minority affairs. [one prepositional phrase—*For years*]

RULE 4: Use commas to set off words that interrupt the flow of thought in a sentence.

Bethune, you might imagine, spent her life improving educational opportunities for African Americans.
Mary McLeod Bethune, of course, served as president of the famous Bethune-Cookman College.

RULE 5: Use commas to set off names used in direct address.

Clarisse, did you know that Ms. Bethune opened a school for girls?
Pardon me, Ms. Moeti, when did she open this school?
Read about Bethune-Cookman College in Florida, Derek.

Teacher's Classroom Resources

The following resources can be used for planning, instruction, practice, reinforcement, reteaching, or enrichment.

Teaching Tools
Lesson Plans

Blackline Masters
Grammar Practice, pp. 42–43
Grammar Reteaching, p. 43
Grammar Enrichment, p. 43

Grammar Workbook
Lesson 72

Exercise 2 **Using Commas**

Write the following sentences, adding commas where needed. Write *correct* if a sentence needs no commas.

1. Mary McLeod Bethune we have learned was the daughter of enslaved persons.
2. Bethune attended a mission school a seminary and the Moody Bible Institute.
3. In the early part of the twentieth century she opened a girls' school.
4. Bethune served in various capacities for presidents Coolidge Hoover Roosevelt and Truman.
5. From 1935 to 1944 she served as President Franklin Roosevelt's special adviser on minority affairs.
6. Mr. Fenster is it true Bethune was the first African American woman to head a federal agency?
7. Yes she was and she also was awarded the Spingarn Medal.
8. Joel E. Spingarn was a leader of the National Association for the Advancement of Colored People and I think an American literary critic.
9. From 1913 to the present the Spingarn Medal has been awarded to African Americans for outstanding achievement.
10. In 1958 the Spingarn Medal was given to the eight young people who were the first African Americans to attend Little Rock Central High School.

Exercise 3 **Identifying Comma Rules**

Write the following sentences, adding commas where needed. Write whether the commas are needed because of *Rule 1, 2, 3, 4,* or *5* on page 456.

SAMPLE Ms. Lamm is it true that Bethune became a friend of Eleanor Roosevelt?

ANSWER Ms. Lamm, is it true that Bethune became a friend of Eleanor Roosevelt? (Rule 5)

1. Yes Mrs. Roosevelt was a great admirer of Bethune.
2. Both women or so I've read worked hard during World War II.
3. Bethune and Roosevelt worked with people who were young poor and illiterate.
4. After her husband's illness in 1921 Eleanor became active on his behalf.
5. Both Bethune and Roosevelt are famous Mr. Branwell for their noble work.

Enabling Strategies

LEP Using Commas in a Series

Students may be accustomed to using commas differently when writing a language other than English. Spanish, for example, does not use a final comma before the conjunction in a series. Explain that in formal English the comma is used before *and* or *or* in a series to prevent confusion. Pair LEP students with non-LEP students. Ask students to write a few simple sentences using a series of three or more items. For example, *I like apples, oranges, and bananas.* Students can then exchange papers and check each other's use of commas.

PRACTICE AND ASSESS

Answers: Exercise 2

1. . . . Bethune, we have learned, was . . .
2. . . . a mission school, a seminary, and the . . .
3. . . . the twentieth century, she . . .
4. . . . Coolidge, Hoover, Roosevelt, and . . .
5. From 1935 to 1944, she . . .
6. Mr. Fenster, is . . .
7. Yes, she was, and . . .
8. . . . and, I think, an . . .
9. From 1913 to the present, the . . .
10. correct

Answers: Exercise 3

1. Yes, Mrs. Roosevelt . . . (Rule 2)
2. . . . women, or so I've read, worked . . . (Rule 4)
3. . . . young, poor, and . . . (Rule 1)
4. . . . in 1921, Eleanor . . . (Rule 3)
5. . . . famous, Mr. Branwell, for . . . (Rule 5)

Independent Practice

Skills Practice

- *Grammar Practice,* pp. 42–43
- *Grammar Reteaching,* p. 43
- *Grammar Enrichment,* p 43
- ***Grammar Workbook,*** Lesson 72

CLOSE

Have students choose a famous person or a period in history they have studied. Invite them to think of sentences about this person or historical period. Their sentences should include examples of the comma rules presented in this lesson. Write the students' sentences on the board as they are presented.

Setting the Purpose

Lesson 19.3 teaches students to use commas correctly in compound sentences, in letters, and for general clarity in writing.

FOCUS

Lesson Overview

Objective: To recognize the correct use of commas in compound sentences, in letters, and for clarity

Bellringer

When students enter the classroom, have this assignment on the board: *Add any necessary commas to the following sentence:*

Phillis Wheatley was a slave and she was also a poet.

Motivating Activity

Discuss the sentence in the Bellringer. Did students add a comma before the conjunction *and*? Ask them to write two compound sentences of their own and remind them of the proper use of the comma.

TEACH

Teaching Tip

Sentence combining is an excellent way to teach the difference between joining two simple sentences with a comma and a coordinating conjunction and joining a compound predicate with a coordinating conjunction but no comma.

19.3 Using Commas II

You need to use commas correctly in compound sentences, after salutations and closings in letters, and to prevent misreading.

RULE 6: Use a comma before *and, or,* or *but* when it joins simple sentences into a compound sentence.

Phillis Wheatley began to write poetry at the age of fourteen, and she became the first important African American poet.
She was born in Africa, but she was enslaved and taken to Boston.
Phillis Wheatley's poems discuss the question of religion, or they treat the issue of slavery.

RULE 7: Use a comma after the salutation of a friendly letter and after the closing of both a friendly letter and a business letter.

Dear Dad, Your friend, Yours truly,

RULE 8: Use a comma to prevent misreading.

Instead of one, two friends visited Phillis.

Teacher's Classroom Resources

The following resources can be used for planning, instruction, practice, reinforcement, reteaching, or enrichment.

Teaching Tools
Lesson Plans

Blackline Masters
Grammar Practice, p. 44
Grammar Reteaching, p. 44
Grammar Enrichment, pp. 44–45

Grammar Workbook
Lesson 73

Exercise 4 Using Commas

Write the following sentences, adding commas where needed. Write *correct* if a sentence needs no commas.

1. Phillis Wheatley was taken to Boston on a slave ship and there she was sold at a slave auction.
2. She was sold to a wealthy family and this family gave her their name and their religion.
3. The Wheatleys recognized Phillis's great talents and they taught her to read and write.
4. They encouraged her to study geography history and Latin.
5. During the day Phillis read the great English poets or she studied the famous Latin writers.
6. She began writing poetry when she was a teenager and many of her poems were published.
7. A book of her poems was published in London in 1773.
8. The title of the book was I believe *Poems on Various Subjects, Religious and Moral.*
9. Ms. Schofield have you read any of her poems?
10. Wheatley traveled to London but she returned to Boston.

Exercise 5 Using Commas

Write each numbered item or sentence. Add a comma or commas where needed.

[1]Dear Phillis

[2]I read your poem today and I thought it showed great promise. [3]You should send it to the local newspaper or maybe a magazine would publish it. [4]You'll be able to travel to London but I know you'll want to return to Boston. [5]Instead of one two people will go to London with you. [6]I suggest that you see Westminster Abbey and Mr. Garns thinks you should visit the Tower of London while you are there. [7]These buildings escaped damage thank goodness during London's Great Fire of 1666. [8]Mr. Garns says that most of the city has been rebuilt and the new buildings are of brick and stone. [9]Of course we all hope that you have a wonderful trip.

[10]Your friend
Hannah

Enabling Strategies

LEP Using Commas in Compound Sentences

Students may be confused about the comma in compound sentences. Point out that since a compound sentence consists of two simple sentences joined by a coordinating conjunction, a comma must be placed before the conjunction. Compare the sentence *I went to the store* and *bought some dessert.* (no comma) with *I went to the store,* and *I bought some dessert.* (comma). In the first sentence, *and* joins a compound predicate; the sentence is simple. In the second sentence, *and* joins simple sentences, making a compound sentence.

PRACTICE AND ASSESS

Answers: Exercise 4

1. . . . ship, and . . .
2. . . . family, and . . .
3. . . . talents, and . . .
4. . . . geography, history, and . . .
5. . . . poets, or . . .
6. . . . teenager, and . . .
7. correct
8. . . . was, I believe, . . .
9. . . . Schofield, . . .
10. . . . London, but . . .

Answers: Exercise 5

1. Dear Phillis,
2. ... today, and ...
3. ... local newspaper, or maybe ...
4. ... London, but I ...
5. ... one, two people ...
6. ... Westminster Abbey, and ...
7. ... damage, thank goodness, during ...
8. ... rebuilt, and ...
9. Of course, we ...
10. ... friend, *Hannah*

Independent Practice

Skills Practice

Grammar Practice, p. 44
Grammar Reteaching, p. 44
Grammar Enrichment, pp. 44–45

Grammar Workbook, Lesson 73

CLOSE

Ask students to write a letter to Phillis Wheatley or some other important person in history. Tell them to make their letters realistic and to use the correct punctuation for letter writing. They should also include compound sentences and sentences that require commas for clarity.

Setting the Purpose

Lesson 19.4 teaches students the correct use of commas for dates, addresses, and other special purposes.

FOCUS

Lesson Overview

Objective: To recognize and use correctly commas with dates, addresses, titles and several other grammatical constructions

Bellringer

When students enter the classroom, have this assignment on the board: *Write a sentence that contains your date of birth and the place (city, state, and country) where you were born. Be sure to use commas correctly.*

Motivating Activity

Discuss the Bellringer activity with students. Ask volunteers to write their sentences on the board. Does the rest of the class agree with the placement of the commas?

TEACH

Teaching Tip

Numbers other than dates usually have a comma after the digit representing the thousands: *More than 1,500 people came to hear Nelson Mandela's speech.* However, do not use a comma in page or date numbers (except for dates of five figures or more) or after a decimal point: *3500 B.C.; p. 2345; 0.76854;* and *35,000 B.C.*

19.4 Using Commas III

Several rules for using commas, including those for punctuating dates, addresses, and titles, are a matter of standard usage.

RULE 9: Use commas before and after the year when it is used with both the month and the day. Do not use a comma if only the month and the year are given.

The flight began on June 18, 1983, and lasted six days.
The flight ended in June 1983 and lasted six days.

RULE 10: Use commas before and after the name of a state or a country when it is used with the name of a city. Do not use a comma after the state postal abbreviation followed by a ZIP code.

People came from as far away as Albany, New York, and Guatemala City, Guatemala, to watch the launch.
The address on the envelope was 42 Campus Drive, Stanford, CA 94305.

RULE 11: Use a comma or pair of commas to set off an abbreviated title or degree following a person's name.

The first American woman to participate in a space mission was Sally Ride, Ph.D.
Norman E. Thagard, M.D., accompanied Sally Ride on that memorable mission.

RULE 12: Use a comma or pair of commas to set off *too* when *too* means "also."

Kathy Sullivan, too, is a famous astronaut.

RULE 13: Use a comma or pair of commas to set off a direct quotation.

Claude said, "Sally Ride received her doctor's degree from Stanford University in 1978."
"I think," said Lotoya, "that Kathy Sullivan became the first woman spacewalker in history."

Teacher's Classroom Resources

The following resources can be used for planning, instruction, practice, reinforcement, reteaching, or enrichment.

Teaching Tools
Lesson Plans

Blackline Masters
Grammar Practice, pp. 46–47
Grammar Reteaching, p. 45
Grammar Enrichment, pp. 46–47

Grammar Workbook
Lesson 74

Exercise 6 **Using Commas**

Write the following sentences, adding commas where needed. Write *correct* if a sentence needs no commas.

1. A letter from a friend in Houston Texas arrived in the mail yesterday.
2. The letter was postmarked March 19 1995.
3. It focused attention on Sally Ride Ph.D.
4. On the June 1983 space mission the other astronauts with Ride were Hauck Fabian and Crippen.
5. Ride and Fabian conducted experiments and they tested the shuttle's remote manipulator arm.
6. They launched a communications satellite for the Indonesian government and one for the Canadian government too.
7. Sally Ride became an astronaut candidate the same year she got her Ph.D. in physics.
8. Yes I think Sally Ride should inspire young women to learn everything they can about math and science.
9. Before her mission in 1983 Sally Ride married a fellow astronaut.
10. "It's true" Lee said in the letter "that Sally Ride is a pioneer and is very brave."

Exercise 7 **Using Commas**

Write each numbered item or sentence in the following letter. Add a comma or commas where needed.

[1]16 Wallace Avenue
[2]Richmond VA 23203
[3]October 4 19__

[4]Dear Monica,

[5]On April 6 1995 my class held auditions for a play. [6]Alice Perri M.A. was our director. [7]"With two students for each part" she said "we can perform the play twice." [8]I won a major role, and my friend Sonia got a part too. [9]We performed the play on May 1 1995 and on May 8 1995.

[10]Your friend
Deling

PRACTICE AND ASSESS

Answers: Exercise 6

1. . . . Houston, Texas, arrived . . .
2. . . . postmarked March 19, 1995.
3. It focused attention on Sally Ride, Ph.D.
4. . . . space mission, the other astronauts with Ride were Hauck, Fabian, and Crippen.
5. . . . conducted experiments, and they tested . . .
6. They launched . . . Canadian government, too.
7. correct
8. Yes, I think Sally Ride . . .
9. Before her mission in 1983, Sally Ride . . .
10. "It's true," said Lee . . . letter, "that Sally Ride . . ."

Answers: Exercise 7

1. 16 Wallace Avenue
2. Richmond, VA 23203
3. October 4, 19__
4. Dear Monica,
5. On April 6, 1995, my class . . .
6. Alice Perri, M.A., was . . .
7. "With . . . each part," she said, "we . . ."
8. . . . got a part, too.
9. . . . on May 1, 1995, and on May 8, 1995.
10. Your friend, *Deling*

Independent Practice

Skills Practice

Grammar Practice, pp. 46–47
Grammar Reteaching, p. 45
Grammar Enrichment, pp. 46–47
Grammar Workbook, Lesson 74

CLOSE

Review the use of commas in this lesson. Then ask students to write a letter to a real or an imaginary person. Students should be attentive both to the way their letters are written and to the placement of commas.

Enabling Strategies

LEP Understanding Commas

Students acquiring English may find comma use confusing. You might help them by explaining that in many cases, commas separate words or phrases that are not essential to the sentence. To show this, write the following sentence on the board: *I, too, am going on the trip.* Tell students you could take the commas, along with the word *too,* out of the sentence and leave the basic meaning of the sentence intact.

Setting the Purpose

Lesson 19.5 introduces students to the proper use of semicolons in compound sentences. It also teaches students the use of a colon to introduce a list, to write the time of day, and to begin a business letter.

FOCUS

Lesson Overview

Objective: To learn the correct use of semicolons and colons

Bellringer

When students enter the classroom, have this assignment on the board: *Correct these sentences by adding words or punctuation:*

The play will begin promptly at seven everyone must be ready. We still need the following props an alarm clock, a camera, and a trumpet.

Motivating Activity

Ask volunteers to tell how they corrected the sentences in the Bellringer activity. Students may suggest making the first item into two sentences, adding the coordinating conjunction *and* or *so*, or using a semicolon. The second sentence requires a colon.

TEACH

Teaching Tip

Explain to students that a semicolon is part period, part comma, and that it indicates that the reader should pause a little longer than for a comma but not as long as for a period. Remind students that the semicolon should be used sparingly and that when it is used, the two compound sentences it joins must be closely related.

19.5 Using Semicolons and Colons

The semicolon and the colon are punctuation marks that separate parts of a sentence that might otherwise be confused.

RULE 1: Use a semicolon to join parts of a compound sentence when a conjunction such as *and, but,* or *or* is not used. Remember that a compound sentence has two or more simple sentences that are joined by a conjunction.

Albert Einstein made many discoveries in science**;** his theory of relativity changed scientific thought.
Einstein was born in Germany in 1879**;** he moved to the United States in 1933.
Einstein liked classical music**;** he played the violin.

RULE 2: Use a colon to introduce a list of items that ends a sentence. Use a phrase such as *these, the following,* or *as follows* before the list.

A list of the greatest scientists in history usually begins with **these** names**:** Newton and Einstein.
Einstein's relativity theory advanced new ideas about **the following:** time, space, mass, and motion.
Einstein wrote his famous equation **as follows:** $E = mc^2$.

Do not use a colon immediately after a verb or a preposition. Either leave out the colon, or reword the sentence.

Einstein **studied** mathematics, physics, and English.
During his lifetime he lived **in** Germany, Switzerland, and the United States.

RULE 3: Use a colon to separate the hour and the minute when you write the time of day.

Einstein's train left Princeton at 10**:**15 A.M. and arrived at New York City at 12**:**33 P.M.

RULE 4: Use a colon after the salutation of a business letter.

Dear Sir or Madam**:** Dear Mrs. Santiago**:**

Teacher's Classroom Resources

The following resources can be used for planning, instruction, practice, reinforcement, reteaching, or enrichment.

Teaching Tools
Lesson Plans

Blackline Masters
Grammar Practice, p. 48
Grammar Reteaching, pp. 46–47
Grammar Enrichment, p. 48

Grammar Workbook
Lesson 77

Exercise 8 Using Semicolons and Colons

Write each sentence. Add any needed semicolons or colons. Write *correct* if the sentence needs no semicolon or colon added.

1. Albert Einstein was an original thinker he changed our view of the universe.
2. His relativity theory contained new ideas about time, space, mass, motion, and gravitation.
3. Einstein speculated about speeds faster than light no object has yet moved that fast.
4. Einstein worked for seven years at the Swiss Patent Office this job gave him the free time to carry out his scientific investigations.
5. Einstein summarized his relativity theory as follows we can never talk about space without talking about time.
6. Einstein's quantum theory led to the development of these inventions motion pictures with sound, television, and sophisticated security devices.
7. Einstein also thought about the problems of his day he wrote a letter to Franklin Roosevelt about developing the atomic bomb.
8. An atomic bomb was dropped on Hiroshima, Japan, at 645 A.M. on August 6, 1945.
9. In the 1950s Einstein was offered the presidency of the state of Israel he insisted he was not right for this position.
10. Einstein lived the last part of his life in Princeton, New Jersey he considered himself a citizen of the world.

Exercise 9 Using Semicolons and Colons

Write each numbered item in the business letter below. Add semicolons or colons where needed.

[1]Dear Ms. Ntinga

[2]I am sorry that I missed your talk on Albert Einstein. [3]I have Glee Club practice at 130 P.M. and could not be there. [4]I am planning to write about Einstein's life I hope you can suggest some good books. [5]I bought these books *The Theory of Relativity* and *Einstein, Profile of the Man.*

Sincerely,
Jerome

PRACTICE AND ASSESS

Answers: Exercise 8

1. ...thinker; he...
2. correct
3. ...light; no object...
4. ...Office; this job...
5. ...as follows: we...
6. ...these inventions: motion...
7. ...day; he wrote...
8. 6:45 A.M.
9. ... Israel; he...
10. ...New Jersey; he...

Answers: Exercise 9

1. Dear Ms. Ntinga:
2. correct
3. I have Glee Club practice at 1:30 P.M. and...
4. ...about Einstein's life; I hope you...
5. I bought these books: *The Theory of...*

Independent Practice

Skills Practice

- *Grammar Practice,* p. 48
- *Grammar Reteaching,* pp. 46–47
- *Grammar Enrichment,* p. 48
- ***Grammar Workbook,*** Lesson 77

CLOSE

Have students look for examples of semicolons and colons in textbooks or magazine articles and present the examples to the class. As each example is presented, ask students to explain why the semicolon or colon was used.

Enabling Strategies

LEP Using Colons to Introduce a List

To help students understand the use of a colon in introducing a list, pair students acquiring English with those who are proficient in the language. Write sentences such as the following on the board: *We bought cereal, milk, and bread. The boys prepared a meal of chicken, salad, and rice. We will study art, science, and history.* Have the paired students work together to change each sentence so that it requires the use of a colon. Encourage students to think of some sentences of their own to demonstrate colon use.

Setting the Purpose

Lesson 19.6 teaches students how to use quotation marks with direct quotations and titles of short works. It also teaches them the correct use of italics (shown by underlining) to identify titles of long works.

FOCUS

Lesson Overview

Objective: To recognize the correct use of quotation marks and italics

Bellringer

When students enter the classroom, have this assignment on the board: *Describe the difference between these two sentences:*

Ana asked Ty what he was doing after school. Ana asked, "Ty, what are you doing after school?"

Motivating Activity

Use the sentences from the Bellringer activity to help students understand direct and indirect quotations. Invite volunteers to provide examples of both direct and indirect quotations.

TEACH

Teaching Tip

To help students understand question marks in quotations, explain that if the quoted sentence itself is a question, the question mark goes inside the quotation marks. (*"Am I late?"*) If the quoted sentence is a statement within a question, the question mark goes outside the quotation marks. (*Who said, "You are late"?*) Ask students to include a famous quotation in a question using correct punctuation. (*Who said, "We have nothing to fear but fear itself"?*)

19.6 Using Quotation Marks and Italics

RULE 1: Use quotation marks before and after a direct quotation.

"Sojourner Truth was born enslaved," said Graciela.

RULE 2: Use quotation marks around each part of an interrupted quotation.

"She was," explained Kazuko, "a great fighter against slavery."

RULE 3: Use a comma or commas to separate a phrase such as *he said* from the quotation itself. Place the comma outside opening quotation marks but inside closing quotation marks.

Victoria said, "Sojourner Truth became free in 1828."
"She finally received her freedom under a New York law," Manny added.

RULE 4: Place a period inside closing quotation marks.

Ms. Yu said, "Sojourner Truth preached concern for the welfare of others."

RULE 5: Place a question mark or an exclamation mark inside the quotation marks when it is part of the quotation.

Chi asked, "Did she find jobs for enslaved persons who escaped?"

RULE 6: Place a question mark or an exclamation mark outside the quotation marks when it is part of the entire sentence but not part of the quotation.

Did Ms. Yu say, "Sojourner Truth visited President Lincoln"?

RULE 7: Use quotation marks for the title of a short story, essay, poem, song, magazine or newspaper article, or book chapter.

"The Open Boat" [short story]   "Shenandoah" [song]

RULE 8: Use italics (underlining) to identify the title of a book, play, film, television series, magazine, or newspaper.

The Grapes of Wrath [book]   *National Geographic* [magazine]

464 *Punctuation*

Teacher's Classroom Resources

The following resources can be used for planning, instruction, practice, reinforcement, reteaching, or enrichment.

Teaching Tools
Lesson Plans

Blackline Masters
Grammar Practice, p. 49
Grammar Reteaching, pp. 48–49
Grammar Enrichment, p. 49

Grammar Workbook
Lessons 78–79

Write each of the following titles. Add the necessary quotation marks or underlining for italics.

1. The Necklace (short story)
2. By the Sea (poem)
3. Newsweek (magazine)
4. A Midsummer Night's Dream (play)
5. Women in Sports (newspaper article)
6. Back to the Future (film)
7. Ivanhoe (book)
8. Treasures of Lascaux Cave (magazine article)
9. Home Improvement (television series)
10. Self-Reliance (essay)
11. Hoop Dreams (film)
12. Amazing Grace (song)
13. New York Times (newspaper)
14. Casey at the Bat (poem)
15. The Morning (book chapter)

Write each sentence. Add quotation marks and other punctuation marks where needed.

1. Sojourner Truth's real name was Isabella Baumfree said Winona
2. Sojourner Truth changed her name said Winona when she decided to preach.
3. Don't you think her talks and lectures have the ring of truth asked Maya
4. That helped make her one of the best-known American abolitionists of her day said Mr. Scruggs.
5. Abolitionists worked to end slavery said Ms. Yu.
6. Bertha asked What is a sojourner
7. Ms. Yu replied A sojourner is a traveler
8. Did Ms. Yu say Sojourner Truth worked to improve the lives of African Americans living in Washington
9. Bertha exclaimed What a brave woman she was
10. Go to the library Ms. Yu said and find a book about Sojourner Truth

PRACTICE AND ASSESS

Answers: Exercise 10

1. "The Necklace"
2. "By the Sea"
3. *Newsweek*
4. *A Midsummer Night's Dream*
5. "Women in Sports"
6. *Back to the Future*
7. *Ivanhoe*
8. "Treasures of Lascaux Cave"
9. *Home Improvement*
10. "Self-Reliance"
11. *Hoop Dreams*
12. "Amazing Grace"
13. *New York Times*
14. "Casey at the Bat"
15. "The Morning"

Answers: Exercise 11

1. "Sojourner . . . Baumfree," said Winona.
2. "Sojourner . . . name," said Winona, "when . . . preach."
3. "Don't . . . truth?" asked Maya.
4. "That . . . day," said Mr. Scruggs.
5. "Abolitionists . . . slavery," said Ms. Yu.
6. . . . asked, "What is a sojourner?"
7. . . . replied, "A sojourner is a traveler."
8. . . . say, "Sojourner . . . Washington"?
9. . . . exclaimed, "What . . . was!"
10. "Go to the library," Ms. Yu said, "and . . . Truth."

Independent Practice

Skills Practice

Grammar Practice, p. 49
Grammar Reteaching, p. 48–49
Grammar Enrichment, p. 49

Grammar Workbook, Lessons 78–79

CLOSE

Have students work in pairs. One partner writes an indirect quotation. (*Carl said he would be late.*) The other partner changes it into a direct quotation. (*Carl said, "I will be late."*) This partner then returns the paper to the original partner, who checks for proper use of quotation marks.

Enabling Strategies

LEP Using Quotation Marks

Students with limited proficiency in English may have difficulty determining which words to enclose in quotation marks in a sentence containing dialogue. To help them with this, have students work in pairs to write dialogue for a cartoon. Encourage them to write the words from the cartoon bubble first, enclosing them in quotation marks, and then to add the words indicating who the speakers are.

Setting the Purpose

Lesson 19.7 teaches students to use apostrophes in possessives and contractions. It also teaches them to use hyphens correctly in their writing.

FOCUS

Lesson Overview

Objective: To recognize the use of the apostrophe in possessives and contractions and the use of the hyphen in word division and compound numbers

Bellringer

When students enter the classroom, have this assignment on the board: *Choose the correct word in the following sentence:*

We learned today that (its, it's) Marie Curie who discovered radium.

Motivating Activity

Discuss the correct answer in the Bellringer activity. Ask students how they decided which form to use. Then have them write two sentences, one using *it's* and the other using *its.*

TEACH

Cross-reference: Hyphens

Tell students that dictionaries usually use hyphens, bullets, or spaces to separate the syllables in each entry word. For instruction and practice with dictionary entries, refer students to Lesson 21.6, pp. 503–504.

19.7 Using Apostrophes and Hyphens

An apostrophe shows possession and points out the missing letters in a contraction. A hyphen divides a word between syllables and joins the parts of compound words.

RULE 1: Use an apostrophe and an *-s ('s)* to form the possessive of a singular noun.

girl + **'s** = girl**'s** Charles + **'s** = Charles**'s**

RULE 2: Use an apostrophe and an *-s ('s)* to form the possessive of a plural noun that does not end in *-s.*

women +**'s** = women**'s** mice + **'s** = mice**'s**

RULE 3: Use an apostrophe alone to form the possessive of a plural noun that ends in *-s.*

girls + **'** = girls**'** cities + **'** = cities**'**

Do not use an apostrophe in a possessive pronoun.

These skates are **hers.** **Theirs** are in the car.

RULE 4: Use an apostrophe to replace letters that have been omitted in a contraction. A contraction is a word that is made by combining two words into one and leaving out one or more letters.

it is = it's you + are = you're

RULE 5: Use a hyphen to show the division of a word at the end of a line. Always divide a word between its syllables.

With her husband, Pierre, Marie Sklodowska Curie dis-
covered radium and polonium.

RULE 6: Use a hyphen in compound numbers.

sixty-five pianos forty-two experiments

RULE 7: Use a hyphen or hyphens in certain compound nouns. Consult a dictionary to be sure.

great-uncle brother-in-law attorney-at-law
editor in chief

Teacher's Classroom Resources

The following resources can be used for planning, instruction, practice, reinforcement, reteaching, or enrichment.

Teaching Tools
Lesson Plans

Blackline Masters
Grammar Practice, p. 50
Grammar Reteaching, p. 50
Grammar Enrichment, p. 50

Grammar Workbook
Lessons 80–81

Exercise 12 **Using the Possessive Form**

Write the possessive form of each word or group of words that follows. Remember to use an apostrophe and an *s* (*'s*) or an apostrophe alone (').

1. men	**6.** horses	**11.** Mrs. Jacobs	**16.** Mr. Sanchez
2. child	**7.** countries	**12.** wolves	**17.** reefs
3. Lois	**8.** babies	**13.** day	**18.** girls
4. Ms. Marie Rossi	**9.** pig	**14.** President Ford	**19.** his
5. oxen	**10.** house	**15.** sheep	**20.** teams

Exercise 13 **Using Apostrophes and Hyphens**

Write each sentence. Add apostrophes and hyphens where needed. Write *correct* if a sentence needs no changes.

1. Marie and Pierre Curie discovered radium in 1898.
2. The daughter of teachers, Marie studied chemistry and physics in Paris.
3. In 1895 Pierre Curie became her husband.
4. The Curies interest in the discovery of radioactivity led to their discovery of radium.
5. The Curies, however, didnt discover radium until two years later.
6. From more than twenty five tons of uranium ore, they isolated radium and polonium.
7. For their work with radium and polonium, the Curies were awarded the Nobel Prize for physics in 1903.
8. Marie Curies work with the chemical properties of radium and polonium won her a second Nobel Prize in 1911.
9. Madame Curies daughter Irene and son in law Frederic Joliot also won a Nobel Prize for chemistry.
10. In 1934 Marie Curie died of leukemia, the same disease that took her daughters life twenty years later.
11. Eve Curies biography of her famous mother has been published in more than twenty languages.
12. Its amazing to think of how much the Curies accomplished.
13. In 1963 Maria Goeppert Mayer became the second woman ever to win a Nobel Prize in physics.
14. Her award followed Marie Curies second Nobel Prize by fifty two years.
15. Goeppert Mayers husband, Joseph E. Mayer, was a chemist.

PRACTICE AND ASSESS

Answers: Exercise 12

1. men's	**11.** Mrs. Jacobs's
2. child's	**12.** wolves'
3. Lois's	**13.** day's
4. Rossi's	**14.** Ford's
5. oxen's	**15.** sheep's
6. horses'	**16.** Mr. Sanchez's
7. countries'	**17.** reefs'
8. babies'	**18.** girls'
9. pig's	**19.** his
10. house's	**20.** teams'

Answers: Exercise 13

1. correct	**9.** Curie's, son-in-law
2. correct	**10.** daughter's
3. correct	**11.** Curie's
4. Curies'	**12.** It's
5. didn't	**13.** correct
6. twenty-five	**14.** Curie's, fifty-two
7. correct	**15.** Mayer's
8. Curie's	

Independent Practice

Skills Practice

Grammar Practice, p. 50
Grammar Reteaching, p. 50
Grammar Enrichment, p. 50

Grammar Workbook, Lessons 80–81

CLOSE

Discuss Exercise 13 with students, especially any parts of the exercise that they found difficult.

Enabling Strategies

LEP Using the Possessive Apostrophe

The possessive apostrophe may puzzle students whose first language is not English, since many languages do not have a possessive form of the noun. Instead they use a phrase with the preposition *of* to show possession.

For example, the English language allows the use of *the building's designer* (possessive noun) or *the designer of the building* (possessive phrase). Some students learning English may find the possessive phrase easier to use.

Setting the Purpose

Lesson 19.8 teaches students to write abbreviations correctly.

FOCUS

Lesson Overview

Objective: To recognize the correct form of abbreviation for common titles, names, and units of measure

Bellringer

When students enter the classroom, have this assignment on the board: *Rewrite the following sentences, spelling out the abbreviations:*

Geo. Washington was the first pres. of our country. Gen. Washington's army crossed the DE River and defeated the British in NJ.

Motivating Activity

As students study correct abbreviations, explain that abbreviations should be used sparingly in writing. All those in the Bellringer sentences are out of place.

TEACH

Teaching Tip

Explain to students that names of organizations—government agencies (CIA), networks (CBS), professional organizations (AMA), trade unions (AFL-CIO)—usually do not have periods with their abbreviations.

Grammar Tip

Tell students that in most formal writing *United States* is spelled out. However, the abbreviation *U.S.* may be used in informal writing as an adjective: *U.S. government.*

19.8 Using Abbreviations

RULE 1: Abbreviate the titles *Mr., Mrs., Ms.,* and *Dr.* before a person's name. Also abbreviate the professional or academic degrees that follow a person's name, as well as the titles *Jr.* and *Sr.*

Mr. Ed Hall **Jr.** Henry Wong, **M.D.** **Dr.** Ann Chu
Juan Diaz, **Ph.D.** **Ms.** Ava Danko, **M.F.A.**

RULE 2: Use all capital letters and no periods for abbreviations that are pronounced letter by letter or as words. Exceptions are *U.S.* and *Washington, D.C.,* which do use periods.

NASA National Aeronautics and Space Administration
MVP most valuable player

RULE 3: Use the abbreviations *A.M.* (*ante meridiem,* "before noon") and *P.M.* (*post meridiem,* "after noon") for exact times. For dates use *B.C.* (before Christ) and, sometimes, *A.D.* (*anno Domini,* "in the year of the Lord," after Christ).

6:15 **A.M.** 5:30 **P.M.** 20 **B.C.** **A.D.** 476

RULE 4: Abbreviate calendar items only in charts and lists.

Mon. Wed. Thurs. Jan. Apr. Aug. Nov.

RULE 5: In scientific writing abbreviate units of measure. Use periods with abbreviations of English units but not of metric units.

inch(es) **in.** foot (feet) **ft.** gram(s) **g** liter(s) **l**

RULE 6: On envelopes abbreviate the words that refer to streets in street names. Spell them out everywhere else.

Street **St.** Avenue **Ave.** Road **Rd.** Court **Ct.**
We live at the corner of Polaris **Avenue** and Maple **Court.**

RULE 7: On envelopes use Postal Service abbreviations for the names of states. Everywhere else, spell out state names.

Indiana **IN** Arizona **AZ** Alabama **AL** Delaware **DE**
Maryland **MD** Georgia **GA** Florida **FL** California **CA**

Teacher's Classroom Resources

The following resources can be used for planning, instruction, practice, reinforcement, reteaching, or enrichment.

Teaching Tools
Lesson Plans

Blackline Masters
Grammar Practice, p. 51
Grammar Reteaching, p. 51
Grammar Enrichment, p. 51

Grammar Workbook
Lessons 82–83

Exercise 14 **Using Abbreviations**

Write the correct abbreviation for each underlined item.

1. Mister Dean Paxton
2. 4000 before Christ
3. March 2, 1988
4. Hugh Hunt Junior
5. 43 Palm Court
6. Sunday
7. anno Domini 63
8. 456 Laguna Street
9. 8 liters
10. Federal Bureau of Investigation
11. Friday
12. 16 inches
13. Tampa, Florida
14. Mister Harold Wong
15. September
16. San Francisco, California
17. Internal Revenue Service
18. 6 feet
19. 109 Van Dyke Road
20. January

Exercise 15 **Using Abbreviations**

Write the correct abbreviation for each underlined item in the following sentences.

1. Representative Mari Ramos plans to speak about Elizabeth Blackwell.
2. Doctor Blackwell received her medical degree in 1849 from a college in Geneva, New York.
3. My National Organization for Women chapter will honor another Blackwell; Antoinette Brown Blackwell was the first ordained woman minister.
4. The first woman elected to the United States Senate was Senator Margaret Chase Smith from Maine.
5. The museum director presented a seminar on ancient Rome from 11:45 in the morning until 1:30 in the afternoon.
6. Juan Bosch Junior is known for giving interesting and lively seminars on various topics.
7. The museum is located at 1680 Sequoia Drive.
8. We learned that the first Roman emperor, Augustus, ruled from 27 before Christ to anno Domini 14.
9. Write to the Organization of American Historians at 112 North Bryan Street, Bloomington, Indiana 47401.
10. If you call, ask for Mister Bosch.

TEACH

Two-Minute Skill Drill

List these words on the board. Have students supply the correct abbreviations.

Illinois	ounces
Captain	Saint
Mount	Associated Press

PRACTICE AND ASSESS

Answers: Exercise 14

1. Mr.	11. Fri.
2. B.C.	12. in.
3. Mar.	13. FL
4. Jr.	14. Mr.
5. Ct.	15. Sept.
6. Sun.	16. CA
7. A.D.	17. IRS
8. St.	18. ft.
9. l.	19. Rd.
10. FBI	20. Jan.

Answers: Exercise 15

1. Rep.	6. Jr.
2. Dr.	7. Dr.
3. NOW	8. B.C., A.D.
4. Sen.	9. IN
5. A.M., P.M.	10. Mr.

Independent Practice

Skill Practice

- *Grammar Practice,* p. 51
- *Grammar Reteaching,* p. 51
- *Grammar Enrichment,* p. 51

Grammar Workbook, Lessons 82–83

CLOSE

Have students write a brief essay about a famous person. They should use at least two abbreviations.

Enabling Strategies

LEP Abbreviating Names of Groups

Explain that abbreviations of the names of organizations usually use only the first letters of capitalized words: *Organization of Petroleum Exporting Countries* is abbreviated as *OPEC,* for example.

Enrichment

Using B.C. and A.D.

Have students look in a history book to see how the abbreviations B.C. and A.D. are used. Do they go before or after the date? The answer may surprise students: B.C. goes after the date (30 B.C.), and A.D. goes before the date (A.D. 30).

Setting the Purpose

Lesson 19.9 teaches students to use numerals and spelled-out numbers correctly in writing.

FOCUS

Lesson Overview

Objective: To recognize the conventions for using numerals and spelled-out numbers

Bellringer

When students enter the classroom, have this assignment on the board: *Study the passage below. Explain why each number is either spelled out or expressed as a numeral.*

> When I was seventeen, Dad let me enlist as a mess boy in the U.S. Coast Guard . . . By 1949 the Coast Guard had made me its first "journalist"; finally, . . . I retired at the age of thirty-seven, determined to make a full-time career of writing . . .
>
> —Alex Haley, *My Furthest-Back Person—'The African'*

Motivating Activity

Discuss students' responses to the Bellringer activity, and refer them to Rules 1 and 8 on page 470.

TEACH

Vocabulary Link

Call students' attention to Rule 6. Explain that the word *ordinal* comes from the Latin *ordo,* meaning "order." Ordinal numbers—*third, fourth,* and so on—indicate order, or position in a series.

19.9 Writing Numbers

In charts and tables you always write numbers as figures. However, in an ordinary sentence, you sometimes spell out numbers and sometimes write them as numerals.

RULE 1: Spell out numbers that you can write in one or two words.

Jackie Robinson helped the Dodgers win **six** pennants.

RULE 2: Use numerals for numbers of more than two words.

The field at Dodger Stadium is **330** feet down the left-field line.

RULE 3: Spell out any number that begins a sentence, or reword the sentence so that it does not begin with a number.

Fifty-five thousand fans turned out on opening day.

RULE 4: Write a very large number as a numeral followed by the word *million* or *billion.*

In 1991 major league baseball attracted more than **56 million** fans.

RULE 5: If related numbers appear in the same sentence, use all numerals even though you might spell out one of the numbers if it appeared alone.

In 1953 the Dodgers won **105** games and lost **49.**

RULE 6: Spell out ordinal numbers (*first, second,* and so forth).

Jackie Robinson was the **first** African American to play in the majors.

RULE 7: Use words to express the time of day unless you are writing the exact time with the abbreviation A.M. or P.M.

Today's baseball game began at **two o'clock.** It ended at **5:15 P.M.**

RULE 8: Use numerals to express dates, house and street numbers, apartment and room numbers, telephone numbers, page numbers, amounts of money of more than two words, and percentages. Write out the word *percent.*

May **16, 1865** **241** Bryant St. Apartment **3G** **50 percent**

Teacher's Classroom Resources

The following resources can be used for planning, instruction, practice, reinforcement, reteaching, or enrichment.

Teaching Tools
Lesson Plans

Blackline Masters
Grammar Practice, p. 52
Grammar Reteaching, p. 52
Grammar Enrichment, p. 52

Grammar Workbook
Lessons 84–85

Exercise 16 Writing Numbers

Use the correct form for writing numbers in the following sentences. Write *correct* if the sentence needs no changes.

1. In the 1930s many baseball games began at three o'clock in the afternoon.
2. Some World Series games began at twelve thirty P.M.
3. A good batter hits safely thirty percent of the time.
4. Jackie Robinson entered major league baseball in nineteen hundred forty-seven.
5. Robinson was born at the end of the 1st World War.
6. Later he gained fame as an all-star 2nd baseman for the Brooklyn Dodgers.
7. Robinson helped the Dodgers win the World Series for the first time in 1955.
8. In that World Series each team won 3 times before the Dodgers won an exciting 7th game.
9. Robinson retired from baseball after his 10th season.
10. In his career Robinson hit 273 doubles, 137 home runs, and fifty-four triples.
11. In Robinson's 1st season in the majors, the average salary was eleven thousand two hundred dollars.
12. In 1992 the average salary for major leaguers was more than 1,000,000 dollars.
13. Satchel Paige was a star pitcher in the Negro baseball leagues for more than 20 years.
14. Paige entered the major leagues in nineteen hundred forty-eight and was elected to the National Baseball Hall of Fame in nineteen hundred seventy-one.
15. Hank Aaron broke Babe Ruth's home run record and hit a total of seven hundred fifty-five home runs in his career.
16. During the 2nd World War many people attended women's league baseball games.
17. A film about the women's leagues titled *A League of Their Own* was made in 1992.
18. Willie Mays led the National League in stolen bases 4 times and in home runs 4 times.
19. In 1961 the New York Yankees hit a record two hundred forty home runs.
20. 23 different teams played in the National League between 1876 and 1900.

Enabling Strategies

LEP Spelling Out Numbers

Give students some practice in spelling out numbers by reading aloud a list of sentences with numbers in numerical form. Have students pair up and together decide which numbers to spell out and which should use figures. They can explain to each other which rule they think applies to each case. Then pairs can exchange papers and check each other's answers.

TEACH

Teaching Tip

Summarize for students as follows: Spell out one- and two-digit numbers (*zero* to *ninety-nine*). Spell out large numbers ending in *hundred, thousand, million,* or *billion* if they can be written in two words—for example, *eight hundred, twelve billion.* Express other numbers ending in *million* or *billion* as a combination of numerals and words—*53 million, 100 billion.* Spell out fractions (*two-thirds*), except in scientific usage.

PRACTICE AND ASSESS

Answers: Exercise 16

1. correct
2. 12:30 P.M.
3. 30 percent
4. 1947
5. First
6. second
7. correct
8. three; seventh
9. tenth
10. 54
11. first; $11,200
12. one million
13. twenty
14. 1948; 1971
15. 755
16. Second
17. correct
18. four; four
19. 240
20. Twenty-three

Independent Practice

Skills Practice

- *Grammar Practice,* p. 52
- *Grammar Reteaching,* p. 52
- *Grammar Enrichment,* p. 52

Grammar Workbook, Lessons 84–85

CLOSE

Invite students to choose their favorite athlete and to discuss their choice in a paragraph. Ask them to use at least three numbers correctly.

TEACH

About the Literature

Explain that the review contains a passage from Langston Hughes's essay about Harriet Tubman, followed by exercises on related topics. Discuss the setting and mood of the passage as well as the character of Harriet Tubman. Then ask students to read the annotations and observe how following the rules of punctuation helps make the passage clear and coherent.

Linking Grammar and Literature

TeachingTip

Dialogue is often used to develop character in literature. Discuss what part punctuation marks play in written dialogue. (Quotation marks set off the words of each speaker.) How does the reader know that a new person is speaking? (Quotation marks close the first speaker's words, a new paragraph is started, and new quotation marks signal the second speaker.)

Critical Thinking

Ask students to think about why the essay has the subtitle *The Moses of Her People.* What did Harriet Tubman have in common with Moses? Some students may know that Moses led his people—the Jews—out of bondage in Egypt and into the Promised Land of Canaan.

UNIT 19

Unit Review

Grammar Review

Punctuation

"Harriet Tubman: The Moses of Her People" by Langston Hughes tells about the African American woman who escaped from slavery and then helped free hundreds of other slaves. The following excerpt from the biographical sketch describes Tubman's activities during the Civil War. The passage is annotated to show some of the rules of punctuation covered in this unit.

Literature Model

from HARRIET TUBMAN:
THE MOSES OF HER PEOPLE

by Langston Hughes

Harriet Tubman's war activities were amazing. She served under General Stevens at Beaufort, South Carolina. She was sent to Florida to nurse those ill of dysentery, small pox, and yellow fever. She was with Colonel Robert Gould Shaw at Fort Wagner. She organized a group of nine Negro scouts and river pilots and, with Colonel Montgomery, led a Union raiding contingent of three gunboats and about 150 Negro troops up the Combahee River. As reported by the Boston *Commonwealth,* for July 10, 1863, they "under the guidance of a black woman, dashed into the enemy's country, struck a bold and effective blow, destroying millions of dollars worth of commissary stores, cotton and lordly dwellings, and striking terror into the heart of rebeldom, brought off near 800 slaves and thousands of dollars worth of property."

Apostrophe to show possession

Comma before a state name when used with a city name

Comma to separate items in a series

Italics for the title of a newspaper

Period inside closing quotation marks

Teacher's Classroom Resources

The following resources can be used for planning, instruction, practice, reinforcement, assessment, reteaching, or evaluation.

Teaching Tools
Lesson Plans

Grammar Workbook
Lessons 71–85
Unit 12 Review
Cumulative Review: Units 1–12

Unit Assessment
Tests with Answer Key
Unit 19 Mastery Test, pp. 75–76
Test Generator
Unit 19 Mastery Test

Exercise 1

Using End Marks Write the correct end mark for each sentence, and then write whether the sentence is *declarative*, *imperative*, *interrogative*, or *exclamatory*.

1. Harriet Tubman was born enslaved in Maryland
2. Why did she serve in the Union Army
3. What an amazing woman she was
4. Read about her heroic actions in Hughes's book
5. Tubman worked in the fields before escaping to freedom in 1849

Exercise 2

Using Commas Rewrite each sentence, inserting commas as needed.

SAMPLE During the Civil War Harriet Tubman served as a nurse a scout and a spy.

ANSWER During the Civil War Harriet Tubman served as a nurse, a scout, and a spy.

1. Tubman served with Colonel Montgomery and she helped him lead a raid on enemy territory.
2. With the help of an African American woman the troops made a successful raid.
3. During the raid Tubman helped destroy houses provisions and cotton.
4. The *Commonwealth* reported her heroic actions on July 10 1863.
5. Yes Tubman was seen as an extraordinary woman even while she was alive.
6. Harriet's husband discouraged her you may be surprised to learn when she wanted to escape to freedom.
7. Harriet settled in Auburn New York and she brought her parents to live there too.
8. Ms. Buchman do you know how many enslaved persons she helped escape?
9. During one military campaign in the war Tubman helped free more than 750 enslaved people.
10. After the war Tubman helped African Americans by establishing a home for the elderly and needy in Auburn New York and by raising money for schools.

PRACTICE AND ASSESS

Answers: Exercise 1

1. period, declarative
2. question mark, interrogative
3. exclamation point, exclamatory
4. period, imperative
5. period, declarative

Answers: Exercise 2

1. ... Montgomery, and ...
2. ... woman,
3. ... houses, provisions, and cotton.
4. ... July 10, 1863.
5. Yes, Tubman ...
6. ... Harriet, you may be surprised to learn, when ...
7. ... Auburn, New York, and ... to live there, too.
8. Ms. Buchman, do ...
9. ... in the war, Tubman ...
10. ... in Auburn, New York, and ...

UNIT 19
Review

Answers: Exercise 3

1. . . . telephone; he . . .
2. . . . film: *The Story* . . .
3. . . . inventor; some . . .
4. . . . 3:15 P.M. . . .
5. correct

Answers: Exercise 4

1. "Rachel Carson was an artist, a poet, a scientist, an author, and a reformer," replied Ms. Erlich.
2. "The journalist Eric Sevareid compared her to Harriet Beecher Stowe," Mr. Santiago added.
3. Severeid said that Carson's book Silent Spring sparked a war against pesticides just as Stowe's book Uncle Tom's Cabin helped start the Civil War. (If students suggest that this could be a direct quote, accept appropriately punctuated answers.)
4. A New York Times article called "*Silent Spring* Is Now Noisy Summer" stirred great interest across the country, and other newspapers picked up the story.
5. In response to the excitement, Rachel Carson said, "As you listen to the present controversy about pesticides, I recommend that you ask yourself who speaks and why."

Exercise 3

Using Semicolons and Colons Rewrite each sentence, inserting semicolons and colons as needed. Write *correct* if the sentence needs no semicolons or colons.

1. Alexander Graham Bell invented the telephone he received the patent for his invention in 1876.
2. I admire Henry Fonda's performance in the following film *The Story of Alexander Graham Bell.*
3. Thomas Edison was a great inventor some of his inventions include the phonograph, the electric lightbulb, the carbon telephone transmitter, and a duplicating machine.
4. I'll pick you up at 315 P.M. to visit Edison's research laboratory in West Orange.
5. Tourists can see Bell's home in Nova Scotia and tour Edison's home in Florida.

Exercise 4

Using Quotation Marks and Italics Rewrite each sentence, inserting quotation marks and underlining for italics as needed.

1. Rachel Carson was an artist, a poet, a scientist, an author, and a reformer, replied Ms. Erlich.
2. The journalist Eric Sevareid compared her to Harriet Beecher Stowe, Mr. Santiago added.
3. Sevareid said that Carson's book Silent Spring sparked a war against pesticides just as Stowe's book Uncle Tom's Cabin helped start the Civil War.
4. A New York Times article called Silent Spring Is Now Noisy Summer stirred great interest across the country, and other newspapers picked up the story.
5. In response to the excitement, Rachel Carson said, As you listen to the present controversy about pesticides, I recommend that you ask yourself who speaks and why.

Exercise 5

Using Apostrophes and Hyphens Rewrite each sentence, inserting apostrophes and hyphens as needed. Write *correct* if a sentence needs no apostrophes or hyphens.

1. Probably Booker T. Washingtons greatest contribution was founding the Tuskegee Institute, a vocational school for African Americans.
2. Washington opened the school when he was twenty five years old.
3. Washington advised President Theodore Roosevelt and President William H. Taft on their racial policies.
4. Its not surprising that W.E.B. Du Bois disagreed with some of Washingtons views on civil rights.
5. Theirs was a disagreement about different ways to achieve a similar end: the improvement of African Americans lives.

Exercise 6

Using Abbreviations and Numbers Rewrite each sentence, correcting the errors in abbreviations and numbers.

1. In 1872 when he was sixteen, he traveled 300 miles to enter an industrial school for African Americans—Hampton Institute.
2. 6 years after he graduated from Hampton, Washington founded Tuskegee Institute in Tuskegee, AL.
3. Washington told about his rise from slavery to national prominence in *Up from Slavery*, published in nineteen hundred one.
4. The autobiography was reprinted 56 years after Washington died.
5. On September eighteenth, 1895, Washington made a speech before a large crowd at the Cotton Exposition in Atlanta, GA.
6. He spoke for less than 20 minutes, explaining his theory that African Americans could accept segregation in exchange for economic advancement.
7. The speech was widely quoted and was the 1st event to make Washington a national figure and adviser to presidents.
8. Today fifty-four percent of the students at Tuskegee are female.
9. The school 1st looks for students with outstanding records.
10. Applications received by March thirty-one are given priority.

UNIT 19
Review

Answers: Exercise 5

1. ... Booker T. Washington's ...
2. ... twenty-five ...
3. correct
4. It's ... Washington's ...
5. ... African Americans' ...

Answers: Exercise 6

1. ... three hundred ...
2. Six ... Alabama.
3. ... 1901.
4. ... fifty-six ...
5. On September 18, ... Georgia
6. ... twenty ...
7. ... first ...
8. ... 54 percent ...
9. ... first ...
10. ... March 31 ...

UNIT 19 Review

Answers: Exercise 7

1. . . . these crops: peanuts, soybeans, and sweet potatoes.
2. . . . the land; they also helped diversify the South's economy.
3. . . . uses for the peanut?
4. . . . the following: a milk substitute, printer's ink, and face powder.
5. Yes, he discovered more than 100 uses for the sweet potato, too.
6. Carver was born enslaved in 1861 on a farm near Diamond, Missouri.
7. . . . education, but he finally graduated from Iowa State Agricultural College in 1894.
8. In 1896, with his master's degree behind him, Carver joined the faculty at Tuskegee Institute in Alabama.
9. . . . mule-driven wagon, and his traveling exhibit helped farmers in Alabama and other states.
10. Carolyn, do you . . . after you graduate on June 6, 1998?

Answers: Exercise 8

Answers will vary, but a sample letter is given below.

[student's street]
[student's city and state]
[date]

Tuskegee Institute
Suite 101
Old Administration Building
Tuskegee, AL 36088
November 11, 1997

Dear Sir or Madam:

I am thinking of applying for admission to Tuskegee on September 1, 1999.

Is Tuskegee still a leading university in agricultural research? Soil erosion is one of my special interests; crop rotation is another. I would like to request information about your classes in these subjects, and I would like information about campus life, too.

Yours truly,

Exercise 7

Using End Marks, Commas, Semicolons, and Colons Rewrite each sentence, inserting end marks, commas, semicolons, and colons as needed.

SAMPLE By overplanting cotton year after year southern plantation owners ruined their land George Washington Carver helped bring the land back to life

ANSWER By overplanting cotton year after year, southern plantation owners ruined their land; George Washington Carver helped bring the land back to life.

1. Carver's radical ideas included rotating these crops: peanuts soybeans and sweet potatoes
2. Carver's innovations helped restore the land they also helped diversify the South's economy
3. Did you know that he discovered more than three hundred uses for the peanut
4. These uses included the following a milk substitute printer's ink and face powder
5. Yes he discovered more than one hundred uses for the sweet potato, too
6. Carver was born enslaved in 1861 on a farm near Diamond Missouri
7. Carver faced many obstacles to getting an education but he finally graduated from Iowa State Agricultural College in 1894
8. In 1896 with his master's degree behind him Carver joined the faculty at Tuskegee Institute in Alabama
9. Carver put his laboratory onto a mule-driven wagon and his traveling exhibit helped farmers in Alabama and other states
10. Carolyn do you plan to visit the George Washington Carver National Monument after you graduate on June 6 1998

Exercise 8

Using Correct Punctuation in a Letter To request information about what Tuskegee Institute is like today, write a sample business letter to Suite 101, Old Administration Building, Tuskegee, AL 36088. Punctuate your letter with end marks, commas, semicolons, and/or colons as needed. For a model letter, turn to pages 461 and 463.

Exercise 9

Using Commas, Quotation Marks, Italics, and Apostrophes

Rewrite each sentence, inserting commas, quotation marks, italics (underlining), and apostrophes as needed.

SAMPLE Mr. Garns answered Du Bois wrote about his disagreements with Booker T. Washington in his book The Souls of Black Folk.

ANSWER Mr. Garns answered, "Du Bois wrote about his disagreements with Booker T. Washington in his book *The Souls of Black Folk.*"

1. Du Boiss other books include Black Reconstruction in America and The Autobiography of W.E.B. Du Bois.
2. I heard he was the first African American to receive a doctorate from Harvard University said Jarell.
3. Du Bois was dissatisfied with the progress of race relations and he moved to Ghana in Africa as a result said the history professor.
4. Du Bois helped found the National Association for the Advancement of Colored People in 1909 and he was editor of its magazine The Crisis.
5. For information on current activities Amanda suggested that we write to the NAACPs national headquarters at this address: 4805 Mt. Hope Drive Baltimore MD 21215.

Exercise 10

Using Apostrophes, Hyphens, Abbreviations, and Numbers

Rewrite each sentence, inserting apostrophes and hyphens as needed and correcting errors in abbreviations and numbers.

1. Thurgood Marshall was chief counsel for the NAACP for twenty three years.
2. As counsel he presented the argument that resulted in the Supreme Courts 1954 decision to end segregation in public schools.
3. For 4 years he was a United States Appeals Court judge.
4. In 1967 he became the 1st African American to sit on the Supreme Court of the United States.
5. Marshall was born in Baltimore, MD, in 1908.

Answers: Exercise 9

1. Du Bois's other books include Black Reconstruction in America and The Autobiography of W.E.B. Du Bois.
2. "I heard he was the first African American to receive a doctorate from Harvard University," said Jarell.
3. "Du Bois was dissatisfied with the progress of race relations, and he moved to Ghana in Africa as a result," said the history professor.
4. Du Bois helped found the National Association for the Advancement of Colored People in 1909, and he was editor of its magazine, The Crisis.
5. For information on current activities, Amanda suggested that we write to the NAACP's national headquarters at this address: 4805 Mt. Hope Drive, Baltimore, MD 21215.

Answers: Exercise 10

1. … twenty-three …
2. … Supreme Court's …
3. … four …
4. … first …
5. … Maryland …

Answers: Exercise 11

Proofreading

This proofreading activity provides editing practice with (1) the current or previous units' skills, (2) **Troubleshooter** errors, and (3) spelling errors. Students should be able to complete the exercise by referring to the units, the **Troubleshooter,** and a dictionary.

	Error (Type of Error)
1.	• one (numbers)
2.	• American (proper adjective)
	• artists (plural noun)
3.	• Douglas's (singular possessive)
	• expressed (spelling)
4.	• sculpture. (end punctuation)
5.	• represent (spelling)
6.	• past, (comma after two introductory prepositional phrases)
	• look (subject-verb agreement)
7.	• following: (colon before a list)

Exercise 11 **Proofreading**

Proofreading The following passage is about African American artist Aaron Douglas, whose work appears below. Rewrite the passage, correcting the errors in spelling, capitalization, grammar, and usage. Add any missing punctuation. There are 10 errors.

Aaron Douglas

[1] Aaron Douglas (1899–1979) is 1 of the best-known artists of the Harlem Renaissance movement of the 1920s. [2] Many African american ➡

About the Art

Aaron Douglas, *Aspiration*, 1936

This painting symbolizes African Americans' struggle for full freedom. Ask students to discuss the image in the painting and how it represents this struggle. (The figures have their backs to the past and are looking toward the future, represented by the city in the background; note the globe, the book, and the builder's tools.)

The 60-by-60-inch oil painting is part of the Evans-Tibbs/Thurlough Tibbs Collection in Washington, D.C.

African american writers and artist's gathered in Harlem during this period to explore and celebrate African American culture. [3]Many of them believed that Douglas' paintings expresed the positive mood of the Harlem Renaissance.

[4]The artist was strongly influenced by the simple forms represented in West African sculpture [5]Douglas used this style in *Aspiration* to reprezent all African American men and women. [6]With their backs to the past the figures in the painting looks toward the future [7]They envision the following freedom, equality, opportunity.

Exercise 12 **Mixed Review**

Rewrite each sentence using correct punctuation. Correct the errors in abbreviations and numbers.

1. Civil rights include the following freedom of speech freedom of the press and freedom of religion
2. During the 12 years after the Civil War Congress passed laws to protect African Americans civil rights
3. In 1883 the Supreme Court ruled that some of these laws were unconstitutional two years later the court upheld a law requiring "separate but equal" accommodations for African Americans
4. Did you know that the "separate but equal" rule remained in effect for more than fifty years
5. The Supreme Court finally ruled segregation unconstitutional in 1954 and 10 years later Congress passed the strongest civil rights bill in its history
6. The Equal Employment Opportunities Commission was established by the Civil Rights Act of nineteen sixty four said Ms Higgins
7. Poll taxes as you may know kept African Americans from voting in many southern states
8. You can learn more about the history of civil right's in the book We Will Be Heard
9. Check it out at the library on Wed.
10. What a fascinating story it is

Answers: Exercise 12

Mixed Review

1. Civil rights include the following: freedom of speech, freedom of the press, and freedom of religion.
2. During the twelve years after the Civil War, Congress passed laws to protect African Americans' civil rights.
3. In 1883 the Supreme Court ruled that some of these laws were unconstitutional; two years later the court upheld a law requiring "separate but equal" accommodations for African Americans.
4. Did you know that the "separate but equal" rule remained in effect for more than fifty years?
5. The Supreme Court finally ruled segregation unconstitutional in 1954, and ten years later Congress passed the strongest civil rights bill in its history.
6. "The Equal Employment Opportunities Commission was established by the Civil Rights Act of 1964," said Ms. Higgins.
7. Poll taxes, as you may know, kept African Americans from voting in many southern states.
8. You can learn more about the history of civil rights in the book <u>We Will Be Heard</u>.
9. Check it out at the library on Wednesday.
10. What a fascinating story it is!

CLOSE

Write the following abbreviations on the board, and discuss with students what phrases they might stand for: AWOL, COD, ESP, POW, R.S.V.P. Write students' suggestions on the board. Invite students to use the dictionary to find out if they were correct.

Punctuation in Writing

This passage with its lively dialogue lends itself to reading aloud. Invite a volunteer to read the passage to the class. Then have the class discuss it with reference to the Techniques with Punctuation section.

Techniques with Punctuation

Discuss the techniques described as they apply to the Uchida passage and then as they apply to the Practice paragraph, which offers good opportunities to use them.

Practice

Answers to this challenging and enriching activity will vary according to how extensively students rewrite. Refer to Techniques with Punctuation as you evaluate student choices. Corrections alone are as follows:

... Natchez, Mississippi ... Chicago, Illinois, ... nineteen. His ... slums. This ... fame. Speaking ... said, "We ... head, so ... young, poor, and black." Wright's ... *The Outsider, The Long Dream,* and his autobiography, *Black Boy*. Much ... States. Wright ... 1937, and ... Paris.

Writing Application

Punctuation in Writing Punctuation helps readers understand what they are reading. Note Yoshiko Uchida's use of punctuation in this passage from *The Invisible Thread.*

> "Honk the horn to let them know we're here," Papa said.
>
> At which point Keiko not only honked the horn, but simultaneously crashed into Jick's dog house, knocked it over on its side, and stopped just inches short of the walnut tree.
>
> "Look out, for heaven's sake," we all shouted. "Look out!"
>
> Jick barked furiously at the sudden assault on his territory, and the chickens scrambled in every direction, screeching and cackling as though the end of the world had come.

Techniques with Punctuation Try to apply the rules of punctuation when you write and revise your own work.

1. Use a comma after items in a series.

Without Commas crashed into Jick's dog house knocked it over and stopped
Uchida's Version crashed into Jick's dog house, knocked it over on its side, and stopped

2. Use direct quotations set off by quotation marks and commas.

Without Quotation We all shouted to look out.
Uchida's Version "Look out, for heaven's sake," we all shouted.

Practice On your paper revise and rewrite the following passage about Richard Wright, an African American author. Add punctuation to make the passage easier to read.

Richard Wright was born near Natchez Mississippi. Wright moved to Chicago Illinois when he was nineteen His second book is a novel about a young African American in the Chicago slums This book, *Native Son*, gained Wright immediate fame Speaking of the book's main character, a reviewer said We get inside Bigger Thomas's head so we can feel the terror and despair of the life of a man who is young poor and black Wright's other books include *The Outsider The Long Dream* and his autobiography *Black Boy* Much of his writing deals with the life of African Americans in the United States Wright moved to New York in 1937 and he lived the last years of his life in Paris

Teacher's Classroom Resources

The following resources can be used for assessment or evaluation.

Unit Assessment

Tests with Answer Key
Unit 19 Mastery Test, pp. 75–76

Test Generator
Unit 19 Mastery Test

You may wish to administer the Unit 19 Mastery Test at this point.

UNIT 20

Grammar Through Sentence Combining

Grammar | Lessons

UNIT GOALS

The goal of Unit 20 is to help students, through example and instruction, to develop an understanding of and an ability to combine groups of short sentences into longer sentences that exhibit greater clarity of thought, conciseness of style, and variety of expression.

Unit Assessment

Tests with Answer Key
Unit 20 Pretest, pp. 77–78
Unit 20 Mastery Test, pp. 79–80

Test Generator
Unit 20 Pretest
Unit 20 Mastery Test

You may wish to administer the Unit 20 Pretest at this point.

Key to Ability Levels

Enabling Strategies have been coded for varying learning styles and abilities.

L1 Level 1 activities are within the ability range of Learning Disabled students.

L2 Level 2 activities are basic-to-average activities and are within the ability range of average students.

L3 Level 3 activities are challenging activities and are within the ability range of above-average students.

LEP LEP activities are within the ability range of Limited English Proficiency students.

Setting the Purpose

Lesson 20.1 teaches students to use compound sentences appropriately.

FOCUS

Lesson Overview

Objective: To combine related sentences using the conjunctions *and*, *but*, and *or*

Bellringer

When students enter the classroom, have this assignment on the board: *Write a brief paragraph about your favorite item of clothing.*

TEACH

Teaching Tip

In grammar the term *compound* refers to the joining of two equal elements of the same type. A compound sentence joins two simple sentences.

Cross-reference: Grammar

For instruction and practice with compound sentences, refer students to Lesson 8.6, pp. 272–273.

PRACTICE AND ASSESS

Answers: Exercise 1

1. … jacket, and his …
2. … jacket, but he …
3. … feelings, or perhaps …
4. … Brownie, and the animal tore a gash in the jacket sleeve, but the boy …
5. … school, and his …
6. … school, and girls …
7. … away, and he pitched it over a fence, but something …
8. … dinner, and he …
9. … cold, and the boy …
10. … jacket, but he …

20.1 Compound Sentences

When you have written a few simple sentences that are closely related in meaning, try combining them to form compound sentences. A compound sentence often states your meaning more clearly than a group of simple sentences does. Also, by using compound sentences, you can vary the lengths of your sentences.

EXAMPLE **a.** The boy wanted a black leather jacket.
b. His mother bought a green vinyl one instead.
[**, but**]

The boy wanted a black leather jacket**, but** his mother bought a green vinyl one instead.

In this example simple sentence *a* is joined to simple sentence *b* with the coordinating conjunction *but*. Note that a comma is used before the conjunction.

A **compound sentence** contains two or more simple sentences. You can combine two or more related simple sentences into a compound sentence by using the conjunctions *and, but,* or *or.*

Exercise 1 Combining Simple Sentences

The sentences below are based on the story "The Jacket" by Gary Soto, which you can find on pages 164–168. Combine the sentences in each numbered item into one new sentence by using a comma plus a coordinating conjunction. In the first few items the coordinating conjunction you should use is in brackets.

1. **a.** The boy had outgrown his old jacket.
b. His mother wanted to buy him a new one. [**, and**]

2. **a.** The boy thanked his mother for the jacket.
b. He actually hated it. [**, but**] ➡

Teacher's Classroom Resources

The following resources can be used for planning, instruction, practice, reinforcement, assessment, reteaching, enrichment, or evaluation.

Teaching Tools
Lesson Plans

Blackline Masters
Sentence Combining Practice, pp. 1–2

Grammar Workbook
Lesson 5

Unit Assessment

Tests with Answer Key
Unit 20 Pretest, pp. 77–78

Test Generator
Unit 20 Pretest

You may wish to administer the Unit 20 Pretest at this point.

3. **a.** His mother did not understand her son's feelings.
   b. Perhaps she simply could not afford a leather jacket. [**, or**]

4. **a.** The boy teased his dog, Brownie.
   b. The animal tore a gash in the jacket's sleeve. [**, and**]
   c. The boy wore his jacket anyway. [**, but**]

5. **a.** The next day the boy wore his jacket to school.
   b. His best friend seemed rude to him.

6. **a.** He got lower grades in school.
   b. Girls seemed to lose interest in him.

7. **a.** One day he decided to throw the jacket away.
   b. He pitched it over a fence.
   c. Something made him pick it up again.

8. **a.** The boy finished dinner.
   b. He went outside with his jacket over his arm.

9. **a.** The night was cold.
   b. The boy soon slipped into his jacket.

10. **a.** He never liked the ugly green jacket.
    b. He had to wear it for three long years.

Exercise 2 **Combining Simple Sentences**

Rewrite the following paragraphs, combining sentences as you think necessary.

The boy wore the jacket for three long years. He was unhappy for most of that time. He wished for a jacket of a different color. His family could not afford a black leather jacket. This was America. Children in America did not wear jackets like this. He wanted another jacket badly. He wore the ugly one.

The boy began to develop muscles. His arms stuck out of the jacket. He repaired the old rip in the sleeve. The gash widened. Stuffing came out of it. Still, he kept the jacket. Perhaps he could not afford another one. Perhaps he had grown attached to his guacamole jacket. The jacket cast a shadow over his life. He would not get rid of it. He called it his "ugly brother." In a sense, the jacket had become part of him.

Enabling Strategies

LEP Combining Sentences

Some students may not understand that only sentences that are closely related in meaning can be combined. Write the following sentences on the board and discuss which can be combined: *Ana was baking bread. I like red roses. Ana's friend Jorge was baking cookies.* Ask students what the first and last sentences have in common. Show how these sentences can be combined using a conjunction.

PRACTICE AND ASSESS

Answers: Exercise 2

The boy wore the jacket for three long years, and he was unhappy for most of that time. He wished for a jacket of a different color, but his family could not afford a black leather jacket. This was America, and children in America did not wear jackets like this. He wanted another jacket badly, but he wore the ugly one.

Then he began to develop muscles, and his arms stuck out of the jacket. He repaired the old rip in the sleeve, but the gash widened, and stuffing came out of it. Still, he kept the jacket. Perhaps he could not afford another one, or perhaps he had grown attached to his guacamole jacket. The jacket cast a shadow over his life, but he would not get rid of it. He called it his "ugly brother," and in a sense, the jacket had become part of him.

Independent Practice

Skills Practice

Sentence Combining Practice, pp. 1–2

Grammar Workbook, Lesson 5

CLOSE

Ask a volunteer to read the original paragraphs in Exercise 2 aloud. Do students hear that the ideas in the paragraphs do not flow well? Ask students to read their revised paragraphs aloud, and compare them to the original. Discuss how sentence combining improves the quality of the paragraphs.

Setting the Purpose

Lesson 20.2 teaches students to use compound elements to combine sentences that share information.

FOCUS

Lesson Overview

Objective: To combine sentences by joining related sentence elements

Bellringer

When students enter the classroom, have this assignment on the board: *Write three sentences about what you do to get ready for school in the morning.*

TEACH

Grammar Tip

Caution students not to confuse sentences with compound parts (which may have two subjects or verbs but only one main clause) with compound sentences (which have two or more main clauses).

PRACTICE AND ASSESS

Answers: Exercise 3

1. … her ears or her mouth…
2. … the color of her arms but not the color of her eyes.
3. … her eyes and teeth.
4. … her own chin and mouth.
5. … different eyebrows but the same ears.
6. … laughed at her, teased her, and compared her face …
7. … eyes and saw two …
8. … clear face with a narrow chin and a wide mouth.
9. … stood up and went back …
10. … mother and father taught …

20.2 Compound Elements

Sometimes several sentences share information—for example, the same subject or verb. By combining such sentences and using compound elements, you can avoid repetition and make your writing more concise. Sentences with compound elements also add variety to your writing.

EXAMPLE
a. Morning Girl looked in the water.
b. Morning Girl **tried to see her own face clearly**. [**and**]

Morning Girl looked in the water **and tried to see her own face clearly**.

Sentences *a* and *b* share information about Morning Girl. The combined version takes the new information from sentence *b, tried to see her own face clearly,* and joins it to sentence *a,* using the coordinating conjunction *and.*

You can avoid repeating shared information by combining and using **compound elements**. Join compound elements with the conjunctions *and, but,* or *or.* A comma is not needed after the conjunction.

Exercise 3 Combining Sentences with Compound Elements

The sentences below are based on a passage from *Morning Girl* by Michael Dorris, which you can find on pages 126–130. Combine the sentences in each numbered item, using compound elements joined by the conjunctions *and, but,* and *or.* As you build on the first sentence in each item, include only the new information from the following sentence(s). In the first few items the new information is in dark type and the conjunctions you should use are in brackets.

1. a. Morning Girl could not see her ears in the water.
b. She could not see **her mouth**. [**or**]

2. a Morning Girl knew the color of her arms.
b. She did **not** know **the color of her eyes**. [**but**] ➡

Teacher's Classroom Resources

The following resources can be used for planning, instruction, practice, reinforcement, reteaching, or enrichment.

Teaching Tools
Lesson Plans

Blackline Masters
Sentence Combining Practice, pp. 3–5

Grammar Workbook
Lessons 4–5

4. **a.** Hay protects the elephants.
   b. It protects them **from sunburn**.
5. **a.** The veterinarians check the elephants' backs.
   b. They check the elephants' backs before the baths.
6. **a.** The keeper sprays water.
   b. She sprays water on the elephants' foreheads and feet.
7. **a.** The elephants' backs are soaked and carefully scrubbed.
   b. They are soaked with green oil soap.
   c. They are scrubbed with brushes.
8. **a.** Scrapes are treated.
   b. The scrapes are on the elephants' backs.
   c. The scrapes are treated with soothing salve.
9. **a.** The elephants' feet are examined.
   b. Their feet are examined in the last part of the bath.
   c. Their feet are examined for pebbles and other irritants.
10. **a.** The keeper has the special ankus stick nearby at all times.
    b. The keeper has the ankus as a sign of authority.
    c. The ankus is a sign of authority to the elephants.

Exercise 6 Combining Sentences with Prepositional Phrases

Rewrite the following paragraphs, combining sentences with prepositional phrases. Make any other changes in wording that you feel are necessary.

One of the Washington Zoo's most colorful elephants is named Shanthi. Shanthi was rescued and raised in an elephant orphanage. She was raised with 21 other elephants. At the age of one, she was sent from Sri Lanka. She was sent to Washington. She was a gift. The gift was to the children of the United States. Her keeper, Sam, came with Shanthi. He came to the United States. Sam slept near his young charge. He slept in the Elephant House. He slept on a cot.

Before going back to Sri Lanka, Sam gave a tape recording to the zoo. The recording was of his special commands. If the zoo-keepers used the commands, they would have no trouble with Shanthi. This was according to Sam. However, the young elephant turned out to be quite a handful. This is in spite of Sam's assurances. She probably misbehaves to get special attention. She wants attention from her keepers.

Enabling Strategies

LEP Recognizing Prepositional Phrases

Students may mistake an infinitive phrase for a prepositional phrase beginning with *to*. Remind them that a prepositional phrase consists of a preposition followed by a noun or pronoun. List some common prepositions, and then let students take turns adding prepositional phrases first to the verb and then to the subject of an incomplete sentence such as the following: *The street leads* ___. (Answers will vary. Sample: *The street leads to the school. The street on the left leads to the school.*)

PRACTICE AND ASSESS

Answers: Exercise 5

Answers will vary, but some suggestions are given below.

1. Elephants in the wild normally bathe themselves in rivers.
2. Elephant baths at the zoo are fun for the keepers and the elephants.
3. Elephants in the wild live in herds, or social groups.
4. Hay protects the elephants from sunburn.
5. Before the baths the veterinarians check the elephants' backs.
6. The keeper sprays water on the elephants' foreheads and feet.
7. The elephants' backs are soaked with green oil soap and carefully scrubbed with brushes.
8. Scrapes on the elephants' backs are treated with soothing salve.
9. In the last part of the bath the elephants' feet are examined for pebbles and other irritants.
10. The keeper has the special ankus stick nearby at all times as a sign of authority to the elephants.

Answers: Exercise 6

Answers will vary, but some suggestions are given below.

One of the Washington Zoo's most colorful elephants is named Shanthi. Shanthi was rescued and raised with 21 other elephants in an elephant orphanage. At the age of one, she was sent from Sri Lanka to Washington as a gift to the children of the United States. Her keeper, Sam, came to the United States with Shanthi and slept near his young charge on a cot in the Elephant House.

Before going back to Sri Lanka, Sam gave the zoo a tape recording of his special commands for Shanthi. According to Sam, if the zookeepers used the commands, they would have no trouble with Shanthi. In spite of Sam's assurances, however, the young elephant turned out to be quite a handful. She probably misbehaves to get special attention from her keepers.

PRACTICE AND ASSESS

Answers: Exercise 7

Answers will vary, but some suggestions are given below.

1. Birch wanted to take a ride in the plane and knew this was her last chance.
2. Her grandfather seemed to have lost his desire for fun, or perhaps he did not want to take any chances.
3. Her grandfather glanced at the sky and decided to fly.
4. Birch grinned with delight, and her grandfather smiled for the first time that afternoon.
5. It was a beautiful day for a flight, and Birch and her grandfather knew it.
6. Birch wanted to go right away, but her grandfather needed to perform a preflight inspection.
7. Her grandfather found no problems with the tires, the gas, or the oil.
8. The old plane sat on the pavement in front of the hangar.
9. Pop steered the plane off the ramp, down the taxiway, and onto the runway.
10. The wind rushed through the open window and blew on Birch's face.

Independent Practice

Skills Practice

Sentence Combining Practice, pp. 9–10

Grammar Workbook, Lesson 42

Exercise 7 Mixed Review

The sentences below are based on a passage from *Coast to Coast* by Betsy Byars, which you can find on pages 84–88. Combine the sentences from each numbered item into one new sentence. Combine sentences and compound elements by using a coordinating conjunction, and add new information as prepositional phrases.

1. **a.** Birch wanted to take a ride in the plane.
   b. She knew this was her last chance.
2. **a.** Her grandfather seemed to have lost his desire for fun.
   b. Perhaps he did not want to take any chances.
3. **a.** Her grandfather glanced at the sky.
   b. Her grandfather decided to fly.
4. **a.** Birch grinned with delight.
   b. Her grandfather smiled for the first time that afternoon.
5. **a.** It was a beautiful day for a flight.
   b. Birch knew it.
   c. Her grandfather knew it.
6. **a.** Birch wanted to go right away.
   b. Her grandfather needed to perform a pre-flight inspection.
7. **a.** Her grandfather found no problems with the tires.
   b. Her grandfather found no problems with the gas.
   c. Her grandfather found no problems with the oil.
8. **a.** The old plane sat on the pavement.
   b. The pavement was in front of the hangar.
9. **a.** Pop steered the plane off the ramp.
   b. He steered it down the taxiway.
   c. He steered the plane onto the runway.
10. **a.** The wind rushed through the open window.
    b. The wind blew on Birch's face.

CLOSE

Divide the class into small groups for a partners activity. Direct the partners in each group to exchange a piece of writing, possibly from a previous assignment or their writing portfolios. Ask partners to underline any sentences they think could be combined to make the writing more concise and to help it flow better.

Part 3

Resources and Skills

PART 3 GOALS

The goal of Part 3 is to help students, through example and instruction, to develop an understanding of the resources available within a library, vocabulary and spelling through context and structural analysis, as well as effective study and test-taking skills.

Unit Assessment

Tests with Answer Key
Units 21–25 Pretests, pp. 81–100
Units 21–25 Mastery Tests, pp. 81–100

Test Generator
Units 21–25 Pretests
Units 21–25 Mastery Tests

See each unit's Teacher's Classroom Resources information for specific Pretest and Mastery Test preferences.

Key to Ability Levels

Enabling Strategies have been coded for varying learning styles and abilities.

L1 Level 1 activities are within the ability range of Learning Disabled students.

L2 Level 2 are basic-to-average activities and are within the ability range of average students.

L3 Level 3 are challenging activities that are within the ability range of above-average students.

LEP LEP activities are within the ability range of Limited English Proficiency students.

Part 3 Resources and Skills

UNIT 21

Library and Reference Resources

21.1 Using a Library

The first free public library in the United States was opened in 1833. It had few books and shared space with a store and a post office. Libraries have changed since then.

Today's libraries contain books of all sorts. They also offer magazines, newspapers, audio recordings, videos, and many other resources. In fact, some libraries are now called resource centers. You can find information about anything from skateboards to Shakespeare, from Persian poetry to pickles.

No two libraries are exactly alike, but all libraries group similar things together. Stories and novels (fiction) are separate from information books (nonfiction). Magazines and audio-visual materials have their own sections. Turn the page to see how a neighborhood library might be arranged.

INTRODUCING Unit 21

Setting the Purpose

Lesson 21.1 teaches students about the organization of libraries and helps them become familiar with basic library research tools.

FOCUS

Lesson Overview

Objective: To become familiar with the library
Skills: locating library resources
Critical Thinking: classifying
Speaking and Listening: discussing

Bellringer

When students enter the classroom, have this assignment on the board: *List four library reference sources you might want to use.*

Motivating Activity

Ask students to draw a map of their school library. Then discuss the contents of that library, comparing its organization with the one illustrated on these pages. Have students identify where they would expect to find the four resources they named in the Bellringer.

Teacher's Classroom Resources

For Lesson 21.1, the following resources can be used for planning, instruction, practice, assessment, reinforcement, or evaluation.

Teaching Tools
Lesson Plans

Blackline Masters
Vocabulary and Spelling Practice, pp. 23–24
Thinking and Study Skills, pp. 23–29

Unit Assessment
Tests with Answer Key
Unit 21 Pretest, pp. 81–82

Test Generator
Unit 21 Pretest

You may wish to administer the Unit 21 Pretest at this point.

TEACH

Guided Practice

L2 Asking for Help

Tell students that the librarian is the best resource that a library has. When they are in doubt, they can always ask for help. Ask volunteers to list some of the materials they might need help finding. Then have them discuss what the librarian might do for them.

Librarian A librarian can be the most important resource of all. He or she can help you use the library wisely and will give you advice when needed.

Young Adult and Children's Section Young readers can find books just for them in a separate area of the library.

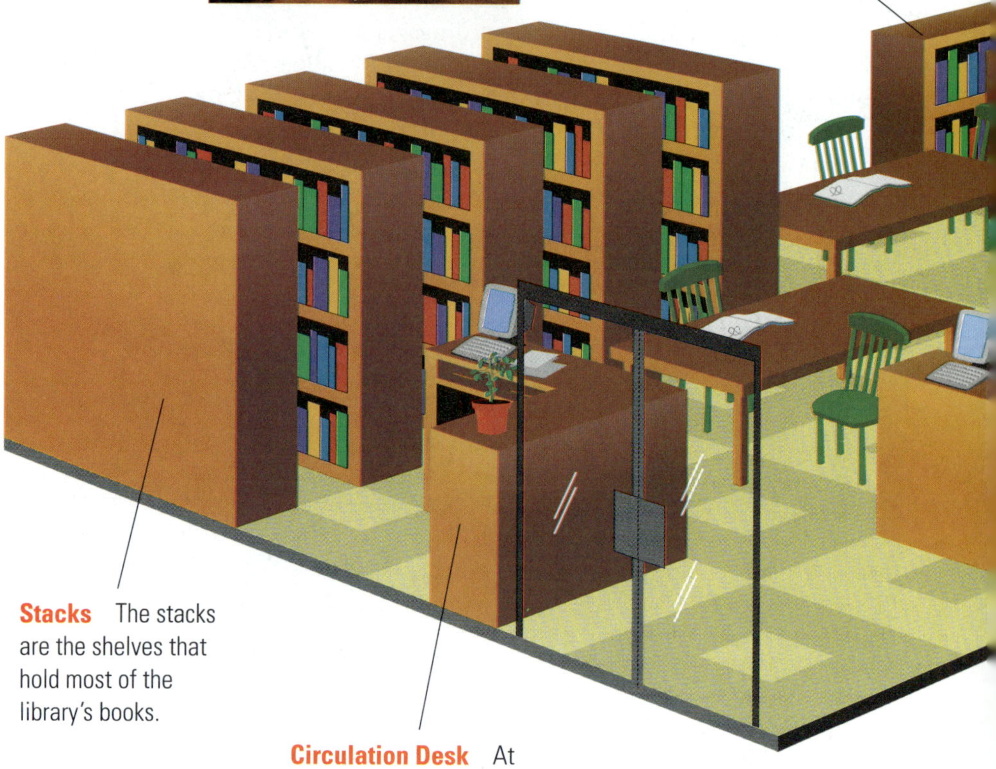

Stacks The stacks are the shelves that hold most of the library's books.

Circulation Desk At the circulation desk you use your library card to check out materials you want to take home.

Reference The reference area holds dictionaries, encyclopedias, atlases, and other reference works.

Audio-Visual Materials Audiotapes, records, compact discs (CDs), and videotapes are in the audio-visual section.

Newspapers and Magazines You can find current issues of newspapers and magazines in a general reading area. A librarian will tell you where you can find old issues.

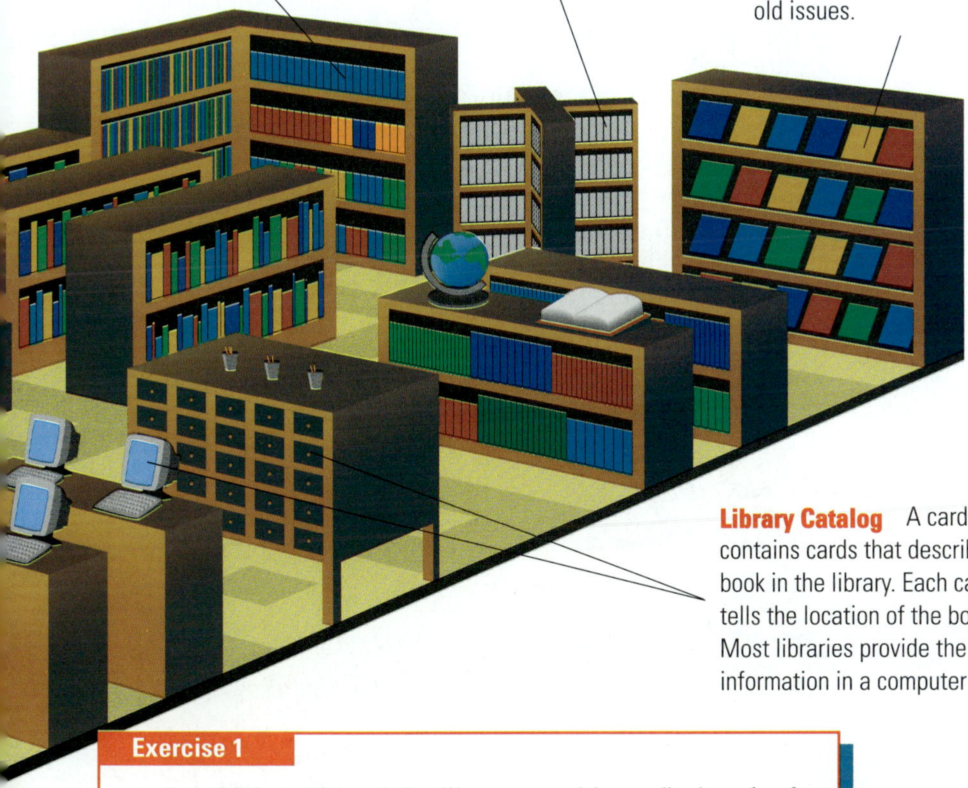

Library Catalog A card catalog contains cards that describe each book in the library. Each card also tells the location of the book. Most libraries provide the same information in a computer catalog.

Exercise 1

In which section of the library would you find each of the following items?

1. The monthly magazine *National Geographic*
2. *Atlas of the American Revolution*
3. The novel *My Side of the Mountain*
4. A video of the movie *Old Yeller*
5. *Encyclopedia of Black America*

PRACTICE AND ASSESS

Answers: Exercise 1

1. Newspapers and Magazines
2. Reference
3. Stacks (general fiction) or Young Adult and Children's Section
4. Audio-Visual Materials
5. Reference

Independent Practice

Skills Practice

Vocabulary and Spelling Practice, pp. 23–24

Thinking and Study Skills, pp. 23–29

CLOSE

Ask students to describe the library resources that they have found the most helpful. You can also have them share any research tips or strategies they know about.

Enabling Strategies

LEP Discussing Periodicals

Students whose first language is not English may not be familiar with common periodicals. Discuss the periodicals carried by your school or local library. You may wish to have some samples of the most useful and interesting periodicals available in class, such as *National Geographic, National Geographic World, 'Teen, National Wildlife, Time, Newsweek,* and *Boys' Life.*

Setting the Purpose

Lesson 21.2 explains the Dewey Decimal System. It also gives students specific examples of how the system works.

FOCUS

Lesson Overview

Objective: To become familiar with the Dewey Decimal System
Skills: using the Dewey Decimal System
Critical Thinking: classifying
Speaking and Listening: discussing

Bellringer

When students enter the classroom, have this assignment on the board: *Write the titles of at least three books you have read.*

Motivating Activity

Discuss the title students have listed in the Bellringer activity. Have volunteers write on the board two or three of the titles they chose. Then ask them to list the classification of these books.

21.2 How Books Are Organized

A large library may have hundreds of thousands of books. How can you find what you want among all those books? In 1876 librarian Melvil Dewey set up a system for organizing books. His system, the Dewey Decimal System, is still used in libraries today.

In this system all nonfiction books are given numbers. Dewey divided the numbers into groups by topic. Books about science, for example, make up the 500s group. A book about magnets would be placed in the science group. One about the English language would go into the language group—the 400s. The chart shows how the Dewey groups are broken into smaller subgroups.

Dewey Decimal System

Numbers	Major Groups	Examples of Subgroups
000–099	General works	Encyclopedias, library science
100–199	Philosophy	Dreams, the senses
200–299	Religion	World religions, mythology
300–399	Social sciences	Law, education, money
400–499	Language	Grammar, foreign languages
500–599	Science	Animals, math, astronomy
600–699	Technology	Tools, medicine, farming
700–799	The arts	Music, painting, sports
800–899	Literature	Poetry, plays
900–999	Geography, history	Travel, biography, U.S. history

Each nonfiction book has a call number on its spine. In most libraries, this is a Dewey Decimal number. It's a short code telling what the book is about. Each digit in the number narrows down the topic. For example, look at the call number for a book called *The Great American Baseball Scrapbook.*

Teacher's Classroom Resources

For Lesson 21.2, the following resources can be used for planning, instruction, practice, or reinforcement.

Teaching Tools
Lesson Plans

Blackline Masters
Vocabulary and Spelling Practice, pp. 23–24
Thinking and Study Skills, pp. 23–29

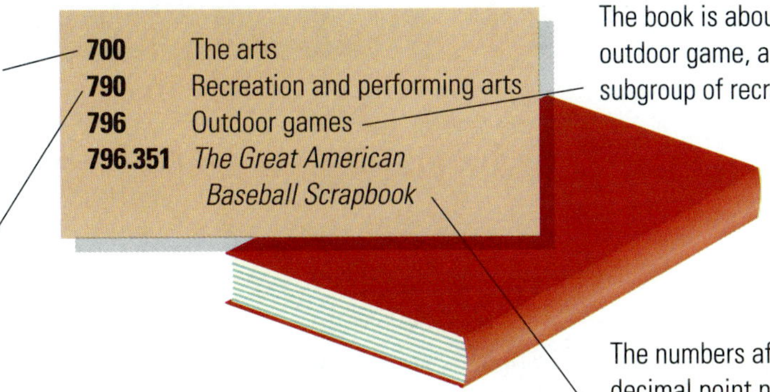

As a student, you don't need to memorize the Dewey code. It's a good idea, however, to learn the main groups in the Dewey Decimal System. Knowing them will make it easier to find the books you need.

Books are shelved by Dewey Decimal number and then alphabetically by author. You might find six books about whales, each book with the number 599.5 on its spine. Within this group a book by Dorothy Hinshaw Patent would appear before a book by John F. Waters.

Fiction works usually don't have Dewey Decimal numbers. They are shelved in alphabetical order by the author's last name. The call number may have *F* or *FIC*, for *fiction,* on the first line. The second line has the first three letters of the author's last name. Different books by the same author are shelved alphabetically by title.

Exercise 2

In what Dewey group would you expect each of the following books to be shelved? Give the main group name and the number in hundreds.

1. A book about the solar system
2. A book with the title *A History of the Ancient World*
3. A book about Greek gods and goddesses
4. A book about the origins of jazz
5. A book of poems by Shel Silverstein

TEACH

Guided Practice

L2 Promoting Discussion

Ask students whether they have at home collections of books, CD-ROMs, video games, or any other articles that could be classified. When might it be necessary to classify such a collection? Ask them to discuss methods that might be used at home to organize the various kinds of collections.

PRACTICE AND ASSESS

Answers: Exercise 2

1. Science, 500s
2. History and geography, 900s
3. Religion (mythology), 200s
4. Arts, 700s
5. Literature, 800s

Independent Practice

Skills Practice

Vocabulary and Spelling Practice, pp. 23–24

Thinking and Study Skills, pp. 23–29

CLOSE

Have students read the titles of the books they listed in the Bellringer and tell how the books would be classified in a library that uses the Dewey Decimal System.

Enabling Strategies

LEP Practicing Alphabetical Order

Students who are new to English may need practice with alphabetical order. Bring in a number of works of fiction, including some books written by the same author. Ask students to arrange the books in alphabetical order by the author's name and where necessary by the book's title. Explain that book titles beginning with the word *a* or *the* are alphabetized by using the second word in the title. Students can discuss why libraries follow this practice. You may prefer to do this activity using three-by-five index cards instead of actual books.

Setting the Purpose

Lesson 21.3 teaches students what a card catalog is and shows the three types of cards: author card, title card, and subject card. It describes the kinds of cards used for works of fiction and nonfiction. Students will learn how to use a card catalog to find a book of their choice.

FOCUS

Lesson Overview

Objective: To become familiar with a card catalog
Skills: using a card catalog
Critical Thinking: categorizing; classifying
Speaking and Listening: discussing; explaining a process

Bellringer

When students enter the classroom, have this assignment on the board: *Write down the titles and authors of a work of fiction and a work of nonfiction that you know. For the nonfiction book, write a word or phrase telling the book's subject.*

TEACH

Guided Practice

L2 Making Cards

Bring into class several library books, including nonfiction works on various topics. Divide the class into small groups, and give each group a book and three three-by-five index cards. Ask each group to create author, title, and subject cards for its book. Encourage students to make the cards as complete as possible using the cards on page 496 as models.

21.3 How to Find a Book

While writing a report, you may need to find a book about a particular topic or you may want to locate a book by your favorite writer. How do you find the books you need? A fast way is to start with the card catalog.

Information on Cards

The card catalog is a cabinet of long, narrow drawers holding cards similar to the ones shown below. Each card has a brief description of a book. The book's Dewey Decimal number is printed in the upper left-hand corner of each card. This number, the call number, is also on the spine of the book.

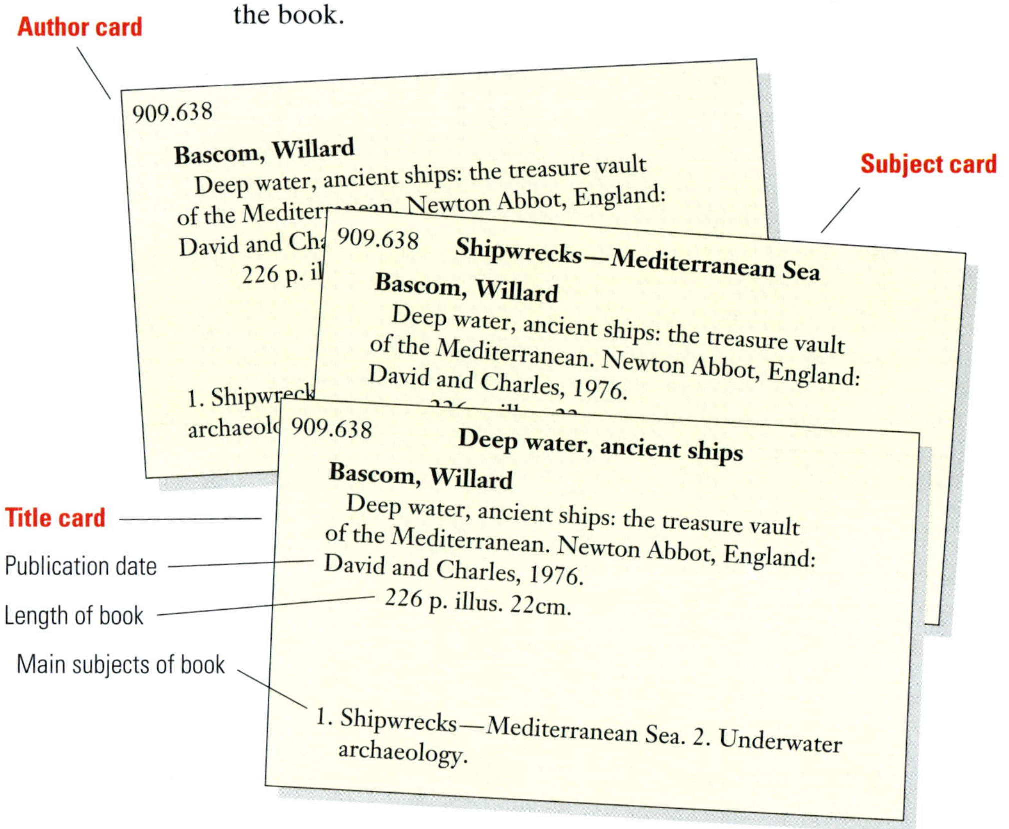

Teacher's Classroom Resources

For Lesson 21.3, the following resources can be used for planning, instruction, practice, or reinforcement.

Teaching Tools
Lesson Plans

Blackline Masters
Vocabulary and Spelling Practice, pp. 23–24
Thinking and Study Skills, pp. 23–29

Most fiction books have two cards: an author card and a title card. A nonfiction book usually has at least three cards: an author card, a title card, and one or more subject cards. The first line on the card shows what type it is. The first line of an author card has the author's name. The first line of a title card has the book's title. The first line of a subject card shows a subject heading.

Many libraries also have a computer catalog that contains the same information. You type an author's name, a title, or a subject into the computer to get the information. A librarian or library assistant can help you learn to use the computer catalog.

Finding a Book

The three types of cards in the catalog are like handles. They allow you to grab onto a book in three different ways. Just look up an author's name, a book title, or any subject in the catalog. Carefully copy down the call number of the book you want. Then go to the shelves to see if the book is available.

The books are arranged in numerical order by call number. You can look at the signs at the end of each row of shelves to see which call numbers are in that row.

Exercise 3

At your school or neighborhood library use the card catalog or computer catalog to find a book as specified in each of the following items. List the author, title, and call number of each book.

1. Endangered animals
2. How to build kites
3. South Africa
4. A book by Jean Craighead George
5. The ocean
6. The American Civil War
7. Musical instruments
8. Women in sports

PRACTICE AND ASSESS

Answers: Exercise 3

Each response should include an author's name, a title, and a call number. Titles and call numbers should reflect the following Dewey Decimal System categories:

1. 600s (Science)
2. 700s (The Arts—Recreation)
3. 900s (Geography and History)
4. Fiction (F or FIC)
5. 500s (Science)
6. 900s (Geography and History)
7. 700s (The Arts—Music)
8. 700s (The Arts—Recreation) or 900s (Biography)

Independent Practice

Skills Practice

Vocabulary and Spelling Practice, pp. 23–24

Thinking and Study Skills, pp. 23–29

CLOSE

Each student can create cards for the books they listed in the Bellringer activity. For the call numbers, they can either give the appropriate number range from the list on page 494 or look up the precise call number when they carry out Exercise 3.

Technology Tip

Using Computerized Catalogs

If your school library or local neighborhood library has a computer catalog, encourage students to investigate its use. You may wish to have computer-literate students help those who are less familiar with computers. You could also have a group of students prepare a presentation on this topic for the rest of the class.

Setting the Purpose

Lesson 21.4 addresses reference sources and teaches students how to use encyclopedias and atlases.

FOCUS

Lesson Overview

Objective: To learn how to use reference sources
Skills: using an encyclopedia; using an atlas
Critical Thinking: evaluating reference sources
Speaking and Listening: oral reporting

Bellringer

When students enter the classroom, have this assignment on the board: *List five reference books you would expect to see in a library.*

TEACH

Guided Practice

L2 Researching Information

Tell students that references can be very helpful, but they must know what topics to look up in order to use these resources effectively. Ask students to name the subjects of papers they have written or are in the process of writing. Discuss entries they could look up in an encyclopedia or other print or CD-ROM reference sources. Suggest that students look up information on the Civil War under the subject categories Civil War, United States Wars, Abraham Lincoln, and Gettysburg. Then ask them to compare the kind of information they find. Point out that they should think about related topics that would give them additional information.

21.4 Using References

You might be curious about a topic and want to know more about it. Or perhaps you need information for a report. Whatever the reason, your first source of information is likely to be a reference work. Reference books make it easy to locate information about a person, a place, or almost any other topic. Encyclopedias and atlases are two examples of useful reference works.

Encyclopedias

Encyclopedias contain articles on many different topics. Major encyclopedias contain a number of volumes. *The World Book Encyclopedia*, for example, is divided into twenty-two volumes.

Guide words at the top of each two-page spread show the first and last entries on that spread.

Articles may contain a list of books you can turn to for more information on the topic.

Encyclopedia entries appear in alphabetical order.

The article or an entry word may refer you to another entry in the encyclopedia.

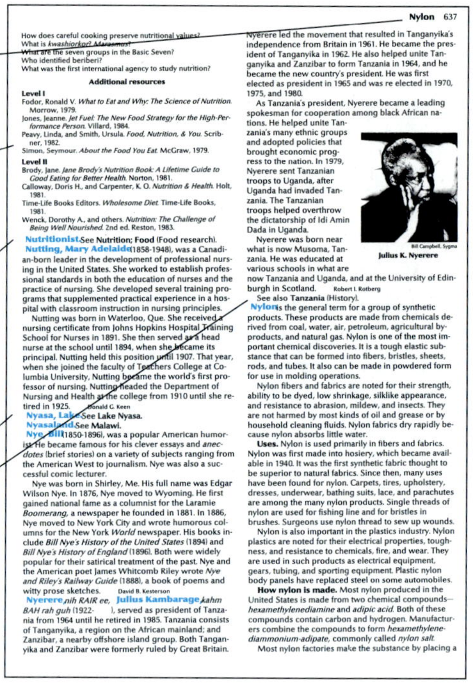
Nylon 637

How does careful cooking preserve nutritional values?
What is *kwashiorkor*? *Marasmus*?
What are the seven groups in the Basic Seven?
Who identified beriberi?
What was the first international agency to study nutrition?

Additional resources

Level I
Fodor, Ronald V. *What to Eat and Why: The Science of Nutrition.* Morrow, 1979.
Jones, Jeanne. *Jet Fuel: The New Food Strategy for the High-Performance Person.* Villard, 1984.
Peavy, Linda, and Smith, Ursula. *Food, Nutrition, & You.* Scribner, 1982.
Simon, Seymour. *About the Food You Eat.* McGraw, 1979.

Level II
Brody, Jane. *Jane Brody's Nutrition Book: A Lifetime Guide to Good Eating for Better Health.* Norton, 1981.
Calloway, Doris H., and Carpenter, K. O. *Nutrition & Health.* Holt, 1981.
Time-Life Books Editors. *Wholesome Diet.* Time-Life Books, 1981.
Wenck, Dorothy A., and others. *Nutrition: The Challenge of Being Well Nourished.* 2nd ed. Reston, 1983.

Nutritionist. See **Nutrition; Food** (Food research).

Nutting, Mary Adelaide (1858-1948), was a Canadian-born leader in the development of professional nursing in the United States. She worked to establish professional standards in both the education of nurses and the practice of nursing. She developed several training programs that supplemented practical experience in a hospital with classroom instruction in nursing principles.

Nutting was born in Waterloo, Que. She received a nursing certificate from Johns Hopkins Hospital Training School for Nurses in 1891. She then served as a head nurse at the school until 1894, when she became its principal. Nutting held this position until 1907. That year, when she joined the faculty of Teachers College at Columbia University, Nutting became the world's first professor of nursing. Nutting headed the Department of Nursing and Health at the college from 1910 until she retired in 1925. Donald G. Keen

Nyasa, Lake. See **Lake Nyasa.**

Nyasaland. See **Malawi.**

Nye, Bill (1850-1896), was a popular American humorist. He became famous for his clever essays and *anecdotes* (brief stories) on a variety of subjects ranging from the American West to journalism. Nye was also a successful comic lecturer.

Nye was born in Shirley, Me. His full name was Edgar Wilson Nye. In 1876, Nye moved to Wyoming. He first gained national fame as a columnist for the Laramie *Boomerang*, a newspaper he founded in 1881. In 1886, Nye moved to New York City and wrote humorous columns for the New York *World* newspaper. His books include *Bill Nye's History of the United States* (1894) and *Bill Nye's History of England* (1896). Both were widely popular for their satirical treatment of the past. Nye and the American poet James Whitcomb Riley wrote *Nye and Riley's Railway Guide* (1888), a book of poems and witty prose sketches. David B. Kesterson

Nyerere, *nih RAIR ee,* **Julius Kambarage,** *kahm BAH rah guh* (1922-), served as president of Tanzania from 1964 until he retired in 1985. Tanzania consists of Tanganyika, a region on the African mainland; and Zanzibar, a nearby offshore island group. Both Tanganyika and Zanzibar were formerly ruled by Great Britain.

Nyerere led the movement that resulted in Tanganyika's independence from Britain in 1961. He became the president of Tanganyika in 1962. He also helped unite Tanganyika and Zanzibar to form Tanzania in 1964, and he became the new country's president. He was first elected as president in 1965 and was re elected in 1970, 1975, and 1980.

As Tanzania's president, Nyerere became a leading spokesman for cooperation among black African nations. He helped unite Tanzania's many ethnic groups and adopted policies that brought economic progress to the nation. In 1979, Nyerere sent Tanzanian troops to Uganda, after Uganda had invaded Tanzania. The Tanzanian troops helped overthrow the dictatorship of Idi Amin Dada in Uganda.

Bill Campbell, Sygma
Julius K. Nyerere

Nyerere was born near what is now Musoma, Tanzania. He was educated at various schools in what are now Tanzania and Uganda, and at the University of Edinburgh in Scotland. Robert I. Rotberg

See also **Tanzania** (History).

Nylon is the general term for a group of synthetic products. These products are made from chemicals derived from coal, water, air, petroleum, agricultural byproducts, and natural gas. Nylon is one of the most important chemical discoveries. It is a tough elastic substance that can be formed into fibers, bristles, sheets, rods, and tubes. It also can be made in powdered form for use in molding operations.

Nylon fibers and fabrics are noted for their strength, ability to be dyed, low shrinkage, silklike appearance, and resistance to abrasion, mildew, and insects. They are not harmed by most kinds of oil and grease or by household cleaning fluids. Nylon fabrics dry rapidly because nylon absorbs little water.

Uses. Nylon is used primarily in fibers and fabrics. Nylon was first made into hosiery, which became available in 1940. It was the first synthetic fabric thought to be superior to natural fabrics. Since then, many uses have been found for nylon. Carpets, tires, upholstery, dresses, underwear, bathing suits, lace, and parachutes are among the many nylon products. Single threads of nylon are used for fishing line and for bristles in brushes. Surgeons use nylon thread to sew up wounds.

Nylon is also important in the plastics industry. Nylon plastics are noted for their electrical properties, toughness, and resistance to chemicals, fire, and wear. They are used in such products as electrical equipment, gears, tubing, and sporting equipment. Plastic nylon body panels have replaced steel on some automobiles.

How nylon is made. Most nylon produced in the United States is made from two chemical compounds—*hexamethylenediamine* and *adipic acid.* Both of these compounds contain carbon and hydrogen. Manufacturers combine the compounds to form *hexamethylene-diammonium-adipate,* commonly called *nylon salt.*

Most nylon factories make the substance by placing a

Teacher's Classroom Resources

For Lesson 21.4, the following resources can be used for planning, instruction, practice, or reinforcement.

Teaching Tools
Lesson Plans

Blackline Masters
Vocabulary and Spelling Practice, pp. 23–24
Thinking and Study Skills, pp. 23–29

An encyclopedia is a good place to check dates and specific facts, such as when Texas became a state or whether a fungus is a plant. You can also use an encyclopedia to get basic information on a topic quickly.

Atlases

An atlas is a collection of maps. A general atlas contains maps of all parts of the world. It may also have special maps that give information about climate or population. Other atlases deal with one part of the world, such as Asia, Zaire, or Oklahoma. Still others cover special topics—for example, an atlas of wildlife. Historical atlases contain maps that show changes over time. Some historical atlases cover lengthy periods of time. Others cover shorter periods, perhaps only a few years. Similarly, they may deal with world history or the history of a single country or region.

Exercise 4

Tell which reference work—an encyclopedia or an atlas—would best answer each question below. Then choose one of the questions to answer. Give the answer and the title of the reference work you used to find it.

1. What countries border the country of Iraq?
2. Which planet has the most moons?
3. How many bones are in a human hand?
4. What sea is between Saudi Arabia and India?
5. What is the average rainfall each year in the Sahara?

PRACTICE AND ASSESS

Answers: Exercise 4

Answers should include the name of the encyclopedia or atlas that furnished the information.

1. atlas; Turkey, Iran, Saudi Arabia, Jordan, Syria, Kuwait
2. encyclopedia; Saturn
3. encyclopedia; 27
4. atlas; Arabian Sea
5. encyclopedia or atlas; less than 10 inches on average, but less than 1 inch in some locations

Independent Practice

Skills Practice

Vocabulary and Spelling Practice, pp. 23–24

Thinking and Study Skills, pp. 23–29

CLOSE

Ask students to describe their experiences using encyclopedias and atlases. Did they find some sources to be more helpful than others? With what types of reference materials did they have difficulty?

Speaking and Listening

Checking References

Ask volunteers to make a list of the atlases and encyclopedias available in their school library. Then ask each student to examine one of these references and report on it to the class. Tell students to respond to questions such as the following: What kinds of information does this reference contain? Does it seem to be up-to-date? How complete is the information provided on a specific topic? Is the information clear and easy to understand? For what kinds of assignments would this reference be useful?

Setting the Purpose

Lesson 21.5 teaches students about three types of dictionaries and different uses for dictionaries and thesauruses.

FOCUS

Lesson Overview

Objective: To learn how to use a dictionary and a thesaurus
Skills: using a dictionary; using a thesaurus
Critical Thinking: comparing; categorizing
Speaking and Listening: discussing

Bellringer

When students enter the classroom, have this assignment on the board: *Name five things you can find in a dictionary.*

Motivating Activity

Bring to class several different types of dictionaries (corresponding to those in the text) for students to examine. Have them compare the dictionaries and tell what is different about them. After students have read the first page of the lesson, have them decide in which category each dictionary belongs.

21.5 Using a Dictionary

The Dictionary

People often speak of dictionaries as though they were all alike. In fact, people often say that they've looked up a word in *the* dictionary. After all, every dictionary is an alphabetically arranged collection of words and their definitions. However, dictionaries come in different sizes and have different uses. They are meant for different users. The chart below shows some of the ways in which dictionaries differ.

Types of Dictionaries

Type	Description	Examples
 **Unabridged Dictionaries** 250,000 or more entries	Detailed word histories and definitions Found mostly in libraries	*Random House Dictionary of the English Language* *Webster's Third New International Dictionary*
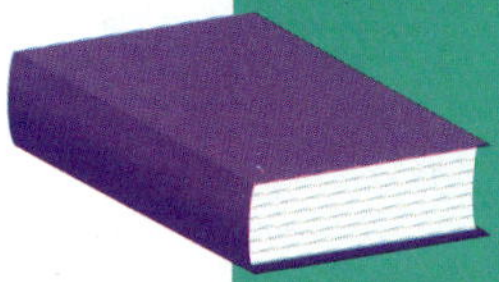 **Desk or College Dictionaries** 130,000–250,000 entries	Detailed enough to answer most questions on definitions and word histories Used in schools, homes, and businesses	*Webster's New World Dictionary* *The American Heritage Dictionary*
 **School Dictionaries** 90,000 or fewer entries	Often in separate versions for primary, elementary, and high school students Definitions suitable for students' grade levels	*Macmillan Dictionary* *Webster's School Dictionary*

Teacher's Classroom Resources

For Lesson 21.5, the following resources can be used for planning, instruction, practice, or reinforcement.

Teaching Tools
Lesson Plans

Blackline Masters
Vocabulary and Spelling Practice, pp. 23–24
Thinking and Study Skills, pp. 23–29

The sample dictionary page shows how the entries on a page are arranged. An entry includes the word, its definitions, and other information about the word. The bold type used for each entry term helps you see what words are defined on each page. The entries are in alphabetical order.

prisoner of war / probe

specifically to one held under arrest in a prison or under guard while on trial or serving a prison sentence: *The prisoner was released on parole.* **Captive** is restricted to prisoners captured and held by an enemy during war or for ransom and suggests a state of complete subjugation rather than imprisonment: *The downed airman was held as a captive by the enemy for six months.*

prisoner of war, person captured or held by the enemy in war.

pris·sy (pris′ē) **-si·er, -si·est.** *adj.* very prim, fussy, or prudish. [Blend of PRIM and SISSY.]

pris·tine (pris′tēn) *adj.* **1.** of or relating to the earliest time, period, or condition; original; primitive. **2.** pure; uncorrupted; unspoiled: *the pristine beauty of freshly fallen snow.* [Latin *pristīnus* former, primitive.]

prith·ee (pri*th*′ē) *interj.* *Archaic.* I pray thee; please.

pri·va·cy (prī′və sē) *pl.,* **-cies.** *n.* **1.** state or condition of being private, secluded, or isolated: *The writer needed privacy to finish his novel.* **2.** right to be free from interference with one's private affairs: *Opening someone else's mail is an invasion of privacy.* **3.** secrecy. —**Syn. 1.** see **solitude.**

pri·vate (prī′vit) *adj.* **1.** belonging or restricted to or reserved for a particular person or persons: *a private driveway, private property.* **2.** personal; individual. **3.** not intended for general or public knowledge; confidential: *a private conversation.* **4.** not holding public office or having an official position: *a private citizen.* **5.** not supported or managed by or connected with the government: *an agency under private control.* **6.** secluded; isolated. —*n.* **1.** in the U.S. Army and Marine Corps, an enlisted man of the lowest rank. **2. in private.** confidentially or secretly; privately. [Latin *prīvātus* apart from the state, belonging to an individual. Doublet of PRIVY.] —**pri′vate·ly,** *adv.* —**pri′vate·ness,** *n.*

private detective, detective who is employed by a private person or group rather than a police force or government agency. Also, **private investigator.**

private enterprise, free enterprise.

pri·va·teer (prī′və tēr′) *n.* **1.** privately owned armed ship commissioned by a government to attack enemy ships, esp. merchant ships. **2.** commander or a member of the crew of such a ship. —*v.i.* to sail on or as a privateer.

private eye *Informal.* private detective.

private first class 1. in the U.S. Army, an enlisted man ranking below a corporal and above a private. **2.** in the U.S. Marine Corps, an enlisted man ranking below a lance corporal and above a private.

private school, school that is supported and managed by a private group rather than by the government.

pri·va·tion (prī vā′shən) *n.* **1.** lack of the comforts or necessities of life or the condition resulting from such a lack. **2.** act of depriving; being deprived. [Latin *prīvātiō* a taking away.]

priv·a·tive (priv′ə tiv) *adj.* **1.** causing deprivation or loss. **2.** *Grammar.* altering the meaning of a word from positive to negative, as by means of a prefix. —*n.* *Grammar.* privative prefix or suffix. [Latin *prīvātīvus* denoting privation, negative, from *prīvāre* to deprive, rob.]

Privet

priv·et (priv′it) *n.* any of a group of evergreen shrubs or small trees, genus *Ligustrum,* widely used for hedges, usually having white flowers and black berries. [Of uncertain origin.]

priv·i·lege (priv′ə lij, priv′lij) *n.* special right, advantage, benefit, or immunity granted to or enjoyed by a certain person, group, or class. —*v.t.,* **-leged, -leg·ing.** to grant a privilege to. [Latin *prīvilēgium* law for or against an individual, from *prīvus* one's own, individual + *lēx* law.]

priv·i·leged (priv′ə lijd, priv′lijd) *adj.* **1.** having or enjoying a privilege or privileges. **2.** confidential; restricted: *privileged information.*

priv·i·ly (priv′ə lē) *adv.* privately; secretly.

priv·y (priv′ē) *adj.* **1.** participating in the knowledge of something secret or private (with *to*): *Only three people were privy to the plot.* **2.** *Archaic.* secret; concealed. **3.** *Archaic.* private; personal. —*n. pl.,* **priv·ies.** outhouse *(def. 1).* [Old French *prive* intimate, private, from Latin *prīvātus* belonging to an individual. Doublet of PRIVATE.]

Privy Council, honorary body appointed by the British sovereign, having about 300 members.

privy seal, in Great Britain, seal affixed to certain documents.

prize[1] (prīz) *n.* **1.** that which is offered or won as a reward, esp. for winning in a competition or in a game of chance. **2.** anything worth striving for. —*adj.* **1.** that has won or is likely to win a prize. **2.** offered or given as a prize. **3.** worthy of a prize; outstanding. [Old French *pris* value, honor, from Latin *pretium* value, reward.] **Syn.** *n.* **1. Prize, award, reward** mean an honor, as a payment, medal, or citation, bestowed on a person in recognition of an achievement. **Prize** is applied to what is bestowed on a victor in a competitive contest: *Frank won the first prize in the chess tournament.* **Award** usually suggests that the honor is bestowed by a judge or panel of judges and that the performers have fulfilled certain conditions: *The publishers have offered an award for the best novel of the year.* **Reward** is restricted to a form of payment earned by someone for his effort: *Jack received a reward for returning the lost dog to its owner.*

prize[2] (prīz) *n.* something seized or captured, esp. an enemy ship captured at sea during wartime. [Old French *prise* seizure, booty, from *prendre* to take, from Latin *prehendere* to seize.]

prize[3] (prīz) **prized, priz·ing.** *v.t.* **1.** to value or esteem highly: *to prize a friend's advice.* **2.** to estimate the value of; appraise: *a man who prizes his honor above his life.* [Old French *pr(e)isier* to value, esteem, from Late Latin *pretiāre* to value, from Latin *pretium* value.]

prize[4] (prīz) **prized, priz·ing.** *also,* **prise.** *v.t.* to raise or force with a lever; pry. —*n.* **1.** instrument used for prying; lever. **2.** leverage. [From PRIZE[2].]

prize·fight (prīz′fīt′) *n.* boxing match between professional boxers. —**prize′fight′er,** *n.*

prize ring, rope-enclosed area, usually on a raised platform, in which boxers fight.

pro[1] (prō) *adv.* in favor of; for. —*n. pl.,* **pros.** reason, argument, or person in favor of something: *The chairman listed all the pros and cons of the proposal.* [Latin *prō* in favor of, for.]

pro[2] (prō) *pl.,* **pros.** *Informal.* *n.* professional; expert. —*adj.* professional. [Short for PROFESSIONAL.]

pro-[1] *prefix* **1.** in favor of; supporting; in behalf of: *proslavery.* **2.** forward; forth; out: *progress, project.* **3.** in place of; acting as; substituting for: *pronoun.* [Latin *prō* in favor of, for, before, instead of.]

pro-[2] *prefix* before in time or place: *prognosis.* [Greek *pro.*]

pro·a (prō′ə) *n.* swift Malay boat having a triangular sail and a single outrigger. [Malay *prāū.*]

prob. 1. problem. **2.** probable; probably.

prob·a·bil·i·ty (prob′ə bil′ə tē) *pl.,* **-ties.** *n.* **1.** quality or state of being probable; likelihood: *A willingness to negotiate increased the probability of an early settlement.* **2.** something probable or likely. **3.** *Mathematics.* ratio of the number of chances favoring the occurrence of an event to the total number of possible occurrences. **4. in all probability.** most probably; very likely.

prob·a·ble (prob′ə bəl) *adj.* **1.** likely to occur or to be true but not certain; that can reasonably be expected or believed: *The experts all agreed on the probable outcome of the boxing match.* **2.** rendering something likely but not certain. [Latin *probābilis* provable, likely, from *probāre* to try, test, approve, demonstrate.]

prob·a·bly (prob′ə blē) *adv.* most likely; in all likelihood.

pro·bate (prō′bāt) *n.* act or process of legally proving a will. —*adj.* of or relating to a probate court or to probate. —*v.t.,* **-bat·ed, -bat·ing.** to establish the authenticity or validity of (a will). [Latin *probātum* thing proved or approved, from *probāre* to test, demonstrate, approve.]

probate court, court having jurisdiction over the probate of wills and over the administration of the property of deceased persons.

pro·ba·tion (prō bā′shən) *n.* **1.** testing or trial of the ability, qualifications, or suitability of a person, as a new employee, usually for a specified period of time. **2.** *Law.* action or practice of allowing a person convicted of a minor or first offense to go free under close supervision and on the condition that his behavior be exemplary. **3.** period of being on probation or the status of one on probation. [Latin *probātiō* a proving, approval.] —**pro·ba′tion·al, pro·ba′tion·ar′y,** *adj.*

pro·ba·tion·er (prō bā′shə nər) *n.* one who is on probation.

probation officer, officer appointed to supervise a probationer.

pro·ba·tive (prō′bə tiv) *adj.* **1.** affording proof or evidence. **2.** serving or designed to test. Also, **pro′ba·to′ry.**

probe (prōb) *n.* **1.** thorough investigation or examination: *The court case led to a Senate probe into prison conditions.* **2.** slender surgical instrument for exploring a body cavity, wound, or similar opening. **3.** device, mechanism, or object used for investigation or exploration, esp. a space probe. —*v.t.,* **probed, prob·ing. 1.** to investigate, examine, or explore thoroughly: *The psychiatrist probed the patient's subconscious in discussing the dream.* **2.** to examine or explore with a surgical probe. —*v.i.* to conduct a thorough investigation or examination: *Scientists probed into the nature of the phenomenon.* [Medieval Latin *proba* ex-

at; āpe; cär; end; mē; it; īce; hot; ōld; fôrk; wood; fōōl; oil; out; up; ūse; turn; sing; thin; *th*is; zh in treasure; ə in ago, taken, pencil, lemon, circus

797

Guide words at the top of each page show the first and last entries on the page. These guide words help you locate an entry.

Illustrations help you understand some definitions.

A pronunciation key appears at the bottom of each page or each pair of facing pages. The pronunciation key gives examples of each pronunciation symbol by using familiar words such as **a**t, **ā**pe, and c**ä**r.

TEACH

Guided Practice

L2 Using the Pronunciation Key

Review the pronunciation key at the bottom of a student dictionary page. Write the phonetic pronunciations for several words on the board, and ask students to identify the words. Then ask students to take turns looking up words and writing only the phonetic spellings on the board. Ask other students to identify the words from those spellings.

L3 Comparing Dictionaries

Emphasize to students that dictionaries differ in ways other than just the numbers of word entries they provide. Even very similar dictionaries—such as various college dictionaries—differ in the order, type, and completeness of information. After students have compared the entries for two or three words in several dictionaries, ask them which dictionary provides the most complete definitions. Which provides word histories that are easy to understand? Which would they prefer to use? Why?

Connections Across the Curriculum

History

The first dictionaries translated words from one language into another. Early English dictionaries translated French and Latin into English. In the seventeenth century, the first completely English dictionaries appeared, but these provided definitions only for difficult words. Authors then wrote more complete dictionaries for scholars only. In 1721, for example, a 60,000-word dictionary was published that assumed readers knew the meaning of common words. The word *horse,* for example, was defined as "a beast well known."

PRACTICE AND ASSESS

Answers: Exercise 5

1. Guide words will depend on the dictionary used.
2. plane, planetarium, plaid
3. grain
4. Examples:
   a. tremble, quake, quiver, vibrate, shiver, shudder, wobble
   b. affluent, wealthy, opulent, well-to-do

Independent Practice

Skills Practice

Vocabulary and Spelling Practice, pp. 23–24
Thinking and Study Skills, pp. 23–29

CLOSE

Have students discuss how dictionaries and thesauruses can help writers improve their writing. Encourage students to share their past experiences in using dictionaries or thesauruses.

The Thesaurus

A thesaurus is a dictionary of synonyms, or words with similar meanings. A thesaurus is a helpful tool when you're revising your writing. You can use it to find a more exact or more colorful word to replace a dull word.

In a dictionary-style thesaurus, entries are arranged alphabetically, as in a dictionary. Several synonyms may be listed for a single definition. A cross-reference to another entry or entries may follow the definition.

Entry word — **lively** *adjective* — Part of speech
1. Very brisk, alert, and high-spirited: *a lively personality* — Definition and example of word in use
Synonyms — **Syns:** animate, animated, bouncy, peppy
Usage label — (*Informal*), pert, spirited, vivacious.—*Idioms* bright-eyed and bushy-tailed, full of life.
2. ENERGETIC.
3. VIGOROUS.

In this thesaurus cross-references to other entries are shown in capital letters. You will find additional synonyms under each entry.

Exercise 5

Use a dictionary or a thesaurus to complete each item.

1. What guide words are on the dictionary page on which *gimmick* appears?
2. Which of the following words would you find on a page with the guide words *plagiarism* and *planetoid*?

plane	plantation	placid
plank	planetarium	plaid

3. Does the word *skein* rhyme with *green, shine,* or *grain?*
4. List three synonyms for the following:
   a. the verb *shake*
   b. the adjective *rich*

Enrichment and Extension

Using Vivid and Precise Words

Write the following on the board:

It's a bad night, and a cold rain is falling. Father watches the bumpy dirt road. We worry that the old car will become stuck. It's extremely muddy. Finally, we arrive at a little cabin. Inside, a nice fire burns in the fireplace.

Have students use thesauruses to replace the underlined words with more vivid and precise words. Discuss how the choice of synonyms affects the paragraph's meaning.

21.6 Understanding a Dictionary Entry

Which is the right spelling: *life style*, *life-style*, or *lifestyle*? How do you divide *environment* into syllables? Is *domestic* a noun, an adjective, or both? These are just a few of the types of questions you can answer with a dictionary.

The Entry Word and Definition

The entry word begins the entry. If the word has more than one syllable, the entry word shows how it is divided, or hyphenated. Notice how *ba•sin* is divided by the dot. A dictionary will show you that some entries are two words, as in *high school*. Other words are hyphenated, as in *runner-up*. Still others are spelled as one word: *lifeboat*.

Most of the time, you probably look up a word to find a definition. Words usually have more than one definition. Some words, in fact, have many definitions. Your dictionary probably includes more than a dozen different meanings for the word *set*. School dictionaries generally list the most common definition first, as in the entry below.

Entry word

ba•sin (bā´sin) *n.* **1.a.** container that is usually round with a wide, flat bottom and sloping sides; shallow bowl, esp. for holding liquids. **b.** bathroom sink. **2.** contents or capacity of a basin. **3.** the entire region drained by a river and its tributaries. **4.** depression in the earth usually holding water, like a pond, but sometimes dry.

Numbered definitions

Other Information in Entries

How do you say *vermicelli*? Where does the word *caribou* come from? Are there any good synonyms for *slow*? Dictionary entries can also answer questions like these. Look at the entry on the next page to locate some of the important parts of a dictionary entry.

Setting the Purpose

Lesson 21.6 teaches students to use the different parts of a dictionary entry.

FOCUS

Lesson Overview

Objective: To become familiar with dictionary entries
Skills: reading a dictionary entry; using word origins
Critical Thinking: analyzing dictionary entries; identifying types of information
Speaking and Listening: discussing; pronouncing difficult words

Bellringer

When students enter the classroom, have this assignment on the board: *List five words that you are not sure how to pronounce.*

TEACH

Guided Practice

L2 Exploring Dictionary Entry Words

As students look at the sample dictionary entry, ask them to describe the types of information given—entry word divided into syllables, pronunciation, part(s) of speech, definitions, and so on. Encourage students to discuss when each of these kinds of information might be useful. Have students look up the words that they would like to know how to pronounce and share their lists with the class.

eacher's Classroom Resources

For Lesson 21.6, the following resources can be used for planning, instruction, practice, assessment, reinforcement, or evaluation.

Teaching Tools
Lesson Plans

Blackline Masters
Vocabulary and Spelling Practice, pp. 23–24
Thinking and Study Skills, pp. 23–29

Unit Assessment

Tests with Answer Key
Unit 21 Mastery Test, pp. 83–84

Test Generator
Unit 21 Mastery Test

You may wish to administer the Unit 21 Mastery Test at this point.

PRACTICE AND ASSESS

Answers: Exercise 6

1. quad • ran • gle
2. Spanish (or Latin by way of Spanish)
3. Examples: *voyage, trip, tour, jaunt, expedition*
4. noun
5. a small bird; one stroke under par in golf

Independent Practice

Skills Practice

Vocabulary and Spelling Practice, pp. 23–24
Thinking and Study Skills, pp. 23–29

CLOSE

Point out to students that different dictionaries may give information in somewhat different ways and that the pronunciation keys may differ. Tell students to look up two or three of the same words in different dictionaries to see how the entries compare. Have students discuss the differences they find.

Pronunciation The pronunciation follows the entry word. Refer to the key at the bottom of the page if you are not sure what the pronunciation symbols mean. Notice that the second syllable of *fragile* can be pronounced two ways.

Part of Speech An abbreviation shows how the word is used as a part of speech. In this entry, *adj.* stands for *adjective* and *adv.* for *adverb.*

Word Origin Many entries include information about the word's origin, or a history of the word.

frag•ile (frag´əl,-īl) *adj.* easily broken, damaged, or destroyed; delicate. [Latin *fragilis.* Doublet of FRAIL.] **—frag•ile•ly,** *adv.* **—fra•gil•i•ty** (fra jil ´ə tē), n.
Syn. **Fragile, frail, brittle** mean tending to break easily. Fragile suggests that the substance of which a thing is made may result in its breaking if it is not handled with care: *The movers carefully packed the fragile china into cartons.* **Frail** implies that a thing is of weak construction and that it will tend to collapse under strain: *The frail wooden bridge cracked and swayed in the heavy winds.* **Brittle** suggests hardness of such rigidity that the thing may easily break if pressure is applied unwisely: *The bones of an aged person are often quite brittle.*

Synonyms Some entries list synonyms, words with similar meanings. Explanations and examples are often included to help you understand the different meanings. For more information on synonyms, turn to page 515.

Exercise 6

Use a school dictionary to answer the following questions.

1. How is the word *quadrangle* divided into syllables?
2. What is the origin of the word *patio*?
3. What synonyms are given for *journey*?
4. Is *bramble* a noun or a verb?
5. What are two different meanings of *birdie*?

Enabling Strategies

LEP Exploring Dictionaries

Students not proficient in English may have difficulty interpreting the symbols and abbreviations used in dictionary entries. Explain the table of symbols and the list of abbreviations in the front matter of the dictionary. Give particular attention to pronunciation symbols. Use common words to demonstrate each sound aloud, and ask students to repeat the words after you. Then read through several dictionary entries that demonstrate the various symbols and abbreviations.

UNIT
22

Vocabulary and Spelling

22.1 Borrowed Words

The English language contains more than 600,000 words, more than any other language. Many of these words have been borrowed from other languages.

Many of the foods you eat originally came from other lands. The names of those foods came from other languages. Think about pizza (Italian), hamburger (German), chili (Spanish), taco (Mexican Spanish), and gumbo (West African). You can probably add more examples of your own. Every time you ask for these foods, you use a borrowed word.

English has also taken in words for clothing, sports, cars, and hundreds of other items in daily use. Parts of words have also been borrowed. Our word *television*, for example, comes from the Greek *tele*, "far off," and the Latin *visio*, "to see."

Often a word passes from one language to another before becoming a part of English. Our word *theater*, for example, began in ancient Greece, where the idea of theater itself began. The word was borrowed by the Romans, who spoke Latin. French later borrowed it from Latin. From French it came into English.

Setting the Purpose

Lesson 22.1 teaches students how new vocabulary is added to English by borrowing words from other languages.

FOCUS

Lesson Overview

Objective: To familiarize students with borrowed words and the development of the English language

Skills: using a dictionary; reading a map

Critical Thinking: classifying; analyzing

Speaking and Listening: oral reporting

Bellringer

When students enter the classroom, have this assignment on the board: *List five foods with names that come from languages other than English.*

Motivating Activity

Point out to students that they really know and recognize many words from other languages, whether they regularly speak another language or not. Have students share the words they listed in the Bellringer activity. Encourage students to speculate on the origins of each word.

Teacher's Classroom Resources

For Lesson 22.1, the following resources can be used for planning, instruction, practice, assessment, reinforcement, or evaluation.

Teaching Tools
Lesson Plans

Blackline Masters
Vocabulary and Spelling Practice, pp. 13–16, 21–34, 41–52

Unit Assessment

Tests with Answer Key
Unit 22 Pretest, pp. 85–86

Test Generator
Unit 22 Pretest

You may wish to administer the Unit 22 Pretest at this point.

TEACH

Guided Practice

L2 Finding Word Origins

Discuss how technology and contact with speakers of other languages have added new vocabulary to English. Have students name words of foreign origin used in sports, films, and games, as well as in the names of dances, music, and imported commercial products. Encourage students to use dictionaries to find word origins.

PRACTICE AND ASSESS

Evaluation Guidelines: Exercise 1

Answers will vary. Students should list a reasonable number of loan words from each language chosen. While French, German, Dutch, Spanish, Italian, Latin, and Greek may furnish examples more easily. Encourage students to use research to locate examples from other languages as well.

Independent Practice

Skills Practice

Vocabulary and Spelling Practice, pp. 13–16, 21–34, 41–52

CLOSE

English has borrowed the largest number of loan words from the French language. Ask students to locate France and England on a more detailed map than that provided in the text. How might the proximity of these countries have contributed to French influence on the English language? Students should identify other nations on the map that have similarly influenced the development of the English language.

The map below shows just a few examples of borrowed words. You have probably used many of them without knowing that they came from another language.

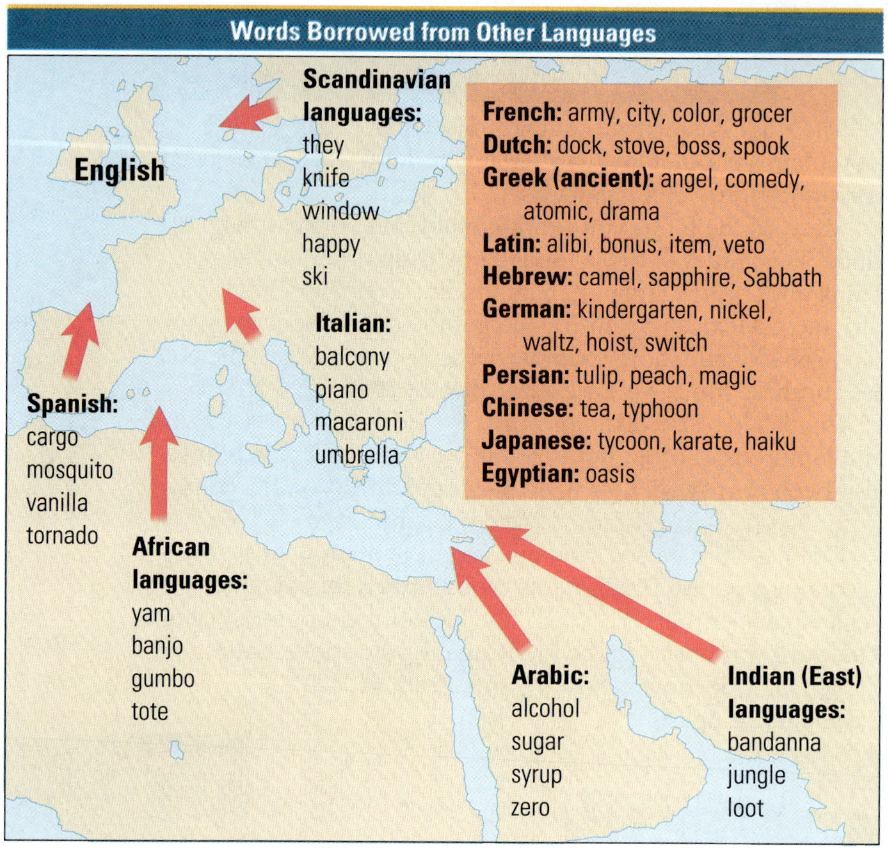

Exercise 1

Working in a group, choose one foreign language. See how many words you can find that came into English from that language. Use what group members already know, interviews, and library resources. Present your list to the class.

Enabling Strategies

LEP Recognizing Borrowed Words

Highlight the advantage of bilingualism by asking students whose first language is not English to supply additional English words borrowed from their first language. Students might create another map on which they write words their first languages have contributed to English.

22.2 Clues to Word Meanings

The surest way to learn the meaning of a new word is to use a dictionary. However, you won't always have a dictionary handy. Try to figure out the meaning of the word yourself. Look for clues in the words and sentences around it. These surrounding words and sentences are called the context.

Specific Context Clues

Definition The meaning, or definition, of an unfamiliar word is often given in the sentence that includes the word. Definitions are usually introduced with clue words.

> The plant has begun to germinate, which means that it is starting to sprout.

The clue words *which means* tell you that the word *germinate* means "to start to sprout."

Example Familiar examples can help a reader understand an unfamiliar word. See how the writer uses examples in the sentence below.

> Felines, such as lions, domestic cats, and leopards, are natural hunters.

The words *such as* introduce examples of felines. From the examples you can guess that *felines* refers to the cat family.

Interpreting Clue Words

Type of Context Clue	Clue Words	Example
Definition: The meaning of the unfamiliar word is given in the sentence.	that is in other words which means	Jerry *inscribed* his name; that is, he wrote his name on the card.
Example: The meaning of the unfamiliar word is explained by familiar examples.	like such as for example including	Some people are afraid of *arachnids*, such as spiders and ticks.

Setting the Purpose

Lesson 22.2 teaches students how to use context clues, such as definition, example, and general context, to figure out word meanings.

FOCUS

Lesson Overview

Objective: To become familiar with clues to word meanings
Skills: using context clues
Critical Thinking: synthesizing
Speaking and Listening: discussing

Bellringer

When students enter the classroom, have this assignment on the board: *Name three different ways you can find out the meaning of a word you don't know.*

Motivating Activity

Let students discuss their strategies from the Bellringer activity. Then have students look in a non-fiction book or textbook from another subject and point out words they don't know. Have students discuss ways of determining the meanings of these words.

Teacher's Classroom Resources

For Lesson 22.2, the following resources can be used for planning, instruction, practice, or reinforcement.

Teaching Tools
Lesson Plans

Blackline Masters
Vocabulary and Spelling Practice, pp. 13–16, 21–34, 41–52

TEACH

Guided Practice

L2 Identifying Context Clues

On the chalkboard, write this sentence: *Grant was so hungry that he grabbed the roll and sooled it, hardly chewing before he swallowed.* Ask students to guess the meaning of the nonsense word *sooled* and identify clues that tell its meaning. (The context words *roll, chewing, swallowed* indicate that *sooled* could mean ate, gulped, or wolfed down.) Ask students which type of context clue they used to figure out the meaning. (general context clues)

PRACTICE AND ASSESS

Answers: Exercise 2

1. a pattern; definition
2. dangerous (or poisonous) snakes; example
3. insect eaters; example (general context is also acceptable)
4. peaceful; general context
5. the art of fine handwriting; definition

Independent Practice

Skills Practice

Vocabulary and Spelling Practice, pp. 13–16, 21–34, 41–52

CLOSE

Begin a discussion of strategies in addition to context clues that students can use to determine the meanings of unfamiliar words. (Use a dictionary or a^k someone what the unknown word means.) Ask students why readers might choose context clues as a strategy to determine word meanings.

General Context

Sometimes there are no special clue words to help you understand a new word. However, you can still use the general context. That is, you can use the details in the words or sentences around the new word. Look at the following sentences:

> Andrea carefully mixed several pigments with an oil base to produce just the right colors. Then she began her painting.

The sentences tell you that pigments have something to do with painting. They also tell you that pigments can be mixed to produce various colors. From those clues you can figure out the meaning. Pigments are a kind of dye or color used to make paint.

Exercise 2

Use context clues to figure out the meaning of the underlined word in each sentence. Write the meaning of the word. Then tell what type of context clue you used to figure out each meaning. The types of context clues will be definition, example, or general context.

1. Brian used a template, or pattern, for cutting the wood he used to build a birdhouse.
2. Vipers, such as rattlesnakes, cobras, and copperheads, can be very dangerous, even deadly.
3. Birds, mammals, and even plants can be insectivores. For example, flycatchers and anteaters are insectivores. So is the Venus's flytrap, a plant that traps flies and then digests them.
4. The scene by the lake was tranquil. There was only a slight breeze, and the surface of the lake was as smooth as glass. Even the birds and insects seemed hushed.
5. Margot is studying calligraphy, which is the art of fine handwriting.

Connections Across the Curriculum

Science

Point out that science writing often uses words that may not be familiar to readers. Have students quickly look through articles or books about science. Encourage them to identify any unfamiliar words. Ask volunteers to use context clues to figure out the meanings of the words. Did students use definition, example, or general context clues?

Wordworks

Oui! French Is Spoken Here

Which do you think would smell better, a perfume called Eau de Cochon or one called Happiness? If you guessed Eau de Cochon, you're not alone. Many Americans associate French names with something fancier or more fashionable. Actually, Eau de Cochon means "aroma of pig."

Although the names of French perfumes have not become a permanent part of our language, English has borrowed many other words from French. This admiration of the French language began more than 900 years ago.

In A.D. 1066 French-speaking Normans conquered England. The people living there spoke a language we now call Old English. The Normans became England's rulers. They controlled the government, the land, the laws, the military, and most of the wealth. Everybody who was anybody spoke French! And people who wanted to be somebody soon began using French words. While English peasants ate the meat of *cows* and *pigs* (words from Old English), ladies and gentlemen of the court dined on *beef* and *pork* (words from French). The Normans were also interested in art, music, and poetry.

CHALLENGE

Based on your reading of this page, under what circumstances do you think one language might borrow words from another?

Parlez-vous français?

Write the word or phrase that completes each sentence.

document *matinee* *petite*
salon *R.S.V.P.*

1. I had my hair cut at the beauty _____.
2. The _____ begins at 2:00 P.M.
3. Angela is very _____.
4. _______ by next Tuesday.
5. The _____ is on my desk.

FOCUS

Lesson Overview

Objective: To become familiar with words borrowed from the French
Skills: using borrowed words
Critical Thinking: defining; clarifying
Speaking and Listening: discussing

TEACH

Discussion

Have students read Wordworks, p. 509, and discuss the following questions: *What language was spoken in England before the Norman Conquest? How did Old English change?*

L2 Finding Word Origins

Supply students with a dictionary that includes word origins. Have students find out as much as they can about the history of the borrowed words on this page. They can find out which language or languages the word came from, how the word was spelled, and the original meaning of the word.

PRACTICE AND ASSESS

Answers: Challenge

The examples given on this page indicate that many speakers of English think of French as a superior, or at least more beautiful, language.

Answers: Parlez-vous français?

1. salon
2. matinée
3. petite
4. R.S.V.P.
5. document

CLOSE

Begin a discussion about how languages change. Ask students why a language might need a new word. Point out that *cyborg* and *rap* are recent additions to English. Ask students to think of some other words that are new to English. The fields of music, science, and computers frequently require new words.

Setting the Purpose

Lesson 22.3 teaches students about the parts of words and gives them practice adding prefixes and suffixes to root words.

FOCUS

Lesson Overview

Objective: To become familiar with word parts
Skills: using prefixes and suffixes; changing the spelling of words when adding suffixes
Critical Thinking: defining and clarifying
Speaking and Listening: discussing; creating riddles

Bellringer

When students enter the classroom, have this assignment on the board: *List five words that have a prefix or a suffix.*

Motivating Activity

Have students choose a paragraph in a book or article. Let them read the paragraph and then scan it for any words with prefixes or suffixes. Begin a list on the chalkboard of words the students find.

22.3 Using Word Parts

You often can figure out the meaning of an unfamiliar word by dividing it into parts. The main part of the word is called the root, and it carries the word's basic meaning. A root is often a simple word in itself. For example, *read* is a word. When a prefix or a suffix is added to it, *read* becomes a root.

Prefixes and suffixes can be attached to a root to change its meaning. A prefix is added to the beginning of a root. A suffix is added to the end. A word can have both a prefix and a suffix.

The **prefix** *non-* means "not."
The **root**
The **suffix** *-er* means "one who."

You know what *ski* means. Look at the meanings of the prefix *non-* and the suffix *-er.* You can easily see that a nonskier is "one who does not ski."

The prefix *non-* and the suffix *-er* can be attached to other roots as well. In each case they will produce the meaning "one who does not [do whatever the root word says]." For example, a *nondriver* is someone who does not drive. A *nonvoter* is a person who does not vote. Try to think of some other root words that would fit between *non-* and *-er.*

Words usually have only one prefix, but may have several suffixes. For example, you can start with *nation,* add *-al* to get *national,* and add *-ity* to get *nationality*. You can see how learning about prefixes and suffixes can help increase your vocabulary. Knowing the meanings of these word parts can also help you understand unfamiliar words.

Teacher's Classroom Resources

For Lesson 22.3, the following resources can be used for planning, instruction, practice, or reinforcement.

Teaching Tools
Lesson Plans

Blackline Masters
Vocabulary and Spelling Practice, pp. 13–16, 21–34, 41–52

Prefixes

The following chart shows some prefixes and their meanings. Notice that some prefixes have more than one meaning. Sometimes two or more prefixes have the same or a similar meaning.

Prefixes

Prefixes	Words	Meanings
in- means "not"	inactive incomplete indirect	not active not complete not direct
non- means "without" or "not"	nonfat nonstop nonreturnable	without fat without stopping not able to be returned
dis- means "opposite of" or "not"	disadvantage disagree disarm	an unfavorable condition to not agree to take away arms (weapons)
un- means "opposite of" or "to reverse"	unable unclean untie unset	not able not clean to loosen not yet firm or set
pre- means "before"	prejudge prepay preview	to judge in advance to pay in advance to view in advance
de- means "remove from" or "reduce"	dethrone defrost degrade	to remove from a throne to remove frost to reduce or make lower

Suffixes

A suffix added to a word can change the word's part of speech as well as its meaning. For example, adding the suffix *-er* to *read* (a verb) makes *reader* (a noun). Adding *-less* to *rain* (a noun) makes *rainless* (an adjective).

TEACH

Guided Practice

L2 Adding Prefixes

On the chalkboard, write the word *prefix*. Remind students that a prefix is a word part added to a root to form a new word. A prefix changes or adds to the meaning of the original word. Ask students how the word *prefix* tells them where the added part can be found. If necessary, point out that *pre-* means "before." A prefix comes before the root. Ask students to name other words that begin with *pre-*. Familiar words include *preview, prepare,* and *preschool.*

L1 Using Word Parts

Before students attempt to read the charts of prefixes and suffixes, help them manipulate word parts. Make flash cards, writing the prefix *un-* on one card and the suffix *-ness* on another. On additional cards write the root words *kind, fit,* and *sound.* Use cards to demonstrate pairing a prefix with a root word to form a new word. Repeat the process with the suffix cards and the suffix chart.

Enabling Strategies

LEP Using Prefixes

Students learning English may have difficulty with prefixes that have similar meanings, such as *in-, non-, dis-, un-,* and *de-*. Suggest that they be alert to the use of these and other prefixes as they read and listen to others speak. You might read the following sentences and ask volunteers to repeat the words that begin with prefixes.

- Lupe was unsure of how to get to the library.
- The magician made the rabbit disappear.
- Sam feels insecure in his new job.

TEACH

Guided Practice

L2 Adding Suffixes

To illustrate how adding a suffix can change a word to a different part of speech, have students work within sentence frames. Write on the chalkboard: *The girl will run fifty yards in the race tomorrow.* Ask a volunteer to add the suffix *-er* to *run.* Can the new word be used in the same place in the sentence? (no) Which word in the sentence can *runner* replace? (girl)

Cross-reference: Vocabulary and Spelling

For more information on spelling rules that apply when adding prefixes or suffixes to words, refer students to Lesson 22.6, pp. 520–523.

Independent Practice

Skills Practice

Vocabulary and Spelling Practice, pp. 13–16, 21–34, 41–52

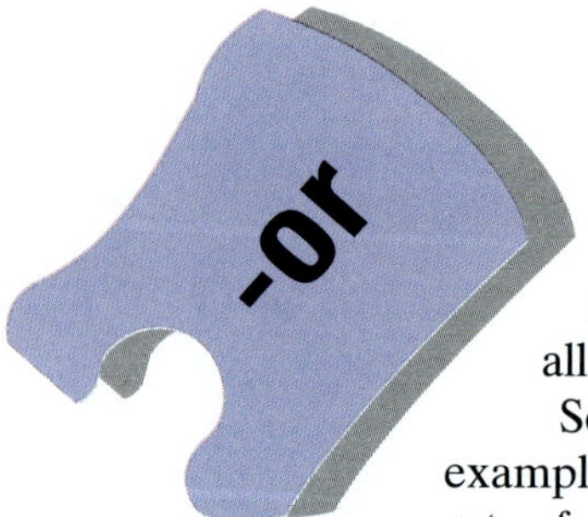

The following chart shows some common suffixes and their meanings. As the examples show, sometimes a suffix has more than one meaning. In addition, two or more suffixes may have the same meaning. For example, the suffixes *-er, -or,* and *-ist* can all mean "one who."

See if you can identify the part of speech of each example word with and without its suffix. You can review parts of speech in Part 2 of this book.

Suffixes

Suffixes	Words	Meanings
-er means "one who," "that which," or "more"	runner baker toaster weaker	one who runs one who bakes that which makes toast more weak
-or means "one who"	actor conductor demonstrator	one who acts one who conducts one who demonstrates
-ist means "one who"	typist violinist scientist	one who types one who plays the violin one who works at science
-less means "without"	hairless spineless merciless	without hair without a spine without mercy
-able means "can be" or "having the quality of"	believable washable valuable	can be believed can be washed having value
-ible means "can be" or "having the quality of"	deductible digestible sensible	can be deducted can be digested having sense
-ness means "quality of" or "state of being"	darkness mildness kindness	being dark quality of being mild state of being kind

Enrichment and Extension

Adding Prefixes and Suffixes

Tell students that with some words, you can add both a prefix and a suffix. Write the following words on the board: *fix, comfort, join, agree, pay, correct*. Challenge students to come up with a prefix and a suffix for each. (unfixable, uncomfortable, nonjoiner, disagreeable, prepayable, incorrectness)

Adding a suffix sometimes changes the spelling of a word. As the chart shows, when adding *-er* to *run,* you also must add another *n* to make *runner.* To learn more about spelling changes when adding suffixes, see pages 520–522.

Exercise 3

Divide the following words. Write their parts in three columns headed *prefix, root word,* and *suffix.* (Note that not all the words have both a prefix and a suffix.) In a fourth column, write another word that uses the same prefix or the same suffix (or both if you can). Check your words in a dictionary to make sure the prefixes and suffixes are correctly used.

1. preteen
2. nondriver
3. unforgivable
4. nonprofit
5. deforest
6. collectible
7. disapprove
8. incompleteness

Exercise 4

To name each person described below, use a word that ends in the suffix *-er, -or,* or *-ist.* You should be able to list more than one word for some of the descriptions. Remember that sometimes the addition of a suffix changes the spelling of the root word. Check your answers in a dictionary to be sure you have the correct spelling and suffix.

1. A person who serves food in a restaurant
2. A person who plays a keyboard instrument
3. A person who instructs others
4. A person who appears in plays
5. A person who rides a bicycle

PRACTICE AND ASSESS

Answers: Exercise 3

(Students' column-four words will vary.)

1. pre-teen — preview
2. non-drive -er — nonjoiner
3. un-forgive -able — unbelievable
4. non-profit — nonskid
5. de-forest — defrost
6. collect-ible — digestible
7. dis-approve — discomfort
8. in-complete -ness — indecisiveness

Answers: Exercise 4

1. waiter, server
2. pianist, piano player
3. teacher, instructor, professor
4. actor, player
5. biker, cyclist, rider

CLOSE

Have students practice writing words with prefixes in sentences. Each student can choose a word with a prefix, a suffix, or both and use it in a sentence. A partner can say the word aloud and identify the root word and the prefix or suffix.

Cooperative Learning

Creating Riddles

Have students use words from the prefixes and suffixes lists on pages 511 and 512 to create riddles for each other like the following:

- What is a story that can be believed? (a believable story)
- Who is a person who bakes cakes? (a cake baker)

Tell students to look at the meaning of the prefix or suffix and use it as a clue in their riddles. For example, *-er* means "one who," so the clue might say "a person who."

Lesson Overview

Objective: To become familiar with word origins
Skills: finding word origins
Critical Thinking: synthesizing
Speaking and Listening: discussing; listening to word sounds

TEACH

Discussion

Have students read Wordworks, p. 514, and discuss the following questions: *How might someone create the meaning of an unfamiliar word? Why might speakers change the pronunciation of a borrowed word?*

L2 Finding Meanings

Write the following etymology for *woodchuck* on the board: folk etymology from the Cree word *otchek.* Ask students what this etymology tells them about *woodchuck.* (It is an invented word that originated from the sounds of the Cree word *otchek.*)

PRACTICE AND ASSESS

Answers: Challenge

Shamefaced comes from Old English *sceamfaest,* which combines *sceamu* (shame) + *faest* (firm). *Shamefaced* suggests a face held firm by shame.

Answers: In Other Words

1. muskrat
2. belfry
3. bridegroom

CLOSE

Have students think of and make a list of words with unusual sounds and look up their word origins.

Wordworks

Sounds Like . . .

"How much wood would a woodchuck chuck if a woodchuck could chuck wood?" You probably remember this tongue twister from your childhood. But if a woodchuck can't chuck wood, how did it get the name *woodchuck*?

When people hear an unfamiliar word, they often try to understand the word by relating it to words they know. Then they create a meaning for the word based on the familiar words. This process of inventing an origin for a word is called folk etymology (et´ə mol' ə jē).

As to *woodchuck*—English speakers new to North America heard the Cree word for the animal, which is *otchek.* They changed its unfamiliar sounds to the familiar sounds of *wood* and *chuck.* People would later guess that a woodchuck had something to do with wood simply because of its name.

Sometimes people change the pronunciation of a word because the word not only sounds like one they know but also seems to be related. For example, you may think that *female* is related to *male.* Not so. During the Middle Ages, the French word for "young woman," *femelle,* was borrowed into English. Because *femelle* sounded like *male* and seemed related to *male, femelle* eventually was pronounced and spelled *female.*

CHALLENGE

Look up the origin of the word shamefaced *in a college dictionary. How did this word get its spelling and pronunciation?*

In Other Words

Figure out the English words related to the following word origins.

1. from the Natick word *musquash* (a North American rodent)
2. from the Middle English word *berfrey* (tower)
3. from the Old English words *brȳd* (bride) and *guma* (man)

Cooperative Learning

Misunderstood Words

Children learning the Pledge of Allegiance often substitute a known word for an unfamiliar one. One small child began:, "Congratulations to the flag . . . ," and another ended with the words: "liver tea and justice for all." In a Think-Pair-Share activity, ask students to recall and list some words they have misunderstood and pronounced incorrectly. They might then work with a partner to share their lists and brainstorm additional words. Then have pairs of students share their recollections with the class.

22.4 Synonyms and Antonyms

Suppose that you were describing a rainy day. Imagine how dull your writing would be if you could use only the word *rain.* Fortunately, the English language has many words with meanings similar to *rain.* In describing the rain, you might use the word *downpour.* You could also choose *flood, cloudburst, shower, sprinkle,* or *drizzle.*

English also contains many pairs of words that have opposite meanings. On a rainy day the streets are *wet.* On a sunny day they're *dry.*

Synonyms

Words that have similar meanings are called synonyms. Knowing synonyms can improve your vocabulary and your writing. It can also help you understand the meanings of unfamiliar words. For example, you may not know what the word *obstinate* means. However, suppose that you knew that its synonyms included *hardheaded* and *stubborn.* Then you'd probably have a pretty good idea of what *obstinate* means.

Synonyms can help you be more precise in your speaking and writing. Synonyms have similar meanings, but they hardly ever have exactly the same meaning. The words *cloudburst* and *downpour* both refer to heavy rain. *Drizzle* and *shower* bring to mind a different, more gentle rain. There's a big difference between a *sprinkle* and a *deluge,* even though both words can mean "rain." When you write about rain—or about anything at all—synonyms help you say exactly what you mean.

You'll find synonyms listed in some dictionary entries. Another place to look for them is in a dictionary of synonyms. Such a dictionary is called a thesaurus. See page 502 for more information on how to use a thesaurus.

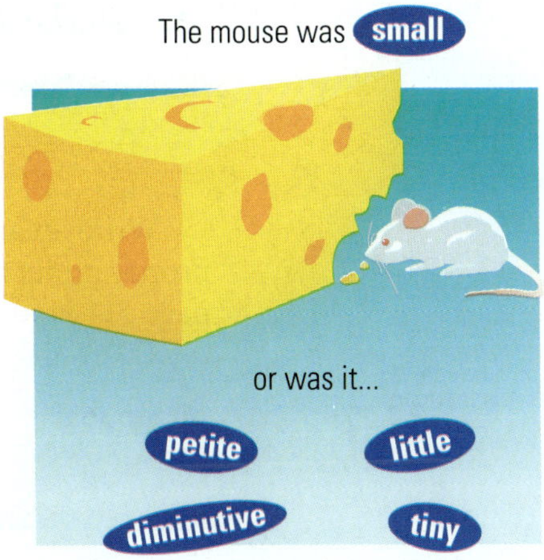

Setting the Purpose

Lesson 22.4 teaches students how synonyms help writers say exactly what they mean and how antonyms can help readers build their vocabularies

FOCUS

Lesson Overview

Objective: To become familiar with synonyms and antonyms

Skills: recognizing and using synonyms and antonyms

Critical Thinking: comparing and contrasting

Speaking and Listening: informal speaking

Bellringer

When students enter the classroom, have this assignment on the board: *Make two lists. In the first list, put words that mean the same as* cold. *In the second list, put words that mean the opposite of* cold.

TEACH

Guided Practice

L2 Teaching Tip

Call on a volunteer to make up a sentence using the word *walk.* Invite other students to repeat the sentence, substituting a synonym for *walk.* If students need prompting, suggest *stroll, amble, stride, march, plod, pace,* or *tramp.* As each sentence is offered, ask a student to act it out and explain how the word differs from other synonyms for *walk.* Ask students how a careful selection of synonyms can help a writer make his or her writing vivid.

Teacher's Classroom Resources

For Lesson 22.4, the following resources can be used for planning, instruction, practice, or reinforcement.

Teaching Tools
Lesson Plans

Blackline Masters
Vocabulary and Spelling Practice, pp. 13–16, 21–34, 41–52

PRACTICE AND ASSESS

Evaluation Guidelines: Exercise 5

Answers will vary. Sentences should demonstrate an understanding of the word's meaning. Examples:

1. Her kindness to the poor showed her to be a benevolent person.
2. He claimed to have seen an apparition of the dead man.
3. His malevolent grin frightened everyone who saw him.
4. The vigorous workout left us fatigued.
5. We must nourish the hungry children.

Answers: Exercise 6

1. disappear
2. nonsense
3. untrue
4. unequal
5. indirect

Independent Practice

Skills Practice

Vocabulary and Spelling Practice, pp. 13–16, 21–34, 41–52

CLOSE

Ask students to write a paragraph explaining what synonyms and antonyms are and tell how synonyms help a writer.

Antonyms

Antonyms are words that have opposite or nearly opposite meanings. Knowing antonyms can help you build your vocabulary and help you understand the meanings of other words. Perhaps you don't know the meaning of the word *taciturn.* Knowing that an antonym of the word is *talkative,* you could guess that *taciturn* describes someone who is silent, or untalkative.

You probably know such common antonyms as *hot—cold, love—hate,* and *short—tall.* One common way to form antonyms is to add a prefix meaning "not" or "the opposite of" to a word. (Page 511 has a list of some prefixes with those meanings.) For example, you can make an antonym of *believable* by adding the prefix *un-*.

Exercise 5

In each pair of synonyms below, the first word may be unknown to you. The second word, however, is probably familiar. Use your knowledge of each familiar word to figure out the meaning of its synonym. Then write a sentence using the first word in each pair.

1. benevolent, good
2. apparition, ghost
3. malevolent, evil
4. fatigued, tired
5. nourish, feed

Exercise 6

Write an antonym for each word below by adding the proper prefix to it. Review the list of such prefixes on page 511 if you need to. Check each word in a dictionary to make sure you used the correct prefix.

1. appear
2. sense
3. true
4. equal
5. direct

Technology Tip

Using the Thesaurus

Many word-processing programs include a thesaurus. Ask students who have used such programs for their writing to compare their program thesaurus to a thesaurus in book form. Is one of the two faster? Easier to use? Do both have a sufficient number of synonyms? Does either provide antonyms?

Wordworks

Word Twins

Identical twins look exactly alike. Some English words called homographs also look identical. They have identical spellings and usually, but not always, identical pronunciations. Unlike identical twins, however, homographs have different parents, that is, different origins.

One example is the word *meal.* *Meal* (ground grain) and *meal* (eating time) are homographs. Since both refer to food, you might think they have the same origin. Actually, the two words are not related.

The meal used in bread comes from the Old English word *melu,* meaning "to grind." The meal that refers to an eating time, such as breakfast or lunch, comes from the Old English word *mael,* meaning "appointed time."

During the Middle Ages (from about A.D. 476 to about A.D. 1450), the word *melu* developed into *meele. Meele* was used as a noun referring to ground grain. By the eighteenth century the spelling had changed to *meal.*

By the Middle Ages, *mael* had developed into *meel,* and its meaning became "appointed time for eating." By the 1700s this word, too, began to be spelled as *meal* and referred to the regular eating times in a day.

CHALLENGE

Using a college dictionary, trace the origins of the homographs lead *(to show the way) and* lead *(a chemical element). List each form, from the most recent to the earliest, and its meaning.*

Reading Double

Write the homographs for each pair of definitions below and for the pair of illustrations at right.

1. inner surface of the hand; a tropical tree
2. to shut; nearby
3. able to; a metal container
4. to move or slide out of place; a small piece of paper

Lesson Overview

Objective: To become familiar with homographs

Skills: recognizing homographs; using a dictionary

Critical Thinking: analyzing

Speaking and Listening: discussing

TEACH

Discussion

Have students read Wordworks, p. 517, and discuss the following questions: How might a word have a twin? How might words that are spelled alike have different origins?

L2 Homographs

Have students brainstorm homographs. List these on the chalkboard. Invite students to make up sentences or sentence pairs using both meanings of selected homographs. You may wish to suggest some common homographs such as wound, tire, wind, and bear.

PRACTICE AND ASSESS

Answers: Challenge

Lead, meaning "to show the way," comes from Middle English and Old English roots meaning "travel" or "go." *Lead* as a name for the chemical element entered English from Irish languages. The old word also referred to the metal.

Answers: Reading Double

1. palm
2. close
3. can
4. slip

CLOSE

Have students write pairs of definitions or draw pictures of homographs similar to those shown in "Reading Double." Students can exchange their definitions and guess the homograph.

Setting the Purpose

Lesson 22.5 teaches students that words that sound alike are called homonyms and sometimes, even though the words sound alike, they are spelled differently.

FOCUS

Lesson Overview

Objective: To become familiar with words that sound alike
Skills: using homonyms
Critical Thinking: defining and clarifying.
Speaking and Listening: telling riddles based on sound words.

Bellringer

When students enter the classroom, have this assignment on the board: *Name five words that have more than one meaning.*

Motivating Activity

Have students share the words they named in the Bellringer activity. Then have students use those words in context sentences that illustrate each meaning.

22.5 Words That Sound Alike

How are a pair and a pear alike? How about a rein and a rain and a reign? The answer, of course, is that these groups of words sound alike. You probably noticed that the words have different meanings and different spellings.

Understanding Homonyms

Words that sound alike but have different meanings are called homonyms. Some homonyms not only sound alike but are spelled alike as well. Such words usually don't cause too many problems. Whether you *ring* a bell or wear a *ring* on your finger, it's still spelled *ring*. You can *file* your nails or *file* some papers. You can even *file* for a job or *file* down the hall with your friends. The spelling of the word *file* remains the same even though its meaning changes.

knight

night

Homonyms that sound alike but are spelled differently can be tricky. These are the ones you need to be careful with. You don't want to write *new* instead of *knew* in a written report. Imagine writing *threw* on a spelling test when you meant to write *through*. The chart on this page has some more examples of such homonyms. Maybe you can think of other examples.

Homonyms
break to crack, split, or smash **brake** to stop a movement
piece a part of something **peace** the opposite of war
holey having holes **holy** sacred **wholly** completely

Using Homonyms

Have you ever been confused about whether to use *their* or *there* in a sentence? Does the difference between *your* and *you're* confuse you sometimes? Because homonyms sound alike, people occasionally don't remember which spelling to use. The chart on the following page shows some common homonyms.

Teacher's Classroom Resources

For Lesson 22.5, the following resources can be used for planning, instruction, practice, or reinforcement.

Teaching Tools
Lesson Plans

Blackline Masters
Vocabulary and Spelling Practice, pp. 13–16, 21–34, 41–52

Common Homonyms	
Words	**Meanings**
their there they're	belonging to them in that place contraction for *they are*
its it's	belonging to it contraction for *it is* or *it has*
to too two	in the direction of also the number
your you're	belonging to you contraction for *you are*
hear here	listen this place
principal principle	the head of a school; most important a rule, law, or truth
who's whose	contraction for *who is* or *who has* the possessive form of *who*

Exercise 7

Write the correct homonym to fit each sentence.

1. The children are concentrating on what (their, there, they're) doing.
2. Be sure to let me know when (your, you're) going to arrive.
3. (Who's, Whose) responsible for this mess?
4. Coffee is one of the (principle, principal) exports of Colombia.
5. I think (it's, its) going to rain today.
6. Mandy heard the noise; John said that he heard it, (to, too, two).

Speaking and Listening

Riddles and Jokes

Discuss riddles and jokes based on words that have the same sound, but different meanings. For example:

- Why are socks and seeds alike? They both come in pairs (pears).
- How did the queen flood her country? She had a long reign (rain).
- Why did the students bring emery boards to school? (They wanted to be ready to file down the hall.)

Ask students whether they know of any other riddles or jokes based on homonyms, or challenge students to make up their own.

TEACH

Guided Practice

L1 Understanding Homonyms

To help students with the concept of words that sound alike but are spelled differently, you might guide them to use both auditory and visual clues. Ask students to close their eyes and listen as you read pairs of homonyms. Next, reread the words and their meanings as students find the words in the chart and copy them onto paper or on the chalkboard. Then ask students to circle or highlight the letters that are different in each pair. They might also draw a cartoon to show the meaning of the words in a set of homonyms and then write each word under a drawing.

PRACTICE AND ASSESS

Answers: Exercise 7

1. they're
2. you're
3. Who's
4. principal
5. it's
6. too

Independent Practice

Skills Practice

Vocabulary and Spelling Practice, pp. 13–16, 21–34, 41–52

CLOSE

Discuss words that sound alike but are spelled differently. Ask students how they know which homonym to use in a sentence. How do they remember which one to use? What kind of memory joggers have they used?

Setting the Purpose

Lesson 22.6 introduces students to some basic spelling rules and teaches students to identify and spell correctly words that are commonly misspelled.

FOCUS

Lesson Overview

Objective: To become familiar with spelling rules

Skills: identifying misspelled words; spelling words with suffixes correctly

Critical Thinking: recognizing patterns

Speaking and Listening: discussing

Bellringer

When students enter the classroom, have this assignment on the board: *List five words that you have trouble spelling correctly.*

Motivating Activity

On the chalkboard, have students group their lists of words according to the source of the spelling problem. For example, list *ie* and *ei* words in one group, and in another group, list words formed by adding a suffix to a root word.

22.6 Spelling Rules I

As a writer, you want to make sure your readers know exactly what you mean. Misspelled words can keep your readers from focusing on your ideas. Improving your spelling, therefore, can improve your writing. You can improve your spelling skills by learning some basic spelling rules.

Suffixes and the Silent *e*

Words that end in a silent *e* can be a spelling problem. They're especially troublesome when you have to add a suffix to them. The rules in the following chart will help you.

Adding Suffixes to Words That End with Silent *e*

Rules	Examples
When adding a suffix that begins with a consonant to a word that ends with a silent *e*, keep the *e*.	pure + -ly = purely grace + -ful = graceful **Common exceptions** awe + -ful = awful argue + -ment = argument
When adding *-ly* to a word that ends with an *l* plus a silent *e*, always drop the *e*.	terrible + -ly = terribly whole + -ly = wholly
When adding a suffix that begins with a vowel or *y* to a word that ends with a silent *e*, usually drop the *e*.	write + -ing = writing shine + -y = shiny **Common exceptions** dye + -ing = dyeing mile + -age = mileage
When adding a suffix that begins with *a* or *o* to a word that ends with *ce* or *ge*, keep the *e* so the word will still have the soft *c* or *g* sound.	change + -able = changeable trace + -able = traceable
When adding a suffix that begins with a vowel to a word that ends in *ee* or *oe*, keep the *e*.	agree + -able = agreeable hoe + -ing = hoeing

Teacher's Classroom Resources

For Lesson 22.6, the following resources can be used for planning, instruction, practice, or reinforcement.

Teaching Tools
Lesson Plans

Blackline Masters
Vocabulary and Spelling Practice, pp. 13–16, 21–34, 41–52

Suffixes and the Final *y*

Adding suffixes to words that end in *y* can cause spelling problems. The chart below shows the rules for changing the *y* to *i* when adding suffixes.

Adding Suffixes to Words That End in *y*	
When a word ends in a consonant + *y*, change the *y* to *i*.	cry + -ed = cried deny + -es = denies
When the suffix begins with an *i*, do not change the *y* to *i*.	cry + -ing = crying deny + -ing = denying
When a word ends in a vowel + *y*, keep the *y*.	joy + -ful = joyful stay + -ing = staying

Spelling *ie* and *ei*

Some writers get confused when spelling words containing *ie* or *ei*. One way to help with these letter combinations is to memorize a simple rhyming rule.

Rhyming Rule	Examples
Put *i* before *e*	believe, chief, grieve
except after *c*	receive, deceit, receipt
and when sounded like *a*, as in *neighbor* and *weigh*.	eight, weight, veil, freight

Fortunately, there are very few exceptions to the *ie* and *ei* rule. The box below lists the only exceptions you need to remember.

Exceptions to the *ie* and *ei* Rule
species, seize, leisure, weird, either, neither, height

TEACH

Guided Practice

L2 Adding Suffixes

List vowels on the chalkboard to help students visualize the final *-y* rule for words ending in *vowel-plus-y*. Tell them to list all the vowels, then cross out *i* and *y*. Dictate four words, each ending in one of the remaining four vowels plus *y* (for example, *stay, obey, toy, buy*). Students can write the words as you dictate them, then write the same words and add suffixes.

Enabling Strategies

LEP Distinguishing Sounds

Some students cannot distinguish certain English speech sounds. Students may not hear the sound differences in such words as *hit/heat, let/late, cat/cot/cut.* They can benefit from practice with minimal pairs of words. Have them practice with sentences such as *Pick up the cap; pick up the cup.* Have a volunteer repeat the sentence several times, varying use of *cap* and *cup*. Then have the student pronounce a list of words while a student who is more proficient in English writes down what he or she hears. Compare the lists.

L1 Understanding Syllables and Accents
Spelling rules for doubling the final consonant involve recognizing the syllables and stress of a word. If students have trouble hearing syllables in a word, or if they cannot always recognize a stressed or accented syllable, suggest that they clap out the rhythm of each word, using soft and loud claps to distinguish the accented and unaccented syllables. Begin by clapping out rhythms yourself; then ask students to clap with you.

Cross-reference: Vocabulary and Spelling
For more information on spelling rules, refer students to Lessons 22.7 and 22.8 on pp. 524–530.

Doubling the Final Consonant

When a word ends in a consonant, you may need to double the final consonant when adding a suffix.

DOUBLE THE FINAL CONSONANT WHEN a word ends in a single consonant following one vowel AND

- the word is one syllable

  sit + -ing = sitting — run + -er = runner
  stop + -ed = stopped — shop + -ing = shopping
  sad + -er = sadder — trap + -ed = trapped

- the word has an accent on the last syllable and the accent stays there after the suffix is added

  prefer + -ed = preferred — reset + -ing = resetting
  occur + -ence = occurrence — control + -ing = controlling
  forget + -ing = forgetting — regret + -ed = regretted

DO *NOT* DOUBLE THE FINAL CONSONANT WHEN

- the suffix begins with a consonant

  forget + -ful = forgetful — pain + -less = painless
  dark + -ness = darkness — part + -ly = partly

- the accent is not on the last syllable

  develop + -ing = developing — offer + -ed = offered
  general + -ize = generalize

- the accent moves when the suffix is added

  prefer + -ence = preference — refer + -ence = reference

- two vowels come before the final consonant

  train + -ing = training — moan + -ed = moaned
  detail + -ing = detailing — pain + -ed = pained

- the word ends in two consonants

  remind + -er = reminder — bang + -ed = banged
  field + -ing = fielding — haunt + -ing = haunting
  drift + -ing = drifting

SPECIAL CASE: When a word ends in *ll* and the suffix *-ly* is added, drop one *l.*

dull + -ly = dully — full + -ly = fully

Connections Across the Curriculum

History

Geoffrey Chaucer, who died about 1400, wrote in Middle English. Speakers of Middle English pronounced the final *e* that is silent in many modern English words. Other vowel sounds and some consonant sounds also differed from those in modern English words.

Many words that come from Old or Middle English conform to the same spelling pattern, such as *eight, weight,* and *freight.* Words from a different language, such as Latin, conform to different patterns, for example, *fate, date,* and *plate.*

Forming Compound Words

Here's the easiest spelling rule of all. When joining two words to make a compound word, keep the original spelling of both words.

school + book = schoolbook   house + fly = housefly

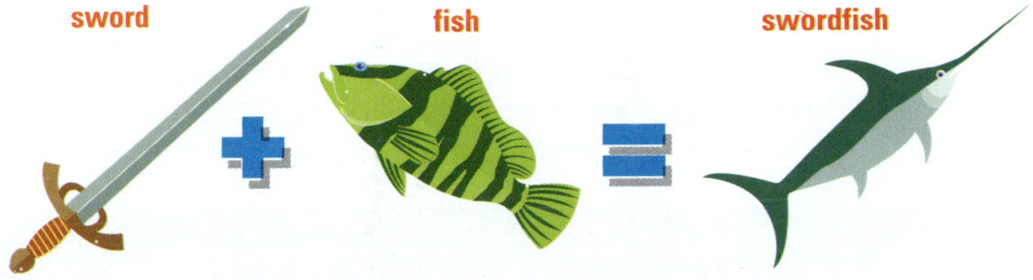

Exercise 8

Carefully examine each set of words below. Find the one word that is misspelled in each set and write it correctly.

1. blackness, roundness, sterness
2. recieve, achieve, veil
3. dullly, purely, rarely
4. stating, shineing, mileage
5. commited, stopped, regretting

Exercise 9

Correctly complete each of the following word + suffix problems.

1. big + -er =
2. supply + -ing =
3. explain + -able =
4. label + -ed =
5. expel + -ing =
6. choose + -ing =
7. occur + -ed =
8. hoe + -ing =
9. differ + -ence =
10. use + -able =

PRACTICE AND ASSESS

Answers: Exercise 8

1. sternness
2. receive
3. dully
4. shining
5. committed

Answers: Exercise 9

1. bigger
2. supplying
3. explainable
4. labeled
5. expelling
6. choosing
7. occurred
8. hoeing
9. difference
10. usable

Independent Practice

Skills Practice

Vocabulary and Spelling Practice, pp. 13–16, 21–34, 41–52

CLOSE

Have students write a list of ways in which learning spelling rules help them to improve their writing.

Enrichment and Extension

Changes in English

Play a recording of a reading from one of Chaucer's *Canterbury Tales* to demonstrate for students how different Chaucer's English was from the English students know today. Ask students to identify words or phrases they can understand. You might write several Middle English words on the board with their modern English equivalents. Ask students to describe how spelling has changed from Middle English to modern English.

Setting the Purpose

Lesson 22.7 provides spelling rules and teaches students how to form plurals for most English nouns.

FOCUS

Lesson Overview

Objective: To become familiar with spelling rules

Skills: forming plural nouns; using a dictionary

Critical Thinking: visualizing

Speaking and Listening: discussing; spelling aloud

Bellringer

When students enter the classroom, have this assignment on the board: *List five plural nouns.*

Motivating Activity

On the chalkboard, work with students to sort into groups the plural nouns that they listed. Have them group or cluster words according to the way the plurals are formed. For example, *lice, mice, men,* and *feet* would be in one group; *cats, boys,* and *skates* in another; and *dishes, matches,* and *foxes* in a third group.

22.7 Spelling Rules II

A handful of spelling rules can help you spell thousands of words. For example, the few rules that follow deal with the spelling of plurals. These rules will help you spell the plurals of nearly every English noun.

Forming Plurals

Most nouns in English form plurals by adding an *-s* or *-es.* However, there are other ways to form plurals. The charts that follow show some general and special rules for plurals.

General Rules for Plurals

If the Noun Ends in	The Rule Is	Example
s, *ch,* *sh,* *x,* or *z*	add *-es*	loss → losses watch → watches bush → bushes box → boxes fizz → fizzes
a consonant + *y*	change *y* to *i* and add *-es*	berry → berries body → bodies baby → babies
a vowel + *y*	add *-s*	key → keys day → days boy → boys
a vowel + *o*	add *-s*	stereo → stereos studio → studios rodeo → rodeos
a consonant + *o*	usually add *-s*	piano → pianos photo → photos solo → solos
	Common exceptions but sometimes add *-es*	potato → potatoes hero → heroes echo → echoes

Teacher's Classroom Resources

For Lesson 22.7, the following resources can be used for planning, instruction, practice, or reinforcement.

Teaching Tools
Lesson Plans

Blackline Masters
Vocabulary and Spelling Practice, pp. 13–16, 21–34, 41–52

General Rules for Plurals		
If the Noun Ends in	**The Rule Is**	**Example**
f or *ff*	add *-s*	reef → reefs cuff → cuffs
	Common exceptions change *f* to *v* and add *-es*	leaf → leaves loaf → loaves
lf	change *f* to *v* and add *-es*	half → halves wolf → wolves
fe	change *f* to *v* and add *-s*	life → lives knife → knives

Special Rules for Plurals	
Special Case	**Example**
To form the plurals of most proper names, add *-s.* But add *-es* if the name ends in *s, ch, sh, x,* or *z.*	Krey → Kreys Jones → Joneses Hatch → Hatches Bush → Bushes Marx → Marxes Sanchez → Sanchezes
To form the plural of one-word compound nouns, follow the general rules for plurals.	textbook → textbooks icebox → iceboxes penknife → penknives blackberry → blackberries
To form the plural of hyphenated compound nouns or compound nouns of more than one word, make the most important word plural.	brother-in-law → brothers-in-law ice cream → ice creams chief of staff → chiefs of staff
Some nouns have irregular plural forms and do not follow any rules.	woman → women ox → oxen foot → feet
Some nouns have the same singular and plural forms.	series → series deer → deer sheep → sheep

TEACH

Guided Practice

L2 Forming Plurals

Encourage students to list additional examples of each spelling rule in the chart. Discuss exceptions as well. Students might take turns naming objects in the room and challenging classmates to spell the plurals.

L1 Tracing Difficult Words

Some students may need to engage a number of senses as an aid for memorizing individual words. Have students use kinesthetic tracing methods. You may wish to pair students. One student should read a word aloud for the other student to write. The reader should then show the word to the listener. Finally, the listener should write the correct spelling of the word, and then spell it aloud while tracing the outline of each letter.

Enabling Strategies

LEP Writing Plural Nouns

Students may have difficulty understanding the concept of plural nouns and developing the habit of changing singular nouns to a plural form. Some languages do not change spelling to form plural nouns. To provide additional practice for students who need it, you may team them with peers who can make up and dictate sentences. Go over the rules for formation of plurals. Ask students to find examples of each rule in available reading materials.

PRACTICE AND ASSESS

Answers: Exercise 10

1. foxes
2. flies
3. elves
4. echoes
5. radios
6. dairies
7. benches
8. troubles
9. Juarezes
10. mosquitoes
11. strawberries
12. zebras

Independent Practice

Skills Practice

Vocabulary and Spelling Practice, pp. 13–16, 21–34, 41–52

CLOSE

Have students discuss strategies for spelling plural nouns. Ask students these questions: *What works best for remembering tricky spellings? What strategies would you like to try in the future?*

Becoming a Better Speller

By following a few simple steps, you can learn to spell new words. Pay attention to unfamiliar words or hard-to-spell words in your reading. As you write, note words that you have trouble spelling. Then use the steps below to learn to spell those difficult words.

Say It
Look at the word on the page, and say it aloud. Say it a second time, pronouncing each syllable clearly.

See It
Close your eyes, and picture the printed word in your mind's eye. Picture how the word is spelled.

Write It
Look at the word again, and write it two or three times. Then write it again without looking at the word.

Check It
Check what you have written. Did you spell it correctly? If not, go through each step again until you can spell the word correctly.

Get into the habit of using your dictionary to find the correct spelling of a word. How do you find it in a dictionary if you can't spell it? Jot down letters and letter combinations that could stand for the sound you hear at the beginning of the word. Try each of these possible spellings as you look for the word in the dictionary. Then *Say It, See It, Write It, Check It,* and learn to spell the word.

Exercise 10

Write the plural form of each of the following words.

1. fox	**4.** echo	**7.** bench	**10.** mosquito
2. fly	**5.** radio	**8.** trouble	**11.** strawberry
3. elf	**6.** dairy	**9.** Juarez	**12.** zebra

Connections Across the Curriculum

History

In Old English, inflections (word endings), rather than syntax (word order), were used to designate changes in grammatical form. However, by the end of the Middle English period, most of the inflections of Old English had disappeared. Among the inflections remaining today are the final *-es* or *-s* for plural nouns and the past tense suffix, *-ed*.

Wordworks

Secret Codes

Suppose that you want to send a secret note to a friend but need to make sure no one else can read it. Do what the ancient Greeks did—code it!

People have sent coded messages, or cryptograms, for thousands of years. Messengers first used codes during wartime, to carry secret messages across enemy lines.

One common code system substitutes letters. Julius Caesar, a Roman general, used such a system. In his system you replace each letter in the message with a letter three spaces to the right in the regular alphabet. For example, the message FIGHT would be written as ILJKW in code. Anyone who knows the code can easily figure out the message. To decode the message, you replace each letter with a letter three spaces to the left in the alphabet.

Another code system reverses the order of letters. Suppose that you want to code the message SUE WILL NOT GO WITH JACK. First, divide the letters of the message into groups of five: SUEWI LLNOT GOWIT HJACK. Then reverse the letters in each group: IWEUS TONLL TIWOG KCAJH. This message would be pretty hard to figure out—unless you knew the code.

CHALLENGE

Working with a friend, experiment with coded messages. Use a system discussed here, or create your own. What fact about language can you learn from your experiments?

Crack the Code

Suppose that you are one of Caesar's messengers. You have just intercepted this coded message from one of Caesar's enemies. All you know is that the numbers in the code stand for letters in the alphabet. Can you crack the code?

Connections Across the Curriculum

History

During World War II, the U.S. Marine Corps used a "code" for sending messages by telephone or radio that the Germans and Japanese never succeeded in cracking. This baffling "code" was simply a spoken Native American language—most often Navajo. Reportedly, only a handful of non-Navajos, none of them German or Japanese, could speak the language. By the end of the war, the Marine Corps included 420 Navajo "codetalkers."

Lesson Overview

Objective: To become familiar with the concept of coded messages
Skills: understanding code systems
Critical Thinking: patterning
Speaking and Listening: discussing

TEACH

Discussion

Have students read Wordworks, p. 527, and discuss the following questions: *Why might someone send a message in a code? How can you create a code?*

L2 Creating a Code

Encourage students to share their experiences with coded language, such as pig latin and other spoken or written code languages. Suggest students work in teams to create an original code and transmit a message. Then have teams exchange their coded messages with other teams and attempt to break each other's codes.

PRACTICE AND ASSESS

Evaluation Guidelines: Challenge

Answers will vary. Students may discover that language is simply a set of symbols that combine to create words that express ideas.

Answers: Crack the Code

The message says: "Attack Caesar at dawn."

CLOSE

Have students discuss how creating codes and figuring out codes can help them learn about language.

Setting the Purpose

Lesson 22.8 teaches students strategies for spelling difficult and easily confused words.

FOCUS

Lesson Overview

Objective: To learn the correct spelling of difficult and easily confused words
Skills: creating a personal word list
Critical Thinking: defining and clarifying
Speaking and Listening: tape recording sentences

Bellringer

When students enter the classroom, have this assignment on the board: *List three pairs of words that are easily confused because they sound alike but have different meanings and spellings.*

Motivating Activity

Form groups and have each group choose a pair of homonyms from their Bellringer lists to use in sentences. Each group member should make up and write one sentence using the wrong homonym. Then students can exchange papers, make corrections, and share their corrected sentences with one another. Groups may then write the original sentences on the chalkboard and challenge other groups to replace incorrect words with the correct homonyms.

22.8 Problem Words

Like most people, you probably have trouble spelling certain words. Some words are harder to spell than others. Some words don't follow basic spelling rules, but there are some ways you can learn to spell even the most difficult words.

Make a personal word list. List the words that you find especially difficult or that you often misspell. Keep your list up-to-date, adding new words as you come across them. Study them by using the steps shown on page 526. When you're sure you can spell a word, you can remove it from your list.

Difficult Words

The following is a list of words that people often misspell. Are any of your problem words on this list? What other words would you add to the list?

Often Misspelled Words

absence	definite	leisure	recommend
accidentally	descend	library	restaurant
adviser	disease	license	rhythm
all right	embarrass	misspell	schedule
answer	environment	molasses	sense
athlete	February	muscle	separate
attendant	foreign	necessary	similar
ballet	forty	neighborhood	sincerely
beautiful	funeral	niece	succeed
beginning	genius	ninety	technology
believe	government	occasion	theory
business	grammar	original	traffic
cafeteria	guarantee	parallel	truly
canceled	height	permanent	usually
canoe	humorous	physical	vacuum
cemetery	immediate	probably	variety
choir	jewelry	receipt	various
colonel	laboratory	recognize	Wednesday

Teacher's Classroom Resources

For Lesson 22.8, the following resources can be used for planning, instruction, practice, assessment, reinforcement, or evaluation.

Teaching Tools
Lesson Plans

Blackline Masters
Vocabulary and Spelling Practice, pp. 13–26, 21–34, 41–52

Unit Assessment

Tests with Answer Key
Unit 22 Mastery Test, pp. 87–88

Test Generator
Unit 22 Mastery Test

You may wish to administer the Unit 22 Mastery Test at this point.

Easily Confused Words

Did you ever get confused over the spelling of *through* and *threw*? How about *hour* and *our*? Would you describe a smell as a *sent,* a *cent,* or a *scent*?

Some words are often confused because they sound alike but have different spellings and meanings. You can review many of these troublesome words on pages 420–423. Following are a few more. You may want to add some of these words to your personal word list.

Words That Are Often Confused

to	toward, in the direction of; as far as *Go **to** the corner, and then turn **to** the left.*
too	also; as well as; more than enough *Mario was **too** tired to dance. His sister Carmen was tired, **too.***
two	the number 2 *The **two** of us were the last pair to arrive.*
principle	a basic rule, truth, or law *The **principle** of free speech is important in a democracy.*
principal	first in rank; the head of a school *The **principal** announced that school would close early.*
desert (dez′ərt)	a dry, barren region *They hoped to cross the **desert** before their water ran out.*
desert (di zurt′)	to abandon; to leave without permission *The soldier was warned not to **desert** his post.*
dessert (di zurt′)	a sweet course served at the end of a meal *I'll have the chocolate cake for **dessert.***
passed	to have moved on or ahead; completed satisfactorily *Donna **passed** the test with only one error.*
past	time gone by; existed earlier *Jake learned from his **past** mistakes.*
weather	the daily conditions of temperature, moisture, wind, etc. *The northern wind brought a sudden change in the **weather.***
whether	conjunction used in indirect questions *Everyone wondered **whether** the plane would leave on time.*

TEACH

Guided Practice

L2 Exploring Misspelled Words

After students look at the list of often-misspelled words, discuss reasons they are often misspelled. Tell students to read a word from the list aloud, such as *absence*, and listen to the way it sounds. The pronunciation doesn't make the second vowel sound clear, since it is in an unaccented syllable. Memorizing the spellings of some problem words is important, since sounds can sometimes be deceiving.

L3 Using Homonyms Creatively

Students may search telephone directories and periodicals for advertisements that show an intentional misuse (or creative use) of homonyms. For example, a secretarial service was called The Write Type. Other business names, logos, or slogans may use homonyms correctly but in clever ways. The editing program RIGHTWriter is one example. After researching and discussing examples, students might invent their own names for products or businesses, using homonyms in creative ways.

Connections Across the Curriculum

History

Some troublesome spelling words are explained by the way the English language has developed. Originally, spelling reflected changes in pronunciation. When printing became common in the late fifteenth century, spelling became more standardized because people saw words in print. The use of dictionaries, starting in the eighteenth century, standardized spellings even more, but pronunciation continued to change. For example, the word *knight* is spelled as it is because people in Chaucer's time pronounced all consonants.

PRACTICE AND ASSESS

Answers: Exercise 11

1. two
2. desert
3. whether
4. too
5. passed
6. principal
7. dessert
8. weather
9. past
10. principal

Independent Practice

Skills Practice

Vocabulary and Spelling Practice, pp. 13–26, 21–34, 41–52

CLOSE

Students may work with partners to write sentences that help them identify and clarify homonyms and other words that can cause spelling problems.

Another way to learn problem words is to use memory devices, or tricks for remembering. For example, do you have trouble remembering the difference between *principal* and *principle*? You might memorize: *Your principal is a pal. A principle is a rule.* Do you confuse *to, too,* and *two*? Perhaps you could remember: *Two horses are one too many for me to tend.* Sometimes these memory devices are little rhymes, such as the following:

Poor little Emma,
*Caught in a dil*emma.

Think of other sentences or rhymes that will help you remember how to spell troublesome words. Do you know any?

Exercise 11

On a separate sheet of paper, write the word in the parentheses that correctly completes each sentence.

1. There were only (to, too, two) of us at breakfast this morning.
2. Camels can travel in the (desert, dessert) better than most other animals.
3. We all wondered (weather, whether) the test would be as hard as the last one was.
4. My parents think I spend (to, too, two) much money on CDs.
5. The helicopter (passed, past) overhead, frightening the animals.
6. My favorite teacher will be the new (principle, principal) next year.
7. I ate so much that I hardly had room for (desert, dessert).
8. Isn't this rainy (weather, whether) ever going to end?
9. I like studying history. The (past, passed) has always interested me.
10. The (principle, principal) purpose of our club is to raise money to help feed the homeless.

Technology Tip

Recording Homonyms

Tape-record students reading sentences containing homonyms. As you play the tape recording back, have students write the correct homonym. Ask them whether they think certain homonyms are more difficult to distinguish than others.

UNIT

23 Study Skills

23.1 Exploring a Book

Imagine that you are researching a report for science class. In the library you find a book that may help you. Can you find out if the book has what you need without reading all of it?

The pictures on this page show some helpful parts of a book. Learning to use these parts will make it easier for you to find the information you need. The chart on page 532 answers some questions you might ask about a book.

The **table of contents** shows the name and the opening page number for each major section of a book.

The **index** is an alphabetical list of the important topics covered in a book. Page numbers are given for each entry.

The **glossary** is an alphabetical list of special terms used in the book. The glossary defines each term and may give pronunciations as well.

Setting the Purpose

Lesson 23.1 provides students with skills for studying and for researching and writing a report.

FOCUS

Lesson Overview

Objective: To become familiar with the parts of a book

Skills: reading a table of contents; using a glossary; using an index

Critical Thinking: analyzing; classifying; evaluating

Speaking and Listening: discussing

Bellringer

When students enter the classroom, have this assignment on the board: *List at least five kinds of information you can find in a book.*

Motivating Activity

Ask students to imagine they are writing a report on a specific topic such as volcanic islands. They have a large stack of books and five minutes to decide what books they need. How would students find out a book's content? What parts of the book would students check?

TEACH

Guided Practice

L1 Providing Support

Ask students to put a ruler under a topic in this book's table of contents. Then have them put a ruler under a subtopic. How are they different? Turn to the index. Have students put a ruler under the topic *Library.* What does that word look like? Have students slide the ruler down, noting subtopics. How are they different?

Teacher's Classroom Resources

For Lesson 23.1, the following resources can be used for planning, instruction, practice, assessment, reinforcement, or evaluation.

Teaching Tools
Lesson Plans

Blackline Masters
Thinking and Study Skills, pp. 30–32, 35–40

Unit Assessment

Tests with Answer Key
Unit 23 Pretest, pp. 89–90

Test Generator
Unit 23 Pretest

You may wish to administer the Unit 23 Pretest at this point.

PRACTICE AND ASSESS

Answers: Exercise 1

1. Three: (1) Composition; (2) Grammar, Usage, and Mechanics; (3) Resources and Skills
2. Unit 10
3. Page 559
4. Page 541
5. Gary Soto, page 164

Independent Practice

Skills Practice

Thinking and Study Skills, pp. 30–32, 35–40

CLOSE

Ask students to describe the three parts of a book they could use for research. Invite a volunteer to demonstrate the use of one section.

Questions	Where to Look for the Answers
Can I find information on my particular topic in this book?	The **table of contents** lists the title of each chapter, lesson, or section. It tells you what topics are covered and shows you how the book is organized.
I may need to find particular words or ideas. Does this book have an index and a glossary?	Look in the **table of contents**. If a book contains an index and a glossary, their page numbers will be given there. You can also look in the back part of the book. That's where those features are located.
Does this book have any maps or graphs I might use in my report?	Some books, especially textbooks, contain lists of maps, graphs, and other special illustrations. Such lists usually appear right after the **table of contents**.
Are the people or places I am writing about mentioned in this book?	The **index** gives the number of each page on which a person or place is mentioned. Events and other important topics are also in an index. You can check the index and quickly find the information you need.
Will I be able to understand the terms used in this book?	Textbooks and other books that contain difficult or technical terms often have **glossaries**. A glossary defines such terms.

Exercise 1

Use the table of contents and index of *this* book to answer the following questions. Tell which feature you used to answer each question.

1. Into how many parts is the book divided? Name them.
2. What unit deals with verbs?
3. On what page does the index begin?
4. On what page or pages would you find information about graphs?
5. Who wrote "The Jacket"? On what page does it begin?

Thinking Skills

Visual Thinking

Ask students to compare and contrast the three images on student page 531. What do they notice about them? (All present information about the book's contents, but each contains a different kind of information, and each is used for a different purpose.)

23.2 Planning Your Study

Some days you may feel that there isn't enough time to learn about all the subjects and skills that interest you. Making a study plan can help you get the most out of the study time you have.

Setting Study Goals

First you need to set study goals. Some study goals can be met in one study session. For example, you could memorize ten spelling words or read four pages of a textbook in one session. Other study goals require more time. Writing a research report would probably take several weeks.

When setting your study goals, decide how long it should take to meet each one. Be realistic about what you can do in one study session. If you have a long assignment, divide it into smaller tasks. If you're planning a report, for example, one goal will be to find library resources. Another goal will be to skim the books or articles for information you can use.

Setting the Purpose

Lesson 23.2 teaches students the principles of task and time planning for more effective studying.

FOCUS

Lesson Overview

Objective: To develop goal-setting and planning skills

Skills: setting study goals; using a calendar; scheduling

Critical Thinking: decision making; evaluating

Speaking and Listening: discussing

Bellringer

When students enter the classroom, have this assignment on the board: *How much time will you spend on homework tonight? tomorrow night?*

Motivating Activity

Ask students the number of hours in a day. Then have them write down the hours they are asleep and the hours they are in school. Do they think there are enough hours left in the day for recreation, chores, and homework?

Teacher's Classroom Resources

For Lesson 23.2, the following resources can be used for planning, instruction, practice, or reinforcement.

Teaching Tools
Lesson Plans

Blackline Masters
Thinking and Study Skills, pp. 30–32, 35–40

TEACH

Guided Practice

L2 Understanding Time

To prepare students to set study goals, discuss how long it takes to do different things. Point out that because of each person's unique skills and interests, the time it takes to do a specific task varies from person to person. Elicit from students that this means they must be aware of their strengths when planning. If someone thinks up ideas for a paper in nothing flat, but has trouble putting the ideas into words, he or she should schedule less time for prewriting and more for drafting.

PRACTICE AND ASSESS

Evaluation Guidelines: Exercise 2

Answers will vary, but completed calendars should reflect a reasonable allocation of study time for each goal and demonstrate an understanding of how to plan each day's work realistically.

Independent Practice

Skills Practice

Thinking and Study Skills, pp. 30–32, 35–40

CLOSE

Ask students how they currently keep track of school assignments, tutoring dates, special class activities, and so on. Emphasize the importance of getting into the habit of recording assignments as they are given.

Using a Calendar

The most important tool for making a study plan is a calendar. As you set your goals, write each one on the calendar. For longer tasks first write the final due date. Then work backward from there, filling in each task. For example, say that a report is due on the 15th. Mark the 14th on your calendar for proofreading the final report. Then set aside the 12th and the 13th to revise your first draft and write the final draft. Continue working backward in this manner through all the needed tasks.

As you schedule your study time, try to keep all your class assignments balanced. Suppose that an English report is due on Friday—the same day you have a social studies test. You'll need to set aside study time for both goals. Also, keep in mind other important activities. You don't want to schedule writing a report on the day you have a track meet.

Exercise 2

Draw a 30-day calendar with the first day falling on a Wednesday. Then set study goals, and schedule the following assignments:

- You must read four chapters (about 80 pages) of your social studies text by the end of the month. You must also review an earlier unit (80 pages) for a test on Friday the 10th.
- A written report for English is due the 17th.
- In science a unit test covering five chapters will be given Friday the 24th.
- You need to review for a short quiz your math teacher gives every Monday.
- You are on the basketball team and have practice every Thursday from 3:30 to 5:00.

Connections Across the Curriculum

History

The calendar now used in the United States and elsewhere is called the Gregorian calendar. It has been in use since 1582. In the past, calendars changed as people learned more about the relation of the earth to the sun and moon. The calendar was changed in 1582 because over the centuries the dates had begun to fall behind the seasons! Other calendars still in use are the Chinese, Jewish, and Muslim calendars. Differences among the various calendars include the names of the months, the number of the year, and how leap year is handled.

23.3 Using a Study Method

Suppose that you could spend less time studying and learn just as much as you learn now—or even more. Wouldn't it be worth taking a little time to learn a method that can help you do that? That's what the SQ3R method can help you do. This method will improve your study habits. You'll learn more and learn it better. What's more, you'll get it done in less time. Look at the diagram below. Can you guess why the method is called SQ3R?

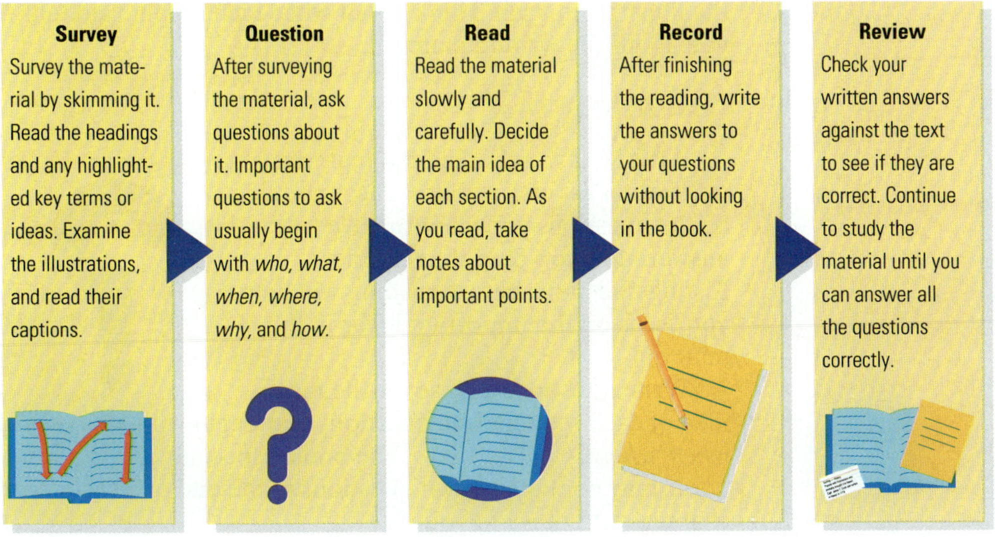

You can use the SQ3R method with any subject. Once you've learned the method and use it regularly, it will become a habit. Effective studying will save you time. In addition, it will help you become better prepared in all your classes.

Survey

To survey means to look something over to get a general view of it. The point of surveying is to get an overview of the material you are studying. You can do that by looking for the main ideas of the material. Read all the headings that divide the material into smaller sections. These headings may help

Setting the Purpose

Lesson 23.3 will familiarize students with a study method that can help make their studying more effective.

FOCUS

Lesson Overview

Objective: To acquaint students with the SQ3R method

Skills: skimming text; generating questions; taking notes; reviewing

Critical Thinking: recalling; main idea

Speaking and Listening: note taking; informal speaking

Bellringer

When students enter the classroom, have this assignment on the board: *Write five questions that you would like answered about this title: "The Last of the Really Great Oompaloompas."*

Motivating Activity

Ask students what they think the abbreviation *SQ3R* stands for. Explain that it is not pronounced as a word but is a memory device for a study method. Write the words *Survey, Question, Read, Record,* and *Review* on the board. Ask a volunteer to come to the board and draw a box around the first letter of each word. Repeat that *SQ3R* stands for these five words and that the abbreviation is designed to make it easier for students to remember the concepts.

Teacher's Classroom Resources

For Lesson 23.3, the following resources can be used for planning, instruction, practice, or reinforcement.

Teaching Tools
Lesson Plans

Blackline Masters
Thinking and Study Skills, pp. 30–32, 35–40

TEACH

Guided Practice

L2 Working Together

You can help students begin to apply the SQ3R method by using an overhead transparency of a page from a social studies textbook. Ask students to brainstorm how they would use SQ3R to study the material. For example, write the word *survey* in the margin, and draw an arrow from it to the chapter head, subheads, or picture captions. Ask students to discuss the benefit of this step. (It provides a quick overview of the material.) Continue with the other SQ3R steps.

L3 Using SQ3R in a Presentation

Emphasize to students that by using the SQ3R study method when listening to a presentation, they can better remember important points. By writing key words, phrases, and ideas from the lecture, students can highlight the speaker's main points and remember important information. They also can note pertinent details that will help them to recall the presentation.

you find the main ideas. They also will show you how the material is organized. Skim the material to find the main idea of each paragraph. In skimming you look over the material rapidly to find its main ideas. You will find a paragraph's main idea stated in the topic sentence. The first sentence of a paragraph is often its topic sentence.

Sometimes important material in the text is highlighted or presented in bold type. Read all such sentences or terms. Look at all the pictures, graphs, charts, and other graphic aids. Read the title and caption for each graphic aid, and examine the illustration itself. Think about what each graphic aid tells you about the written material.

Question

After you've surveyed the material, write out a list of questions. These should be the questions you want to have answered as you read the material. Listing questions before reading will help you focus on the important ideas in the material.

Write questions that cover the main idea of each section. Use questions that begin with *who*, *what*, *when*, *where*, *why*, and *how*. The book, especially if it is a textbook, may contain its own questions at the end of a section or chapter. Add those to your list.

Read

Read through the material carefully. As you read, write each main idea in your own words. Look for answers to your questions. You may also add additional questions to your list as you read. Make sure you understand each paragraph or passage. If the ideas are complicated, you may need to read passages more than once. Make sure you understand each idea before you move on to the next one.

Enabling Strategies

LEP Writing Questions

Students learning English may require some practice turning heads or main ideas into questions. Write these headings on the board and help students practice by formulating questions on these science topics:

- The Vast Universe
- Superclusters
- Our Solar System
- Venus: A Sizzling Planet
- Finding Your Weight on Jupiter

Record

After you've read the material carefully, write the answers to your list of questions. If the material you're studying is long, divide your reading into smaller sections. Stop after each section to record the answers to your questions about it. Rely only on your memory of what you've read when you write your answers. In this way you'll test whether you've really learned the material.

Review

After you finish answering the questions, check your answers against the material. If you answered any questions incorrectly, review the section covering that material again. Write new questions that cover the same material. After reviewing the material again, answer the new questions and check your answers. Continue to question, read, record, and review until you can answer all questions correctly. Keep your review questions and answers in your notebook for later study and review.

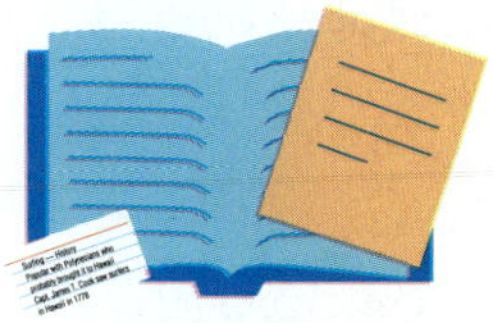

Exercise 3

Choose a short chapter or section from one of your textbooks. You can also select a short article from a magazine. Study the material, using the SQ3R method. After you have studied the material, answer the following questions:

1. Where can you find clues about the main ideas of the selection?
2. What are the main ideas of the selection?
3. List your review questions and your answers to them.

PRACTICE AND ASSESS

Evaluation Guidelines: Exercise 3

Answers will vary, but responses should reflect that students can do the following:

- find the main ideas of a selection
- ask relevant questions about the material
- read for comprehension
- take notes
- construct and answer questions about a selection and evaluate the answers

Independent Practice

Skills Practice

Thinking and Study Skills, pp. 30–32, 35–40

CLOSE

Ask students to write a paragraph outlining how they would begin reading a chapter or an article for research purposes. Have them think back to the Bellringer: now that they know SQ3R, would they ask the same questions about "The Last of the Really Great Whangdoodles"?

Beyond the Classroom

Analyzing News Articles

Newspaper writers often answer the questions *who, what, when, where, why,* and *how* in the first paragraph of a story. This technique gives readers vital information right away—they get the main idea quickly and can scan the article for details. It also allows editors to cut paragraphs from the end of the article if it is too long. Invite students to find an article from a newspaper that comes close to this style. Ask them to circle the main idea and underline the sentences or phrases that answer the *who, what, when, where, why,* and *how* questions.

Setting the Purpose

Lesson 23.4 teaches students how to take notes on note cards and how to use those notes to create an outline.

FOCUS

Lesson Overview

Objective: To become familiar with notes and outlines

Skills: taking notes; creating an outline

Critical Thinking: observing and organizing; summarizing

Speaking and Listening: discussing

Bellringer

When students enter the classroom, have this assignment on the board: *List five questions that you would research to write a report on Aesop's fables.*

Motivating Activity

Create an overhead transparency or a handout by drawing a box about the size of a 3-by-5-inch or 4-by-6-inch note card. Ask students how they might organize notes about the animals in Aesop's fables. (The names of the fable and the animal might appear at the top of the card; the animal's traits and other details can appear below.) Have each student create a sample card.

23.4 Notes and Outlines

While working on a report, you'll find many facts and ideas. Most people can't count on memory alone to keep track of everything they read. You need to make notes of the facts and ideas you might use in your report.

Taking Notes

Use a separate note card for each piece of information. The cards will allow you to organize your notes easily. Write the name of your source on the card. (Use the sample note card below as a model.) Then, in your own words, summarize the information from your research.

Write only the details and ideas that relate to your topic. Use a quotation if a sentence or phrase is especially interesting. You may also need to use the words of an authority to strengthen your report. When you do quote something from a source, copy it word for word. Enclose it in quotation marks. The quotation marks will make clear which ideas are yours and which are someone else's.

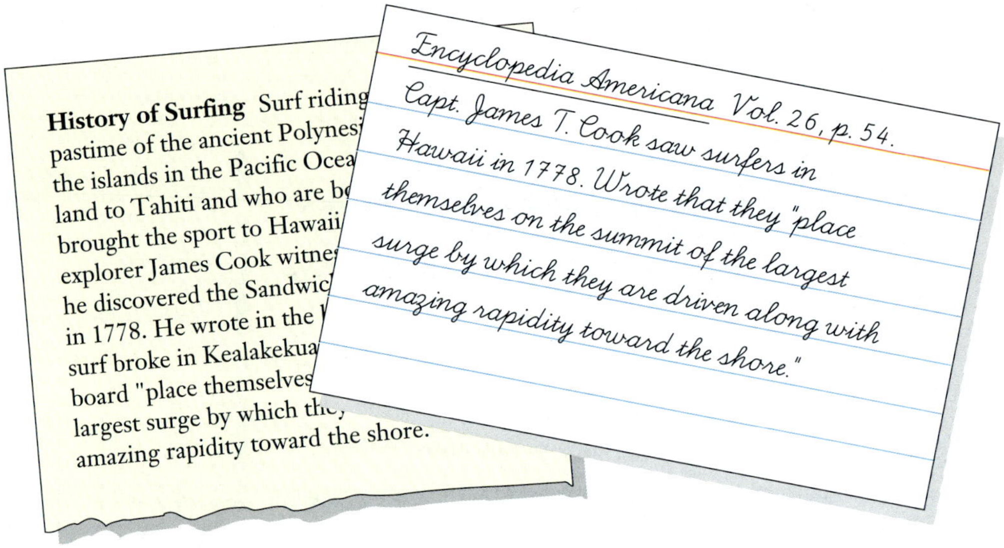

Teacher's Classroom Resources

For Lesson 23.4, the following resources can be used for planning, instruction, practice, or reinforcement.

Teaching Tools
Lesson Plans

Blackline Masters
Thinking and Study Skills, pp. 30–32, 35–40

Tips on Taking Notes

1. Use a new 3 x 5 card for each important piece of information.
2. At the top of each card, identify the source of the information (the reference you used).
3. Summarize information in your own words.
4. Use direct quotations only when the words are especially useful or come from an important source.

Outlining

After completing your research, you're ready to organize the information in an outline. Look through your note cards and write down the main ideas you want to cover. Then decide on the right order for presenting them. For example, suppose that you're writing about the history of ballooning. You'll probably use time order—from earliest event to latest event. For other kinds of topics, think about how you can best group your ideas.

Write your outline. Begin by listing main ideas. Then fill in the supporting details. Look at the outline below.

Each main topic is one of the big ideas of your subject. Suppose that your subject is surfing. The first main topic could be the history of surfing.

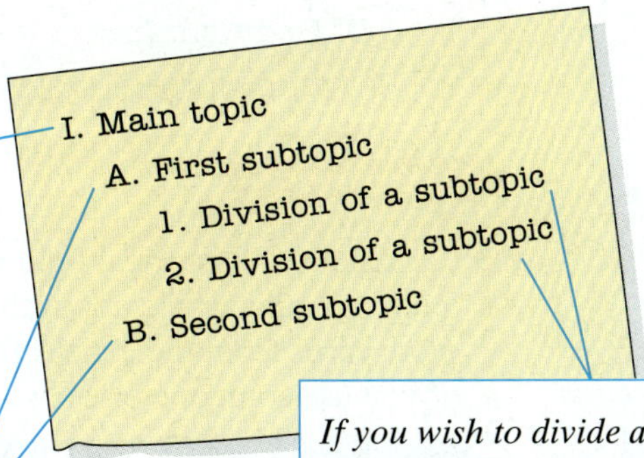

If you have subtopics under a main topic, there must be at least two. They must relate directly to the main topic.

If you wish to divide a subtopic, you must have at least two divisions. Each division must relate to the subtopic above it.

Technology Tip

Writing Note Cards

If students have access to computer software with an outline option, they can write their note cards using the computer. When they organize their outline, they may want to use the Search function to locate information on a particular topic.

TEACH

Guided Practice

L1 Organizing Note Cards

Show students how to manipulate note cards before writing an outline. Tell them to place the main topic note card at the top of their desk, and then to group together the subtopic cards. They should arrange the group of subtopic cards below their main topic card. They should then do the same with the divisions cards, placing them below the subtopics. When they have arranged the cards in descending order, they can create an outline.

L3 Organizing an Outline

Ask students to think of events they have heard or read about in the news in recent months. They might make an outline showing each event (main topic), the date and people, country, or group involved (subtopics), and details (divisions of subtopics). Students may think of other original ways to organize the information.

Cross-reference: Note-taking

For more information on notetaking, refer students to Lesson 3.2, pp. 102–104.

PRACTICE AND ASSESS

Evaluation Guidelines: Exercise 4

Answers will vary, but check that students have followed the Tips on Taking Notes on page 539. Emphasize the need to use quotation marks around any material that is copied directly from a source.

Independent Practice

Skills Practice

Thinking and Study Skills, pp. 30–32, 35–40

CLOSE

Some students may feel that making up note cards is an unnecessary step in their research. Ask students to discuss the pros and cons of using note cards. (Pro: Note cards allow them to organize and outline information, encourage them to keep notes brief, and keep them focused on the main topic and important details. Con: Note cards take time to write; it might be difficult to fit all information on one card; cards can get separated, lost, or out of order.)

Put your note cards in order according to your outline. You may not need all the information you've found. Don't try to include ideas that don't fit your outline. An example of a completed outline follows. Notice that you don't have to use complete sentences in an outline.

Main topic

Divisions supporting subtopic A

Subtopics of main topic III

Surfing

I. History of surfing
  A. Ancient Polynesians
    1. Began surfing in Pacific islands
    2. Brought it to Hawaii
  B. Discouraged by New England missionaries
  C. Became popular again around 1908
II. Surfboards
  A. Size and shape
  B. Materials
III. How to surf
  A. Safety factors
  B. Taking off and riding the wave
  C. Special moves
  D. Body surfing

Exercise 4

Choose a historical figure who interests you. Read an encyclopedia article about that person. Make at least five note cards from the article. Be sure to use quotation marks if you use someone else's words.

Enrichment and Extension

Using Topics and Outlines

Give students topics, such as surfing in the 1950s, analyzing waves, movies about surfing, and wooden surfboards. Ask them to decide how each topic would fit into the outline shown on this page. Ask students to suggest other possible topics for their classmates to fit into the outline.

23.5 Using Graphic Aids

Sometimes you need to present complicated information. You'll find that words don't always provide the best way to do it. Certain kinds of information call for graphic aids, such as tables, graphs, time lines, and maps.

Tables

Tables show pieces of information in a way that makes sense of them. Tables use columns and rows to organize information, which often includes groups of numbers. Look at the table below. Notice how easily you can tell which groups of animals include the most endangered species.

The title identifies the table's topic.

The left column names the groups of animals that are endangered.

Numbers of Endangered Species in the United States and the Rest of the World

Group	U.S.	Rest of World
Mammals	36	249
Birds	57	153
Reptiles	8	58
Amphibians	6	8
Fishes	51	11
Insects	12	1

Source: Fish and Wildlife Service, U.S. Department of Interior, 1991

Columns 2 and 3 divide the world into two areas. One column shows figures for the United States. The other gives figures for the rest of the world.

Each row gives the numbers of endangered species for one group.

You can read this table from left to right or from top to bottom. Suppose that you want to know how many species of birds in the United States are endangered. To find out, you don't have to read the whole table. First find the row that shows birds. Then move your eye across the row to the column for the United States. The table also makes it easy to compare numbers for the United States with those for the rest of the world. The numbers for each group of animals are side by side in columns 2 and 3.

Setting the Purpose

Lesson 23.5 teaches students how to read and interpret graphic aids, such as tables, graphs, time lines, and maps.

FOCUS

Lesson Overview

Objective: To gain proficiency with graphic representations

Skills: interpreting tables; reading bar graphs and line graphs; reading time lines; using maps

Critical Thinking: synthesizing; categorizing; relating images to concepts; summarizing; comparing

Speaking and Listening: questioning; informal speaking

Bellringer

When students enter the classroom, have this assignment on the board: *On a sheet of paper, give directions on how to get to your house from school.*

Motivating Activity

Ask students if they wrote the directions to their house in words or if they made a map. Have volunteers explain why they gave directions the way they did. Then point out that sometimes it is simpler and more effective to explain things graphically instead of verbally. Write the number 255,000,000 on the board. Elicit from students that it represents two hundred and fifty-five million. Tell them that is about how many people live in the United States. Write the numbers 26,000,000, and 4,000,000 on the board and explain that they represent the populations of Morocco and Nicaragua, respectively. Ask students which of these countries has the most people. Which has the least? What would be the easiest way to tell someone about these population figures?

Teacher's Classroom Resources

For Lesson 23.5, the following resources can be used for planning, instruction, practice, assessment, reinforcement, or evaluation.

Teaching Tools
Lesson Plans

Blackline Masters
Thinking and Study Skills, pp. 30–32, 35–40

Unit Assessment

Tests with Answer Key
Unit 23 Mastery Test, pp. 91–92

Test Generator
Unit 23 Mastery Test

You may wish to administer the Unit 23 Mastery Test at this point.

TEACH

Guided Practice

L2 Formulating Questions

Divide the class into groups with two sets of partners. Have one pair in each group formulate at least three questions based on the television viewing graph. (For example, How many hours a week do children ages six to eleven watch television?) The second pair should formulate questions about the United States population graph. The pairs will then try to answer each other's questions. The groups should conclude by discussing their questions and answers.

L1 Graphing Knowledge

To make the use of graphs more accessible, help students create their own graph. On the board draw the bottom axis and label it "Students." Draw the side axis and label it "Height." Mark height in six-inch segments, explaining what you are marking. Ask for volunteers to tell how tall they are, or if possible, measure them in the classroom. Have volunteers write their names on the bottom axis and draw lines up from their names to the level of the number representing their heights. When all volunteers are finished, discuss what they have recorded on the graph (for example, Yoko is taller than Reggie; Ken and Elizabeth are the same height).

Graphs

Graphs always deal with numbers of some kind. They can show the same kinds of information that tables show. However, graphs organize information differently.

Bar Graphs Numbers in a bar graph appear as bars. The bar graph below shows the number of hours young people spend watching television. Notice how easily you can see the highest bar and find the group that watches the most television. You also can easily compare the viewing times of all the groups.

To find the number a bar represents, use the scale along the left side. You can see that three of the groups watch close to 15 hours of television per week. Which group watches about 19 hours per week?

The left side contains a scale divided into hours.

The height of each bar shows the amount of time one group watches television.

Labels along the bottom identify the groups. Each bar stands for one group.

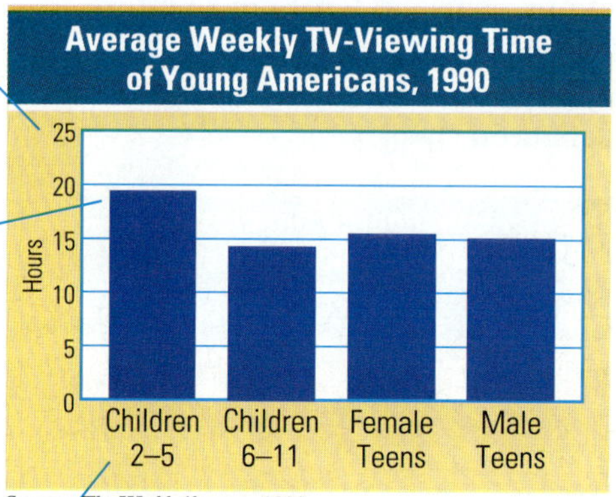

Source: *The World Almanac*, 1992

Line Graphs A line graph shows changes in numbers or amounts over a period of time. For example, a line graph can show the rise and fall of daily temperatures. A line graph can also show any other numbers that change over time. Read the title of the line graph below. What does it show?

*The **graph scale** is along the left side. Since the numbers are in millions, 150 stands for 150 million people.*

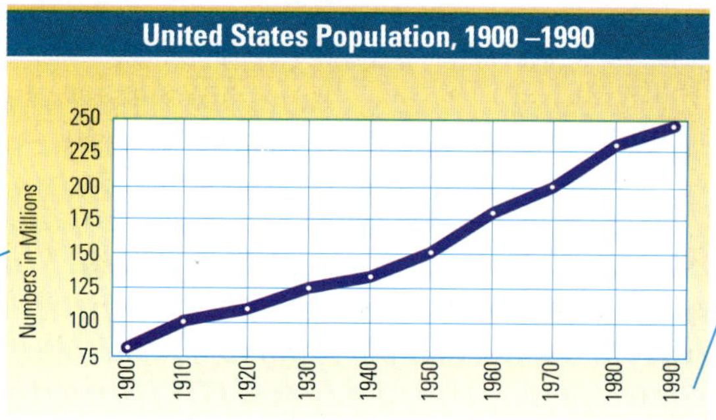

Source: *Statistical Abstract of the United States*, 1991

The years are shown along the bottom of the graph. In what year did the U.S. population go over 200 million?

Enabling Strategies

LEP Using a Time Line

Students from other cultural backgrounds who have recently moved to the United States may not be familiar with the events shown on the time line. You might have them make a time line of events related to their country of origin.

Time Lines

A time line shows events that happened over a period of time. Time is shown along a line or sometimes a bar. The amount of time shown on a time line can be anything from seconds to eons. A time line allows you to see easily the order in which the events occurred. You can also see how much time passed between certain events. On the time line below, for example, which two events occurred closest in time?

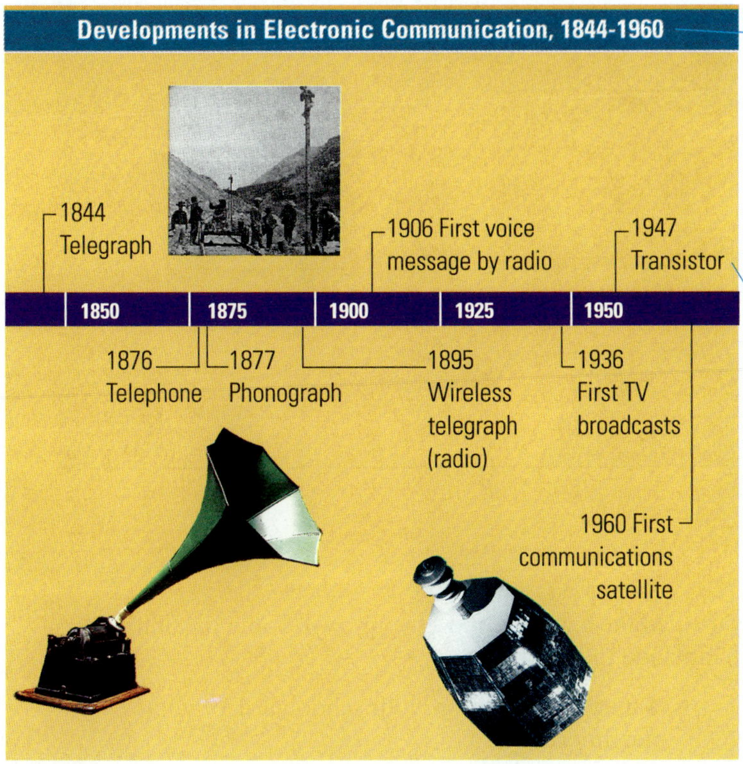

The title shows the subject of the time line. It also may include the dates covered.

Space between events shows the amount of time that passed between them. Which two events came closest together?

Maps

Maps show some part of the earth's surface. The area shown can be as small as a playground or as large as the entire world.

TEACH

Guided Practice

L3 Exploring Careers

Ask students to describe jobs in which a person might rely on tables and graphs. How would people in those professions use them? (A meteorologist might use a graph to record changes in temperature or rainfall; a truck driver might use a chart to record times and locations of deliveries; a nurse might use a chart to record a patient's temperature, pulse, and other vital signs.) Encourage students to choose a profession and create a "mock-up" of a table, chart, or graph that would be used in a work setting.

Independent Practice

Skills Practice

Thinking and Study Skills, pp. 30–32, 35–40

Visual Thinking

Making a Time Line

After students have looked at the time line on this page, tell them to make their own time lines that focus on a topic of interest to them. An individual's time line might show the history of a favorite sports team, the development of a musical ability, a scouting career, volunteer work, a hobby, or another area of that person's life.

PRACTICE AND ASSESS

Evaluation Guidelines: Exercise 5

The graphic aids will vary but should demonstrate a mastery of the concepts and skills introduced in the lesson.

CLOSE

Ask students to find examples of tables, graphs, time lines, and maps in their Social Studies textbooks. Discuss the various types of information shown. Ask students what other ways they might visually show dates and events (lists, charts).

Maps are drawn to scale. That is, a certain distance on the map stands for a certain distance on the earth. Maps usually contain a line or bar scale that you can use to measure distances. Use the scale on the map to see if you can tell the distance between New York City and Chicago.

*A **map key** explains the symbols and sometimes the colors used on the map. How many U.S. cities have more than 1 million people?*

*The **top line** of the map scale shows miles. The bottom line shows kilometers.*

Exercise 5

Make a graphic aid of your own. Some possibilities include the following:

- a map of your room, your schoolyard, or your neighborhood
- a bar graph that compares the heights or weights of four or five classmates
- a line graph showing the batting averages of your favorite baseball player over several years
- a time line of your life or the life of a historical figure you admire

Connections Across the Curriculum

History

The oldest known map was made about 2300 B.C. It is a small clay tablet from Babylonia that appears to show a man's estate in a valley. The Egyptians made maps as early as 1300 B.C. One of the few remaining ancient Egyptian maps shows the route from the Nile Valley to the gold mines of Nubia. The Greeks made maps in the early 300s B.C. and were among the first to realize that the earth is spherical. The Romans used maps for taxing land and to assist in military campaigns.

UNIT
24 Taking Tests

24.1 Tips for Test Taking

"There will be a test on Friday." Do those words throw you into a panic or are you usually well-prepared? Either way, you can probably improve your test-taking skills. This lesson will help you learn a few strategies for taking tests.

Preparing for a Test

Preparing for a test can get you off to a good start. Here are some simple but effective strategies:

- Allow plenty of time to study. Don't wait until the day before the test. Several short review sessions are better than one long one.
- Gather information about the test. When will it be given? How long will it take? Exactly what material will it cover?
- Review material from your textbook, class notes, homework, quizzes, and handouts.
- Make up some sample test questions, and answer them.
- Study with a partner or a small group. Quiz one another on topics you think the test will cover.

Setting the Purpose

Lesson 24.1 teaches students about strategies for improving test-taking skills.

FOCUS

Lesson Overview

Objective: To improve test-taking skills
Skills: preparing for a test; planning your time
Critical Thinking: evaluating
Speaking and Listening: discussing

Bellringer

When students enter the classroom, have this assignment on the board: *List five hints for doing well on a test.*

TEACH

Guided Practice

L2 Getting Ready for a Test
Ask students to think about a test that they have coming up, in any subject. Have them write down the subject and what the test is on. Then have them write the strategies from the list on page 545 that they think will help them prepare for it. Now ask students to be as specific as possible: When will they have time to study? Can they arrange to study with classmates? What types of materials will they need to look at? Have them write a few questions that they think might be on the test.

Teacher's Classroom Resources

For Lesson 24.1, the following resources can be used for planning, instruction, practice, assessment, reinforcement, or evaluation.

Teaching Tools
Lesson Plans

Blackline Masters
Standardized Test Practice
Thinking and Study Skills, pp. 41–42

Unit Assessment

Tests with Answer Key
Unit 24 Pretest, pp. 93–94

Test Generator
Unit 24 Pretest

You may wish to administer the Unit 24 Pretest at this point.

PRACTICE AND ASSESS

Evaluation Guidelines: Exercise 1

Statements 1, 2, 5, 6, 8, and 9 are bad advice. Examples of rewritten sentences follow. Accept other valid revisions.

1. Don't put off studying until the night before you take a test.
2. Study alone, with a friend, or with a small group.
5. Use your textbook to review for a test.
6. Save the difficult questions for last.
8. Answer the easy questions first.
9. Guess at answers only if guessing is not penalized.

Independent Practice

Skills Practice

Standardized Test Practice
Thinking and Study Skills, pp. 41–42

CLOSE

Ask students to tell which tips for preparing for a test and planning their time they already knew and have used. Also ask students to discuss which new tips they think will be most helpful to incorporate into their test-taking strategies. See if they have other test-taking tips they would like to share with classmates.

Planning Your Time

You normally have a limited amount of time to take a test. Using your time wisely will help you do your best work. Before you begin, plan a general amount of time for each section of the test.

Tips for Using Time Well

- Read all test directions carefully. Understanding the directions will keep you from making mistakes.
- Answer the easier items first. By skipping the hard items, you give yourself time to answer all the easy ones.
- In whatever time is left, return to the items you skipped. Answer them as best you can. If you won't be penalized for doing so, guess.
- Save some time to check your answers before you turn in your test.

Exercise 1

The following statements give advice on taking a test. Which statements give *bad* advice? Write their numbers. Then rewrite each statement so that it gives *good* advice.

1. Do all your studying for the test the night before you take the test.
2. Always study alone for a test.
3. Review your homework and quizzes.
4. Try to learn what the test will cover.
5. Try to study without using your textbook.
6. Always avoid answering any of the difficult test questions.
7. Read the test directions carefully.
8. Answer every test question in order.
9. Never guess at an answer.
10. Check your answers carefully before turning in your test.

Thinking Skills

Visual Thinking

Ask a small group of volunteers to make a poster on "How to Prepare for a Test" or on "How to Plan Your Time on a Test." Remind students that these strategies can be used for tests in any of their classes. You might suggest that the students use color and illustrations to highlight key ideas. When the poster is complete, display it in the classroom so that students can refer to it.

24.2 Test Items

The best way to prepare for a test, of course, is to learn the material that will be tested. You can also help yourself by mastering the different types of test items.

True-False Items

A true-false item gives only two choices, true or false. An answer is true only if the *entire* statement is true. If any part of the statement is false, you must mark it *false*. Look at the statement below.

The earth circles the sun once each day.

The earth does circle the sun. However, it does so once each year, *not each* day. *The statement is false.*

Multiple-Choice Items

In a multiple-choice item you must answer a question or complete a sentence. You do so by picking the *best* response out of the three or four given.

What is included in our solar system?
a. the earth and the sun
b. all the sun's planets
c. asteroids and moons
d. all of the above

Item a *seems true, but be sure to read all the choices before answering.*

Reading all responses is especially important when one choice is "all of the above" or "none of the above." The answer is d.

Matching Items

In the matching test format, you have two groups or lists of items. You must match each item from the first group with an item in the second group. Complete the easy matches first. That will leave fewer items to choose from when you get to the difficult ones.

Setting the Purpose

Lesson 24.2 teaches students to identify different types of test items and presents specific strategies for approaching each type.

FOCUS

Lesson Overview

Objective: To become familiar with test items
Skills: applying appropriate strategies for solving true-false; multiple choice; and matching items
Critical Thinking: evaluating
Speaking and Listening: discussing

Bellringer

When students enter the classroom, have this assignment on the board: *Write down as many different kinds of test questions as you can think of.*

Motivating Activity

Survey student responses to the Bellringer activity. Have students give examples of each type of item and name situations in which those items are likely to occur.

Teacher's Classroom Resources

For Lesson 24.2, the following resources can be used for planning, instruction, practice, or reinforcement.

Teaching Tools
Lesson Plans

Blackline Masters
Standardized Test Practice
Thinking and Study Skills, pp. 41–42

TEACH

Guided Practice

L2 Scanning Questions

Point out to students that when they take reading comprehension tests, it often helps to look at the questions before reading the selection. That way students will know what they should look for as they read. Tell them to practice this strategy as they work on Exercise 2.

PRACTICE AND ASSESS

Answers: Exercise 2

1. false
2. b
3. 1. b; 2. a; 3. c

Independent Practice

Skills Practice

Standardized Test Practice
Thinking and Study Skills, pp. 41–42

CLOSE

Ask students which types of test items they find easy and which they find difficult. Encourage them to discuss why this might be. Do they have better strategies for a certain type of test item? Have students make up test questions on a topic that interests them (for example, cars or music). They can exchange tests with a partner for extra practice on any problem areas. Remind them to "talk through" the strategies they use to answer each question.

Complete the items you are sure of first. Doing so will increase your chance of choosing correctly from the remaining items.

Notice that column 2 has more items than column 1. One item in column 2 will not be used.

Match each river with its continent.

1. Rhine River	a. North America
2. Nile River	b. South America
3. Mississippi River	c. Africa
4. Amazon River	d. Asia
	e. Europe

Exercise 2

Read the passage below. Then use your test-taking skills to answer the questions.

Kilauea is one of the most active volcanoes in the Hawaiian Islands. Since 1983 it has erupted dozens of times. When Kilauea erupts, it rarely explodes. Instead, fast-running lava pours out from cracks and vents. Sometimes it shoots up in fountains hundreds of feet high. Usually the lava runs down the sides of the mountain and cools. These layers of lava have formed Mt. Kilauea's long, gentle slopes. When the lava reaches the ocean, it quickly cools into rugged black rock.

1. Kilauea is an explosive volcano. True or false?
2. The lava from Kilauea
   a. forms mile-high fountains.
   b. has created the mountain's gentle slopes.
   c. is driven back by the ocean.
   d. none of the above
3. Match the terms in column 1 with the descriptions in column 2.

1. Kilauea	**a.** a sudden release of lava
2. eruption	**b.** a volcano
3. lava	**c.** melted rock

Speaking and Listening

Telling Tales

Write on the chalkboard the titles of some familiar folk or fairy tales, such as "The Ugly Duckling," "Beauty and the Beast," and "The Three Little Pigs." Call on one or more volunteers to retell briefly one of the tales. Then have students help you write several true-false, multiple choice, and matching test items related to the tale. Write these items on the board, and then call on students to give the answers. Ask them to discuss the strategies they used to arrive at each answer.

24.3 Standardized Tests

In addition to classroom tests, you will sometimes take standardized tests. Students all over the country take these tests.

Taking Standardized Tests

There are different kinds of standardized tests. Some tests measure your abilities or how well you think. Other tests measure how much you have learned in such subjects as English, math, and science. Taking a standardized test is a chance for you to find out about your abilities or some of the things you do best. You probably would like to do as well as you can on such a test. The following tips can help you.

Tips for Taking Standardized Tests

1. Sleep well the night before the test. Eat well in the morning.
2. Try to arrive early for the test. Relax.
3. Listen carefully as directions are given before the test. Ask questions if you don't understand the directions.
4. Complete all the easy items first. Leave hard items until the end.
5. On standardized tests you will mark your answers on a separate answer sheet. Compare the numbers for test items with the numbers on your answer sheet. Be sure your answers are in the right place.
6. If you can, find out whether points are subtracted for wrong answers. If they are not, you should guess at questions you aren't sure of.

Analogies

Do you ever think about how the meanings of words compare? For example, *stop* and *go* have opposite meanings. Analogy items test how well you can compare the meanings of words. You can improve your test scores by practicing analogies.

Setting the Purpose

Lesson 24.3 teaches students tips for taking standardized tests, emphasizing strategies for approaching analogy items.

FOCUS

Lesson Overview

Objective: To become familiar with standardized tests
Skills: taking standardized tests, doing well on analogy items
Critical Thinking: analyzing
Speaking and Listening: discussing

Bellringer

When students enter the classroom, have this assignment on the board: *Think of a standardized test you have taken. Write down three kinds of problems that were on the test.*

TEACH

Guided Practice

L2 Creating Analogies

Direct students to create several analogy items like those in Exercise 3. Each student will then meet with another student to exchange and complete each other's analogies. If some analogies are particularly difficult to solve, write them on the board. Encourage other class members to solve the analogies. Ask some students to explain their solutions to the class.

Cross-reference: Vocabulary

For more information on the use of synonyms and antonyms, refer students to Lesson 22.4, pp. 515–516.

Teacher's Classroom Resources

For Lesson 24.3, the following resources can be used for planning, instruction, practice, assessment, reinforcement or evaluation.

Teaching Tools
Lesson Plans

Blackline Masters
Standardized Test Practice
Thinking and Study Skills, pp. 41–42

Unit Assessment

Tests with Answer Key
Unit 24 Mastery Test, pp. 95–96

Test Generator
Unit 24 Mastery Test

You may wish to administer the Unit 24 Mastery Test at this point.

PRACTICE AND ASSESS

Answers: Exercise 3

1. b
2. b
3. c
4. c

Independent Practice

Skills Practice

Standardized Test Practice
Thinking and Study Skills, pp. 41–42

CLOSE

Ask students to discuss how classroom tests and standardized tests are similar and how they are different. Which type of test do most students prefer to take? Why? Ask students to discuss which of the tips on page 549 they usually follow when taking standardized tests. Which others do they think would help them improve their performance on such tests? Encourage them to explore how these tips could work for them.

First figure out the relationship in the first pair of words. Eyes are used for seeing.

Then complete the second pair with the same kind of relationship. You use eyes to see and ears to hear. The correct answer is b.

A typical analogy item shows one relationship and asks you to complete another. To start with, you need to know how to read analogy items. They are often written as follows.

```
eyes: seeing:: ears:________

a. smelling    b. hearing    c. touching
```

The single colon (:) stands for "are to" or "is to." The double colon (::) stands for "as." So you would read the top line as "eyes are to seeing as ears are to ___."

Common Types of Analogies	Examples
Antonyms One word means the opposite of the other.	light : dark
Synonyms Two words have the same general meaning.	tired : sleepy
Use The thing named by one word uses or is used by the other.	rider : horse
Cause and effect One item causes or results from the other.	cold : shiver

Exercise 3

Write the letter of the answer that correctly completes each analogy.

1. down : up :: short : ___
   a. heavy **b.** tall **c.** far **d.** tiny
2. calm : still :: hurry : ___
   a. peaceful **b.** rush **c.** hurt **d.** yet
3. sweeper : broom :: writer : ___
   a. artist **b.** reader **c.** pen **d.** work
4. adult : child :: dog : ___
   a. young **b.** baby **c.** puppy **d.** bark

Enabling Strategies

LEP Following Tips and Asking Questions

Students who lack confidence in their English skills may be especially intimidated by standardized tests. Language is likely to be an added burden for these students. Emphasize the importance of following the tips listed in the chart on page 549. Explain that it is particularly important to ask questions if they do not understand all the directions given before the test. Students could also work as partners to practice analogy test items.

UNIT

25

Listening and Speaking

25.1 Listening

Imagine yourself taking a trip and using a map for directions. How would you know where to go if a part of your map were missing? Traveling without a complete set of directions can be difficult. The same is true in listening. You must listen for *all* the important "road signs." Miss one, and you may not understand what you hear.

Following Instructions

You often receive instructions in class. Understanding exactly what your teacher expects of you begins with listening to instructions. The following suggestions can help you improve your listening skills.

Listening to Instructions in Class

1. First make sure you understand what you are listening for. Are you receiving instructions for homework or for a test? What you listen for depends upon the type of instructions being given.
2. Think about what you are hearing, and keep your eyes on the speaker. This will help you stay focused on the important points.
3. Listen for word clues the speaker is using. Examples of word clues are expressions such as *above all, the most important,* and *the three basic parts.* These clues can help you identify important points you should remember.
4. Take notes on what you hear. Write down only the most important parts of the instructions.
5. If you don't understand something, ask questions. Then, if you're still unsure about the instructions, repeat them aloud to your teacher to receive correction on any key points you've missed.

Teacher's Classroom Resources

For Lesson 25.1, the following resources can be used for planning, instruction, practice, assessment, reinforcement, or evaluation.

Teaching Tools
Lesson Plans

Blackline Masters
Speaking and Listening Activities, pp. 6–11, 17–18
Thinking and Study Skills, pp. 33–34

Unit Assessment

Tests with Answer Key
Unit 25 Pretest, pp. 97–98

Test Generator
Unit 25 Pretest

You may wish to administer the Unit 25 Pretest at this point.

Setting the Purpose

Lesson 25.1 teaches students the importance of good listening skills. It also teaches them how note-taking can be used as a listening aid.

FOCUS

Lesson Overview

Objective: To improve listening skills
Skills: listening to instructions; taking notes
Critical Thinking: evaluating; determining important information
Speaking and Listening: listening to instructions; discussing

Bellringer

When students enter the classroom, have this assignment on the board: *List five situations when it would be important for you to listen carefully to instructions or information.*

TEACH

Guided Practice

L2 Listening to Instructions

Draw a simple design on a piece of paper. Have one student study the design and then give instructions to the class on how to draw it. Suggest that other students try to duplicate the original design, using the instructions given. Then have them compare their drawings to the original design. Ask students why there are differences in their drawings. Were the instructions clear and complete? Did students listen carefully to the instructions?

PRACTICE AND ASSESS

Evaluation Guidelines: Exercise 1

Answers will vary. Responses should reflect an understanding of the listening and note-taking skills introduced in the lesson. Each student should

- take brief notes on the program's key ideas
- include graphic aids, if useful
- present an effective summary of the program's content
- use descriptive words and phrases that help group members "see" the program

Independent Practice

Skills Practice

Speaking and Listening Activities, pp. 6–11, 17–18

Thinking and Study Skills, pp. 33–34

CLOSE

Explain to students that part of being a good listener is letting the speaker know that you are really listening. Invite students to list ways to listen actively, such as making eye contact, nodding your head, and asking good questions.

Taking Notes

Taking notes as you listen is a good way to sort out main ideas and supporting details. The process of taking notes also helps you remember what you've heard. You may already have your own way of taking notes. Here are a few useful note-taking tips you may want to keep in mind:

- **Key ideas** are the ones you want to remember. Listen for them.
- **Don't be in a hurry** to start writing. It can take time to complete an idea. Make sure the speaker has completed a key idea before you write it down.
- **Keep listening** as you take notes. Stay alert so that you don't miss important information as you write.
- **Keep your notes brief.** Don't try to take down everything the speaker says. You don't need to write complete sentences. A few words are usually enough to help you remember a key idea. Remember, your notes are for you. All you need to write is something that will jog your memory later.
- **Use graphic aids** to organize information clearly. Charts, pictures, tables, or even arrows and lines can help you understand and remember how points are related. You can review the information about graphic aids on pages 541–544.

Exercise 1

Working with a small group, pick several programs to watch on television. Choose different types of programs, such as news, comedy, drama, science, and sports. Each group member should watch one program and take notes on it. Afterward, share with the group your notes on the program you watched. Try to help the group members "see" the program you describe for them.

Enabling Strategies

LEP Summarizing

Students who are just learning English may have difficulty understanding and summarizing verbal information. You might suggest that as they listen to people speak they notice nonverbal as well as verbal cues. Demonstrate examples of nonverbal communication. Show how stress and intonation can change meaning. Ask students to suggest their own examples of nonverbal cues.

25.2 Informal Speaking

Did you know that you're already an expert in at least one type of public speaking—informal speaking? Most of your talking with other people is informal. There are many ways to speak informally. Examples include talking with friends, speaking in small groups in class, and communicating on the telephone.

Using the Telephone

When you call someone on the telephone, always identify yourself right away. Don't make the person on the other end try to guess who you are. You might say, "Is Gabriel there? This is Maria calling."

Here are some more tips for using the telephone:

- Speak clearly. Make sure the person on the other end can understand you easily. If a listener keeps asking you to repeat what you're saying, you may be mumbling.
- If the person you called is not there, try to leave a message. First ask if you can do so. Then give the person who answered time to get a pencil and paper.
- Speaking clearly becomes especially important if you must leave a message on an answering machine. Remember, the machine can't ask you to repeat something.
- Deliver your message clearly. Give your name and your phone number. Then tell what information you'd like to leave for the person you've called. Try to make your message short and to the point.
- Be polite. Good telephone communication depends on how willing the other person is to listen to you. Good manners can help keep the other person interested.

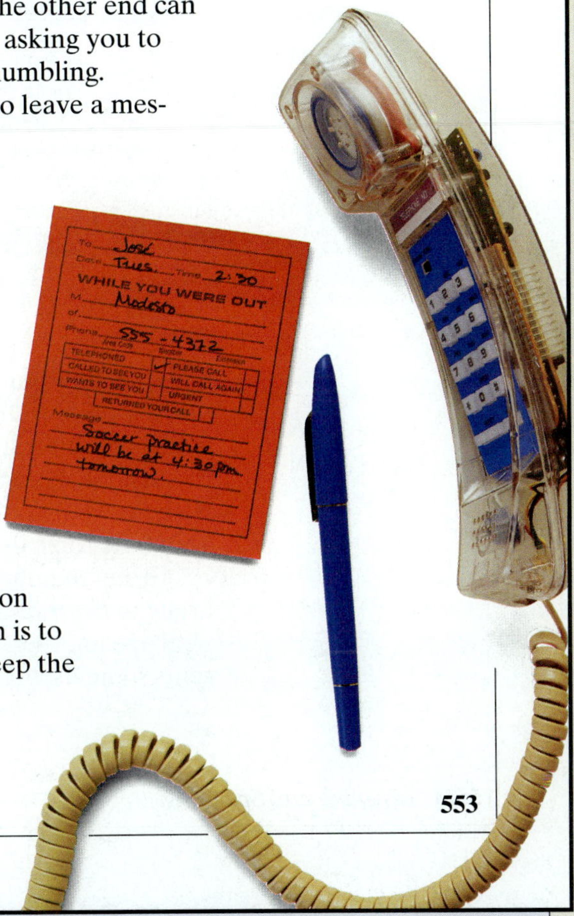

Setting the Purpose

Lesson 25.2 teaches students how to give and receive telephone messages, how to give clear directions, and how to participate in an informal discussion.

FOCUS

Lesson Overview

Objective: To become familiar with informal speaking

Skills: using the telephone; giving directions; taking part in informal discussions

Critical Thinking: clarifying; evaluating

Speaking and Listening: leaving and taking messages; giving directions; discussing

Bellringer

When students enter the classroom, have this assignment on the board: *Think of five informal, or casual, conversations you recently had either on the phone or in person. List the subject or purpose of each conversation.*

Motivating Activity

Ask students to imagine they are new to the school and unfamiliar with the layout. Invite volunteers to give directions to the main office, library, gym, cafeteria, and so forth. Ask other students to evaluate the directions. Were the directions clear and complete?

Teacher's Classroom Resources

For Lesson 25.2, the following resources can be used for planning, instruction, practice, or reinforcement.

Teaching Tools
Lesson Plans

Blackline Masters
Speaking and Listening Activities, pp. 6–11, 17–18
Thinking and Study Skills, pp. 33–34

TEACH

Guided Practice

L2 Participating in Discussions

Encourage the students to get involved in discussion. Stress that in an informal discussion everyone's opinion is valid; there may be differences of opinion, but everyone's ideas should be listened to. Ask volunteers to suggest do's and don'ts of participating in a discussion, such as "Do be an active listener," "Do ask questions," "Don't interrupt."

L1 Keeping Direction Steps in Order

Students may need suggestions for ordering steps when giving directions. Suggest that they actually go through the steps needed to complete a process, such as entering a computer program, setting up a telephone answering machine, or programming a VCR. Have students complete the first step, and then write what they did on a piece of paper. Instruct them to follow this procedure until they complete all steps.

Giving Directions

When someone asks you for directions, it's important to give detailed and exact information. You want to be sure that the person listening understands exactly what you're saying. The examples in the following chart will help you understand how to give clear directions.

Giving Directions		
Unclear	**Clear**	**Remember to**
Go a few blocks, then turn, and go two more blocks.	Go straight ahead for three blocks. Then turn left, and go on for two more blocks.	**Be precise.**
Mix the eggs and milk and the flour.	First mix the eggs and milk. Next sift the flour, and then combine it with the eggs and milk.	**Use proper ordering.**
Graham stopped by. He wants you to meet him later.	Graham stopped by at noon. He wants you to meet him in the library at about seven tonight.	**Give complete information.**
That's how you do it. Now you try it.	Before you try it yourself, do you have any questions about what I've said?	**Make sure you've been understood.**

Taking Part in an Informal Discussion

A small-group meeting in class is one example of an informal discussion. Other examples include planning a party with friends or discussing vacation plans with your family. Informal discussions should be relaxed. You usually don't have to prepare for what you'll say. You should, however, be ready to talk about the topic the group wishes to discuss.

Group members should express their own opinions and argue in favor of them. Members should feel free to disagree with one another, but in a polite way. The following chart presents some useful tips on taking part in an informal discussion.

Connections Across the Curriculum

History

The telephone was invented in 1876 by Alexander Graham Bell. The first commercial telephone exchange opened in New Haven, Connecticut, on January 28, 1878. According to the *Guinness Book of Records*, the United States has the greatest number of telephones, more than 130 million. The United States also holds the record for the greatest number of calls made in a year, over 400 billion.

Tips for Informal Discussions

1. Be sure you've listened carefully to what other people have said. To respond well, you should have a good idea about what points have already been made.
2. Decide what ideas you want to get across when you speak. You need not have the wording completely planned ahead of time.
3. Help the discussion move forward. Make sure each comment adds something important to the topic.
4. Take turns listening and speaking without interrupting other speakers.
5. Speak in a normal tone of voice. Feel free to use gestures to stress a point you want to make strongly. The idea in informal speaking is to express yourself as naturally as you can.
6. Accept and evaluate criticism of your ideas.

Exercise 2

Working in pairs, take turns pretending to speak to each other on the telephone. Each caller should leave a short, clear message after asking for someone who is not available. The person receiving the call should write an accurate, complete message. Calls might be made to the dentist, to a friend, to a grandparent or other relative, or to a teacher or instructor.

Exercise 3

Work with a small group. Use a topic from the list below or one of your own choosing and hold a ten-minute discussion on it.

- Skateboards at school
- Eliminating the long summer vacation in schools
- Watching television versus reading a book

PRACTICE AND ASSESS

Evaluation Guidelines: Exercise 2

Answers will vary. The caller should
- identify him- or herself immediately
- speak clearly and politely
- ask if he or she can leave a message
- give a brief, clear message that includes his or her name and phone number

The listener should
- speak clearly and politely
- record the message clearly and accurately
- repeat the caller's name and phone number to verify their accuracy

Evaluation Guidelines: Exercise 3

Answers will vary. In group discussions, each student should
- listen carefully in order to avoid repeating points already made
- make comments that move the discussion forward
- speak naturally and expressively
- listen politely to other members without interrupting
- accept criticism of his or her ideas

Independent Practice

Skills Practice

Speaking and Listening Activities, pp. 6–11, 17–18
Thinking and Study Skills, pp. 33–34

Enabling Strategies

LEP Following Directions

Many students acquiring English can be helped when giving or listening to directions if they pay attention to some basic elements: verbs (*draw, write*), transition (*next, then*), directional words (*above, left*) and non-verbal communication. Have students discuss these tips and then practice giving and following simple directions (for example, how to get to the principal's office, how to draw a cube.) Ask students to take notes when they are listening and provide non-verbal clues when they are speaking.

Setting the Purpose

Lesson 25.3 teaches students how to prepare an oral report. It also provides students with hints for effectively presenting an oral report.

FOCUS

Lesson Overview

Objective: To become familiar with giving oral reports
Skills: preparing and presenting oral reports
Critical Thinking: determining main points
Speaking and Listening: oral reporting

Bellringer

When students enter the classroom, have this assignment on the board: *Your friend is nervous about having to present an oral report tomorrow. List five pieces of advice you would give so that your friend will be better prepared and less nervous.*

TEACH

Guided Practice

L2 Preparing to Speak

During prewriting, work with students to narrow their topics. They should be able to state in a sentence what they will cover in the report. Before students revise reports, remind them that speakers usually use shorter sentences than writers do, and that they should include transition words to show how they organized their material. These techniques help listeners follow the main idea of an oral report. Suggest that students practice speaking from their notes.

25.3 How to Give an Oral Report

Speaking in front of an audience can be exciting. You can make sure your talk goes smoothly by taking care as you prepare it. Good planning also will help your audience gain the most from what you say.

Preparing an Oral Report

The following five-step plan can help you prepare and deliver an oral report. You'll find the plan familiar. It's very much like the one you use to do a written report.

1. Prewriting Decide on your topic. Make sure it's narrow enough to cover in a short oral report. Do research, take notes, and outline as you would for a written report.

2. Drafting Write out your report just as you'd like to deliver it orally. Let your thoughts flow, but keep to your outline. Make sure all the details help support your main ideas.

3. Revising Review what you've written. Do your ideas flow from one to another? Is there a better way to organize your material? Is it the right length? Does it need revision for style? Rework your draft as needed. Keep reworking it until you're satisfied it's right.

Teacher's Classroom Resources

For Lesson 25.3, the following resources can be used for planning, instruction, practice, assessment, reinforcement, or evaluation.

Teaching Tools
Lesson Plans

Blackline Masters
Speaking and Listening Activities, pp. 6–11, 17–18
Thinking and Study Skills, pp. 33–34

Unit Assessment
Tests with Answer Key, Unit 25 Mastery Test, pp. 99–100

Test Generator
Unit 25 Mastery Test

You may wish to administer the Unit 25 Mastery Test at this point.

4. Practicing Practice giving your report in front of a mirror. Try not to read from your written copy. Use it only as notes for your talk. You might ask a friend or relative to listen to you and offer suggestions. You can also tape-record your talk.

5. Presenting Relax! If you've prepared well, you can trust that your oral report will go smoothly.

Presenting an Oral Report

Actually, it's not unusual to feel a bit nervous when speaking before an audience. Even well-known actors feel nervous, no matter how often they've performed. Here are some suggestions for giving an oral report.

Tips for Effective Speaking

1. Speak slowly, clearly, and in a normal tone of voice. Raise your voice a bit or use gestures to stress important points.
2. Pause a few seconds after making an important point. This lets your audience think about what you've said.
3. Use words that will help your audience picture what you're talking about. Visual aids such as pictures, graphs, charts, and maps can also help make your information clear to the audience.
4. Stay in contact with your audience. Make sure your eyes move from person to person in the group you're addressing.

Exercise 4

Work with a small group. Each member should select a topic and write a two- to three-minute oral report about it. Be sure to narrow your topic before you begin. Practice giving your talk before your group. Allow group members to suggest improvements. Group members may give their oral reports later before the entire class.

PRACTICE AND ASSESS

Evaluation Guidelines: Exercise 4

Answers will vary. Oral reports should be evaluated according to the following criteria:

- topic is narrow enough to cover in a short oral report
- all details support the main idea
- ideas flow logically
- report is presented clearly and in a normal voice
- speaker uses voice, gestures, and visual aids to make points clear
- speaker maintains eye contact with the audience

Independent Practice

Skills Practice

Speaking and Listening Activities, pp. 6–11, 17–18

Thinking and Study Skills, pp. 33–34

CLOSE

Have students explain in writing what they would do to prepare a short oral report on a topic such as "How to Listen to Instructions" or "How to Use the Telephone." You may want to have volunteers use their plans to give a short, impromptu report.

Enabling Strategies

LEP Practicing for a Report

Encourage students who are acquiring English to practice their oral reports with a more fluent partner. Students should continue to practice until they feel comfortable with their delivery.

L3 Videotaping for Review

If possible, videotape students as they present their oral reports. Students can review the tapes within their groups and use them to make constructive criticisms, emphasize effective speaking skills, and adjust their own presentations.

Index

A

B

C

D

E

F

G

H

I

J

L

M

N

O

P

Q

T

U

V

W

Y

Acknowledgments (continued from page iv)

Text

10 From *Breaking Ice* by Terry McMillan, Preface by John Edgar Wideman. Copyright © 1990 by Terry McMillan, Preface, copyright © 1990 by John Edgar Wideman. Used by permission of Penguin, a division of Penguin Books USA Inc. **18** From *The Ups and Downs of Carl Davis III* by Rosa Guy. Copyright © 1989 by Rosa Guy. Published by Delacorte Press. **22** *William Carlos Williams: The Collected Poems of William Carlos Williams, 1909–1939, vol. I.* Copyright © 1938 by New Directions Publishing Corporation. Reprinted by permission of New Directions Publishing Corp. **25** *William Carlos Williams: The Collected Poems of William Carlos Williams, 1909–1939, vol. I.* Copyright © 1938 by New Directions Publishing Corporation. Reprinted by permission of New Directions Publishing Corp. **27, 30** From *The Invisible Thread* by Yoshiko Uchida. Copyright © 1991. Used by permission of the publisher, Julian Messner, A Division of Silver Burdett Press, Simon & Schuster, Englewood Cliffs, NJ. **51** From *Meet the Authors and Illustrators: 60 Creators of Favorite Children's Books Talk About Their Work* by Deborah Kovacs and James Preller. Copyright © 1991. Published by Scholastic, Inc. **53** From *Root River Run* by David Kherdian. Copyright © 1984 by David Kherdian. Published by Carolrhoda Books, Inc. **64** From *The Complete Beginner's Guide to Backpacking* by Richard B. Lyttle. Copyright © 1975 by Richard B. Lyttle. Published by Doubleday & Company, Inc. **65** From *The Sierra Club Wayfinding Book* by Vicki McVey. Copyright © 1989 by Vicki McVey. Published by Little, Brown and Company. **68** Reprinted with the permission of Charles Scribner's Sons, an imprint of Macmillan Publishing Company from *The Yearling* by Marjorie Kinnan Rawlings. Copyright © 1938 Marjorie Kinnan Rawlings; copyright renewed © 1966 Norton Baskin. **81, 84** From *Coast to Coast* by Betsy Byars. Copyright © 1992 by Betsy Byars. Used by permission of Delacorte Press, a division of Bantam Doubleday Dell Publishing Group, Inc. **98, 99** From *Julie of the Wolves* by Jean Craighead George. Copyright © 1972 by Jean Craighead George. Published by HarperTrophy, a division of HarperCollins Publishers. **102** From *I Know Why the Caged Bird Sings* by Maya Angelou. Copyright © 1969 by Maya Angelou. Published by Bantam Books. Reprinted by permission of Random House, Inc. **106** From *Chitty Chitty Bang Bang: The Magical Car* by Ian Fleming. Text copyright © 1964 by Gildrose Productions Ltd. Reprinted by permission of Random House, Inc. **110** Reprinted with permission from *Great Days of the Circus,* Copyright © 1962 by American Heritage, a division of Forbes, Inc. **116** Reprinted with the permission of Macmillan Publishing Company from *Thunder Country* by Armstrong Sperry. Copyright © 1952 by Macmillan Publishing Company; copyright renewed 1980 by John A. Sperry and Susan S. Burns. **118** From *Nilda* by Nicholasa Mohr. Copyright © 1973 by Nicholasa Mohr. Published by Harper & Row, Publishers, Inc. **124, 126** From *Morning Girl* by Michael Dorris. Copyright © 1992 by Michael Dorris. Published by Hyperion Books. **141** From *A Place Called Ugly* by Avi. Copyright © 1981 by Avi Wortis. Published by Pantheon Books, a division of Random House. Reprinted by permission of McIntosh and Otis, Inc. **148** From "The Greatest Prank," from *In the Shade of the Chestnut Tree* by Benjamin Tene. Copyright © 1981. Published by The Jewish Publication Society of America. **152** Reprinted by permission of *Cricket* magazine, January 1987 Vol. 14, No. 5, © 1987 by Open Court Publishing Company. **156** © 1990 Kai Friese. Used by permission of Silver Burdett Press. All rights reserved. **161, 164** "The Jacket" from *Small Faces* by Gary Soto. Copyright © 1992. Published by Arte Publico Press. **176** From "How Does Michael Fly?" from *Chicago Tribune* Page 10, Section 4, Tuesday, February 27, 1990. **178** From *Eyewitness Books: Invention* by Lionel Bender. Copyright © 1991 by Dorling Kindersley Limited, London. Reprinted by permission of Alfred A. Knopf, Inc. **180** From *The Music of Africa* by Dr. Fred Warren with Lee Warren. Copyright © 1970 by Dr. Fred Warren and Lee Warren. Reprinted by permission of the publisher, Prentice Hall, A division of Simon & Schuster, Englewood Cliffs, NJ. **180** From *Eyewitness Books: Music.* Copyright © 1989 by Dorling Kindersley Limited, London. Reprinted by permission of Alfred A. Knopf, Inc. **188** From *Henri Matisse: Paper Cut-Outs* by Jack Cowart. Copyright © 1977. Published by The Saint Louis Art Museum and The Detroit Institute of Arts. **191** From "Sharks: Magnificent and Misunderstood" by Eugenie Clark from *National Geographic,* Vol. 160 No. 2, August, 1981. Copyright © 1981. Published by National Geographic Society. **199, 202** From "Bathing Elephants" from *Keepers and Creatures at the National Zoo* by Peggy Thomson. Copyright © 1988 by Peggy Thomson. Published by Thomas Y. Crowell. **216** From *101 Questions and Answers About Pets and People* by Dr. Ann Squire. Copyright © 1988 by Ann Squire. Published by Macmillan Publishing Company, a division of Macmillan, Inc. **224** From *Lovebirds, Lizards, & Llamas: Strange and Exotic Pets* by Leda Blumberg and Rhoda Blumberg. Copyright © 1986 by Rhoda and Leda Blumberg. Published by Julian Messner, A Division of Simon & Schuster, Inc. **233, 236** From *Keepers of the Earth: Native American Stories and Environmental Activities for Children* by Michael Caduto and Joseph Bruchac. Fulcrum Publishing, 350 Indiana St., #350, Golden, CO 80401. 303-277-1623. **274** From *A Tree Grows in Brooklyn* by Betty Smith. Copyright © 1981. Published by Buccaneer Books. **282** From *Nilda* by Nicholasa Mohr. Copyright © 1973 by Nicholasa Mohr. Published by Harper & Row, Publishers, Inc. **290** From *Black Star, Bright Dawn* by Scott O'Dell. Copyright © 1988 by Scott O'Dell. Reprinted by permission of Houghton Mifflin Company. All rights reserved. **296** From *Keepers and Creatures at the National Zoo* by Peggy Thomson. Copyright © 1988 by Peggy Thomson. Published by Thomas Y. Crowell. **316** From *All Stories Are Anansi's* retold by Harold Courlander. Copyright © 1988. Published by Holt. **324** From *Julie of the Wolves* by Jean Craighead George. Copyright © 1972 by Jean Craighead George. Published by HarperTrophy, a division of HarperCollins Publishers. **336** From *The Wise Old Woman* by Yoshiko Uchida. Copyright © 1994. Published by Macmillan. **342** From *Morning Girl* by Michael Dorris. Copyright © 1992 by Michael Dorris. Published by Hyperion Books. **352** From *Giants of Jazz* by Studs Terkel. Copyright © 1992. Published by Harper Collins. **358** From *The Invisible Thread* by Yoshiko Uchida. Copyright © 1991. Used by permission of the publisher, Julian Messner, A Division of Silver Burdett Press, Simon & Schuster, Englewood Cliffs, NJ. **370** From *Across Five Aprils* by Irene Hunt. Copyright © 1987. Published by Berkley Pub. **378** From *Coast to Coast* by Betsy Byars. Copyright © 1992 by Betsy Byars. Used by permission of Delacorte Press, a division of Bantam Doubleday Dell Publishing Group, Inc. **394** From *One Writer's Beginnings* by Eudora Welty. Copyright © 1984. Published by HUP. **402** Reprinted with permission from *Great Days of the Circus,* Copyright © 1962 by American Heritage, a division of Forbes, Inc. **410** From *John Muir* by Eden Force. Copyright © 1990 by Gallin House Press, Inc. Published by Silver Burdett Press, Inc., a division of Simon & Schuster, Inc., Englewood Cliffs, NJ. **418** From "Bathing Elephants" from *Keepers and Creatures at the National Zoo* by Peggy Thomson. Copyright © 1988 by Peggy Thomson. Published by Thomas Y. Crowell. **424** From *Exploring the Titanic* by Robert Ballard. Copyright © 1991. Published by Scholastic Inc. **428** From "The Jacket" from *Small Faces* by Gary Soto. Copyright © 1992. Published by Arte Publico Press. **446** From "A Secret for Two" by Quentin Reynolds from *Short Stories As You Like Them.* Copyright © 1940. Published by Harcourt Brace & Co. **452** From *Keepers of the Earth: Native American Stories and Environmental Activities for Children* by Michael Caduto and Joseph Bruchac. Fulcrum Publishing, 350 Indiana St., #350, Golden, CO 80401. 303-277-1623. **472** From *Harriet Tubman: The Moses of Her People* by Sarah Bradford. Copyright © 1961. Published by Citadel Press. **480** From *The Invisible Thread* by Yoshiko Uchida. Copyright © 1991. Used by permission of the publisher, Julian Messner, A Division of Silver Burdett Press, Simon & Schuster, Englewood Cliffs, NJ. **502** From *Roget's II: The New Thesaurus.* Copyright © 1984 by Houghton Mifflin Company.

Published by Berkley Books by arrangement with Houghton Mifflin Company. **503–504** From *Macmillan Dictionary for Students.* Copyright © 1977, 1973 by Macmillan Publishing Company. Published by Macmillan Publishing Company.

AL=Allan Landau; **AW**=Art Wise; **BET**=The Bettmann Archive, UPI/Bettmann; **RJB**= Ralph J. Brunke

Cover Co Rentmeester/The Image Bank; Aaron Haupt. **4** AW. **5** AW. **6** AW. **7** AW (l); Copyright © 1992 Mike Andrews/ Earth Scenes (r). **8** Copyright © Tobias Everke/Gamma-Liaison. **9** AW. **10** RJB. **11** RJB. **12** RJB. **13** Copyright © The Detroit Institute of Arts, City of Detroit Purchase. **14** RJB. **15** RJB. **16** RJB. **18** Copyright © 1992 Ralph A. Deinhold/Animals Animals. **20** RJB. **23** Nathaniel Bruns. **25** Copyright © Erich Lessing/Art Resource, NY. **26** Deborah Kahn-Kalas/Stock, Boston. **29** Jeff Persons/Stock, Boston. **31** Cezanne, Paul French, 1839–1906 *Farmhouse and Chestnut Trees at Jas-de-Bouffan* c. 1885. Oil on canvas 36 x 29 inches F.1969.38.2.P The Norton Simon Museum. **32** Copyright © 1980, Helen Oji. Collection of Prudential Insurance Co., Newark, NJ. **38** Courtesy National Railroad Passenger Corp. **39** RJB. **40** RJB (bl); Copyright © Charles O'Rear/West Light (t). **41** Courtesy National Railroad Passenger Corp. (b); RJB (t). **42** National Portrait Gallery, Smithsonian Institution, Washington D.C./Art Resource, NY. **43** David Barnes. **44** AL. **48** RJB. **50** RJB. **52** RJB. **56** RJB. **59** Courtesy of Tina Dunkley. **60** RJB. **61** RJB. **62** Historical Pictures/Stock Montage. **67** Private Collection, Photo courtesy of Joshua Baer & Company, Santa Fe. **68** Copyright © Steven Frame/Stock Boston. **69** RJB. **71** Joan Lebold Cohen. **72** AL. **74** RJB. **76** RJB. **80** FPG International. **83** FPG International. **85** Giraudon/Art Resource, NY. Copyright © 1992 ARS, New York/ADAGP, Paris. **86** Scala/Art Resource, NY. **89** AL. **92** Copyright © John Boulanger. **94** Copyright © John Boulanger (t); AW (b). **95** Copyright © Fritz P. Mueller. **96** AW. **97** AW. **98** Copyright © 1991 Lawrence Migdale/ Stock Boston. **99** Copyright © Matthew McVay/Stock Boston. **102** RJB. **103** Janice Fried. **104** AL. **105** Edition Leipzig, Germany. Courtesy of the Library of the Academy of Sciences of St. Petersburg, Russia. **106** Copyright © Thomas R. Fletcher/Stock Boston. **107** AL. **108** AL. **109** Tony Shafrazi Gallery, New York. Collection Mr. and Mrs. K. Scharf. **110** Culver Pictures. **113** Salander-O'Reilly Galleries. **114** Copyright © Jose Carrillo/Stock Boston. **118** AL. **119** RJB. **120** AL. **122** Copyright © Myrleen Ferguson/PhotoEdit. **125** Copyright © Stephan Frisch/Stock Boston. **127** Giraudon/Art Resource, NY. Copyright © 1992 ARS, New York/SPADEM, Paris. **129** Scala/Art Resource, NY. **131** RJB(l); AL(r). **134** Victoria Walker. **135** BET. **136** RJB. **137** RJB. **138** RJB (l); Copyright © Christiana Dittman/Rainbow (r). **139** RJB. **140** AL. **144** From the Collection of The Portland Art Museum, photo by Edward S. Curtis (b); Frans Lanting/Minden Pictures (t). **147** Asian Art & Architecture/Art Resource, NY. **148** Copyright © Bill Aron/PhotoEdit. **149** Calvin and Hobbes. Copyright © 1992 Watterson. Reprinted with permission of Universal Press Syndicate. All rights reserved. **151** Scala/Art Resource, New York. **152** Copyright © Charles Palek/Animals Animals. **156** BET (r, l). **158** BET. **160** Tony Freeman/PhotoEdit. **165** Acervo Partrimonial de la Secretario de Haciende y Credito Publico, Mexico, D.F. **166** Courtesy of Carmen Garza. **169** AL(t); RJB(b). **172** AL. **173** AL. **174** AL. **175** AL. **176** AL. **177** AL. **178** Copyright © Peter L. Chapman/Stock Boston. **179** AL. **181** The Butler Institute of American Art, Youngstown, Ohio. **182** Copyright © DC Comics, Inc. **185** Courtesy Gallery Hans Meyer, Dusseldorf Private collection, Germany. Copyright © 1992 The Estate of Keith Haring. **186** Copyright © AFP. **189** Los Angeles County Museum of Art, gift of Mrs. Homer Kripke. **194** Janice Fried. **196** AL. **198** Copyright © Diane Graham-Henry/Tony Stone Worldwide. **201** Tony Stone Worldwide. **203** AL. **205** Copyright © 1983 Andy Warhol/Ronald Feldman Fine Arts, courtesy Ronald Feldman Fine Arts, New York. **206** Courtesy of Nancy Schutt. **210** Tad Merrick (t); AW (b). **211** RJB. **212** AL (l); Copyright © Randy Brown/Alaska Stock Images (r). **213** AW. **214** RJB (r); Courtesy Children's Television Workshop (l). **215** William Jordan. **216** AW. **217** AW. **218** AW. **219** Copyright © Jasper Johns/VAGA, New York 1992. Collection Albright-Knox Art Gallery, Buffalo, New York. **222** Copyright © Mike Okoniewski/ The Image Works (l); Myrleen Ferguson/PhotoEdit (r). **223** National Museum of American Art, Smithsonian Institution/Art Resource, Transfer from the Museum of Modern Art. **224–225** AL. **226** AL. **228** AW. **230** AW. **235** RJB. **235** Copyright © David Young-Wolf/PhotoEdit. **237** Courtesy Elaine Horwitch Galleries, Scottsdale, Arizona. **262** Photo: Murray Close. Copyright © 1991 TriStar Pictures, Inc./PhotoFest. All Rights Reserved. **280** Giraudon/Art Resource, NY. **322** Courtesy of Nancy Schutt. **328** David Young-Wolff/Photo Edit. **340** National Museum of American Art, Washington, D.C./Art Resource, NY. **356** Collection of the Artist. **376** Phylis Kind Gallery, New York/Chicago. **388** AL. **392** Calvin and Hobbes. Copyright © 1986 Watterson. Reproduced with permission of Universal Press Syndicate. All rights reserved. **400** Robert Miller Gallery, New York. **416** National Museum of American Art, Smithsonian Institution/Art Resource, Bequest of Henry Ward Ranger Through the National Academy of Design. **426** Courtesy Frumkin/Adams Gallery, New York. **450** Copyright © The Phillips Collection, Washington, D.C. **458** Library of Congress. **478** Evans-Tibbs Collection, Washington, D.C. **491** AL. **492** Copyright © Cathy Ferris. **498** From *The World Book Encyclopedia*. Copyright © 1992 World Book, Inc. By permission of World Book, Inc. **499** Hammond Incorporated, Maplewood, NJ, photo by AL. **501** Courtesy of Macmillan Publishing. **505** Copyright © Bob Daemmrich/Stock Boston (c); Copyright © 1992 E.R. Degginger/ Earth Scenes (r); Copyright © Bob Daemmrich/The Image Works (l). **509** RJB. **514** Neal Mishler/Natural Selection. **518** Copyright © 1985 Vernon Doucette/Stock Boston (b); BET (t). **531** RJB. **533** Copyright © Mark Burneti/Stock Boston. **534** AL. **543** BET (t); Copyright © Bill Gallery/Stock Boston (bl); NASA (br). **545** AL. **553** AL. **556** AL. **Back Cover** Aaron Haupt